The Great Ideas

Man	Reasoning
Mathematics	Relation
Matter	Religion
Mechanics	Revolution
Medicine	Rhetoric
Memory and Imagination	Same and Other
Metaphysics	Science
Mind	Sense
Monarchy	Sign and Symbol
Nature	Sin
Necessity and Contingency	Slavery
Oligarchy	Soul
One and Many	Space
Opinion	State
Opposition	Temperance
Philosophy	Theology
Physics	Time
Pleasure and Pain	Truth
Poetry	Tyranny
Principle	Universal and Particular
Progress	Virtue and Vice
Prophecy	War and Peace
Prudence	Wealth
Punishment	Will
Quality	Wisdom
Quantity	World

Encounter, oil on canvas by Jean Paul Riopelle, 1956.
In the Wallraf-Richartz Museum, Cologne, Germany

*"Police activity marks the point at which society interferes
with the conduct of the individual."* —*Ramsey Clark*

The Great Ideas Today

1972

William Benton, *Publisher*

Encyclopaedia Britannica, Inc.

Chicago • London • Toronto • Geneva • Sydney • Tokyo • Manila • Johannesburg

The Great Ideas Today 1972

Contents

PART ONE   **The Civil Police: A Symposium**

Introduction   2
Police That Serve Society   *Ramsey Clark*   4
The Proper Role of the Criminal Law   *Norval Morris*   22
Changing Conceptions of the Police
  Jerome H. Skolnick   40
Democratic Control and Professional Restraint
  James F. Ahern   58
The Problem of Power   *Casamayor*   72
Law, Authority, and the Limits of Law Enforcement
  in Great Books of the Western World   90

PART TWO   **The Contemporary Status of Three Great Ideas**

Modern Philosophies of Law   *Shirley Robin Letwin*   104
The Great Anti-School Campaign   *Robert M. Hutchins*   154
The Discipline of History   *Henry Steele Commager*   228

PART THREE   **A Special Feature**

The Idea of Freedom — Part One   *Charles Van Doren*   300

PART FOUR   **Additions to the Great Books Library**

The Duration of Life   *August Weismann*   394
Benito Cereno   *Herman Melville*   416

A NOTE ON REFERENCE STYLE

In the following pages, passages in *Great Books of the Western World* are referred to by the initials *'GBWW,'* followed by volume, page number, and page section. Thus, *'GBWW,* Vol. 39, p. 210b' refers to page 210 in Adam Smith's *The Wealth of Nations,* which is Volume 39 in *Great Books of the Western World.* The small letter 'b' indicates the page section. In books printed in single column, 'a' and 'b' refer to the upper and lower halves of the page. In books printed in double column, 'a' and 'b' refer to the upper and lower halves of the left column, 'c' and 'd' to the upper and lower halves of the right column. For example, 'Vol. 53, p. 210b' refers to the lower half of page 210, since Volume 53, James's *Principles of Psychology,* is printed in single column. On the other hand, 'Vol. 7, p. 210b' refers to the lower left quarter of the page, since Volume 7, Plato's *Dialogues,* is printed in double column.

Gateway to the Great Books is referred to by the initials *'GGB,'* followed by volume and page number. Thus, *'GGB,* Vol. 10, pp. 39-57' refers to pages 39 through 57 of Volume 10 of *Gateway to the Great Books,* which is James's essay, "The Will to Believe."

The Great Ideas Today is referred to by the initials *'GIT,'* followed by the year and page number. Thus *'GIT* 1968, p. 510' refers to page 510 of the 1968 edition of *The Great Ideas Today.*

PART ONE

The Civil Police

A Symposium

Introduction

It is a commonplace that the police, who until recently were taken for granted, at least in the United States, have become one of the troublesome and uncertain institutions of contemporary society. In Europe, in Japan, in South America, there is evidence that the business of maintaining what we like to call law and order has become both difficult and dangerous. It is not merely that crime rates are on the rise and that violence is everywhere reported. The quiet consent with which police operations were carried on in the past seems to have disappeared, replaced by sharp hostility, on the one hand, and on the other, by fervent support. Thus at the very time when some segments of the public feel that the police have become a menace far more threatening than the social disorders they are supposed to control, other groups that feel insecure demand greater police power than already exists, and urge that it be exercised with less restraint than the law now prescribes.

In undertaking to survey this situation—or more exactly, the police institution that the situation involves, and more exactly still, the informing idea by which the institution exists—the editors of *The Great Ideas Today* have recognized that the term *police* is ambiguous. According to one tradition, it signifies all those operations by which the power of government is asserted and maintained, whatever kind of government it be and however its power is derived; in this sense of the term, the "police" combine administrative and judicial responsibilities, are charged with seeing to it that society functions in a safe and orderly manner, and make, administer, and enforce such regulations as are necessary to that end.

The other meaning of *police* is much narrower. It refers to the agency of government that is charged with the enforcement of the laws and the maintenance of peace and order. This limited sense of *police* is possible only with a government *of* laws—a government, that is, which is duly constituted by those to whom the laws apply, and which remains accountable to them. Such a police has no legislative powers and no judicial authority of any kind, but in the exercise of its proper function it enjoys a monopoly of legitimate coercive force.

In common usage these two senses of *police* are often confused, or the distinction between them is ignored, and in practical application they often mean the same thing—as when, for example, a criminal arrest or

2

the direction of vehicular traffic is involved. Yet the distinction between them is important, for it is only the second kind of police that can properly be called a civil police, and it is only a civil police, considered as an institution, that is a matter of public concern. It is a matter of public concern because it is responsible to the public, who through the processes of government accord it limited powers for limited ends. As such it is quite different from the other kind of police, which is not circumscribed in the same way—which indeed is responsible only to the regime that employs it, and which is limited only by the capacity of that regime to sustain itself. The question with police of this kind is simply one of efficiency, however strict the procedures according to which it functions, and it is of concern only to those who hold power.

For reasons which the editors endeavor to make clear in the review that begins on p. 90, there is little if anything in the intellectual tradition embodied in the great books that bears upon the civil police, or on the question of law enforcement generally. It was thought appropriate, therefore, to make such matters the subject of this year's Symposium, so they could be discussed by persons eminent in the field, and in this way be put before the readers of *The Great Ideas Today*.

The contributors to the Symposium, who were asked to address themselves to different aspects of the subject rather than to attempt to encompass it as a whole, are Ramsey Clark, the former United States attorney general, who suggests what the character of a true democratic police might be; Norval Morris, co-director of the Center for Studies in Criminal Justice at the University of Chicago, who discusses the possibility of decriminalizing what are called victimless crimes; Jerome H. Skolnick, of the Center for the Study of Law and Society at the University of California at Berkeley, who reminds us of some police history; James F. Ahern, who was chief of police at New Haven, Connecticut, and who considers the relationship between democratic procedures and police professionalism; and Casamayor (Serge Fuster), a French jurist who is well known for his writings on the criminal justice system, and who writes with special concern about its impact on society.

The essay on the idea of law enforcement in the great books is by William Gorman, contributing editor of *The Great Ideas Today*.

Police That Serve Society

Ramsey Clark

Ramsey Clark was born in Dallas, Texas, in 1927. He attended public schools there and in Los Angeles and Washington, D.C., before going on first to the University of Texas and later to the University of Chicago, from which in 1950 he received both an M.A. in American history and an LL.B. Admitted to the State Bar of Texas in 1951, he engaged in the private practice of law at Dallas until 1961, when he was named assistant attorney general of the United States by President John F. Kennedy. Four years later, in 1965, he was nominated deputy attorney general by President Lyndon B. Johnson, whom he served subsequently as acting attorney general (1966–67) and as attorney general (1967–69). Since 1969 he has been a member of the law firm of Paul, Weiss, Goldberg, Rifkind, Wharton, and Garrison. He is the author of a widely discussed book, *Crime in America* (1970), and of various articles on the subjects of crime, law enforcement, and civil liberties. This year, among other legal commitments, he undertook to defend the Reverend Philip Berrigan, who, with six co-defendants, was on trial at Harrisburg, Pennsylvania, charged with conspiring to kidnap presidential adviser Henry Kissinger.

Too often, when we are confronted with the necessity of stating the idea behind the most common and essential functions in society, we realize that we have no idea. We do the things we do mainly because we have done them before, adding new usages to old ones as our immediate needs change. So it is with civil police. Where among the great ideas do we find a clearly developed concept of civil police? Not within the dialogue on constitution, government, or law. Where among the great books is there a significant treatment? Not in Aristotle, Tacitus, Montesquieu, or Marx. Are ideas only manageable for things remote? Are police activities too close to us, too pervasive in our lives to be encompassed by a concept? Is the subject too complex, too much like the totality of human conduct to yield to the constraint of the idea? Or does it involve an inherent variance between form and function that frustrates all attempts at definition? But if we begin without some notion of what it is we intend, how can we know where we want to end?

In matters of importance, a society must have a clear impression of its purpose if it seeks to shape its destiny. The performance of the police has a profound effect upon freedom, the rule of law, the quantity of violence and antisocial conduct, the safety of persons and property, and the quality of justice within a society. As long as men have the capacity to injure one another, some kind of police, interfering with individual conduct, will be necessary. However noble the word of the law and the stated purposes of a people, the police is what they do. Police activity marks the point at which society interferes with the conduct of the individual. We shall be known by the kind of interference we require—and permit. A truly civil police is a hallmark of a truly civilized people.

There will be no rule of law where there is not a general voluntary compliance with its word. Even there, the rule will fail if the police do not faithfully and uniformly enforce it. The Magna Carta, the Bill of Rights, modern international conventions of human rights—these are mere homilies where police do not obey their mandates. Freedom, privacy, civil liberty, and human dignity all fall before an unrestrained constabulary. Police who act by force, violence, and cunning stamp the imprimatur of the people on such practices, and leave those they seek to subjugate with little alternative but to reply in kind. In this way, by acting violently and criminally, the police are the cause of further crime

5

"Injustice will prevail among a people policed by a force that does not seek justice as its fundamental purpose"

and violence. Injustice will prevail among a people policed by a force that does not seek justice as its fundamental purpose. It is within the power of the police to destroy freedom, diminish safety, make force sovereign, and maintain an order of injustice.

The function of the police has evolved from a relatively primitive exercise of organized force into something that incorporates the refined techniques and some of the immense power of the modern military. This evolution makes our continued failure to conceptualize the police role a perilous affair, given our interdependent, urban, technologically advanced society. If we are to know freedom, safety, and justice in the years ahead, we must create a civil police clearly conceived and understood, fiercely self-disciplined in the performance of a lawfully delegated function, and faithfully supported by the public it serves—but only when properly engaged in the performance of its duties.

America is not alone in its failure to analyze the nature and role of a civil police. The most libertarian and democratic of modern nations have

left their police institutions largely undefined, or have made them contradictory. France, a country passionately devoted to freedom and popular
government, is served by police designed in the main by a royal monarch
and a military dictator—Louis XIV and Napoleon Bonaparte. England,
with its long traditions of civil liberty and elective government, has a
police service derived from the mutual pledge system of Alfred the Great;
the shire reeve, constable, and "watch and ward" of Edward I; and the
military structure, command, and uniform devised by Sir Robert Peel almost a century and a half ago. The idea of a civil police has only slowly
and often capriciously developed.

A civil police is comprised of persons employed in the public service who
are an integrated part of the citizenry they serve, and who participate
fully and equally as individuals in the common society. It is, and should
conceive of itself as, a social service under civilian control, deriving its
power from the people and answering to the people for the quality of its
performance. It is the antithesis of the military or paramilitary in concept, authority, organization, and function. Hence the existence within
police departments of military organization, rank, command, authority,
deployment, uniform, weaponry, and technique represents more than
merely the vestiges of military inception. It manifests the dominance of
a paramilitary concept of the police and their function, segregating them
physically and rendering them socially and psychologically isolated, antagonists of the public.

A civil police is an essential component of a government of laws. Its
purpose is the equal enforcement of those laws. It cannot be commanded
or influenced by any particular power or special interest, only by a duly
constituted government seeking to maintain the rule of law. Such a government need not have a written constitution delegating certain powers
to its various branches and levels while reserving others to the people,
but there must be an accepted system for the promulgation, enforcement,
and adjudication of rules of uniform and general application. Without a
written constitution or some other binding commitment allocating the
powers of government and reserving inviolable rights to the people,
government has authority for totalitarian conduct and the rule of law
will fail.

It is possible to have a civil police within a government that does not
have separate law-making, law-enforcing, and law-adjudicating branches.
But if the police make, enforce, and interpret the law without uniformity,
truth, and fairness, again the rule of law fails. Nor may civil police act in
any way except strictly in accordance with the rule of law. That is their
delimitation—and their strength.

Within the scope of police powers is the enforcement of laws designed
to protect life, property, and freedom from the antisocial conduct that is
determined by law to require government intervention. The enforcement
of such laws is primarily a matter of preventing their violation, since

". . . the dominance of a paramilitary concept of the police and their function, segregating them physically and rendering them socially and psychologically isolated, antagonists of the public"

this offers society the best protection and the most efficient use of limited resources. Other elements of enforcement are the direct control of conduct that threatens or commits violations of criminal statutes, the detection of persons who have committed past criminal acts, and the apprehension and arrest of persons who there is adequate cause to believe have committed such acts.

A civil police in any society that values freedom and seeks to protect it through the rule of law will enforce laws that are designed to preserve freedom as vigilantly as those that preserve life and property. Police will be not only prohibited by law but restrained by the best traditions of their function and the clear and ardent feeling of the public from any conduct violative of the basic elements of freedom. These will include all those liberties that deal with the spirit of humanity—the right to have privacy, to be free of arbitrary interference by authority, to think, to speak, to write, to publish, to broadcast, to petition government, to assemble, to dissent, and to pray. The law will forbid discriminatory, arbitrary, unfair, and violent conduct by police. It will authorize only the minimum use of force necessary to accomplish a lawful purpose. Purposes for which any use of force is permitted will be severely limited.

In any society that places a high value on freedom and human dignity, the civil police, by virtue of their lawfully vested powers and social service purpose, will protect the feared and the despised and the powerless equally with the mighty and the wealthy and the beloved. They will neither seek nor take unfair advantage of any citizen, even when they are convinced he is guilty of the most heinous crime. They will understand their duty to assure equality to the poor, the sick, and the ignorant in the enforcement of their rights. Such a police will be sensitive to the customs, needs, fears, and hopes of all segments of the society, and will understand its obligation to protect the dignity of all. It will not be aligned with a particular group or interest except as directed by law.

There is no contest in a free society between freedom and safety. The obligation of the civil police to protect the liberties of the individual is as great as its obligation to protect the safety of society. In the performance of its duties, a true civil police will always seek ways to enlarge both liberty and safety, knowing that each can be increased without diminishing the other, and that one must never be sacrificed in the false hope of thereby securing the other. Such a police will vigorously enforce safeguards against wrongful arrest, physical and psychological abuse of persons under arrest, and unlawful detention. Equally, it will enforce safeguards against self-incrimination and against unreasonable searches and seizures of the premises where a person lives, of his person and papers, and of those places where he has a reasonable expectation of privacy.

True civil police will understand the very limited capacity they have to control social unrest. Knowing with Plato that poverty is the mother of crime, and with Aristotle that the chief and universal cause of the revolutionary impulse is the desire for equality, they will never seek to segregate and confine the ravages of poverty by brute force. Nor will they seek by force and violence to continue a state of inequality that can only give rise to revolutionary violence beyond the power of any police to contain. Rather they will seek to fulfill the rule of law which promises equality and justice. They will be an educator of the people constantly reminding us of the presence of poverty and injustice with which they must deal daily, appealing to our conscience in the name of humanity, justice, and our own safety to address them with our might. The real causes of antisocial conduct can never be contained by police power alone, they will tell us.

Unwilling merely to confine the effects of poverty and other conditions that create crime, determined to act under the rule of law rather than from motives of vengeance or contempt, a civil police will expose the containment of such conditions as ignoble and contrary to the spirit of laws that should be supported in a democracy. Such police will refuse to control our urban ghettos by force and fear as though they were colonies of a larger society. They will not use force in excess of law, and because they will not, they will find that their acts no longer provoke the violent reaction of the people. Within this kind of civil police it will be possible to abide by rules prohibiting the use of force capable of causing death or serious injury except where necessary to protect life, thus saving hundreds of lives and thousands of injuries annually.

There are large areas of human conduct that police can never control. The classic illustration in the American experience is the use of alcohol. Other examples include gambling, drug abuse, addiction, drunkenness, prostitution, sexual activity among consenting adults, abortion, sales on Sunday, pornography, and profanity. Attempts to use criminal sanctions against such conduct result in discriminatory and selective enforcement, which leads to police corruption and loss of respect for the rule of law. As a result, police performance suffers in activities of importance where it can be effective. This consequence will not be conceded by a paramilitary department. Such police, given as they are to the use of force and not committed to the rule of law, may indulge the public and claim credit for themselves with sensational and violent enforcement efforts. A true civil police, on the other hand, will refuse to engage in such activities and will endeavor instead to demonstrate that certain laws cannot be enforced —that the rule of law will be undermined and police integrity eroded if the attempt is made.

The corruption that pervades large segments of our paramilitary police departments is caused in great measure by the hypocritical attempts of

". . . poverty is the mother of crime, and . . . the chief and universal cause of the revolutionary impulse is the desire for equality"

society to control conduct in which millions will nevertheless engage. Police corruption more often arises from a rotten barrel than a rotten apple. The good apple placed in such a barrel will quickly spoil. Among the paramilitary forces of our urban ghettos, an honest officer can operate only in fear of ridicule or reprisal. The laws he is supposed to enforce are unenforceable, yet he cannot admit the fact. It is his accommodation to the reality of the conflict between the stated rule and the irrepressible conduct that corrupts him. The resulting loss of both public confidence and self-respect tragically impairs the capacity of the officer to perform his proper functions.

A civil police must be organized so as to devote its resources, which consist basically of manpower, to the areas where antisocial behavior occurs most often. Crime is human conduct. We are an urban society. Present police jurisdictions are the happenchance of history. Nearly 40,000 police jurisdictions exist in the United States. Single metropolitan areas often have scores of police departments within them. Not only do these jurisdictional lines, rooted in history and irrelevant to the present, defy rationality, they prevent effective performance. To be effective, the police organization should comprehend and cover the patterns of the population it serves, adapting itself to shifts in population and changing needs. If they are to cope with the problems of the society they serve, police must be allocated to the groups and neighborhoods in which the problems exist. Officers must understand and live among the young, the poor, the minorities, the slum dwellers, and other residents of high-crime areas.

To be part of the community, rather than to be imposed on it, is both the essence of the civil police and the condition of its effective performance. Most crime in America today is never reported to the police. At the very threshold of their opportunity to enforce the law, the police are denied the knowledge essential to success. This will ever be so where the police role is military, because the police are then regarded as an army of occupation, alien and mistrusted. To know what the community knows, one must be part of it. The community knows the psychotic who assaults, the drug peddler who sells heroin, the youth gang that mugs, the fence who sells stolen property, the boy who has dropped out of school and will live a life of crime, the father who beats his child until someday the child has the capacity to murder, the tormented family slowly breaking up, the burglar, and the thief. A paramilitary police, segregated from society as a whole, will learn too late, if at all, what it needs to know to prevent the conduct that flows inevitably from these conditions. A civil police, fully integrated into and part of the society it serves, alone can be an effective early-warning system alerting social services with the capacity to solve social problems.

Above all, a civil police can exist only with the consent of the governed. Such consent will not be forthcoming unless the laws are fair, de-

"To know what the community knows, one must be part of it"

signed from generous motives for just ends. An abiding respect for law is essential to its fulfillment; it cannot be coerced or be expected to endure from childhood teachings when the law in fact is unjust. To be respected, law must be worthy of respect. If the law has a substantial and permanent effect on a people, it is through moral leadership. The rule of law will always depend upon the voluntary observance of the overwhelming majority of a population. It is only a small part of the citizenry that a police can hope to prevent from criminal acts, assuming this minority has both the capacity and the will to commit those acts. If police do not act fairly, and if they do not respect the dignity of every citizen and make it clear that they serve the public, they will lose the public's support.

In a free democratic society there is no cause for the use of military personnel against civilians, except when a breakdown of order beyond the capacity of civil police to contend threatens substantial loss of life and property. The United States Constitution, recognizing the implied risk to self-government, permits the federal government to intercede in state and local violence only on application of the state legislature, or of the governor when the legislature cannot be convened.

The use of military police in civilian surveillance, intelligence gathering, investigation, or law enforcement should be impermissible. When military resources are so used, democracy, civil government, the rule of law, freedom, and safety are all imperiled. Societies that justify enormous expenditures for military defense but fail to provide the bare essentials for a civil police create a threat to civilian government from the resulting military capacity—and from industrial dependence upon it. It is a threat that is not easily curtailed. The abundance of resources possessed by the military will always seek ways to increase military power.

A secret police, unless it is carefully segregated from domestic activity under clear and direct civilian authority, will always pose a risk to the rule of law, to respect for the law, and to individual liberty. In a society that has created an effective civil police, there is neither a need nor a place for a secret function within its domestic jurisdiction. Traditions of secrecy and intrigue have invariably undermined the rule of law and its support among the people.

Nor is there a place in a free society for a private police force. Police work entails activity of the highest public importance. It must not be left to private discretion or private means. Discriminatory enforcement, the particular interests of the private enforcer, inability of the poor to provide private protection, and the loss of public control over personnel standards, training requirements, and discipline all dictate against placing any public power of police in private hands. While some uses of private resources for property management, custodial purposes, night watchmen, and similar functions can be appropriate, persons so engaged cannot be

"In a free democratic society there is no cause for the use of military personnel against civilians"

allowed to use force in excess of that authorized for a private citizen under the same or similar circumstances. The right of the private guard to carry or use a gun should be no greater than the right of the citizen generally. Even for such purposes, private police activities should not be favored in a free society because they will lead to unequal police protection. Those with wealth and power will protect themselves, insensitive to the needs of the poor, who suffer most crime. Excellence in civil police will then be diminished.

*   *   *

The general qualities of civil police and the nature of their role in society can be described with some assurance that we are dealing in fundamentals that are relatively durable. Thus, guidance by the rule of law, the full involvement of the police officer as citizen and individual in the common society, the self-image of social service, the careful determination of enforcement priorities among problems capable of solution by police service, the clear limitation on police power fully described in law, the role of law in providing moral leadership, the peril of segregation of the police, and the destructiveness of the assignment of functions that cannot be successfully performed by the police are elemental considerations through changing societies and through different government structures. But the precise functions of the civil police within the general scope of the civil idea are more transitory. Greater care in definition, tentativeness in commitment, and sensitivity to changing needs are required if police are to perform effectively under the rule of law.

The great paradox of police performance in America today is that society's vast overreliance on police to control conduct it merely does not desire exists simultaneously with its incredible failure to support the police in their efforts to control conduct that is a clear threat to society's safety and well-being. One wonders whether we really want to prevent crime. Our failure to provide supportive measures, combined with our insistence that behavior of which we disapprove be suppressed, is the cause of the general failure of the police at the present time. Victims equally of neglect and overreliance, they have an impossible assignment.

The police function in a mass, technologically advanced society is essentially different from what it was in the past. Indeed, its character has changed rapidly in our time, and continues to change. This change, which permeates our total existence, is the cause of what is called the police crisis, rather than any defect in the police performance as such. Change is the fundamental fact of our time. We experience more change in a generation today than came in a millennium heretofore. The police, like other institutions in our society, must make attitudinal change among its personnel and the public, and institutional change both within its organization and in its relationships with other institutions of society, its major science.

Society, and the police who enforce its rule of law, must learn to distinguish between turbulence and disorder. Turbulence is a natural product of change. It is a manifestation of change. There will be vast turbulence in the years ahead. This turbulence cannot be suppressed any more than social change itself can be stopped. To confuse change with disorder and to seek its suppression by force can only tend toward revolution. The police, like other institutions, must see change as desirable, as

"Victims equally of neglect and overreliance, they have an impossible assignment"

the opportunity for something better, as the chance to improve the human condition and the quality of life.

Civil police, rapidly changing individual attitudes, and police departments sensitively changing institutional forms and functions can help preserve freedom and provide safety in an epoch of change. The primary police function will be to prevent conduct that has been explicitly defined through appropriate social procedures as criminal. Society must constantly reexamine this conduct to decide again whether it is undesirable, and if it is still so considered, to determine whether police coercion is an effective way of preventing it.

Protection of life, liberty, and property will remain the chief function of a civil police in a technologically advanced society. A civil police will strive for measures more effective than mere attempts to suppress grave social problems. It will know that prison cannot cure alcoholism, addiction, or psychosis, and will seek to remove the control of persons so afflicted from the system of criminal justice. Treatment of these illnesses as the complex medical and social problems they are is required if their incidence is to be materially reduced. They are not problems the police can effectively resolve. Nor are many other social ills.

In the 1960s, nearly one-third of all nontraffic arrests involved people under the influence of alcohol. This is a problem that cannot be solved by police, who waste an enormous amount of their time, aggravate their relationship with the public, and compound the difficulties of the already difficult life of the alcoholic in the effort to do so. Comprehensive counseling, detoxification facilities adequate to need, family assistance, employment opportunities, and rehabilitation of alcoholics can relieve police of responsibilities they cannot successfully discharge and which should never have been given to them in the first place.

Nor can the police be effective problem solvers for the drug addict. It is impossible to beat heroin from the bloodstream of a human being. A civil police, illuminating the real nature of the narcotics problem and the grave peril it poses for a mass society in a troubled time, can help to motivate us toward the medical research that must be undertaken if we are to develop the synthetic chemistry that will finally relieve a human body of physical dependency on opium and its derivatives. Treatment of addiction outside the criminal justice system, with adequate resources for care and cure of those addicted, vesting in addicts the right to the most effective medical-social treatment that is known, can relieve society of the enormous burden of the antisocial conduct of the addict. Most crimes against property in several of our major cities are committed by addicts who are driven by their need for drugs. Society can begin to relieve itself of the dehumanization and the vast antisocial conduct caused by this phenomenon when it takes the problem of addiction out of the hands of paramilitary police, who can never coerce addicts from their habit.

17

Another substantial part of antisocial conduct is committed by people with mental illness, brain damage, or retarded intelligence. These, too, are problems that police power cannot solve. The majority of inmates in penal institutions suffer from mental illness. Yet prisons cannot treat such problems; they only aggravate them. More mental illness is released from prison than enters it. A sizable fraction of all prison populations are mentally retarded, but there is no way that police can help the retarded by arresting and imprisoning them. This is a profound social problem. Our failure to deal with it reflects deeper failures of our society illustrated in a way by our failure to create better police. As long as we continue to put off on the police all of these difficult social problems, which are created by the nature of our society and reflect its character, we cannot hope to have a true civil police. We can only have what we do have, which is a police *force*. Force will fail.

We also tend to impose on police problems that are basically economic. Often police are empowered to enforce building, safety, and health ordinances. This makes them the enemy of the poor. Strict enforcement will cost them their homes. Failure to enforce may cost health, or life itself. At best, such laws cause landlords to invest the minimum of funds that are necessary to meet the law's requirements. They thus escape the cost of more fundamental improvements, which would entail the investment of billions of dollars in decent housing for the poor. Until these investments are made, strict enforcement of the law can do nothing but deprive the poor of the miserable housing that they now have. It cannot give them housing that is essential to the maintenance of their dignity and the binding together of their families. Other laws of an economic nature, which are specifically designed to protect the poor and are often ignored, should be vigorously enforced. These include the laws against consumer fraud, overpricing, sale of defective goods, sale of impure foods and drugs, excessive rent, wrongful eviction, pollution, and excessive noise. Police could also be more active in cases of white-collar crime, civil rights violations, and other antisocial conduct of the privileged.

Beyond such activities, police can be a major element in the early detection of human need. Family breakdown is an important factor contributing to violence in America. Seventy-five percent of our juvenile offenders come from broken homes. Family breakdown is often first known to the police. If their concept of their role is one of social service and not of paramilitary activity, the police can serve as an early-warning system for society. On first discovering trouble, they can direct a family to the social services that are available to help it. Family counseling, Alcoholics Anonymous, churches, various charities, hospital care, legal aid, psychological and psychiatric counseling and assistance, remedial help in school, employment guidance, and job training are some of the social services to which police can guide the public they serve.

Police themselves must possess many skills. The range of professional knowledge required of them exceeds what is needed by members of any other institution in our society. Law enforcer and lawyer; scientist in a broad range of physical sciences, including chemistry, physics, and electronics; medic, nurse, and doctor; psychologist, social worker, human relations and race relations expert; marriage counselor, youth adviser, athlete, and public servant—these are but a few of the skills a member of a major police department may be called on to exercise many times each day. Police must have within their complement persons in adequate numbers to provide such services.

Yet while there is a great demand for professional skills, there will always remain within any civil police a large area of activity that is nonprofessional in character, requiring relatively little skill and no great intelligence. To attract, develop, and retain the professional, it will be necessary to use trainees, aides, and nonprofessionals to perform these routine, nonprofessional functions.

Indeed, the careful division of activity among professional, semiskilled, and unskilled manpower will be essential to the performance of the civil police. For the professionals, high standards will be necessary. A true civil police will have to bring to the service the best skills within our society, involving people of high initiative and competence. Constant training will be necessary to assure the quality of their service and the relevance of their assignment. A police youth corps, providing opportunity for ongoing education and on-the-job training, can give employment, a livelihood, a chance for social service, and the opportunity to become a professional officer to many of our youth who otherwise might become criminals themselves. We cannot afford to be afraid of professionalism in police. A firm commitment to the idea of a civil police will protect the liberties of our people, and only a professional capacity within the police can provide the quality of service that is necessary to sustain both freedom and safety.

A professional police need not and should not be elite. It must be drawn from all segments of society, and generally in proportion to the need for police service that those segments of society reflect. This means police must be drawn from the poor, the uneducated, the young—from blacks, Chicanos, and other minorities—in greater proportion than such persons by their mere numbers would require. The police should include ethnic groups and religious faiths of every type, reflecting all backgrounds and experiences within our society. This will give the police an understanding of the problems people have, a sense of identity with them in their plight. It will assure a primary loyalty to the people themselves and not to the power of police. It will provide the basis for a civil police.

In the stormy years of change ahead, we must realize what is really involved in the difference between a civil police and a paramilitary police.

The one contemplates a social order based on force, the other a condition of freedom based on the will of the people. The difference between them is the difference between authoritarianism and democracy, between a government of men and a government of law. Only where the police serve with the wide cooperation and support of the public is there government of, by, and for the people. Where police maintain order only by force, there is totalitarianism. The question is whether we are to have a government that subjects its people or a government that serves them. One controls through fear, the other by the confidence of the people. Where the police are paramilitary in concept, they and the interests they serve are the state. Where the police are civil in concept, the people are the state. Thus, one is a police state, the other a free society.

The Proper Role
of the Criminal Law

Norval Morris

Norval Morris was born in Auckland, New Zealand, in 1923. After serving
with the Australian army in the Pacific theater during World War II, he studied
law at Melbourne University, and in 1949 he received a doctorate in law
and criminology from the University of London. Since then he has lived and
held academic positions in England, Australia (where he was also a barrister
and solicitor of the High Court), Japan, and the United States, and has
served on numerous councils and commissions, as well as two UN com-
mittees, that have made studies and produced reports on various aspects
of his chosen field. In 1964 he was appointed Julius Kreeger Professor of
Law and Criminology at the University of Chicago, where he is also co-
director of the Center for Studies in Criminal Justice. Widely known for his
work in crime prevention, delinquency, and corrections, he has been
particularly concerned with what is called victimless crime and the current
movement to decriminalize it. He is the author of *The Habitual Criminal*
(1951), *Studies in Criminal Law* (with Colin Howard, 1964), and *The Honest
Politician's Guide to Crime Control* (with Gordon Hawkins, 1970), among
other works. His home is in Chicago, where he lives with his wife and
three sons.

Insofar as certain serious crimes are concerned, there is broad agreement among the world's many criminal law systems on what behavior to punish. Thus, though somewhat differently defined in different countries, murder, manslaughter, assault, rape, robbery, burglary, theft, and major threats to or interferences with governmental processes (treason, perjury) form the common staple of serious crime. But there agreement stops; great divergence is to be found between legal systems on what further behavior should fall under the prohibitions of the criminal law. Thus, centrally important questions in criminal law policy are these: Beyond the traditional grave crimes, what is the criminal law good for? What more are police, criminal courts, and corrections good at? What can the criminal justice system achieve, and at what social and economic costs?

In the United States of America there is a long-standing tendency to rely on the criminal law not only to try to protect our persons and property and our governmental processes but also to try to lead men away from vice and sin, including those vices and those sins which injure only the actor—and, of course, since few men are islands, those who depend on him. The typical statute book of most states of America purports to punish a wider swath of human behavior than has been proscribed anywhere else since John Calvin left Geneva.

This use of the threat and actuality of criminal punishments to try to coerce men to the good life seems to many commentators to be a gross overreach of the criminal law. They argue that in seeking to control much "victimless crime," the criminal law is not only ineffective but injures rather than protects the community. Some have even suggested that insofar as the criminal law is concerned, the adult man or woman not certified as insane has an inalienable right to go to hell in his own way; that other agencies of society—not the police and the criminal courts but rather the home, the school, the church, and the social welfare agencies—are more appropriate than the criminal justice system to help him to achieve the good life and salvation. And they suggest that we pay heavy collateral costs for our reliance on the criminal law to reach these ends.

This problem is of practical importance as well as of theoretical interest. The present use of the criminal law for the purported control of public drunkenness, much narcotics and drug abuse, gambling, disorderly conduct and vagrancy, a sweep of consensual sexual crimes, and the juvenile court's jurisdiction over neglect, truancy, incorrigibility, and other non-criminal behavior of youth account for over half the arrests of adults and juveniles per year in this country.[1] The jails and courts are cluttered with those who are merely nuisances and not social threats; they pre-occupy a great deal of police time and effort. And this in a country with no lack of other serious problems to concern the criminal justice system. The United States suffers luxuriant rates of serious crime; in particular, violent crime flourishes in comparison with all other industrialized, developed countries. Indeed, to the student of international criminal statistics, America may or may not be the land of the free but it is certainly the home of the brave! In that situation it is surely paradoxical that so much else besides serious crime is thought to fall within the proper purview of the criminal law.

"Victimless crime" is the rubric under which much of the debate is being conducted. A definition may help. Herbert Packer has defined such crimes as "offenses that do not result in anyone's feeling that he has been injured so as to impel him to bring the offense to the attention of the authorities."[2] This definition, setting aside its inapt application to some homicides and abortions, carves out a sufficiently distinct area of the criminal law for its consideration apart from other crimes.

Let me acknowledge at once that this essay advocates a substantial reduction in the present role of the criminal law and a diversion of several social problems from the criminal justice system to other mechanisms of social control and social assistance. Indeed, my view is that the present overreach of the criminal law is both its leading defect and a major obstacle to the creation of a socially protective, reasonably efficient criminal justice system that respects individual freedoms and constitutional rights. This view reflects the opinions of an increasing number of influential commentators (*see* Bibliography) and is already having a perceptible effect on new criminal codes and other statutory amendments designed to create more modest and, it is hoped, more achievable roles for police, criminal courts, and corrections.

Political leaders and senior police administrators increasingly support these projected reforms. Thus, at a recent national conference on the criminal courts, President Nixon said: "We have to find ways to clear the courts of the endless stream of 'victimless crimes' that get in the way of serious consideration of serious crimes. There are more important matters for highly skilled judges and prosecutors than minor traffic offenses, loitering, and drunkenness." And even before the crisis of public confidence in the New York City Police had occurred following the Knapp Commission's inquiry into corruption in that police force, the city's police commissioner, Patrick V. Murphy, said: "By charging our police with the responsibility to enforce the unenforceable, we subject them to disrespect and corruptive influences, and we provide the organized criminal syndicates with illicit industries upon which they thrive."

So much, then, for the general position that I and others take on the question of a reduced role for the criminal law: now to a closer analysis of the arguments for this.

Regulation *v.* prohibition

A traditional and excellent departure point for any consideration of the proper role of the criminal law is the well-known principle enunciated by John Stuart Mill in his essay *On Liberty*.

> *That principle is, that the sole end for which mankind are warranted, individually or collectively, in interfering with the liberty of action of any of their number, is self-protection. That the only purpose for which power can be rightfully exercised over any member of a civilised community, against his will, is to prevent harm to others. His own good, either physical or moral, is not a sufficient warrant. He cannot rightly be compelled to do or forbear because it will be better for him to do so, because it will make him happier, because, in the opinions of others, to do so would be wise, or even right. These are good reasons for remonstrating with him, or reasoning with him, or persuading him, or entreating him, but not for compelling him, or visiting him with any evil in case he do otherwise.*[3]

Mill is careful to exclude children and the mentally ill or incompetent from the ambit of this principle, but he offers it unqualified for all others "in the maturity of their faculties."

What would be involved in the acceptance of this principle? What would it imply for the criminal law? The answers would vary from state to state, but public drunkenness, much narcotics and drug abuse, most forms of gambling, much disorderly conduct and vagrancy, much sexual misbehavior (including prostitution), and a substantial part of juvenile delinquency as at present defined would fall outside the control of the police. (The juvenile delinquency reduction flows from Mill's principle, though he did not address that question in *On Liberty*.)

In some states there is a clear and strong movement in this direction. State-run lotteries have recently been established in New Jersey, New Hampshire, and New York; Massachusetts and Connecticut are planning to follow suit. There is legal off-track betting in New York. In many states there is experimentation with diversion of addicts and public drunks from the criminal justice system, with methadone maintenance programs and detoxification centers expanding and their work becoming better organized. The courts and a National Commission on Obscenity and Pornography have led the criminal justice system away from its impassioned but irrelevant concern with pornography. States as a matter of law

25

or practice are much less inclined to punish the consenting homosexual and prefer to confine their enforcement of legislation against extramarital sex to situations of force, fraud, or gross disparity of age. The reduction of the reach of the criminal law is perceptible; but the overreach remains.

One rhetorical difficulty in advocating the decriminalization of conduct is this: The advocate of withdrawing the criminal sanction from, for example, consensual adult homosexual conduct is frequently understood to be unopposed, or not sufficiently opposed, to that conduct. To argue for a withdrawal of the law's sanction is often to be interpreted as favoring the behavior previously punished. This is, of course, nonsense, since what is primarily at issue is the efficacy and collateral costs of the criminal law, not the desirability or undesirability of the sinful or self-destructive behavior; but the confusion presents a substantial obstacle to reform.

There is a further, similar, political and rhetorical impediment to reform, analytically more difficult, which merits mention. "You want," I am told, "to legalize drugs, to legalize gambling." Not at all. It is better regulation and not blanket legalization that the thoughtful law reformer now pursues. And this strikes to the heart of the argument. *It is impossible to regulate behavior that you prohibit.* The proper role of the criminal law in this area of victimless crime is to back up rational regulatory efforts by criminal sanctions. An example or two may assist in making this point.

The Volstead Act was prohibitory, not regulatory. Its repeal led to a reasonably enforceable regulatory system, with defects, true, but inflicting nothing like the societal damage caused by Prohibition.

Likewise, the present gambling laws in most states are in substance prohibitory (though opportunities for the middle class to gamble legally are widely available). In the result, the numbers racket flourishes in the ghettos; and illegal off-course betting on horse races and illegal betting on a wide variety of sporting events fill the coffers of organized crime to no apparent societal benefit. Regulation, backed up by the criminal law, should supplant prohibition.

A third obstacle in this movement from prohibition to regulation in the area of morals and social welfare deserves more consideration than the previous two. It has been thoughtfully offered by Sir James Fitzjames Stephen and Sir Patrick Devlin.[4] They point out that the criminal law intends by its punishments and threats of punishment to speak to three groups in the community: first, to the convicted criminal, to persuade him not to repeat his crime; second, to like-minded potential criminals, to persuade them not to commit crime, or that crime; and third, insofar as we are a group different from the first two, to the rest of us, to forcefully affirm minimum standards of conduct, to educate us in the right, to dramatically affirm the punishment of wickedness and vice. To withdraw the sanctions of the criminal law from what is described as victimless crime, so they argue, quite overlooks a vitally important purpose of the criminal law. It is a dramatic educative system. Criminal trials and the

"It is impossible to regulate behavior that you prohibit"

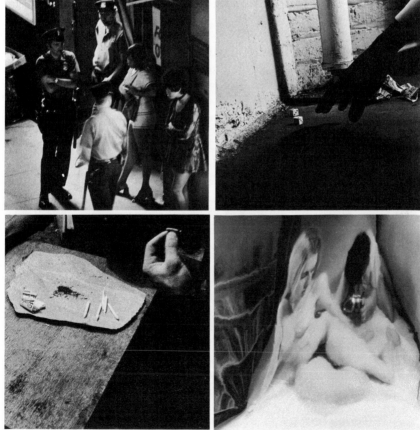

imposition of criminal punishments constitute the modern morality plays. They help to shelter society from the unfettered permissiveness of man's self-indulgence. This argument clearly cannot be lightly dismissed. It is grappled with in several of the books referred to in the reading list appended to this essay. But it may be cast into a better perspective when we later consider the social costs of its acceptance.

Perhaps more important than these rhetorical and political obstacles to reducing the reach of the criminal law is the belief, sincerely held by many people, that to do so would increase the frequency, the incidence, of the behavior previously criminally prohibited, and that social malaise and individual suffering would flow from that increase. The opposing position is that these criminal sanctions are ineffective, that the only behavior affected is man's capacity for hypocrisy. Data on this question are certainly elusive, nor do speculation and common sense—notoriously unreliable guides—carry us far. But, for what it is worth: It seems clear that some persons will be deterred by the criminal prohibition; on the other hand, some will be attracted by it, by the belief in the peculiar sweetness of forbidden fruit. It seems likely, though data are again quite lacking, that in some cases the former group will exceed the latter, and substantially so, since the relaxation of the criminal prohibition also expands the sources of supply of the goods or services previously prohibited. Whether, overall, this increase impinges significantly on social stability and individual suffering is an open question.

Again, for what it is worth in the absence of empirical data, I do not believe there is a larger proportion of saints and a lesser proportion of sinners in America than in those countries with less extensive criminal sanctions. My experience is that the mixture is about the same in every country. I doubt that sexual behavior has been rendered more confined or circumspect in America by virtue of a statute book that prohibits under threat of criminal punishment any sexual behavior other than the intramarital missionary position. The statistical chasm between adultery as a ground for divorce and adultery as a crime is indication enough that such laws are ineffective. It would surprise me indeed if there was much less gambling in America than in those countries that do not prohibit gambling; at judicial sentencing institutes I make a practice of checking with judges if in their view illegal bets are placed in their very courthouses: the replies are predominately affirmative! I doubt that either the Volstead Act or our present criminal laws concerning public drunkenness have reduced alcoholism or the vast sufferings flowing from the abuse of alcohol. And so on, throughout the whole field of victimless crime, with the point becoming starkly clear in relation to vagrancy, where one can hardly take the criminal law seriously as a means of decently assisting the pathetic indigent and geriatric cases swept up under that medieval criminal proscription.

The ineffectiveness of the criminal law's reach into morality and social

The police-jail-court-jail system has neither
deterred nor solved the problems of the public
drunk and the vagrant. Members of the Manhattan
Bowery Project (right) provide an approach that
is designed to reform and regulate by providing
derelicts with detoxification and rehabilitation
facilities

welfare tends to bring the whole system into disrepute. Much of this law is not taken seriously; it is mostly unenforceable and unenforced; when it is enforced it creates many problems, to which we shall now turn.

Results of the enforcement of overreach

Those favoring a reduced definition of the role of the criminal law lay heavy stress on certain collateral disadvantages of our many prohibitions of victimless crime. Apart from the ineffectiveness and hypocrisy of these laws, it is argued that insofar as they are enforced, they waste scarce resources, create black markets, corrupt police and local politicians, are criminogenic and racially discriminatory, raise constitutional difficulties, and allow our political leaders effective means to distract themselves from the serious business of crime control. These arguments will be considered *seriatim,* with occasional critical comments, though it would be less than candid on my part to pretend to impartiality or objectivity of judgment. The essay will conclude with a discussion of some means of diverting victimless crimes from the criminal justice system and some reference to the need of the police for a better guide to the exercise of discretion in these difficult areas.

Waste of resources

Eugene Doleschal has studied the extent of victimless crime and concludes: "More than half of all arrests in the United States are for crimes without victims. . . . Victimless offenders constitute the majority of all inmates in local correctional institutions but only small numbers are sent to prison."[5]

Any acquaintance with the work of the police, of the local and city criminal courts of first instance, and of the jails will confirm that very substantial resources of men, money, and materials within the criminal justice system are devoted to the victimless and social welfare areas of the criminal law. To give only one example: a Washington, D.C., prison committee recently published a special report on the records of six habitual drunks. According to the report, the six have been arrested for public drunkenness a total of 1,409 times and have collectively served 125 years in the city's penal institutions. On a purely monetary level, the arrest, prosecution, and incarceration of just these six alcoholics have cost Washington more than $600,000. A powerful argument can be made that these resources should be liberated for the better pursuit of the primary work of the police, courts, and corrections, which is, or should be, the control of serious crime. But there is this difficulty in such an argument: Other resources will need to be applied to our public drunks and to other welfare and minor nuisance cases currently treated as criminals, and those other resources may well not be cheaper than the present police-jail-court-jail system. Hence the case for overall social economics cannot be confidently made, and the waste-of-resources argument becomes circular in that it returns us to an analysis of the proper role of the police and the courts and the jails. It is the waste of the resources of the criminal justice system, not the amount of economic resources of the community as a whole (which must be expanded anyway, through some agency) that is the problem.

In the period between 1960 and 1971, police "clearance rates" of serious crime, as reported by the FBI, declined from 31 per 100 to 20 per 100. ("Clearance" does not require a court conviction, or even, in every case, an actual arrest; it merely indicates that the police are satisfied that they know who the perpetrator of the crime is, or was.) And this acknowledged drop in police efficiency, which came about for reasons that were largely beyond police control, occurred at a time of political stress on the importance of law and order, when there was allegedly much political support for better-paid, better-trained, and more effective police. Likewise, the pressures on our courts and jails increased over that decade; the courts fell further in arrears in their calendars and the jails became further overcrowded. Hence any liberation of police, court, and jail resources for the more effective processing of serious crime should have high social priority. The enforcement of the overreach of the criminal law certainly wastes scarce criminal justice system resources.

The black market

Where the supply of illegal goods or prohibited services—narcotics, gambling, prostitution—is concerned, the criminal sanction operates as a "crime tariff" that makes the supply of such goods and services profitable for the criminal by driving up prices and discouraging competition from those who would enter the market were it legal to do so. Hence, large-scale organized criminal groups form, and these tend, as in legitimate business, to extend and diversify their operations, financing and promoting other criminal activity.[6]

This analysis would seem accurately to reflect experience during the Volstead Act era and our continuing experience with gambling prohibitions. The effect of such black markets on legal enterprise, into which for a variety of reasons they also seek to diversify, has been far from economically or socially desirable. The expansion of organized crime is a heavy price to pay for so doubtful a benefit.

Corruption

All black markets are corruptive, whether produced by national shortages of demanded goods as in time of war or by the artificial stimulus of the criminal law prohibition. To function, those who operate them must bribe; they must be both open and clandestine, known to their potential of demanded goods as in time of war or by the artificial stimulus of the police of the world are subjected to these temptations. And when the pro-

31

hibitions they are supposed to enforce do not strike them as particularly injurious to anyone, the temptation to turn a venally veiled eye is frequently overwhelming. The same is true for local political and administrative officials. The sanctimonious overreach of the criminal law inflicts a serious cost on the body politic by its pervasive pressure toward corruption. In 1971 the Knapp Commission in New York City laid bare some of these pressures in that city, but it would be a mistake to see them as peculiar to New York; they are a problem wherever black markets in legally prohibited goods and services are to be found. It is a problem that becomes intractable when the law enforcers do not share the values of the lawmakers, or at any rate the values expressed by the lawmakers for political purposes.

Inducement to crime

Upon goods and services for which the demand is relatively inelastic—and it is suggested that this is particularly true of narcotics—the criminal prohibition has a secondary criminogenic effect insofar as it causes persons to resort to crime in order to obtain money with which to pay the high prices that are artificially maintained by the law. It is, of course, peculiarly difficult to measure the strength or incidence of this criminogenic effect; but it is the settled experience of law enforcement authorities, particularly in those cities where heroin addiction is a serious problem, that most addicts must steal to support their habit, unless they be female and young enough to support it by working in another legally proscribed market, prostitution.

When alternative techniques of supporting an addiction or of lessening the impact of withdrawal are made available, as in the increasing number of methadone maintenance clinics (supporting addicts on an ambulatory basis in the community and without a craving for heroin), the rate of non-drug crime as well as drug crime committed by treated addicts dramatically declines. Here the criminogenic effect of the prohibition is demonstrable and the wisdom of providing systems of treatment and control other than under the inescapably punitive aegis of the criminal law would seem clear.

Discrimination

The overreach of the criminal law is usually enforced, if it is at all, on terms that indicate racial and class bias. Few of the middle class are arrested for public drunkenness, though the phenomenon of their appearing drunk in public is not entirely unseen. But it is in the area of gambling that discriminatory enforcement along the lines of class and race is most apparent. Research by Marvin Wolfgang and Bernard Cohen[7] revealed that, in the last year studied, for every one white person arrested for gambling, nearly twenty-five blacks were so arrested. Now blacks probably gamble more than whites; poverty and overcrowding are positively cor-

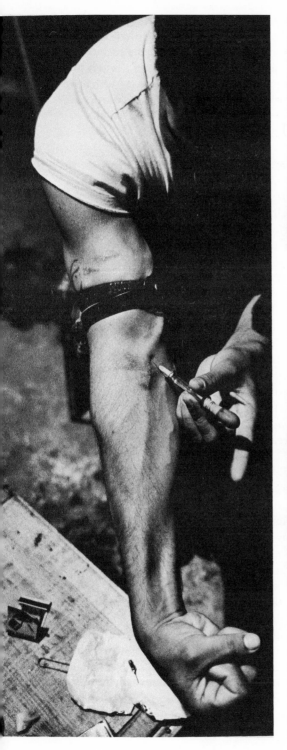

Police agree that crimes committed to finance the habit of drug addiction are a symptom, not the root, of a serious social problem. Policewoman Sister Mary Cornelia counsels drug offenders and gives lectures on drug abuse to schoolchildren. Synanon, designed and staffed by ex-addicts, offers a socially responsible rehabilitation program outside the criminal justice system related with gambling, and blacks are disproportionately poor and over-crowded; but does anyone think that blacks gamble twenty-five times as much as whites? The criminal law, certainly in its enforcement, does not appear to object to gambling as such; what is prohibited, practically speaking, is certain types of people gambling in certain ways of which we disapprove, the money going to other people of whom we disapprove even more!

Constitutional difficulties

The area of overreach and the area of the victimless crime coalesce. By definition, police work is much more difficult in these cases, since there is no injured citizen complaining to the police, seeking protection, and telling his story of the alleged criminal offense. The police here lack willing witnesses. They must therefore manufacture them by the support of dubiously reliable and often corrupted informers, by undercover work, by "tapping" and "bugging," by the use of questionable entrapment and decoy methods, by swift seizure of incriminating evidence, by forceful interrogative techniques. Drug cases account for most of our constitutional difficulties with search and seizure. Organized crime cases and gambling cases account for most of our constitutional difficulties with wire-tapping and other law enforcement invasions of privacy.

Skewing constitutional doctrines to meet the unusual problems of these difficult areas of law enforcement has lessened the protection of constitutional rights generally for the rest of us. In the long run, this enervation of constitutional protections to meet the exigencies of law enforcement in these special problem areas may not be the least of the collateral disadvantages flowing from the overreach of the criminal law.

Distraction

In the language of the activists, the overreach of the criminal law provides excellent opportunity for a political "cop out." The better protection of our persons and property from criminal depredation that now begins to seriously affect the quality of life in this country will require large investments of funds and intelligence in the reorganization of police recruitment, training, operations, and administration; it will require a massive investment in the development of our judicial processes, particularly in the city criminal courts of first instance, with their excessive reliance on plea-bargaining to scramble through their overcrowded calendars; it will also require a much larger allocation of resources to our correctional systems. All these improvements are both expensive and slow, earning few votes and inviting superficial but damaging political attack. If the politician balks at such an uninviting prospect, he can nevertheless give an appearance, an illusion, of responding to the crime problem and to people's genuine anxieties, and with little cost, even with popular support, though the springs of those anxieties will not be tapped: he can declare war on bookmakers and their organized crime, can mount a march against marijuana, can powerfully condemn pornography, can bewail galloping permissiveness. Strike vigorously at the branches, at the symptoms, but do not risk attacking the tree at its roots! Though this will not touch crime in the streets or houses, it will do no harm, and it will gain votes.

To round out this prejudiced argument for a retrenchment of the criminal law, two steps that would facilitate such a retrenchment should be indicated. First would be the development of "diversionary" techniques by which categories of offenders may gradually be removed from the criminal law. Second would be the clarification of diversionary processes that we must and do entrust to the police, and that require better definition and control.

Diversion

There is already wide experimentation in many states and in the federal system with diversionary techniques—that is to say, with methods of keeping those who could properly be defined as criminals, as the law now stands, out of the criminal justice system. The most common technique is, of course, mere nonenforcement of the law, the police eye being discreetly or sometimes corruptly averted. But more carefully planned and socially responsible methods are being devised. Prosecutors are increasingly being permitted to direct addicts to ambulatory treatment programs, sometimes methadone maintenance programs, and to advise them that they will not be prosecuted for the offense for which they were arrested provided they continue in treatment and abstain from crime. Police are increasingly being permitted to take public drunks to detoxification centers instead of to jail, thus completely bypassing the rest of the criminal justice system.[8]

The point that emerges is that there is no single method of cutting down the overreach of the criminal law and of diverting from the criminal justice system those who previously fell within its scope but continue to need social assistance in or out of the community; the problems of public drunks, of addicts, of vagrants, of prostitutes, and of uncared-for homeless youth are profoundly different and call for a variety of noncriminal solutions. Likewise, we must have diversionary techniques not only at the police level but available also to prosecutors, to defense counsel, to jailers, to judges, and to correctional officials. There is a central principle to all these diversions—the avoidance of the use of the ponderous hammer of the criminal law on problems of social welfare and individual incompetence—but the principle does not provide a simple or single alternative to that heavy hand.

The historical path of diversion often follows a pattern, currently well exemplified in relation to drug addiction. The criminal prohibitions

35

come to seem excessive to police, counsel, and courts, particularly as groups with which they can easily identify are swept into their net. The marijuana prohibitions and middle-class white youth offer a prime example. The legislature and the courts pursue different policies, with the legislature reaching for ever increasing sentences—and sometimes mandatory minimum sentences—and the courts by a variety of means rarely and reluctantly carrying out the legislative mandate. Pressure grows for legislative change; gradually legislatures perceive the need to make greater distinctions between drugs as to their dangerousness, and between users and pushers (though the two often overlap), and thus move to reduce the severity of the sentences that have been permitted or prescribed. Like cautious generals they lead from behind. At the same time there is experimentation with alternative treatment techniques for addicts—if jail and prison can be described as treatment techniques at all. California and New York, followed by the federal criminal justice system, experimented with compulsory civil commitment as an alternative either to prosecution or to imprisonment. Other states and the military experimented with methadone maintenance, cyclazocine, and similar medical ambulatory treatments. Addicts themselves, in the Synanon movement, developed treatment methods that clearly help certain addicts to avoid crime and continuing addiction. These various treatment modalities for addicts are used by police, prosecutors, judges, and correctional administrators. What gradually emerges is a complex system of treatment modalities that meets society's needs and the needs of the addict better than our previous simplistic hammer of the criminal law. Of course, the criminal law and the criminal justice system stand as threats behind all these treatment methods for the time being, but their roles are sensibly and substantially reduced.

The problem of the public drunk and of his diversion from the criminal justice system has followed a different path. The drunk who steals, who attacks another, or who destroys property or drives a car, properly belongs in the criminal justice system; but does the alcoholic who is merely drunk in a public place, weaving on the sidewalk or fallen in the gutter? Several courts, on constitutional grounds, had doubted the state's legislative capacity to prohibit such behavior, the argument being that it was behavior over which the alcoholic had no control, and that to punish it would be to punish illness (not volitional wickedness, which is the business of the criminal law) and hence would be a cruel and unusual punishment, prohibited by the Eighth Amendment to the Constitution. In *Powell* v. *Texas* in 1968 the United States Supreme Court in a 5–4 decision upheld the constitutional right of the state of Texas to use its criminal justice system against public drunks, certainly until it could be established that anyone so treated completely lacked the capacity to control his drinking. The Court was also moved by the lack of available medical alternatives. There has followed a period of experimentation with such alternatives.

Five major cities now have detoxification centers as alternatives to the police-jail revolving door, with its stage army of pathetic drunks. Many other cities are following suit. It is clear that we are in a period of gradual eviction of the two million annual arrests of such people from the criminal justice system.[9]

It is sometimes suggested that in this area we have a choice between the criminal law model and the medical model, and all members of the Supreme Court in *Powell* v. *Texas* pursued that analysis. Of course, the fallen drunk cannot be allowed to lie in his vomit in the gutter; on humanitarian as well as aesthetic grounds he must be picked up and cared for. Hence, if not a police van, should we not use an ambulance? Though this is a minority view, let me suggest that such an either-or choice reflects a false dichotomy. We have a wider choice. Some fallen public drunks may need an ambulance and protracted medical treatment, for disease closely accompanies their way of life. But for many others a social welfare response—as distinct from a medical response—may, in the present state of medical knowledge, be preferable to either the criminal law or medical model. It may be that we should be as reluctant coercively to treat as coercively to punish. One suggestion of this nature may merit consideration:

> *For the police lockups, courts, and jails we would substitute community-owned overnight houses capable of bedding down insensible or exhausted drunks. For the police and the paddy wagons we would substitute minibuses, each with a woman driver and two men knowledgeable of the local community in which the minibus will move. A woman is preferred to a man as the driver–radio-operator because it is our experience that the presence of a woman has an ameliorative effect on the behavior of males, even drunken males.*
>
> *The minibus would tour the skid row area, picking up the fallen drunks and offering to help the weaving, near-to-falling drunks. If there be a protest or resistance by a drunk, cowardice and withdrawal must control our team's actions; if there be assaults or other crimes, a police transceiver will call those who will attend to it; if there be unconsciousness or drunken consent, the minibus will deliver the body to the overnight house.*
>
> *If there be talk by the drunk the next day of treatment for his social or alcoholic problem, let him be referred, or preferably taken, to whatever social assistance and alcoholic treatment facilities are available. Indeed, let such assistance be offered if he fails to mention them; but let them never be coercively pressed.*[10]

The social welfare model is also clearly more appropriate than the criminal law model to many of those pathetic nuisances now swept into

Delinquent but noncriminal youth could be regulated outside the jurisdiction of criminal sanctioning and law enforcement

the criminal justice systems by the loosely defined crimes of disorderly conduct and vagrancy. Apart from the collateral disadvantages of the use of the criminal law for over 700,000 such arrests each year, it is a sad commentary on our social sensitivities that we continue to deal with the problems of the inadequate poor in this harsh way.

Further to underline this diversity of methods of diversion from the criminal justice system: Since 1967 there has been a steady and growing movement to exclude from the juvenile justice system those children and youths who are charged with acts that would not be criminal were they adult. These cases of neglect, of lack of care and protection, of truancy, incorrigibility, and similar offenses account for about half the business of the juvenile courts; they should be treated, as the National Crime Commission recommended, by youth service bureaus, community based, more akin to welfare boards than to courts, and having less coercive power than juvenile courts.

Police discretion

As we move to reduce the role of the criminal law to its central social protective functions, as we lop off its moralistic and social welfare excrescences, the role of the police will take on clearer dimensions and, it can be anticipated, will be more efficiently performed. Nevertheless, the police are likely to remain in the front line of the community's response not only to crime but also to a wide variety of other social problems.[11] For the latter, however, instead of bearing the burden alone, they will be the activators of other societal responses. This will require more, not less, training than they now receive, and a higher professionalism than they now enjoy. More diagnostic and judgmental skills will be expected of them as we develop methods of treating public drunks, addicts, vagrants, and children in need that are better than our present simple jail-court or detention home-court responses. Police already exercise a largely uncontrolled discretion in the whole area of victimless crime: as their discretion is better defined and circumscribed, it should be possible to develop a true professionalism in policing.

To date, a professional police has been seen merely as a paramilitary force that eschews corruption and obeys orders—honest, unreflecting law enforcement—whereas the leading characteristic of any true profession is the defined and wise exercise of discretion. It is time the police and the public moved to that view of a professional police skilled in exercising complex social choices. They can do so only if the role of the criminal law is reduced essentially to that recommended by John Stuart Mill.

1 *See* Eugene Doleschal, "Victimless Crime," *Crime and Delinquency* (June 1971), pp. 254–69.

2 *The Limits of the Criminal Sanction* (Stanford, Calif.: Stanford University Press, 1968), p. 151.

3 *GBWW*, Vol. 43, p. 271.

4 *See* Stephen, *Liberty, Equality, Fraternity* (1873), reprint ed., Cambridge Studies in the History and Theory of Politics (New York: Oxford University Press, 1968); and Devlin, *The Enforcement of Morals* (New York: Oxford University Press, 1965).

5 Doleschal, "Victimless Crime," p. 258.

6 *See* Packer, *Limits of the Criminal Sanction;* and Norval Morris and Gordon Hawkins, *The Honest Politician's Guide to Crime Control* (Chicago and London: University of Chicago Press, 1970).

7 *Crime and Race* (New York: Institute of Human Relations Press, 1970), p. 32.

8 *See* Raymond T. Nimmer, *Two Million Unnecessary Arrests* (Chicago: American Bar Foundation, 1971).

9 *See* Nimmer, *Unnecessary Arrests.*

10 Morris and Hawkins, *Honest Politician's Guide,* pp. 7–8.

11 *See* Packer, *Limits of the Criminal Sanction;* H. L. A. Hart, *Law, Liberty, and Morality* (Stanford, Calif.: Stanford University Press, 1963); and Albert J. Reiss, Jr., *The Police and the Public* (New Haven: Yale University Press, 1971).

BIBLIOGRAPHY

BITTNER, EGON. *The Functions of the Police in Modern Society.* National Institute of Mental Health, U.S. Public Health Service Publication No. 2059. Washington, D.C.: U.S. Government Printing Office, 1970.

DUSTER, TROY. *The Legislation of Morality.* New York: The Free Press, 1970.

KADISH, SANFORD. "The Crisis of Overcriminalization." *Annals of the American Academy of Political and Social Sciences* 374 (November 1967): 157–70.

KAPLAN, JOHN. *Marijuana—The New Prohibition.* New York: World Publishing Co., 1970.

NATIONAL COUNCIL ON CRIME AND DELINQUENCY. *Crimes Without Victims.* New York: National Council on Crime and Delinquency, 1971.

SCHUR, EDWIN. *Crimes Without Victims: Deviant Behavior and Public Policy.* Englewood Cliffs, N.J.: Prentice-Hall, 1965.

Changing Conceptions
of the Police

Jerome H. Skolnick

At scarcely over forty, Jerome H. Skolnick has become one of the leading
figures in his chosen field of the sociology of law. Educated at the City
College of New York, from which he graduated in 1952, he received a Ph.D.
in sociology from Yale in 1957, and taught at both the Yale and Harvard
Law Schools, among other places, before his appointment as professor of
criminology at the University of California, Berkeley, where since 1970 he
has also been research criminologist at the Center for the Study of Law and
Society. In 1968–69 he was director of the Task Force on Violent Aspects
of Protest and Confrontation for the President's Commission on the Causes
and Prevention of Violence (the Kerner Commission), which produced a
report entitled *The Politics of Protest* (1969) that received wide notice. In
addition, he is the author of *Justice Without Trial: Law Enforcement in
Democratic Society* (1966), a standard work on the conduct, functions, and
personality of the police that are manifested in contemporary law enforcement, and of numerous articles concerned with criminal or socially deviant
behavior and the contemporary effort to understand and control it.

The civil police is a social organization created and sustained by political processes to enforce dominant conceptions of public order. The same definition would apply to the military forces of a society, with an important difference. Unlike the military, police operate through and are governed by the instrumentality of the criminal law.

This definition of the civil police, however, is far more complicated than it may initially appear. The major components of the definition—social organization, political process, public order, and criminal law—are all capable of assuming a variety of shapes, postures, and meanings. Accordingly, a sensible approach to the idea of the civil police would not regard the police as an immutable conception or form of organization but rather as an idea and a structure shaped by time, by social conditions, and above all by the interests and values of those who exercise or have access to political power. Even when examination of the civil police is restricted to England and the United States, change and variety are evident.

Great Britain

The Statute of Winchester (1285) authoritatively guided English courts and writers for several centuries. It provided for the appointment of specific numbers of night watchmen for every city and borough, according to population; for the system of "hue and cry"; and for the responsibilities of individual citizens for maintaining policing equipment according to their individual wealth. This medieval system began to break down by the seventeenth century, out of both apathy and corruption. The combination of the breakdown of feudal social structure and industrial expansion resulted in enormous crime and in what contemporary writers of the eighteenth and nineteenth centuries called a "criminal" or "dangerous" class. John J. Tobias writes of that period:

> In the last half of the eighteenth century and the first half of the nineteenth century . . . society was in violent transition. The towns were growing rapidly, and the facilities available to their rulers were very limited and their knowledge of how to use them even more limited. Their population, ever increasing, was pre-

dominantly a young one, and the young town-dwellers were faced with a whole host of unfamiliar problems, problems for which their background and training provided them with no answer. The towns, and especially London, had always had a criminal problem different from and larger than that of other areas, and there were groups of people, living in distinctive areas, who had evolved a way of life of their own based on crime. Many young town-dwellers, faced with these problems and receiving no assistance from their families or their employers (if they had families or employers) or from the municipal authorities, found solutions by adopting the techniques, the habits and the attitudes of the criminals. There was thus, in London and the other large towns in the latter part of the eighteenth century and the earlier part of the nineteenth century, an upsurge of crime which was the fruit of a society in rapid transition.[1]

The problem of security and protection of persons and property was paralleled by frequent working-class rioting, beginning with the anti-Catholic Gordon riots of 1780 and marked by the Peterloo massacre of 1819 in which hundreds of people were injured and eleven killed during a protest against high wheat tariffs, food prices, and other parliamentary abuses. Following the Napoleonic wars, there was a severe economic depression. One English historian, Asa Briggs, has recorded that in 1816 and 1817 nearly a fifth of the population was receiving weekly relief at Birmingham; in the iron-producing areas of the Black Country there was "the silence of unmingled desolation" inside many of the great ironworks, and the cries of angry men outside; in Lancashire, weavers were complaining that "now, when the waste of war is over, our sufferings are become more general and deeper than ever"; at Newcastle upon Tyne, the colliers were rioting in the same grim mood as the farm laborers at Ely and the townsfolk of Bridport.[2] All over the country, as Samuel Bamford, a social activist of the time, put it, "Whilst the laurels were yet cool on the brows of our victorious soldiers . . . the elements of convulsion were at work amongst the masses of our labouring population."[3] These economic hardships often precipitated riots and demonstrations that were an important element of working-class power.

Working-class unrest and agitation led to a backlash on the part of a "silent majority" of the middle class and a sharp law-and-order response by Parliament. As to the "silent majority" backlash, Halévy comments:

We have depicted the irritation of the masses growing more in-intense every day towards the close of 1816; but the picture requires its complement. We must also depict the hostility which the agitation aroused among all those who possessed any property, and whose fear of the tax collector's demands was outweighed by their

"The civil police is a social organization created and sustained by political processes to enforce dominant conceptions of public order"

greater terror of the confiscations which a revolution would entail. No bookseller or innkeeper wished or dared to sell Cobbett's Political Register. *Publicans who signed a petition or allowed signatures to be collected at their bar were threatened by the magistrates with the withdrawal of their license. A reign of terror was estab-*

lished throughout England by the nobility and middle class—a terror more formidable, though more silent, than the noisy demonstrations conducted by Hunt and Cobbett.[4]

The parliamentary response to the Peterloo massacre was to increase the army by 10,000 men and to pass the six acts known as "gag acts." Yet these incursions into civil liberties did not, according to the leading historian of British police, Charles Reith, solve the problem of civil unrest for the government. Indeed, they only created greater mistrust. As he writes:

The Six Acts prohibited drilling and limited public meetings; imposed a fourpenny stamp on all periodical publications, including newspapers; authorized the seizure of anything that could be called a seditious or blasphemous libel; and allowed magistrates to search houses for arms. Their net effect was to suppress the reading of all forms of political expression and complaint of any kind of privilege of the powerful. They greatly increased the prevailing indignation against the Government, and together with the general effect of Peterloo, did much to shake faith in the principles of old-fashioned Toryism in thinking circles, especially those of the younger generation at the universities.[5]

If the "gag acts" were Parliament's answer to civil unrest, the answer to crime was the supposed deterrent effect of an extremely severe penal code. As Melville Lee writes in his *History of the Police in England:*

The penal laws were written in blood. Colquhoun estimated that there were 160 different offenses which were punishable by death, without benefit of clergy. . . . Such indiscriminate infliction of the extreme penalty of the law could serve no useful purpose, on the contrary it undoubtedly aggravated the very offenses it was intended to check.[6]

Strenuous efforts were first made by Jeremy Bentham and later by Sir Samuel Romilly to persuade the government to reduce the number of offenses punishable by death, but with little immediate success. In a similar vein, Sir James Mackintosh in 1822 urged Parliament to adopt measures that would increase the efficiency of the criminal law by mitigating its vigor. Although Sir Robert Peel initially opposed the position advocated by Romilly and Mackintosh, he was soon to realize that police can be neither effective nor just if the laws they are required to enforce are so sweeping in their scope and so onerous in their penalties that they do not receive wide public support. The savagery of the penal code defeated its own ends. Witnesses refused to give evidence that might condemn a man to the barbarous sanctions proposed by the penal code, and juries would not always convict even when the evidence that was given was perfectly clear. Accordingly, Peel came to understand, as Charles Reith puts it:

> ... that Police reform and Criminal Law reform were wholly inter-
> dependent; that a reformed Criminal Code required a reformed
> police to enable it to function beneficially; and that a reformed
> police could not function effectively until the criminal and other
> laws which they were to enforce had been made capable of being
> respected by the public, and administered with simplicity and
> clarity. He postponed for some years his boldly announced plans
> for police, and concentrated his energies on reform of the law.[7]

The major thrust of Peel's reform of the criminal law was to limit its scope and to reduce penalties drastically. For example, he abolished the death penalty for over 100 offenses and removed numerous criminal penalties entirely. So behind the idea of the London Metropolitan Police was the notion that the criminal law should not seem unjust or irrational to large segments of the public.

The salience of public relations represented a second governing understanding behind the organization of the new police. The army, which had formerly been responsible for public order, was often hated by the masses of people who were engaging in rioting or public demonstrations. Soldiers usually had no understanding or sympathy for the causes of demonstrations, and were apt to be extremely brutal. Peel and Colonel Charles Rowan, whom Peel appointed commissioner of the new police, strongly urged moderation in the actions of the police. Thus, the "instructions" to constables that were officially published in 1829 contain the following statement reminding the constable that:

> ... there is no qualification more indispensable to a Police Officer
> than a perfect command of temper, never suffering himself to be
> moved in the slightest degree, by any language or threats that may
> be used; if he do his duty in a quiet and determined manner, such
> conduct will probably induce well-disposed by-standers to assist
> him should he require it.[8]

The policeman's command of temper was prominently displayed in management of crowds. One writer offers the following as the best hard evidence of police restraint:

> During the first forty years of its existence, the peace was so well
> maintained that the damage done to property by rioters was quite
> insignificant and this without the intervention of the military;

> *whilst in witness of the moderation of the methods employed by the police in the attainment of this result, it need only be stated, that in every conflict which occurred during the same period, personal injuries sustained by the aggressors were invariably less severe than those suffered by the constables, though the latter were all men of exceptionally fine physique, and were armed with truncheons.*[9]

Such restraint was doubtless influenced by the considerable political opposition against the formation of the new police. Despite rising crime rates, parliamentary commissions considered and rejected instituting a police force in 1770, 1793, 1812, 1818, 1822, and 1828. As T. A. Critchley comments:

> *It is one of the most remarkable facts about the history of police in England that, after three-quarters of a century of wrangling, suspicion and hostility towards the whole idea of professional police, the Metropolitan Police Act, 1829, was passed without opposition and with scarcely any debate.*[10]

Chateaubriand's tracts against the French police system were eagerly read and quoted in England, and it was felt by many that London could not avoid the interference with individual liberty that characterized the French police. The idea of a police truly responsible to the citizenry was not believed realizable in practice. As E. P. Thompson writes:

> *The Parliamentary Committee of 1818 saw, in Bentham's proposals for a Ministry of Police "a plan which would make every servant of every house a spy on the actions of his master, and all classes of society spies on each other." Tories feared the over-ruling of parochial and chartered rights, and of the powers of the local J.P.s; Whigs feared an increase in the powers of Crown or of Government; Radicals like Burdett and Cartwright preferred the notion of voluntary associations of citizens or rotas of householders; the radical populace until Chartist times saw in any police an engine of oppression. A quite surprising consensus of opinion resisted the establishment of "one supreme and resistless tribunal, such as is denominated in other countries the 'High Police'—an engine—invented by despotism. . . ."*[11]

Peel's success may be attributed to: (1) his political adroitness—he excluded the City of London from his plans, and won the support of the Whigs; (2) an increasingly frightening crime problem; and (3) a philosophy of police geared to assuaging anxiety over possible despotism. As Lee comments:

> *The strength of the Man in Blue, properly understood, lies in the fact that he has behind him the whole weight of public opinion; for he only wages war against the lawbreaker, and in this contest can claim the goodwill of every loyal citizen. If a police constable is in need of assistance, he can call upon any bystander, and in the King's name demand his active cooperation; should the bystander refuse without being able to prove physical impossibility or lawful excuse, he can no longer be considered as a loyal citizen, but is guilty of an indictable offense and becomes liable to punishment.*
>
> *The basis upon which our theory of police ultimately rests, is the assumption that every lawful act performed by a police officer in the execution of his duty, has the sanction and approval of the great majority of his fellow-citizens; and under our constitution it would be impossible for any constabulary force to continue in existence, if its actions persistently ran counter to the expressed wishes of the people.*[12]

From the above it seems evident that although the social organization and norms surrounding the London Metropolitan Police did not derive from any single idea, but rather from a fairly complete set of developing historical events and interests, the ideas of minimum force, respect for law, and responsibility to the public were paramount. While the purpose of the police was to protect private property and to maintain public order, there was a clear understanding that police power would be restrained by the rule of law and public opinion. The new police did not spring full-blown from the mind of Sir Robert Peel, but developed from the thinking of a number of persons who sought to preserve the existing social order through the use of measured and limited force, and who felt that a repressive police might well promote rather than inhibit both crime and insurgency. By disarming the police, by putting them in distinctive uniforms with tall hats, by stressing exemplary public conduct even during times of riot, Peel's police were able to convey a sense of benign and sensible authority. Even very recently the discipline and restraint of the London Metropolitan Police was noted, during a Vietnam war protest in London. According to the *New York Times* report:

> *. . . the police never drew their truncheons and never showed anger. They held their line in front of the embassy until, as the attackers tired, they could begin to push the crowd down South Audley Street and away from the square.*
>
> *Americans who saw the Grosvenor Square events could not help drawing the contrast with the violence that erupted between the Chicago police and demonstrators at the Democratic Convention in August.*[13]

47

The London police and the Chicago police have had different methods of dealing with "the conflict between order and legality" they face at public protests and demonstrations

The United States

The police in the United States are perhaps even more complicated, both historically and ideologically, than the police in England. Certainly, the theory of the police in the United States mirrors the conflict between order and legality found in English conceptions of police. But America is geographically more complex, with greater regional and urban differentiation. Besides, no police department in America has been so carefully thought through and organized as the London Metropolitan Police. As Roger Lane comments in his history of the Boston police, "The employment of police in municipal administration was governed not by theory but by convenience."[14] In early nineteenth-century Boston, for example, the major problem was not crime but public order. Boston established its first full-time police in 1837 after roving bands of Protestants destroyed nearly every Irish home on Broad Street.[15] The police also performed what we think of today as nonpolice functions—enforcing laws governing refuse and sewerage. When the sewer, health, street, and building departments were created, the role of the police diminished considerably.

In American cities there has been a progressive exchange of functions between the citizenry and the police. At first, the citizenry were primarily responsible for guarding themselves against criminals through a watch system. As other agencies took over other areas of municipal administration, the police began to be increasingly concerned with crime. All this, however, was not dictated by a governing plan or idea but came as a response to historical circumstances. Accordingly, it makes more sense to discuss characteristic problems and issues of American society as these influenced the development of police in America.

". . . a characteristic problem of American public order has been ethnic conflict, in which the police themselves have sometimes been involved"

The combination of immigration, expansion, and slavery stand behind the contradictory images of America as a land of promise and of oppression. The indigenous Indian population was often slaughtered by white settlers. Riots involving blacks occurred even in colonial days: James F. Richardson, in *The New York Police,* describes brutality against the black slaves who made up one-fifth of New York City's population in the 1740s:

> *From the 1740's on, New Yorkers thought themselves engulfed in a rising tide of crime and disorder. The simplest explanation, aside from the presence of the military, was that foreigners and Negroes were responsible. Immigration from non-English sources did rise rapidly in mid-century, and to contemporaries this accounted for the difficulties. Actually, more native Americans engaged in criminal activities than did the foreign born. The New York authorities contributed to the city's criminal population by failing to make adequate provision for the poor, and there were fewer private benefactors to compensate for public indifference than there were in the other colonial towns. Negro slaves, a despised and degraded group who made up one-fifth of the town's population in the 1740's, were an unstable and unruly element often treated with great brutality.*[16]

The themes of brutality against blacks, of discrimination against immigrants, of immigrant hostility toward blacks—all set against a turbulent background of social and class conflict—arise time and again in American history. Richardson describes a paradigmatic American riot of the year 1900 in New York City that grew out of the competition between Irish and blacks for jobs and living space in the West 30s.

> *After the classical precipitating incident of a fatal fight between a black civilian and a white policeman, rampaging crowds moved up and down Eighth and Ninth avenues beating Negroes. Policemen swarmed over the area, cracking the heads of Negroes and doing nothing to restrain the Irish mob. Frank Moss and others carefully collected testimony concerning the police brutality and pressured the commissioners to take proper disciplinary action. In every case the commissioners refused to allow counsel for the Negro plaintiffs to cross-examine witnesses favoring the police, and whenever there was conflicting testimony they accepted the word of the police. As they explained in their report to the mayor the police witnesses testified in an impartial manner while the witnesses for the plaintiffs "displayed a strong and bitter feeling while under examination." That the Negroes were bitter is hardly surprising seeing that the police not only did not protect them against a white mob, did not arrest any of the whites involved, but also indulged in gratuitous clubbing. The police did not stop the white rioters, they joined them.*[17]

So a characteristic problem of American public order has been ethnic conflict, in which the police themselves have sometimes been involved. They have also been involved in labor disputes, often uncomfortably, especially when drawn from the same social class as the workers.

Another characteristic issue affecting the development of the American police is the legislative tendency to coerce morality through the criminal law. For example, the attempt of the New York Police of the Seventeenth Ward to enforce the Sunday closing laws in 1855 led to three days of rioting between the police and the predominantly German residents of the ward. The Germans accused the police of being unduly harsh, of using their clubs indiscriminately, and of shooting to death an innocent man who was walking with his wife. "The incident," says Richardson, "pinpointed the gap between the standards of the Sabbatarian legislature and the beer-drinking Germans, and again it was the police who were in the middle of the quarrel."[18] Even today, most criminal arrests involve violations of moral norms or incidences of annoying behavior, rather than acts of dangerous crime.

The attempt to enforce conventional morality produces several closely related consequences. One is to make the policeman's job more difficult, both by extending the scope of his responsibilities and by enlarging the size of the "criminal" population. As a representative of the FBI stated to the President's Commission on Law Enforcement and Administration of Justice:

> *The criminal code of any jurisdiction tends to make a crime of everything that people are against, without regard to enforceability, changing social concepts, etc. . . . The result is that the criminal code becomes society's trash bin. The police have to rummage around in this material and are expected to prevent everything that is unlawful. They cannot do so because many of the things prohibited are simply beyond enforcement, both because of human inability to enforce the law and because, as in the case of prohibition, society legislates one way and acts another way. If we would restrict our definition of criminal offenses in many areas, we would get the criminal codes back to the point where they prohibit specific, carefully defined, and serious conduct, and the police could then concentrate on enforcing the law in that context and would not waste its officers by trying to enforce the unenforceable, as is done now.*[19]

Such an expansion of the policeman's jurisdiction not only makes him the guardian of public morality but also makes his work seem more dangerous, rendering him more watchful and suspicious. When his jurisdiction is enlarged, the policeman comes to perceive his environment as more threatening because there are, in fact, more potential lawbreakers. Moralistic law also encourages the growth of social organizations—a criminal underworld—for satisfying and creating illicit demands. This has been the American experience following the prohibition of alcohol, opiates, and gambling. Forbidding an activity offers a "protective tariff" to those engaged in the sale of illicit goods and services, thereby increasing the profits of their activities.[20]

Moralistic laws are related to another classic theme in American police history, official corruption. Corruption operates at a number of levels ranging from systematic complicity with organized crime to the acceptance of small bribes and gifts for favors and service. Although it is often claimed that police corruption may be traced to a few "rotten apples" who wear the uniform, it is difficult to understand how police corruption can occur without the knowledge and often the complicity of high police and government officials. For example, a "numbers" racket depends on thousands of small daily bets and scores of "runners." For this sort of widespread organized gambling to occur, the police and city officials must be either extraordinarily naïve or complicitous.

Corruption is not a minor issue for American police. A recent study supported by the President's Commission on Law Enforcement and Ad-

THE NEW YORK METROPOLITAN POLICE.

A PICTORIAL ANALYSIS OF THE REPORT TO THE LEGISLATURE.

1. These gentlemen, finding the garroting business on the decline, resolve to become guardians of law and order, and enter the Metropolitan Police.

2. Policemen are but men, and when young and fascinating women happen to get into the police-stations, who can blame them if they are civil and gallant?

3. As to poor devils, houseless wretches, with no good looks, and steeped in poverty and misery, can a high-bred policeman be expected to cringe to such as these? No, no; let them eat the bread of sorrow.

4. If a rowdy who votes with the Republicans happens to stick his knife into his neighbor's midriff, the judicious Metropolitan policeman instantly discovers a fight between two small boys at the next corner and hastens to interfere on behalf of law and order.

5. But if a poor wretch of a Democrat steals a loaf for his starving family, the zeal and fury of the Metropolitan police know no bounds, and the fellow is lucky if he be not brained on the spot.

6. A high-minded Commissioner scorns the idea of accepting a house bought by the members of the force; but somehow the house *is* bought, and the title-deeds are slipped into somebody's pocket without his knowledge and tremendously against his will.

7. The powers that be ask no favor; but when they want new clothes a friendly captain goes round with the hat, and as for the patrolman who declines to put in a quarter, he had better emigrate to California by the next steamer.

8. The consequence of which is, that the poor patrolman is unable to procure the food which his sick wife requires, and his children go without stockings and without new frocks.

9. The police service continues, however, to be admirably efficient, and quite a number of back-carriages are actively employed on pressing police duty, as above depicted.

ministration of Justice, carried out by Professor Albert J. Reiss, Jr., of Yale University, found that roughly one in five officers in the cities of Chicago, Boston, and Washington, D.C., was observed in criminal violation of the law by a research team that looked at thousands of police responses to telephone calls for assistance. This figure was obviously minimal. It does not include complicity with organized crime but only routine acts that working policemen permitted to be observed. Reiss's account is as follows:

> *The types of opportunities and situations that give rise to officers violating criminal statutes are relatively few. Opportunities arise principally in connection with the law-enforcement roles of officers, particularly in relationships with businesses and businessmen, policing traffic violators and deviants, and controlling evidence from crimes. Obtaining money or merchandise illegally is the principal officer violation. A striking fact is that few officers were observed committing crimes against the residential property of citizens, although this may be a function of the fact that they usually were observed policing low-income residential areas. The major exception is the violation of criminal statutes by controlling evidence illegally, as by swearing false testimony or carrying additional weapons for the sole purpose of using them as evidence against citizens. These additional weapons were obtained from previous searches of the person, and are used as evidence against other citizens who were injured or killed, thereby buttressing the officer's argument that he injured or killed a citizen in self-defense.*[21]

Reiss is not here describing merely minor improprieties, because he also distinguishes a "gray area" of offending. He says that many businessmen engage in exchanges and practices with police that could well be construed as a form of bribery. He writes:

> *A variety of such practices were uncovered in our observations of the police including almost daily free meals, drinks, or cigarettes, the profferment of gifts marking anniversaries and holidays, and discounts on purchases. Such practices are specifically prohibited by the rules and regulations of any police department and subject to disciplinary action if "officially" discovered.*[22]

Every observer of police in America has noted the considerable discretion police enjoy in carrying out their duties. What mainly determines police conduct in any particular department is a police subculture, and if the department is large, its traditional "gray areas" may be difficult to contain even by the most well-motivated and skilled of police administrators. Since large police departments in the United States such as the ones

". . . large police departments in the United States . . . tend to develop their own internal norms regarding deviance and conformity"

studied by Reiss tend to develop their own internal norms regarding deviance and conformity, the police are to a large extent exempted from law enforcement. This fact, combined with a variety of pressures on police to deviate from legal and departmental rules, renders such deviance an everyday reality for many police throughout the United States.

Whether "professionalism" is an effective appropriate remedy for police misconduct is uncertain. The employment of that term may easily confuse the issues. Clearly, it is desirable to offer support to those policemen who by dint of education and persuasion are committed to the enforcement of law through constitutional means. Yet this goal is becoming increasingly difficult to achieve because the police are not always disinterested technicians, simply repairing defects in a machinery of social order. On the contrary, a number of observers have pointed to a growing body of evidence showing that rank-and-file police officers in the United States in the late 1960s generally supported radical right politics and particularly those candidates who exploited student or racial unrest. Such political activity is increasingly linked to the fraternal organizations of police. For example, the New York City Policeman's Benevolent Association allied itself with the Conservative Party of New York and the John Birch Society to campaign openly for a referendum on the Citizens Review Board.

Professionalism may be able through training and education to improve performance by teaching restraint, respect for the law, skill, and honesty. Often, however, professionalism has been equated with technical innovation—shiny cars, sophisticated weaponry, communications systems, computerization—rather than with legality and social service. The "professional" police notion is as easily assimilated to the military model as to the medical or legal one.

Aside from the military, the police exercise a practical monopoly on the legal use of force in our society. The recent emergence of police as themselves an active political force raises questions about the idea of the role of police in a society governed by principles of constitutional democracy. Since police are closer to the day-to-day workings of the political process and interact quite frequently with the citizenry, the political activities of police pose at least an indirect threat to the political freedom of others.

The importance of the police to our legal processes can scarcely be overestimated. The police interpret the legal order and make low-visibility decisions allowing the exercise of considerable discretion that is not subject to the review of higher authorities. The policeman's actions are often regarded by the public in the same way that the law is, and with reason. Citizens who feel that the law is unfair and oppressive are apt to regard its enforcement by the police as harassment. In the same way, when the police are corrupt, the law is corrupt. When the police are political, the law is political. It is difficult to reconcile the stance of an impartial legal official with the stridency of a political activist.

Historically, the police emerge as a significant agency of social control in periods of social and economic transition accompanied by crime and social unrest. But, in a free society, the existence of such an agency continually poses a problem. Broadly and ultimately, the question to be answered is whether the police shall be public servants controlled by the citizenry or whether they are to have a relatively free hand in the use of force. More immediately, controversies in the United States will arise over trends, practices, and suggested reforms—constitutional restraints, decriminalization, "professionalization," or decentralization of authority—and whether the tendency of these is to erode or enhance police responsibility to citizens at all levels of society. For, in a democracy, the ultimate responsibility of the police is to be accountable to their fellow citizens. It was in this understanding that the Commissioners of the New Police showed their clearest prescience in 1829. As T. A. Critchley describes their policy:

> *Among the flood of applications which poured into Scotland Yard, those from military men of senior rank and from people with influence in Government were generally turned down. From the start, the police was to be a homogeneous and democratic body, in tune with the people, understanding the people, belonging to the people, and drawing its strength from the people.*[23]

---

1 *Crime and Industrial Society in the 19th Century* (New York: Schocken Books, 1967), p. 37.

2 *The Making of Modern England, 1784–1867* (New York: Harper & Row, Harper Torchbooks, 1959), p. 207.

3 *Passages in the Life of a Radical* (1844 ed., vol. 1, p. 6), quoted in Briggs, *Making of Modern England.*

4 Elie Halévy, *A History of the English People in the Nineteenth Century*, trans. E. I. Watkin, vol. 2, *The Liberal Awakening, 1815–1830*, 2d rev. ed. (New York: Barnes and Noble, 1961), p. 19.

5 *The Police Idea: Its History and Evolution in England in the Eighteenth Century and After* (London: Oxford University Press, 1938), pp. 203–4.

6 Captain W. L. Melville Lee, *A History of the Police in England* (London: Methuen & Co., 1905), pp. 204–5.

7 Reith, *The Police Idea*, p. 236.

8 Reith says that the only copies that appear to be in existence are with the Chadwick Papers, in University College Library, London, and at Scotland Yard. The quoted portion is in Reith, *A New Study of Police History* (London and Edinburgh: Oliver and Boyd, 1956), p. 140.

9 Lee, *History of Police in England*, p. 327.

10 *A History of Police in England and Wales, 900–1966* (London: Constable and Co., 1967), p. 50.

11 *The Making of the English Working Class* (New York: Random House, Vintage Books, 1966), p. 82.

12 Lee, *History of Police in England*, p. 328–29.

13 *New York Times*, October 28, 1968, p. 3.

14 *Policing the City: Boston, 1822–1855* (Cambridge, Mass.: Harvard University Press, 1967), p. 221.

15 Michael S. Hindus, "A City of Mobocrats and Tyrants: Mob Violence in Boston, 1747–1868," *Issues in Criminology* 6 (Summer 1971).

16 *The New York Police: Colonial Times to 1901* (New York: Oxford University Press, 1970), pp. 4–5.

17 Ibid., p. 277.

18 Ibid., p. 110.

19 Task Force on Administration of Justice, President's Commission on Law Enforcement and Administration of Justice, *Task Force Report: The Courts* (Washington, D.C.: U.S. Government Printing Office, 1967), p. 107.

20 Herbert L. Packer, "The Crime Tariff," *The American Scholar* 33 (1964): 551–7.

21 *The Police and the Public* (New Haven: Yale University Press, 1971), pp. 156–60.

22 Ibid., p. 161.

23 *History of Police in England and Wales.*

Democratic Control and
Professional Restraint

James F. Ahern

James F. Ahern is by profession a policeman. Born in New Haven, Connecticut, in 1932, he joined the police force there as a patrolman in 1954 and
rose through the ranks until 1968, when he was made chief. In that position,
which he held for two years, he gained national recognition for his handling,
without violence, of the demonstration that was organized in New Haven
in May 1970 against the murder trial of Bobby Seale and other members
of the Black Panther Party. Shortly afterward, he was appointed to the
President's Commission on Campus Unrest (the Scranton Commission),
which eventually produced a report highly critical of the violence committed
by the authorities at Kent State and Jackson State universities in 1970.
Since 1971, Mr. Ahern has been director of the Insurance Crime Prevention
Institute, with headquarters in New Haven, which investigates white-collar
crime. He is a member of or a consultant to many commissions and organizations, among them the Ford Foundation, on matters connected with law
enforcement, is a lecturer on the subject of police at Branford College,
Yale University, and has recently written a book, *Police in Trouble: Our
Frightening Crisis in Law Enforcement* (1972).

When I became a policeman in 1954, police were not controversial. While the social status of the individual policeman was clearly low, the operation of the institution was nearly universally accepted. It is inconceivable, for example, that a symposium such as this would have been thought useful or interesting twenty years ago.

The quality of policemen and police work have not declined in those twenty years, yet police are now and have been for the past decade subjects of mounting controversy and contention. It is not the police that have changed but the social context in which they operate.

Two factors have contributed to the present ferment regarding police. The first is the emergence of real concern for the people that society has formerly passed over: the poor, the black, the elderly, and the criminally accused. The determination to bring about changed societal priorities that in the early sixties led to John Kennedy's civil rights proposals, the Medicare bill, and the 1963 march on Washington underlay also the famous Warren court decisions, *Gideon* v. *Wainwright* (legal counsel for indigent defendants), *Mapp* v. *Ohio* (illegal searches), and *Escobedo* v. *Illinois* (coercive interrogations). Enthusiasm for Great Society liberal reform waned in the late sixties. The erosion of that spirit brought these newly defined legal rules surrounding criminal process into question. In the area of what is now commonly called law and order, as in education, welfare, and racial integration, we have come to see a retreat from liberal solutions, the espousal of radical alternatives by some, and a newly respectable hostility to any change in the character and procedures of institutions.

The second contributing factor is the breakdown of the former consensus of society and government that has existed with only brief interruptions throughout our national history. This consensus has traditionally been a very "liberal" one in the classic nineteenth-century sense. America's fundamental political and social thoughts emerged from the European tradition that aimed at limiting institutional roles, reflecting a belief that men are moral, autonomous, and rational beings. The danger to be guarded against was thought to be the excesses of the state, not of the individual. What made America unique in the world was the extent to which doctrines of individual autonomy and social equality had here actually been translated into reality. The core of the consensus that sur-

"... the emergence of real concern for the people that society has formerly passed over"

rounded these doctrines was fixed early in our national experience, and there was never an extended debate over social philosophy in the United States. Attempts to offer doctrines of the right, by proponents of aristocratic and authoritarian role, or of the left, by the believers in collectivism, were alike frustrated by the promise and fact of personal opportunity.

Prior to the twentieth century, the American consensus was broken down fundamentally only once, in the slavery dispute that led to the Civil War. That dispute divided the country along regional lines, so that police departments, which in any event were rare, small, and undeveloped in the 1850s, were not substantially affected. Indeed, the Fugitive Slave Act of 1850, which did introduce the slavery issue in very direct terms into the North, placed United States marshals and private persons designated by them in what today would be a typically untenable police position: that of arresting persons with whom most citizens were in sympathy for actions which most persons did not regard as crimes. However, municipal police were not involved.

The Great Depression of the thirties came close to confronting American police with a divided society. The image of police emerging from well-publicized bonus marches, from literature such as *The Grapes of Wrath,* and from governmental studies such as the 1931 National Commission on Law Observance and Enforcement did not differ substantially from the image that developed in the late sixties. The difference, of course, was that the New Deal and the gradual return of prosperity restored consensus and avoided fundamental crisis for the police, as for many other social institutions. How great the potential was for trouble is illustrated by the often inappropriate reaction of police to the aggressive union organizational drives of the late thirties and the forties.

While disturbances have subsided somewhat in recent months, the broad philosophical chasm that opened up in our society in the late sixties is not likely to be quickly closed. Whatever course society takes on almost any fundamental issue is likely to be vehemently opposed by a substantial minority of citizens for the foreseeable future. This is not to say that political leaders should not attempt to restore consensus where they can, but only to note that the general agreement regarding matters affecting police that once was prevalent will not soon return.

It is only when consensus breaks down and when society becomes concerned with those outside its main current that the proper operations of the police become a difficult question. So long as police departments dealt only with persons universally regarded as evil, and primarily with people generally regarded as unimportant, the function of the police was not a public issue. It is because such persons are no longer so unsympathetically regarded, and moreover, because they have been joined by the more socially advantaged in being caught up in police operations, that the scope and control of those operations has over the past few years become very much a new question in the American context.

Perhaps the best way to begin an examination of such operations is to look at what American municipal police actually do today. Police in many cities today perform myriad, inappropriate, and sometimes arbitrary tasks. For many years the police in New York City manually turned on the street lights. While this is no longer the case, there still are police chauffeuring public officials, operating garbage trucks, licensing bicycles, and collecting taxes. However, the basic police functions can be viewed in four categories.

The first of these is the detection and apprehension of persons committing major violent crimes, such as murder and robbery. This is the classic police role of television and movies and certainly one of the most important. No one contends that it can be done without. However, this aspect of the police function has become a model of how our society balances the rights of the individual against those of society at large. It can be contended with some justice that society's attitudes toward individuals are tested by how it treats accused murderers, rapists, and thugs. These are persons accused of despicable crimes, who on a statistical basis are almost certain to be guilty, who typically come from society's lowest and least influential rungs, and who are likely, viewed as individuals, to be exceptionally unappealing people. If such people are treated with humanity and fairness then the rights of all of us are more secure. Conversely, if such men are dealt with arbitrarily, we may not be able to contain that arbitrariness. Society cannot allow such extreme and uncontroverted criminal acts as murder and robbery. Its entire fabric would be threatened, for the most basic function for which individuals look to government is, after all, physical safety. Thus, a difficult social question is presented. Although it has technical aspects, it is essentially a question of values and therefore ultimately a political one. And, by virtue of the imprecise and continuously shifting nature of the area to which it extends, it is more a problem of public administration than of legal rules, despite all the recent emphasis on Supreme Court actions.

The second function of police today is the solution of a sufficient proportion of crimes against property to deter potential offenders in this category, and thus to limit the cost of such crimes to a level that society can absorb. Many of the civil liberties questions alluded to with regard to violent crimes carry over into this area as well, although often with somewhat diluted force. However, there is here also a second range of problems regarding the allocation of limited available resources, and ultimately there is a question as to what kinds of misconduct regarding property should be deemed to be criminal. It is one thing to say we must allocate the resources to investigate virtually every murder, rape, and serious assault; it is another to contend that we can and should build a criminal justice system capable of detecting every theft and swindle and every

"It is only when consensus breaks down and when society becomes concerned with those outside its main current that the proper operations of the police become a difficult question"

". . . on this practical level, the continuously made decisions regarding what crimes are worth pursuing are far more important than the abstract determination of what theoretically constitutes 'crime'"

padded expense account, and of dealing with each of them as a criminal matter. Simply to state that proposition is to demonstrate its absurdity. We clearly lack resources of this character. We are unwilling to accept the intrusion into our private lives and personal business dealings that would inevitably result from such an approach, and if we were, we would still not be prepared to regard all kinds of wrongdoing affecting property as crimes.

Consequently, those in charge of the criminal process must continually make judgments as to whether certain acts are strictly criminal, whether they are more or less serious, whether they are prosecutable with available resources, and so on. Only one limited part of this process is a police responsibility. The legislatures decide what basic categories of activity can be construed to be criminal, and the courts provide some small measure of specificity to these characterizations. But such formulations cannot be strictly applied. Most of the laws formally defining crimes are far more broad than we really intend. Judging by the face of the statute, evading a transit fare or obtaining an item for free from a malfunctioning vending machine is a criminal act. Thus, as a practical matter, the critical decisions about what conduct is deemed criminal are made by the law enforcement agencies, for the most part by the police. Obviously, on this practical level, the continuously made decisions regarding what crimes are worth pursuing are far more important than the abstract determination of what theoretically constitutes "crime." The Intelligence Division of the Internal Revenue Service, to cite an exceptionally clear-cut example, knows that many taxpayers commit violations of tax laws and regulations that arguably are criminal and that a smaller but still substantial proportion of taxpayers commit clearly criminal offenses. Its policy, as I understand it, is to avoid criminal investigations of uncertain offenses and, among clear-cut crimes, to choose those that involve the greatest amount of revenue for criminal prosecution. However, this basic approach is modified to the extent that where clearly immoral actions (e.g., racketeering, fraud) have resulted in technical violations of the tax laws, these cases are also pursued. Whether or not we concur in the substantive conclusions reached, the Internal Revenue Service is obviously right in setting forth clear-cut and thoughtful policies in determining how law enforcement objectives are to be pursued.

In fact, there have long been inarticulated and frequently unintentional policies in most police departments to the effect that the crimes against property committed by low- and moderate-income individuals are the ones that are to be pursued, and the crimes against property committed by those with more wealth, power, and subtlety are those that are to be disregarded. The police department concentrates on the drug addict burglar and disregards the chiseling landlord, the dishonest attorney who defrauds his client and the insurance company as well, and the contractor who bribes municipal officials to obtain preferential treatment in bidding for government work. To put the matter mildly, this is not an adequate approach to the problems in this area. Yet it is the operative one.

I do not mean to suggest that police have reached this approach principally through class or race prejudice. Police have often resisted extraordinary pressure from the local power structures in this regard. While attitudes are certainly one factor, it is as important that police lack the support to deal with other kinds of property crimes, and often lack the resources. The issues thus created, now slowly emerging into the public eye, are exceptionally complex ones. And as with the handling of major violent crimes, they are value-related and imprecise questions, and therefore necessarily political issues of a kind that can only be resolved through the vehicle of public administration.

The third basic role of the municipal police is the enforcement of prohibitions against consensual crimes such as drug abuse, obscenity, gambling, and prostitution. This is an exceptionally difficult area for the police administrator. Many liberal observers would propose to resolve

"Clearly what he needs is an enlightened sensitivity to shifting societal values as well as a commitment to maintaining fairness and avoiding discrimination"

issues in this area with the sweeping adage, "you can't legislate morality." The issue is not that simple. Laws against murder and theft are also derived from moral conclusions. Indeed, what seems to underpin our notion that an activity should be characterized as a crime is a near universal concurrence that the activity represents a serious moral transgression. In modern society at least, basic to this conclusion is almost invariably a notion of victimization. The victims are obvious in murder and theft situations. But from some perspectives, victimization can be seen also in activities that others would characterize as "victimless." The chronic alcoholic may impose extreme hardship and anguish on his family. The pandering pornographer may cause deep offense to many people. The heroin addict is likely to become dependent upon the public dole. The difficulty of these more subtle theories of victimization is that public acceptance of them is tied to prevailing social values, which may shift relatively quickly. Of course such shifts in attitude may be evident long before legal rules are revised. Police departments were under pressure to harass saloonkeepers long before Prohibition. Adultery remains a criminal offense in most jurisdictions today.

Compounding the difficulty is the fact that changes in the public regard of these matters are confused, gradual, and loudly debated. Surely every police chief would appreciate a reference point from which he could determine whether he should continue operationally to regard adultery, homosexual conduct, and possession of marijuana as appropriate targets for law enforcement. He is hardly likely to do well if he relies on either public opinion polls or the statute books as his guide, for both notoriously lag behind changing attitudes. On the other hand, he can hardly be expected to stop enforcing every law to which someone has an objection. Clearly what he needs is an enlightened sensitivity to shifting societal values as well as a commitment to maintaining fairness and avoiding discrimination. Thus, here as well, we return to theme that the underlying issues are political, that the laws evolved by the legislature and courts are too imprecise a device for resolving them, and again that the necessary vehicle for reflecting political determinations is public administration through the structure of representative officials.

The fourth and final central role of the police is the maintenance of public order. Essentially this includes three separate tasks: controlling and monitoring large-scale public events; enforcing a variety of relatively minor regulatory schemes such as parking prohibitions, street vendor licensing, and juvenile curfews; and controlling the wide variety of actual and potential disruptions that disturb citizens on the streets, in their homes, or elsewhere. Criminal law gives the police coercive authority in these situations and is their ultimate recourse. Yet as every competent policemen recognizes, these are problems far more of human interaction than of true law enforcement. Even the statutes involved recognize implicitly that their sanctions are to be invoked almost wholly at the discretion of the police officer. The following is a typical example:

> *Any person who, by offensive or disorderly conduct, annoys or interferes with any person in any place or with the passengers of any railroad car, ferry boat or other public conveyance, or who disturbs or offends the occupants of such railroad car, ferry boat or public conveyance, by any disorderly conduct, although such conduct may not amount to an assault or battery, shall be fined not more than two hundred dollars or imprisoned not more than six months or both.*

The invidious way in which laws such as this have generally been applied has made them vulnerable on constitutional grounds of vagueness to recent challenges in the federal courts. Nevertheless, while this attempt to seek more exact legal definitions is undoubtedly healthy, much of the law's vagueness is inherent in its function. A police officer, responding to a neighbor's complaint about a drunken husband abusing but not really injuring his drunken wife, must exercise a large measure of judgment in determining what action, if any, should be taken. Indeed, it is desirable to expand the range of services such as counselling and psychiatric treatment that the police can evoke, perhaps even with coercive authority, in such situations.

Inevitably, the police officer working in this context, whether controlling a political demonstration, a boisterous drunk, or a rowdy teenage gang, must in every case endeavor to strike a balance between public

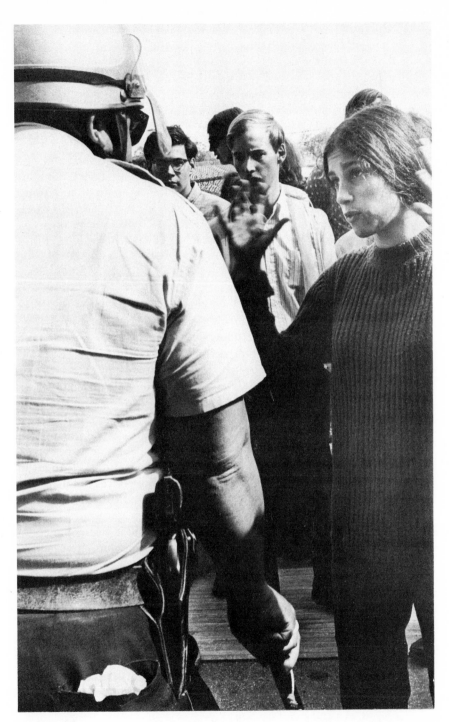

"Yet as every competent policeman recognizes, these are problems far more of human interaction than of true law enforcement"

order and individual freedom. Where the First Amendment guarantees of freedom of speech are involved, he operates in increasingly circumscribed areas, since the law so clearly mandates the preference of individual liberty. But this is a special case, though an exceptionally important one. More typically, a policeman is weighing the right of a group of teenagers to be rambunctious against that of a merchant and his customers to conduct their business without disruption. While this is not a constitutional question, when multiplied hundreds of thousands of times it constitutes, in a very real sense, a determination of how open and how ordered a society we are to have. Since technical legal violations are almost always present in these situations, such a determination becomes a police affair. Again we have the police making what are ultimately important social formulations that can only be arrived at through the exercise of administrative machinery, whatever the political control of the machinery may be.

What emerges then from this survey of the principal police functions is the realization that the truly critical questions posed by the police functions arise from the day-to-day workings of police, and not from the formal legal framework within which those workings are conducted. This is not particularly a new insight, though it is one that has frequently been disregarded in the last decade's preoccupation with Supreme Court decisions and legal definitions. To the extent that attention has been given to institutional questions, proposals have centered on the fancied solutions of community control and external discipline.

The call for community control derives from the realization that large bureaucratic governmental structures become isolated from and insensitive to the people they supposedly serve, as on some of the issues previously outlined in this discussion. The goal is to convey the attitudes of each small community to those in charge of public services for that community by exercising control of such services locally, in the belief that personal interaction and localized politics can keep government policy in line with local wishes. Obviously, this approach is not confined to police work. It is proposed for all governmental functions—from education to garbage collection—now performed on the municipal level.

Whatever its applicability in other areas, community control is not an appropriate approach to law enforcement. Its inevitable impact is to divide communities. While this may be acceptable (though perhaps undesirable) with regard to schools, given the coercive power of criminal law, the divisive impact becomes extreme. If one community within a metropolitan area decided to legalize heroin, or refused to enforce laws against vandalism, or required American flag pins in the lapel of every adult male, the effect would obviously be to fragment and polarize our whole society to an unacceptable degree.

As for external discipline, it ends up as just another form of legalistic control, since punishment can only be meted out for demonstrated

"... the truly critical questions posed by the police functions arise from the day-to-day workings of police, and not from the formal legal framework"

wrongdoing, and wrongdoing must be proved through adversary proceedings very much like those in a courtroom. Consequently, civilian review boards and similar outside disciplinary agencies are not likely to assure that police conduct reflects the political decision-making process.

It seems evident that only when elected public officials, intended as the principal implementers of the collective political judgments of citizens, are in control of the police operation can the police continually reflect public judgment on essential issues affecting their work. When the mayor of a municipality directly and unambiguously oversees the work of the police chief, there is at least the possibility that, through proper administrative procedures, the police department can be made to hold its police to acts that are in accordance with prevailing societal judgment regarding the ordering of society. No system of external checks or regulatory agency is as well suited for this purpose as is reliance on the democratic process.

Yet this solution is, by itself, clearly inadequate. The enforcement of the criminal law in society is so significant in its impact that we cannot permit it to be drastically revised from election to election, as is fiscal policy. The power of police requires that the exercise of administrative control over the police work occur in the framework of ongoing and slowly evolving values, much as the power of the legislature requires a similar framework, in this case the Constitution, to encompass and structure their work.

This framework cannot really be a system of law. The legal rules relating to the police function, while certainly important, cannot provide the needed restraints derived from basic principles of ethics and judgment that are required. Rather, this function must be performed by the concept of police work as a profession. Certainly, police work meets the characteristics of a profession in everything but social and economic status. Police exercise independent judgment regarding the reputations and often the lives of citizens. Police have access to highly confidential information and are charged with responsibility for extraordinary human situations that they are expected to be able to handle on the basis of their particular expertise. Moreover, policemen, unlike most professionals, are placed in a position comparable to that of soldiers concerning the use of deadly force, and may well be thought to come under the Nuremberg principles.

But if police have professional responsibilities, they do not act as a profession. While many of the organized professions in the United States today are not adequately performing their functions, they at least, as police do not, recognize the maintenance of standards within their group as their collective obligation. For example, attorneys who fail to adhere to ethical standards or who are demonstrably incompetent are supposed to incur from their colleagues penalties ranging from informal censure to removal from the profession. The standards operative here are not

"Professional police would be in a position . . . . to condemn police excesses such as the shootings at Orangeburg and Jackson State colleges"

formulated with statutory precision, and rely a great deal on the understanding among professionals of what good legal work or medical work or accounting encompasses. Police must have a comparable sense of obligation to professional ethics, to their colleagues, and to the public if they are to be effective in opposing corruption, in refusing the use of police for narrowly partisan purposes, and in resisting unethical demands upon them. A structure of genuinely professional policemen would be able to identify and formulate policy decisions for the political system, and would enable police to implement those decisions in a manner consistent with fundamental principles. Professional police would be in a position to resist any excesses by political leaders such as the "shoot to kill" orders in the 1968 Chicago riots and to condemn police excesses such as the shootings at Orangeburg and Jackson State colleges.

Within the framework provided both by a true police profession, able to bring to bear moral and expert judgment, and by the law, it would be possible for elected public leaders to determine the policy direction of law enforcement agencies without undermining public safety or individual freedom. Only police of this kind, professional in operation and democratically controlled, can maintain effectiveness and legitimacy in a society no longer bound by general philosophical consensus.

The Problem of Power

Casamayor

Casamayor is the pseudonym of Serge Fuster, a magistrate of the French judicial system in Paris who has gained a reputation as a writer and sociologist. The author of a dozen books, among which have been novels as well as essays, he is best known for his efforts to bring about a reconsideration of the relations of the citizen with the law and the police—relations he regards as full of prejudice and unsuited to modern conditions. For long isolated and opposed in this work, he is today widely recognized, especially by the young French magistrates, who in sympathy with his ideas have for the first time formed a professional association. He has also, as a doctor of law, taught courses in judicial sociology at L'École Pratique des Hautes Études and on civil rights at the University of Vincennes. In addition to his books, he has written numerous articles for the newspaper *Le Monde* and the review *L'Esprit*. A former aviator, he was born in 1911.

History

The history of policing, in the sense of civil measures that have for their purpose the maintenance of order and security in public and private affairs, is part of the history of civilization. That is to say, it can only be understood as a function of the continuous evolution of human societies. Within this evolution we can distinguish three stages, each of which is characterized by a way of looking at the world, of attempting to understand it, of learning to survive in it. Together these stages represent the long human effort to discard illusion, to recognize and come to terms with reality.

The first stage, which we can only imagine since we long ago left it behind, might be called one of "mystical empiricism." Turning the same face to both the earth and the sky, man is confronted with an infinite variety of objects and sensations. He is incapable of judging in advance which of these can harm him and which can be useful to him, which warn and which enlighten him, and which can mislead and which destroy him. Since he cannot make any predictions about the future, he must base his conduct on his immediate reactions. Unfortunately, the results are sometimes astonishing, and he cannot tell whether out of the mélange of his impressions he has acted from experience or superstition—each of which, to be sure, can have its value.

We come to the second stage, in which man exploits all his resources, both those that derive from his knowledge, from what he has learned, and those that derive from his personality, from what he has become. It is in this period that he constructs systems, purely intellectual products that purport to explain the world, but that often have no other purpose than the reassurance of those who contrive them. For curiously enough, it is precisely when man begins to fulfill his potential that he enters what we might call the realm of fear. This fear is more than a sense of danger. Danger can be at the source of fear—although some fears exist without it —but it can never be the full measure of fear. Rather is it that as man becomes aware of his situation and his resources, he becomes afraid of advancing blindly. He invents an artificial light and constructs, alongside

the real universe to which he belongs and in which he struggles, a fictitious, docile universe over which he has well-defined powers. In the course
of time this creative function, encouraged by its discoveries, is developed
further, and man begins to assign more reality to his imaginings than to
his experiences, to emphasize theory more than practice. Operating on
the assumption that his senses are deceiving him, he regulates his conduct
on his ideas. But these too can deceive him. If we take a few floating sticks
for an armada, the fault lies with our brains, not our eyes. Optical illusions exist, but they are not the illusions that lead us astray. That is done
by intellectual illusions, which have brought men now living to an unprecedented level of civilization and at the same time to an unprecedented
degree of cruelty and insecurity.

Emerging from the realm of fear, we come to the third stage—that of a
reality uncluttered with preconceptions. We proceed with less pride and
no longer make choices in advance. We attempt to understand in all its
details the situation that confronts us on earth. As a result, we are no
longer afraid of the unknown. We have somewhat assuaged our desperate
thirst for knowledge, which made us fabricate systems to conceal our ignorance. We realize that it is better to advance on a narrow but solid path
than on a vast avenue where the ground threatens to dissolve at any
moment under our feet. It remains difficult, however, to rid ourselves
of the illusions that have formed part of our beliefs for so long.

In the effort to accomplish this, which is the effort that is being made
and must be made in our time, it is helpful to keep the idea of policing
and the institution of police in mind. For if there is any antidote to illusions, it is the police. They, more than anyone else, must force themselves
to remain on firm ground, to work always with the concrete, to confront
the reality of day-to-day life. It is not by chance that police forces have
been expanding more and more throughout the world, even though the
Utopians could once think that as civilization advanced, the role of the
police would diminish accordingly. Such an expansion is a requirement
of the evolution I have just described, but it can also become a serious
impediment to it, with the gravest consequences, if it is directed to the
wrong ends.

Definition

In order to study the police, we have to extricate from the tangled net-
work of administrative structures and social services those which are
specifically designed to protect the public against crimes committed by
individuals or groups. We will concern ourselves here with only the simplest types of crime, those which public opinion and current usage know
as misdemeanors and felonies and resent as such. Distinctions between

types of crime tend to blur after a little basic research. However, they are practical on the level of the ordinary citizen and his immediate reactions and opinions. In effect, we are talking here about crimes in which the policeman is pitted against the criminal.

Both uniformed and plainclothes policemen are paid to defend society as it is. It is up to the voters to change its form if they so desire; such is the law under a democratic government. Once the decision of the voters has been made, it is the duty of the government to see that it is carried out and the duty of the police to put down any obstacles to this process. However, the police themselves, as voters, have also made a choice. If their choice has been successful, if, in other words, they belong to the majority party, there is no conflict. If however their beliefs put them in the ranks of the opposition, will they, as policemen, devote themselves to enforcing laws to which they, as citizens, are opposed? It is a serious problem, which moralistic statements cannot help solve. The ideal solution is to have all policemen agree to enforce laws which none of them question. Fortunately, this is what happens in most cases. Everyone is agreed that murderers should be arrested, for example, and there is no reason to fear that, with rare exceptions, the police will hesitate to do so. The same applies to stealing, rape, drug abuse, and the like. From this we conclude that governments should not use the police in all kinds of situations but should choose carefully the area in which they are most effective. As this area may change with historical circumstances, it is essential for the government to remain clear-sighted and alert. Let us take a look at what happens in actual practice.

Force

There are aspects of a policeman's job that are peculiar to it—functions of its twofold mission of repression and investigation. We recognize some of these aspects in the simple situation that arises when an offender is caught red-handed. In such cases—a pickpocket rifling the pockets of a passerby, a burglar forcing a door or safe, an angry man hitting another— the policeman's task is a straightforward one. He has simply to be present, and stronger than the offender, in order to intimidate or arrest him. This is his repressive or coercive role, in which he is allowed and even required to use force, if necessary.

Other aspects of repression are not so obvious. In fact the repressive function, even in clear cases, may take different forms and has certain requirements. It demands a sufficient quantity of personnel, but the number required depends on the state of society. If this is calm, few policemen are needed, because there is nothing for them to do, and because in excessive numbers they give an impression of martial law and insecurity that prevents the community from developing to its fullest. Since the police are also a preventive element, however, it is reasonable that they be somewhat more numerous than strictly necessary. They must also have powerful resources: if gangsters are operating out of an armored car, policemen need similar equipment and, consequently, a budget that increases with technical advances.

Unhappily, the size of the police force and the resources it is given are not always determined by such sensible considerations. In actual practice, those who govern tend to cut down or expand the power of the police according as they feel optimistic or pessimistic about social conditions. For their part, policemen tend to demand more men and money than they need. Deals are made as often in government as they are in private business. To insure the success of their demands, police can even at times aggravate the situation vis-à-vis law and order and provoke disturbances. Opposing policies are likely to be followed, one by the corrupt, the other by the uneasy. Those with ties to the criminal world prefer a weak police force, while those who are afraid exaggerate their requirements. But within this basic division a complication can arise in cases where the police force is itself corrupt. Criminals will be the first to want an expanded force if it is their ally. The larger it is, the more they will be in control of the entire society, the freer they will be to commit crimes.

Secrecy

The second, more subtle mission of the police, which is virtually impossible to supervise, is that of investigation. In this, a society takes very great risks. For if it is sometimes dangerous to hand over the use of force to certain people, it is equally dangerous to confide to them the task of gathering information. The greatest danger occurs when the man responsible for obtaining information has force at his disposal as well and realizes that he has more privileges and rights than other citizens and is exempted from normal obligations.

The search for information often leads to secret intelligence and betrayal. No one is ever a police informer with impunity. We can say what we like about the necessity for such work and its danger and make films and novels about those who undertake it, but such spies still are scorned for the very good reason that they cannot operate without treachery, lies, disguises, and deceptions, practices that go against the grain of the most basic and natural need in human relations: trust. Such practices almost inevitably debase those who employ them. Anyone who spends his life inducing others to betray takes a grave risk of becoming accustomed to betrayal, of betraying people himself if he thinks it necessary for his personal security or gain. Indeed, he may succeed in lowering still further the criminal standards by which he justifies his acts. Those who undertake operations that require them to be both dishonest and disloyal, if not also

brutal and vicious, descend below the moral level of most of their criminal victims. Then their relations with the innocent tend also to deteriorate.

People in intelligence are nowadays becoming less and less scrupulous about their choice of means, claiming excuse for what they do by the results they get from doing it or by the general tenor of the times. But dividing lines can easily be crossed and distinctions can quietly disappear. It would once have been unthinkable to use the devices of espionage and military intelligence, such as sophisticated monitoring equipment, except against an international danger. Yet such devices are now regularly used in the domestic area against common criminals who break everyday laws. Among the results are greatly increased opportunities for police corruption—for certain policemen to take advantage of the information they acquire in this way.

Of course, much, perhaps most, secret information about criminals is of a concrete, uncomplicated nature: their identity, domicile, numbers,

"... in excessive numbers they give an impression of martial law and insecurity that prevents the community from developing to its fullest"

plans, and so forth. In order to unearth these details—which he must do—the policeman makes himself invisible, so far as possible, to those he watches. But other, more diffuse information can also exist, offered by those who are motivated by fear or malice, and has the opposite effect, making the figure who is known (or thought) to have received it widely recognized. He becomes like the donkey carrying religious relics in the fable. People prostrated themselves in front of the relics, and the donkey thought it was in front of him. Current research in psychology has shown that he was not totally mistaken. Whether relics or donkey, the spectacle acted as a machine to set genuflections in motion. Through the process of kneeling down, men become used to servitude, and others become used to being served. This is why the expansion of the idea of secret intelligence work is dangerous and why those who live with it are dangerous.

Finally, secret intelligence is antidemocratic by definition, because it cannot be publicly debated. People often joke, and with reason, about state secrets but always stand in awe of the men privy to them. Conspirators and wizards have no place in a healthy society. A policeman who thinks he is either should be removed from his profession.

Protection

There would be no police force if there were no threat to society, but the notion of what is threatening is a very elastic one and depends on how courageous or fearful the men are who decide it. The police are always on the watch: vigilant, available, there. They seek out information about everything and can intervene everywhere. They are a true state within the state. Almost all the branches of government nowadays are tending to become states within states, but most of them still have a long way to go and competitors to deal with along the way. The police, however, have a monopoly and are firmly entrenched. The reality and scope of police work are very different from what its originators foresaw; they believed that the forms of democracy would create a real democracy. Who is going to define the dangers from which the police protect us? We ourselves, the ordinary citizens? And how will this protection be exercised?

In theory, the police are at the service of the law. In France, for example, the magistrates require the police to make inquiries, but when they proceed to act, the police do not wait for an order. They intervene, just as any citizen may, as soon as they spot an infraction of the law. We also recognize their right to make investigations on their own. In so doing we are simply sanctioning an established fact of life—it cannot be otherwise. The police, to be effective, must be everywhere at all times. They follow the nation and the citizen throughout their existence, whatever may occur along the way. They must be unobtrusive when they want information, conspicuous when they need to reassure, strong when they need to protect. Yet is this not too much to ask of them? And does not society, by its very nature, constitute something beyond the capacity of police to control?

Control

In principle, the police protect honest people from criminals. This is their basic function in every country and is the reason the differences between political systems, with their differing ideologies and economic systems, do not translate into significant differences between their police systems. Estimates of policemen may vary, but their position within a country is virtually the same everywhere. Authority has sometimes been used as a barometer: the more authoritarian the political system, some say, the greater the power of the police. But we must be careful how we define authority. If we are talking about imposing the will of one person or a small group of people, we have to say that a dictatorial or even a very centralized regime has more authority than a democratic government. If however we define the authority of a state as the faithfulness with which the will of the nation is transmitted by the structures it has created, we would say that the true authority is that of a democratic government. Those who think that a dictatorship is stronger than a democracy will say that the police in a dictatorial regime are stronger than the police in a democratic government. Those who disagree, those for whom force is not the decisive factor, will say that the police are stronger in a democracy, because instead of deriving their authority from one or a few, they derive it from all.

In the real social and political situation, the police combine a capricious authoritarianism with a measure of reasonable authority. The latter should dominate, but there will always be a struggle between the two. To be effective, as we have said, the police must be strong; but if they are strong, how do we control them? Of course this would not be a problem if the social situation were calm. Then the government would pay its police, the police would arrest the criminals, the law would condemn them, and everybody would be satisfied, sometimes even the criminals, who after having served their term might say: "I sinned, I've paid, I'm quits." But that situation could only occur in a society that was without serious problems, in which there was no movement, where time had stopped. Such societies do not exist. Every real society is the seat of active forces, and these forces exist in the police as well.

Again the problem of force arises. Force alone is not enough. The police operate as much by what they are as by what they do. Suppose that policemen succeed in arresting criminals but are themselves brutal, ignorant, and unchecked? Would they not have an unhealthy influence on the populace as a whole, whom they protect against criminals but to whom they set a bad example? If these policemen in addition enjoy privileges which arouse envy, they may provide the spark for revolt and thus contribute to the destruction of law and order, even though they incapacitate the official enemies of law and order.

On the other hand, policemen who are respected have a wholly positive role. It is sometimes more useful for the police to be well-regarded, to be admired, and if at all possible, to be liked, than to be feared. Law and order will be better protected by the presence of men who have proven themselves to be good men and good citizens than by a gang of masked, helmeted, excitable unknowns. A particularly violent disturbance may require violent methods to put it down, but it is a mistake to confuse the problem of violence, which is only an exaggeration of the problem of force, with the problem of the police. In the case of great social upheaval, the policeman's job will naturally become one of the most important to the government, and the best paid, but can we still call policemen the

"Every real society is the seat of active forces . . ." (Above) Troops were used in Chicago during the 1968 Democratic National Convention. (Below) In 1971, Paris police started a campaign to improve their public image; students responded by protesting a recent police tear-gas attack in which a youth lost an eye. During the protest they managed to paste an advertisement for an outlawed Maoist newspaper onto a policeman's back

men who merely do certain work? Are they not rather mercenaries paid to kill and beat up people?

Revolutions are rare in our times, and the greatest of our criminals are not those given to acts of violence. For this reason, policemen should be well educated as well as muscular. But education always creates a further problem of government. For quite as much as force itself, it allows people to escape from certain kinds of bondage. Then government, no longer assured of blind obedience, must cast about for new means with which to assert and maintain itself.

The government has various devices for maintaining control over the many people and the multifarious situations with which it must deal. Among these devices are some that have to do with specific areas and one that affects the system as a whole. Those used for specific ends are all based on the old adage "divide and rule." Branches of the police are established, and more resources are committed to some of them than to others. For example, men in charge of maintaining order in the street and of making sure that cars can circulate freely during demonstrations will be provided with more material resources than detectives who arrest burglars and murderers. It is extremely important to the authorities that streets not be used by hostile demonstrations. Burglars are less important, except when they are so numerous that public opinion becomes aroused.

Specially qualified or elite corps may also be created within the police force, recruited in such a way that political affiliations or favoritism carry more weight than professional merit. The expression *police parallèle,* or "para-police," is applied to policemen in France who do not entirely belong to the police force, but there can be "para-police" groups within the force as well. Moreover, as I have indicated, in extreme cases when their backs are to the wall, the authorities can recruit men willing to do anything for pay, whom they can supply with uniforms or animal skins—it makes little difference, since they are still hired killers.

The above tactic involves only a sector of the police force and is used only in response to emergencies. However, the authorities also pursue a policy that requires more continuity and attention than the hiring of a few warped and highly paid killers, and that affects the entire society. It involves maintaining the police in what might be called a state of almost total compromise. The same authorities who frequently boast about the purity of their police force are not anxious for it to be too pure, lest they no longer be free to employ it for corrupt ends. Almost all police chiefs, and particularly ministers of the interior, play up to government officials, attack their critics, and feign great indignation when public opinion expresses doubt or hostility about police actions. They appeal to the public's sense of justice, say that it is unfair to think badly of men to whom everyone is indebted for maintaining order and who should be thanked, not criticized. This is simply a pretense, however. Under the camouflage, where the unpleasant truths reside, the government congratulates itself on this state of affairs because it is to its advantage. The proof is the resistance the authorities offer to any efforts that are mounted to free the police and make them more responsive to the country, less so to their chiefs.

A sociologist may receive the impression that the police are caught in a trap from which the only opening leads directly to the authorities. But the example of countries in which the police are strictly subordinate to the government is a dangerous one for other countries in which the police have popular support. In the latter, instead of separating themselves from the people, the police make every necessary effort to enter into the lives of the people, because they are aware of the dangers that their power and the secret nature of their intelligence work entail. Such a police force recognizes that these are disadvantages inherent in its work that must not be concealed but compensated for by greater efforts to be courteous, available, and broadminded. It is this kind of police force that everyday citizens and policemen-as-citizens must build.

Law and order

It is a kind of first principle, which should be clearly stated though it is hardly likely to be controverted, that the police are only good in a good society. But it is equally true that there cannot be a *bad* police in a good society, or a bad society with a good police. The relationship between a government and its police, as with its other structures, is always one of kindred; there cannot be a clash between them that results in victory for the stronger of the two. If such a thing were possible, a powerful and good police force could raise up an evil and weak nation, and a powerful and good nation could keep down an evil and weak police force. Conversely, a strong and evil police force could destroy a good nation.

If we wish to change the police (or society) we must substitute the idea of mixture for the idea of opposition, the idea of influence for the idea of obedience. This conflicts with the traditionalist concept particularly strong in European countries still suffering from the legacy of Roman law, which continue to believe that distinctions are always clear and relations always stable. The gold standard is supposed to be stable, as are fortunes, contracts, and institutions. In France people talk about "frameworks," which contain or delimit a picture, or of "jurisdictions," the surfaces comprised within the frame. People are now beginning to admit that the superficial and flat image conjured up by these ideas should be replaced by the global image of centers of radiating influence, or spheres of activity, which reflects sociological reality far better and which helps to counteract simplistic notions. Unfortunately, too many people still believe that ukases and categorical orders are the answer to all disorders. They still think that it is enough to command and to obey. This is no longer true. And it is dangerous. By trying to remain a century behind the times, they may hasten the catastrophes they attempt to avert.

Up until now, people have thought of the police as a counterweight and have repeatedly and self-righteously called them a "necessary evil." But if the police are an evil, they should be suppressed. An evil is never necessary and must never be tolerated. The truth of the matter is that this mechanistic idea of the counterweight, of an equilibrium, should be considered only as a pedagogical image, a kind of jumping-off point where we can gather our forces in order to go further. The equilibrium of societies is not a static equilibrium, but an equilibrium in motion. Policemen do not embody all that is best in society. Nor are criminals all that stand in the way of its perfection. Every society reckons on a certain amount of criminality and therefore must take certain actions, but it would be facilely reassuring, and therefore disturbing, to believe that society could be made perfect simply by confronting a group of criminals with a group of policemen. Society would probably be no more perfect if it had neither policemen nor criminals.

As matters stand, we have to take society, crime, and the police as the imperfect entities they are. This means that we must go on dealing with each of them as best we can. Perhaps in a different society police would have no gangsters to pursue and would act rather as social workers helping the needy. Policemen in every country would be delighted. But in today's world, the realities are different. In today's world, indeed, everyone is afraid, first, that the police may not be capable of doing their job, which consists of uncovering criminals and turning them over to the courts; second, that the police are diverting to their own exclusive use the resources they monopolize; and third, that the police may fall into the hands of a government that will use them in order to dominate.

What kind of police do we need?

Either a society is tyrannical, and the tyrant has a free hand, or a society is democratic, and everything is theoretically possible for everyone. We can only have the kind of services that are appropriate to our society. In a democratic society, an enslaved, regimented, "robotized" police force would constitute a foreign element. Far from insuring that everything would function, it would jam up the entire mechanism, preventing all movement. Then either it would have to become democratic or the society tyrannical before things could start up again.

Democracies should not deceive themselves and make the mistake of demanding a strong police force, at least as that phrase is usually understood. As I have pointed out above, those who believe that the regimented, absolutely obedient, and, as it were, mechanized police force is the strong one take a risk of becoming the victims of such a force. On the other hand,

"In a democratic society, an enslaved, regimented, 'robotized' police force would constitute a foreign element"

those who consider that "force" means first of all comprehension, intelligence, and education will not be panic-stricken if the police cannot immediately bring criminals to justice. For this is the argument used to discredit the liberal viewpoint: "You can see perfectly well that your police force lets criminals get away. It's inefficient. We're no longer safe." It takes courage to answer that it is better to have a police that is profoundly in tune with the nation, composed of high caliber men fully aware of their role, the needs of their fellow citizens, and the future of their country than a police that is invincible and beats down every obstacle in its path, but is devoid of a political conscience, or even of any conscience at all.

The police have to be a stabilizing element in the country, not a machine to enslave some for the benefit of others, even if the some are criminals and the others are victims. The stabilizing function is more important than the repressive function, but its fulfillment is more difficult for a policeman than for another official. First of all, a policeman has so many routine jobs that require no thought or special knowledge that he ends up doing without either. Also, the seemingly easy aspect of his daily work conceals the importance of the police function. It has long been believed that the police, as a kind of central office for informers, devote themselves to elementary, and, what is worse, degrading activities. And it is true that police personnel were once recruited without much difficulty, since the requirements were not much greater than for a day laborer; any job demanding more skill and discretion fell to a suspect type over whom the police had some hold. Over the years, the police force has often been made up of men having more in common with society's leftovers than with its more successful products.

Nevertheless, we must guard against seizing upon the oversimplistic alternatives that are offered to us. To blindly substitute the trained specialist for the ordinary officer is to forget that both have their virtues as well as their defects. It is dangerous to distinguish between easy tasks and difficult tasks and to believe that humble laborers are incapable of higher thoughts and even less of political action. It has generally been in the latter category that they have revealed their true mettle and have even changed the course of history.

Keeping traffic moving at a busy intersection can require as many talents as writing a report in a government ministry, and is also more dangerous if the air at the intersection is polluted. Finding and arresting a criminal is far more difficult than keeping a government dossier up to date. It is always unfair to set up hierarchies; there are only individual cases. One man is gifted in human relations, another in mathematics. The important thing is not to put one in the place that belongs to the other.

By treating police work as second-rate, we have often prevented it from improving. After the period of "manual laborers" in the police force came that of the "intellectuals," whose main concern has been to separate themselves from their less gifted or less well-educated comrades. They live a sophisticated life, pride themselves on their scientific knowledge. Thus two classes of policemen have emerged, a development with which the authorities are well pleased, for they can use one to put pressure on the other. This may represent an advance from the sociological and political point of view, but it also presents a new danger, as is true each time a class rises above the others. We must move beyond such a stage and make sure that there is first a democracy within the police force so that there may be a genuine police force in the democracy. This is why the police must never be a private matter. There is no police but a public one; it is the prototypical public duty.

Methods of influencing people have become extraordinarily refined of late, and the simplest problems turn out to be full of complications. However, these complications should be known by every police officer, and should not be reserved for certain echelons in the hierarchy. Arresting even a loiterer is no longer a cut-and-dried operation. Whoever performs the arrest does not confine himself to carrying out an order, but has his own ideas on the problem of loitering, and depending on whether the loiterer is young or old, the policeman will follow his own convictions on

"Keeping traffic moving at a busy intersection can require as many talents as writing a report in a government ministry"

the problems of youth and age, jobs and unemployment, retirement and welfare—problems that are aired every day on the radio, on television, and in the newspapers. Similarly, if a policeman is responsible for clearing a street blocked with pedestrians, he will ask himself why they are there: is it a parade, a political campaign, a rights campaign? Like his fellow citizens, he will think about the implications. It is one of the consequences of civilization for which we should be grateful.

A policeman is not an object: he lives and acts continuously. When he is not fighting criminals or uncovering information he does not cease to breathe or think; he calculates the possibility, the form, and the consequences of future conflicts. He trains and develops his strength.

The police have become more and more intelligent, and as they have become aware of the difficulties of the jobs which have devolved upon them, they have also become aware that they are not alone in ensuring law and order. Law and order are no longer their exclusive property. The entire administration of the society is concerned in the maintenance of law and order. Organizing transportation, education, health, or finances is being involved with law and order, with improving it, and therefore with reinforcing it. The ordinary officer or foot-patrolman should be aware of this, and should understand that, far from restricting his own role, such a complex social background gives him the flexibility he needs. Then he will grasp that his role is not confined to his jurisdiction, nor defined by a specific task to be carried out, but is rather measured by the idea formed of his job by whoever accomplishes it. There are very highly placed officials who work with no more imagination than it takes to break up stones for a road. There are also road workers who break up stones realizing that their work is needed by all mankind.

Law, Authority, and the Limits of Law Enforcement in Great Books of the Western World

> *The dread of disturbance and the love of well-being insensibly lead democratic nations to increase the functions of central government as the only power which appears to be intrinsically sufficiently strong, enlightened, and secure to protect them from anarchy. . . . All the particular circumstances which tend to make the state of a democratic community agitated and precarious enhance this general propensity and lead private persons more and more to sacrifice their rights to their tranquillity. . . . The love of public tranquillity becomes . . . an indiscriminate passion, and the members of the community are apt to conceive a most inordinate devotion to order.*
>
> Alexis de Tocqueville, *Democracy in America*

It has been a custom in *The Great Ideas Today* to attach a sort of coda or appendix to its contemporary symposium, which would briefly recall the attention given to the symposium's subject in the tradition represented by the *Great Books of the Western World*. This custom has reflected the editors' conviction that vital address to issues in their current context is aided by a sense of tradition about those issues.

Over the years the relevance of that tradition, as suggested by the appendices, has varied with the different symposium subjects. However, in the editors' judgment the tradition has never failed the kind of test involved in their notion of such an appendix. Thus it is worth noting that, at first glance, the failure in relation to this year's symposium subject appears to be total. No penetrating, enduring, provocative moments on the subject of law enforcement in the Great Conversation are to be found. There is almost literally no mention of the subject, not even in purely descriptive passages.

This fact has to be considered something startling, since the Great Conversation is notably strong on ideas and issues in political philosophy that are proximately regulative for any reflections on the idea of law enforcement. Indeed, discussions of these regulative matters are organized in something like fifteen chapters of the *Syntopicon*—chapters, in varying degrees of proximity to the idea of law enforcement, on Law, Liberty, Justice; on Government, State; on Citizen, Constitution; on Duty, Punishment; on Tyranny, Monarchy, Aristocracy, Oligarchy, Democracy; on Revolution; and on Virtue and Vice.

In the long traditional discussion of the idea of law, which, of course, is directly proximate to this year's symposium subject, basic issues have turned up, but they have never been resolved in such a way as to give dominant direction to historical development. Those issues are decidedly not resolved in the political philosophy and jurisprudence of our time. It seems possible that the state of irresolution that has prevailed as to the nature of law may have contributed in the past to the remarkable inattention in the tradition to the subject of law *enforcement*. The same irresolution may be contributing to current difficulties in reflection about law enforcement, which is widely declared to be in a critical condition.

This appendix proposes to explore those possibilities—briefly, and so, perforce schematically.

A fundamental split in the tradition regarding the very definition of law underlies the question asked by Aquinas in the first of the four articles in the first question of his *Treatise on Law*.[1] Following the canons of Aristotle, who regards a good definition as one that comprehends the four causes of the thing being defined, Aquinas asks about the formal cause of law (what is it?), the efficient cause (who is it that brings it to be?), the material cause (out of what is it constituted?), and the final cause (why was it produced, or what is its purpose?). At the end of these four articles, Aquinas sets down his definition of law: "an ordinance of reason for the common good, made by him who has care of the community, and promulgated." The question in the first article is about the formal cause: whether law is something (in the order) of reason or something (in the order) of will. Aquinas argues that law is something in the order of reason.

A different answer to this question is provided in the first book of Plato's *Republic*, the founding book for Western political philosophy. There, Thrasymachus, in offering a definition of justice as "the interest of the stronger,"[2] places law as something in the order of will. The same result would appear to be accomplished by the fundamental formula of the Roman Empire: "That which pleases the emperor has the force of law."[3] It would be the effect also of this definition by Sir Robert Filmer in his *Patriarcha* (1680): "Law is nothing else but the will of him that hath the power of the supreme father."

Coming forward in the tradition, the theories of law of Kant and Hegel, though they do not have the same view of practical reason that Aquinas does, hold law to be essentially something in the order of reason. But Hobbes gives the other answer: "And first it is manifest that law in general is not counsel, but command; nor a command of any man to any man, but only of him whose command is addressed to one formerly obliged to obey him."[4] And John Austin, writing in 1832, follows Hobbes. His word for the formal cause of law is "command." Laws, he says, "are a species of commands." He explains the term in this way: "If you express or intimate a wish that I shall do or forbear from some act, and if you will visit me with an evil in case I comply not with your wish, the *expression* or *intimation* of your wish is a *command*."[5]

It is not hard to discover variant versions of this opposition that exists as to the essence of law in Shirley Letwin's account of three modern theories of jurisprudence—realism, pure theory, and analytical jurisprudence—that appears in the present volume.[6]

It would be something of interest had the impact of the opposing definitions of law on the organization and character of law enforcement been developed in subsidiary treatises.

There is agreement on both sides that the idea of law somehow includes coercive power for the enforcement of law. But the status of that coercive power is not the same in the two types of theory. Indeed, coercive power is not present as a constitutive note in Aquinas' definition of law quoted above. Rather, it is something like a property deduced from the definition, from the reasonable need toward the end of law that its ordinances be efficacious, and from the likelihood, given the weakness of human nature, that some measure of disordering disobedience will occur. Aquinas would have agreed with Hegel's argument that of course compulsion is bound up with law, but is so, not because force is the primary essence of law, but because it is something belonging to law as a consequence of injustice.[7] Hegel places it according to the order given in this text from Aquinas: "The notion of law contains two things: first, that it is a rule of human acts; secondly, that it has coercive power."[8]

By contrast, the note of coercive power is primary in the other type of definition. To be sure, reason is used to formulate what the interest of the stronger, or the will of the emperor, or the content of a command is. But it is reason in service to the will. The primary thing is that it is a command being formulated, a command in Austin's meaning of the term.

There is a tension between the idea of an ordinance of reason intending obedience because its reasonableness can be seen, and the use of force to compel obedience. There is no such tension between a declaration of what someone who is stronger declares he *wants done* and the use of force to compel obedience. Indeed, Austin is at pains to be explicit on the point.

He writes that *"command, duty* [to obey], and *sanction* are inseparably connected terms: each embraces the same ideas as the others, though each denotes those ideas in a peculiar order." Or again, "each of the three terms *signifies* the same notion; but each *denotes* a different part of that notion and *connotes* the residue."[9]

The two opposed types of definition would seem to have different consequences regarding what would be said about law enforcement. That the enforcement should be steadily efficacious would presumably be a point of agreement. The voluntarist definition would not seem to require any further principles regarding the organization, procedures, and quality of law enforcement. The other type of definition, declaring law essentially an act of reason, would seem to require a carry-through on the note of reason, a concern that the enforcement be conformed to what law is and to the purpose of law, a concern that law enforcement itself be lawful (reasonable), that its processes be rationally articulated and examined.[10] The one type of definition would seem not to require moral concern about the proper forms for the authorized use of coercive power. Questions about that could be posed in amoral, purely technical terms (as they are, for example, in Machiavelli's advice to his prince).[11] The other type of definition would seem to require a moralization of the means of law enforcement.

If such different consequences are indeed implicit, then any society simultaneously influenced by both of the conflicting definitions of law would perforce show some serious confusion about law enforcement.

If we turn to the efficient-cause question about law, which is the second one that Aquinas considers, it similarly appears that unresolved issues characterize the tradition and persist into the present, and that the irresolution can affect reflections about law enforcement.

The efficient-cause question is not just about who makes law, but by what right he does so. Throughout the tradition, the key term for the question has been the term *authority*. The question has been about the source of the authority claimed by those who make law.

This question is not always accepted. Power for rule has been sometimes declared to derive only from the fact of its possession and to be self-authenticating in the results of its use for rule. But such a "might-makes-right" view amounts to a refusal of the question about authority. In modern times, extreme positivist doctrines dismiss that question, holding that the term *authority* is an abstraction that cannot designate anything real.

Among doctrines that accept the question, a basic division can be made between doctrines asserting that, in one way or another, authority is derived from the people who are to be subject to the laws, and doctrines that do not hold it to be so derived. There are many different types of doctrine on both sides of that division. The variety of these doctrines can only be schematically indicated in the brief space here.

Authority has been sometimes held to derive from a source outside the whole body politic, as in the case of the Eastern divine kings or of the early modern absolute kings with a divine hereditary right to rule. In other doctrines, authority is held by prescriptive possession, established by a sort of consuetudinary law or immemorial custom. In still others, the authority is believed to inhere in the rulers because of some qualities relevant to rule with which they are uniquely endowed—superior age, wisdom, virtue, or wealth. Modern variants of the forms of government, as the ancients classified them, have turned up. In Lenin's doctrine of authority, the claim of the communist party to rule rests on its superior capacity to interpret a science of history—the regime, conforming in type, then, to what the ancients meant by aristocracy.

Doctrines that agree that authority for rule comes from the consent of the governed nevertheless have decisive differences about the mode of transmission and the scope or jurisdiction and the modality of the authority that is transmitted. A few examples can show the importance of such differences. The jurisprudents of the Roman Empire, mindful that Rome had once been a republic, rested the authority of the empire on a constitutional fiction that, in Justinian's statement of it, reads this way: "The will of the emperor has the force of law because the people conceded to him and into his hands all its authority [*imperium*] and all its power [*potestas*]."[12] The authority transmitted is total in scope and final in intent. There are no limitations on the powers conceded, and there is to be no sort of dependency on, or accountability to, the people for the exercise of such powers. In Hobbes's version of a social contract, the results are the same. The transmission to an absolute monarch is total in scope, and final.

Doctrines in the *constitutionalist* tradition are alike in differing from those in the family of Justinian and Hobbes. Aquinas' answer to the efficient-cause and authority question reads as follows:

> *A law, properly speaking, regards first and foremost the order to the common good. Now to order anything to the common good belongs either to the whole people, or to someone who is the vicegerent of the whole people. And therefore the making of a law belongs either to the whole people or to a public personage who has care of the whole people, for in all other fields the directing of anything to the end concerns him to whom the end belongs.*[13]

Nothing further is there said about the notion of "vicegerency," though just by itself the term suggests some dependency in the mode of holding the authority transmitted to the vicegerent. But Aquinas was writing in the context of medieval constitutionalism. In that tradition, legal limitations were thought of as constitutionally placed upon the powers of the ruler. If the vicegerent was a constitutional king, he swore in his oath to uphold, and not to violate, certain immemorial rights of the people. His oath placed him under judgment by the people as to his fidelity, even though no institutions existed that could effectively bring him to trial for violation. The authority transmitted is not total in this medieval tradition, and there is a suggestion in Aquinas' undeveloped doctrine that the power that is transmitted is to be exercised in a fiduciary way—a suggestion underlined elsewhere in his reflections on the right to disobey a gravely bad law.[14]

One famous section of Locke's *Second Essay Concerning Civil Government* brings into full view a constitutionalist and social-contract doctrine of authority that clearly states points about the modality of the transmission, the limitations on what is transmitted, and the non-finality of the transmission. The whole section deserves to be quoted:

> *Though in a constituted commonwealth standing upon its own basis and acting according to its own nature—that is, acting for the preservation of the community, there can be but one supreme power, which is the legislative, to which all the rest are and must be subordinate, yet the legislative being only a fiduciary power to act for certain ends, there remains still in the people a supreme power to remove or alter the legislative, when they find the legislative act contrary to the trust reposed in them. For all power given with trust for the attaining an end being limited by that end, whenever that end is manifestly neglected or opposed, the trust must necessarily be forfeited, and the power devolve into the hands of those that gave it, who may place it anew where they shall think best for their safety and security. And thus the community perpetually retains a supreme power of saving themselves from the attempts and designs of anybody, even of their legislators, whenever they shall be so foolish or so wicked as to lay and carry on designs against the liberties and properties of the subject. For no man or society of men having a power to deliver up their preservation, or consequently the means of it, to the absolute will and arbitrary dominion of another, whenever any one shall go about to bring them into such a slavish condition, they will always have a right to preserve what they have not a power to part with, and to rid themselves of those who invade this fundamental, sacred, and unalterable law of self-preservation for which they entered into society. And thus the community may be said in this respect to be always the supreme power, but not as considered under any form of government, because this power of the people can never take place till the government be dissolved.[15]*

Locke, as the apologist for the "glorious revolution," had attacked, in his *First Essay on Civil Government,* Filmer's doctrine about the divine right of kings. In the above passage from his *Second Essay,* he explicitly adds the democratic note to the ancient English constitutionalist tradition. Not only is it to be understood that the authority for government delegated to Parliament is limited to action "for certain ends" and Parliament instructed not "to lay and carry on designs against the liberties and properties of the subject," but further, the authority transmitted is fiduciary in quality and revokable, and "thus the community may be said in this respect to be always the supreme power."

In effect, however, the England that emerged from the revolution was something like a constitutionalist oligarchy, since, because of limitations on the franchise, it was effectively the propertied class, not the people, which stood as "the supreme power."

The American revolution led, though still with some lingering limitations on the franchise, to a democratic-constitutionalist regime, appearing in the explicitly legal mode of a founding constitution. In that constitution, the "people" is explicit about the powers it transmits to government and the powers it "retains"; explicit about laws that can *not* be made and rights that can *not* be violated; explicit about rights retained that ensure political accountability of the government to the governed, rights that ensure concurrent criticism by the people of the performance of government, and rights that ensure electoral replacement of the officers of government; and, further, it at least appears to impart to the judiciary the right to review "the laws of the United States." The authority constitutionally transmitted is thus not only not the whole of that inherently possessed by the people, but further, that which is transmitted is to be held participatively and instrumentally. All subsequent governments would hold authority from the initial constitutional consent of the governed and from the continuing political consent.

As in the case of the differences about the formal cause of law, it would be something of interest had the import for law enforcement of opposing doctrines of authority been developed in subsidiary treatises. A few points can be here made supposititiously about what that import might be seen to be.

There would, of course, be law enforcement in all regimes on both sides of the fundamental question as to whether the source of authority is or is not "the people." But the differences between them might well seem so consequential that the term "police force," as used for agencies in both kinds of regime, would verge toward equivocality.

In all the doctrines that construe authority as coming from a superior being or some superior endowment, the police would be the government's police ("the king's men"), its authorization for the use of coercive power immediately delegated from that government. Whatever the unlikelihood of its actually happening, given historical evidence, such a government *could* confine its use of the police to the enforcement of its well-intentioned particular laws. But, as a consequence of the underlying doctrine about authority, there would be an intrinsic temptation to use the police force "politically," that is, to use it to support the regime itself and to suppress any motions that could bring its claim to authority into doubt. Indeed, since regimes of this kind hold their claim to authority to be sound, why should they not enforce obedience to their governorship as such, as well as to their governance?

The same sort of consequence would seem to follow for the doctrines of total transmission on the other side of the division. If the people have transmitted authority to an emperor or an absolute ruler totally and irrevocably, something like an abdication has taken place. The people have not retained any title to concern or complaint about police activity. The police are again the government's police, and the government may consider itself entitled to use the police *politically* to maintain the regime the people have allegedly brought into being.

Perhaps no separate juridical treatise on the police need or could appear in regimes that construe governmental authority as not being from the people, or as being totally and finally transmitted by the people. In such regimes, the police is not a differentiated body. When the police is the government's police, it is caught up, in an undifferentiated way, in the overall governance and in the whole political process.

Matters would seem to be radically different in the constitutionalist tradition involving legal limitations on the powers of government. The constitutionally placed limitations would extend to the uses of coercive power, only *mediately* delegated by the government to a police force. Certainly, a government would have no authority for using coercive power to bring about something it was denied authority to bring about by law. Further, some of the constitutionally placed limitations could go explicitly substantively to what the police cannot legally do, and to a requirement that a police force be politically neutral.

When the regime was a full-fledged democratic one, in addition to being constitutionalist, the differences would appear more sharply. In such a regime, the people has not abdicated when it makes constitutional arrangements for government. As the standing principal ruler, it electorally authorizes its instrumental governments. A police force authorized to use coercive power has that power principally from the people, and only mediately from its government. It is a people's police. A police force composed of citizen-members of the people is a *civil police*. It would appear unthinkable that an instrumental government would be allowed to use the police "politically" to maintain its power. The people, ruling by its own judgments in the political process, would decide about who maintains governmental power, and would tolerate no use of coercive power that could render those judgments unfree. In a constitutionalist and democratic regime, the police force would be legally limited and politically accountable.

On the first of those two notes—legal limitations—there is, in fact, something like a great book. Its chapters lie in the tradition of the common law. The very nature of that tradition, the way doctrine is developed in that tradition, precluded the appearance of a treatise.

An important incident in this nation's period of gestation involved an appeal to this common law tradition—the famous debate in Boston, in 1761, concerning the issue of writs of assistance to revenue officers, empowering them, *in their discretion,* to search suspected places for smuggled goods. In that debate, James Otis pronounced such writs "the worst instrument of arbitrary power, the most destructive of English liberty and the fundamental principles of law, that ever was found in an English lawbook," since they place "the liberty of every man in the hands of every petty officer." Of that debate, John Adams said: "Then and there was the first scene of the first act of opposition to the arbitrary claims of Great Britain. Then and there the child Independence was born."[16]

Only two years later, in a case involving searches for evidence of seditious libel, Lord Camden pronounced a judgment considered a landmark of English liberty and thereafter something permanent in the unwritten British constitution. His judgment declared "illegal and void a warrant to seize and carry away the party's papers in the case of a seditious libel."[17] There thus never has been any mystery about where the founding fathers found the Fourth Amendment. In an opinion in a 1948 case, Justice Felix Frankfurter echoes Otis and Camden:

> *The security of one's privacy against arbitrary intrusion by the police—which is at the core of the Fourth Amendment—is basic to a free society. . . . The knock at the door, whether by day or by night, as a prelude to a search, without authority of law but solely on the authority of the police, did not need the commentary of recent history to be condemned as inconsistent with the conception of human rights enshrined in the history and the basic constitutional documents of English-speaking peoples.*[18]

The Warren Court acted vigorously in this ancient tradition of protecting individual liberties by placing restraints on the uses of power. In a variety of Fourth, Fifth, and Sixth Amendment cases, its judgments set forth doctrines and rules touching the legal limits of police action.

The Warren Court enlarged the concept of privacy and acted to stiffen the enforcement of the Fourth Amendment's "search and seizure" clause. Undeterred by Justice Benjamin Cardozo's famous "so the criminal is to go free because the constable has blundered," it ordered the judicial exclusion of illegally obtained evidence. In *Gideon* v. *Wainwright* (1963), determining that indigence should not entail inequality before the law, it directly overruled a 1942 decision and held that the Sixth Amendment right to counsel is a fundamental right made obligatory on the states by the Fourteenth Amendment. It proceeded to draw out the implications of that case by extending the right to counsel to pretrial stages—to preliminary hearings, arraignments, and to *in-custody interrogations*. In a variety of cases it placed new restraints on police efforts to obtain confessions, restraints designed to protect the Fifth Amendment right against self-incrimination. Finally, in *Miranda* v. *Arizona* (1966), this line was consummated. Delivering the opinion of the Court, Chief Justice Earl Warren made a preliminary statement of the holding in this way:

> *Our holding will be spelled out with some specificity in the pages which follow but briefly stated it is this: the prosecution may not use statements, whether exculpatory or inculpatory, stemming from custodial interrogation of the defendant unless it demonstrates the use of procedural safeguards effective to secure the privilege against self-incrimination. By custodial interrogation, we mean questioning initiated by law-enforcement officers after a person has been taken into custody or otherwise deprived of his freedom of action in any significant way. As for the procedural safeguards to be employed, unless other fully effective means are devised to inform accused persons of their right of silence and to assure a continuous opportunity to exercise it, the following measures are required: Prior to any questioning, the person must be warned that he has a right to remain silent, that any statement he does make may be used as evidence against him, and that he has a right to the presence of an attorney, either retained or appointed.*[19]

This line of decisions from the Warren Court precipitated what it does not seem excessive to call "a constitutional crisis"—an epiphenomenon of the primary "social crisis," caused by convulsive conflicts about social justice, about the incidence of crime, and about the frightening speed of social change. A quick review of this "constitutional crisis" can serve to indicate what the dimensions would be of a normative treatise on the idea of a civil police in a democratic-constitutionalist regime. The elements involved in the crisis seem to be beyond dispute.

First of all, the minority opinions of the Supreme Court in these cases are an important part of the whole situation. Often in a spirit of near outrage, the dissenting judges protested that the majority, stretching out to protect civil rights, had produced an unbalanced and unnecessary threat to the public and the governmental interest in the value that should be attached to effective law enforcement.[20] Most decidedly of interest are the 1968 side-line opinions of Warren E. Burger, at that time a judge in the United States Court of Appeals in Washington, D.C. In a conference on criminal justice, he stated a challenge, "overstated," he said "to evoke a challenging response" to the proposition that "while our adversary system may be inefficient, it is still the best that could have been devised." He reported his experience that enlightened judges and lawyers in Europe, with as much compassion and concern for human dignity as we have, are baffled by the exclusionary rule in the American system, the rule that excludes evidence from a trial if it has been obtained by a procedure that violates a statute, a regulation, or a basic constitutional right. He said in the conference that the line of Court decisions referred to above involved "a grave mistake in methodology. They have undertaken to rewrite the code of criminal procedure on a case-by-case basis, without evidence of the impact over the broad spectrum of the administration of criminal law. They have confined themselves to the needs of each particular case." His most far-reaching statement in the conference was this:

> *I hope I am making it clear that I do not want simply an efficient system that convicts more people. My settlement point would be the British system, which, though highly adversary, is handled entirely by skilled professionals. But beyond and apart from efficiency, I think the system in some of the northern European countries is more humane. It is fairer across the board than it is in our country. I would suppose that a system of criminal justice ought to be judged by these three questions: Is it fair? Is it humane? Is it efficient? I put efficiency last.*[21]

That statement about the order of concern by the now chief justice of the Supreme Court should prove to be something consequential.

In the public forum, the standing principal ruler—which is to say, the people—has been bitterly, indeed angrily, divided. Those with a standing bias that uncurbed police power is a threat to liberty and justice have endorsed the Warren Court's decisions. Conservatives, not indifferent to traditional liberties, but worried that convulsive conditions of crime and violence would make the rate of social change something unmanageable, have denounced the decisions. They have followed the dissenting judges in predicting serious diminutions in the effectiveness of law enforcement. Fervent radicals consider the agitation about the Court decisions something in the main diversionary, because it obscures attention to the social crisis, but of some use as revealing the impotence of the liberal tradition to alter the historical direction of police harassment and violence—from the propertied to the poor, from the white to the other-colored—and useful as revealing the stake established interests have in the police as the enforcers of the status quo.

From the police, the reaction has generally been one of outrage that they should be hampered in their efforts toward effective law enforcement at a time when they take the principal ruler of the nation to be crying out for it as something unusually needed now. With that sentiment, the police have to a degree flirted with the notion of organizing as an interest group in the political order, to press police views on the public and on political parties taking particular views about police affairs.

A traditional phrase, "law and order," was badly battered on both sides of a presidential campaign, which to a degree pivoted on the promise of a new attorney general and a new Supreme Court. The Congress, by overwhelming votes in both houses, passed three comprehensive pieces of crime control legislation. The legislation included arrangements for police entrances without knocking; arrangements for limits on the immunity given to witnesses compelled to testify; authorizations for the use of illegally obtained evidence after five years have passed; provisions for "preventive detention" of defendants with a record of "past conduct" alleged to be "dangerous"; and authorizations for wire-tapping and electronic surveillance. No one claims that this legislation does not entail a reduction in civil liberties. And it seems to a degree probable that if crime does not get more efficiently controlled with the help of this legislation, the search for efficiency at the expense of civil rights will be intensified—in the public forum and in all branches of government, including, perhaps, the new Supreme Court.

From this review, then, it would appear that all parties in the polity are deeply involved in the constitutional crisis about "law and order" and "support your local police."

In all this turmoil, it should be remembered that the issue about the nature of law, with which this note began, has not been firmly resolved in the history of this nation, and is not resolved in extant theories of jurisprudence and political science. Is a "sovereign people" a new kind of absolute ruler, getting the laws it wants as expressions of its majority *will*? Can the majority will rightly get whatsoever it wants, because whatever pleases it has the force of law? Or, does a sovereign people subject itself to the rule of reason, bind itself to want only laws that are right, laws in decent conformity to natural rights? Did it so bind itself when it declared its best sense of those rights in the constitution that founded the nation?

There can be no question that the majority will of the people could in fact prevail—could in fact prevail as regards the law enforcement it wants and the price it would be willing to pay in a search for total efficiency.

In convulsive times, a people, even though it had lived its life in the constitutionalist tradition, could turn away from the commitment to reason implicit in that tradition. The prediction of Tocqueville at the head of this note has a chilling plausibility.

1 *Summa Theologica* I–II, Qu. 90; *GBWW*, Vol. 20, pp. 205–8.

2 *GBWW*, Vol. 7, p. 301.

3 Justinian *Institutes* 1. 2. 6.

4 *Leviathan*, bk. 2, chap. 26; *GBWW*, Vol. 23, p. 130.

5 *The Province of Jurisprudence Determined* (New York: Noonday Press, 1954), pp. 13–14.

6 *See* pp. 104–53.

7 *The Philosophy of Right*, pt. 1, sec. 94; *GBWW*, Vol. 46, p. 36.

8 *Summa Theologica* I–II, Qu. 96, art. 5; *GBWW*, Vol. 20, p. 234.

9 *Province of Jurisprudence*, pp. 17–18.

10 *See* Kenneth Culp Davis, *Discretionary Justice* (Baton Rouge: Louisiana State University Press, 1969), pp. 80–96.

11 *The Prince; GBWW*, Vol. 23, pp. 3–37.

12 *Institutes* 1. 2. 6.

13 *Summa Theologica* I–II, Qu. 90, art. 3; *GBWW*, Vol. 20, p. 207.

14 Ibid., Qu. 96, art. 4; *GBWW*, Vol. 20, p. 233.

15 *GBWW*, Vol. 35, p. 59.

16 Quoted in the decision in *Boyd* v. *United States* (1886), in Paul A. Freund et al., eds., *Constitutional Law* (Boston: Little, Brown & Co., 1961), p. 1156.

17 Ibid., p. 1158.

18 Ibid., p. 1168; from the decision in *Wolf* v. *Colorado* (1949).

19 Quoted in William B. Lockhart, Yale Kamisar, and Jesse H. Choper, *Constitutional Law* (St. Paul, Minn.: West, 1967), p. 672.

20 Cf. Justice John Harlan in his dissent in the Miranda case: "I believe the decision of the Court represents a poor constitutional law and entails harmful consequences for the country at large. . . . The Court's opinion in my view reveals no adequate basis for extending the Fifth Amendment's privilege against self-incrimination to the police station. . . . What the Court largely ignores is that its rules impair, if they will not eventually serve wholly to frustrate, an instrument of law enforcement that has long and quite reasonably been thought worth the price paid for it. . . . Society has always paid a stiff price for law and order, and peaceful interrogation is not one of the dark moments of the law."

21 Report on the Conference on Criminal Justice held at the Center for the Study of Democratic Institutions, Santa Barbara, Calif., in *The Center Magazine*, November 1968, pp. 69–77.

PART TWO

The Contemporary Status of Three Great Ideas

Modern Philosophies
of Law

Shirley Robin Letwin

Shirley Robin Letwin, who took her M.A. and Ph.D. in the Committee on
Social Thought at the University of Chicago, has taught at Chicago, Cornell,
Brandeis, Harvard, and the London School of Economics, and has been
a fellow of the Radcliffe Institute. She has published *The Pursuit of Certainty:
Hume, Bentham, J. S. Mill, and Beatrice Webb* (1965), *Human Freedom:
Topics and Texts* (1952), and essays and reviews in *Review of Politics,
Cambridge Journal, Encounter, Government and Opposition,* and most recently
in *The Human World* and *The Spectator. The Dictionary of the History of
Ideas* will shortly be publishing her monograph on the history of the idea of
certainty since the seventeenth century. She now lives in London, is working
on philosophy of law, and is preparing a book on Victorian morality and
Anthony Trollope. She is married to William Letwin, whose essay, "Social
Science and Practical Problems," appeared in *The Great Ideas Today,* 1970.

Contents

I   Some basic questions about law   105

II The foundations of modern jurisprudence   106
    1. Natural law and its critics   106
    2. Kant   109
    3. Bentham   112
    4. Savigny   115

III Positivist theories of law   117
    1. Realism   117
    2. The pure theory of law   130
    3. Analytical jurisprudence   136

IV Authority, constitutional justice, and substantive justice   142

I Some basic questions about law

Modern legal philosophy rests on the premise that law is nothing but a human artifact. It has rejected the view that prevailed before the seventeenth century, in which the lawmaker appeared to be an under-craftsman of the Supreme Architect, who had provided an eternal blue-print for the universe and disclosed it to man through reason or revelation. Legal philosophy has been left with two alternatives: to discover within the world of human artifacts another sort of objective standard for laws, or to renounce the need for any standard to distinguish lawful coercion from brute force. The exploration of these possibilities constitutes modern jurisprudence.

All jurists agree that laws are regulations made by the ruler, that laws should establish peace and order in social life, and that laws are to be obeyed by the ruled. The differences among jurists refer to the following questions:

How is the ruler to be recognized? Is anybody who commands force sufficient to impose his will on the community an authentic ruler, or must the ruler satisfy certain requirements, possess certain qualifications, be installed according to certain procedures? What must he do in order to cease being a legitimate ruler?

How are the laws made? Can they be, and should they be, deduced from general principles, as the conclusion of a geometrical proof is deduced from axioms? If so, how are these principles discovered? Are they true necessarily? Or are laws arrived at by some other form of reasoning? Or are they rather to be understood as acts of will, which may be determined by the unreasoned preferences of the ruler?

How do the ruled recognize whether a regulation is a law? Is it enough that the regulation has been declared a law by the ruler and published in the appropriate form? Must a law have been made by previously accepted procedures? Must it meet other criteria of form, such as that it be a general rule rather than a specific order, or that it apply only to future actions of the ruled; or of content, such as that it must be just?

How are different laws related to one another and to decisions based on them? Must the laws of a given legal order form a logical system deducible from a set of basic principles? Or may they be coherent and consistent in some other manner? If consistency is essential to law, how is it possible to change any law; how can any one law be changed without changing all or many other laws as well? Does consistency in the law imply that no two judges can give different decisions for the same case? What makes a decision coherent or consistent with preceding ones?

What do laws tell the ruled? Do they issue orders: "You must do this"? Or do they inform the ruled of considerations or consequences that must be taken into account: "If you do this the following consequences will ensue"? Or do they regulate social behavior in some other fashion altogether?

How can a law be known to be a good law? Is any law whatsoever desirable simply because the ruler has declared it to be law? Are there any other criteria by which the goodness of a law may be discerned? Are they criteria of morality, justice, or expediency? Are they accessible to rational inquiry, in whole or in part? Are they certain and universal or rationally justified in some other fashion?

Why should laws be obeyed? Must every pronouncement that can be identified as a law be obeyed, or only some of them? Are the appropriate reasons for obeying the fear of punishment, the subject's agreement that the law is desirable, or his readiness on quite different grounds to follow rules with which he does not agree?

The various theories of jurisprudence assign these questions different priorities and relationships—by ignoring some or dismissing them as irrelevant, or by making one or a few the foundation for the rest.

II The foundations of modern jurisprudence

1. Natural law and its critics

The traditional doctrine of natural law contains answers to all these questions, even though it fails to distinguish some of them. In the most complete account of natural law doctrine, that of Aquinas, there is a clear order of descent from divine law to natural and positive law. Natural law, Aquinas tells us, is "nothing else than the rational creature's participation of the eternal law"[1] and "every human law has just so much of the character of law as it is derived from the law of nature. But if in any point it differs from the law of nature, it is no longer a law but a corruption of law."[2] This left room for dispute over the justice of a law, for it is not true, as some modern writers have claimed, that those who believed in natural law supposed they could deduce from it "a divinely certain system of law" in which "all doubt disappeared and man bowed to the infallible decision."[3] Positive law was understood to be a "determination of," not a deduction from, divine law. The human lawmaker was understood to work not as a geometrician but as a craftsman, who "needs to determine the common form of a house to the shape of this or that house." Thus, though exponents of natural law believed that one of its principles dictates "that the evil-doer should be punished," they did not believe that anybody could *deduce* from this principle the punishment that fits any crime; appropriate punishment could only be "determined," and different degrees and kinds of punishment could be equally just. In general, Aquinas held, it is impossible "to give the reason for all the legal enactments of the lawgivers"[4] because these are decided by prudential not demonstrative reasoning. Therefore even when a positive law is accepted as just, it cannot be shown to be necessarily just or to exclude all other alternatives, which a deduction from universal principles would do. This is what Aquinas meant by saying that positive law is a "determination of" natural law.

Nevertheless the subordination of positive law to a given nonhuman superior order implies that the human makers of legal artifacts cannot claim to be the sole judges of their products. They are obliged to ask: Does this artifact conform to the "natural" standard? There may be difficulties about understanding precisely what "conform" means, whether the artifact is supposed to be an emanation of the model, an embodiment, or a further specification. The question, whether a particular human law agrees with natural law, cannot therefore in Aquinas' view be answered with demonstrative certainty.

But because a ruler who sets out to make a law is an actor within a cosmic order, to whose rules he is subject as all men are, the fundamental question to be asked about any regulation made by man is whether it satisfies a universal standard, which men do not make but can discover. All other questions about human law are, in the view of Aquinas, subordinate to that one.

In a Christian society given to deference and to keeping traditional ways of understanding and behaving, it was relatively easy to agree on what conformity to natural law required. But when the sanctity and hence the authority of the king was called into question and when consensus about moral and social questions became less clear in the modern secular state, the gap between natural law and positive law became more impressive. Indeed, to men who had no belief in a rational cosmic order and who were acutely aware of the diversity in positive laws, appeals to a natural law appeared to be intrusions of arbitrary decisions, conjuring up awesome but meaningless mystical phrases to justify usurped powers.

Nevertheless the belief that human law is not wholly self-sufficient continued to be reflected in the theories of jurists and the decisions of judges throughout the nineteenth century, and has still not wholly disappeared from the courts. There has, moreover, grown up a school of natural lawyers, especially in the United States and also in France, who have concerned themselves with reformulating the doctrine of natural law independently of a theological context or foundation. It has been proposed that natural "law" be replaced by natural "principles of law" that can be recognized as universally acceptable and so can provide a standard of justice for all laws, without requiring that they all be uniform.[5] Like their ancient and medieval predecessors, modern natural lawyers are chiefly concerned with the relation between justice and law, and they assert that law must be understood in terms of both reason and will, of both nature and convention.

What is known as positivist jurisprudence begins from a different concern than that underlying the natural law tradition. The latter answers the questions that can be raised about law by asking first how a law can be known to be good; the positivist tradition starts by asking how a law can be recognized at all. The first and still the classic formulation of the positivist tradition was by Hobbes, who declared that the fundamental question about a law was whether it had been made by someone duly authorized. The justice of a law, he concluded, depended on the authority of the lawmaker; if that authority were granted, the command of the lawmaker was necessarily not might but right.

As the extensive literature on Hobbes testifies, Hobbes himself did not keep strictly to this argument. He spoke also of equity as a quality that law ought to have and gave the subjects of a duly authorized sovereign leave to renounce the sovereign's authority if he failed to keep peace and order. But none of these qualifications detract from Hobbes's insistence that though the sovereign might make better and worse laws and be answerable to God in the hereafter, for his subjects—concerned above all with escaping from the war of each against each—the sole reason for obeying a rule was that the sovereign had made it. The justice of a law is derived from its source, that is, its authority.[6] Because arguments based on natural law asserted that a positive law that conflicts with natural law is not truly a law and gave rise, Hobbes believed, to division, dissent, and civil war, he opposed the doctrine of natural law as the source of a basic and dangerous confusion about what constitutes law.

Positivist jurists have accepted Hobbes's diagnosis of the confusion in natural law without wanting to accept his remedy. The alternatives they have proposed have been built on foundations laid principally by Kant, Bentham, and Savigny, and can be divided into three main varieties: the pure theory of law, analytical jurisprudence, and realism.

Though in different degrees and manners, all of these, unlike natural law theory, imply that law is to be understood exclusively as a matter either of reason or of will, either of necessity or of contingency.

2. Kant

The radical alternative to natural law suggested by Immanuel Kant has the deceptive appearance of being closest to it. Because he derived the obligatory character of law wholly from reason, Kant is regularly classified as a believer in natural law. But in fact the relation between law and reason on Kant's view is nothing like that described by Aquinas, for Kant understood something very different by reason.

As Kant described it, reason is a faculty wholly independent of sensation. Its activity consists in disclosing the system of laws underlying empirical phenomena. But these laws are not discovered in a reality external to reason. They constitute the structure of reason, whereby reason imposes order on the flux of sensation and so makes it possible for experience to become an object of understanding. Knowing, according to Kant, means therefore becoming aware of what is inherent in reason, or, in other words, the subject of knowledge is the a priori structure that reason gives to experience. Knowledge then necessarily takes the same form as this structure. As Kant believed the structure of reason to be that of a logical system derived deductively from universal principles, it follows that where no such system has been disclosed there is no knowledge.

What reason prescribes as the foundation for all morals and justice is the categorical imperative: "Act according to a maxim which can be adopted at the same time as a universal law."[7] This means that a moral action must be derived from a principle that is valid for all men at all times and in all places. It follows that "every action is *right* which in itself, or in the maxim on which it proceeds, is such that it can coexist along with the freedom of the will of each and all in action, according to a universal law."[8] The universal law of right, which is concerned with the external behavior of men rather than their motives, follows directly from the moral law and constitutes the fundamental principle of jurisprudence: "Act externally in such a manner that the free exercise of thy will may be able to coexist with the freedom of all others, according to a universal law."[9] That is to say, every human being is a person of unique value, never to be treated as a thing or used by another.

On the basis of this principle, Kant defined a "juridical state" as an association of beings none of whom is subordinated to any purpose other than what he makes his own: "The juridical state is that relation of men to one another which contains the conditions under which it is alone possible for every one to obtain the right that is his due."[10] In such an association no one is a subordinate and all are "co-ordinated" and "mutually equal, in so far as they stand under common laws." This emphasis on the equality of all men under law has given Kant the venerable status of inventor of the idea of the *Rechtstaat,* a state under the rule of law. Philosophers and jurists have accordingly paid homage to Kant for formulating the essence of justice in a manner acceptable to men who had renounced metaphysical knowledge of the Aristotelian kind.

What has received less attention, though it has had a greater influence on modern jurisprudence, is the manner in which Kant used his universal principle of right. For Kant's conception of reason led him to suppose that just as he could derive Newton's laws of physics from the a priori principles of pure reason, so he could derive all the principles of law from his a priori principle of right. He thought of both the fundamental law of right and the subordinate concepts of law as perfectly analogous to the laws of physics because he believed reason has furnished the understanding with "intuitive presentations *a priori*" on which both geometry and the science of right are based.

Just as geometry can unequivocally define a straight line, so can the science of right determine "what every one shall have as his *own* with mathematical exactness."[11] Kant accordingly proceeded to "unfold analytically" a system of fundamental legal conceptions that descend so far into the realm of the particular as to declare that sexual relations with a member of the opposite sex necessarily must be sanctioned by a marriage contract—"If a man and a woman have the will to enter on reciprocal enjoyment in accordance with their sexual nature, they *must* necessarily marry each other; and this necessity is in accordance with the juridical laws of pure reason."[12]

No law, according to Kant, can be right merely by convention. The whole legal system constitutes a rational unity, by which Kant meant a logical unity. All the rules he deduces are, Kant affirmed, "to be regarded as necessary *a priori*—that is, as following of themselves from the conceptions of external right generally—and not as merely established by statute."[13] Even the relations of the different branches of government can and must be determined by demonstrative reasoning. In short, the purpose of Kant's *Science of Right* was to eliminate and to deny the propriety of any element of contingency in the law.

Because the content of the law can be known by reason even in the natural state there is no need to give anyone authority to determine what the law should be. Neither need the law stand on authority in order to require obedience. What reason dictates is intrinsically obligatory. As the rationality of law is based on universally valid laws and wholly uncontaminated by any individual act of will, to recognize law as rational is to recognize an obligation to obey it. The purpose of civil society according to Kant is not then to provide for the determination of positive laws from rational principles, as Aquinas believed, or to give a sovereign authority to make rules, as Hobbes says, but merely to establish compulsion for enforcing the laws made by reason.

Though by removing contingency from law Kant made law inseparable from justice, his manner of doing so inspired his disciples to sever law from justice. From Kant's conclusion that law can only be deduced from a priori principles of reason and right and that law necessarily has the only valid logical form of any rational system, Kant's juristic disciples drew the implication that there is no need to be concerned with the justice of law if one discovers a logical structure in it. For this, by insuring its rationality, at the same time insures its justice. The law can then be understood as a self-sufficient logical system, and the jurist's only concern is with the question: How are laws related to one another? The answer would disclose the systematic structure that constitutes law.

In quite another fashion the conclusion that justice is irrelevant to law appeared to be supported by Kant's equation of knowledge with propositions that have universal validity, coupled with his insistence on the autonomy and sanctity of the individual person. To those impressed with the latter, any denial of worth to what an individual values would seem to violate his autonomy. If then men cherish diverse conceptions of what constitutes justice, this diversity must be respected. But as rational knowledge consists only in universally valid propositions, the variety of values to be found in the human world could not belong to the realm of knowledge. So Kant's disciples came to divide the world between "facts" and "values," the former constituting knowledge, the latter irrational preferences. From this it followed for them that as there is disagreement about what constitutes justice, it must lie outside the world of reason.

Kant thus suffered the ironic fate of becoming the patron saint of those who deny that there are rational standards for judging the law. They concluded, as Gustav Radbruch—a twentieth-century disciple of Kant— put it (but came to qualify after World War II), that the only valid approach to law is "methodological dualism," which recognizes two wholly different spheres of action. To preserve its objectivity, law has to be kept free from contamination by "values." And anyone who refuses to consider law apart from values is obliged to deny that rationality and objectivity belong to law. By isolating one of these diverse implications of Kant's philosophy and building a theory of law on it, German jurists have produced many varieties of Kantian jurisprudence, all of which refuse, however, to see law as a blend of rationality with contingency.

The influence of Kant on recent legal philosophy came by way of Rudolf Stammler, who led a neo-Kantian revival in jurisprudence toward the end of the nineteenth century.[14] He disavowed Kant's attempts to present "specific detailed propositions of absolute validity" as inconsistent with Kant's own understanding of philosophy. What was needed, he said, was a critical theory of law such as Kant should have written. This theory would be distinguished by its attempt to differentiate between the form and matter of law, a purely analytic distinction designed to disengage the eternal and rational in law from what is contingent and irrational. The new critical jurisprudence proposed to understand law by discovering the hierarchy of forms headed by the "pure forms" that constitute the idea of law, just as the ideas of cause, space, and time constitute the idea of nature. This means that although law is a human artifact, it is made not by reasoning about how to achieve certain human objectives, as Hobbes described it, but by the structure of man's reason. It remained for Hans Kelsen to draw out the extreme implications of this understanding of law.

3. Bentham

An understanding of law that appears to be much further from natural law than Kant's was proposed by Jeremy Bentham. But though Bentham regularly expressed contempt for natural law, he was more disposed than Kant to allow for both reason and contingency in law, in the manner of theories of natural law.

Bentham accepted Hobbes's identification of law—a law is what a sovereign commands. He also agreed that whatever the legislative authority commands, however undesirable it might be, continued to be law until it is repealed by that authority. But Bentham insisted besides that there should be a criterion for what a good law is. Refusing to subordinate justice to authority as Hobbes had, Bentham wanted to convert the exercise of authority into acts that could be justified and assessed by objectively conclusive arguments. While natural law offered no such criterion, according to Bentham, providing only a disguise for despotism by allowing anyone to claim the sanctity of a natural standard for his opinion, the principle of utility constituted a truly objective criterion for assessing the law.

The principle of utility assumes that men are bundles of desires, for which they seek satisfactions which, when obtained, yield pleasure, and when denied, produce pain. Pleasures and pains are, Bentham believed, reducible to sensations and are therefore concrete empirical realities, not metaphysical fantasies such as the theory of natural law conjured up. Moreover, these pleasures and pains can be measured and compared according to a "calculus" that Bentham constructed, thereby providing the legislator with an exact criterion for judging the consequences of a law. Above all, while the principle of utility offers a guide for choosing among alternatives, it imposes nothing on anyone, for it permits every man to balance his pleasures and pains as he experiences them, without directing him to seek or forego anything. To impose one man's will or tastes on others constituted injustice for Bentham.

The legislator who guided himself by the principle of utility would be in no danger of imposing his views of how best to live on anyone else. If he took into account all the pleasures and pains of all the members of the community impartially, no person or group interest would be favored above any other. The greatest happiness would be achieved for the greatest possible number. Justice would be secured because the only just concern on Bentham's view is the greatest happiness regardless of the effects on any particular interest or set of interests.

That the certainty and justice of Bentham's calculus was a delusion has by now been pointed out repeatedly. Apart from its failure to provide any moral criterion for how to order our desires, it does not tell us how to decide between people who are more and less sensitive to pain. As an event only mildly upsetting to some causes others extreme distress, we are left with the question—should the less disciplined and self-indulgent members of the community be rewarded more than those who are better able to bear pain? Nor does utility tell us how to decide between maximizing pleasure and minimizing pain. It says nothing about the difficulty of judging whether what people report of their pleasures is correct, whether a man knows himself well enough to judge, whether he may not be willfully deceiving us. If, on the other hand, we take the expression of wants at their face value, as Bentham probably intended, we are left with a society in which the most strident voices always win out. Bentham's magic formula then turns out to justify government by competition among pressure groups where success depends on the capacity to frighten others into yielding to one's demands, which is in effect rule by force covered by the euphemism *pressure*. Nevertheless, the identification of justice with impartiality as to competing interests has remained a more or less explicit assumption of analytical jurisprudence.

But in addition, Bentham also equated justice with certainty in the law. The requirement that there ought to be no doubt about what the law is, was given a new importance by Bentham. His arguments on this point were directed at what he considered an outrageous contemporary abuse, "judge-made law," by which he generally meant decisions based on common law. Whereas Hobbes had insisted that in order to make the right decisions judges must have great latitude in interpreting the law, Bentham saw in such latitude the destruction of rule by law, which requires perfectly clear and fixed rules. Certainty in the law meant, according to Bentham, a law that could be pointed to and would yield unequivocal decisions. A series of judicial opinions stretching back several hundreds of years provided no such object. Only a statute passed by a legislative body at a particular time and place and duly inscribed in a book of laws constituted a genuine law. If all the laws of a country were to be clearly visible in this way, they had to be part of a strictly organized code of laws deduced from a single ruling principle. Bentham therefore suggested that certainty in the law could not be had without codification.

If codification were done in a perfectly rational fashion, it would dispense with any reference to the past; indeed a good code is obliged to free itself of the burden of history. The principle of utility provided a basis for such rational codification. Once the code was available, a father could produce a verdict simply by referring to the code book. Bentham thus broke with the tradition that distinguished between analogical reasoning, which cannot produce necessarily true conclusions but is appropriate in applying law to particular cases, and demonstrative reasoning, which can produce certainty but cannot be used in applying law to cases. Bentham, on the contrary, suggested that unless the judgment on any particular case is unambiguously specified by the law the judgment would be incurably arbitrary.

At the same time, Bentham's attempt to discover unambiguous criteria for supporting or favoring a law led him to make coercion central to the concept of law. If every law had to be identified in terms of pleasures and pains, it followed that every law had a detrimental effect on someone, either by authorizing the inflicting of pain directly or indirectly by granting someone pleasures that thereby became inaccessible to others, as in bestowing privileges and honors. In this respect Bentham admitted an element of contingency in the law. For though a law might satisfy his formula for resolving conflicts among men, it could not prevent those conflicts from occurring. Laws could not then be universally desirable, because they necessarily inflict more pain on some than on others. For Bentham this analysis had the virtue of underscoring the drawbacks of every act by government. For his successors, it identified law as necessarily a threat of coercion and denied that some laws may have a different purpose, to regulate voluntary private activities.[15]

All these suggestions became the central themes in the jurisprudence of Bentham's disciple John Austin, who in 1826 became the first professor of jurisprudence in the University of London. Whereas Bentham began from Hobbes's definition of law as the command of the sovereign and ended by proposing the principle of utility as a rational ground for the obligation to obey the law, Austin never gave the principle of utility such prominence. He restored the emphasis placed by Hobbes on the source of law, but without Hobbes's painstaking account of the authorization of a sovereign. Whereas Bentham recognized that the impartiality of the law is morally desirable, Austin took this impartiality to indicate the amorality of law. Law then became quite simply a command backed by force.

Austin also gave more importance to the mode of analyzing the law employed by Bentham—in terms of acts, circumstances, subjects, objects, extent, duration, that is, in terms of entities that supposedly could be clearly identified. From Bentham's insistence that mandates, decrees, orders, edicts, and regulations are all laws because anything commanded by the sovereign is law, Austin arrived at a definition of law as a command that ignored any distinction between a general rule stipulating conditions to be met and an order to perform a particular act. In addition, Austin opposed Bentham's insistence on the importance of separating judging from legislating.

Nothing was left then of Bentham's conception of the connection between a legal system and the freedom it was meant to serve. Instead, Austin gave the central place to a logical distinction between the law as it "is" and the law as it "ought" to be. This, combined with his emphasis on analyzing the law as it is, made it the task of the jurist to discover within legal institutions and practice a formal pattern of the law uncontaminated by any considerations of why a legal system is desirable, or of the goodness or badness of laws, and this came to be known as analytical jurisprudence.

4. Savigny

An altogether different theme in modern jurisprudence was suggested by Friedrich Karl von Savigny, the founder of the so-called historical school of jurisprudence. He opposed the disposition to liken law to a system of mathematics that can be deduced from axioms, an analogy that appealed to those who saw in codification the universal remedy for all defects in a legal system. The character of law is rather, Savigny argued, like that of a language, about which rules can be formulated but whose complexity can never be fully expressed by such rules.

Against the codifiers who believed that there were abstract principles from which law could be deduced, Savigny insisted that law can only be understood as a development over time. This does not mean that Savigny substituted principles drawn from history for principles drawn from reason. Although he advised his contemporaries to acquaint themselves with Roman law, it was not in order to discover the essential principles of law but to become familiar with the texture of a peculiarly rich and orderly legal system.

Because Savigny rejected the entire notion of an essence of law consisting of abstract principles, he understood the development of law in a manner totally different also from that of Hegel. For Hegel, law was the concrete embodiment of reason in history, and progress meant the increasing incorporation of reason in concrete human institutions. Hegel therefore contrasted the rationality, objectivity, and permanence of the law to the irrationality, subjectivity, and contingency of individual acts of will.[16] Although Hegel had no use for attempts such as Kant's to deduce law from formal universal principles, he saw in codification an advanced effort to give reason objective embodiment, and condemned Savigny's views as an insult both to the nation and to the legal profession.[17]

But if Savigny did not regard law as an embodiment of reason or deduction from reason, he neither denied its rationality nor opposed changing the law. He even praised some attempts at codification. His arguments were directed against those who would jettison a legal heritage by assuming that its subtlety and variety could be comprehended by any one set of men at any given time and place, or by thinking that, as Thomas Jefferson said, "every law naturally expires at the end of 19 years."[18]

Savigny's thesis was that the law, like all human institutions, had been made by the "footprints of thinkers and statesmen who knew which way to turn their feet without knowing . . . the final destination."[19] The law of the present had been developed over many centuries by men working in a variety of circumstances for a variety of purposes. The unintended consequence of numerous acts with more particular intentions was the blending of rules of law into an organic whole that could not be deduced from any simple set of principles. Therefore, both in its structure and in its mode of change, law is not at all like mathematics or logic but more like language.

This implied that law is to be understood as an abstraction from a totality of ideas and habits and procedures that constitute the life of the community that Savigny described as the *Volksgeist*. By this he did not mean to imply either that there is a generic difference between the laws of different countries attributable to a national spirit or that justice could be dispensed directly from the *Volksgeist* by a leader, as the Nazi jurist, Carl Schmitt, maintained. Lawmaking rightly understood, according to Savigny, is an act of self-conscious articulation of what has previously been imbedded in the custom of the community. It does not follow that the law cannot be changed, but that it does not change by acts of creation out of nothing. There can be no absolute beginnings or ends to law; insofar as they are conversant with the law, all jurists must carry in their modes of thought legal concepts and practices of the past, and if they attempt to change the law by applying the dissecting knife, they run the risk of cutting through sound flesh and producing a monstrosity.

There can be nothing mechanical about the law in interpretation any more than in legislation. No code and no command can relieve the judge of an obligation to interpret the law. This was described by Savigny as an act of imagination in which the judge has to reproduce within himself the activity of the legislator. And he warned that any attempt to tie the judge to a mechanical application of a text or to give him leave to make the law for every case would destroy the security of law against the encroachments of caprice and dishonesty.[20]

Savigny's contribution to modern jurisprudence lay in his effort to make plain how contingency is combined with stability in the law. He denied that contingency could be eradicated, but believed that nevertheless stability is possible. The stability of the law, he tried to show, is based on continuity. This is not, however, what his admirers and would-be disciples drew from him. Some of the disciples converted his emphasis on the historical development of law into a source of immutable historical principles. Others were mainly impressed by what he denied—that a legal system could be spun out of reason by legislators who have purely abstract knowledge of what is right. His emphasis on the relation between a legal system and its cultural context was made the basis for legal realism by those who concluded that if rules of law are not perfectly self-sufficient and decisive, then they have no meaning at all. His emphasis on the constant change in the law was converted into a denial that there can be or should be any stability in the law.

III Positivist theories of law

1. Realism

By a twist of intellectual fate, Savigny's effort to explain how the law combines continuity with change has been used by later philosophers as a basis for arguing that neither reason nor stability can be attributed to law. This transformation was achieved by the realist school, currently in great favor with forward-looking lawyers and laymen. Realism began in Germany during the second half of the nineteenth century with Rudolf von Ihering; it was given a distinctive shape by the American jurist John Chipman Gray; and it reached maturity in the works of the American judge Jerome Frank.

The derivation of legal realism from the connection that Savigny tried to establish between law and its social context followed a very indirect route. Out of the historical principles of law discovered by Savigny, his disciple G. F. Puchta constructed a formal system for which he claimed not merely historical truthfulness but universal philosophical validity. This way of looking at law struck Puchta's student, Ihering, as "jurisprudence in the air," and he set himself to producing a "jurisprudence of realities." The moral he drew from the connection Savigny had disclosed between law and other aspects of social life was that law had been produced by efforts to realize a social purpose. Such a purpose was always of a practical order. Law had then to be understood as a means of realizing an objective that was both social and practical.

What Ihering found wrong with the cult of the abstract advocated by *Begriffsjurisprudenz,* as he called both analytical and historical jurisprudence, was that they considered law as if it were an end in itself to be brought to some static perfection or else they denied that law could be shaped by purpose. Their talk about legal logic and the science of law had no connection with real life. What matters, Ihering said, is not the structure or development of the law but its adjustment to changing social conditions. Law is not to be understood as the product of reason but of will, and this will is not that of any individual but of a social whole seeking to perfect itself as a whole. The jurist's task is to consider what the social needs are and how law can best serve them.

Although he emphasized that "the good of the individual is never an end in itself but only a means for accomplishing a social purpose," Ihering nevertheless admired Bentham's attempts to found legislation on social utility, and thought of his own system as belonging to the utilitarian tradition. But Ihering disapproved of the individualist and hedonist implications of the principle of utility as Bentham had formulated it and rejected its use for calculating the priorities among competing purposes. Any such attempt was to be condemned for an unconscious reversion to a doctrine of natural rights. There could be no standard for measuring the value of ends.

Unlike his realist successors, Ihering was explicit about his presuppositions. He assumed that there was no problem about discerning the social purpose and that the social purpose always took precedence over any that was merely individual. The differences in how individuals conceived of the social purpose, he said, were insignificant compared with their agreement. In any case, "ideals" could not be hostile to one another; nor could the legislator have any problem in determining what constituted the moral consciousness of the nation. He had only to consider the consequences of any course of action to discover whether they served the social purpose.

Thus Ihering returned to accepting, in another guise, what he had started by rejecting. He had argued in his first publication, *The Struggle for Law* (1872), against what he took to be the "myth of the folk-spirit" propagated by the historical school, that law was not produced by the silent work of a folk-spirit but by the struggle of everyone for his right. The "idea of the personality" of the individual depended, he said, on retaining the notion of struggle, though he also stipulated that the "right" should be right "on principle." But by 1877, when he wrote *Law as a Means to an End*, the notion of struggle had become unimportant. Indeed, the objective of the law had become entirely a social, not at all an individual, purpose, and what this consisted in appeared to be a truth self-evident in the moral consciousness of the community. The general criterion that should guide the legislator was obvious. The practical aim of justice is to establish equality, for, Ihering said, "when the burdens which society imposes upon its members are distributed unequally . . . the centre of gravity is displaced, the equilibrium is disturbed, and the natural consequence is a social struggle for the purpose of the re-establishing equilibrium . . . always a shock to the existing social order."[21] And he defined the equality desired as a "relative, geometrical equality which measures every share in accordance with each one's contribution . . . ." Only when the members of society were compensated for their devotion could the society flourish. Thus the principle of equality came to be something dictated by the "practical interest in the continuance and success of society" and not any "*a priori* categorical imperative."[22]

Progress, Ihering predicted, would bring with it a continuous increase in the demands of the state on the individual.[23] In return, the individual would receive not merely sensuous and material goods but also an improved quality of life. Although private property and the right of inheritance would always remain (socialistic and communistic notions of removing it were "vain folly"[24]), the state would constantly encroach more on private property in order to distribute burdens and privileges equally throughout the social body, so that no one part of it would be unduly weakened or strengthened at the expense of the other parts.

A conflict between social and individual purposes is impossible in these terms because society is not, as Kant had said, an association for the purpose of realizing the equal freedom of all, but an association with "a common purpose," in which every individual finds his place and himself by working for the good of the whole. Therefore, setting limits to the activities of the state, or thinking in terms of the disadvantages of state action, as Mill and Humboldt did, was futile. Humboldt and Mill were still wedded to the law of nature for which the individual, Ihering said, "is the cardinal point of the whole law and the State . . . an atom without any other purpose in life than that of maintaining itself alongside of the innumerable other atoms." And they accepted the Kantian formula according to which the state and the law have the task of "dividing off the spheres of freedom" of the individual members "in the manner of cages in a menagerie."[25] But contrary to both Mill and Humboldt, Ihering asserted, the state in the future would not "measure restrictions of personal liberty . . . according to an abstract academic formula but according to practical need."[26]

In making law subservient to purpose, Ihering did not mean to emphasize the contingent character of law. On the contrary, the historical relation of purposes was a necessary one:

> One legal purpose is produced out of the other with the same necessity with which, according to the Darwinian theory, one animal species is developed from the other. And if the world should be created a thousand times as it was once created—after milliards of years the world of law would still bear the same form; for purpose has the same irresistible force for the creations of the will in law as cause has for the formation of matter. . . . Law obeys this compulsion willingly or unwillingly. But the compulsion proceeds step by step.

Ihering drew from this necessary progression of purposes the conclusion that therefore "it is not the sense of right that has produced law, but it is law that has produced the sense of right."[27]

Unlike his successors Ihering saw and admitted the consequences for freedom of the will. The notion that the will "could set itself in motion spontaneously without a compelling reason" is, he said, "the Munchausen of philosophy," who thinks that he can "pull himself out of a swamp by his own hair. . . ."[28] The notion of purpose in relation to the will is parallel to the notion of cause in relation to mechanical events. The stone falls because it is pulled by the earth; the will acts because it is pulled by a purpose. Free choice has then nothing to do with law. Whereas Kant had removed contingency from law by making it wholly a product of reason, Ihering achieved the same result by making law wholly a product of will, understood to be totally subservient to a historically given social purpose.

In Ihering's terms, it makes no sense to judge law by ethical standards because for him "ethical" describes whatever is required to adjust the individual to desirable social conditions. It is the function of law to define what constitutes such conditions and such an adjustment. In that sense the law determines what is ethical. But in another sense, Ihering preserved a degree of independence for ethics. Moral development consisted for him in the progress of human beings from egoism to a recognition of themselves as part of a social organization. As a legal system could be preserved only by men ready to renounce their private desires, the legal system was dependent on the morality of its subjects. There was then a circular relationship between law and ethics—law depended on the social devotion and discipline of individuals but such qualities could not be developed without the law.

Ihering emphasized that precisely what was required either for the conquest of egoism in the individual or for the achievement of the social purpose was never fixed and could never be known a priori. What was required at any given time had to be left for the legislature to decide. Of course it was morally bound to use its power in the interest of society, but to do so well it had to be left free to change the law when and how it considered fit. There could not then be any limit on the right of the legislature to make what laws it considered desirable. Like Hobbes's sovereign, the legislature could never commit an unjust act because the legislature decides what constitutes justice and so stands above the law.

In Ihering's work the attack on the idea that permanence or stability was intrinsic to the law was only a minor theme that led him to place the legislator above the law. It became the central thesis of the American school of realists. They seasoned Ihering's theory with suggestions made by J. H. von Kirchmann, some years before, in *The Worthlessness of Jurisprudence as a Science* (1848), which declared a science of law to be impossible because the law was constantly changing, depended on feeling as well as knowledge and understanding, and rested not on nature but on human will. The American realists moved from emphasizing that the law is constantly changing to asserting that in order to destroy any pretense that the law is stable, as well as to insure that this constant change should be deliberately and rightly forwarded, it should be recognized that not only the legislature but also the judge is above the law.

The line that the American realists were to take is generally traced from the definition of law given by Justice Oliver Wendell Holmes in his lecture on "The Path of the Law": "The prophecies of what the courts will do in fact, and nothing more pretentious, are what I mean by the law." It has been suggested[29] that Holmes did not intend this to be a comprehensive definition of the law but a mark for distinguishing between law and ethics. Nevertheless, Holmes's definition expresses an attitude to the law that regularly distinguishes all his pronouncements and underlies all realist jurisprudence. This is an attitude of doubt about the use, meaningfulness, and reality of general rules.

The first exposition to display this tendency, though in a moderate form, was given by John Chipman Gray in *The Nature and Sources of the Law* (1909).[30] Although he is one of the few jurists who rightly understood Savigny's emphasis on the history of law, Gray's interest lay elsewhere—in how rules of law, and what officers of law do, affect the conduct of ordinary people.

What matters to the ordinary man is not, Gray concluded, what the legislator has said, but what the judge decides. Any law that the courts fail to adopt is not law. To claim otherwise shows confusion of an ideal with reality. For law "is not that which is in accordance with religion, or nature, or morality; it is not that which ought to be, but that which is."[31] What the law is cannot be discovered by reading a statute because the same statute can result in two contrary decisions. This possibility means that whether, for instance, a man has a property right at law cannot be known until a court has pronounced.

Gray attributed the futile and mistaken insistence on "discovering" or "finding" the law to an "unwillingness to face the certain fact that courts are constantly making *ex post facto* Law," and thus exercising a highly unpopular power. In reality "the Law, except for a few crude notions of the equity involved in some of its general principles, is all *ex post facto*."[32] People go about their business without the vaguest notion of what the law is, Gray maintained, and "the Law of which a man has no knowledge is the same to him as if it did not exist."[33] And if a case comes up for which there seems to be no law and no precedent, as the judge's business is to "maintain the peace by deciding controversies," he will produce a rule of law for the occasion. "That rule is the Law, and yet the rights and duties of the parties were not known and were not knowable by them. That is the way parties are treated . . . by the courts. . . ."[34] Thus the true lawgiver, Gray goes on to say, is not he who utters the words of a law, but as Bishop Hoadly said, "whoever hath an *absolute authority to interpret* any written or spoken laws. . . ."[35] It is futile to look for the "sources, purposes, and relations of the rules themselves, and to call the rules 'The Law'."[36]

The problem then for jurisprudence is to consider how the judge arrives at his rules and what gives his rules authority. In many areas of law, Gray pointed out, it is the judges themselves who decide whether other judges are acting properly. The state may also indicate that the judges are to obtain their law from certain sources, and that acts of legislation shall take precedence over all other sources. In addition judges may draw their rules from "judicial precedents, opinions of experts, customs, and principles of morality (using morality as including public policy)."[37] Acts of legislation seem to be different from these other sources only because the limits set by a statute are more definite than those set by other sources. Nevertheless, because a statute must be interpreted, though the judge's powers of interpretation are restricted within limits, "these limits are almost as undefined as those which govern them in their dealing with the other sources."[38] A statute then guides the conduct of the community not directly but in the shape of a judicial interpretation. Therefore, Gray said, "the Law of the State or of any organized body of men is composed of the rules which the courts, that is, the judicial organs of that body, lay down for the determination of legal rights and duties."[39]

Radical as it was, Gray's doctrine of the law still had "more than a trace of the old philosophy," Jerome Frank complained in *Law and the Modern Mind*.[40] Frank found no more reality in the judge's rules than in statutes. For, after all, rules are merely words, and "words can get into action only through decisions; it is for the courts in deciding any case to say what the rules mean, whether those rules are embodied in a statute or in the opinion of some other court."[41] Law, according to Frank, consists neither in statutes nor in precedents or rules, but simply in verdicts:

> *For any particular lay person, the law, with respect to any particular set of facts, is a decision of a court with respect to those facts so far as that decision affects that particular person. Until a court has passed on those facts no law on that subject is yet in existence. Prior to such a decision, the only law available is the opinion of lawyers as to the law relating to that person and to those facts. Such opinion is not actually law but only a guess as to what a court will decide.*[42]

Thus Frank consigned the judge's rules, along with all other rules, to "some among many of the sources to which judges go in making the law of the cases tried before them."[43] The law is reduced to a set of acts by judges. A legal statement is a prediction of what the judge will *do*.

This is indeed the only notion of law compatible with Frank's understanding of general ideas. For Frank, as for his philosophical ally John Dewey, an idea represents not an "understanding" of the world but an "instrument" for changing it. An idea is not a response to other ideas but to problems, needs, hopes, fears, or aversions, and is designed to reconstruct an unsatisfactory situation. All ideas are like legal fictions.

The connection between the true character of ideas and legal fictions had been suggested to Frank by Hans Vaihinger's *The Philosophy of As If* (1911), where fictions are described as "constructions of thought, thought-edifices deviating from and even contradicting reality but invented and interpolated by this very thinking in order to attain its end more expeditiously."[44] Vaihinger had been inspired, as Ihering was, by Kant's view that thought is creative rather than passive, and Vaihinger was also anxious to tie this creativity to an empirical rather than a rational reality. He found this reality in activity directed to changing the world. The function of ideas was to serve as instruments of change. A clear recognition of how ideas are used for transforming the undesirable present to the desired future appeared, Vaihinger believed, in the legal concept of "fictions." Vaihinger accordingly praised lawyers for their acceptance of fictions, which had only to be broadened to include all general ideas to make the relation between thought and action clear.

Frank, however, saw in the notion of legal fictions an unintended achievement. Lawyers did not recognize their true value but misused them as "semi-myths to conceal the actualities of legal change and adaptation." What is needed, Frank said, is "liberated fictional thinking" that would recognize "the correct use of valid fictions" and acknowledge "that all legal rules are relative and instrumental." This progress depends on the willingness of lawyers to accept nominalism, "the first step towards knowledge of the provisional or relative character of all concepts."[45] Only by adopting a nominalist view of human understanding, Frank believed, could lawyers come to see how naïvely they have been using general ideas, and come to recognize the truth pointed out by Vaihinger: "General judgments, when connected with a general subject, only represent convenient methods of expression. There is no such thing as a general subject in reality. . . ."[46] Jurists such as Bentham who denounced fictions did not distinguish, according to Frank, between "legal lies . . . designated to deceive others" and "legitimate legal fictions," which are undisguised instruments for changing the world.[47] Thus Frank appeared to align himself with jurists of the natural law school who regard legal fictions as salutary ways of stretching established legal concepts to cover new circumstances. But whereas the latter value fictions for preserving the efficacy and stability of rules of law, Frank valued them for destroying the pretense that there are rules of law.

Other realist jurists moved from the belief that legal rules are irrelevant to the conclusion that what matters is something "more real" that determines the behavior of judges: Hessel Yntema found that the "most salient" thing to say about "the mystery of the judicial process" is "that decision is reached after an emotive experience in which principles and logic play a secondary part. The function of juristic logic and the principles which it employs seems to be like that of language, to describe the event which has already transpired."[48] A truly scientific study of the law, according to

Herman Oliphant, would completely devote itself to a genuinely scientific subject, "which way they decide cases."[49] Karl Llewellyn pointed out that judges have no monopoly on making law. In the first edition of *The Bramble Bush* he declared quite simply: "This doing of something about disputes, this doing of it reasonably, is the business of law. And the people who have the doing in charge, whether they be judges or sheriffs or clerks or jailers or lawyers, are officials of the law. What these officials do about disputes is, to my mind, the law itself."[50] (In the next edition he pronounced these "unhappy words . . . . at best a very partial statement of the whole truth" because they failed to take "proper account" of law as "an instrument of conscious shaping."[51] But how this praiseworthy recantation fits into his general view of the law remains unclear.)

All the realists echo the views of Bertrand Russell, Ludwig Wittgenstein, and the Vienna Circle when they were still trying to discover the pure sensory core of knowledge. But the strictest juristic disciples of logical positivism have been the Scandinavian realists, most notably Anders Lundstedt, Karl Olivecrona, and Alf Ross—all disciples of Axel Hägerström. They have addressed themselves to disclosing the meaninglessness of all legal notions, even that of legal validity, along with the logical distinction between "is" and "ought" revered by the analytical jurists. If a word cannot be shown to refer to some act or sensation, they agree, it is metaphysical and meaningless. Legal concepts have no common factual core to them. The concept of marriage, for instance, Olivecrona pointed out, describes an imaginary condition because the life of every married couple is different. Even the idea of cohabitation signifies nothing because all husbands do not live with their wives. Legal concepts are therefore to be condemned and abjured because they compound superstition, myth, magic, and confusion. Similarly, any talk of the "ends" of law is nonsense because "ends" cannot be known scientifically and are merely irrational declarations of feeling: "We like an end or we don't. We strive for it. We are uninterested. We strive against it. That is all," Olivecrona wrote.[52] Therefore the proper study of law has to do with relations between cause and effect, just as in natural science, for this is the only object of rational discourse. A practical implication of Olivecrona's view was drawn in a book with the ironic title of *On Law and Justice,* where Alf Ross advocated that jurists should concern themselves with "legal politics" that would study not the ends of law but how to make law correspond to changing "ideological" conditions.[53]

Whatever variations they suggest, all realists are agreed on denying the rationality of the law. Some have reduced it to mere acts of will, others to apparent acts of will really determined by chemical or physiological processes. Yet their characterization of a legal order has appeared to be plausible even to many who do not accept it.

One reason for this, Mortimer Adler has suggested, is that the realists are confusing "law as official action" with "law in discourse." In the former sense, law "designates all of the actual processes which take place in time, the prosecution of litigation, the advisory work of the law office, the judicial administration of disputes, and so forth; 'law' in the second instance is an academic subject-matter, a body of propositions having certain formal relations capable of analysis. . . . The science of law as official action is an empirical observational science; it includes a study of sociological and psychological phenomena as well as knowledge of 'law' *in the second sense* as a subject-matter in discourse." [54] From the standpoint of "official action," it can rightly be said that judicial decisions are laws and decide only the particular case because "until the decision is uttered in the particular case, the law does not exist as an instance of official action. . . ." [55]

That the realists have drawn attention to the historical aspect of legal institutions may indeed constitute part of their appeal. But, besides, their insistence that this aspect is the whole of the law gains credence because it seems to do justice to something that jurists, especially of the analytical school, appear to neglect. This is the element of contingency in the law. What makes the law so difficult to understand is that it is a changing permanency.

Superficially the law appears to consist of a set of known rules applied by a judge which, because they are stable and enforced by a government, give security to certain expectations. A concern with increasing this security led Bentham to his preoccupation with codification, which he hoped would eliminate all uncertainty about the law. But despite the monumental efforts of Bentham and others, students of the law have become increasingly aware of how much any legal system differs from a set of known rules applied by a judge. Therefore the stability of the law has been dismissed as a pretense and even jurists who are not of the "realist" persuasion, such as Benjamin Cardozo and Roscoe Pound, praise realism for voicing what is described as a useful protest against the dogma that the law consists in rules applied with mechanical certainty.

The realists believe themselves to be opposing a myth that made the law appear to be fixed and certain, a myth supposed to have been fostered by medieval theologians and preserved because men yearn for a universe "free of chance and error due to human fallibility." [56] In fact, however, the realists are not arguing against a medieval or ancient myth but against a modern one, perpetrated by Kant, which their protests continue to reflect and reinforce—the myth that there is only one rational activity, consisting of demonstrative reasoning from universally valid laws.

That human law cannot produce certainty was taken for granted by ancient and medieval theories of natural law, and Aristotle's *Rhetoric* remains the basic text for understanding the character of legal reasoning. But it is only recently that the relation between the logic of the law and its capacity to combine stability with change and uncertainty has been more fully explored. In the classic modern work on the subject, *An Intro-*

duction to Legal Reasoning, Edward Levi says bluntly that the law operates under a pretense: "The pretense is that the law is a system of known rules applied by a judge. . . ."[57] He goes on to explain that it is a pretense because no rule of law can absolutely specify a decision. This gap between general rules and particular decisions means that rules of law are always ambiguous. The ambiguity is inescapable because of the logical relationship between any general proposition and a more particular one. Any given particular can be fitted into a variety of general statements, and the particulars that could be implied by a general statement cannot be exhaustively stated. Thus the character of the logical relationship between a general rule and a particular instance makes it impossible for any general rule, however clear, to yield only one correct decision.

Take a law that says, "Any driver found driving over forty-five miles an hour in city limits will be fined." Ordinarily cases arising under such a law are settled easily once the speed of the car is established. But that there will be no doubt cannot be known in advance. The vehicle being driven might have been an ambulance. Or the driver might have been fleeing from a would-be murderer. Or the car might have suddenly developed a defect that made it impossible to slow down. Thus even where there is no doubt that the car was moving at more than forty-five miles an hour, it remains for the judge to decide whether the person behind the wheel constitutes the "driver" intended by the law. Only with general statements of a perfectly abstract nature, as about figures the sum of whose angles is 180 degrees, can the particulars fitting under it be unambiguously identified. In the law, the rules are general but not abstract. To identify the particular instances that fit under a law, we must always abstract from a cluster of perceptions. And while we can and do make rules for a proper manner of abstracting, any attempt to eliminate all uncertainty would lead us into an infinite regress of rules.

But this ambiguity in law, Levi points out, also contributes to the stability of the law. Where laws are made by an assembly of men or must be acceptable to more than one person and at more than one instance, a degree of ambiguity makes agreement and acceptance easier. Differences of view, at least within certain areas, can be reconciled under ambiguous words and the ambiguity can then be left for the court to resolve as each case arises. Such ambiguity is indispensable for civil peace.

Moreover, the ambiguity in laws makes it possible for the law to remain stable while adapting to changing circumstances. Not only do new situations arise but in addition peoples' wants change.

> *The categories used in the legal process must be left ambiguous in order to permit the infusion of new ideas. And this is true even where legislation or a constitution is involved. The words used by the legislature or the constitutional convention must come to*

> *have new meanings. Furthermore, agreement on any other basis*
> *would be impossible.*[58]

What makes this flexibility possible without destroying the stability of the law is reasoning by example, or analogical reasoning. A legal decision can be formulated in a syllogism and the syllogism is not a deception. But the premises are never self-evident. The problems in legal reasoning arise out of the difficulty of discovering the premises of the syllogism that is designed to conclude in a decision. The major premise is in question until it is decided what rule of law applies. If there is agreement about what rule of law is relevant, as there may be from the outset in some cases, the court still has to establish whether the action in dispute is of the sort designated by the rule or how this case compares with other cases that have come under the rule.

If even a simple speed law can spawn many awkward questions, a law forbidding "combinations in restraint of trade" provides an inexhaustible subject for argument. Moreover, once a number of cases have been brought under a statute, the judge is faced with the problem of precedent. He must decide whether the case before him most resembles this or that case in the past if he is to see the law as a consistent whole. In deciding such questions, the judge and the lawyers arguing before him must proceed by analogical reasoning in order to establish the minor premise of the syllogism concluding in the verdict. The question constantly being answered is: When is it reasonable to treat different cases as though they were the same? This problem is not, as Bentham said, peculiar to the common law. Nor can it be resolved by any definition of precedent. A precedent is binding on a subsequent case because the court finds the cases to be similar. But as no two cases are ever identical, what constitutes a precedent and how a rule applies to this case is not known until the court has pronounced. This is what makes the realists sound plausible when they say that the judge cannot "find" the law.

It does not follow, however, that the judge's decision is arbitrary or to be explained only by some irrational cause, as the realists suppose. The judge arrives at his decision by reasoning; his decision has reasons, not causes. And the system of law dictates that only certain kinds of reasons are appropriate. The judge ought not to ask himself: "Which of the parties is handsomer, more virtuous, has suffered most, will pay me more?" Or: "What decision will strengthen the government?" Or: "Whom can I make happier?" The questions appropriate for a judge to consider are on the order of: "What rule applies to this case? How does this case compare with other cases like it? Which of the analogies presented before me is most persuasive?" In answering such questions, a judge will be concerned only with applying the law as it exists in statutes and precedents, and he does this by considering whether his decision is consistent with past decisions. His concern with preserving the law will inhibit him from doing justice in this case at the cost of destroying the consistency of the law.

It is therefore just as misleading to think that the judge "makes" the law as that he "finds" it. He does not make the law in the sense of giving effect to his will or to arbitrarily selected requirements. What issues from the court is a decision, not a personal fiat. The judge supports his decision with a legal argument; he may not say, "I think him so because I think him so."

Those who insist that these arguments are spurious and look for some "real" cause for the decision, as realist jurists are doing, are exhibiting a fallacy that is endemic today, the fallacy of supposing that there are only three alternatives—certainty, science, and irrationality. Either we must arrive at an indubitable answer of the sort possible within Euclidean geometry, or justify our answer in terms of an established scientific theory, or else we must, on this fallacious view, fall into irrationality. If the reasoning of the judge is neither certainly infallible nor scientifically valid, it must be condemned as illusory.

But rational activity is not confined to deductive reasoning from indubitable premises such as mathematical constructs, or from universally acceptable premises such as scientific theories. Analogical reasoning cannot produce certainty or even the degree of consensus generally found among scientists in stable areas of research; it can only persuade a given audience that one conclusion is more "reasonable" than another. Only a critic grossly ignorant about the law will criticize a verdict for ignoring the "facts" in favor of "abstractions." What is at issue in any case, even if settled easily, is deciding what constitutes the "facts." An appropriate criticism will offer reasons for considering one set of "facts" more reasonable or relevant than another possible construction. But no construction can be indubitable.

Because analogical reasoning cannot reach a conclusion from which no man could rationally dissent, it lacks perfect impersonality. When this lack of impersonality is confused with irrationality, it gives credence to realist theories of law. But the personal element in analogical reasoning does not render its rationality spurious. A decision is rational because it has reasoned antecedents, not social, psychological, or physiological causes. There is an order appropriate to the reasoning, and impersonal criteria for judging it. It is therefore rational though not certainly right. What emotions the judge may have experienced before or during the trial, or in what order the various ideas in his opinion occurred to him should worry his biographer, not the jurist. What matters for the law is that other reasonable men conversant with the statutes, decisions, and procedures of the land should find his decision and reasoning plausible even if they themselves might have reached another verdict.

The dependence of law on analogical reasoning also explains what the realists assert to be desirable and possible though they cannot show how it comes about—the relation between the law and the moral convictions of the governed. For when a judge finds some analogies more reasonable than others, however objectively he tries to see analogies, he must see them with his own eyes. And a judge, like all other people, has inherited beliefs, acquired convictions, an outlook on life, in short, a "mental background." His judgment always incorporates assumptions about what constitutes a reasonable interpretation of certain words or what constitutes reasonable conduct in a reasonable man. His verdict necessarily incorporates judgments about whether conduct is negligent or responsible, malicious or well intentioned, reasonable or unreasonable. In other words, the judge cannot decide what accords with the law in a moral vacuum. He decides in accordance with his understanding of moral conduct, in terms of which he necessarily interprets the words of the law and understands the arguments presented to him. Though the judge is not meant to be and should not be a one-man public opinion poll nor a student of public opinion, he is obliged to exercise his discretion in the manner of a reasonable man of his time, and this implies that he reflects unselfconsciously the morality of his time. But he does so in the course of attempting to apply the law as it is. The notion that the judge "finds" the law, while incorrect as a description of the law, is a useful practical maxim that directs the judge to keep his attention fixed on the appropriate considerations.

Once the character of analogical reasoning is recognized, it becomes obvious, as Levi has said, that a controversy with the realists about

> *whether the law is certain, unchanging, and expressed in rules, or uncertain, changing, and only a technique for deciding specific cases misses the point. It is both. Nor is it helpful to dispose of the process as a wonderful mystery possibly reflecting a higher law, by which the law can remain the same and yet change. The law forum is the most explicit demonstration of the mechanism required for a moving classification system.*[59]

The realists deny this because they are bedeviled by the very demon they mean to exorcise. They have equated rationality with certainty and demonstrative reasoning. Having discovered that neither exists in the law, they feel obliged to deny the rationality of the law.

Yet for all their insistence on the value of uncertainty, the realists have smuggled a new kind of monarch onto the throne they affect to despise. In one fashion or another, all realists advocate that everything done in the name of "law" should be ruled by "real social needs." These, they assume, as Ihering said explicitly, can be known with certainty whether by direct

129

intuition or through scientific expertise. From decisions based on this new myth about social needs, the realists, unlike their timid ancient and medieval predecessors, can promise consequences whose desirability is certain.

2. *The pure theory of law*

Kelsen's pure theory of law is wholly opposed to realism or any other form of sociological jurisprudence. The reasons he gives suggest that the pure theory recognizes a fundamental difference between the natural and the human world, which sociological jurisprudence denies by being concerned only with facts and causes rather than norms and "meanings of acts of will." But the distinction vanishes as Kelsen refutes the charge, made by sociological jurists, that the pure theory is ideological.

Pure theory is accused of being "ideological," Kelsen explains, because it concerns itself with legal norms rather than with legal acts and the causes of legal acts. But such charges assume that whatever is not natural reality or its description is "ideology." If, however, ideology is used correctly to refer to a "nonobjective presentation of the subject influenced by subjective value judgments and . . . disfiguring the subject of cognition," then the pure theory of law can be acquitted of being an ideology.

For it is uncontaminated by any illicit considerations of justice. It aims only to discover the essence of law by analyzing its structure: "The Pure Theory desires to present the law as it is, not as it ought to be; it seeks to know the real and possible, not the 'ideal' and the 'right' law. In this sense, the Pure Theory is a radical realistic theory of law, that is, a theory of legal positivism." [60] Traditional jurisprudence, unlike pure theory, consciously or unconsciously serves as an ideology to justify or oppose an existing social order. All ideology is rooted in "wishing" rather than "knowing," that is, in "subjective values" and interests other than the pursuit of truth. It is therefore concerned either to preserve or to attack reality, and in order to achieve its end it will either glorify or denigrate reality, but will never present it undistorted.

The pure theory of law, Kelsen is confident, escapes any such danger by denying all "value" to positive law. He believes it to be a true science of jurisprudence with the same object as the social science of ethics. But both, he explains, are normative sciences, not because they prescribe norms for human behavior and thereby command, authorize, or positively permit a certain conduct, but because they describe certain man-made norms and the relationship between men that is thereby created.[61] By describing norms, Kelsen means analyzing the logical relationship between the rules governing men without any reference to the purposes they might be designed to serve, other than peace or survival, which are biologically given, not man-made, ends. This exclusion of any relation between law and purposes it might be expected to serve removes any possibility that positive law as it appears in pure theory can either conform to or violate an ideal law. Therefore Kelsen argues that neither supporters nor critics of the existing order could find a weapon in pure theory.

The objectivity of pure theory comes of recognizing, Kelsen says, that justice is merely an "irrational ideal." It may be an ideal that men need in order to will and to act, but it is not a subject of "rational cognition." The latter knows only "interests" and "conflicts of interests." These may be satisfied by sacrificing some to others but that one alternative is "just" cannot be established by rational cognition. If, however, justice is thought of as "neutrality," it might be admissible. It would then require only that the government remain indifferent to the various conflicting interests and aim to bring about a compromise between them. Such neutrality, Kelsen argues, has the "objective" justification that "only a legal order . . . which brings about such a compromise between opposing interests as to minimize the possible frictions has expectation of relatively enduring existence . . . [and can] secure social peace on a relatively permanent basis."[62]

But when justice is used in the ordinary sense, it signifies nothing but a rationalization of personal preferences pretending to a spurious universality, or what Kelsen calls "subjective judgment of value." A norm can be "just" or "unjust" only for those who do or do not desire what the norm prescribes, although whoever pronounces a social institution to be just or unjust may be unaware that he is expressing a merely private interest. This is especially obvious in appeals to "natural law," which pretend that the norm of justice is immanent in nature, thus displaying a typical illusion due to an "objectivisation of subjective interests."[63] Even the claim that men have a natural right to be free or treated equally is really a self-deception "or—what amounts to much the same thing—an ideology," because it pretends that "a subjective judgment of value" proceeds from some indubitable source such as "nature."[64]

The only correct sense of justice in Kelsen's terms is "legality." It is therefore " 'just' for a general rule to be actually applied in all cases where, according to its content, this rule should be applied."[65] Used in this way, justice is related not to the "content of a positive order, but to its application" and it is compatible with any legal order, capitalist or communist, democratic or autocratic. A statement that the behavior of an individual is "just" in the sense of legal has the same character logically "as a statement by which we subsume a concrete phenomenon under an abstract concept." It is therefore "an objective judgment of value" to be clearly distinguished from subjective judgments.[66]

Justice in any moral sense does not enter into Kelsen's preference for a *Rechtstaat*. He uses the holy term to describe a legal order but for a very different purpose from Kant's. Insofar as Kant's *Rechtstaat* is an association defined by nothing but the rules governing it, Kelsen would appear to echo Kant when he says:

> *If it is asked why an individual together with other individuals does belong to a certain state, no other criterion can be found than that he and the others are subject to a certain, relatively centralized coercive order. All attempts to find another bond that holds together and unites in one unit individuals differing in language, race, religion, world concept, and separated by conflicts of interests, is doomed to failure.*[67]

Kelsen is not, however, asserting that the members of a *Rechtstaat* are autonomous persons, but that there is no reality to any notion of national character or spirit, nor to any "ideology," "metaphysics," or "mysticism" about the state. His reason is not to establish the incompatibility of a "common objective" with "freedom" but to destroy any impediment to a world state and to eliminate any ground for passing judgment on the existing legal order. He is concerned to identify an object of legal cognition that is untainted by "values" and therefore is a proper subject for scientific investigation.

The pure theory of law accordingly discovers what the law "is" and not what it "ought" to be. Kelsen regards this distinction as a departure from Austin's command theory; what he and Austin share he confines to a disposition to proceed solely by analysis of positive law.[68] But there can be no doubt that Kelsen significantly differs from Austin when he substitutes the concept of a "norm" for that of a "command" to explain the character of a law.

Law cannot be a command, Kelsen argues, because a command is the expression of the will of an individual directed to the conduct of another individual. There is a command only so long as both the will and its expression are present. But legal rules remain valid even if the individuals who made them have ceased to be. In fact, some legal obligations that exist probably do not represent the "real will of anyone." When the members of a legislature die, the statutes enacted by them remain in force, and although a statute is directly contrary to the will of those legislators who voted against it, the statute is regarded as an enactment of the whole legislature. Moreover, a large proportion of the members of a legislature who vote for a bill either do not know its content or know it very superficially.[69]

At most, then, to call a law a command is, Kelsen says, only a figurative expression. It is based on the analogy between enacting or prescribing and commanding. But the former two occur "without any psychic act of will." Therefore, law is better described as a "depsychologized" command. More precisely it is a "norm." Whereas a command prescribes a particular act, a norm prescribes a manner of conducting oneself. To think of laws as commands is to introduce a "superfluous and dangerous fiction of the 'will' of the legislator or the state."[70]

The concept of the norm makes it possible, Kelsen believes, to keep clear the distinction between "is" and "ought," as Austin failed to do. A norm states what "ought" to be done. But to describe the law as a system of norms is to say not what it ought to be, but only what it is. Thanks to the concept of "norm" it is possible to describe the law without either leaving out its prescriptive character or entering into the realm of "ought." His new concept also enables Kelsen to reject Austin's characterization of a law as "enforcible" without denying that coercion is central to the law. A law does not, Kelsen argues, force men to obey its commands. Nor is it at all certain that the lawful behavior of individuals is brought about by fear of the threatened sanction. Rather, a law is a "norm which provides a specific measure of coercion as sanction." This sanction follows upon a "delict," that is, illegal conduct.[71] Or, in other words, the law says that certain consequences "ought" to follow upon certain sorts of behavior.

A legal system consists of a hierarchy of norms. The hierarchy has the character of a series of more and more confining frames. Interpretation of legal norms, or movement from a more general to a less general norm, consists in fitting a smaller frame into a larger one. When the judge applies the law to an individual case, he fits the particular case into an appropriate frame.

Kelsen opposes this conception of the law as a frame to what he takes to be the traditional view that law can render certain decisions by an "act of cognition." At the same time, he dismisses analogical reasoning as a worthless description of interpretation because analogies can lead to diverse results and "no criterion exists to decide when the one and when the other should be applied."[72] As he cannot therefore credit analogical reasoning with rationality, Kelsen assumes that the traditional insistence on the rationality of law must mean, as it does for Kant, that there is only one logically correct interpretation of the law. This, he argues, is a fiction which, though useful for supporting legal security, is not a legitimate part of a scientific description of positive law.

The act of interpretation is not, Kelsen emphasizes, an act of cognition, because there is always more than one possible object that will fit into a given frame. The designation of one of several possibilities must then be, according to the Kantian dichotomy between reason and will, an act of will. And it is an act of will that "creates" law. If the interpretation is being done by a "law-applying organ" it is an "authentic creation of law."[73] Thus by a strange route Kelsen unwittingly arrives at the same conclusion as the realists. By describing every movement to a more particular norm as an act of interpretation, which "creates" law, he converts the whole legal order into a creation of will.

But the view of law as a creation of will contradicts Kelsen's notion of validity, which he treats as a logical criterion. The validity of a norm is always derived from a higher norm, and in this context Kelsen describes the relation between higher and lower norms as that between a major premise and the conclusion derived from it.[74] This means, Kelsen believes, that the whole legal order can be understood as a logical system. Yet at the same time Kelsen felt obliged, as Kant had not, to explain the uncertainty of the law. To solve this problem he introduced the notion of law as a "frame." The result is a self-contradictory account of a legal system that unwittingly describes it both as a chain of deductive reasoning and as an act of will.

Kelsen proposed a more consistent and ingenious solution to the problem of explaining the ultimate justification of the norms that constitute a legal system. A valid law should be obeyed, according to Kelsen, because it has been issued by someone who is authorized by a higher norm to make such a law. But this leads to an infinite regress of norms that could never give validity to the system as a whole. What is needed then at the base of the legal system, Kelsen concluded, is a norm that is not enacted. This ultimate norm cannot be "directly evident" in the sense that it emanates from reason, "because the function of reason is knowing and not willing, whereas the creation of norms is an act of will."[75] As the validity of the ultimate norm can neither be derived from a higher norm nor its reason questioned, it must then be a "hypothetical" norm or, in other words, the presupposition of a "law-making authority whose norms are, by and large, observed, so that social life broadly conforms to the legal order based on the hypothetical norm."[76] This presupposition Kelsen calls the "basic norm."

It has the same epistemological character as the categories of Kant's transcendental philosophy. Just as the categories are not data of experience but conditions of experience, the basic norm is a condition of juridical science. The hypothetical basic norm answers the question: "How is positive law possible as an object of cognition, as an object of juridical science; and, consequently, how is a juridical science possible?"[77] A legal system can then be identified as a hierarchy of norms whose validity can be traced to the same basic norm, which also constitutes their unity.

But Kelsen is not content with a merely formal solution. He adds an empirical conditional for the validity of the legal system as a whole. The norms of a valid system remain valid, Kelsen tells us, "only on the condition that the total order is efficacious; they cease to be valid, not only when they are annulled in a constitutional way, but also when the total order ceases to be efficacious."[78] This saves the efficacy of the legal system from being questioned because a particular law or laws have become ineffective. But it introduces a significant uncertainty. Kelsen appears to suppose that whether or not a legal order is "efficacious" is self-evident. Yet the difficulty of deciding after World War II whether the legal order in Nazi Germany could be said to have broken down or whether it was sufficiently in effect to justify acts accepted as valid by it, suggests that Kelsen's ultimate criterion of "efficacy" may yield judgments not wholly uncontaminated by "subjectivity." More important, to say that the validity of a legal system as a whole rests on its "efficacy" is to equate right with might.

All these difficulties arise out of Kelsen's anxiety to disengage the concept of norm from any suggestion that it has to do with acts of deliberation or choice. Although he distinguishes the world described by natural science from that described by a science of norms, he refuses to attribute free will to men. Free will, he believes, denies that a man's will is "causally determinable." The law need make no such assumptions. Indeed it cannot make such assumptions because a "normative behavior-regulating order" would not be possible if human behavior were not determined by causes. For a norm "commanding certain behavior" can only signify "the cause of a norm-conforming behavior."

The law needs to assume only that a man may be held responsible for what he does. This means, according to Kelsen, that a man's will may be considered the end point of a relationship of "imputation," which is as central to the normative sciences as causality is to the natural sciences. Thus a criminal act may be "imputed" to a man when he has violated a norm. A punishment is then "imputed" to his crime; "by imputation we understand every connection of a human behaviour with the condition under which it is commanded or prohibited in a norm."[79] In this fashion, by substituting cause and imputation for choice and deliberation, Kelsen believes himself to have given a pure scientific account of the law without any illegitimate references to human purposes or understanding.

Nevertheless Kelsen recognizes that he must explain an apparently serious difference between imputation and causation. Whereas in a causal relationship described by a law of nature the effect necessarily follows the cause, in a relationship by imputation the connection may or may not come about because the judge may or may not find the defendant guilty. Kelsen solves this difficulty by saying that when a man lies or speaks the truth, he is causally determined. But he is not determined by a law of nature "according to which one must always speak the truth or always lie." He is determined by "another law of nature," for example, by "one according to which man chooses that behavior from which he expects the greatest advantage."[80] Causality then is not incompatible with uncertainty about the relation between two events. Imputation is not then essentially different from causation.

The only shortcoming in Kelsen's solution is that this second "law of nature" is a rhetorical flourish covering a self-contradiction. For if a man "chooses," he is not determined by a law of nature; he deliberates and decides. If he is "determined" by a law of nature, he is not understanding and considering alternatives and so he cannot be choosing.

Kelsen has succeeded in giving an account of law that uses all the words traditionally associated with human beings, but in a manner that dissociates them entirely from creatures that can imagine, interpret, deliberate, and decide. His attempts to make credible the relationship between his account and the phenomenon it is meant to explain lead him into self-contradiction. But he has made it clear that the law can only be understood as the product of beings who can do something more than perform logical demonstrations and create acts of will.

3. Analytical jurisprudence

H. L. A. Hart, one of the most prominent living philosophers of law and until recently professor of jurisprudence at Oxford, might seem to have set himself the same task as Kelsen. He has, however, phrased it in more matter-of-fact terms: "to give an account of what it is for a legal system to exist." [81] And his style reflects the fact that his affinity is with Bentham rather than Kant, which saves him from annihilating law with "pure theory."

Although Hart accepts Kelsen's criticism of Austin, he offers different corrections. The command theory of law, he says, affords no way of distinguishing the gunman's order from the policeman's warrant. What matters for Hart is that although the gunman may get his way, his victim feels no obligation to obey him but only a need to do so in order to avoid being shot. For the same reason Hart rejects the realist's view that a legal system makes it possible to predict when one is likely to suffer. On the realist view, he points out, any obligation to obey the law would disappear whenever one could confidently expect to avoid punishment.[82] Hart argues, to the contrary, that the existence of a legal system implies that the citizen has an obligation to obey regardless of whether he will or will not in fact be punished for disobeying. This obligation cannot be explained by what citizens do but only by how they understand their relation to the laws. A description from an "external point of view" necessarily ignores this "internal aspect" of rules because it can only indicate regularities of conduct. It cannot show why a man who commits a crime may not only predict a "hostile reaction" but may also recognize a "reason for hostility." [83]

Hart criticizes Austin and Kelsen for having too restricted a view of what law does. The former, in his command theory of law, thinks all law consists in effect of a policeman halting a motorist at an intersection; Kelsen thinks all law consists of telling officials what to do if somebody commits a crime. Hart regards Kelsen's view as an improvement on Austin's but holds that Kelsen too has fallen far short of an adequate analysis, having failed to distinguish two further types of law, which Hart now proceeds to analyze.

The first kind gives private persons the security of knowing that the contracts, wills, and other private arrangements they make in accordance with such laws can be enforced in the courts. They are enabling acts granting new powers to private persons rather than making any behavior criminal or obligatory. They set conditions for engaging in certain activities, but they command nothing. By treating such laws as parts of an order to officials to apply sanctions, Kelsen obscures the fact, so Hart argues, that such rules are "an additional element introduced by the law into social life over and above that of coercive control." They are designed not for the "bad man" but for any "man who wishes to arrange his affairs." [84]

Besides, Hart distinguishes rules of a totally different kind because they are rules for making or recognizing rules. Primitive societies make do with only "primary rules," which govern the activity of the members directly. But a legal system appears only when primary rules are supplemented by "secondary rules," whose function is to eliminate the uncertainty that arises as soon as primary rules become at all complicated. Hart identifies three kinds of secondary rules. A "rule of recognition" is fundamental because it specifies some marks by which rules may conclusively be known to have the force of primary rules. By connecting what would otherwise be "discrete unconnected" rules into a unified set, the rule of recognition introduces the idea of a system. Second, when the rule of recognition is supplemented by "rules of change," it becomes possible to alter old primary rules or introduce new ones in a deliberate fashion. Third, there are "rules of adjudication," [85] which empower certain persons to determine authoritatively whether a primary rule has been broken. They indicate who is to decide and according to what procedures. In other words, they define conceptions such as judge, court, jurisdiction, and judgment.

All these distinctions enlarge the notion of law from that of a ground for private litigation or prosecution to a manner of controlling, building, and planning "life out of court." [86] The old notion of law as coercive orders or rules makes it impossible to see this larger function of law; for the coercive aspect of law, in Hart's view, is only incidental to its general task of introducing or modifying "general standards of behaviour to be followed by the society generally." [87]

Another crucial contribution of the category of secondary rules is its capacity to explain the idea of validity, which is as central to the concept of law for Hart as it is for Kelsen. Whereas Kelsen resorted to a mystical "basic norm," which is itself not a legal phenomenon but a "presupposition" of legal phenomena, Hart can point to definite rules or procedures on which the validity of laws in a given legal system is based. Moreover, this enables Hart to keep the validity of a legal system independent of its efficacy. For Kelsen, the obligation to observe the laws of a legal system disappears once the legal system ceases to be effective; Hart argues that laws remain valid, if they have been made in accordance with established secondary rules, even when the legal system is no longer efficacious.

In these respects, Hart's theory is more nearly "positivist" in the sense connected with the Vienna Circle, inasmuch as he stays closer to phenomena that can be "observed." But by emphasizing the "internal" aspect of law, he is saying that what matters is not only how laws are made, but how laws are understood to be made. This suggests that "beliefs" about law are as important as "observable phenomena" such as orders and acts, and carries intimations of a concept of "authority."

In another way too Hart departs from positivism by admitting considerations of justice to the concept of law, despite his emphasis on the distinction between "is" and "ought." The Scandinavian realists are wrong, he believes, when they declare words such as "just" and "unjust" to be devoid of meaning. The fact that "concepts like justice" depend on "implicit varying and challengeable criteria," Hart says, "does not render them meaningless when applied to law." They are like other variable standards such as those indicated by "long," "short," "genuine," "false," and "useful." [88] The idea of "fairness," that is, "treat like cases alike and different cases differently," Hart considers essential to law.

Besides, Hart admits that something can be salvaged from theories of natural law. But it has to be disentangled from the "teleological point of view" which is "latent in our identification of certain things as human *needs* which it is *good* to satisfy and of certain things done to or suffered *by* human beings as *harm* or *injury*." [89] A minimum natural law can be constructed without resort to metaphysical notions simply by considering "contingent" facts "which could be otherwise" but in general are not.[90] Such a fact is the desire of men to survive. We cannot, Hart says, demonstrate the necessity of this desire but can agree that it persists.

There are a number of such "natural facts" that have a "rational connection" with certain legal and moral rules. This connection, Hart is careful to point out, is "not mediated by *reasons;* for they do not relate the existence of certain rules to the conscious aims or purpose of those whose rules they are." [91] But as men are vulnerable creatures, they must exercise mutual forbearance and compromise if their lives are not to be nasty, brutish, and short. As their altruism is limited and the things they need to survive relatively scarce, it follows that some form of property arrangements must exist. Then, too, the division of labor brings with it a "need for dynamic rules enabling men to transfer, exchange or sell their products," and recognize promises. And as human understanding and strength of will are limited, there must also be "sanctions" to "*guarantee* that those who would voluntarily obey shall not be sacrificed to those

138

who would not."[92] These conclusions are all untainted by metaphysics or reasons or purpose; they are "simple truisms," Hart maintains, that "disclose the core of good sense in the doctrine of Natural Law." They can be admitted to a positivist theory because they modestly recognize the rational connections of certain facts, contingent though persistent, with certain laws.[93]

All this helps to carry Hart well beyond his positivist colleagues in giving an account of what we understand by a legal system. But it is not enough. He is handicapped by a conception of reason that cannot allow for a proper understanding of rules of law, let alone of the purpose of law.

The difficulty is most obvious in his attempt to reply to the realists. For Hart will have none of the realists' scepticism about rules of law, yet he feels obliged to answer their charge that rules of law must be meaningless because they do not produce perfectly predictable decisions. His reply rests on a distinction between the "core" and "penumbra" of a law. By the "core" he means those particulars that are clearly known to belong to the class of acts or things designated by a rule of law—what he calls "the standard cases"; in the "penumbra" he includes those particulars that were not in the minds of the legislators but are offered later as new candidates for inclusion. The realists make the mistake, according to Hart, of neglecting the "core" in every rule of law and supposing that a rule consists only of the "penumbra," although he agrees that what the realists say about a law applies rightly to the penumbra.

Unfortunately there is an unintended resemblance between Hart's view on this point and the realist one he means to refute. For if the core of a law consists of "standard cases," a law appears to have the character of a class of particulars rather than a general concept. If a law is no more than that, it would seem reasonable to conclude, as the realists do, that rules of law have no independent claim to attention. Furthermore, in drawing out the implications of the "penumbra" Hart takes over the realists' reliance on judicial intuition of social needs. When the judge is faced with a case in the penumbra, as he cannot, Hart says, decide in terms of logic, he can only consider which decision would produce the most desirable social consequences. In such cases, judges who pretend to be applying the law as it "is" are really enemies of social progress. Hart consequently interprets the decision of Justice Rufus Peckham in *Lochner* v. *New York* (1905)—that regulating bakers' hours of labor by state legislation was an unprecedented interference with the right of free contract— as an attempt to "give effect to a policy of a conservative type." What is taken to be an excessive use of logic in law, Hart explains, consists in giving "some general term an interpretation which is blind to social values and consequences (or which is in some other way stupid or perhaps merely disliked by critics)."[94] Thus in cases belonging to the penumbra, justice or morality and law intersect in a way not allowed for by utilitarian theory. The qualification on utilitarianism that he proposes, Hart believes, can save the reality of rules of law while allowing for the truth that inspires some jurists to disown them.

But in saving the reality of rules of law by distinguishing between a "core" and a "penumbra," Hart has failed to provide a genuine alternative to realism. He misrepresents legal reasoning and assumes that general rules can sometimes produce a certainty that they can never produce. At the same time he unwittingly joins the realists in denying the possibility of separating the powers of judge and legislator, which, as Bentham insisted, is vital for preserving the rule of law. For the realists are much more perceptive in recognizing that if judges are permitted to decide cases in terms of what they consider desirable social consequences, then a man cannot know what the law is until his case has been decided.

Nor is Hart's notion of "validity," for all its superiority to Kelsen's, competent to explain why rules of law are obligatory. Here again Hart is handicapped by his allegiance to positivist understanding of knowledge, which rejects abstract ideas that cannot be traced to sense perceptions. This prevents Hart from admitting to his understanding of law the only ideas that could solve the problem that concerns him.

The clue to his difficulties appears in the curious importance he attaches to the logical distinction between propositions about what "is" the case and propositions about what "ought" to be, which he declares to be the foundation of all positivist jurisprudence. Critics of Hart's theory, such as Lon Fuller, deny that law and morality can be separated in the manner advocated by positivist jurists. But this does not mean that they refuse to recognize the logical distinction between "is" and "ought." They disagree rather about the significance for jurisprudence of making the distinction.[95]

In attempting to clarify his own allegiance to positivist jurisprudence, Hart appears to be accusing Fuller of refusing to recognize that a law may be binding, that is, valid, even if not desirable. But as Fuller is a distinguished jurist and is not a notorious revolutionary, he is unlikely to be advocating that a citizen should disobey any law he considers undesirable. Fuller, for his part, believes that Hart does not regard the purpose of law as one of the primary criteria in judging it. But this too seems odd. For Hart never suggests that it was irrelevant to consider the purpose of Nazi laws designed to consign part of the population to gas chambers. In fact the issue between Hart and Fuller is about what the notion of validity entails.

Hart is arguing, as Kelsen did, that validity depends entirely on a logical standard that requires law to be logically consistent with other "higher" laws. Fuller believes validity to involve a moral standard as well. Both arguments are plausible because "validity" is one of those apparently "neutral" or "valueless" scientistic words in vogue now that obscure important distinctions. The "is/ought" distinction is irrelevant because Fuller's case can be stated perfectly well entirely in terms of "is" propositions: a law is valid if and only if it is made in conformity with higher laws and is just. Hart's position can be shown to derive an "ought" from an "is": if this law is valid, then it ought to be obeyed. (Kelsen recognizes this problem and attempts to solve it with a verbal trick by saying that as a law is a "norm" that prescribes what *ought* to be done, an assertion that what the law commands ought to be obeyed merely describes what the content of a normative proposition *is*.)

Everyone agrees that if a law is said to be "valid," that makes observing it obligatory. But to say that a valid law is obligatory does not indicate anything about why it is obligatory. For the concept of validity only pushes the question back onto a prior or higher law—this law should be obeyed because it conforms to other laws. That, however, leads to an infinite regress. Besides, the real difficulty is present at every stage of the regress. As the concept of validity according to positivist jurists makes a law obligatory when it conforms to other laws, and independently of whether it is desirable, the real question raised by making "validity" the source of legal obligation is: Why should I obey any law that has consequences I consider undesirable? This is the question being raised regularly today by demonstrators and marchers.

The question can be rendered irrelevant only if we take the view that a law can be shown to be desirable by a demonstration from indubitable premises. Then the desirability of the law becomes a necessarily true conclusion that is irresistible to any rational creature. Indeed, after such a demonstration it would be superfluous to say that a law is obligatory, because a man cannot be obliged to accept what he necessarily cannot reject (though perhaps a law might still be "obligatory" for men who are not perfectly rational and prevented by their passions from recognizing rational necessity). The realists replace obligation with social necessity. If men must adjust to or change social reality in order to survive, and if a judicial decision attuned to social needs indicates what is necessary to achieve this result, then men who wish to survive are obliged to obey the orders enabling them to do so. Thus the realists make a practical rather than a rational necessity the ground for accepting the law.

If, furthermore, a political association is not thought of as an association of individual human beings, but as an organism of which the members constitute organs, as many realists suggest, all the questions that the idea of authority is designed to answer become irrelevant. For these questions arise from the supposition that the purpose of a political association is to promote the well-being of its members, individually considered. This is what gives its members the right to ask: Why should I obey a law? But if the end of a political association is independent of the ends of its members, then the latter have no rights. They can but serve and suffer. Then all the questions raised by jurists concerning validity of laws belong to the world of fantasy, and need concern no one.

If, however, laws are intended to regulate the behavior of persons as individuals, and if no law can be shown to be necessarily desirable, then even good and wise men may deny the desirability of any particular legal prescription. Then the question, Why should I obey a law that I consider undesirable? must be answered. Hart and other positivist jurists attempt to dodge this question by playing on the distinction between "is" and "ought." But in doing so they merely assert that a law must be obeyed when it is made in a certain fashion, regardless of whether it is desirable in content. To say that the concept of validity is central to the law is not to explain why a valid law that is not necessarily desirable is nevertheless necessarily obligatory.

How does this necessity get there? It is put there by lawmakers observing the prescribed procedures. But if the lawmakers' acts cannot claim the sanction of a divine or eternal law, what obliges me to recognize this man-made necessity? The only answer is that the lawmakers have been given the authority to make rules obligatory. It is the idea of authority that is missing from Hart's account. Though he speaks of secondary rules giving an "authority to legislate,"[96] he does not explore the meaning of authority and its place in law. Because of this he cannot make clear the relation between law and justice. His difference with Fuller is about the relationship between the authority of a law and its justice. Hart's argument is in effect that the authority of a law is independent of the justice of its content. Fuller appears to be insisting that the two are inseparable. He might, however, find it easier to agree with Hart and to avoid the appearance of advocating anarchy if he were to distinguish between constitutional and substantive justice. In short, the controversy between Hart and Fuller summarizes the difficulties of understanding law as a human artifact without reference to authority, without reference to justice, and without distinguishing between constitutional and substantive justice.

IV Authority, constitutional justice, and substantive justice

Authority must be exercised whenever men must choose among alternatives, none of which is either demonstrably correct or universally preferred. Authority is not needed to establish the conclusion of a geometrical demonstration, because everyone who understands geometry will recognize that one particular conclusion is proved to be correct and that every alternative conclusion is thereby proved to be incorrect. Neither is authority necessary to settle speculative questions, where men may be left free to differ, because no action need be taken. But in practical matters authority is sometimes indispensable, because although reasonable men may reasonably disagree about which practical policy is preferable, there are some circumstances in which all must pursue only one of the alternative policies. In such cases, authority must be used to designate one of the alternatives as the binding choice, so that practical action can be taken.

Authority establishes fixity by fiat. It fills an ineradicable gap between reasoning and deciding. If someone in authority is asked by someone subject to his authority, Why must I do as you say? the correct answer is, Because I say so. He may go on to explain why he has chosen to say so, but that explanation will give his reasons for issuing the order; it will not furnish his subject with the reason for obeying it. A legal order of any sort—that is, rules that serve to bring order into a social situation—do so by putting beyond question a decision that cannot be shown to be necessary by reason and could reasonably be otherwise.

Just as an authorized legislator has been given the right to make rules that have an irremovable element of arbitrariness, so accepting the judge's decision is obligatory because the judge has been authorized to interpret the law in particular cases. Some systems of secondary rules provide for appeals to other judges, until the highest tribunal of the land is reached. But there, as in all other courts, the judge's decision must be obeyed because he is authorized to make it and not because it is the correct or only possible one. The judge adds necessity to an otherwise contingent conclusion by an act of will. If, however, he has reasoned in the manner appropriate to a judge his decision is neither irrational nor arbitrary.

The positivist insistence on the distinction between "is" and "ought" would seem then to be a mysterious and misleading way of saying: that the authority of a law is independent of whether what it prescribes is desirable; that every law is arbitrary in the sense that it cannot be justified conclusively; and that a law need not be justified in terms of its rightness because it is justified by the right of the authority to issue it. The coercion used by the law is an exercise of right rather than might, not because it is recognized in every case to be desirable but because it is exercised by an authorized agent in an authorized manner. That is why it remains true, as Hobbes put it, that anyone who violates the law wills his own punishment even if he refuses to punish himself. By refusing to consider what the purpose of a legal system is, positivist jurists have obliged themselves to pretend that a logical distinction can explain why obedience to the law is obligatory. They have removed any ground for answering those who mean to destroy the law by creating confusion about its authority. And it has become plausible to think that there is no difference between the policeman's truncheon and the hooligan's cudgel. Right is thus reduced to might, and the realists are left holding the field.

The masking of authority with logic has made it impossible to see how complex is the relation between authority and justice. It has encouraged a false belief that recognizing authority is tantamount to accepting absolute government. But it does not follow from the fact that social life depends on authority and that the authority of a rule or order does not rest on its desirability, that there is nothing further to be said about authority. It was the great achievement of Hobbes that by eliminating all considerations other than maintaining peace he made plain the idea of authority. At the same time, however, political practice was developing a conception of a particular sort of authority suitable to an association concerned with matters other than peace. For authorities may be constituted in a great variety of ways, and some ways may be preferable to others.

Hobbes's only concern was to establish peace; he therefore gave the sovereign absolute authority. Absolutism was rejected by Hobbes's successors; but why it should be rejected is not made clear by contemporary jurists who propose no grounds other than Hobbes's for accepting the sovereign's commands. Peace appears to be Hart's only criterion for judging a legal system, just as it is Kelsen's. The preservation of peace underlies all Hart's suggestions for a minimum natural law, and he could not consistently provide arguments against absolutism without moving beyond "facts" into the kind of assertions excluded from rational discourse by the positivist theory of knowledge. Yet unlike Kelsen, Hart believes that a legal order must include rules for deciding who should make rules. These secondary rules are introduced, Hart tells us, to give more certainty about primary rules. But he neglects to notice that they also do the contrary. In the West, a political dissident may or may not, after a lengthy legal battle, be found guilty. In countries where secondary rules are primitive or disregarded, a man charged with a political crime can be more nearly certain of being condemned. It is misleading to make certainty the only virtue of law. Those who complain about the uncertainty produced by appeal procedures forget that the purpose of allowing appeals is to increase the justice, not the certainty, of the law. It is not a preference merely for certainty that is satisfied by secondary rules, but for a particular manner of constituting authority, or what may be called constitutional justice.[97]

Constitutional justice becomes relevant once it is recognized that social life "originating in the bare needs of life, and continuing in existence for the sake of a good life"[98] not only remedies a deficiency in man, but also enables him to realize his capacities. Men want to act in concert with other men not merely to survive but in order to live well. What they understand this to mean will affect how they choose to constitute authority.

The preference for defining authority in accordance with constitutionalism, which has been perfected in England and the United States, depends on a distinction that has emerged in modern Europe between two sorts of association—a "civil association" and an "enterprise."[99] It is this distinction rather than any between rule by the one, the few, or the many, that is the most fundamental in political life. It resembles but is more refined than Aristotle's distinction between a despotism and a polity. The crucial question for Aristotle was whether the subjects were treated as ends rather than means, and whether they were ruler and ruled in turn. The modern distinction emphasizes that treating men as ends leaves them free to shape their lives for themselves, as opposed to their being shaped, even if for their own good, by the laws. The object of the laws in a civil association is not then to make men good, but to protect the freedom of each person to pursue his own projects or, in other words, to preserve his self-determination. Of course the first concern of a civil association must be to maintain civil peace without which civilized living is impossible. But what the laws are expected to do beyond keeping the peace—the concern with freedom for self-determination rather than common objectives—distinguishes a civil association.

Whereas the government of an "enterprise" association acts as though it were the manager of a factory, the director of a hospital, or the headmaster of a school, the government of a civil association is responsible for nothing beyond enabling the members of the civil association to remain responsible for themselves while submitting to rules. As a factory is concerned with producing efficiently, the management sets certain hours, determines what equipment is needed, distributes the various tasks. Similarly, a hospital imposes on its patients courses of treatment, diet, sleep, and exercise in order to restore them to health. A school is designed to initiate immature human beings into their intellectual heritage and therefore prescribes certain courses of study and whatever activities are deemed helpful for preparing students to recognize and appreciate their heritage. In all these enterprises the decisive consideration is not how to allow the workers, patients, or students freedom to run their own lives, but how to further whatever purpose the enterprise is designed to serve.

But in a civil association, what the members have in common is neither a purpose nor a pool of interests, but a public good understood as the conditions that they regard as necessary or helpful to the pursuit of their private projects. A civil association is constituted by nothing other than its rules and the recognition by its members of the meaning and desirability of living by rules. The members may have much else in common, such as culture and language. They may also be associated in a variety of other ways, in enterprises of different sorts. But what is distinctive about the unity of a civil association is that it rests on the acceptance by its members of a common set of rules rather than of a common objective.

Although the sort of procedures that are desirable for constituting authority in a civil association cannot be deduced from pure reason, as Kant supposes, such procedures have been discovered in the course of long political practice and are summed up by the term *constitutionalism*. Thus constitutional justice has come to be thought of as requiring not only that there be some secondary rules, such as Hart describes, but that the rules should be of a certain sort. They must govern even those empowered to change secondary rules—that is, no one is to be above the law. They should provide security for the independence of the judicial authority, both to keep it from being used as an instrument of social policy by the executive or legislature and to prevent judges from usurping the legislative power in order to make arbitrary changes in the law. They should provide securities against arbitrary action by the authorities, such as the interdiction against retroactive or secret laws, the writ of habeas corpus, a definition of what constitutes "due process" in the law, and the right to appeal against search and seizure by officers of the law. They should encourage decentralization of authority and establish means by which any monopoly of economic or other resources by either the rulers or the ruled may be prevented. Just what form such provisions take will, and does, vary with time and place, because they are determinations of, and not deductions from, more general requirements of constitutional justice.

Most fundamental to constitutionalism are the distinction between laws and orders and the restriction of powers to issue orders or decrees rather than laws. Orders determine the action to be performed. That they may be general in the sense of applying to a class of persons does not change their character. The clearest example of laws that are "orders" are tax "laws" that direct the citizen to fill out returns and to send in payment. On the other hand, a true law does not command the subject to perform anything. It either designates the manner in which certain activities are to be carried out by those who wish to engage in them, with sanctions for a failure to comply—the most obvious instance being the law governing contracts. Or it designates a manner of performing certain actions that will subject the performer to penalties. Thus a law against murder does not command the citizens to do anything; it does not even prohibit all killing. It says that whoever causes the death of another in a certain manner under certain conditions will be subject to certain penalties. This is not to say that a law is merely a piece of advice, a counsel, or a recommendation. But neither is it an order. Strictly speaking, a civil association should be governed by laws only and not by orders.

Although the distinction between laws and orders is crucial for constitutionalism, its importance was long neglected. Bentham, who was concerned with making constitutionalism incorruptible, not only ignored but opposed the distinction because his attention was fixed on emphasizing the element of coercion in all authoritative rules, however general or conditional. Today the importance of restricting the use of orders to preserve constitutionalism has become more obvious as the sort of freedom that constitutionalism is designed to protect is increasingly destroyed by the proliferation of administrative decrees needed to conduct the welfare activities of contemporary governments.[100]

Questions that are attributed by positivist jurists to a conflict between law and morality—such as the problem faced by someone subject to Nazi or Communist laws—are really questions about the acceptability of a given authority. For we may ask whether an authority has been established in accordance with constitutional justice. If it has not, then the next question is whether it should nevertheless be accepted because peace in any form is better than anarchy, or in other words, whether constitutional justice should be sacrificed for peace. Because answers to such questions cannot be given in the abstract it does not follow that considerations of constitutional justice are irrelevant in deliberating about the desirability of any particular authority.

There is still another question that may be raised about an authorized ruler: whether the rules he makes are in accordance with substantive justice. The distinction between constitutional and substantive justice has not been emphasized in discussions of constitutionalism because the tradition of individualism, which has been the principal source of constitutionalism, has tended to equate substantive justice with neutrality of government in the manner of Bentham. But now that the moral consensus based on Christianity has wholly broken down, it has become uncomfortably clear that the commitment of a civil association to protecting the freedom for self-determination of its members is not a morally neutral commitment.

In the first place, it has become obvious, as Devlin has argued,[101] that not only censorship laws have moral assumptions imbedded in them. To allow nothing but primogeniture or to prohibit entailing of estates, to refuse property rights to women or insist that they have half an interest in all their husbands' property, to allow money to be left away from natural heirs or disallow its being left to homes for cats—all these decisions reflect moral notions of what constitutes decent and reasonable behavior just as much as obscenity laws do. Similarly how we treat various crimes will depend on our view of different passions. In the law of torts, the branch of law designed to answer the question, Who is to pay if things go wrong? the concept of negligence is central. And although it has been said that "gross negligence is only negligence with the addition of a vituperative epithet," even the notion of bare negligence implies a conception of how a reasonable man behaves and what constitutes the exercise of reasonable care.

The difference between law in a civil association and in a theocracy is not that between neutral and moral legislation but between the kinds of morality expressed or enforced by the law. The dichotomy between a "closed" and an "open" society is simple-minded. In an important

147

sense every society is closed. What matters is in what respect, manner, or degree it is closed. Just what ideas of substantive justice are compatible with a civil association remains to be explored. What can be said now is that the commitment of a civil association is not morally neutral; it is a commitment to a conception of what a civilized life implies, however great the variety of its forms. It is this commitment that constitutes substantive justice in a civil association.

The fact that our conceptions of constitutional and substantive justice cannot be demonstrated to be correct does not make them, as Kelsen maintains, "irrational." They are no more irrational than the arguments in a court of law or the judge's reasoning in giving his opinion. Sometimes agreement on what constitutes justice may remain implicit. It tends to become explicit as soon as someone begins to question what had until then been generally accepted. All this is part of the rational life of human beings, understood not to depend on "pure reason" and certain knowledge of universal laws, but on observing a certain order in discourse, considering evidence and arguments with regard to their truth and consistency rather than their use. As long as we try to defend our conclusions by giving reasons that are relevant and consistent and respectful of distinctions, we are not making random arbitrary assertions. The law need not shun considerations of constitutional or substantive justice in order to preserve its rationality.

Constitutional and substantive justice cannot conflict with one another because they are independent of one another. Neither then is there any natural connection between them, as theories of natural law assume. As they have different subjects—constitutional justice pertains to authority, substantive justice to the content of law—either may appear without the other. A law duly enacted in a legal system of impeccable constitutional justice may introduce an unjust social policy. A just social policy may be put into effect by gross violations of constitutional justice, as by judges giving decisions that violate every precedent in order to establish a rule that cannot get passed in the legislature.

There is no need to impugn legal procedures in order to establish that they have authorized an unjust law. Nor can it be said that judges who consider it their professional duty to enforce the established law and not to make law serve social policies they consider just, are willing instruments of injustice. Such an attitude makes the introduction of new social policies slower. But it also protects a constitutional order against its enemies. It is often forgotten that a disrespect for the established law by its appointed guardians, through allowing the law to be perverted, might have enabled the Nazis to replace the established constitutional order with a tyranny even more quickly and easily than they were in fact able to do. The readiness of judges to make the law subservient to "just" social policies may just as easily let tyrants take over as the readiness to enforce a law instituted by entrenched tyrants may perpetuate tyranny.

The moral question for a judge is never: Is this law so unjust that I must refuse to enforce it? but: Is the legal order so unjust that I can no longer help to perpetuate it? For in a legal order that conforms to constitutional justice and regularly to substantive justice, there not only may but must be many laws and many decisions that some members of the community will find objectionable. Every judge must sometimes reach decisions that are distasteful to him on the grounds of substantive justice. But as long as he remains on the bench he must render such decisions as a necessary part of his duty. When the established order is so far from just as it is in a Communist regime, a judge is likely to be faced regularly with the duty of enforcing heinous laws, apart from being compelled to ignore the law so as to further some immediate tyrannical design. At what point a moral judge is obliged to resign cannot be decided for him. But he can be certain that as long as he remains on the bench he is in effect deciding that the legal system he is helping to operate is preferable to its destruction and the attending risks.

He must also remember that when, in a legal system such as that of the United States or England, he ignores precedent in order to introduce quickly "social justice" he is acting as a revolutionary out to destroy the established order.* If it is true that the legal profession in Nazi Germany showed little disposition to oppose the Nazis, it could not have been because they were too disposed to respect established legal procedures but because they had refused to reflect on the purpose of those legal procedures and so failed to recognize when they were being perverted. It is not the positivists' emphasis on validity that makes them ready accomplices of the enemies of constitutionalism but their ready use of "validity" to discourage reflection on the reasons for wanting and venerating a legal order. So they are disposed to praise realist jurists for having discovered an important truth about the law rather than to censure them for being declared enemies of the rule of law.

Those who imagine a progress toward greater justice and who fret because a stable law fetters us to "outmoded" ideas may find comfort in the character of analogical reasoning. For it is nothing but the continuous tradition of analogical reasoning that constitutes the stability of the law. Of course this means that we can never wholly emancipate ourselves from the past. But then anyone who pretends that he is the first man on earth

---

* Violating precedent in order to establish "social justice" should be distinguished from violating precedent in order to correct what a judge considers to be legally improper decisions by his predecessors. In the latter case, the judge is concerned not to impose policies he considers desirable but to establish a more correct interpretation of the law, whether a statute or a decision. Of course a long line of "mistaken" decisions establishes expectations, and a break with precedent, whatever the motive, threatens the stability of the law. Whether it is more desirable to allow a "mistake" to continue or to avoid violating established expectations constitutes still another question. But allowing previous decisions to be reversed in order to preserve the integrity of the law is entirely distinct from allowing judges to violate precedent in order to make law.

must either be renouncing civilization or convicting himself of hypocrisy or delusion. The continuous tradition of analogical reasoning gives the law its flexibility as well as its stability and protects us against suffering from any "tyranny of the dead." It means that if Americans in the twentieth century prefer that judges decide in accordance with and not in defiance of the Fourteenth Amendment, they are not recommending subservience to "what a few senators of varying intellectual caliber may have intended—or hinted they intended—during the remote and unattractive year of 1868," as Edmund Cahn dolefully proclaims.[102] For a continuous tradition of judicial interpretation has brought the Fourteenth Amendment to the present not in the shape of a rule rigid with age, but as a living standard that has steadily been shaped by changing ideas and circumstances. We have no need to be "emancipated by fact scepticism," for we were never enslaved. And if a rule as it now stands appears to be undesirable, there are constitutional arrangements that provide procedures for changing it. Those who find these procedures too slow would do well to recollect that even Cardozo, who said that the judge had a duty to "raise the level of prevailing conduct," and not to be "indolent" or "passive in the face of injustices tolerated by the law," also urged the importance of safeguarding the law against the "assaults of opportunism, the expediency of the passing hour, the erosion of small encroachments, the scorn and derision of those who have no patience with general principles."[103]

Any judgment about the justice of law is part of a range of reasonable alternatives that cannot be conclusively ruled out. This latitude is inescapable in a contingent existence. But recognizing the contingency in human affairs is not equivalent to reducing human life to a chaos punctuated by random acts of will. It means recognizing that human life, both private and public, is shaped by a respect for limits to the exercise of choice. A respect for legal procedure implies a degree of passivity, a willingness to accept qualifications on one's own judgment, to suspend the response of the moment, and to recognize that men cannot consider or decide all things at once.

The infatuation of positivist jurists with logical gadgets has encouraged us to forget that the problem of human life consists not in unscrambling logical puzzles but in bringing order into a world of contingencies. For the latter task, there can be no neat formulas, simple answers, or ingenious solutions. Through legal institutions developed over two thousand years, men have found a way of fending off disorder by means of the changing permanency of the law. But to preserve it requires a nice appreciation of how, under the aegis of authority, stability and justice may live with uncertainty and change. Where there is no such appreciation, the lawful coercion that guards civilization can be slandered, blackmailed, and destroyed.

1 *Summa Theologica* I–II, Qu. 91, art. 2; *GBWW,* Vol. 20, p. 209.

2 Ibid., Qu. 95, art. 2; *GBWW,* Vol. 20, p. 228.

3 Josef Kohler, *Philosophy of Law* (1914), quoted in Jerome Frank, *Law and the Modern Mind* (New York: Brentano's, 1930), p. 198.

4 Justinian *Digests* 1. 2., quoted in *Summa Theologica* I–II, Qu. 95, art. 2; *GBWW,* Vol. 20, p. 227.

5 *See* Mortimer Adler, "The Doctrine of Natural Law in Philosophy," *University of Notre Dame Law Institute Proceedings,* vol. 1 (Notre Dame, Ind.: University of Notre Dame Press, 1949), pp. 65–84.

6 *Leviathan,* pt. 2, chap. 26; *GBWW,* Vol. 23, pp. 130–38 *passim.*

7 Kant, *General Introduction to the Metaphysic of Morals; GBWW,* Vol. 42, p. 392.

8 Kant, *The Philosophy of Law, trans. W. Hastie* (Edinburgh, 1887), p. 45. Reprinted in *GBWW,* Vol. 42, as *The Science of Right.* Cf. p. 398.

9 Ibid., p. 46; *GBWW,* Vol. 42, p. 398.

10 Ibid., p. 155; *GBWW,* Vol. 42, p. 433.

11 Ibid., p. 49; *GBWW,* Vol. 42, p. 399.

12 Ibid., p. 110; *GBWW,* Vol. 42, p. 419.

13 Ibid., p. 165; *GBWW,* Vol. 42, p. 436.

14 *See* Rudolph Stammler, "Fundamental Tendencies in Modern Jurisprudence," *Michigan Law Review* 21 (1923), pp. 623–54, 765–85, 862–903; idem, *The Theory of Justice,* trans. Isaac Husik, ed. François Gény and John C. H. Wu (New York: The Macmillan Co., 1925).

15 For Bentham's view of law, *see* the new Athlone Press editions of *An Introduction to the Principles of Morals and Legislation,* ed. J. H. Burns and H. L. A. Hart (London: University of London, 1970), and *Of Laws in General,* ed. H. L. A. Hart (London: University of London, 1970).

16 Hegel, *The Philosophy of Right,* par. 219; *GBWW,* Vol. 46, pp. 72–73.

17 *See* Gustav Radbruch in *The Legal Philosophies of Lask, Radbruch, and Dabin,* trans. Kurt Wilk, 20th Century Legal Philosophy Series, vol. 4 (Cambridge, Mass.: Harvard University Press, 1950), p. 63.

18 Letter to James Madison, September 6, 1789.

19 Michael Oakeshott, *Rationalism in Politics* (London: Methuen & Co., 1962), p. 131.

20 *See* Savigny, *System of Modern Roman Law,* 2 vols. (Madras, 1867), 1:171; *see also,* ibid., pp. iv–v, 13, 16; idem, *The Vocation of Our Age for Legislation and Jurisprudence,* trans. A. Hayward (London, 1831), esp. pp. 64ff., 96, 101, 106, 108, 135, 139, 182. For a common misinterpretation of Savigny, *see* Roscoe Pound, *Interpretations of Legal History* (Gloucester, Mass.: Peter Smith, 1967), pp. 12–20.

21 Ihering, *Law as a Means to an End,* trans. Isaac Husik (New York: The Macmillan Co., 1924), p. 276.

22 Ibid., p. 277.

23 Ibid., p. 381.

24 Ibid., p. 396.

25 Ibid., p. 399.

26 Ibid., p. 409.

27 Ibid., p. lviii.

28 Ibid., p. 2.

29 *See* A. L. Goodhart, "Some American Interpretations of Law," in *Modern Theories of Law* (London: Oxford University Press, 1963), pp. 1–20, esp. pp. 9–10.

30 Gray's view became current in England through Sir John Salmond's *Jurisprudence.*

31 Gray, *The Nature and Sources of the Law* (New York: The Macmillan Co., 1909), p. 90.

32 Ibid., p. 97.

33 Ibid., p. 98.

34 Ibid.

35 Ibid., p. 100.

36 Ibid.

37 Ibid., p. 118.

38 Ibid., p. 119.

39 Ibid., p. 82.

40 *Law and the Modern Mind,* p. 123.

41 Ibid., p. 125.

42 Ibid., p. 46.

43 Ibid., p. 127.

44 Ibid., p. 318.

45 Ibid., p. 315.

46 Ibid.

47 Ibid., p. 320.

48 "The Hornbook Method and the Conflict of Laws," *Yale Law Journal* 37 (1928): 480.

49 "A Return to Stare Decisis," *American Bar Association Journal* 14 (1927): 159.

50 *The Bramble Bush* (New York: Columbia University School of Law, 1930), p. 3.

51 Ibid., 2d ed., p. 9.

52 *Interpretations of Modern Legal Philosophy,* ed. Paul L. Sayre (New York: Oxford University Press, 1947), p. 543, quoted in Geoffrey Marshall, "Law in a Cold Climate," *Juridical Review* n.s. 1 (1956): 261.

53 *On Law and Justice,* trans. Margaret Dutton (London: Stevens & Sons, 1958), p. 327. *See also* H. L. A. Hart, "Scandinavian Realism," *Cambridge Law Journal* (1959): 233–40.

54 "Law and the Modern Mind," *Columbia Law Review* 31 (1931): 103.

55 Ibid., p. 104.

56 *Law and the Modern Mind,* p. 34.

57 *An Introduction to Legal Reasoning* (Chicago: University of Chicago Press, 1970), p. 1.

58 Ibid., p. 4.

59 Ibid.

60 Hans Kelsen, *The Pure Theory of Law,* trans. Max Knight (Berkeley and Los Angeles: University of California Press, 1967), pp. 105–6.

61 Ibid., p. 86.

62 "The Pure Theory of Law and Analytical Jurisprudence," *Harvard Law Review* 55 (1941): 49.

63 *General Theory of Law and State,* trans. Anders Wedberg, 20th Century Legal Philosophy Series, vol. 1 (Cambridge, Mass.: Harvard University Press, 1945), p. 49.

64 "Pure Theory and Analytical Jurisprudence," p. 47.

65 *General Theory,* p. 14.

66 Ibid.

67 *Pure Theory of Law,* p. 287.

68 "Pure Theory and Analytical Jurisprudence," p. 54.

69 Ibid., p. 56.

70 Ibid., p. 57.

71 Ibid., p. 58.

72 *Pure Theory of Law,* p. 352.

73 Ibid., p. 353.

74 Ibid., p. 194.

75 Ibid., p. 196.

76 *General Theory,* p. 437.

77 Ibid.

78 Ibid., p. 119.

79 *Pure Theory of Law,* p. 92.

80 Ibid., p. 95.

81 Hart, *The Concept of Law,* Clarendon Law Series (London: Oxford University Press, 1961), p. 110.

82 Ibid., p. 82.

83 Ibid., p. 88.

84 Ibid., p. 39.

85 Ibid., p. 94.

86 Ibid., p. 39.

87 Ibid., p. 43.

88 "Scandinavian Realism," p. 235.

89 *Concept of Law,* p. 186.

90 Ibid., p. 188.

91 Ibid., p. 189.

92 Ibid., p. 193.

93 Ibid., p. 194.

94 "Positivism and the Separation of Law and Morals," *Harvard Law Review* 71 (1958): 610.

95 Cf. Hart, "Positivism and the Separation of Law and Morals," and Lon L. Fuller, "Positivism and Fidelity to the Law—A Reply to Professor Hart," *Harvard Law Review* 71 (1958): 630–72.

96 *Concept of Law,* p. 57.

97 See Judith Shklar, *Legalism* (Cambridge, Mass.: Harvard University Press, 1964), where a similar conclusion is arrived at and characterized differently.

98 Aristotle *Politics* 1. 2. 1252^{b}27; *GBWW,* Vol. 9, p. 446.

99 I owe this distinction to Prof. Michael Oakeshott, who has developed it in a number of lectures and unpublished essays.

100 *See* F. A. Hayek, *The Constitution of Liberty* (Chicago: University of Chicago Press, 1960), especially pt. II.

101 Patrick Devlin, *The Enforcement of Morals* (New York: Oxford University Press, 1965).

102 *Confronting Injustice* (Boston: Little, Brown & Co., 1966), p. 288.

103 Benjamin N. Cardozo, *The Nature of the Judicial Process* (New Haven: Yale University Press, 1921), p. 108.

NOTE TO THE READER

The questions raised in this essay arise from a tradition that is well developed in the great books. See in the *Syntopicon* Chapter 46, LAW, along with the references cited under Topic 1, where law is defined; under Topics 4a–f, which treat of natural law; under Topic 5g, where writings concerned with the judicial process are listed; under Topic 6a, which deals with the terms of individual obedience to law; and under Topic 9, which has to do with the legal profession and the study of law. Chapter 42, JUSTICE, is also instructive. And consult the readings listed under GOVERNMENT 3d(2), concerned with judicial institutions and procedures; under REASONING 5e(2), which deal with the rational processes that are involved in legal thought; and under WILL 10b, where the relation of law to will is considered.

Readers who own *Gateway to the Great Books* may read "A Full and Faithful Report of the Memorable Trial of Bardell against Pickwick," by Charles Dickens, which is in *GGB,* Vol. 2, pp. 387–448; and for one of the great examples of forensic argument in American history, look at Lincoln's "Address at Cooper Institute," in Vol. 6, pp. 733–46.

The Great Anti-School Campaign

Robert M. Hutchins

The great campaign against the American public school has now reached the stage of overkill. It is impossible to believe that anything new can be added to the attacks already delivered, for the schools have been assailed from every conceivable direction, with every conceivable motive. The coalition against them is such as to suggest that the one thing on which our people have reached unanimity is the evils of our system of public education. The coalition is a strange one, because the critics would not agree with, or even speak to, one another on any other subject. Softhearted revolutionaries and hardheaded businessmen join in arguing that the public schools should be abolished. A critic is now regarded as moderate if he proposes merely that the system be instantly, drastically, and thoroughly reformed. Everybody wants to have education available. Everybody wants it paid for by taxes. But nobody has a kind word for the institution that was only the other day the foundation of our freedom, the guarantee of our future, the cause of our prosperity and power, the bastion of our security, the bright and shining beacon that was the source of our enlightenment, the public school.

The signs of overkill are not merely that the critics are repeating themselves. Some of them are beginning to question solutions advanced by members of their own groups, such as the abolition of all schools whatever. Recoiling from this proposal, questioners have asked what problems of the community, or of children, it would solve. They have gone on to point out that poverty, slums, racial discrimination, disorganized families, disease, injustice, and television[1] would remain, and have thus inferentially let us know that if the schools are bad, or if children do not learn in school, or if they have a hard time there, some of the fault may lie with the community and the environment in which children live rather than with the schools alone.

Other critics appear to be preparing for a strategic withdrawal. Some of those who have told us that schools are prisons and teachers tyrants are now hinting that some schools are joyous and some teachers humane.

Donald McDonald has helped me in the preparation of this article from the beginning. Mortimer J. Adler, Stringfellow Barr, Clifton Fadiman, William Gorman, Milton Mayer, Joseph J. Schwab, and John Van Doren have been good enough to criticize the manuscript.

Some who led us to believe that all we had to do was to follow the whims of children now want to make sure we understand that a curriculum, with teachers in charge, is required.

On the side of the hardheaded businessmen, the voucher plan sponsored by the Office of Economic Opportunity contains so many restrictions on free enterprise and so much governmental control that it cannot be looked upon with much favor by the free-enterprise economists who were its principal sponsors at the outset. And those who announced that performance contracting, in which commercial corporations take over teaching and are paid for "results," was the remedy for the inefficiency of the academic bureaucracy are now rebuffed by their erstwhile advocates in government.

Whether or not the campaign against the schools subsides, it will leave traces for years to come. The wrecks of bond issues and proposals for tax increases for the schools are scattered all over the landscape. What is more significant, the value of universal, free, compulsory education, supported by taxes and controlled by the political community, has been called in question for the first time in our history. If we cannot give a clear answer, we may take irreversible steps downhill. So we should try to answer. The political community should be required to justify the prolonged detention of children in an educational system. This essay is an attempt to inquire into the possibility of such justification. It seeks to answer the question whether public education, as defined above, is any longer useful. If so, on what terms? If not, what is the alternative?

The idea of public education

As the *Syntopicon* says, "Education is not itself so much an idea or a subject matter as it is a theme to which the great ideas and the basic subject matters are relevant. . . . There can be no philosophy of education apart from philosophy as a whole."[2]

T. S. Eliot made the same point in "Modern Education and the Classics":

> *If education today seems to deteriorate, if it seems to become more and more chaotic and meaningless, it is primarily because we have no settled and satisfactory arrangement of society, and because we have both vague and diverse opinions about the kind of society we want. Education is a subject which cannot be discussed in a void: our questions raise other questions, social, economic, financial, political. And the bearings are on more ultimate problems even than these: to know what we want in education we must know what we want in general, we must derive our theory of education from our philosophy of life.*[3]

The confusion of which Eliot speaks is nothing new. It seems to have prevailed in societies we are accustomed to think of as much simpler than our own. Aristotle says in the *Politics:*

> *As things are, there is disagreement about the subjects. For man-kind are by no means agreed about the things to be taught, whether we look to virtue or the best life. Neither is it clear whether education is more concerned with intellectual or with moral virtue. The existing practice is perplexing; no one knows on what principle we should proceed—should the useful in life, or should virtue, or should the higher knowledge, be the aim of our training; all three opinions have been entertained.*[4]

Since any free society is likely to be engaged in controversy about the kind of society it ought to be, confusion about the kind of education it ought to have seems inevitable.

No believer in free speech can object to argument, however heated, about issues of this sort. On the contrary, most Westerners have been brought up to regard such discussion as essential to the progress of the political community. But the task of educational statesmanship is made infinitely complicated by the shifting balance of power among competing doctrines and by the difficulty of distinguishing between public convictions and passing fads. The more rapid the pace of social and intellectual change, the harder the task becomes. The difficulty is accentuated by the power of the mass media, which gain and hold their audience by presenting a kaleidoscope of novelties. The extraordinary proliferation of new or seemingly new educational theories may result as much from the new opportunities to get attention through the media as it does from any failure of the schools.

Until recently the contemporary Western world has regarded free schools maintained by taxes and controlled by the political community as one of the indispensable requisites of an advancing or even a lasting society. We are likely to forget that this idea is new. Rousseau, after saying that public education, under regulations prescribed by the government and under magistrates established by the sovereign, is certainly the most important business of the state, and that only the Cretans, Spartans, and Persians had such education, goes on to remark: "Since the world has been divided into nations too great to admit of being well governed, this method has been no longer practicable, and the reader will readily perceive other reasons why such a thing has never been attempted by any modern people."[5]

Although Plato had laid it down in the *Laws* that education should be compulsory and public,[6] and Martin Luther and Rousseau had made similar pronouncements, it was not until the social and political changes of the eighteenth century that such a thing was attempted on any considerable scale. Yet by the time the twentieth century opened, universal, free, compulsory education controlled by the political community had been largely realized all over the West, and wherever Western ideas were dominant.

This rapid development seems to be associated with industrialization and democracy. Adam Smith, for example, insisted that everybody must have some education and that the state must see to it that he gets it, in order to rescue the mass of the population from the evil effects of dawning industrialization. He says:

> *In the progress of the division of labour, the employment of the far greater part of those who live by labour, that is, of the great body of the people, comes to be confined to a few very simple operations, frequently to one or two. But the understandings of the greater part of men are necessarily formed by their ordinary employments. The man whose whole life is spent in performing a few simple operations, of which the effects are perhaps always the same, or very nearly the same, has no occasion to exert his understanding or to exercise his invention in finding out expedients for removing difficulties which never occur. He naturally loses, therefore, the habit of such exertion, and generally becomes as stupid and ignorant as it is possible for a human creature to become. The torpor of his mind renders him not only incapable of relishing or bearing a part in any rational conversation, but of conceiving any generous, noble, or tender sentiment, and consequently of forming any just judgment concerning many even of the ordinary duties of private life. Of the great and extensive interests of his country he is altogether incapable of judging. . . . But in every improved and civilised society this is the state into which the labouring poor, that is, the great body of the people, must necessarily fall, unless government takes some pains to prevent it.*[7]

Smith wanted small schools established. His reason for having the schoolmaster paid in part by the parents is characteristic. He says if the teacher were paid wholly, or even principally, by the public, "he would soon learn to neglect his business." He went on to say that the intervention of the public would take place through a system that would oblige "every man to undergo an examination or probation" in the most essential parts of education "before he can obtain the freedom in any corporation, or be allowed to set up any trade either in a village or town corporate."[8]

Smith had little occasion, in 1776, to consider the uses of education in preparing the citizen to take his part in the political community. Those in what he calls "the inferior ranks" had no part in that community, and it was not supposed they ever would have. His emphasis, therefore, is on the needs of the individual.

"Since any free society is likely to be engaged in controversy about the kind of society it ought to be, confusion about the kind of education it ought to have seems inevitable"

> *A man without the proper use of the intellectual faculties of a man,*
> *is, if possible, more contemptible than even a coward, and seems*
> *to be multilated and deformed in a still more essential part of the*
> *character of human nature. Though the state was to derive no ad-*
> *vantage from the instruction of the inferior ranks of people, it*
> *would still deserve its attention that they should not be altogether*
> *uninstructed. The state, however, derives no inconsiderable ad-*
> *vantage from their instruction.*[9]

This advantage turns out to be less superstition, less disorder, less disrespect for superiors, less factious and wanton opposition to government,
and less rash and capricious judgment of public affairs.

John Stuart Mill, the apostle of diversity, insists on education for everybody, at the cost, if necessary, of the public treasury. He says:

> *It is in the case of children that misapplied notions of liberty are*
> *a real obstacle to the fulfillment by the State of its duties. . . . Is it*
> *not almost a self-evident axiom, that the State should require and*
> *compel the education, up to a certain standard, of every human*
> *being who is born its citizen? Yet who is there that is not afraid to*
> *recognise and assert this truth? . . . But while this is unanimously*
> *declared to be the father's duty, scarcely anybody, in this country,*
> *will bear to hear of obliging him to perform it. . . . It still remains*
> *unrecognised, that to bring a child into existence without a fair*
> *prospect of being able, not only to provide food for its body, but*
> *instruction and training for its mind, is a moral crime, both against*
> *the unfortunate offspring and against society; and that if the parent*
> *does not fulfil this obligation, the State ought to see it fulfilled, at*
> *the charge, as far as possible, of the parent.*[10]

The role of the state must ostensibly be limited to paying the expenses
of the educational system. Mill's program is:

> *If the government would make up its mind to require for every*
> *child a good education, it might save itself the trouble of providing*
> *one. It might leave to parents to obtain the education where and*
> *how they pleased, and content itself with helping to pay the school*
> *fees of the poorer classes of children, and defraying the entire*
> *school expenses of those who have no one else to pay for them. The*
> *objections which are urged with reason against State education do*
> *not apply to the enforcement of education by the State, but to the*
> *State's taking upon itself to direct that education; which is a totally*
> *different thing. That the whole or any large part of the education*
> *of the people should be in State hands, I go as far as anyone in*

deprecating. . . . A general State education is a mere contrivance for moulding people to be exactly like one another. . . .[11]

On one point Mill differs drastically from Smith and that is in the effects state examinations are to have. Whereas Smith sees them as excluding those who do not pass from the chance to earn a living, Mill, perhaps anticipating the later growth of credentialism, would allow them no influence whatever. How he would accomplish this, or just what he expected to accomplish, remains obscure. His intention, to prohibit the state from affecting the careers of individuals by means of its examination system, is clear. He says:

> *It would be giving too dangerous a power to governments were they allowed to exclude any one from professions, even from the profession of teacher, for alleged deficiency of qualifications: and I think, with Wilhelm von Humboldt, that degrees, or other public certificates of scientific or professional acquirements, should be given to all who present themselves for examination, and stand the test; but that such certificates should confer no advantage over competitors other than the weight which may be attached to their testimony by public opinion.*[12]

We know now that the weight attached to degrees and certificates by public opinion can be just as exclusionary as any that might be imposed by law.

The essay *On Liberty* appeared in 1859, and England moved decisively toward free, compulsory education eleven years later. It came in essentially the form in which we know it, with schools supported by taxes and controlled by political entities. Mill's proposal, the ancestor of the voucher plan put forward in the United States today, was not accepted. Parliament was unwilling to have taxing bodies put up the money and allow the parents to dispose of it as they saw fit for the education of their children.

This result was to have been expected. In the first place, in Mill's own terms he was striving for an unattainable ideal. He wanted education paid for by the state but free from its control. Yet his plan requires examinations given by the state on subjects selected by it and with standards set by it. The power to select subjects and set standards gives a large measure of control, and this is apart from the general proposition that he who pays the piper calls the tune. Some form of inspection, approval, and accreditation by the state would have been inevitable.

In the second place, Parliament did not share Mill's confidence in parents. The report of the Children's Employment Commission of 1866, cited by Marx, said, "It is unhappily, to a painful degree, apparent throughout the whole of the evidence that against no persons do the children of both sexes so much require protection as against their parents."[13] So Mill's contemporary Hegel declared that he would no more trust parents to get their children educated than to get them vaccinated.[14] One argument for child labor was that manufacturers would relieve children of the oppression and exploitation they were enduring at home.

But it seems likely that the principal reason why Mill's recommendations were not adopted was that the motives of those who carried through the establishment of public education in England were different from his. He was concerned with the individual and saving him from mutilation through failure of a chance to develop his intellectual powers. Mill sees the state, in this connection, only as a necessary evil.

But Lord Sherbrooke expressed the prevailing mood of the country after Reform when he said, "Now we must educate our masters." Education appeared to be necessary for the maintenance of a society that admitted large new groups and classes to the franchise. The education of all had been required by similar considerations in the Massachusetts Bay Colony long before; it ran through the statements of the Founding Fathers; it was officially set forth in the Northwest Ordinance. The people, however "people" was defined, had to be educated in a self-governing state. The common schools, as their name implied, originated in and for the community. Their object was to maintain and increase the common good, that good which accrued to every member of the community because he belonged to it and which he would not enjoy if he did not belong to it.

James Russell Lowell pronounced the general judgment when he said, "It was in making education not only common to all, but in some sense compulsory on all, that the destiny of the free republics of America was practically settled."[15] In 1954 the Supreme Court spoke in the same tone in rejecting racially segregated public schools. The unanimous opinion of the Court held:

> *Today, education is perhaps the most important function of state and local governments. Compulsory school-attendance laws and the great expenditures for education both demonstrate our recognition of the importance of education to our democratic society. It is required in the performance of our most basic public responsibilities, even service in the armed forces. It is the very foundation of good citizenship.*[16]

Smith and Mill spoke almost exclusively of the individual and the necessity of educating him in order to prevent him from becoming a clod, or to help him realize his full human potential. They talked of the value to him of education that would rescue him from stupidity, ignorance, and torpor, that would enable him to enjoy and conduct a rational conversation, to conceive elevating sentiments, to form just judgments, and to learn to use his mind. Neither argued that education ought to be a way of getting ahead. Mill's limitations on the professional effects of examinations originate not merely in his fear of the state, but also in his fear that its examinations would be used to advance the careers of those who passed them. Yet this notion of the aim of education was as popular in England in the hundred years from Smith to Mill as it was in Germany in Kant's time; and Kant had felt called upon to repudiate the idea that the object of education was to help young people make their way in the world. He protested that "parents usually educate their children merely in such a manner that, however bad the world may be, they may adapt themselves to its present conditions."[17] Their purpose should not be to adjust to the environment, but to change it.

By the time of the Civil War and the passage of the Morrill Act establishing the land grant colleges "to teach such branches of learning as are related to agriculture and the mechanic arts . . . in order to promote the liberal and practical education of the industrial classes in the several pursuits and professions in life," the doctrine that the purpose of education was to give the individual a leg up the economic and social ladder was widely accepted in the United States. The last of the self-made men had to disappear before it became the universal creed; but with the departure of such figures as Thomas Edison and Henry Ford, who thought education a waste of time, the proposition that it was a means to the achievement of economic rewards was generally agreed to. The Supreme Court, in *Brown* v. *Board of Education,* evidently thought the rhetoric of community and the rhetoric of getting ahead could be effectively combined. After its resounding statement that education was the very foundation of good citizenship, the Court added: "In these days, it is doubtful that any child may reasonably be expected to succeed in life if he is denied the opportunity of an education." Whatever may be said of the rest of the opinion, in this statement the Court was up-to-date. A report of the Carnegie Commission on Higher Education published in the fall of 1971 said, "Education has increasingly become *the* bridge to better status. . . . Income, occupation, and education are related, but education is increasingly the key factor."

The concern of Smith and Mill with the individual was now transformed. The slogan came to be "equality of opportunity." This did not mean that everybody's full human potential was to be developed, but that everybody should be admitted to school and have a chance to compete for such rewards as schooling could offer. In view of what we know now about the effects of family background and socioeconomic status on success or failure in school, it is not surprising that poor children lost out in this competition. For these children, schooling was not the path to success in life. It helped most those who needed it least. And, since the poor have always borne a disproportionate burden of taxes, they paid a large part of the cost of the education of those richer than themselves. Nevertheless,

Free and Cantril report that when Americans were asked to choose among the reasons explaining "success," 71% named education, more than the 66% for "initiative, effort, hard work" and the 59% for "character, will power." Seventy-six percent said lack of education was the prime cause of human failure.[18]

Associated with the rhetoric of success in life is the rhetoric of national strength or success in the life of the nation. This came into use after World War II, in which the scientists seemed to establish once and for all that knowledge was power. When the Russians sent up Sputnik, suggesting that they had more knowledge and hence more power than we, an educational frenzy swept the country. Only by pouring billions more into educational institutions could we hope to defend ourselves against a nation with such resources.

President John F. Kennedy proclaimed the causal connection between education, prosperity, and power in a message to Congress in 1963:

> *This nation is committed to greater advancement in economic growth; and recent research has shown that one of the most beneficial of all such investments is education, accounting for some forty percent of the nation's growth and productivity in recent years. In the new age of science and space, improved education is essential to give meaning to our national purpose and power. It requires skilled manpower and brainpower to match the power of totalitarian discipline. It requires a scientific effort which demonstrates the superiority of freedom.*

Sputnik was a shock we quickly forgot in the excitement of our own lunar exploits. But other surprises have been in store for us; we have discovered that other nations, even some formerly regarded as lesser breeds without the law, are able to challenge our economic, technological, scientific, industrial superiority, and, in such matters as medical care, to leave us far behind.

The beginnings of confusion and doubt

The reader will note that, though the rhetoric has shifted through the years, it has always come out at the same place. Everybody ought to be educated. This means everybody ought to go to school. If some schooling is good, more is better. Therefore the school-leaving age should be as high as possible. The state of the nation—of any nation—can be judged by the proportion of its income spent on schools and the proportion of the relevant age groups that is attending them. By this standard the United States has led the world. Education has been the palladium of our liberties and the symbol of our progress. It is the key to our future. Universal, free, compulsory education, supported by taxes and controlled by the state, has made us what we are today and will make us even better tomorrow.

Unfortunately, we do not much like what we are today, and we are not convinced any longer that education will solve the problems in our future. Almost every citizen born in this country has now had extensive acquaintance with its educational system. With our vast and varied resources, our admirable Constitution, and our elaborate and expensive schools, colleges, and universities, we should lead the world, not merely in school population and expenditure, but also in all the qualities self-government demands.

On the contrary, all our policies are in question and all our institutions in disarray. We are no longer the only superpower in the world. It looks as if instead of dominating everybody we would have to make our way by playing off Russia and China against each other. The war in Asia, which has disillusioned us about our political leaders and our military power, drags on. The young people and the minorities who have borne the brunt of the war are in revolt against it, and many of them are rebelling against the system that made it possible. After billions spent on urban "rehabilitation," our metropolitan centers are becoming uninhabitable, and the slums are as bad as ever. We have been told on high authority that we are enjoying an affluent society, but we have discovered that millions are living in poverty and that those who have affluence don't know what to do with it. Meanwhile the devastation and pollution of the natural environment proceeds at a faster and faster pace, and we cannot make up our minds to pay the price for past sins or future self-denial. It has occurred to a good many people that we should have been saved from these conditions by our educational system and that, if we have not been saved by it, the system cannot be much good. It is often said to be irrelevant—it cannot remedy the ills at which it has connived. We have an even less settled and satisfactory arrangement of society than the one T. S. Eliot saw in 1932. Education is for the first time in this country generally regarded as chaotic and meaningless and, worse still, as positively damaging.[19] *Newsweek* magazine has referred to a feeling that, it says, has gnawed at many Americans for a long time—the uneasy sense that most U.S. elementary schools are actually harmful to a child's development.

Many of the negative criticisms of the public schools are justified, though some of them are stated in rather intemperate language. Nobody who has attended an American public school will deny that it is afflicted with boredom, authoritarianism, bureaucracy, inefficiency, and ineffectiveness. It always has been. But it is now much more expensive than it ever has been. It includes a higher proportion of the population than ever. Success in school and getting credentials to prove it are thought to be indispensable to social mobility; and we have discovered that the school, contrary to our expectations, does not provide it. We have learned

"Everybody ought to be educated. . . . everybody ought to go to school"

that socioeconomic status and family attitudes and background impose constraints upon the child that the school seems powerless to overcome. The earliest years, even days, of life, long before school has a chance to be of influence, leave an imprint upon a child that may never be erased.[20]

Brown v. *Board of Education* hastened the flight from the cities and from their public schools. The school systems in many cities are overwhelmingly black. Meanwhile the Coleman Report has shown that black pupils are markedly affected by the presence of white pupils. It says:

> *For example, a pupil attitude factor, which appears to have a stronger relationship to achievement than do all the "school" factors together, is the extent to which an individual feels that he has some control over his own destiny. . . . While this characteristic shows little relationship to most school factors, it is related, for Negroes, to the proportion of whites in the schools. Those Negroes in schools with a higher proportion of whites have a greater sense of control.[21]*

White people discovered the ghetto and the consequences of the ghettoized school at the same time. The ghettoized school did nothing to confirm our faith in public education.

Taxes have been going higher and higher. The property tax, which supplies 52 percent of the current annual support of the schools, has been felt to be more and more burdensome and inequitable; the courts of California and Minnesota and a federal district court in Texas have cast doubt on its constitutionality when it results in gross inequities among school districts.[22] If these decisions are upheld, the whole process of financing schools will have to be thought out again: the states may be faced with the alternatives of reducing the cost of their "best" schools or greatly increasing the total expenditures on the whole system. The dilemma is disturbing.

The question is now raised whether the educational system has much, or indeed, any, effect, whether it has any function except a custodial one, whether it does much of anything except keep children out of worse places until they can go to work. Some critics suggest, in fact, that any place the child wanted to go would be better than school, where he is "imprisoned" against his will. The slogan of one recent book is, "Let Our Children Go," and one of the authors intimates that truancy offers the only hope of salvation to the rising generation.[23] If an institution is accomplishing little and that little is bad, if it is both conspicuous and expensive, if it directly involves almost everybody in the country (as pupil or parent, teacher, or taxpayer), then summary execution would seem to be the only punishment that would fit its crimes.

One other question may be more important than those I have mentioned, and that is what has happened to the purposes for which the schools have been thought to exist. In recent years these purposes have been the material and social improvement of the individual and the establishment and maintenance of self-government in the community. The first of these, helping the individual get ahead, has suffered, as we have seen, at the hands of scholars who have shown that family background and attitudes and the influences of the earliest years may make it almost impossible for schools as we have known them to help the individual get out of the station in which he was born. Evidence of another, but no less disturbing, kind has been piling up that the whole idea of getting a better job by getting more credentials may be absurd.

At the moment of writing this, the current issue of *Life* carried the following letter:

> *Sirs: Mitchell Roland is easily discouraged ("Doesn't Anyone Need a Ph.D. Chemist?" Nov. 5). Only 250 rejections after 19 years of study? I find that after 28 years of study, five earned degrees (including two M.A.s and a Ph.D. due in March), and seven years of teaching experience, I am not wanted either. My school has sent my résumé to over 200 colleges but there has been nary a nibble.*
>
> *My advice to graduate students: Drop out and get a job before you make yourself unemployable!*

Those who have been hardest hit by the current unemployment in the United States are those who have the most credentials.[24]

If one lives long enough one may expect to see the dilution of one's credentials going on before one's very eyes. When I graduated from college half a century ago, only two percent of the population could boast of the same distinction. My advantage has been undermined by the same process that has made the high school diploma less and less valuable: too many people have been receiving it. How can schooling confer status when it is universal? When everybody's somebody, nobody's anybody.

There is a law about credentials, a law by which the spread of one credential requires the invention of a "higher" credential having the distinctiveness the old one has lost. When I was graduated from law school forty-five years ago, I was handed an LL.B. degree, and I was glad to get it. But other law schools had already begun to degrade me by awarding a doctorate, the J.D., for the same work. It took the Yale Law School a long time to get around to it, but finally I received a notice, forty-five years later, that for a small fee I could obtain a certificate from Yale saying I was the holder of a J.D. degree and that for a slightly larger sum I could get a J.D. diploma all written out in Latin.

In India, we are told, "B.A. Failed" will appear after a man's name, for this credential is thought to be better than none; and it is even re-ported that "B.A. Failed (Twice)" has been seen on an office door. In Africa and Japan and the Soviet Union various shades of the same super-stition appear. The Open University in Britain, one of the most hopeful educational projects of the modern age, may ruin itself and its students by its adoption of the American credit system and its dedication to what is known as "upgrading professional qualifications," which means getting credentials into the hands of those who are without them.

In the United States the value of credentials has been upheld by gov-ernmental regulations that distinguish among students on the basis of whether or not they are seeking credentials. One cannot receive some forms of federal aid unless one is after a degree. Hence institutions that want their students to be eligible for such aid—as all institutions do—must concoct degrees to which they may aspire.

Student deferments from the draft have the same effect; they give the degree a charm that has nothing to do with the education it is supposed to stand for. Some part of the reduction in the number of freshmen in the country by 100,000 in the autumn of 1971 may be accounted for by the suspension of student deferments. At any rate, the members of a committee of professors from a large state university who met in Santa Barbara a short time ago reported a dropout rate of 45 percent in the freshman year. They attributed it to the abolition of student deferments. The degree was no longer thought worth the effort.

If this is the way students are thinking, they are correct, for little pre-tense is made that there is any relationship between the certificate, di-ploma, or degree that an applicant for a job must display and the work that is to be done. Ivar Berg's book, *Education and Jobs: The Great Training Robbery* (1970), shows that credentials have only a ritualistic function. They simplify the labors of personnel officers. Berg points out that in the armed forces it was found that high school graduates were not uniformly and markedly superior to nongraduates, and that training on the job was more important than educational credentials.

The tide may be turning. A preliminary report issued by the Commis-sion on Post-secondary Education in Ontario in January 1972 asks, "Why should there be any formal links between educational requirements and occupations? Why, indeed, do we use degrees and diplomas for certifica-tion purposes?" The Commission adds: "Certification, in fact, is probably one of the greatest causes of rigidity and inequality in education. It is therefore imperative that we take a new look at the need for and justifica-tion of certification and its coupling to education."[25]

A headline in the *New York Times* for November 6, 1971, said "Study Finds School Dropouts Do Not Appear to Suffer." The study, directed by Dr. Jerald Bachman of the Institute for Social Research at the University of Michigan, covered four years in the lives of 2,213 boys who at the outset were in the tenth grade in high schools across the country. The study showed that the dropouts' self-esteem rose after they left school and that they received slightly higher incomes than those of their contemporaries who went on to graduate. Dr. Bachman said his findings did not support the stay-in-school campaign, which was based on the supposition that remaining long enough in school to get a diploma improved a young person's lot in life. Dr. Bachman argued the campaign should be stopped: "It's giving dropouts a bad name."

If educational credentials turn out to confer no benefit on the individual who acquires them, and none on the firms that employ those who hold them, the question arises whether schooling confers any practical benefits at all, and if it does not, why the costly and elaborate system should be maintained. If your object in going to school was to get ahead, and you don't get ahead, why should you have gone? Why should others go? The principal effect of connecting schooling with getting ahead seems to be to discourage those having difficulty in finishing school. These are chiefly the underprivileged, the disadvantaged, the poor, and the black. One is sometimes tempted to think this is why educational requirements are popular with employers: these requirements help relieve them of the embarrassment of saying they don't want underprivileged, disadvantaged, poor, or black people around.

Adam Smith's and John Stuart Mill's concern with the development of the individual as a human being, saved from stupidity, ignorance, and torpor, able to carry on a rational conversation, conceive elevating sentiments, form just judgments, and use his mind, has passed through various stages of degradation until nothing is left but an exhortation to acquire a piece of paper, however meaningless, the magical powers of which as a passport to a brighter future seem to be declining. Insofar as the schools have cooperated in building up the impression that years of schooling confer economic advantage in proportion to their number, the schools could expect to suffer from the rage and disappointment of those who put in the years without reaping the advantage.

The loss of purpose

In the *Politics* Aristotle says, "The state, as I was saying, is a plurality, which should be united and made into a community by education."[26] The other day Carl Weinberg wrote, "A democratic nation requires an enlightened electorate, and with universal suffrage, all citizens need to be educated." He then wryly adds, "Unfortunately, the only aspect of fulfilling this requirement has been compulsory attendance."[27]

The statement of the Supreme Court in *Brown* v. *Board of Education* about education as the foundation of good citizenship has an anachronistic ring. Such a statement has meaning if there is a political community, if the citizens think of themselves as such, and if they have something on their minds beyond survival and prosperity. Perhaps the last epoch at which the schools were seriously regarded as the agency of good citizenship was that of the great Americanization campaign at the high tide of immigration. Seventy-five and more years ago, an issue hotly debated was that of "assimilation"; persons born in other countries were rated in terms of their "assimilability." (Orientals were regarded as highly suspicious characters because they were set in their ways.) I can remember in 1914 taking part in a long, hot argument tending to show that immigrants from countries other than those in northern and western Europe should be excluded or subjected to special restrictions on the ground that certain nationalities were clearly less assimilable than others. This doctrine was involved in the quota system adopted thereafter.

Those were the days of the melting pot. The compulsory public school was the institution by which the children of the foreigner were to be made into good Americans. In only one generation, we thought, this transformation would take place.

The passion for Americanization died down, to be revived in an unpleasant form whenever political capital could be made by claiming that some elements in the population were likely, because of their ancestry, to be disloyal. The role of the schools in the maintenance and the development of the political community or citizenship therein became a topic limited to Fourth of July oratory. On other occasions the rhetoric of the individual reigned supreme.

Brown v. *Board of Education* had the unintended effect of promoting a new definition of the community. The community was no longer everybody; it was not united for the common good of all. The community became people of my race, my neighborhood, my economic class. The rhetoric of the community now asserted that the school belonged to the community as redefined. "Pluralism" became a popular war cry. The black and white racists, the poor and the rich, the city dweller and the suburbanite all demanded that the school their children attended should be theirs. They would control it if they could; if they could not, they would at least insist that it be attended only by children of the same color and background as their own. This led to the opposition to busing, an attitude endorsed by the president of the United States. The neighborhood school, meaning a school that ignored the existence or importance of the wider political community, became a sacred object.

This is not what *Brown* v. *Board of Education* meant. And where race has been involved, the courts have had some success in repelling attempts to give this meaning to that decision. Civil rights legislation, by forbidding racial discrimination in housing, may gradually change the patterns of neighborhoods so that residential divisions will not result in segregation. But what has happened to the public school in the course of the argument is that its purpose as the builder of good citizenship in the political community has been forgotten. As we shall see later on, this role of the school is now seldom mentioned. The field is left to the rhetoric of the individual, neighborhood, or the group, or the race, or the class.

A school is truly public if it belongs to the public and if its aim is to form and maintain the public. As Werner Jaeger put it in *Paideia*,[28] education is the deliberate attempt to form men in terms of an ideal. The aim of the American public school originally was to form men as independent, self-governing members of a self-governing community. That community was as wide as each of the thirteen original states. After the passage of the Fourteenth Amendment, it became as wide as the nation, in the sense that the states were not permitted to violate national standards in any of their important activities, of which education was one. That the political community extends beyond the boundaries of the state is evident in the judicial regulation of education in the states and in congressional appropriations for support of education, which are becoming commonplace.

The growth of technology is shrinking the planet at such a rate that we must already think of a world community, no matter how far off a world political community may be. Hence it is alarming that American educational discussion either omits the community from consideration entirely or refers to it only in a dwarfed and trivial form, as the selfish interest of neighborhoods, groups, or classes. Such a redefinition of the community is defensible only if its self-centeredness is mitigated as it would be in the context of a carefully worked out theory of decentralization or subsidiarity, in which each smaller unit made its contribution to and carried its share of the burdens of the whole. As Senator William Fulbright has said, "The essence of any community—local, national, or international—is some degree of acceptance of the principle that the good of the whole must take precedence over the good of the parts."[29]

A large, conspicuous, elaborate, expensive institution on which the hopes of a nation have been pinned cannot hope to escape attack in a period of national distress unless it can show that it has intelligible purposes and that it is achieving them. The American educational system cannot make the required demonstration. This is not altogether the fault of the schools. The reader will remember that the failure of educational philosophy reflects the failure of our philosophy in general. It is not the schools that make their purposes, but the people who control them. For example, credentialism is not the fault of the schools but of parents and employers. The unfortunate new definition of community did not originate in the schools but in the propaganda of those who wished to use them for their purposes. We are not here allocating praise or blame. We are attempting to understand why the institution we have thought most dear to American hearts should suddenly lose its grip on the affections of our citizens and arouse instead feelings of hostility and remorse.

We turn now to the proposals of those who in varying degrees share these feelings. I have summarized their criticisms in the previous parts of this paper. One must agree with much of what they say. The trouble with these authors is that the alternatives they offer are either trivial or unworkable.

Should schools be abolished?

The first set of charges is that the schools harm the child. They repress his individuality. They destroy his spontaneity. They do this, according to some critics, merely by requiring him to be in school at all. He should not be there if he prefers to be somewhere else. These writers, though they are sometimes obscure on the point, seem to favor the abolition of schools of every kind. Their argument is psychological: that child develops best who is not subject to any kind of coercion. Compulsory education is therefore a crime against the young.

Others add a political argument to the psychological one. They see the school as the instrument of tyranny, of that oligarchical conspiracy which runs the world, which has set up its institutions, and which keeps everybody in his place. In this view, a political, social, and economic revolution is necessary: any school, even a so-called free school, originating with and controlled by groups of parents and dedicated to following the interest of the children, is an intolerable makeshift because it is a school. As such it is likely to have grades and credentials the effect of which is to degrade and disqualify those from poor homes.

No alternative to school is offered by those who oppose compulsory schooling on psychological grounds. They believe that children will learn what they ought to learn—assuming that they ought to learn anything—as they feel the need to learn it. Compulsion will merely thwart learning, because learning can only take place when the pupil wants to learn. How and what these children will learn does not appear. The picture is one of the child, with such guidance as he asks for (if he can find a guide to ask), working out the times, places, and methods of his own education.

An important assumption is also involved here, and that is that all learning is of equal worth. The child who goes fishing when he feels like it learns what he wants to know at the time and therefore what he needs to know. George Dennison, who is not a man to oppose schools as such, feels free to put forward the proposition that wishes = needs = rights. He says, "Why is it, then, that so many children fail? Let me put it bluntly: it is because our system of public education is a horrendous, life-destroying mess." He asks, "Now what is so precious about a curriculum (which no one assimilates anyway), or a schedule of classes (which piles boredom upon failure and failure upon boredom) that these things should supersede the actual needs of the child?" He goes on to say, " . . . we trusted that some true organic bond existed between the wishes of the children and their actual needs. . . ." As Dennison is not opposed to schools, he is not opposed to a course of study. He says, "Naturally we want a coherent curriculum (we need not impose it in standardized forms)."[30] But the wishes of children, which may be expected to vary from child to child, from time to time, and from place to place, can hardly form the basis of a "coherent" curriculum unless the children are somehow tricked into wishing for what the teacher wishes them to have.

So the course announcement of a seminar offered by Ronald and Beatrice Gross at New York University, "Free Learning: Non-institutionalized Education in Theory and Practice," begins:

> The realization that the most important learning can, does, and should go on outside of schools and colleges, is beginning to revolutionize American education. Ivan Illich, Paul Goodman, John Holt, and others have argued that the resources available for learning—media, tools, money—should be wrested from the established institutions that currently "provide" education and put in the hands of consumers—students.

No doubt the notion that learning can take place only in an institution is a delusion. It does not follow that a consumer's movement would bring about favorable changes. Some experience and some reflection would seem required for the formation and exercise of enlightened judgment on the subject. If education cannot take place in an institution purporting to be educational, then of course it should be abolished. But the task of proposing a sensible alternative remains.

The principal standard favored by those who propose to turn the schools over to the children is whether or not the children are interested in, excited by, and cheerful about what is going on. If the children entertain these sentiments, their school is good; if they do not, it is bad. A popular book[31] was applauded by *Newsweek* for showing, by the example of the British infant schools, that "learning can be fun."[32]

Aristotle said, "Now obviously youths are not to be instructed with a view to their amusement, for learning is no amusement, but is accompanied with pain."[33]

Hegel[34] condemned the "play theory" of education in the following words:

> The necessity for education is present in children as their own feeling of dissatisfaction with themselves as they are, as the desire to belong to the adult world whose superiority they divine, as the longing to grow up. The play theory of education assumes that what is childish is itself already something of inherent worth and presents it as such to the children; in their eyes it lowers serious pursuits, and education itself, to a form of childishness for which the children themselves have scant respect. The advocates of this

177

> method represent the child, in the immaturity in which he feels himself to be, as really mature and they struggle to make him satisfied with himself as he is. But they corrupt and distort his genuine and proper need for something better, and create in him a blind indifference to the substantial ties of the intellectual world, a contempt of his elders because they have thus posed before him, a child, in a contemptible and childish fashion, and finally a vanity and conceit which feeds on the notion of its own superiority.[35]

In his *Autobiography* John Stuart Mill writes:

> It is, no doubt, a very laudable effort, in modern teaching, to render as much as possible of what the young are required to learn easy and interesting to them. But when this principle is pushed to the length of not requiring them to learn anything but what has been made easy and interesting, one of the chief objects of education is sacrificed. I rejoice in the decline of the old brutal and tyrannical system of teaching, which, however, did succeed in enforcing habits of application; but the new, as it seems to me, is training up a race of men who will be incapable of doing anything which is disagreeable to them.[36]

T. S. Eliot adds, in the work I quoted at the beginning,

> As soon as this precious motive of snobbery evaporates, the zest has gone out of education; if it is not going to mean more money, or more power over others, or a better social position, or at least a steady and respectable job, few people are going to take the trouble to acquire education. For deteriorate it as you may, education is still going to demand a good deal of drudgery.[37]

Without accepting Eliot's view of man, implying an aversion to exertion for any but the most commonplace rewards, we can ask whether there is any way in which learning can be fun. Certainly some learning can be. But the notion that all learning can be all the time seems extreme and will appear so to everybody who ever tried to learn anything—that is, to every member of the human race.

One recent book brings together several critics who have achieved fame through their attacks on the schools.[38] Jonathan Kozol says they destroy the minds and hearts of our children. John Holt remarks that school is a place where children learn to be stupid. Peter Marin announces that the schools are the means by which we deprive the young of manhood. Edgar Friedenberg claims that the schools condition students to be dutiful, complacent, and consumer-oriented. Theodore Roszak refers to the public schools as coercive institutions: Blake's drawing of Age cutting the wings of Youth shows what our present education is all about, what any education must be all about in schools financed by church or state and forced upon the young by compulsion.

Roszak's statement is explicit: compulsory education financed by taxes and controlled by the political community must ruin children. What is the evidence? The fact that some children have been ruined by some schools would not prove that schools *must* ruin children; still less that all schools must ruin all children. If it turned out that there was some inherent inescapable path to ruination running through the school, then the institution should of course be abandoned. But compulsory attendance or state control or tax support does not seem *a priori* a sufficient ground for that conclusion.

And what of the alternative? The only one I can imagine is wholly voluntary arrangements, such as those advocated by Ivan Illich, in which one young person who wants to learn seeks out another who wants to learn the same thing. Together they may seek out others and form with them a kind of network or web of learning. Apart from practical questions to be taken up later, this brings us back to interest as the determinant of the order and content of education.

How can a person be interested in something he knows nothing about? How long should he be interested in it when he finds out—in a preliminary way—what it is? (I once said to Bertrand Russell that his educational theories would have the effect of depriving the young of their cultural heritage. I asked him whether every boy shouldn't read Shakespeare. Lord Russell replied that he would make every boy read one play: if he didn't like it, he would not insist that he read another. Here Russell went further toward a curriculum than Paul Goodman, who remarked to me that it was "arrogant" for anybody to tell anybody else, or at least any child of school age, what he ought to study.)

If we appeal to common experience, we see that the interests of childhood are evanescent, that many people abandon interests once very strong and dedicate their lives to activities formerly unattractive to them. What children ought to learn (if at this stage we may assume that there exists something answering to this description) cannot be wholly determined by their interest in it. What they ought to learn should be made as interesting as possible—everybody ought to have as much fun as he can. But the art of teaching would seem to consist in large part of making what ought to be learned interesting to learners who bring little interest with them to the task.

A curriculum is simply a way of saving lost motion. It is an attempt to profit by the most obvious mistakes of the past and to make it unnecessary for the child to commit every last one of them all over again. Learning how to read is not a simple matter, or one that seems obviously desirable to every child, and it is not fun all the time. But George Dennison, who asks what is so precious about a curriculum, says that when he decided

José was ready to read, and José refused to do so, he gave José lessons in reading, and José learned to read. This is having a curriculum in mind, if not in the catalogue.

Joseph Featherstone, Charles Silberman, and Lillian Weber have popularized the British infant school in the United States. (Featherstone's latest article in the *New Republic* is entitled "Tempering a Fad," which suggests that he may be having second thoughts.[39]) Some of the consequences are indicated in *Scholastic Teacher,* May 1971.

> *Something strange is happening up on the third floor at* [Philadelphia's] *John Bartram High. . . . Students sprawl about aqua-carpeted floors playing with tinker toys. Blindfolded boys are led through mazes of chairs. Others are sculpting with junk, giving voice and movement to their creation. . . . A teenage troupe role-plays a pregnant woman, a 70-year-old minister, an armed policeman, an athlete, and other human types in a bomb shelter, deciding whom to eliminate. . . . What's happening at John Bartram? Affective education. Elsewhere it's called humanistic education. . . .*[40]

The British infant school is designed for children five to seven years old. Its tone and spirit are markedly different from the rest of British education, which is in general more "formal" and more "intellectual" than the elementary and high schools in the United States. The British infant school has not been free from controversy in its native land, but it has been going on for twenty years and more and has a definable character that can be understood—and imitated. The American imitations, which, as the example of John Bartram High School shows, are not limited to pupils who have not yet begun what the British would call serious schooling, sometimes seem to overlook two constituents of the British infant school that are essential to any analysis of it and perhaps to such success as it has had. The British infant school has a curriculum, and it has teachers who possess and exert authority.

Thus in *Children Come First,* Casey and Liza Murrow point out that although the children in a British infant school make a good many decisions about the way they allocate their time

> *This does not mean that the teachers avoid planning. On the contrary, classrooms that appear totally free are really skillfully engineered. They must be if they are to succeed. The teacher needs to be clear about what each child has accomplished and what sort of work he needs to become involved in during the coming days.*[41]

I cannot imagine that anybody is in favor of inhumane or tyrannical teachers. I cannot imagine that anybody supports curriculum that has no

". . . everybody ought to have as much fun as he can. But the art of teaching would seem to consist in large part of making what ought to be learned interesting to learners who bring little interest with them to the task"

meaning. But, if nobody can tolerate a school that is a prison, it is hard to see how anybody can propose a school that is a playpen in which children amuse themselves with assorted toys until they can escape to the serious business of life. It is still more difficult to believe that the situation will be improved by simply turning children loose to shift for themselves. George Dennison and, in some moods, John Holt both recognize that school is the least unattractive of the alternatives available, though Holt, in all moods, appears to be hostile to compulsory attendance. Their object is to transform the school, not to abolish it. The same is true of the proponents of the "open school." They want the school to have an atmosphere of warmth and friendliness. They want children treated as human beings. They correctly believe that there are many ways to learning and that those which are pleasanter may also be more productive. Since no sensible person differs with this conclusion, it is hard to see why the statement of it should arouse excitement. The changes it would make in the schools can hardly be called fundamental.

Many members of the group bringing the first set of charges, who hold that the child's interest should determine what he studies—the great word is *relevance*—are compelled to take the next step. That is the step to the doctrine that any bit of learning or knowledge is as good as any other bit. They must take this step, because otherwise they might not be able to answer the question, what do you do if the child does not learn what you (secretly) believe he ought to know? They have to say, as some of them do, that the child will eventually feel the need to learn what he should know and will learn it, or that whatever he learns is as valuable as anything a teacher or a curriculum could propose to him.

As to the probability that the child will eventually feel the need to learn what he should know, there is no evidence that he will and some likelihood that he will not; for, as we shall see, some of the things he ought to know, if I may use the expression, are not within his ken and not necessarily within that of his parents or associates. He may, of course, come to feel the need of reading, writing, and arithmetic, but when, and after how much loss and pain? And how can he be certain that when he feels the need to learn these indispensable subjects, he can find a person or an institution that will help him learn them? I repeat: a curriculum is a way of saving waste motion and profiting by the mistakes (and the discoveries) of others.

The notion that one bit of any kind of learning is as good as a bit of any other kind is very handy. It is an all-purpose answer to any suggestion that schools may be preferable to no schools. For if one asserts this proposition one can say that whatever interests the child, whatever seems relevant to him, no matter what its intellectual content may be, is just as educational as anything else. But there is a difference between learning and education. For example, we probably would not call a course of study in learning how to be a safecracker, an occupation for which skill and train-

*". . . a curriculum is a way of
saving waste motion and
profiting by the mistakes
(and the discoveries)
of others"*

ing are required, educational. On this we would agree, because burglary is a crime. But here the argument ends. John Holt would regard taking a job, presumably a legal one, as a substitute for school.

An announcement in the *Chronicle of Higher Education* extrapolates this program to the colleges and universities:

> *About 1,000 college students from 31 U.S. campuses will soon be combining activism with academic credit, at government expense .... the students will work in urban and rural poverty projects for a year while earning full academic credit and drawing subsistence allowances of about $175 a month.*[42]

A feeling is abroad that the knowledge dealt with in educational institutions, and hence the educational opportunities to be found in them, is actually inferior to that which may be acquired by contact with "real" life. John Holt has no compunctions about saying that the resources of the city are infinitely larger than those of the school. There are two answers to that. The first is that the resources of the school include the whole of human history and human knowledge; they include the resources of all the cities that have ever been. The second is that the value of the resources of the city depends upon the stage of the student's development at which he tries to avail himself of them.

Morris B. Abram, a former president of Brandeis University, has expressed himself on this subject in a way directly applicable to the program of combining activism with academic credit. He says:

> *Chemistry students instinctively know that without a grounding in basic theory, practical exercises are merely piddling. Social science students, however, in many cases totally unprepared for what they experience in their "lab"—the streets—are apt to think they are engaged in the real thing. I think they, too, are piddling, for without the benefit of the theoretical literature in their field, they will be unable to assimilate or conceptualize what it is they see or try to do.*
>
> *Experience is undeniably an adjunct to knowledge if it comes after and in addition to conventional study and if the experience is interpreted and analyzed. Do-goodism in the streets, however, is not a substitute for education. The student who experiences an alien and impoverished environment is no more entitled to credit for simply having done so than are the victims who are forced to live their lives in such circumstances.*[43]

Anybody who remembers the tours of industry he made as a school child will agree: he may have been frightened, as I was of the steel plant in Lorain, Ohio, but he did not understand anything any better for the visit.

The pressure on those who are responsible for any educational institution is always to "relate it to life." The necessity of gaining public support for the institution will often suggest the desirability of making that relationship obvious and direct. When I was dean of a law school, eager for the favor of the Bar, I was sometimes tempted to try to make the law school program an out-and-out vocational scheme, designed to produce men who would fit readily into the law offices that employed them because they had learned in law school the technical skill the practice required. I came to the conclusion that this was no business for a university, and that the object of a university law school was to teach lawyers what they ought to know about the law that they would never have a chance to learn in practice. The technical skills they needed they could rapidly acquire in the practice itself. What they would never have a chance to learn in practice was what the law was all about: the philosophy of law, its relation to other disciplines and other institutions, its history, its purpose, and its prospects. Lawyers trained only in technical skills would be stuck with them and would have nothing that would help them get out of their rut as law and society changed. The man who understood the law would be able to anticipate change in the law and would know how to take part in making it change for the better.

As long ago as 1828 the Yale College faculty said in a famous report: "There are many things not taught in colleges, because they may be learned elsewhere."[44] The unique function of educational institutions, if any such function exists, and if we can discover what it is, is likely to be so complicated and so time consuming as to require the full attention of those who are responsible for them.

Substitutes for schools

A serious charge against the schools is that they support and reflect an unjust political, economic, and social system. Ivan Illich's book *Deschooling Society* is explicit on the point. He says, "School is the advertising agency which makes you believe that you need the society as it is."[45] Credentialism, which Illich attacks, is, as I have said, not the fault of the schools, but of the community. The elimination of credentials in the present society would merely lead to the invention and substitution of other credentials, along with another bureaucracy to administer them. Illich proposes an "edu-credit card" provided to each citizen at birth. This is another credential: some authority must decide when the card is to be punched; some employer is bound to ask to see the applicant's card and reject him if the desired mosaic of punches does not appear.

The consumer society, which is Illich's bête noir, was not created by the schools. It would not be exorcised if the schools were abolished. Illich's program of webs and networks formed by those eager to learn would be likely in the present state of affairs to bring together people who were looking for some product they wanted to consume but could not find. Illich believes that the life of the city is educational, but how can this be good education if that life is what he says it is? His collection of "educational artifacts" is based on the view that all learning is equally valuable and that haphazard learning of anything you chance to be interested in will in some way add up to education. It would seem that one of Illich's desiderata, critical judgment, is as likely to emerge from schooling as from the kind of intermittent miscellany he seems to favor.[46] An adult who had already grasped the principles and acquired the tools of liberal education might find ways to supplement or enlarge his learning through the maze of "educational artifacts" proposed by Illich, but it is hard to imagine that a child could do so.

Illich proposes an educational system. It is a different system from the extant one; but it is still a system. Presumably it would be paid for by taxes. Some public authority would have to sponsor, manage, and control it. Therefore the system would reflect the society in which it operated. It is self-evident that any educational system must do so. A society that wants to change its ways can use its educational system to do it, but an educational system cannot openly set out to achieve goals the society does not accept.

It seems a little absurd of Peter Schrag to complain that the public school cannot "become a subversive enterprise,"[47] and to advocate on that ground the substitution of private schools paid for by public funds on a voucher plan. No society will knowingly pay an institution to subvert it, whether the institution is called public or private. It will not tolerate subversive institutions even if they are paid for by private funds. Schrag's estimate of what the American people would regard as subversive reflects an unusually low opinion of his fellow countrymen. The public school would be subversive, he says, if it were "designed to encourage children to ask real questions about race or sex or social justice or the emptiness and joys of life."[48] But if we accept that estimate and that definition of subversion, we can hardly conclude that these people will allow their money to be used for these purposes, or that they will be deceived by a change in the name and organization of the institution.

If, as Illich intimates, we are all bent on consumption, any educational system supported by us will reflect our misguided passion. The money comes from us; the teachers come from us; so do the school boards. The values of the society are ours. The only way Illich could hope to separate education from us would be to have no system at all. And still the result might not be far different from what we have today. On the hypothesis that we are a consumer society and that we like being one (otherwise we would not be one), such education as we gave our children if we could decide what kind we wanted might be no less "consumer-oriented" than what the public schools now are giving them. We have 16,000 more or less independent school boards, in 50 states that are still more independent. We have some 3,000 institutions of higher learning, so-called, almost all of them independent of one another. What strikes the observer is not the variety of the schools, colleges, and universities of the country, it is their uniformity, a uniformity not required by law but derived from the uniformity of American society from coast to coast.

We may recall that Mill thought leaving education to the whims of parents was more dangerous to the individual and society than the uniformity that might result from state support.

Those who want to abolish compulsory attendance at public schools fail to make their case because they cannot show that the school must necessarily lack interest, spontaneity, joy, or fun. A school does not have to destroy the minds and hearts of children. If some schools do so, it is because they are bad schools. Those who want to retain compulsory attendance at public schools but make them pleasanter places for children to spend their time in have said something useful, though hardly sensational. Remarks like these made by Joseph Featherstone seem eminently sensible:

> *Still another confusion on the American scene lies in the notion that liberalizing the repressive atmosphere of our schools—which is worth doing for its own sake—will automatically promote intellectual development. It won't. We need more humane schools, but we also need a steady concern for intellectual progress and workmanship. Without this, it is unlikely that we will get any sort of cumulative development, and we will never establish practical standards by which to judge good and bad work.*[49]

Featherstone also succeeds in keeping interest, informality, and spontaneity in their place in relation to other educational and social issues. He says,

> *A final word on the faddishness of our educational concerns. The appearance of new ideas such as the clamor for open, informal schools[50] does not cancel out old ideas. "Open education" will be a sham unless those supporting it also address themselves to recurring, fundamental problems, such as the basic inequality and racism of our society. The most pressing American educational dilemma is not the lack of informality in classrooms: It is whether we can build a more equal, multi-racial society.*[51]

This last remark suggests that Featherstone has some notion of the possible relationship between the educational system of a community and the formation and maintenance of that community. So has George Dennison. He believes in tiny schools, as informal as possible, and also in a curriculum and in the value of adult guidance (teaching) to children. With his emphasis on the individual child and the child's immediate environment, he might be expected to omit the larger community entirely. On the contrary, he widens it in time and space. He says that by community he does not mean the neighborhood and adds: "But in fact no community need want for wisdom. The greatest of minds are, in effect, its permanent residents. . . . All philosophers are of the community. All scientists are. All artists are. . . . Or put it this way: a community is not a true community unless, in principle, it is universal."[52] That is an excellent way to put it and one that critics of the schools might ponder.

Those who would abolish schools give no sign of having this relationship in mind. They do not mention community except in a pejorative context: the present society is bad. Since the society is bad, the schools are necessarily bad, for they necessarily support the society. Is there a possibility that a bad society can have good schools? Probably not. Can the schools, whether or not they are the place to begin, make a contribution to a better society? Probably they can. In the last part of this essay we shall try to discover what they can do.

Aristotle said in the *Politics:*

> *No one will doubt that the legislator should direct his attention above all to the education of youth; for the neglect of education does harm to the constitution. The citizen should be moulded to suit the form of government under which he lives. . . . And since the whole city has one end, it is manifest that education should be one and the same for all, and it should be public, and not private— not as at present, when every one looks after his own children separately.*[53]

Rousseau adds:

> *. . . and as the reason of each man is not left to be the sole arbiter of his duties, government ought the less indiscriminately to abandon to the intelligence and prejudices of fathers the education of their children, as that education is of still greater importance to the State than to the fathers. . . . Families dissolve, but the State remains.*[54]

We have seen that these sentiments are not shared by the softhearted revolutionaries: they ordinarily do not mention the state at all except in terms of reprobation. They consider the ends of individuals, who are alleged to be threatened by the environment or deformed by it. Though many of them think, in apparent contradiction to their estimate of the environment, that it is more "educational" than the schools, so that it would be better for children to be roaming around in it than to be tied down in a classroom, they do not consider that the community has an end that may be worth talking about or that the common good may have some value to the individual.

When we turn to the hardheaded, no-nonsense critics of the schools we find them uninterested in these questions. They want more for their money, by which they mean greater efficiency in teaching. Or they want to redefine the community as my group, my class, my neighborhood—people like me—and they want the schools controlled by the community as redefined. The present administration in Washington has supported both of these positions through the Office of Economic Opportunity.

Philip V. Sanchez, director of OEO, spoke in November 1971, appropriately enough, to a committee of the National Association of Manufacturers. He told the group of OEO's experiments with vouchers and performance contracting and assailed teacher's organizations for opposing them. In commenting on his speech, John J. Kilpatrick, a conservative columnist, said, "Both programs feature certain elements of the free enterprise system, which doubtless accounts for their appeal to the NAM."[55]

On January 31, 1972, Mr. Sanchez announced that the OEO's experiment with performance contracting had failed: "In all cases, the average achievement level of children in the experimental group was well below the norm for their grade and in all cases, in terms of grade equivalents, the average slipped even further behind during the year." Dr. Thomas K. Glennan, Jr., one of his assistants, said the conclusions were consistent with the Coleman Report,[56] which found that a child's family background and the background of his classmates seemed to be the major factors in academic performance, as opposed to differences in facilities, instruction, or class size.

The experiment with performance contracting involved 6 private firms, engaged to teach mathematics and reading to 23,000 pupils in 18 communities. The contracts totaled $5.6 million, or about $200 a child. The compensation of the contractor depended on the success of his pupils in reaching national averages. If they did not reach that level, he was not paid. Of this arrangement Mr. Kilpatrick says, "Parents everywhere, aroused and angry, are demanding better performance in terms of their investment in educational institutions."

It is said that in 1970–71 some fifty-five schools entered into performance contracts including those financed by the OEO. These have usually covered reading and mathematics. Gary, Indiana, turned over the Banneker School to Behavioral Research Laboratories, Inc., a corporation for profit, on a money-back guarantee. The superintendent of schools in Gary has called the first year a success. The American Federation of Teachers has disputed the superintendent's claim: it says that if the figures are correctly interpreted no money was saved and no intellectual progress made through "free enterprise."

The results foreshadowed by Polly Carpenter of the Rand Corporation are no less ambiguous. The corporation was retained by the Department of Health, Education and Welfare to examine performance contracting. It followed some twenty-three programs, eight of them in depth. To what she calls the "key question," whether performance contracting had better than average effects on student learning as measured by standardized tests, Mrs. Carpenter is unable to give a clear answer. The question is a "key" one, because if the pupils did not do better than they would otherwise have done, the taxpayers did not get more for their money.

Even on the Gary superintendent's interpretation of the results in that city there is no convincing evidence that the program was a success there. The pupils did better than most in mathematics, but comparisons are difficult because the contractor controlled the whole school and was able to concentrate almost exclusively on mathematics and reading during the first semester. With so much additional time to devote to the subject they should have been able to do better than those who had to spread themselves over more fields. Another important difference, according to Mrs. Carpenter, was that Gary parents were deeply involved in their children's education, "in contrast to most of the parents of students in other programs."

Only two of the corporations fulfilled their performance guarantees in 1970–71, and nobody knows whether or not they made money. They may have decided to forgo a profit in the first year in order to obtain further contracts and a wider market for their teaching materials.

Mrs. Carpenter concludes that "performance contracting will continue for at least a few years, in spite of some of the poor showings on student achievement. . . . Whether the techniques will have any lasting benefit we cannot say." She does feel, however, that it is a "helpful change agent and does provide the emphasis on accountability that is currently in vogue." The large amount of individualized instruction given under these programs bears out the suggestion that the profit motive may induce desirable changes that might not be made by tenured teachers.

The Rand report from which I have been quoting says that "considerable work will be needed to develop measuring instruments before performance contracting can be of wider use." Robert Feldmesser of Educational Testing Service makes the same point. He says that one of the gravest criticisms of the plan is that "it stresses the development of a few narrowly defined skills, merely because they are measurable, at the expense of broader educational objectives." He thinks performance contracting, "even if it is not an enduring innovation," will have been valuable if it stimulates us to develop our capacity to measure progress toward the broader educational objectives he has in mind.[57]

191

It seems more likely that the attempt to measure "broader educational objectives" will result in narrower ones. We shall tend to select those aims the achievement of which can be readily measured. We are all familiar with the phenomenon, which has at times been particularly noticeable in France, of a curriculum formulated not in terms of what the student ought to study but in terms of what he can be most easily examined upon. The contractor in Gary had a whole school and its program at his disposal. He chose to concentrate on reading and mathematics because he knew that whatever results he got would be measurable. Measurable results of efforts to attain "broader objectives" have been sought for decades in this country. The search has tended to trivialize "broader objectives." All we have to do is to think of such measures as time spent, classes attended, and grades received to understand what insistence upon such results has done and can do to education.

One thing has to be watched with all new ventures in education, and that is the so-called Hawthorne effect, discovered by Elton Mayo and his associates half a century and more ago. They found that the introduction of novelties, involving as it did new attention to the group among which the novelties were introduced, increased production. As the novelties became routine, production reverted toward the original figure. Performance contracting carries with it new methods, new materials, and new faces. Nobody knows whether good results, if they are obtained, come from the superiority of the new methods, materials, and people, or from their novelty. In the nature of things, novelty is a waning asset.

A second general observation is in point. There is a difference between learning and education. A student can learn many things—perhaps he could even learn everything—without being educated. He can learn how to read, but, if he does not read anything thereafter, or if he has no judgment about what he reads, if the ability to read does nothing to civilize him, we should be hard put to it to say that any education had taken place.

This observation is illustrated by a kind of performance contracting I engaged in fifty years ago. I was a master in a preparatory school dedicated to getting boys through the College Board examinations. Most of our pupils had failed at other schools. This was their last chance. Their parents paid us very large sums on the understanding that we would get them into Harvard, Yale, or Princeton if it was humanly possible to do so. We accomplished this highly measurable result by deliberately refusing to educate these children—we did not want to confuse them. We crammed them for the examinations. Instead of teaching them to spell, we taught them not to use a word they did not know how to spell. We gave them no outside reading. But we made sure they could answer every question that had been asked on the College Boards since those examinations were instituted in 1909. As I remember it, our pupils all got into college and all of them flunked out at the end of the first semester. But we had performed our contract. A good deal of learning went on in that school, but very little education.

A third general observation. Efficiency, at least as the word is used by efficiency experts, may be a useful criterion for learning a subject: one wants to learn that subject without waste of time, effort, or money. Learning a language, for example, requires a great deal of drill. (Learning is accompanied by pain.) But one does not "learn" literature or philosophy or history or science in this way, though admittedly learning any subject may require some drill. But if drill alone were employed to teach the subjects I have mentioned nobody would think any education in them had taken place. The reason is that no understanding would have been communicated or achieved. For understanding reflection is required, and reflection takes time. There is a sense in which education goes on between classes. Efficiency, as measured by the stopwatch and the budget, can have little application to this process.

Performance contracting raises one final important question: Should corporations for profit be entrusted with the education of our children? If it could be proved that they were more effective, as well as more efficient, should we substitute profit for the motive of public service? The present standards are political; that is, they are arrived at by the democratic process, and they reflect what the political community has decided it wants from its schools.

It may be said that many people are now making money by selling everything from chalk to buses to the schools. Almost all the learning materials used in the schools are now prepared by corporations for profit. If such a corporation can without objection sell its textbooks to the schools, why should it not move in and teach reading, too?

The answer is that it is one thing to supply what the schools want and another to take them over. If the object of the Banneker School in Gary were to become that of making a profit for Behavioral Research Laboratories, Inc., then the object would no longer be to educate the children of Gary, or, in John Dewey's phrase, to put them in possession of all their powers. Some efforts in this direction might not be profitable. If they were not, they would be dropped. If education is entitled to the high place in the American hierarchy that we have traditionally accorded it, then the question whether it can be made to pay is, as the lawyers say, incompetent, irrelevant, and immaterial. It is worse than that: it is demoralizing, in the literal meaning of that word.

The market is the foundation on which rests the other hardheaded proposal to which I have referred, educational vouchers, by which parents receive public funds and provide for the schooling of their children. I hasten to say that enthusiasm for the plan is not limited to businessmen or free-enterprise economists. Some softhearted reformers, disgusted with the public schools, embrace the voucher plan as a "consumer" movement, taking control away from torpid bureaucracy and turning it over to

"... to put them in possession of all their powers"

parents. Others, like Peter Schrag, see voucher schools as a way of escaping from the vulgar prejudices and aspirations that in their view must dominate the public schools. Schrag says, "Any single, universal public institution—and especially one as sensitive as the public school—is the product of a social quotient verdict. It elevates the lowest common denominator of desires, pressures, and demands into the highest public virtue."[58] Hence good public education is an impossible dream, and one that is now at an end. It should be replaced by schools paid for by public funds but organized, operated, and controlled by private persons.

Other reformers, though they are not classical economists, believe in the virtues of competition and think the public schools would profit from more than they have now. So Christopher Jencks has said,

> Either tuition grants or management contracts to private organizations would, of course, "destroy the public school system as we know it." When one thinks of the remarkable past achievements of public education in America, this may seem a foolish step. But we must not allow the memory of past achievements to blind us to present failures. . . . If the terms of the competition are reasonable, there is every reason to suppose that it is healthy. . . . And if, as some fear, the public schools could not survive in open competition with private ones, then perhaps they should not survive.[59]

So formulated, the voucher plan would not only destroy the public school system as we have known it, but would also perpetuate and exacerbate the injustices in American society. An unregulated voucher system would raise the question whether all schools could escape the commands of the Constitution on the ground that they were private and not public. For example, public schools may not discriminate against students or teachers. Such discrimination is held to be state action violative of the Fourteenth Amendment. Private schools are not within the purview of the amendment, because no state action is involved. Are voucher schools public or private? If they are all private, the Supreme Court's prohibition of racial segregation would not apply to them. If they are all public, parochial schools would have to obey the constitutional ban on religious instruction in public schools.[60]

An unregulated voucher plan would mean that the rich and experienced would be able to get superior education for their children. They would know how to organize a school, or they could hire competent persons to do it for them. They might even have some idea of what a good school was. But it is unlikely that they would insist that the children of the poor must be admitted to their schools. The support for the voucher plan in the country comes from those who do not want their children compelled to associate with those of other races or economic and social status.

Unregulated vouchers have been advocated by Virgil Blum, who urged that parents should be in complete control of schools,[61] and by Milton Friedman, who saw them as extending free enterprise.[62] But the obvious dangers of turning money over to parents to spend as they like on the education of their children have led to the formulation of numerous voucher plans designed to avoid the dangers and preserve the principle.[63] Vouchers in any form are opposed by Americans United for Separation of Church and State, who do not want public funds used to support parochial schools; by the American Civil Liberties Union; by organized labor; and by the California Congress of Parents and Teachers. Harvey B. Scribner, chancellor of the New York City public schools, testified in opposition to the plan put forward by the OEO. Appearing before the House Education and Labor Committee, he said, "The unregulated marketplace has never been known as a friend of the poor and unsophisticated."

This is true. But the OEO plan contains many important regulations, and the question is whether they are adequate to overcome the objections to a program of giving money to parents to use as they wish for the education of their children.

The plan was worked out by the Center for the Study of Public Policy, Cambridge, Mass., on a grant from OEO. Christopher Jencks has described and argued for it in an article in the *New Republic*,[64] and the center has published a 220-page exposition of it.[65]

In his magazine article Jencks first attacks an unregulated voucher system, saying it

> *would have all the drawbacks of other unregulated markets. It would produce even more racial and economic segregation than the existing neighborhood school system. It would also widen the expenditure gap between rich and poor children, giving the children of the middle-classes an even larger share of the nation's educational resources than they now get, while reducing the relative share going to the children of the poor.*

"Fortunately," he says, "OEO has shown no signs of funding a completely unregulated voucher system." Instead, OEO would require that schools accept all applicants. If a school had more applicants than places, it would have to fill at least half its places by a lottery among the applicants, and it would have to show that it "had accepted at least as high a proportion of minority group students as had applied. Thus no school would be able to cream off the most easily educated children or dump all the problem children elsewhere."[66]

The redemption value of a middle- or upper-income family's voucher would approximate what the local public schools are currently spending on upper-income children. Vouchers for children from low-income families would have a somewhat higher redemption value. Participating

197

schools would have to accept every child's voucher as full payment for his education, regardless of the redemption value of the voucher. "Otherwise, parents who could afford to supplement their children's vouchers would inevitably have a better chance of getting their children into high cost schools than parents who could not supplement the voucher."[67]

A new bureaucracy, the Educational Voucher Agency, would be established in every community to receive the money from federal, state, and local sources for the schools and to oversee the voucher plan. It would lay down eligibility requirements, "regulate the newly created marketplace," and pay transportation costs so that every family would have equal access to every participating school.

> *So instead of telling schools whom to hire, what to teach, or how to teach it, the EVA will confine itself to collecting and disseminating information about what each school is doing. . . . This should ensure that families are aware of all the choices open to them. It should also help discourage misleading advertising, or at least partially offset the effects of such advertising.*[68]

In addition the EVA would set up uniform standards governing the suspension and expulsion of students.

This is the barest outline, with many important details omitted, of the plan now being pushed by the federal government, so far with indifferent success. Only three experimental programs have been announced and only one seems to be getting under way. The reason is not wholly, though it may be in part, the opposition of those who have vested interests in the public schools. An effort designed to offer some competition to the public schools ends up as an enormously complicated, expensive mechanism, another public school system. The restrictions on the participating schools are such that an existing private school would have to be desperate indeed to accept them, and a new private school might prefer to go it alone rather than submit to them.

What is the superiority of the proposed new public school system over the old? Virgil Blum and Milton Friedman had a clear idea, defensible in their terms. I think it incompatible with the Constitution and with justice and humanity; but at least I can understand it. But the Jencks-OEO program is an attempt to allow the market to operate without letting it operate, to minimize bureaucracy by setting up another bureaucracy, and to give parents a control over the education of their children that is not much more real than the control they have today.

Every step in the voucherizing process presents a trap for the unwary. The constitution of the EVA is unclear, but crucial. Do we know that the Supreme Court would allow parochial schools to receive public funds in this way? Can we be certain that the Court will hold voucher schools to the same standards of nondiscrimination and academic freedom that have been applied to public schools? If we assume that the OEO will see to it that its experiments are managed in a spirit of justice to the poor and to minorities, can we make the same assumption about the state legislatures that will have to support any continuing voucher plan?

Professor George R. La Noue, in his admirable critique of vouchers, says,

> *The point is that marketplace analogies do not fit well to the educational world. In the first place, public schools are not a non-competitive monopoly like the postal service. They are highly decentralized and they do compete, both with private schools, which enroll 15 to 35 percent of the students, and with each other. . . . Pinning the reform of American schools on a series of ad hoc regulations to be enforced by a yet-to-be defined EVA seems to be an enormous risk. . . . A system of financing that runs the risk of undermining all constitutional rules in education in favor of ad hoc regulations seems to me to be too great a price to pay. . . . As a vehicle for reform, vouchers are a very inefficient device. They would prove costly by adding to existing state and local budgets the expense of (1) all private school tuitions, (2) the EVA administrative bureaucracy, (3) new buildings and inefficient use of existing structures, (4) inefficient use of existing tenured personnel, and (5) greatly increased transportation costs.*[69]

La Noue's final warning is this:

> *Those who advocate ideal or model vouchers don't seem to fully recognize the true nature of the voucher constituency. There is a latent coalition prepared to support vouchers, and it won't be led by the gentlemen scholars from Cambridge and Berkeley. The coalition is the one Kevin Phillips proposed in* The Emerging Republican Majority. *It is composed mainly of Southern Protestant nativists and Northern Catholic ethnics—plus, I would add, a touch of the far right and the far left. . . . The danger is, then, that while the intellectual debate focuses on ideal vouchers, the true voucher coalition will rise up to take command of the idea. Once united, that coalition might be able to bring about the kind of unregulated, noncompensatory, constitution-free vouchers that would lead to the social disaster Jencks himself warns about.*[70]

The schools and the community

Let us accept all we have heard about genetic limitations, the restrictions that are imposed by socioeconomic status, family background, parental attitudes, and the conditions of the earliest years of life and those further influences that are exerted by the neighborhood, the home, and television —in short, all the waves of every sort that beat upon the child from birth on, and even before. We cannot assume that all these forces are permanent or that they leave irreversible effects. If society is bad, and hence a bad educator, let us by all means struggle to improve it, and let us not imagine that we can do so solely by improving the educational system. If we have no philosophy in general, because we do not know what we want, or our philosophy is defective, because we want the wrong things, let us try to straighten ourselves out; and let us recognize that we cannot do this solely by straightening out our educational system. The limitations within which an educational system operates are severe. It is a means of accentuating and perpetuating accepted values, not of raising a nation by its own bootstraps into a different and better world. This is true of any system of education under any form of government.[71]

Education is not a panacea. My colleague Harry S. Ashmore has called it the last refuge of the scoundrel, because it is often resorted to by those who do not want to do anything about a problem. Education takes a long time. Meanwhile, they can forget the problem without feeling any sense of guilt. This course is especially attractive to those whose prosperity or social standing would be adversely affected by an energetic attack on the problem. No matter what an educational system does, it is not in our time going to get rid of war, disease, poverty, slums, or crime. Its contributions, if any, to the elimination of these and other plagues will be indirect, through helping people learn to be as intelligent as they can be.

It may be that in many countries such an aim for an educational system would be impossible. In some, the sheer magnitude of the task would be too much for the nation's resources. In others, helping people to become intelligent may be contrary to public policy: the state may want people to have technical skill—to be efficient rather than intelligent. It may not want them to think or to exercise critical judgment. Such a country may produce experts of every kind, including experts in indoctrination, called teachers. But the system of "educational" institutions it has will be dedicated to training rather than to education. Education is a process of civilization. To this end it aims at intellectual development. It excludes indoctrination. In the phrase I have already quoted from John Dewey, it tries to put the child in full possession of all his powers. Educated people may also be trained, and trained people may be educated, but the two objects can be confused only at the risk of failure to achieve one or both. Since training is usually easier and more easily measurable than education, it is usually education that suffers from the effort to combine them.

The United States may be a bad society: it is certainly far worse than it ought to be. Its educational system reflects the atmosphere of crass materialism and anti-intellectualism in which it operates. But the people of this country have some commitments that may make it possible for edu-

"Education is a process of civilization"

cation to take place, even in schools maintained by taxes and controlled by political entities.

The basic commitment is that of the First Amendment, which lays it down that Congress shall make no law abridging the freedom of speech.[72] This provision, which is now applicable to the states as well as the federal government, means that every American is encouraged to express himself on public questions—or on any other subject. The notion is that of a self-governing community of self-governing citizens locked in argument. This was the kind of community the founders wanted. They could not hope to have one of this kind without an educated people. They had to have citizens who could think, and think for themselves.

Is this a sufficient basis for a political community? I think it is when combined with universal citizenship and universal suffrage. Does it justify compulsory schooling in institutions supported and controlled by the state? I think it does.

Every child must be given the chance to become the kind of citizen the First Amendment demands. This obligation is too important to be left to parents. The community must compel them to allow their children to have this opportunity either by offering the education itself or by making it available through institutions it approves.

It may be argued that this is all highly abstract and unrelated to the actual situation in American public schools today. We shall be reminded of the litany of horrors repeated by the softhearted revolutionaries and the charges of delinquency brought by the hardheaded businessmen. But the question is whether we shall give up the principle of compulsory universal public education. To answer that question in the affirmative requires a conviction that the public schools of America cannot be made what they ought to be and that there is a valid alternative to them. We have already seen that the alternatives that have been offered are not attractive. They are either that we should have no schools at all and let children run free, or that we should turn the schools over to parents or private businesses to be operated under their direction at public expense.

Can the American school be made what it ought to be? I cannot share Peter Schrag's estimate of his fellow countrymen. According to the Supreme Court, it would be unconstitutional to prevent the kind of discussion in public schools that he says would be regarded as "subversive." The Court has ruled that children have all the rights of other Americans and that they do not shed these rights at the schoolhouse gate.[73] In the case in which the Court used this language it held that children in elementary school could not be prevented from wearing black armbands to protest the war in Vietnam; the prohibition would violate their rights under the First Amendment. The decisions of the Court also protect the teacher by guaranteeing his freedom of criticism even if his target is the school board that employs him. The kind of discussion Shrag says is impossible is sanctioned and encouraged by the Constitution.

"Every child must be given the chance to become the kind of citizen the First Amendment demands"

If this seems too legalistic a view, if the answer is that popular preju-dice will prevent what the Constitution allows, one answer is that changes have occurred in popular prejudices, sometimes under pressure from the Court. Professor La Noue, in the article I have already cited, says,

> *In 1960 the median school year completed by nonwhites in the United States was 10.8; by whites, 12.3. By 1968 the gap had nar-rowed to 12.2 for nonwhites and 12.6 for whites. Furthermore, the number of black students in colleges doubled between 1964 and 1969, and black youngsters are now more likely to be enrolled in preschool programs than are whites.*[74]

The United States is trying, with some success, to outlaw race as a dis-tinction upon which any difference in the public treatment of individuals or groups may be based. Public policy is now moving to outlaw distinc-tions based on sex. There are signs that distinctions founded on money will suffer the same fate. The decisions I have cited holding the property tax violative of the equal protection of the laws when it results in gross inequalities in public expenditures among school districts are evidence that the law is going to try to equalize the public position of the rich and the poor. The long list of cases in which the Supreme Court has held that poor defendants charged with crime must be accorded legal assistance at public expense is to the same effect. I am reasonably confident that some of my readers will live long enough to applaud a decision by the Supreme Court that a man may not be thrown in jail pending trial merely because he has not the money to put up bail. There are even some faint stirrings suggesting that the control of money over the electoral process may be diminished by limiting campaign expenditures; there are some slight indications that these expenditures may eventually be assumed by the public, and private campaign contributions made illegal.

The Constitution of the United States contemplates government by discussion, with all citizens participating in it. The motion toward this goal may be slow and erratic. But it is not trivial or irrelevant. The rule of one-man–one-vote and the extension of the franchise to eighteen-year-olds are steps in the same direction, toward an inclusive national com-munity based on the equality of all the people in it, all of whom are taking part in the consideration of public affairs.

Nothing in these tendencies excludes such values as "cultural plural-ism" has to offer. But cultural segregation is another matter. The prin-ciple of subsidiarity, which is a good rule leading to decentralization, holds that small groups should so far as possible have control over their own affairs and have the right to be heard on matters that concern them. The argument for cultural segregation of blacks or whites or ethnic groups is that no "outsider" should have anything to say about the behavior of a subcommunity. *Brown* v. *Board of Education* should have put the quietus on this doctrine. The interests of the larger political community, and in particular the standards established by the Bill of Rights, set limits to the desires of any subcommunity.

It is not necessary for the members of a political community to agree with one another. The First Amendment assumes Americans will not. But it is necessary that they understand one another. The aim is twofold, unity and diversity, an aim we see reflected in John Stuart Mill's argument for public education.

If this is the ideal, what part does public education have to play in it? Those who have been leading the great anti-school campaign have ignored this question. Yet it is, after all, *the* question. It cannot be answered by saying that we should have no schools at all, or that we should let our children go, or that we should encourage them to pursue their own interests, or that we should have schools they could drop into and out of as they pleased, or that the schools should be turned over to parents or private businesses; for such decisions would promote cultural, social, and economic segregation and the kind of individualism Tocqueville saw as a danger to every democracy.

Tocqueville said,

> Individualism *is a novel expression, to which a novel idea has given birth. Our fathers were only acquainted with égoïsme (selfishness). Selfishness is a passionate and exaggerated love of self, which leads a man to connect everything with himself and to prefer himself to everything in the world. Individualism is a mature and calm feeling, which disposes each member of the community to sever himself from the mass of his fellows and to draw apart with his family and his friends, so that after he has thus formed a little circle of his own, he willingly leaves society at large to itself. Selfishness originates in blind instinct; individualism proceeds from erroneous judgment more than from depraved feelings; it originates as much in the deficiencies of mind as in the perversity of heart.*
>
> *Selfishness blights the germ of all virtue; individualism, at first, only saps the virtues of public life; but in the long run it attacks and destroys all others and is at length absorbed in downright selfishness. Selfishness is a vice as old as the world, which does not belong to one form of society more than to another; individualism is of democratic origin, and it threatens to spread in the same ratio as the equality of condition.*[75]

Tocqueville's conclusion is:

> *Thus not only does democracy make every man forget his ancestors, but it hides his descendants and separates his contemporaries from him; it throws him back forever upon himself alone and*

> *threatens in the end to confine him entirely within the solitude of his own heart.*[76]

Tocqueville considered that the Americans of his day had subdued the individualism attendant on democracy by means of political freedom. He says, "The free institutions which the inhabitants of the United States possess, and the political rights of which they make so much use, remind every citizen, and in a thousand ways, that he lives in society."[77] One of the institutions that most powerfully reminds us of this important proposition is the public school. It is the only institution erected by the society for the specific purpose of helping the citizen learn to live in it and, if I am correctly interpreting the First Amendment, of helping him learn how it may be improved.

Mill feared more than anything else the pressure toward conformity that is exerted by any society. We know his fears were justified; the memory of Senator Joseph McCarthy is still green; the Cold War is not yet over and may flare up again at any time. Only the other day opponents of the war in Vietnam were suspected of treason; and a little earlier it was proposed to unseat Justice William O. Douglas because he favored friendly relations with Communist China. But the demands of the community cannot be ignored or suppressed without running into the extremes of individualism that Tocqueville describes. On balance, if we have to choose between an education that expands our individuality and one that draws out our common humanity, we should at this juncture prefer the latter. Fortunately, as I hope to show, we do not have to choose.

The doctrine of every man for himself, or every nation for itself, loses its charm in an interdependent world. This doctrine has to give way before the idea of a world community. We have to understand and rely on our common humanity if we are to survive in any condition worthy to be called human. Everything else sinks into triviality in comparison with this task. To hear the United States commissioner of education talk about "career education"—he has rechristened vocational training—or to read all the new programs, based on the whims of children, that one finds in the trade papers of what satirist Tom Lehrer calls the "ed biz," or to think about whether or not we should invent new combinations of letters to put after the names of students who have spent a certain time in a certain school, or, in short, to consider most of the topics of current educational discussion, is irrelevant, to borrow a word, to the real issue we face. So is the great anti-school campaign, except that if it succeeds we shall be deprived of the one institution that could most effectively assist in drawing out our common humanity.

Democracy is the best form of government precisely because it calls upon the citizen to be self-governing and to take his part in the self-governing political community. This is the answer to the individual-community dilemma. The individual cannot become a human being without the democratic political community; and the democratic political community cannot be maintained without independent citizens who are qualified to govern themselves and others through the democratic political community.

Political life in a democracy in which the people truly participate has tremendous educational force. In *Representative Government*, John Stuart Mill argues from a somewhat idealized version of the American example:

> *Among the foremost benefits of free government is that education of the intelligence and of the sentiments which is carried down to the very lowest ranks of the people when they are called to take a part in acts which directly affect the great interests of their country. . . . People think it fanciful to expect so much from what seems so slight a cause. . . . Yet unless substantial mental cultivation in the mass of mankind is to be a mere vision, this is the road by which it must come. If anyone supposes that this road will not bring it, I call to witness the entire contents of M. de Tocqueville's great work; and especially his estimate of the Americans. Almost all travellers are struck by the fact that every American is in some sense both a patriot, and a person of cultivated intelligence; and M. de Tocqueville has shown how close the connection is between these qualities and their democratic institutions. No such wide diffusion of the ideas, tastes, and sentiments of educated minds has ever been seen elsewhere, or even conceived as attainable. . . . It is by political discussion that the manual labourer, whose employment is a routine, and whose way of life brings him in contact with no variety of impressions, circumstances, or ideas, is taught that remote causes, and events which take place far off, have a most sensible effect even on his personal interests; and it is from political discussion, and collective political action, that one whose daily occupations concentrate his interests in a small circle round himself, learns to feel for and with his fellow-citizens, and becomes consciously a member of a great community.*[78]

The primary aim of the educational system in a democratic country conscious of the impending world community is to draw out the common humanity of those committed to its charge. This requires careful avoidance of that attractive trap, the ad hoc, that which may be immediately interesting, but which is transitory, or that which is thought to have some practical value under the circumstances of the time, but which is likely to be valueless if the circumstances change.

For example, vocational training, or "career education," has never had a place in education that could easily be defended. It was most often used to accommodate those who could not legally leave school but who did not take to the regular curriculum. These were most often the children of the poor. It amounted to saying that they had to be educated to the station to which they were born. It was an abandonment of any duty to try to draw out their common humanity or to prepare them for participation in the political community. As Karl Mannheim put it,

> The wrong type of democratic education will tend to transform everything into terms of vocational training and adjustment to an industrial order. It will be so concerned to bring about a compatibility with the contemporary that its sense of heritage, of history and tradition will be cut at the root.[79]

These children would have fared better if they had been allowed to drop out of school and go to work, because then they would have been trained on the job and not deluded into thinking the school had prepared them. If any technological change at all is going on, the training for industry given in schools must be in some degree obsolescent. In a period like the present, in which, we are told, every boy must expect to follow three or more different careers during his working life, training in a vocation becomes farcical: when he completes his training the student may find there are no jobs in the field for which he has been trained, or that the machines and methods have been so changed that his training is a handicap to him.

The same may be said of anything else that must rest on current practices or events. These may have value as illustrations, but they have none as the stuff of education. This is because they will not remain current. They lead to the affliction known as presentism, which lulls its victims into ignoring yesterday and extrapolating today.

The most elementary truth about education is the one most often disregarded. It takes time. The educator must therefore remember that unless he wants to be a custodian, or a sitter, or a playmate, he must ask himself whether what he and his pupils are doing will have any relevance ten years from now. It does not seem an adequate reply that they are having fun, any more than it would be to say they were learning a trade. Nor would it be much more adequate to say they were learning what their parents wanted. The community includes parents but is not confined to them. Taxes for the support of schools are paid by bachelors, spinsters, childless couples, and the elderly on the theory that the whole community is interested in and benefits from its common schools.

The barbarism, "communication skills," is the contemporary jargon for reading, writing, figuring, speaking, and listening—arts that appear to have permanent relevance. These arts are important in any society at any time. They are more important in a democratic society than in any other, because the citizens of a democratic society have to understand one another. They are indispensable in a world community; they are arts shared by people everywhere. Without them the individual is deprived, and the community is too. In a technical age these are the only techniques that are universally valuable; they supply the only kind of vocational training a school can offer that can contribute to vocational success. They are the indispensable means to learning anything. They have to be learned if the individual hopes to expand his individuality, or if he proposes to become a self-governing member of a self-governing community. Learning these arts cannot be left to the choices of children or their parents.

The first object of any school must be to equip the student with the tools of learning. These are the arts to which I have referred. With these arts at his command the citizen can learn all his life.

The second object of any school—and this is vital to a democratic community—should be to open new worlds to the young, to get them out of the rut of the place and time in which they were born. Whatever the charms of the neighborhood school, whatever the pleasures of touring one's native city, whatever the allure of presentism, emphasis upon the immediate environment and its current condition must narrow the mind and prevent understanding of the wider national or world community and any real comprehension of the present itself. Hence those who would center education on the interests of children and on their surroundings, though these critics may seem up-to-date, are working contrary to the demands contemporary society is making upon any educational system.

The third object of any educational institution must be to get the young to understand their cultural heritage. This, too, is in the interest of the individual and the community.[80] The individual ought to see himself in the community, a community having a tradition, which perhaps ought to be rejected, but not unless it is first understood. Comprehension of the cultural heritage is the means by which the bonds uniting the community are strengthened. The public school is the only agency that can be entrusted with this obligation. Its performance cannot be left to chance.

These obligations, teaching the arts of communication, opening new worlds, helping children learn how to learn, and transmitting the cultural heritage, rest upon the public schools, but it cannot be said that the American public schools are discharging them—or any one of them. In many American public schools the children are simply in custody. In many, boredom and frustration are the characteristics of school life. In many, the pupils are simply waiting out their time. It is sometimes said that this must happen in any institution. James Herndon wrestles with this question in his book *How To Survive in Your Native Land*. He first says: "An Institution Is A Place To Do Things Where Those Things Will Not Be Done." He then adds,

> *There is no law any more that people must go to church or pay attention to the church, and so many people don't, while others do.*

"to open new worlds to the young, to get them out of the rut of the place and time in which they were born"

> *That is the best you can expect, and good enough. You can appar-*
> *ently get one institution to combat another, and it would be most*
> *useful to get rid of the law that all kids have to go to some school*
> *or other until age x or any other age. The public school is the*
> *closest thing we have in America to a national established church,*
> *Getting-An-Education the closest thing to God, and it should be*
> *possible to treat it and deal with it as the church has been treated*
> *and dealt with. This treatment has not really changed the existence*
> *of the one institution and will not harm the other, but it has al-*
> *lowed the growth of alternatives to it and that is what is wanted,*
> *even if some of those alternatives have become, and will become,*
> *institutions themselves.*[81]

Having favored alternatives to the public school even if they are institutions, Herndon seems to take it back by saying alternative institutions
would be equally harmful. "Public schools are irrelevant; free schools
(whether invented by parents or children) are irrelevant. . . . All irrelevant
and harmful, like much else in this country, to the lives of people."[82]
This seems to dispose of every present or possible kind of school.

Herndon then goes on to describe a minor triumph in a public school,
teaching a class to read. First he sets forth the grounds on which the
decision to teach reading was reached.

> *It is O.K. for the adults to decide what's going to go on. To be*
> *authoritarian. Decide, simply because no one else can do so. What*
> *other use is there for adults, if not to decide things for kids? . . .*
> *We decided that we would teach reading because the kids couldn't*
> *read well, and because you had to be able to read in America in*
> *order to be equal.*[83]

Or more elaborately:

> *We considered these questions: How come some kids couldn't*
> *learn in school? How come some other kids could? What was it*
> *that everyone in America could agree on that kids needed to learn?*
> *Why did they need to learn it, or did they? We came to no conclu-*
> *sions about the first questions; even though we all felt we knew all*
> *about it, all we could say was that some kids were defeated by*
> *school, diminished by it. On the latter questions we had no such*
> *problems. We had all lived in America, in the West, South, Middle-*
> *west and East. No one could doubt that the parents and uncles and*
> *big brothers of every class and of every conviction in America ex-*
> *pected kids to learn to read and write. We thought that good*
> *enough for us, and why not? Were we in America or not? Why had*
> *public schools been started at all if not to see that kids learned to*

read and write who otherwise—if their parents couldn't read, or if their parents were too poor to hire a tutor or couldn't teach them themselves—might not be able to do it? As for why—they needed to learn it in order to become equal *in the country.*[84]

The reader will note that Herndon first rejects all institutions. Then he rejects all educational institutions, and in particular the public school. Then he proves that the public school is an institution indispensable to the kind of community America purports to be, because without the public school many children might not learn to read and without learning to read could not hope to be full participating citizens of this democracy. No alternative can be suggested, because none can work.

I have quoted Herndon at length because I think he points to conclusions to which any honest critic of the public schools must come, namely, that, bad as they are, we cannot do without them. If that is so, the question is how can they be made better, which is another way of asking how can we grow citizens worthy of the First Amendment? How can we conduct a deliberate attempt to form men in terms of this ideal?

Here I do not propose to repeat the general observations I have made about the purposes of basic education: to teach the arts of communication, to open new worlds, to help the young learn how to learn, and to transmit the cultural heritage. I intend rather to deal with the institution through which these things are to be done and to suggest how its organization and methods might be reformed with these ends in view. It is perhaps unnecessary to point out that the ends must be clear and supported by the community if any effort to achieve them is to succeed.[85] It will also be understood that inclusion in the program of the public schools of material not pertinent to these ends will confuse the enterprise and make it difficult if not impossible to tell whether or not it is succeeding.

The importance of adult education

As T. S. Eliot said in the passage already quoted, "Education is a subject which cannot be discussed in a void: our questions raise other questions, social, economic, financial, political." The answer to questions about what the schools can do depends in large part on what other institutions are doing. For example, the family seems to have great influence on the education of its members. This was the finding of the Plowden Report in Britain.[86] This report and other studies led the Tanners to conclude: "No matter how well-conceived, well-financed, and well-intended, an educational program for children alone can not counteract the adverse cultural effects of the home."[87] In the absence of some reasonable standard of health and some sort of financial resources and security, families are likely to have neither the inclination nor the energy to change their atti-

215

tudes toward their children's schooling. Socioeconomic status has some correlation with parental views of and interest in education. But it is not conclusive, as the cases of Jewish and Oriental children, who are likely to do better in school than other children of the same status, suffice to show. If socioeconomic status were decisive, the school would be limited to preparing children for the station to which they were born.

The Tanners say,

> *While many educational and social theorists are debating such meaningless dichotomies as cultural pluralism vs. assimilation (the members of the opposing sides invariably are, themselves, well-assimilated in the prevailing culture), our new urban immigrants and their children are remaining, through no fault of their own, at an educational and cultural level too low to function successfully in the real world. If they are given every possible opportunity to gain the language facility, skills, attitudes, and knowledge to assimilate into the prevailing culture, then we also have given them the choice of cultural identity and/or assimilation. Without education, the choice might not be theirs. The kind of pluralism they will have is the kind they now have and do not want for their children.*[88]

In this view one of the country's greatest needs is for a comprehensive program for the education of adults. It is true that adults, after trying it, may not like the taste of education, but they might at least have a better idea of what their children are up against than they have now. The hope would be that parental attitudes might change; if they did, one of the principal obstacles to the education of the disadvantaged would disappear.

A second reason for a comprehensive program of adult education lies in the effects it might have on the curriculum of the schools. That is at present organized, from the primary school on, in accordance with the principle that the student must learn in childhood and adolescence everything he is going to need for the rest of his life. The proliferation of courses throughout the educational system demonstrates the force of this principle. If the chance to learn were continuously open to the citizen, no one could claim that everything had to be packed into him during his school days, a time at which, incidentally, he cannot have much comprehension of those subjects which become comprehensible only as the learner acquires enough experience and maturity to understand them.

A third advantage of increased emphasis on the education of adults is that it would make it possible to lower the school-leaving age. If the only chance at systematic learning occurs in childhood and adolescence, then the argument for a packed curriculum, extending over many years, may stand up; detention in school for a decade and more may be justified. But how is it possible to justify such detention if the pupil, at any stage of life, can find the means of learning ready to his hand? Nothing we know about biology or society suggests that much of what is now taught between fourteen and eighteen has to be learned in that period. The attention that has been focused on the influence of the earliest years of life is bound to lead to greater and greater public interest in nursery schools and kindergartens. In these institutions early beginnings may be made in subjects now taught later on. In eight or nine years more, if the time were well spent, it ought to be possible to provide the rising generation with the knowledge and skill needed for its self-preservation and the maintenance of the society.

The reduction of the length of compulsory education would require the educators of this country to reexamine the curriculum and get rid of the extraneous elements that have been forced upon it by the demands of those parents and legislators who have come to regard the school as an all-purpose instrument for doing to or for children whatever may cross their benefactors' minds.

The school is now primarily a custodial institution. The answer to the suggestion that the length of compulsory full-time schooling be cut down will doubtless be, what shall we do with our children? First, there is part-time schooling. The continuation school, in session in the late afternoon and evening, can be made compulsory up to a certain age. Then there would be adult education. As Arnold Toynbee has said,

> *But, in the poverty-stricken civilizations of these first few thousand years, formal education, even for a privileged minority, has usually come to an end at the close of adolescence, if not earlier; and this has had an unfortunate consequence. The student has been surfeited with book learning at a stage of life at which he has not yet acquired the experience to take advantage of this, and he has then been starved for book learning at a later stage in which, if he had been given the opportunity, he could have made much more of it in the light of his growing experience. In the rich society of the future, we shall be able to afford to offer part-time adult education to every man and woman at every stage of grown-up life.*[89]

Toynbee relies on the example of Denmark, which has a low school-leaving age and a system of continuation schools:

> *Already, in Denmark, a highly civilized people that has had the intelligence to carry out an agricultural revolution has used some of its modest profits, Greek fashion, for providing voluntary adult higher education for itself in the admirable Danish high schools (which are schools for grown-up persons, not for children). A Danish farmer will save money for years to enable himself to take a six-months' or a twelve-months' course, and he will make it a point of honor to choose his subject with an eye to raising the*

217

level of his culture and not with an eye to improving his economic position. In this present-day Danish institution we have a foretaste of an educational advance that will be open to the whole of mankind in the coming age of "atoms for peace," automation, and the leisure that will be generated by an abundance of scientifically directed mechanical power.[90]

One aspect of the Danish tradition of adult education should be emphasized. The Danish farmer does not go to a folk high school in order to learn how to be a better farmer, but to be a better man. Much discussion nowadays revolves around the technological revolution and the need for periodic retraining or "refresher" courses to learn new techniques suddenly required on an old job or demanded by a new one. The necessity for such training and retraining is clear enough, though it is by no means equally evident that this should be the responsibility of the state rather than of industry. Whatever the method of supplying the training that is needed, it will be supplied in response to the deep national concern about unemployment, technology, and industrial power. Few Americans today make it a point of honor to choose their subjects of study at any stage with an eye to raising the level of their culture and not with an eye to improving their economic position.

What John Stuart Mill said about the university bears on the aims and content of adult education today. In his Inaugural Address at St. Andrews in 1867, he remarked:

> *Men are men before they are lawyers, or physicians, or merchants, or manufacturers; and if you make them capable and sensible men, they will make themselves capable and sensible lawyers or physicians. What professional men should carry away with them from an University is not professional knowledge, but that which should direct the use of their professional knowledge, and bring the light of general culture to illuminate the technicalities of a special pursuit. Men may be competent lawyers without general education, but it depends on general education to make them philosophic lawyers—who demand, and are capable of apprehending, principles, instead of merely cramming their memory with details.*[91]

Mill goes on to take the same attitude to nonuniversity, nonprofessional education. He says, "And so of all other useful pursuits, mechanical included. Education makes a man a more intelligent shoemaker, if that be his occupation, but not by teaching him how to make shoes; it does so by the mental exercise it gives, and the habits it impresses."[92]

The advance of technology makes this observation even more pertinent than it was 100 years ago, and in two ways. In the first place, technology remorselessly simplifies—or eliminates—skill; its object is to get the operation down to the point at which it would be conducted by a child who had had only a few hours' instruction, or even to get rid of labor altogether. As the managing director of a fully automatic biscuit factory in West Germany said, "Here the skill of the baker dies." No doubt in a cybernated society the need for technical training and retraining will exist, but it will exist for a declining proportion of the work force, and the work force will be a declining proportion of the population. As the present plight of scientists and engineers suggests, they, rather than the work force they have been accustomed to direct, require at this moment retraining on a large scale.

In the second place, as technology decreases the demand for skilled labor, or labor of any kind, it increases the demand for intelligent citizens. It puts constant strains on a democratic society, presenting it with new problems every day. If, as Mill says, education makes a man a more intelligent shoemaker, perhaps we can expect it to make him a more intelligent citizen. I think everybody will agree that if ever the United States needed more intelligent citizens, it needs them now.

Reform of the public school system

This brings us back to the beginning. At the outset it appeared that there could be no philosophy of education apart from philosophy as a whole, that to know what we want in education we must know what we want in general, and that we derive our theory of education from our philosophy of life. As Mill called for philosophic lawyers, doctors, physicians, merchants, manufacturers, and shoemakers, men who would demand and be capable of apprehending principles, we might yearn for philosophic citizens, men and women who learn from the beginning to demand and apprehend principles instead of merely cramming their memory with details. If we had such citizens, we should be able to put an end to the great anti-school campaign. Philosophic citizens would understand the reasons for the public schools; and they would support those reforms in the schools which were dictated by the principles on which the schools were based. They would not, for example, pay much heed to the United States commissioner of education, Sidney P. Marland. He says that high school graduates go either to work or to college; three out of ten go to college; one-third of those drop out.

> *That means that eight out of ten present high school students should be getting occupational training of some sort. But only about two of these eight students are, in fact, getting such training.*

> *Consequently, half our high school students, a total of approxi-*
> *mately 1.5 million a year, are being offered what amounts to*
> irrelevant general educational pap![93]

Mr. Marland's statement that general education is irrelevant to anybody who is not going to college is as undemocratic a pronouncement as
has come out of Washington in a long time. No hope here of philosophic
citizens. We may get a few from the colleges—the best that can be said of
the rest is that they will have adjusted themselves to the industrial machine; or, more accurately, they may think they have adjusted themselves
to it, when in fact they will be maladjusted. The shoemakers of Mill's
day, like the buggymakers of this century, have disappeared. Whether or
not they could shift to other occupations must have depended in large
part on whether or not they were narrowly trained or had some general
education, with the mental exercise it gives and the habits it impresses.

If I left the matter here, I could properly be accused of the crime I have
charged against others, using education as a means of avoiding a problem.
So far I have proposed to solve the problems of public education by means
of education. Give us educated citizens and the public school will become
what it ought to be. This is probably true, but in the meantime the school
is far from what it ought to be, and, to paraphrase Keynes, in the meantime we may all be dead. Immediate steps have got to be taken to make
the schools more adequate to their task. These steps must be taken within
the boundaries set by the Constitution and, unfortunately, as in the case
of the property tax, we cannot always be sure what those boundaries are.
The property tax is not the only example. We cannot be certain whether
the Supreme Court will adhere to its decision that lower courts may order
busing if it is necessary to desegregation, even though the Coleman Report suggests that busing, which is an old American tradition, is necessary
on educational grounds.

These views limit decentralization, which has an attractive, cozy sound.
The word calls up a picture of small schools watched over by small communities that have firsthand knowledge of the schools, the teachers, and
the pupils. In practice, as we have seen, decentralization has usually been
a disguise for cultural segregation.

Nevertheless, the problem of bureaucracy must be dealt with. Although
Dennison's remarks on this subject are exaggerated, they will arouse some
sympathy. He says, "The present quagmire of public education is entirely
the result of unworkable centralization and the lust for control that permeates every bureaucratic institution."[94] The one-room school has disappeared, and large consolidated school districts have been built up, not
because of the lust for power, but because a larger tax base and larger
institutions were thought to give a chance for better education, and they
probably did. Any large institution has to operate bureaucratically, that

is, in accordance with established routines; otherwise it could not operate at all.

Within the limits set by the Constitution and by the necessity of allocating resources in the most economical way, school districts, schools, and classes should be as small as possible. Even if, according to the Coleman Report, such changes would not materially affect the achievement of children, they would facilitate variety and experimentation, and they would make schools less formidable to those who must attend them.

Ways must be found to break the lockstep, the system by which all pupils proceed at the same pace through the same curriculum for the same number of years.[95] The disadvantages of small schools can be overcome by building them in clusters, each with somewhat different courses and methods and permitting students to avail themselves of anything offered in any one. This is an extension of the idea of dual enrollment or shared time, which now exists everywhere, and which allows students in one school to take advantage of what is taught in another, even if one of the schools is private and the other public.

Variety in the methods and curriculum is one way of breaking the lockstep. Another is allowing the student to proceed at his own rate of speed. Under the present system the slow learner is eventually thrown into despair because he cannot keep up, and the fast learner is in the same condition because he has "nothing to do." If we are to have a graded curriculum, we can overcome some of the handicaps it imposes by substituting examinations for time spent and by encouraging the student to present himself for them whenever in his opinion he is ready to take them.

It is self-evident that if a course of study is designed to provide the minimum requisites for democratic citizenship, nobody can be permitted to fail. If, then, the basic curriculum is revised as proposed above, so that it is limited to studies essential to the exercise of citizenship, it follows that grades would be eliminated and with them the degrading distinction between winners and losers. If parental attitudes are, as the Plowden Report intimates, profoundly influential in producing this distinction, then the grading system makes the children pay for the sins of their parents. We have reason to believe that everybody is educable. The rate and method of education may vary; the aim of basic education is the same with all individuals, and the obligation of the public schools is to achieve it with all. On this principle, if there is failure, it is the failure of the school, not of the pupil.

I take for granted the adoption or adaptation of many of those reforms about which so much noise has been made of late. The critics of the schools have performed a public service in calling attention to shortcomings that can be repaired by keeping them in mind and working on them. Interest, for example, can be restored to schooling without coming to the indefensible conclusion that whatever is not immediately interest-

221

ing to children should be omitted from their education. About some other matters the elementary and secondary schools can do little or nothing. They cannot do much to change parental attitudes, though they should certainly try by keeping in touch with the families of pupils. They can do nothing about the socioeconomic status or the slum environment of the children in their charge. The present efforts in preschool education have a trifling effect in improving the conditions of the earliest years in the lives of slum children. The schools can do nothing about the high taxes that infuriate their no-nonsense, hardheaded critics. They can see to it that money is not wasted, but the definition of waste depends upon an understanding of the purpose of the activity and the best methods of accomplishing it. For example, I would say that buying uniforms for the school band was a waste of money, even though they were bought after competitive bidding, whereas buying good books for the library was not, even though they were not required by the curriculum.

The purpose of the activity is the crucial question. The purpose of the public schools is not accomplished by having them free, universal, and compulsory. Schools are public because they are dedicated to the maintenance and improvement of what the philosopher Scott Buchanan called the Public Thing, the *res publica;* they are the common schools of the commonwealth, the political community. They may do many things for the young: they may amuse them, comfort them, look after their health, and keep them off the streets. But they are not public schools unless they start their pupils toward an understanding of what it means to be a self-governing citizen of a self-governing political community.

---

1 On January 2, 1972, *Parade* reported (p. 5) that the average American preschooler spends 64 percent of his time watching television. By the age of 14 he will have seen 18,000 murders on TV, by the age of 17, some 350,000 commercials. In the course of his life television will have consumed 10 years of his time. Dr. Gerald Looney of the University of Arizona says the American preschool child spends more time watching television than he would in the classroom during four years of college.

2 *GBWW,* Vol. 2, pp. 376, 377.

3 *Selected Essays* (New York: Harcourt, Brace & Co., 1950), p. 452.

4 *GBWW,* Vol. 9, p. 542.

5 *A Discourse on Political Economy; GBWW,* Vol. 38, p. 377. Rousseau seems to have forgotten Prussia, where in 1717 Frederick William I ordered all children to attend school where schools existed; and he overlooked the American colonies.

6 *GBWW,* Vol. 7, p. 721. Aristotle seems to favor private education in the *Ethics* and public in the *Politics.* In the time of Plato and Aristotle, Athenian education was entirely private.

7 *The Wealth of Nations; GBWW,* Vol. 39, pp. 340–41.

8 Ibid., p. 342.

9 Ibid., p. 343.

10 *On Liberty; GBWW,* Vol. 43, pp. 317–18.

11 Ibid., p. 318.

12 Ibid., p. 319.

13 *Capital; GBWW,* Vol. 50, p. 241.

14 *The Philosophy of Right; GBWW*, Vol. 46, p. 140.

15 *Among My Books* (Boston: Fields, Osgood & Co., 1870), p. 239.

16 *Brown* v. *Board of Education* (1954). The Supreme Court has also held (*Pierce* v. *Society of Sisters*, 1925), and will doubtless continue to hold, that "the child is not the mere creature of the state" and that parents may send their children to private schools regulated by the state. The First Amendment protects the free exercise of religion against interference by government; 95 percent of the students in private schools are in institutions connected with churches. The balance represents what we may call the John Stuart Mill strain in American thought, which works out to the notion that people who have money are free to obtain for their children, under the supervision of the state, the "best" education their money can buy. It should be noted in passing that the Supreme Court holds that the Constitution forbids the states to cooperate in the establishment of private schools if they are organized for the purpose of preventing the education of different races in the same school. But *South Today* reported (December 1971) that enrollment in private schools in North Carolina had almost tripled since 1964.

On December 20, 1971, the Supreme Court entered a summary judgment denying tax-exempt status to private schools that practise racial discrimination and refusing to allow contributions to such schools to be classed as charitable contributions.

17 *Education* (Ann Arbor: University of Michigan Press, 1960), p. 14.

18 Lloyd A. Free and Hadley Cantril, *The Political Beliefs of Americans* (New Brunswick, N.J.: Rutgers University Press, 1967), pp. 193–94.

19 The only faithful voice I have heard lately is that of Clark Kerr, former president of the University of California. In June 1971 he wrote: "The hopes that Benjamin Franklin and Thomas Jefferson had so long ago for the contributions of education to American society have been largely realized. Their faith still remains well justified in modern circumstances." On the other hand, *Educational Leadership* reported in October 1971 a study of school budget elections in New York State that found that one-half the dissenting votes opposed the proposed expenditures not because of the money but because of doubts about the effectiveness of the schools.

20 On January 4, 1972, the Associated Press reported the results of the National Child Development Study in Britain, following the lives of 17,000 children born in March 1958. It found that middle-class children have a 17-month lead over their working-class schoolmates. Those from upper-middle-class homes with two cars, color TV, and household labor-saving gadgets are even further ahead, if their parents are happy and limit their children to two or three. Children whose parents left school as soon as they could are six months behind those whose parents remained in school as long as they could.

21 James S. Coleman et al., *Equality of Educational Opportunity* (Washington, D.C.: Government Printing Office, 1966), p. 23.

22 A New York court has declined to follow these cases. See *U.S. Law Week*, February 1, 1972.

23 Ronald Gross and Paul Osterman, eds., *High School* (New York: Simon and Schuster, 1971).

24 Cf. Dael Wolfle and Charles V. Kidd, "The Future Market for Ph.D.'s," *Science*, August 27, 1971, pp. 784–93.

25 Mark Hopkins College in Vermont made the front page of the *Wall Street Journal* on February 2, 1972, by announcing that its guiding principles are: "No teachers, no classes, no lectures, no examinations, no grades, no credits. Above all, no accreditation and no degrees."

26 *GBWW*, Vol. 9, p. 459.

27 "Schools and Social Change," *School and Society*, December 1971, p. 488.

28 *Paideia: The Ideals of Greek Culture*, 3 vols., trans. Gilbert Highet (New York: Oxford University Press, 1943).

29 J. William Fulbright, "In Thrall to Fear," *New Yorker*, January 8, 1972, p. 59.

30 *The Lives of Children* (New York: Random House, Vintage Books, 1970), pp. 74, 17, 21, 73.

31 Charles E. Silberman, *Crisis in the Classroom* (New York: Random House, 1970).

32 A report in the *American School Board Journal* for February 1971 shows what can happen. "Daytime soap operas televised in the classrooms of public schools? Why not? says a Michigan State University communications specialist. In fact, Bradley Greenberg believes he has come up with two convincing reasons why commercial television should

be incorporated into the classroom: because television presents more of a real life situation to children than does the schoolroom, and because children watch TV voluntarily." The reader should not be surprized at this suggestion. Critics of the schools can get almost anything into print these days. For example, "In this technological age, it is difficult to understand why literacy has maintained such importance. With education focusing almost solely on a curriculum based on literacy, we are excluding a sizable number of potentially capable citizens from an opportunity to be educated, informed and employed in meaningful jobs. . . . Can't we teach children about the world around them, their own and other cultures, the similarities and differences of other peoples, the social and ecological needs of people, past, present, and future? The child's right to learn these things should outweigh his right to read." Norman and Margaret C. Silberberg, "Reading Rituals," *Trans-action,* July-August 1971, p. 49.

33 *Politics; GBWW,* Vol. 9, p. 544.

34 *Philosophy of Right; GBWW,* Vol. 46, p. 61.

35 I asked my eight-year-old grandson how he liked his riding master. He said, "Mr. Cathcart is a very nice, strict man. He doesn't get mad at you unless you do something you're not supposed to do." Somebody should write a Ph.D. dissertation on the difference in attitude toward athletic coaches and other teachers in American educational institutions.

36 *GGB,* Vol. 6, pp. 30–31.

37 *Selected Essays,* p. 453.

38 *See* note 23.

39 September 25, 1971, pp. 17–21.

40 Karen Branan, "I Get a Very Different Feeling in That Class," *Scholastic Teacher,* May 3, 1971, p. 8.

41 *Children Come First* (New York: American Heritage Press, 1971), p. 34.

42 November 15, 1971, p. 7.

43 "The Debasement of Liberal Education," *Chronicle of Higher Education,* October 18, 1971, p. 8.

44 "Original Papers in Relation to a Course of Liberal Education," *American Journal of Science and Arts,* January 1829.

45 *Deschooling Society* (New York: Harper & Row, 1971).

46 "If the goals of learning were no longer dominated by schools and schoolteachers, the market for learners would be much more various and the definition of 'educational artifacts' would be less restrictive. There could be tool shops, libraries, laboratories, and gaming rooms. Photo labs and offset presses would allow neighborhood newspapers to flourish. Some storefront learning centers could contain viewing booths for closed-circuit television, others could feature office equipment for use and for repair. The jukebox and the record player would be commonplace, with some specializing in classical music, others in international folk tunes, others in jazz. Film clubs would compete with each other and with commercial television. Museum outlets could be networks for circulating exhibitions of works of art, both old and new, originals and reproductions, perhaps administered by the various metropolitan museums." Ibid., p. 84.

47 "End of the Impossible Dream," *Saturday Review,* September 19, 1970, p. 70.

48 Ibid.

49 "Open Schools," *National Elementary Principal,* October 1971, p. 24.

50 It would surprise old-time members of the Progressive Education movement to learn that the idea of open, informal schools was new.

51 Ibid., p. 25.

52 *The Lives of Children,* p. 280.

53 *GBWW,* Vol. 9, p. 542. But in the *Ethics* he says: "Further, private education has an advantage over public, as private medical treatment has . . . . It would seem, then, that the detail is worked out with more precision if the control is private; for each person is more likely to get what suits his case." *GBWW,* Vol. 9, p. 435.

54 *Discourse on Political Economy; GBWW,* Vol. 38, p. 376.

55 *Santa Barbara News-Press,* December 9, 1971.

56 *See* note 21.

57 *Education Summary,* December 24, 1971.

58 "End of the Impossible Dream," p. 70.

59 "Is the Public School Obsolete?," *The Public Interest,* Winter 1965, p. 27.

60 On this point cf. Walter McCann and Judith Areen, "Vouchers and the Citizen—Some Legal Questions," *Teachers College Record,* February 1971, p. 401.

61 *Freedom of Choice in Education* (New York: The Macmillan Co., 1958).

62 *Capitalism and Freedom* (Chicago: University of Chicago Press, 1962).

63 *See,* for example, John E. Coons, William H. Clune III, and Stephen D. Sugarman, *Private Wealth and Public Education* (Cambridge, Mass.: Harvard University Press, Belknap Press, 1970); and Leonard Ross and Richard Zeuckhauser, "Education Vouchers," *Yale Law Journal,* December 1970, p. 451.

64 "Education Vouchers," *New Republic,* July 4, 1970, pp. 19–20.

65 *Education Vouchers: A Preliminary Report on Financing Education by Payments to Parents* (Cambridge, Mass.: Center for the Study of Public Policy, 1970).

66 "Education Vouchers," p. 20.

67 Ibid.

68 Ibid.

69 "The Politics of Education," *Teachers College Record,* December 1971, pp. 314, 315, 318.

70 Ibid., p. 318. To the same effect *see* Robert Lekachman, "Vouchers and Public Education," *New Leader,* July 12, 1971, p. 1. ". . . I simply do not believe the scheme will end as anything other than some variant of free-market, conservative vouchers. The overriding social fact is that most parents who favor vouchers do so for reasons quite different from any aspiration toward racial or economic integration."

71 Cf. "It is impossible to escape the realization that our society, like any society, rests on common beliefs and that a major task of education is to perpetuate them." *General Education in a Free Society: Report of the Harvard Committee* (Cambridge, Mass.: Harvard University Press, 1945), p. 46.

72 I am not suggesting that this commitment is one of which all Americans are conscious. Norman E. Isaacs, former executive editor of the *Louisville Courier-Journal,* has cited a survey by the *Corpus Christi Caller-Times,* December 15, 1969, showing that of 199 persons asked to sign a petition supporting the Bill of Rights, only 19 could correctly identify the document: 143 refused to sign. Obviously something is wrong with our educational system. Nevertheless, the commitment is there and is binding on all governments in the United States.

73 *Tinker* v. *Des Moines Independent Community School District* (1969).

74 "The Politics of Education," p. 304.

75 Alexis de Tocqueville, *Democracy in America,* tr. Henry Reeve, vol. 2 (New York: Random House, Vintage Books, 1962), p. 104.

76 Ibid., p. 106.

77 Ibid., p. 112.

78 *Representative Government; GBWW,* Vol. 43, pp. 381–82.

79 Karl Mannheim and W. A. S. Stewart, *An Introduction to the Sociology of Education* (London: Routledge & Kegan Paul, 1962), p. 23.

80 Cf. John Dewey, *Experience and Education* (New York: The Macmillan Co., 1938; Collier Books, 1963, p. 77). ". . . the achievements of the past provide the only means at command for understanding the present. Just as the individual has to draw in memory upon his own past to understand the conditions in which he individually finds himself, so the issues and problems of present *social* life are in such intimate and direct connection with the past that students cannot be prepared to understand either these problems or the best way of dealing with them without delving into their own roots in the past. In other words, the sound principle that the objectives of learning are in the future and its immediate materials in present experience can be carried into effect only in the degree that present experience is stretched, as it were, backward. It can expand into the future only as it is also enlarged to take in the past."

81 *How to Survive in Your Native Land* (New York: Bantam Books, 1972), p. 100–101.

82 Ibid., p. 118.

83 Ibid.

84 Ibid., pp. 116–17.

85 Cf. "To use school children as shock troops in attacking social inequities and injustices, and to use the schools as means to non-educative ends, will serve only to undermine the constructive and generative capability of the schools to educate children so that they may develop the power to improve their lives." Daniel and Laurel N. Tan-

ner, "Parent Education and Cultural Inheritance," *School & Society*, January 1971, p. 23. This was said in comment on the tendency of some groups to close down schools in the effort, for example, to obtain larger welfare allowances for children's clothing.

86 Bridget Plowden et al., *Children and Their Primary Schools: A Report of the Central Advisory Council for Education*, vol. 2, Appendix 9 (London: Her Majesty's Stationery Office, 1969), pp. 381–82.

87 "Parent Education and Cultural Inheritance," p. 23.

88 Ibid.

89 "Education in the Perspective of History," in *The Teacher and the Taught*, ed. Ronald Gross (New York: Dell Publishing Co., Delta Books, 1963), p. 135.

90 Ibid.

91 *GIT* 1969, p. 387.

92 Ibid.

93 Undated press release from the U.S. Department of Labor, Manpower Administration, advertising its magazine, *Manpower*.

94 *The Lives of Children*, p. 9.

95 The *New York Times* of July 11, 1971, gives an account of various alternatives proposed for the high schools of New York City, including satellite academies, "mini-schools," and independent study. Twelve new kinds of high schools are called for, to be established "as soon as possible." It must be said that some of them sound like make-work programs designed to fill out the time until the student can legally get a job. It might be better to lower the school-leaving age than to exhaust our imaginations trying to figure out how to keep children amused in school until they are eighteen or, as is sometimes suggested, until they have finished the first two years of college.

NOTE TO THE READER

The matters treated in this essay by Mr. Hutchins are widely discussed in *GBWW*, as his quotations will serve to indicate. See, in the *Syntopicon*, the references under Chapter 20, EDUCATION, in particular Topic 5c, which deals with the nature of learning; 5d, which is concerned with the organization of curriculum; and 5e, which is devoted to the emotional aspect of learning—the function of pleasure, desire, and interest.

For the political implications of the subject, consult the entries under Topic 6 of both Chapter 11, CITIZEN, and Chapter 16, DEMOCRACY, as well as those under STATE 7d, which have to do with the educational task of the state and the trained intelligence of the citizen. See also, for further psychological aspects of learning, the entries under PLEASURE AND PAIN 4c(2), which are devoted to the pleasure and pain of learning and knowledge.

The Discipline of History

Henry Steele Commager

In the field of American historians, which is full of specialists, and which tends always (there have been notable exceptions) to be parochial, Henry Commager has for forty years been an untypical and distinguished figure. He has read everything that bears upon the American past and much besides, until there is hardly any literature on any subject that can be said to have been quite beyond his interest. This immense and various learning, which he has never let grow stale or academic, has been evident in the courses he has taught at New York University, Columbia, Amherst College, as well as Cambridge and Oxford universities, and in the long succession of books and essays that he has written. Among the latter have been studies of Theodore Parker and Justice Story, several works on Constitutional matters, an authoritative collection of *Documents of American History* (1934), *The American Mind* (1950), *The Nature and the Study of History* (1965), and a two-volume survey, *The Growth of the American Republic* (with Samuel Eliot Morison), for many years the best and most readable account at any comparable length of the American past. Now formally retired, Professor Commager nevertheless continues to teach half of each year at Amherst. He was recently awarded the Gold Medal for historical writing by the American Academy of Arts and Letters.

I What is history?

When we approach the spacious realms of History we stumble at the very threshold on the word itself. For the term *history*, unlike *art*, let us say, or *philosophy*, is inescapably ambiguous. It means the Past—let us capitalize that—and all that happened in the past. It means, too, the record of the past—all that men have said or written, all that they have built or fashioned, whatever they have, consciously or unconsciously, left behind them that may help us to reconstruct how they lived and what they thought and did.

This is not the simple matter one might suppose, for man has neither remembered nor recorded more than a very small fraction of his past. This should not surprise us: after all, how much of our own lives do we remember, how much that we have fashioned with our hands do we preserve, how much of our thoughts and actions have we recorded? The collective memory of man is even more fragmentary and arbitrary than the individual memory, the collective record more complete but probably more capricious. And—just as with the individual—the further back we go, the more evanescent is the memory, the more fragmentary the record. Yet there is a past, stretching back not 5,000 years, but 50,000. Life was just as real, what happened just as important, to the men huddled in their caves along the banks of the Dordogne, or perched precariously in the lake dwellings of Switzerland, or to the Tartars who crossed from Siberia to Alaska 25,000 years ago, as it is to us. Unlike us they left no memories and few records, except fossils and artifacts and here and there some astonishing paintings, yet they are just as legitimate a part of the past as are the Vikings or the Founding Fathers. Merely because we know little or nothing about them does not blot them out of existence. But it does pretty much exclude them from History, for History is dependent on memory and record. Perhaps we should say that History is dependent on record alone, for unless memory gets itself recorded in myth or fable or song, or perhaps in art, it too slips away like a dream.

It is History as memory and as record that concerns us in this little essay and, for the most part, History as the memory and the record of

Western man, for though of all of the peoples the Chinese probably have the most exact record, it is chiefly the West that has preoccupied itself with what we call History. But merely to say "the record" does not get us very far. There are many kinds of records, and not all of them are of equal interest or significance in the history of History.

The physical record is natural and archaeological. It is natural in the changes in the structure of beaches whose ridges reveal so much of the movements of the oceans; in the ebb and flow of the ice caps that once covered such vast areas of the earth; in the flood of oceans that broke through continents and created islands and altered both the geography and the climate of the earth; in the draining away or evaporation of inland seas; the creation of swamps, the alteration in the courses of rivers, the spread of desert sands. It is archaeological in the recovery of the many artifacts that ancient man left behind him—pottery, stone and iron weapons, instruments and utensils fashioned of bone, medals of iron and bronze, gems and beads, timber that went into the making of ships—and, eventually, in the uncovering of great temples and palaces and monuments, such as those of Knossos or Nineveh or Chichén Itzá, long buried beneath the sands of the desert or the deposits of the jungle.

The oral record, long out of fashion, is now enjoying something of a revival. It was, no doubt, the first form of History; it was also, in all likelihood, the first form of literature, for it preserved the traditions of the past over the centuries until they could be written down in the Homeric lays, the Icelandic sagas, and the songs and myths of primitive peoples that James Frazer collected to make his *Golden Bough,* or that have been reinterpreted by the genius of Claude Levi-Strauss. In a more sophisticated form, oral history is now formally organized, mechanized, and institutionalized, and a new generation of clerks has grown up who record history directly from the mouths of those who make it and preserve it on imperishable tapes.

A third form of record is that of art. That the artistic record is the most faithful of all was the conclusion of the great art historian John Ruskin, whose *Stones of Venice* (1851) was, in its day, a moral as well as artistic bible to his generation. "Great nations," he observed pontifically, write their autobiographies in three manuscripts,

> *the book of their deeds, the book of their words, and the book of their art. No one of these books can be understood unless we read the two others, but of the three the only quite trustworthy one is the last. The acts of a nation may be triumphant by good fortune, and its words mighty by the genius of a few of its children, but its art only by the general gifts and common sympathies of the race.... Art is always instinctive, and the honesty or pretense of it are therefore open to the day.*

Certainly the record here is incomparably full, from the wall paintings in the caves of the Dordogne and Altamira to the pictorial record bequeathed us by the painters of the Renaissance or by the nineteenth-century impressionists; from sculptures and decorations of the primitive Africans or the Mayan and Aztec peoples to the tools and machines and fabrics and glass of our time; from the palaces uncovered at Nineveh and in the Yucatán to the Acropolis, the cathedral of Chartres, the Palladian villa "La Malcontenta," and the modern skyscraper.

Most familiar, and most voluminous, is of course the written record—most voluminous especially since the invention of printing in 1440. It is this that comes most naturally to mind when we think of the historical record. The written record is customarily divided into two large categories, of which the first comprises what are called original sources—diaries, journals, letters, eyewitness accounts, and public documents such as court reports, legislative proceedings, census statistics, and military dispatches. (Whether the now vast accumulation of photograph, motion picture, and television film belongs in this category or should be considered as part of the pictorial and artistic record is a difficult, but not an important, question.) The second category of written History is that which most of us think of when we think of History at all—the textbooks we read in school, the biographies, the histories of nations and peoples and institutions with which we fill our leisure time. These range from the narratives of Herodotus to the chronicles of Froissart, the interpretations of Voltaire and the epic surveys of Gibbon to the masterly re-creations of the past by Winston Churchill or George Macaulay Trevelyan.

We are not yet done with our distinctions, for here, too, there are two familiar kinds of History, which are distinctive though often overlapping and blended. One kind, the simplest, may be symbolized by the daily newspaper; the other consists of the formal treatise, the learned monograph, or the ambitious interpretation. These two may be called, for convenience, History as record and History as reconstruction.

In its simplest form, History as record is exemplified by the day by day, sometimes year by year, listings of dramatic events that happen to appeal to an Egyptian stonecutter (or his master), a medieval monk, or a modern diarist: a storm, an earthquake, a famine, a pestilence, the ravages of an invading army, the death of a monarch, the birth of an heir to the throne, the interposition of some god to save his chosen people. This kind of record is still very much with us in the almanac or the newspaper; in more elaborate form it ranges from the genealogical listings of Genesis to the Icelandic sagas. These, while they have great poetic merit, fulfill at the same time the requirement that Henry Adams laid down for History, that it provide, "by the severest process of stating, with the least possible comment, such facts as seemed sure, in such order as seemed rigorously consequent, . . . a necessary sequence of human movement"[1]—"necessary" to

Burnt Njal, for example, or to Egil because it was so decreed by fate. In its current form, this kind of densely packed factual record can be found in such popular books as Jim Bishop's *The Day Lincoln Was Shot*.

It is the second and more sophisticated form of History—that which constitutes a reconstruction of the past rather than the mere record of it— that commands the broadest interest and fulfills the deepest need. This kind of History embraces all that is put together artificially, by the historian. Indeed the very concept of *History* is itself of this nature. The past, as distinct from History, is not dependent on the historian for its existence, but exists quite independently. Geologists, paleontologists, zoologists have revealed to us a past of millions of years before man made his belated appearance on the earth. No one now doubts the reality of that past, though there were none there to record it. No such thing as *History* is known to nature. History is like other abstract concepts such as philosophy and art, which exist because men have invented them, nourished them, given them life and meaning, conferred History (we might almost say) upon them. We all recognize this when we consider the innumerable segments of history that we have endowed with life and individuality—the ancient world, for example, or the Renaissance, or the Enlightenment, or the *ancien régime,* or the Old South. Socrates and Aristotle did not know that they were living in the ancient world, Petrarch and Leonardo did not know they were Renaissance men, nor was Louis XV aware that he was a representative of the *ancien régime* or John C. Calhoun that he was a spokesman for the Old South. No, these and a thousand other chapters in history are contrivances of the historian —admirable contrivances to be sure—designed to bring order out of what otherwise might be chaos.

The overwhelming majority of books that most of us read as History belong in this category: History recreated by the historian, who imposes upon it a pattern of coherence, logic, and meaning. Merely to state, for example, that in 1781 Thomas Jefferson wrote some *Notes on Virginia* is of no interest whatever; merely to record that on July 2, 1863, the Twentieth Maine fought at Little Round Top means nothing at all, not even when we locate Little Round Top and identify the Twentieth Maine. If the historian expects his readers to make any sense of such statements he must explain them, and as soon as he starts explaining them he is forced to reconstruct history. To explain why it is important that Jefferson wrote some *Notes on Virginia* the historian must introduce us to the great debate over the meaning of America then raging in Europe, the attack on the New World by the *philosophes,* Jefferson's role as a defender of America, why he commanded a hearing and prestige in France, the effect of the *Notes* throughout Europe, and Jefferson's use of history for national and moral purposes. If he is to interest us in the Twentieth Maine, the historian must explain why soldiers from Maine were fighting soldiers from North Carolina at Gettysburg, Pennsylvania, what the importance was of Little Round Top to the battle and of the battle to the war and of the war to the survival of the Union and the end of slavery—a large order, this. Fortunately the historian does not need to do this sort of thing with every statement, any more than a sportswriter has to explain the law of gravity every time he records that a ball landed in left field; most of these things we can take for granted.

It is clear that whenever the historian deals with more than discrete facts, whenever he puts facts together in logical rather than in chronological order, or imposes some pattern on them, he is reconstructing, even recreating, the past. If he is an historian of America, he will inevitably write about the evolution of American nationalism, the development of the presidency, the emergence of judicial review, the westward movement, the plantation system, imperialism, the growth of democracy, and much more that is familiar. Now all of these things are creations of the contriving mind. There is no such thing by itself as nationalism, or judicial review, or the westward movement, or the plantation system. These are philosophical, or intellectual, concepts thought up by the historian to help him give meaning to a vast body of miscellaneous and intractable facts. If the historian were actually to tell all that he knew or could find out about what happened hour by hour and day by day and year by year, he would be like a sadist torturing his victims with the "water cure," dropping facts relentlessly on his readers' minds until he drove them mad. Instead the sensible historian comes along with an organizing idea and applies it to his otherwise chaotic materials. Let us, he says, gather together 1,000 or 100,000 facts under some controlling principle—the evolution of the power of the Supreme Court, or the idea of progress—and present this as History. What is presented is not the past, but a selection, an organization, an interpretation of the past.

But if general terms like *nationalism* or *imperialism* or *the Enlightenment* or *the church* or *the westward movement,* which are the coinage of the historical realm, are in reality abstractions or inventions or (as Toynbee says) myths, what purpose do they serve? Perhaps the simplest answer is that we cannot get along without them. What, after all, are we to substitute for such terms as *nationalism* or *the Renaissance* or *the Old South?* Yet it is important that we keep in mind the symbolic rather than the scientific character of these and similar words. They are agreed-on fictions, as the value of the dollar bill is an agreed-on fiction, or a passport or a marriage license. They differ from such fictions in that they do not possess a universally agreed-on character. Everyone knows what a dollar bill or a passport stands for and when we use these things as symbols they are everywhere accepted on their merits, as it were. But when we use such words as *nationalism* or *Renaissance* or *Old South,* we cannot be sure that any two people mean the same thing by them. Are we then to say of historians what Humpty Dumpty said to Alice: "When *I* use a word, it means just what I choose it to mean"?

This situation, however, is by no means as awkward as it might seem, for it is one in which we are all familiar with almost all of the terms. We can and do speak of the *beauty* of a sunset, the *melody* of a Mozart trio, the *fragrance* of a rose, the *virtue* of a saint, without scientific agreement on the meaning of any of these nouns, yet their elusiveness gives us no trouble. So when over the years scholars have worked out a general agreement on what is meant by such words as *Renaissance* or *Old South,* we need not quarrel with them, nor, for that matter, with their idiosyncratic preferences. We do, after all, study Florence in the fifteenth century, not Odense; we study art and letters and philosophy rather than basket weaving or advertising; we acquiesce in a loose vocabulary and in fictions about what is interesting and significant; over the years those things have proved themselves profitable and enjoyable. Men have found that there is a lift to the spirit and an excitement to the mind in studying fifteenth-century Florence that is not, on the whole, to be found in studying the Madagascar of that time. And perhaps *"de gustibus non est disputandum"* applies more persuasively to collective than to private taste.

There is, then, no such thing as History independent of those who remember it and put it together in story or myth, poetry or drama, annals or chronicle, graph or chart, or who celebrate it in painting or in stone. This means that while we can make a stab at saying what History (by which we mean, of course, historians and their associates) does, what function it fills, what purposes it serves, we cannot define it. Not, to be sure, that men have failed to try: the literary landscape is littered with the *disjecta membra* of definitions of History and aphorisms about History ranging from Edward Gibbon's somber "register of the crimes, follies and misfortunes of mankind" to Professor John Bagnell Bury's magisterial "a science, no more and no less"; from Matthew Arnold's sardonic "huge Mississippi of falsehood" to Jacob Burckhardt's "record of what one age finds worthy of note in another"; from Johann Huizinga's somewhat Hegelian "spiritual form in which a civilization gives to itself an account of its past" to Charles A. Beard's disillusioned "noble dream."

The difficulty of defining History should not discourage us; it is a difficulty that History shares with art, education, law, philosophy, and similar concepts. It does not get us very far to say that art is the portrayal of the true and the beautiful, or that law is the search for justice, or that education is the imaginative communication of ideas from one generation to another, or that philosophy is the love of wisdom. All of this is no doubt true. But if it is understanding that we want, we must ask of History what purposes it serves, what uses it meets, what objectives it fulfills—in short what it does and how it works.

II The uses of history

The first and most elementary thing to be said of History is that it is, or serves as, the collective memory of mankind. Just as individual man would be lost without memory, or even (in more sophisticated form) without records—uncertain who he was or how he should use his tools, forced to evolve a new language, to create a new religion, to fashion new customs and laws—so without History mankind would be lost. Justice Oliver Wendell Holmes put the matter with characteristic brevity: "Continuity with the past is not a duty, it is only a necessity." Without such continuity, society as we know it would collapse. How could government function if no one remembered, or could find out, what laws had been enacted or by what authority they were enforced? How could the courts function if there were no records of judicial proceedings, no collections of precedents, no memory of contracts? Would not all formal education falter without records of the knowledge that had been accumulated in the past, and with it all training for medicine or theology or law? These, and others that rush readily into the mind, are somewhat lurid examples: after all, society managed to survive for uncounted thousands of years with no other records than those in the memories of priests and bards, or such as were inscribed, perhaps on a stone. But no civilized society has ever flourished without records—which is to say, without History—and when civilized societies lose the records of the past, as they do in time of war or of ruin, they are zealous to replace them. One of the first tasks that engaged the energies of the German people after the catastrophe of the Great War was the restoration of the past, the reprinting of the scholarly, scientific, and literary records of the past—learned journals, encyclopaedias, law reports, historical documents—on a vast scale.

But the preservation of the past is not purely a practical matter; it is sentimental as well. "Every archaeologist," writes the English archaeologist Geoffrey Bibby, "knows in his bones why he digs. He digs in pity and humility, that the dead may live again, and that what is past may not be lost forever." What motivates the archaeologist and the genealogist, the biographer, and the historian is a deep, almost ineradicable sense of responsibility to and sympathy for those who have gone before, and who made what we have inherited, and a corresponding sense of obligation to the future. "Take care of me when I am dead," wrote Thomas Jefferson to his old friend James Madison, just a few months before his dramatic death precisely fifty years after the Declaration of Independence. It is the *cri de coeur* of mankind—take care of us when we are dead—and all who realize that they will soon join the innumerable throng of the dead echo the wistful plea.

So universal is the instinct to be remembered, the fear that we and everything we know shall fade "and leave not a rack behind," that for two thousand years, whether by graffiti on the walls of Pompei or by

"Kilroy was here" scrawled on fences and stones throughout the globe in World War II, ordinary men have made some gesture, however vain, toward immortality. Historians, conscious of the fragility of the individual life and of the tenacity of the life of the race, of the ephemeral character of so much of the physical world and the enduring quality of the artistic and the intellectual, have taken it as their special responsibility to rescue men and their works from oblivion.

Memory serves not only to gratify vanity but to stimulate emulation and fire ambition, and from the beginning historians have acknowledged a special obligation to provide models for succeeding generations. This was what inspired the greatest of historians, Thucydides: "it will be enough for me if these words of mine are judged useful by those who want to understand clearly the events which happened in the past and which at some time or another and in much the same ways will be repeated in the future";[2] it was perhaps the chief purpose of Plutarch's *Parallel Lives* of the Greeks and the Romans; it animated both Jean Froissart and Sir Thomas Malory. It has always had a special appeal to biographers for, as the most popular of American poets made clear:

> *Lives of great men all remind us*
> *We can make our lives sublime,*
> *And, departing, leave behind us*
> *Footprints on the sands of time.*[3]

Second, History enormously extends our perspective and enlarges our experience. It permits us to enter vicariously into the past, to project our vision backward over thousands of years, and sympathetically to embrace the whole of mankind. "Through History," wrote Friedrich Nietzsche, who did not always think well of it, "the man of reverent nature . . . surveys the marvellous individual life of the past, and identifies himself with the spirit of the house, the family, and the city. He greets the soul of his people from afar as his own, across the dim and troubled centuries." Through the pages of History we can hear Pericles deliver that incomparable Funeral Oration which Thucydides has preserved for us; look with excitement as Scipio and Hannibal lock forces on the field of Zama; sail with Columbus past the Pillars of Hercules and to a new world; fight with Cortés as he topples the fabulous empire of Montezuma; kneel with the Pilgrims on the sandy shores of Cape Cod as they give thanks for safe arrival after a perilous voyage on the *Mayflower;* stand beside General Washington in New York's Fraunces Tavern as he takes leave of his companions-in-arms on that cold December day of 1783; share with Goethe and Schiller and Wieland and Herder the cultural riches of the little court of Weimar; listen to those stirring debates in the dusty prairie towns of Illinois that sent Stephen Douglas to the Senate and Abraham Lincoln to the White House; fight at the barricades in the streets of Paris in the uprisings of 1871; listen to Winston Churchill as he rallies the people of Britain to their finest hour. All this can be—and usually is—a sober scholarly experience; it can be, as with Whitman, almost mystical:

> *I am possess'd!*
> *Embody all presences outlaw'd or suffering,*
> *See myself in prison shaped like another man,*
> *And feel the dull unintermitted pain,*
> *For me the keepers of convicts shoulder their carbines and*
>   *keep watch,*
> *It is I let out in the morning and barr'd at night.*
>
> *Not a mutineer walks handcuff'd to jail but I am handcuff'd to*
>   *him and walk by his side . . .*
> *Not a youngster is taken for larceny but I go up too, and am tried*
>   *and sentenced.*
> *Not a cholera patient lies at the last gasp but I also lie at the*
>   *last gasp . . .*
> *Askers embody themselves in me and I am embodied in them,*
> *I project my hat, sit shame-faced, and beg.*
>
> * * * * * *
>
> *I am the man, I suffer'd, I was there.*
>
> *The disdain and calmness of martyrs,*
> *The mother of old, condemn'd for a witch, burnt with dry wood,*
>   *her children gazing on,*
> *The hounded slave that flags in the race, leans by the fence,*
>   *blowing, cover'd with sweat,*
> *The twinges that sting like needles his legs and neck, the murderous*
>   *buckshot and the bullets,*
> *All these I feel or am.*[4]

History enlarges the sense of place as well as the sense of time. When we look at ancient towns through the eyes of History they take on a deeper meaning and a richer texture. Nestling between its ancient hills, cut by the sluggish Arno flowing under the Ponte Vecchio and the Ponte Sta. Trinita and the Ponte alla Carraia, its domes and campaniles piercing the skies, Florence is beautiful even to the eyes of the untutored visitor. How it springs to life when we people its piazzas and its streets with the men and women of the past! We conjure up Savonarola burned in the great Piazza della Signoria where the mighty *David* stands, Brunelleschi building the spacious Duomo, Ghiberti fashioning the incomparable bronze doors of the Baptistry, Giotto and Fra Filippo Lippi and Raphael and Leonardo painting the pictures that hang in such crowded profusion on the walls of the Uffizi and the Pitti palaces, Machiavelli pondering the history of the Medici as he writes *The Prince,* and Galileo seeing a new universe through his telescope. It is a city that lives in literature as in history, for from Dante and Boccacio to Henry James and E. M. Forster, storytellers and novelists have painted it, not just as a backdrop but as an integral part of their works of art.

Or consider the town of Salem on the North Shore of Massachusetts. It is a lovely town, there by the sea and the rocks, its handsome houses still standing sedately along Chestnut and Federal streets, which have some claim to be thought the most beautiful streets in America. As we look at it through the eyes of history we see a straggling village busy with fishing and theology, and remember that Roger Williams preached here those heresies that earned him banishment, and so too Mistress Anne Hutchinson. We revisit Gallows Hill and recall the dark story of witchcraft that haunted the imagination of Nathaniel Hawthorne, who grew up here, and who made the House of the Seven Gables part of the architectural history of every American town. We see it again in its heyday when its captains sailed the seven seas and its flag was thought to be that of an independent nation, and the spoils of the China and India trade glittered in all the great drawing rooms. For in the early years of the nineteenth century, when Hawthorne was but a boy, Salem was like one of the storied city-states of Italy or Germany. It had its own architects—Samuel McIntire, who built the stately mansions of the captains and the merchant princes; its own preachers—the Reverend William Bentley of the East Church, for example, reputed to be the most learned man in America; its own jurists—Joseph Story, who was named to the Supreme Court of the United States at thirty-two; and three chief justices of the Commonwealth of Massachusetts. It had scientists such as Nathaniel Bowditch, who as a boy played on the India wharf and watched the great ships sail in from the distant waters of the globe, and who wrote *The Practical Navigator* (1802), which was the Bible of all sailors for a hundred years; or such as Benjamin Thompson, who grew up to be prime minister of Bavaria and Count Rumford of the Holy Roman Empire and who founded the Royal Institution in London and the Rumford Chair of Natural Science at Harvard University. Then another generation and Salem entered its long decline, its harbors silted up, its wharves falling into decay, its Custom House silent, its merchant princes and lawyers and statesmen moving to Boston. It is all there for us to recapture in the pages of History and of literature and in the monuments of architecture and the heirlooms of art.

As History serves to extend the dimensions of experience it also serves to define and explain that experience. It helps us to identify the individual, the community, the nation, the race. It supplies the chronology, maps the latitude and longitude, provides the grammar and the language through which men identify themselves and their groups. For almost all men define themselves in their history and in their institutions, which are of course a product of history. We are the people who wrote the Magna Carta and defeated the Spanish Armada, say the British; we are the people who spread our race and our language and our law throughout the globe; we are those

> *who speak the tongue*
> *That Shakespeare spake; the faith and morals hold*
> *Which Milton held.—In everything we are sprung*
> *Of Earth's first blood, have titles manifold.*[5]

Or, we are the descendants of the Puritans who were, in turn, the "sifted grain," say the Americans. We are those who fought and won independence for this people, and those who braved the deserts and the mountains and planted the Stars and Stripes on the gleaming shores of the Pacific; we are those who beat a trail to Deseret, singing

> *Come, Come ye saints, no toil nor labor fear,*
> *But with joy wend your way, though hard to you,*
> *This journey may appear*
> *All is well! All is well!*

and who built a new Zion in the wilderness. We are those "huddled masses yearning to breathe free" who fled the pogroms of Russia and Poland; we are the children of bondage, and have not forgotten the long road to freedom that stretches behind us as it stretches before us.

Perhaps the deepest and most satisfying of all the uses of History is precisely this, that it enables men to belong to something bigger than themselves, something that unites them with the whole of mankind and provides, if not immortality, then the sense of an illimitable past and future. Here History can provide a secular substitute for religion.

Though History can liberate, it can also imprison; along with the sense of the past goes the burden of the past. Sometimes that burden is almost too much for men to bear. Just as the individual, especially when young, feels the urge to liberate himself from his family and his forebears and work out his own destiny, so whole peoples and nations sometimes feel a compulsive need to free themselves from their past and start anew. Some even of the Jewish people, who have perhaps the deepest and most profound sense of the past of any modern people, revolt against the burden that their long and tragic past imposes upon them, and reject at least its outer and formal manifestations: thus no matter how loyal American Jews are to their heritage, not many of them have thrown in their lot with Israel. Sometimes the past—especially an immediate past— carries with it an intolerable burden of guilt, as with the present generation of Germans who must somehow escape the nightmare knowledge of

Buchenwald and Auschwitz. And sometimes, too, the past imposes unacceptable responsibilities—thus with peoples or nations that have lost or forfeited their former glory; this was the theme of Wordsworth's sonnet "On the Extinction of the Venetian Republic" (1802):

> *And what if she had seen those glories fade,*
> *Those titles vanish, and that strength decay;*
> *Yet shall some tribute of regret be paid*
> *When her long life hath reach'd its final day:*
> *Men are we, and must grieve when even the Shade*
> *Of that which once was great is pass'd away.*

The most nearly universal and perhaps the most powerful of all forms of identity that History provides is nationalism. The nationalism that we know is relatively new—it may be dated from the American and the French revolutions—but the sense of belonging to a special or a privileged group is as old as the Jews who knew that they were the Chosen People, or the Hellenes who regarded the rest of mankind as barbarians. Has there ever been a more ardent pride of place and of people than that which animated the Athenians of the fifth century B.C. and inspired Pericles' Funeral Oration of 430 B.C.?

> *We are lovers of beauty without extravagance, and lovers of wisdom without unmanliness. Wealth to us is not mere material for vainglory but an opportunity for achievement; and poverty we think it no disgrace to acknowledge but a real degradation to make no effort to overcome. Our citizens attend both to public and private duties, and do not allow absorption in their own various affairs to interfere with their knowledge of the city's. We differ from other states in regarding the man who holds aloof from public life not as "quiet" but as useless; we decide or debate, carefully and in person, all matters of policy, holding, not that words and deeds go ill together, but that acts are foredoomed to failure when undertaken undiscussed. For we are noted for being at once most adventurous in action and most reflective beforehand. Other men are bold in ignorance, while reflection will stop their onset. But the bravest are surely those who have the clearest vision of what is before them, glory and danger alike, and yet notwithstanding go out to meet it. In doing good, too, we are the exact opposite of the rest of mankind. We secure our friends not by accepting favours but by doing them. And so we are naturally more firm in our attachments: for we are anxious, as creditors, to cement by kind offices our relation towards our friends. If they do not respond with the same warmness it is because they feel that their services will not be given spontaneously but only as the repayment of a debt. We are*

*alone among mankind in doing men benefits, not on calculations
of self-interest, but in the fearless confidence of freedom. In a word
I claim that our city as a whole is an education to Greece, and that
her members yield to none, man by man, for independence of spirit,
many-sidedness of attainment, and complete self-reliance in limbs
and brain.[6]*

No people have used History more self-consciously to create and nourish
nationalism than the American and the German. Confronted with the unprecedented task of forming a nation out of thirteen independent states
that lacked not only a common monarch, a common government, a common people, and a common church, but even that common history that
had been so vital an ingredient in nourishing a sense of unity in Old
World nations, Americans set out energetically to make good this latter
deficiency by conjuring up a common past. In remarkably short order
they provided themselves with a respectable history—history as myth
and legend, monument and symbol, heroes and villains, song and story, in
addition to history as politics and war. They demonstrated that even in
modern times myth could serve not merely as an echo or a symbol of history, but as a creator of History: myths about Pocahontas and the Pilgrims,
about Betsy Ross and Mad Anthony Wayne, about Franklin and Jefferson,
about Daniel Boone and Indian captivities, helped mold a people into
a nation, who became thereby, themselves, the stuff of History. Though
the whole of American history lies within the era of the printing press,
and its records are therefore more nearly complete than those of any other
nation, history and myth are nevertheless interfused in America, and what
passes for American history is a combination of myth and reality.

The problem that confronted the Germans as they set themselves to
convert a hundred or more independent principalities into a single nation
was different from that which had faced the Americans. The common
denominators were already there—territory, language, religion, even the
myths and legends from the *Nibelungenlied* to the folk tales of the
Brothers Grimm. The task, in Germany, was to overcome centuries of
particularism and win allegiance to a common nationalism, and here it
was formal History that played a decisive role. No sooner had Waterloo
freed the Germanies from the grip of Napoleon and his henchmen, than
statesmen, lawyers, philosophers, and historians turned to the task of
rebuilding the shattered land and giving it a new unity. In 1819 the states-
man Baron von Stein, the archivist Georg Heinrich Pertz, and the scholar
Johann Böhmer combined to launch that greatest of all historical enterprises, the *Monumenta Germaniae Historica,* with its almost religious
motto, *Sanctus amor patriae dat animum.* In the next generation almost
every major historian in Germany was enlisted in the enterprise that was
as much political as historical: Leopold von Ranke, Johann Gustav
Droysen, Friedrich Christoph Schlösser, Georg Waitz, Heinrich von Sybel,

Heinrich von Treitschke. Every one of them might have endorsed Böhmer's pious confession that he was "inspired by love of the Fatherland, the conviction that the knowledge of the past could be instructive for the present, the hope that the true might lead to the good." Together they provided a new historical basis for a nationalism that in time developed a mystical character of terrifying intensity.

Fortunately, History provides an antidote to excessive nationalism, as it provides an antidote to religious fanaticism. It reminds us that nations, as we know them, are relatively new on the historical stage, and that national pride and ethnic arrogance have been responsible for more wars and conquests, rapine and destruction, misery and hatred than any other force in history unless it is religious zeal. History enables us—or should—to see beyond the particular and the parochial to the general and the cosmopolitan. While it records the fanaticisms that have driven sects and nations into religious wars, it makes clear, too, that religious faith of some kind is a universal experience. It celebrates what is particular in government and law, education and social customs, but it demonstrates too how nearly universal is the search for order, the yearning for justice, the faith in education, the tenacity of family and community ties. In all this it provides the evidence that should enable us to transcend political chauvinism, religious fanaticism, and cultural provincialism. That we so rarely act upon this evidence is one of the reasons for the current disillusionment with History.

Finally History, like literature, conjures up for us a sense of the past. Not, mark you, the past itself; for the past, the whole past, nothing but the past is irrevocable. Indeed if by some miracle we could recover it, we would find ourselves buried beneath it. History gives us a sense of the past by stimulating and then nourishing the imagination. It is to this that Shakespeare appeals in one of the greatest of his historical plays:

> *Piece out our imperfections with your thoughts . . .*
> *Think, when we talk of horses, that you see them*
> *Printing their proud hoofs i' the receiving earth;*
> *For 'tis your thoughts that now must deck our kings,*
> *Carry them here and there; jumping o'er times,*
> *Turning the accomplishment of many years*
> *Into an hour-glass: for the which supply,*
> *Admit me Chorus to this History . . . .*[7]

A risky thing this, no doubt, for imagination misused threatens the integrity of the historical record. Yet it is clearly impossible to exclude imagination from our reconstruction of History; all we can hope to do is to control it. After all every step in the writing of History is affected by the imagination—the choice of the subject, the selection of the actors and the events we admit to our pages, the play of emphasis, the scope and the style of the narrative, the structure of the drama itself. It is the imagination that enables us to clothe the bare bones of history with life, and to assign to it conduct that is not wholly fortuitous or irrational. Imagination infuses even a statistical table with meaning and romance: who can read the statistics of nineteenth-century immigration to America without seeing in his mind's eye the tidal wave of the poor and the oppressed flowing from the Old World to the New—the flight of the Irish from the Great Famine; the coming of the refugees and exiles from Germany, seeking to establish in Pennsylvania and Wisconsin and Missouri new outposts of German culture; the outpouring of Mormons from the Scandinavian countries, seeking freedom to worship at new altars and to try new experiments in communal living; the armies of Poles and Hungarians and Italians crossing the Atlantic in miserable immigrant packets and crowding onto Ellis Island and into the tenements of the great cities with a sense that they have reached the Promised Land. It is imagination, too, that infuses History with poetry. "The curtain of cloud that hides the scenes of the past," wrote the Cambridge historian George Macaulay Trevelyan, who had himself the mind of a poet,

> *is broken here and there, and we have magic glimpses into that lost world, which is as actual as our own, though placed on another step of the moving staircase of time. Forward we cannot see at all; backward we can see fitfully and in part. In that strange relation of past and present, poetry is always inherent, even in the most prosaic details, in Greek potsherds and Roman stones, in Manor rolls and Parliamentary reports, all hallowed in our imagination by the mere passage of the years.*[8]

It is imagination, Woodrow Wilson asserted in his tribute to the Roman historian Theodor Mommsen, that is "the patent of nobility in the peerage of historians. . . . Not the inventing imagination, but the conceiving imagination." Or listen to Francis Parkman, who possessed, beyond any other American historian, the conceiving imagination, as he introduces to us the paradox of the Jesuits in the forests of Canada:

> *The French dominion is a memory of the past; and, when we evoke its departed shades, they rise upon us from their graves in strange romantic guise. Again their ghostly camp-fires seem to burn, and the fitful light is cast around on lord and vassal and black-robed priest, mingled with wild forms of savage warriors, knit in close fellowship on the same stern errand. A boundless vision grows upon us: an untamed continent; vast wastes of forest verdure; mountains silent in primeval sleep; river, lake, and glim-*

mering pool; wilderness oceans mingling with the sky. Such was the domain which France conquered for civilization. Plumed helmets gleamed in the shade of its forests, priestly vestments in its dens and fastnesses of ancient barbarism. Men steeped in antique learning, pale with the close breath of the cloister, here spent the noon and evening of their lives, ruled savage hordes with a mild, parental sway, and stood serene before the direst shapes of death. Men of courtly nurture, heirs to the polish of a far-reaching ancestry, here, with their dauntless hardihood, put to shame the boldest sons of toil.[9]

Or hear Parkman's successor, Samuel Eliot Morison, himself a master-mariner, as he recreates Salem in the days of its glory:

Whenever a Salem lad could tear himself away from the wharves, he would go barefoot to Juniper Point or pull a skiff to Winter Island, and scan the bay for approaching sail. . . . The appearance of a coaster or fisherman or West-India trader caused no special emotion; but if the stately form of an East-Indiaman came in view, then 't was race back to Derby Wharf, and earn a silver Spanish dollar for good news. The word speeds rapidly through the town, which begins to swarm like an ant-hill; counting-room clerks rush out to engage men for unloading, sailors' taverns and boarding-houses prepare for a brisk run of trade, parrots scream and monkeys jabber, and every master of his own time makes for cap-sill, roof-tree, or other vantage-point.

Let us follow one of the privileged, an old-time provincial magnate now in the East-India trade, as with powdered wig, cocked hat, and scarlet cloak, attended by Pompey or Cuff with the precious telescope, he puffs up garret ladder to captain's walk. What a panorama! To the east stretches the noble North Shore, Cape Ann fading in the distance. No sail in that direction, save a fisherman beating inside Baker's. Across the harbor, obscuring the southerly channel, Marblehead presents her back side of rocky pasture to the world at large, and Salem in particular. Wind is due south, tide half flood and the afternoon waning, so if the master be a Salem boy he will bring his ship around Peach's Point, inside Kettle Bottom, Endeavors, Triangles, and the Aqua Vitæs. We adjust the glass to the outer point where she must first appear, and wait impatiently. A flash of white as the sun catches foretopgallant sails over Naugus Head; then the entire ship bursts into view, bowling along at a good eight knots. Her ensign's apeak, so all aboard are well. A puff of smoke bursts from her starboard bow, and then another, as the first crack of a federal salute strikes the ear. Fort William replies in kind, and all Salem with a roar of cheering. Every one recognizes the smart East-Indiaman that dropped down-harbor thirty months ago.[10]

Granting all the power of these imaginative reconstructions, have we not omitted what is commonly considered the primary function of History —to explain the past and to answer questions about it? Explanation in history, one of the most chewed-up of problems, we must deal with later, but what of the responsibility of the historian to answer our importunate questions? May we not say that it is more important for History, or for historians, to ask questions than to answer them if only because, except in the most obvious and elementary matters like "Who won the presidential election of 1896?" historians cannot really answer questions at all? Just what Goethe said,

Also fragen wir beständig
Bis man uns mit eine Handvoll
Erde endlich stopft der Mund
Aber ist das eine Antwort?

[So we go on asking questions
Until God closes our mouth
With a handful of earth
But is that an answer?]

The question who won the election of 1896 may be fairly simple (though even it has its complexities if we take a long view), but consider the difficulty of explaining who won the election of 1876, when an electoral commission decided all contested votes in favor of Hayes and against Tilden who had won a clear majority of the popular vote and appeared to have a majority of the electoral college as well. Nor is this the whole of it: Hayes was installed in the White House, but was not his Reconstruction policy a victory for the Democratic party, and might it not then be said that the Democrats won the election after all?

History consists primarily in asking questions that range over all human experiences—and some natural experience—and skill in History begins with asking the right questions. But what do we mean by the "right" questions? We mean, on the whole, questions that are fundamental rather than superficial, general rather than particular, and consequential rather than trivial—in short in asking questions that are *useful*. But useful for what? Useful to enable us to get on with the job of understanding the past and the present, useful to ride on. This does not mean that all questions must be broad and philosophical; sometimes very particular questions have wide implications—thus such a question as why the Spanish Armada was scattered and dispersed, in 1588, or whether slavery was ever profitable

245

in the Old South. But the questions that have, over the years, excited the interest of historians and philosophers are those involving such things as the rise and decline of empires, the nature of nationalism, the explanation of racial intolerance, and even the meaning of History itself. And the reason it is important to ask such questions is that they open up new lines of thought, suggest new areas of investigation, inspire new and original interpretations, not of History alone but of the life of man.

Only rarely do we get answers to these larger questions of philosophy or of art. You can get final answers to a good many scientific questions such as what is the speed of light, or what are the permissible limits of fever or of heartbeat, but you cannot expect final answers to questions of history or of philosophy. But merely formulating and probing them illuminates our concepts of past and present, and perhaps even of the future. We cannot ask questions about the fateful Sicilian expedition that all but destroyed Athens in the Peloponnesian War without exciting speculations about the American expeditions to Vietnam, which present so many analogies. We cannot ask questions about the rise of military dictatorships in Prussia and Japan without suggesting parallels with the American drift toward a war-oriented politics and economy. We cannot study the Luddite destruction of machinery in 1811 without raising in our own minds the issue of the cost society has paid and is paying for the Industrial Revolution and for modern technology.

History, it was confidently believed for perhaps one thousand out of twenty-five hundred years, was philosophy teaching by examples. Whether it teaches or not is a question that does not lend itself to an easy answer, but who can doubt that one of its indispensable uses is to encourage and stimulate philosophy?

III History in disrepute

At the turn of the last century the dignity of History was beyond challenge, and so, too, its influence. Speaking at the St. Louis world exposition of 1904, Woodrow Wilson proclaimed exultantly that "we have seen the dawn and the early morning hours of a new age in the writing of history, and the morning is now broadening about us into day." At almost the same time, the greatest of American historians, Henry Adams, observed in his presidential address to the American Historical Association (sardonically to be sure) that almost every student of that generation felt that he stood on the verge of some discovery that should do for history what Darwin had done for nature, and that "science would admit its own failure if it admitted that man, the most important of its subjects, could not be brought within its range." History was almost everywhere acknowledged to be, after philosophy, the sovereign study, the one that mediated between art and science, the humanities and the social sciences. The great masters from the world of History—Admiral Mahan and Henry Adams in the United States, Lord Bryce and Lord Acton in England, Treitschke in Germany, Croce in Italy, and Brandes in Denmark—commanded universal respect, and the two men who occupied the White House for most of the first twenty years of the new century were both historians, and both presidents of the American Historical Association.

But by mid-century the clouds had drawn over these promising skies. History was banished to the shadows; it was in retreat; it was on the defensive. Now, a quarter-century later, History is in disgrace, and historians themselves can write of the death of the past. On the surface, to be sure, History still flourishes. More History is being written by more historians than ever before, though whether it is as widely read or even as widely taught as half a century ago is debatable. But whatever the indices of overt popularity, History no longer commands the prestige, attracts the following, or exercises the influence that it once did.

How explain the decline of History? We should keep in mind that this is not the first time that History has come under suspicion or suffered disrepute. From Dio Cassius in the third century to the poets and bards and skalds of the twelfth and thirteenth—those who composed the *Nibelungenlied* and the *Chanson de Roland* and the *Poetic Edda* and the great Icelandic sagas—History languished in the shadow of theology, and three more centuries were to elapse before the Florentines, Machiavelli and Guicciardini, returned to the great tradition of secular History. The Enlightenment, to be sure, produced magisterial historians—Gibbon and Robertson, Hume and Voltaire, Raynal and Filangieri, John Adams and Thomas Jefferson, too—but of all of them only Gibbon was by profession an historian or thought the writing of History an end in itself. We need not assume therefore that the eclipse of History that we now witness is permanent.

We should keep in mind, too, that History shares its disfavor not only with other social sciences (who now has the influence that Adam Smith exercised, or Henry T. Buckle, or Auguste Comte, or Herbert Spencer, or John Stuart Mill?) but with much of traditional art, literature, music, and education. Disenchantment with History is part of the larger disenchantment with tradition and precedent, and (as George Steiner makes clear in *Bluebeard's Castle*) "The Death of the Past" is even more dramatic in the realms of philosophy and morals than it is in History. Students display little interest in the historic function of the university; a new school of jurisprudence looks with suspicion on the great slag heaps of juridical practices and precedents; society is busily destroying its architectural and artistic heritage—destroying quite deliberately, as in the bombing of Dresden or the mining of the bridges over the Arno or of the burning of the Royal Library in Naples, destroying mindlessly as in wiping out ancient

247

villages and landmarks to make way for superhighways. Even the Roman Catholic Church, which has a longer history than any other Western institution, is turning from historic teachings on matters such as clerical celibacy, for example, or the ritual of the Latin mass. It is scarcely to be expected that History should escape the ravages of the war on the past.

Yet the current crisis of History has its own special explanations. It is rooted in the pervasive ambiguity about history as past and History as the record of the past. It is primarily the past that is in disfavor, but just as primitive tribes killed the bearer of bad news, so in our more sophisticated society the young, and not the young alone, symbolically reject the historians who come to them with bad news, and to most of them all the news about the past is just what Gibbon said it was: a register of the crimes, follies, and misfortunes of mankind. The past, then, is something we should reprobate! It committed sins that we would not commit; it made mistakes that we would not make; it precipitated the problems with which we have to struggle, and gave us neither warning nor guidance for our desperate task. Nor are these crimes decently buried in a past so distant we can allow it to sink into oblivion; they are crimes within the memory of living men. Alas, those responsible for making a shambles of the past are no longer here to incur our displeasure: the wicked slaveholders and their successors who persisted in racialism, the pioneers who mined the soil and burned down the trees, the "robber barons" who exploited the natural resources of the earth for their own selfish profit, the ideologues who sowed misunderstanding and hatred among the peoples of the earth, the militarists who only yesterday plunged the whole globe into war. We must content ourselves, then, with contempt and disdain for those who come to us with the shameful tale and who have the effrontery to try to explain it all away: the historians!

What is more, History has failed to live up to its glittering promises. The first of its promises was that it would serve as philosophy teaching by examples, but it is not philosophy at all, and it has palpably failed to teach anything. Consider the Germans. For over a hundred years (from Ranke to Meinecke) no people cultivated History more assiduously or took it more seriously, none produced so many distinguished historians or so vast a library of historical records. Yet what did they learn from their almost fanatical study of History, what but national pride and racial prejudice, the glorification of militarism and of war?

Or consider the *ignis fatuus* of Progress, which for two centuries now History has held before our enraptured gaze. How hollow that promise in the light—perhaps we should say the glare—of the bombings of Warsaw and Rotterdam, Dresden and Hiroshima, the gas chambers of Auschwitz and Belsen, the systematic destruction of Vietnam! And how confusing even the concept of progress as we realize that the conquest of disease leads to an overpopulation that may spell disaster and convulsions; that the triumph of technology leads to the ravaging of the earth, the pollution of water and air; and that the emergence of new nations leads to racial, religious, and ideological wars.

To a self-confident society, History acts as a kind of religion, nourishing that self-confidence and providing faith in the future. Such a society looks to the legendary heroes of the past—an Alfred, a Barbarossa, a Joan of Arc, a Valdemar Victorious—as a devout one looks to the Scriptures; in such a society a Washington can assert that "the fate of unborn millions" will depend on the Continental Army, and a Churchill can appeal proudly to the opinion of the British people a thousand years hence. But loss of faith in the past—just such a loss of faith as we are now experiencing—carries with it a loss of faith in the future, too, for when people conclude, however illogically, that they have been betrayed by the promise of progress unfulfilled, of greatness unrealized, of divine favor withheld, they transfer their sense of frustration and betrayal from the past to the future.

Nineteenth-century History made another promise, one that has not so much been betrayed as drained of much of its significance. That was the promise, made with the full support of science, that it would recreate for us the past *as it actually was*. It has indeed recreated chapters of that past with marvelous authenticity, but it has failed to persuade our generation that this was an enterprise worth performing except as an artistic one.

Nor does History now fulfill with anything like its former effectiveness or enthusiasm what was for so long its most familiar function—that function set forth by William Caxton in his preface to Thomas Malory's *Morte Darthur*, wherein, he wrote, the reader

> *shall find many joyous and pleasant histories, and noble and renowned acts of humanity, gentleness, and chivalries. For herein may be seen noble chivalry, courtesy, humanity, friendliness, hardiness, love, friendship, cowardice, murder, hate, virtue, and sin.*[11]

Contemporary historians are no longer greatly concerned to provide what is "joyous and pleasant," nor even humanity, to say nothing of "virtue and sin." They feel no compulsion to tell a story, provide a storehouse of anecdotes, analogies, and allusions, conjure up a sense of the past, or excite the imagination. Instead they often look upon such objectives as beneath the dignity of History, as the great Sir Lewis Namier, the most influential of contemporary British historians, looked upon biography as unworthy the attention of scholars. This attitude, needless to say, historians share with the most representative novelists, dramatists, painters, sculptors, musicians of our day. It is all part of the revolt of the humanities against what is human, a kind of nihilism in which we are always waiting for Godot, or wandering in the nightmare world of a Kafka, or suffering the masochistic humiliations of a Genet, or entranced by the illusions of a Robbe-Grillet, or bemused by the abstractions of a Jackson Pollock. It is not astonishing that much of History should embrace the impersonal and rely on the technical and accord the highest distinction to the new methods of quantification.

Professionalization of History began in the German universities in the eighteenth century. We can date it with some precision from the founding of the University of Göttingen in the 1730s and the emergence there of the first professional school of history under men like Johann Gatterer and August Schlözer; even the first serious historian of America, Christoph Ebeling, who produced seven stout volumes on the geography and history of the United States, was trained at Göttingen. From that famous university professionalism spread throughout the German world, but elsewhere in Europe History kept its amateur character well into the next century. Nowhere was the amateur tradition more strongly entrenched than in England—there were Regius professors of History at both the ancient universities, but they did not bother to teach or to write. Only in the twentieth century did the professionals finally take over. The amateur tradition flourished in the United States too; none of the major historians —Bancroft, Prescott, Motley, Parkman,* Henry Adams—was formally trained to History, and none, except Adams for a few years, was attached to a university. The academic take-over of History began tentatively in the 1870s with scholars like Moses Coit Tyler at the newly opened Cornell University, and Herbert Baxter Adams at the newly opened Johns Hopkins, and with the manufacture of the first Ph.D.'s in history—a German importation, this—at Yale and Harvard. By the opening of the twentieth century, however, the professionals were in command, and with every passing year they have become more firmly entrenched.

The shift from amateur to professional History and historians meant that gradually the writing of History ceased to engage statemen and men of affairs (there were always striking exceptions like Winston Churchill and Charles de Gaulle) and became the province of academics; that history itself was fragmented into ever smaller units that lent themselves to intensive research; and that historians tended more and more to write for each other rather than for the larger public that had delighted in Macauley and Carlyle and Prescott and Parkman. It meant that responsibility for synthesis often went by default to outsiders like H. G. Wells, whose *Outline of History* boldly pushed back the frontiers of history by a million years; or Oswald Spengler, whose *Decline of the West* inaugurated a spate of inquests into the decline, or the death, of the only society that had ever taken History seriously; or Will Durant, whose ten-volume *Story of Civilization* filled a need that the professionals were inclined to disregard or disdain. It meant too that History assimilated

---

* Parkman was for a few years professor of horticulture at Harvard University.

the standards and the interests of the "behavioral sciences," borrowed their vocabulary and their concepts, imitated their reliance on quantitative data, and tended to substitute, for the kind of philosophical analysis that Henry Adams had presented in the famous opening chapters of his history of the administration of Thomas Jefferson, quantitative analyses supported by statistics and charts.

"Technical history"—the term coined by Herbert Butterfield of Cambridge University—is the culmination of a trend under way since the era of Ranke in the mid-nineteenth century. It has many virtues, among them the shining virtue of authenticity, but literary grace is not conspicuous among them, and what it has gained in professional acceptance it has forfeited in public interest. One explanation of the disfavor that History now confesses is to be found in this development.

The general and popular disappointment with History is matched by a more radical professional disillusionment. History, it is alleged, is always sycophantic, always on the side of authority and power. It is, as the poet Paul Valéry has said, "the most dangerous product evolved from the chemistry of the intellect, for it will justify anything." It is the apologist for every cause, if victorious; for every government in power; for every ruling class, until it is supplanted. It celebrates liberty and justifies tyranny with equal effrontery, makes a case for the *ancien régime* and a case for the Revolution, explains slavery and the plantation system and glorifies the Lost Cause while it makes clear the necessity of Emancipation and of Union. It is the ever-ready spokesman for nationalism and stands prepared to prove that each particular nation is peculiarly the favorite of Providence and each particular national culture superior to all others. It glorifies war and warriors and is the camp follower of victorious armies. It delights in the pomp and circumstance of royalty and prefers to take up residence at a court or a capital and to associate with the rich and the powerful and the well bred rather than with *hoi polloi*. How illuminating that Edmund Burke rested his case for conservatism on three stout pillars—the Church, the Monarchy, and History—and that he thought History was the most important of these, for it provided the credentials for the other two. And how illuminating too that Tom Paine, who thought every man was a new Adam in a new world, had no use for History. For History is instinctively conservative; it gives preferential treatment to any institution or practice that has been around long enough. It traces the authority of the greatest of churches back to St. Peter; it presides over that constitution that "broadens down from precedent to precedent"; it underwrites the titles to property.

All this is no doubt natural enough, but contemporary critics are not prepared to concede that. Historians, like lawyers, want to make the best possible case for their faith, their country, their race, even their party; in such matters their advocacy is for the most part unconscious. How else explain that Protestant and Catholic historians do not give the same account of the wars of religion; that honorable historians of Germany and England, using the same documents, do not agree on the question of responsibility for World War I; that even today scholars of undoubted integrity provide very different versions of the origins of the Cold War.

Closely associated with this objection that History is almost always "official" is the charge that History instinctively represents the past as order, reason, and logic and tries to impose these upon the palpitating stuff of the past. The instinct for tidiness, as Arthur Schlesinger has observed, is the professional vice of the historian. The order that History imposes upon the past is not inherent in the stuff itself, nor is it merely the product of the historian's imagination; it is an order that almost invariably reflects the political, religious, social, and economic establishment of which he is a part. Thus the historian requires the past to fit into an order whose structure is dictated by tradition and by the dominant forces of his own time and place. The historian of the United States, for example, begins with the assumption that the creation of a single nation from the Atlantic to the Pacific was dictated by some inner logic—perhaps by Providence itself—and he almost inevitably requires American history to articulate itself to that logic: thus the destruction of the Indian civilizations, the westward movement, the defeat and dismemberment of Mexico, the frustration of particularism and the imposition of unity upon all sections of the continental domain are all effortlessly subsumed under this general law.

This is the real Manifest Destiny that presides over history, one that few are inclined to challenge. It ascribes to the pattern of American history, for example, a misleading simplicity and a spurious continuity. The philosopher Hayden V. White has leveled this indictment against almost the whole of History as it is now written:

> *Since the second half of the nineteenth century, history has become increasingly the refuge of all those "sane" men who excel at finding the simple in the complex, and the familiar in the strange. This was all very well for an earlier age, but if the present generation needs anything at all it is a willingness to confront heroically the dynamic and disruptive forces in contemporary life. The historian serves no one well by constructing a specious continuity between the present world and that which preceded it. On the contrary we require a history that will educate us to discontinuity more than ever before; for discontinuity, disruption, and chaos is our lot.*[12]

The logic of this will not bear close examination if it means that the best preparation for dealing with chaos is chaotic education, but the animus is unmistakable.

The attack from what might be called the new left is acrimonious; the younger social scientists and philosophers give no quarter. Outraged by the "bad faith" of History in claiming the privileges of both art and science, "while refusing to submit to the standards of either," they are prepared to assert that History is essentially "trivial." It is, they charge, hopelessly amateurish. It does not respect or use the tools of research that the other sciences have provided, nor does it know what to do with such meager data as it has. It has no standards of its own, and wobbles foolishly between those of the artist and the scientist, conforming to neither. It does not respect facts, but plays fast and loose with them, taking refuge in generalizations that it cannot support; it fails to perform the most elementary functions of science, like counting; it ignores the contributions of sister sciences like statistics, economics, linguistics, and psychiatry. Worst of all, after twenty-five centuries, History is no closer to solving the central problem of causation than was Thucydides or Tacitus, or for that matter St. Augustine, who at least knew where he stood.

Finally there is the impeachment we have heard before: that as History is neither independent, original, nor creative, it neither attracts nor inspires great minds and therefore cannot, in the nature of things, achieve the kind of greatness that art, science, and philosophy have achieved. The seminal thinkers of the past three centuries who have contributed most to History itself, we are reminded, have all come from outside the ranks of historians: Newton and Leibniz, Voltaire and Turgot, Hume and Bentham, Humboldt and Goethe, Comte and Tocqueville, Darwin and Spencer, Marx and Nietzsche, Lester Ward and John Dewey, Sigmund Freud and Bertrand Russell among them. Perhaps the philosopher Santayana was right: History, he concluded, "is an imperfect field for the exercise of reason. . . . Its values, with mind's progress, would empty into higher activities."

The decline in the influence and prestige of History, so widespread in the Western world, has a special and perhaps less acrimonious character in the United States. History undoubtedly played a significant role in the evolution of American nationalism in the nineteenth century, but it has never been part of the American heritage of experience as it has been of the European. To Americans, History tends to be symbolic rather than real, even prospective rather than retrospective. It is not, as we say, in the blood. This is no doubt what Henry James had in mind when he wrote that Emerson had dwelt for fifty years "within the undecorated walls of his youth," or in that famous passage in his essay on Hawthorne where he contrasted the "denser, richer, warmer European spectacle" with the bleak prospect that Hawthorne viewed:

> *No sovereign, no court, no personal loyalty, no aristocracy, no church, no clergy, no army, no diplomatic service, no country gentlemen, no palaces, no castles, nor manors, nor old country houses, nor parsonages, nor thatched cottages, nor ivied ruins; no cathedrals, nor abbeys, nor little Norman churches; no great*

Universities nor public schools—no Oxford, nor Eton, nor Harrow;
no literature, no novels, no museums, no pictures, no political so-
ciety, no sporting class—no Epsom nor Ascot![13]

Such a list, James added, would have appalled the English or the French
imagination. Doubtless true enough, but what is more to the point is that
it did not and still does not appall the American imagination. Quite the
contrary: the characteristic American response to what James calls "such
an indictment" is rather one of complacency that America has missed so
much that is anachronistic or iniquitous.

Nor did Americans develop those institutions that carry History along
with them as a swollen river carries the debris that has accumulated over
the long winter. James was quite right: it was History that gave significance to the monarchy, the church, the remnants of the feudal order, the
ancient universities, the artistic inheritance, and these in turn nourished
the sense of History. But what, in the New World, nourished the sense of
history? Salem—yes, and Williamsburg and Charleston and perhaps Saint
Augustine, but what in Indiana or Kansas or Nevada? Nor had Americans
contrived new institutions to take the place of those they had abandoned,
or developed new traditions. Even their mythology always had about it a
curious contemporaneity: Washington was a legend in his own lifetime,
and Daniel Boone, too, while both the Alamo and Buffalo Bill belong to
the era of the Industrial Revolution. It is doubtless this juxtaposition of
the conventional and the legendary that Thomas Beer had in mind when
he penned that opening sentence of *The Mauve Decade:* "They laid Jesse
James in his grave and Dante Gabriel Rossetti died immediately."

There are other reasons scarcely less compelling why Americans have
not, on the whole, felt history in their bones. Those who came over to
the New World—and all Americans (except the Indians) are immigrants
or the descendants of immigrants—left history behind them, and many of
them, like Crèvecoeur or Tom Paine, regarded it as good riddance. For
to them history was not so much a Church as an Establishment from
which they wished to escape; the monarchy and the class system not
something to venerate but something to reject; and their very flight to
America constituted not only a rejection of traditional institutions but of
traditional history. What was true of immigrants from the Old World to
the New was true, to only a lesser degree, of the immigrants who left
the settlements along the Atlantic seaboard and struck off into the trans-
Appalachian wilderness. Walt Whitman spoke for all of them:

All the past we leave behind,
We debouch upon a newer mightier world, varied world,
Fresh and strong the world we seize, world of labor and the march,
Pioneers! O pioneers![14]

Many of the earlier settlers from the British Isles and Germany were able to bring with them some of their *lares* and *penates,* and to set up in the New World communities not unlike those they had fled. What shall we say of the "new" immigrants, the "uprooted" Italians and Poles and Russian Jews whose coming Thomas Bailey Aldrich lamented in elegaic lines:

> *Accents of menace alien to our air,*
> *Voices that once the Tower of Babel knew!*[15]

What but that their flight from history was more desperate, their revolt against the past more complete, than those of earlier migrations. Except in the religious arena they did not try to recreate the Old World in America (as some Germans had, for example, or Norwegians and Swedes) or even to hang on to their native languages. What history they knew, they forgot; what history was available to them in America they rarely bothered to learn. Their children, to be sure, acquired a smattering of American history in school, but it was rarely part of their lives as Joan of Arc was part of the life of every French child, or Drake and Nelson of every English.

Indifference to the past had philosophical roots as well as historical. "I like dreams of the future better than the history of the past," wrote their greatest political philosopher, Thomas Jefferson. He knew history well enough—especially the history of the ancient world—but he had come to the conclusion that it had little to teach that was relevant to the needs of the new America. Far better to wipe the slate clean and start over. Where many of Jefferson's contemporaries—John Adams, for example— were sure that as men were always the same, they were doomed forever to repeat the errors of the past, Jefferson rejected the notion that man was a prisoner of the past. "Shake not your rawhead and bloodybones at me," he said, and affirmed that in America, at least, men could triumph over history. That is what, for a time anyway, Americans proceeded to do. And this cavalier attitude toward the past, rationalized by philosophy and nourished by experience, was confirmed by another Jeffersonian conviction—the belief that America was, after all, unique, and that the lessons of the past, or of other societies, did not apply to her.

There are, of course, countervailing forces, as there were from the beginning. The New England clergy, and the clergy of many of the immigrant churches, was eager enough to preserve the heritage of learning that they felt was part of the heritage of religion. Unregenerate Irishmen, devout Jews, Swedes and Norwegians proud of their heritage, these and others organized to preserve their own cultures in the New World. Scholars in and out of universities cultivated Old World history and literature with piety and zeal: two of the first four major American historians, Prescott and Motley, wrote the histories of Old World countries, and the third, Francis Parkman, gave more attention to the French and the Spanish in America than to the English. All true enough, but it remains true, too, that while the ordinary American may boast some knowledge of the past, he has little sense of the past nor does he care deeply about it.

IV The new history

There is always a "new" history, and there are always new viewpoints in history. Herodotus wrote social history and Tacitus' *Germania* is a pretty good example of what we call cultural anthropology, while Plutarch gave us psychological, if not precisely psychiatric, portraits of illustrious Greeks and Romans. Perhaps the "new" history really began with Machiavelli and Guicciardini in that sixteenth-century Florence that was in so many ways the harbinger of the modern world; these two were the first truly secular historians of any stature since the unimportant Ammianus Marcellinus of the fourth century. Or perhaps it began with Montesquieu's *Spirit of Laws* in the mid-eighteenth century, or with Giambattista Vico down in Naples, or with the obscure Justus Möser in Osnabrück, who anticipated much of what we have come to call historicism—the study of the past in *its* own terms rather than in *our* own terms. In any event the New History is firmly established by the mid-eighteenth century when, for the first time since Augustine, it has fully emancipated itself from religion, and concerns itself with the City of Man rather than with the City of God.

For secularization is surely the most fundamental and far-reaching revolution in historical thinking and writing since the Middle Ages; without it we would not have, or be able to comprehend, any of the great philosophical and scientific concepts that have so profoundly altered our thinking about History (and about everything else), such as evolution, economic determinism, and psychology. With the advent of secularism, for the first time in more than a thousand years, the center of gravity shifted back from the heavens over which an omnipotent God presided to that earth in which man seemed so powerless, but perhaps was not. For the first time since the Renaissance, historians permitted themselves to inquire into secular causation rather than merely to record the Providential. Under the auspices of secularism, the new History burst the doors of cathedrals and monasteries and moved out into courts and marketplaces and battlefields. Or perhaps we should simply say that the new History proved vulnerable, or hospitable, to a series of explosive concepts, all drawn from secular science.

For modern History, though it provides so much of the connective thought of the arts and the sciences, is an intellectual dependent, almost a parasite. It is imaginative rather than original; it draws on all the stuff of history provided by past experience to create what Jacques Barzun has called a "panorama of continuity in chaos." The great seminal ideas that illuminate and inform it come almost entirely from the outside—from science, philosophy, sociology, law. Even its growth and expansion have come from without rather than from within, come because geography and archaeology and ethnology have forced it to embrace ancient and primitive peoples, or because economics and sociology, psychiatry and linguistics have required it to entertain new ideas and employ new tools. History persistently reflects ideas more than it contributes to them. In the long Middle Ages it faithfully reflected the ideas of the Christian church; in the age of the Enlightenment it reflected the ideas of science and natural law; in the past two centuries it has reflected the ideas of evolution, materialism, and technology. As it faithfully served the church in the Middle Ages, it has loyally served the nation-state in modern times, and at all times it has been the servant of supernational ideologies like the divine right of kings or Manifest Destiny, democracy or communism.

Once the mind of man was emancipated from the theological prison in which it had languished for so many centuries, it could substitute reason for faith and science for fate and inquire fearlessly into all the operations of nature and of man, all the institutions of government and society, all the enterprises of art and labor. Science took command. In the words of the most representative of Enlightenment poets:

> *Nature and Nature's laws lay hid in night:*
> *God said, Let Newton be! and all was light.*[16]

In a Newtonian universe order presided over the laws of nature and nature's God, directing both the wheeling of the constellations of stars in the heavens and the circulation of blood in the veins. Order presided too over the institutions of government, the functioning of the economy, the administration of the law, the rules of grammar, the standards of art, and the character of History.

Now for the first time History was expected to inquire critically into the "causes of things," to eschew miracles, wonders, and divine interventions, and to provide explanations that were reasonable in the light of science. For the first time History was brought within the scope of law and required to adapt its records, explanations, and interpretations to a logical pattern; that did not mean that History now had its own laws, but merely that it was subject to the same laws that controlled everything else in the known universe. It was freed, at last, from the biblical chronology, or at least from that worked out by the good Bishop Ussher, who had so conclusively demonstrated that the creation of Adam occurred on

257

October 28, 4004 B.C. Now a Comte de Buffon, greatest of scientists, could publicly estimate the age of the earth at 75,000 years and privately at 3,000,000. Now History could acknowledge nature rather than God as the force to which it of necessity responded; now it could reject the notion—still lingering on into the nineteenth century—that (it is Karl von Raumer speaking) "the New Testament is the foundation and the living heart of the history of the world," and boldly submit the history of comparative civilizations from China to Peru. Now it could speculate on the rise and fall of civilizations in secular terms, a subject that has fascinated historians from Montesquieu and Gibbon to Oswald Spengler and Arnold Toynbee.

This was the third revolutionary concept that transformed the character and the study of History: that the history of man was conditioned by his natural environment. It was, more than anything else, the eighteenth-century discovery of a whole galaxy of new worlds that had dramatized this idea, for that century, even more than the fifteenth, was preeminently the age of discovery of both nature and man. *Universal History,* as written by Bishop Bossuet in 1681, confined itself almost exclusively to the history of the Jewish and Christian peoples, but when, in 1756, Voltaire published the first version of his *Essai sur les moeurs et l'esprit des nations,* he started out with a chapter on China!

How, after all, account for the extraordinary variations in the customs and manners, to say nothing of the *esprit,* of peoples and nations? How account for the three-thousand-year-old civilization of China and the abiding savagery of the Hottentots, for the Hurons who were so like the Trojans, and for the giants of Patagonia or the pygmies of Brazil? How fit into the annals of History the decline of what was once the great civilization of Egypt, the expansion and retreat of the Arab civilization, the explosive energy of the Vikings, the peculiar felicity of the Tahitians, the rich variety of civilizations in the great subcontinent of India—how account for all these once you have unthroned God as the moving force? "Climate" was the answer, climate, by which the Enlightenment meant the whole of environment as it affected and conditioned the life of man.

Soon History absorbed geography, or was absorbed by it, in terms of "one glorious principle of universal and undeviating regularity"—the geographic.

Nowhere was the geographical interpretation of history cultivated more assiduously than in America, nowhere did its claims seem more irresistible. From the beginning, the history of America took the form of geography—in John Smith's *History of Virginia,* for example; in much of Bradford's *Plimmoth Plantation;* in William Byrd's delightful *History of the Dividing Line;* in that astonishing tour de force by the Jesuit priest, Father Joseph Lafitau, on the *Customs of the American Savages,* which has some claim to be the first essay in cultural anthropology in our literature; and in the vast literature of exploration which culminated in *Notes on Virginia* and the *Journals* of the Lewis and Clark expedition, both products of Thomas Jefferson's fertile imagination. Consciously or unconsciously—and a bit of both—the generation of the Founding Fathers were almost all cultural geographers: thus Crèvecoeur's *Letters From an American Farmer*, or Jefferson's classic *Notes on Virginia*, which were a curious mélange of geography, ethnology, history, politics, and sociology. Thus too the first formal histories of the American states—the Rev. Jeremy Belknap's *History of New Hampshire*, which was as much geography as was his novel, *The Foresters*; or Hugh Williamson's remarkable *History of North Carolina*, which was prefaced by a long study of climate, geography, and native races. And how revealing that the first, and for long the best, history of America, that by the prodigious German scholar Christoph Ebeling, in seven enormous volumes, was called *Geography and History of the American States*! The tradition persisted, and came in time to dominate American historical thought. It was manifest in George Perkins Marsh's classic *Man and Nature*, for example; in Francis Parkman's twelve volumes on the struggle for a continent, which he envisioned as a history of the American forest; in Frederick Jackson Turner's "Significance of the Frontier in American History," with its insistence that all American history was to be interpreted in terms of open land; in Theodore Roosevelt's stirring volumes on *The Winning of the West*; and even in more recent literature such as Walter Prescott Webb's pioneering interpretation, *The Great Plains*, or William Goetzmann's *Exploration and Empire*, which is almost a history of American thought about nature.

Out of Newtonian science and the study of environment came a fourth seminal idea that was to add a new dimension to history, perhaps the only one of the major ideas that owed much to History itself: the idea of progress. It was, of course, a very secular idea and thus, at an earlier time, an exotic. After all, if life on this earth was but a preparation for life to come, and if the whole purpose of man was to know the will of God and to do it, then there could be no such thing as progress in society, or in history. Only secularism put a premium on improvement, or even left room for it; the improvement was not spiritual but material or artistic, or humane—the very word states the case.

Then came Newtonian science, which pointed pretty clearly to progress, though always, of course, within the fixed framework of nature. But progress, in the era of the Enlightenment, did not mean improving on the laws of nature, which was impossible, but penetrating them and conforming to them. This was the thrust of so much of the literature of the time, from Montesquieu's *The Spirit of Laws* to Diderot's great *Encyclopédie*, and Blackstone's *Commentaries* on the Constitution; this was part of the controversy between the mercantilists and the physiocrats; this was the Reason of State that animated a Frederick the Great or a Joseph II and their ministers—a Turgot in France, a Sonnenfels in Austria, a Struensee in Denmark.

The promise or at least the suggestion of nature was now reinforced by the revelations of geography and ethnology. For, say what you will about the uniformity of mankind, and romanticize as you will the noble savage of America or of the South Seas, it was clear that mankind had somehow progressed from the savagery of the Brazilian or the Australian aborigines to the society that graced the court at Weimar or gathered in the salons of Paris. Out of comparisons such as these, and out of the curious but vigorous debate between the ancients and the moderns, which left victory pretty much with the moderns, came those speculations that in a Turgot, a Chastellux, a Condorcet, or a Thomas Paine replaced the "Dark Ages" with the Enlightenment, and rejected the cyclical interpretation of history for the progressive.

Nowhere was the doctrine of progress more clearly vindicated than in America. But American statesmen, philosophers, and historians adopted it not as a revolutionary idea, which it was, but as an axiom so obvious that it did not need to be demonstrated: the whole of American history was nothing but a prolonged demonstration. This was the argument of Tom Paine's *Common Sense* and of his *Rights of Man,* as it was also of Jefferson's *Notes on Virginia,* which proved by exact measurements how prodigious was the sheer physical progress in the New World—the spread of antlers on a bull moose, the weight of a sow, the productivity of the soil, the physique of men, the vital statistics of birth and death—and which claimed a comparable intellectual and moral progress. This was the argument of Crèvecoeur's *Letters,* of Joel Barlow's poetic *Vision of Columbus* (perhaps the most sustained vision on record, for it lasted for twenty years and stretched through 8,000 lines), and of a score of histories and biographies that recounted the glorious story of the birth and progress of the new nation and asserted the moral superiority of its leaders. Indeed some of these works—Parson Weems's *Washington,* for example—came full circle by demonstrating that progress in America was not so much the achievement of American genius as the working out of a Divine Plan.

The idea of progress was reinforced by what is, since secularization, incomparably the most influential of all the ideas that have fertilized History: Darwinian evolution. Darwin himself made no attempt to apply his all-embracing theory outside the biological area, but evolution could no more be confined to that area than could the concept of environment, with which it was closely associated, be limited to geography. For now that man had been translated from the religious orbit to the natural, and from the Adam created by God to the *Homo sapiens* evolved over millions of years from lower biological forms, what applied to all other living organisms applied to him. And evolution, it quickly appeared, could be made to apply to collective man as well as to individual man. What is more, it applied to man's institutions as well as to his body and mind. Evolution soon came to dominate the whole body of historical thought, which now concluded that all social institutions—the family, the church, government, the university, art, language, and even History—must be studied organically.

Evolution introduced a dramatic shift in the study of history, as of all of the political and social sciences, from the static to the dynamic, from the formal to the functional, and from change through catastrophe or fortuity to change through organic evolution. It forced history to look to the consequential rather than to the dramatic, and put a premium on institutional analysis rather than on narrative. It required that each segment of history be placed in a larger framework than the immediate or the local, and be interpreted as part of the evolution of society, thus shattering the artificial distinctions between history, economics, sociology, religion, art, science, and even morals. It ended the theological explanation of history as effectively as it did the Scriptural chronology, and made clear that change is the pervasive principle of the universe.

It was the English philosopher Herbert Spencer who made himself the spokesman of the secular version of Darwinian evolution; his vast *System of Synthetic Philosophy*, which embraced science, the social sciences, and ethics, attempted to do for these what Darwin had done for biology, and in large measure succeeded, at least to the satisfaction of his contemporaries. What emerged was a new reading of history as an organic process that functioned through the Darwinian principle of the "survival of the fittest." History, as it unfolded in the sombre pages of Spencer's *First Principles* and his *Principles of Sociology,* took on a character at once exhilarating and desperate. It was exhilarating because it demonstrated that over the centuries and the millennia, the same inexorable forces of nature that had produced fish and fowl and animals perfectly adapted to their environment, thereby fulfilling the functions that nature intended, operated on man and his society, and that in time, therefore, man too, and all his institutions, would adapt themselves to their environment and would attain such perfection as nature intended. Here was a new reading of progress, one that for the first time appeared to provide solid scientific support for confidence in the future of the human race. For "progress is not an accident, but a necessity," Spencer wrote. The Spencerian reading of evolution was discouraging and even desperate because it promised progress and perfection on two implacable conditions: first, that there be no interference by man or government with the grand processes of nature, and second, that man contain himself patiently for some thousands or tens of thousands of years while the processes of evolution worked themselves out.

Thus the century-long search for law had ended with the law of evolution, but, as interpreted by Spencer, it was for human purposes a negative end. Man was, indeed, distinguished by reason and will, but reason taught that his highest wisdom lay in treading the path that nature had marked out for him and, as for will, its most solemn exercise was the passive one of refraining from interference with nature's laws.

Here was, in a sense, a new determinism and one that, if accepted literally, might turn History into antiquarianism. For it left no play for human purpose or genius but, on the contrary, warned that, if set by the contumacious will of man against the majestic purposes of nature, these might prove deterrents to orderly evolution.

This Spencerian version of history and of progress was promptly challenged by Lester Ward, one of the ablest scientists of his generation and the most distinguished of American social thinkers. Ward rejected as radically unsound Spencer's assumption that social evolution was governed by the same laws that governed biology, and insisted that for man the "psychic" factors—that is, those of the mind—were more important than the biological. For while all other creatures on the globe were subject to nature, man and man alone was in command of nature. Man had survived not by being "fit" in nature's terms, but by imposing on nature his own concept of fitness. All progress, Ward demonstrated, from the most primitive state of society to the most civilized had been achieved by interference with the processes of nature and by defiance of the principle of the "survival of the fittest." Every implement or utensil, he pointed out,

> *every mechanical device, every object of design, skill and labor, every artificial thing that serves a human purpose, is a triumph of mind over the physical forces of nature in ceaseless and aimless competition. The cultivation of plants and the domestication of animals involve the direct control of biological forces and the exemption of these forms of life from the operation of the great organic law which dwarfs their native powers of development. All human institutions—religion, government, law, marriage, custom—are only so many ways of checkmating the principle of competition.*[17]

Thus progress would be achieved not by blind conformity to nature but by imposing the mind and will of man upon it.

Ward's reading of the operation of the *Psychic Factors of Civilization* (the title of his most important work) gave, logically at least, a new vigor to history and to politics, economics, sociology, and law, for it rejected determinism and restored to history its traditional function, that of philosophy (or as Ward himself would say, of facts) teaching by examples. As it required men, at their peril, to take charge of their own evolution, it made it necessary for them to know and to build upon the past.

The doctrine of psychic forces capable of overcoming natural forces was shortly to win one great victory after another throughout the Western world, in the emergence of the welfare state. It was nevertheless seriously challenged from a new quarter, and by a new determinism, one closer to that of Buckle than to that of Spencer. This was historical materialism as formulated by Karl Marx and Friedrich Engels. Marx, who had lived and worked in London while Darwin was writing his *Origin of Species* in his house in nearby Down, thought of himself as the Darwin of the historical world:

> *Darwin has interested us in the history of Nature's technology* [he wrote], *i.e., in the formation of the organs of plants and animals, which organs serve as instruments of production for sustaining life. Does not the history of the productive organs of man, of organs that are the material basis of all social organization, deserve equal attention?*[18]

Indeed it did, and Marx and his faithful associate worked out a philosophy of history that differed from the Spencerian one chiefly in the choice of the dynamic forces that were to control the functioning of human nature and society—a decisive difference, to be sure. Georg Friedrich Hegel (Marx had been trained in Hegelian philosophy) had located this force in some vague world spirit which, notwithstanding its transcendental qualities, turned out to have German citizenship. Hegel had indeed asserted that "passions, private aims, and the satisfaction of selfish desires are . . . most effective springs of action,"[19] but he never allowed this insight to distract him from the *Zeitgeist* to reality. Marx was revolted by what he thought a perverse denial of this reality and located the controlling force in the earth.

> *In direct contrast to German philosophy which descends from heaven to earth* [he wrote], *here we ascend from earth to heaven. That is to say, we do not set out from what men say, imagine, conceive . . . in order to arrive at men in the flesh. We set out from real, active men, and on the basis of their real life-process we demonstrate the development of the ideological reflexes and echoes of this life-process. . . . Life is not determined by consciousness, but consciousness by life.*[20]

The character of history, and of civilization, is not to be found, then, in abstractions, but in the soil, labor, machinery, production and consumption, markets and exchange. As Engels later wrote:

> *In every historical epoch the prevailing mode of economic production and exchange, and the social organization necessarily follow-*

> ing from it, form the basis upon which is built up, and from which alone can be explained, the political and intellectual history of that epoch . . . . the final causes of all social changes and political revolutions are to be sought not in men's brains, but in changes in the modes of production and exchange. They are to be sought not in philosophy but in the economics of each particular epoch.[21]

For all its apparent realism, Marxist historical philosophy, like the Hegelian, is deductive rather than inductive; for all its reliance on material phenomena that are measurable, it is *a priori* rather than experimental. Its significance and its prodigious influence lie not in its theory, which has not on the whole been vindicated, but in its point of view. That point of view has conditioned, perhaps dominated, much of historical and social thought for the past century, maintaining that economic interests and issues explain more of the course of history than any others, and that history should therefore be interpreted in predominantly economic terms. At first gradually, then with increasing urgency, this view invaded and conquered the minds of economists and historians until, by the turn of the century, it came to be more widely accepted than any other theory of history. As late as 1887 Professor Thorold Robers of Oxford University could give a series of lectures on the Economic Interpretation of History without mentioning Marx, but by the time of World War I that was no longer possible. With such books as Werner Sombart's *Modern Capitalism,* Jean Jaurès' *Socialist History of the French Revolution,* Richard H. Tawney's *Religion and the Rise of Capitalism,* and Charles A. Beard's *Economic Interpretation of the Constitution of the United States,* the seminal ideas of Marx and Engels entered the mainstream of History. If the more ostentatious influence of Marxist philosophy seemed to wane after World War II, that was not because it was ignored, or rejected, but rather because it had so entered into the texture of social thought that it ceased to command attention or excite controversy.

The influence of Marx is very different from Marxist interpretation. The first has been, and is, pervasive; the second is rare. In the United States, the Marxist influence on the interpretation of history has concentrated pretty heavily on the issue of class. That the new nation was supposed to have a classless society was long an article of faith with historians as with politicians. That is the way Benjamin Franklin described it, that is the way Jefferson imagined it, that is the way the Constitution-makers planned it. All ignored slavery in their analyses, and all assumed that the forces of environment, the political arrangements for equality among whites, and the economic potentialities of a free market on a continental scale would inevitably eliminate whatever class distinctions there were. It was easy to forget that it did not work out that way by confining attention to whites and forgetting blacks, and that is what most historians and even political philosophers did, at least until the publication (in 1935) of W. E. B. Du Bois's *Black Reconstruction*. Nor was Marxist philosophy applied with any rigor to the exploitation of the resources of the continent by private enterprise, or to the growth of corporate capitalism; these developments could be explained, after all, as natural outgrowths of laissez-faire liberalism.

It was the remarkable Norwegian-American economist Thorstein Veblen who challenged these assumptions most effectively, but not so much on Marxist as on quite independent grounds. Repudiating the classical economists, Veblen refused to associate himself with Marxism; inscrutable and sardonic, he stood aloof from most of the currents of thought that swirled around him and worked out his own, highly original, interpretations of economy and culture. His epoch-making *Theory of the Leisure Class* (1899) interpreted class not so much in Marxist as in cultural terms, and though he apparently was not familiar with the insights of Sigmund Freud, his approach to the economic manifestations of culture was profoundly psychological. If he did envision a class, it was neither the exploited poor nor the bumbling and miscellaneous rich, but rather the "engineers"—the managerial technocrats who, he thought, would do a far better job with the economy than did the willful, greedy, and untutored corporate owners. Those engaged in business, he argued, were addicted to "anthropomorphic explanation of phenomena in terms of human relations, discretion, choice, and precedent, to de jure rather than de facto arguments"; they made facts conform to doctrine, exalted tradition, and took refuge in abstractions or in illusions rather than in economic realities. Veblen concluded that the triumph of American capitalism could not be explained by the business acumen of corporate owners nor by the conscious control of an exploited proletariat, but by "the sentimental deference of the American people" to business leaders and to the notion of private enterprise.

When in the course of the new century younger historians turned their attention to some of the crises of American history—the making of the Constitution, the emergence of Jacksonian democracy, the rise of plantation slavery, the coming of the Civil War, the frustration of Reconstruction, the struggle between labor and business and the exploitation of immigrants in the last quarter of the nineteenth century, the expansion of "dollar diplomacy," and so forth—they found much that was similar to the class conflicts of the Old World, and that could be illuminated, if not wholly explained, in Marxist terms. Yet few of those who drew on the insights of Marxist philosophy were themselves Marxists. Most influential of the economic interpreters was Charles A. Beard, whose *Economic Interpretations of the Constitution* and *Economic Origins of Jeffersonian Democracy* (1913 and 1915) created and even gave respectability to a new school. Soon Marxist analyses were directed on such institutions as the Supreme Court, the corporation, the political party, imperialism, slavery, and Reconstruction. Some of the more striking and valuable contributions in these areas were Louis Boudin's attack on the practices of judicial review in his *Government by Judiciary;* John R. Commons' profound analysis of the *Legal Foundations of Capitalism;* W. E. B. Du Bois's frankly Marxist *Black Reconstruction,* which successfully challenged two generations of academic interpretations of the Reconstruction process; and by implication at least, Vernon L. Parrington's great *Main Currents in American Thought,* in many ways the most brilliant study of the American mind that has been written. More frankly Marxist in their approach are some of the younger historians who even now contest leadership in the American historical profession: William Appleman Williams, who has concentrated pretty much on American foreign policy; Eugene Genovese, whose learned and original studies throw a flood of light on slavery and plantation capitalism; and Staughton Lynd, who has challenged all the orthodoxies in his studies of the Revolution and the Constitution.

Secularization, the laws of nature, the idea of progress, the influence of climate, the all-encompassing force of evolution, economic determinism—to these great ideas that did so much to shape the character of History were joined, in the early years of the twentieth century, the insights of psychiatry, which we associate with one of the intellectual giants of our age, Sigmund Freud.

Psychology is very old, though not by that name. Psyche herself appears in Greek mythology as the beloved of Eros; her conquests and her empire have expanded enormously in modern times. The term *psychology* appeared first in 1749, in David Hartley's *Observations on Man;* it was another hundred years until the emergence of the term *psychiatry,* and then it was in connection with medicine; it will not be forgotten that both William James (whose great book on psychology in 1890 inaugurated the modern study of that subject) and Sigmund Freud were trained in medicine. Actually, what we now call "psycho-history," in one form or another, is very old and familiar. Thucydides' account of the appeals by Nicias and Alcibiades to the passions of the Athenians in the debate over the Sicilian expedition is a little masterpiece of psychology. Plutarch's portraits of the Greeks and the Romans sought to penetrate to the psyches of these illustrious men; in his sketches of the Caesars—the sadism of Caligula, the hysteria of Claudius, the perverseness of Nero—Suetonius anticipated something of modern psychiatry. And since Machiavelli's subtle analysis of the nature of power, many modern historians—Gibbon, Carlyle, Karl Lamprecht, and Henry Adams among them—have indulged themselves and their readers in rich psychological speculations. In 1904 James Harvey Robinson of Columbia University asserted that "the progress of history must depend largely, in the future as in the past, upon the development of cognate sciences . . . perhaps above all psychology," and that same year Henry Adams wrote in *Mont-St.-Michel and Chartres* of the intellectual and artistic life of the High Middle Ages as a kind of sublimation of the love for the Virgin. But until Freud, none of these commanded the techniques of psychiatric research.

Freudian psychiatry grew out of Freud's experiences with his patients, and so was long confined to the individual. Therefore, its insights were, and remained, more useful in biography than in History, and today it is most evident in such studies as Erik Erickson's *Young Man Luther* and *Gandhi,* Leon Edel's magisterial *Henry James,* David Donald's *Charles Sumner,* Halvdan Koht's *Life of Ibsen,* or Hjalmar Helweg's psychiatric study of that tortured soul, *Hans Christian Andersen.* Gradually, Freud came to believe that the life of the race recapitulated the psychological life of the individual, and that what was conscious in primitive man persisted as unconscious in civilized man. As the sexual drive was the most universal and powerful of all forces operating on human beings, their development could be understood in terms of the efforts of organized society to control, direct, express, and repress that drive. It was to explore the implications of these theories that Freud wrote many of his later works: *Totem and Taboo* (1913), *Civilization and Its Discontents* (1929), and the highly controversial but enormously influential *Moses and Monotheism,* in 1939, the year of his death.

What this meant not only for psychiatry and philosophy but for the behavioral sciences can be read in the educational psychology of G. Stanley Hall, who brought Freud to America in 1909:

> *The mind stretches far beyond the limited experience of the individual. It contains within itself all the past and all the future. It has grown up in the race, step by step, and has passed through stages as different from its present form as we can conceive. It is so vastly complex that it is never twice alike in the same individual nor are ever two minds the same. It is a product of millions of years of struggle. Its many experiences with light and dark and with heat and cold have established many of its rhythms. A long apprenticeship in aquatic and arboreal life has left deep and indelible marks. ... It has been shocked and molded into its present form by labor and suffering, and it shows in every function the marks of the process through which it has passed. Although it is by far the most wonderful work of nature, it is still very imperfect, full of scars and wounds, incompletely coordinated and but poorly controlled. .·.. Its old forms appear at every turn; and every trait of mind as well as of body, is full of indications of its origin. So close is the past to the present in all we think and feel, that without referring to what has gone before in the race, the human mind, as we know it, is utterly unintelligible and mysterious; while many if not most of its mysteries become clear, when the mind is studied with reference to the past.*[22]

If much that was unconscious but powerful in civilized man was conscious and overt in the ritual and magic of primitive societies, then those who wanted to understand what appeared irrational or inexplicable in modern man could turn with profit to the study of primitive peoples. The great James Frazer of the *Golden Bough* had already seen something of this, and so had psychologist-anthropologists like Bronislaw Malinowski, with his pioneering studies of the sexual life of the Trobriand Islanders, or E. A. Westermarck, whose *History of Human Marriage* was almost the first scholarly work of anthropology and psychology to bear on the sexual life of both primitive and civilized peoples. Soon a new school of cultural anthropologists, including Franz Boas, Ruth Benedict, Margaret Mead, and Alfred Kroeber were concentrating on the study of the American Indian or the natives of the South Sea islands, with new insights borrowed from the realms of psychiatry of contemporary peoples. Clearly those now classic studies by Alfred Kinsey, *Sexual Behavior in the Human Male* and *Sexual Behavior in the Human Female,* owe an immense debt to the new school of cultural anthropologists.

If Freud's impact on conventional History has been meager, his influence on the study of culture has been prodigious. It has contributed greatly to our understanding of irrationalism, mass hysteria, paranoia, the prejudices about class, sex, and race. Most of these contributions have come from psychologists and sociologists, to be sure: thus Erich Fromm's penetrating study of the *Escape From Freedom,* which cast so much light on the psychology of totalitarianism; thus Hannah Arendt's classic essays on *The Origins of Totalitarianism* and *On Violence;* thus Jay Lifton's sobering study of the impact of disaster on a community, *Death in Life: Survivors of Hiroshima;* thus David Riesman's *Lonely Crowd,* with its perspicacious analysis of the shift in the American character from inner- to outer-directed man. Contributions of historians have tended to focus increasingly on the more ostentatiously irrational chapters of American history—Salem witchcraft, for example, or fanaticism, North and South, that paved the way to open conflict in 1861, or the hysteria of the 1940s that made possible the Japanese concentration camps, or the phenomenon of mass paranoia that partially explains the success of Senator Joseph McCarthy in the fifties. Yet how does one ultimately explain the state of mind and emotions that sustained the institution of Negro slavery, the theory of white supremacy, and the persistence of the myth about Southern Womanhood (which has figured so prominently in Southern fantasies for a century and a half), all of which linger in, and contribute so much to, the irrationality in the current discussion on the issue of school busing? Thomas Jefferson, who saw everything, observed that "the whole commerce between master and slave is a perpetual exercise of the most boisterous of passions," and sexual fantasies about the relations between black and white disturbed the thinking of Southern apologists and of Northern Abolitionists in the decades before the Civil War. Certainly Wilbur J. Cash's *Mind of the South,* Winthrop Jordan's *White Over Black,* and Stanley Elkins' *Slavery,* with its suggestive analogies between plantation slavery and the concentration camp, have drawn heavily upon the findings of psychiatry. Psychiatry has illuminated, too, such miscellaneous chapters of American history as the role of the cowboy as a symbol of virility, the persistence of anti-intellectualism, the nature of the search for identity vis-à-vis the mother country in the first half of the nineteenth century, and the persistence of the paranoid style in American politics—a subject to which the gifted Richard Hofstadter contributed so richly.

Psycho-history has not yet, however, vindicated its claims to have added a distinctly new dimension to historical (as distinct from biographical) understanding. It provides insights, but those insights are perceptive rather than conclusive. A gifted psychiatrist like Erik Erikson can probe deeply into the motivations of a Luther or a Gandhi, but it is not so easy to probe the motivations of a hundred thousand or a million people, especially when (as is commonly the case) the data is fragmentary and elusive, and can never be submitted to scientific tests. The historian stands on firm ground when he is aware of the forces of irrationality and assigns to them a role in history, but he is on treacherous ground when he tries to explain the origins or the motivation or the impact of irrationality. Nor is it entirely clear that fascination with motivation is advantageous rather than distracting to the student of history. Even our own motives for the simplest of actions—let us say the choice of a college, a career, a spouse —are almost infinitely complex; how difficult it is to be sure of the motives of a Henry VIII or a Napoleon, a Leonardo or a John D. Rockefeller. Again, whether Henry VIII was motivated by lust, caprice, religious convictions, or reasons of state and whether John D. Rockefeller's benefactions were inspired by ambition, vanity, or the desire to distract public attention from his predatory activities makes really but little difference: what does make a difference is what happened.

It is difficult to know whether quantification should be considered as a new idea or only a new technique, or even whether it is new. In one sense it is very old indeed. Historians have always counted—the years of a dynasty, the number of soldiers in an army, the drachmas or livres or pounds in the treasury—and they have always recognized, too, the importance of counting. More than a century ago Henry Thomas Buckle wrote, in the opening chapter of *History of Civilization in England,* that the

> *proofs of our actions being regulated by law, have been derived from statistics; a branch of knowledge which, though still in its infancy, has already thrown more light on the study of human na-*

> *ture than all the sciences put together. But . . . the statisticians*
> *have been the first to investigate this great subject by treating it*
> *according to those methods of reasoning which in other fields have*
> *been found successful. . . . they have, by the application of num-*
> *bers, brought to bear upon it a very powerful engine for eliciting*
> *truth. . . .*[23]

Quantification is new neither in practice nor in philosophy. What is new is, first, that the historian now has available to him prodigious quantities of statistical data drawn from census, social security, welfare, military, medical, commercial, and financial records; and second, that thanks to new mechanisms like the computer he is able to use this data—use it and master it—with efficiency, accuracy, and rapidity. Taken together, these developments constitute a change analogous to (though not equal to) the changes introduced by the invention of printing in the fifteenth century, the emergence of scientific library classification in the nineteenth, and electronic devices like the tape recorder in the twentieth. What this amounts to is a quantitative advance so remarkable that it achieves qualitative significance. For historians now have at their command a body of empirical data vastly greater and incomparably more readily available than at any time in the past, and along with this they have mechanisms to assure a rigor, an accuracy, and a concreteness heretofore unknown in historical writing. "To have any validity at all," Lawrence Stone has said, "conclusions about social movements must have a statistical basis," and the conclusions now coming out of the famous Sixième Section of the French historical institute, which addresses itself so energetically to problems of demography and statistics, and from similar groups in England and the United States, have an authority acknowledged by scholars everywhere.

Yet for all its revolutionary techniques, quantification was, philosophically, a return to the ideal that inspired Leopold von Ranke and his followers to believe that they could reconstruct the past "as it actually happened." Indeed, what had been merely a romantic hope became instead a scientific possibility. For—so the quantitative historians believed—with the aid of the computer, the IBM card, the tape recorder, and other technical devices, it was possible to reconstruct some segments of the past brick by brick, as it were, and stone by stone. Now historians could substitute facts—hard facts, authenticated facts, well-mannered and well-disciplined facts—for the mixture of speculation, inference, and conjecture that had passed for History among uncritical historians of earlier times. Now, for the shadowy and subjective past of the classical and romantic schools, the quantifiers were prepared to substitute a past born of the marriage between the data bank and the computer and guaranteed, what is more, to be objective. It was, once again, that "noble dream" against which Charles

A. Beard had fulminated, but it was a dream that the technicians proposed to realize.

And it was true that in some areas, most of them real and public, the quantifiers could discover almost everything they needed of a quantitative nature. Quantification could recover statistics of births and deaths, disease and longevity, marriage and family, from a thousand parish records; it could give an accurate table of voting, county by county and precinct by precinct, in all modern elections; it could trace the vicissitudes of farm production and farm prices, mortgages and foreclosures, and correlate these with voting or migration; it could record the increase in literacy, and the great number of functional illiterates that remain; it could determine how many hours children spent in front of a television screen, and what the public thought it thought about the impact of television on its children. It could explore both horizontal and vertical mobility in discrete populations, or the relationship of revolutions and counterrevolutions to religious affiliations, or the correlations of union membership with voting patterns, or levels of education with sexual habits and prejudices. What could it not do? What it did not even pretend to do was to explain the statistics that it so hopefully submitted. But then, that was the business of the philosopher.

Even as the new school of quantifiers were intoxicated with their triumphs, doubts and misgivings emerged. Quantification was all very well, but its usefulness, so it was asserted, was limited, and it might even prove "counter-productive." Though it is as yet too soon either to vindicate or to refute the criticism, we must take note of it.

First, it is asserted that the quantitative approach to historical problems is lacking both in subtlety and in sophistication and in the all-important comparative dimension, and that while it no doubt provides an impressive body of accurate facts, it often points to misleading conclusions. Consider, for example, the flood of monographs on voting in the American colonies and states in the eighteenth century. Some of these reveal that most adult white males (and in New England there were few who were not white) were entitled to vote in New England town meetings, and substantial numbers in colonial or state elections; others suggest that only 15 or 20 percent of these males could or did in fact vote. Now if you take your stance in the present, when all men and women over eighteen are (in law at least) permitted to vote (though notoriously they do not), that looks like a pretty limited democracy. But if you take your stance in the eighteenth century and do not confine yourself to the American scene, you note at once (what you do not need quantifications to reveal) that on the European continent no one voted at all—except in the Swiss cantons, anyway—for there were no elections, and that even in Britain less than 200,000 persons were entitled to vote and far fewer in fact did. Thus, left to themselves, your computerized figures might lead the unwary to the conclusion that eighteenth-century America was a very limited democracy, whereas in fact it was incomparably the most democratic society in the world. To be sure, the quantifiers would point out here that it is the business of historians to educate the "unwary"; to make clear that laws are not always rigorously enforced, or that considerations other than those of legal qualifications affect voting, or that an examination of voting in New England towns or Virginia counties is not supposed to be an exercise in comparative Western history. Alas, the responsibility of explaining these things often goes by default.

Or consider another and more highly technical application of quantitative tests: the analysis of the voting patterns of judges of the Supreme Court. The computer can faithfully record all the votes of all the judges in all cases, and distinguish these by some predetermined test as "liberal," "center," or "conservative," and lo, we know just where to place each judge on our scale of liberalism or conservatism. But the tests themselves are worthless, for they ignore such fundamental considerations as that judges are rarely in a position to give free rein to their political or social sentiments; that they are bound by the existing law, or by the facts presented by counsel, or by precedents; that they may sincerely suppose it more liberal to observe judicial continence than to impose judicial views of wisdom or virtue on misguided majorities; and that technical considerations may get in the way of a philosophical consideration of a particular case.

Second, it is alleged that while quantification may provide the data for judgment, it is no substitute for judgment, and that those who use it are almost irresistibly tempted to believe that if there are only enough facts, the facts will speak for themselves. Thus quantification puts a premium on the continuous accumulation of data. In this it ignores the law of diminishing returns. Certainly microfilms of ten midwestern newspapers of the Populist era are a great deal more valuable than microfilms of only two or three, but it does not follow that microfilms of one hundred are ten times as valuable as microfilms of ten. The accumulation of data can in fact be self-defeating; there is, in any event, no very impressive correlation between quantitative accumulation and qualitative interpretation. Thus, to take two very different examples, Tocqueville's interpretation of equality in Jacksonian America, arrived at entirely by the deductive method, is still more valuable than any of the more scientific studies of class structure produced with the aid of quantification; Troels-Lund's enchanting fourteen volumes on *Daily Life in the North,* written in the last quarter of the nineteenth century, wholly without benefit of any of the new techniques, remains almost a century later incomparably the best study of its kind in any historical literature.

To be sure, in the hands of skillful quantifiers—the members, for instance, of the famous Sixième Section in Paris, who have so successfully explored problems of demography in medieval France, the fluctuations in the production of grain, and the causes of the Vendée counterrevolution of the 1790s—the use of statistics is both critical and judicious, and the results illuminate areas of history heretofore in shadow. So, too, with Alfred Kinsey's masterly use of the techniques of the interview, and of statistical analyses in his now classic volumes on the sexual behavior of the human male and the human female—reports that have had a profound and lasting influence on the public attitude toward sexual habits, and on legislation. But the Kinsey reports, which appeared in 1948 and 1953, were without benefit of computers, and nothing of equal importance has emerged in the last two decades.

Third, quantification tempts the historian, almost irresistibly, to concentrate on the modern or even the contemporary scene, for it is in the modern period that he is sure to find an abundance of records. There is, to be sure, data for quantification in the town records of colonial New England (*see* John Demos' study of the Plymouth colony) or in the parish records of seventeenth-century England (*see* Peter Laslett's *The World We Have Lost*); it is possible to draw important conclusions from a study of votes in the state and national legislatures in the Federalist era (*see* David Fischer, *The Revolution of American Conservatism*), and as far back as 1939, Lawrence Harper's intensive analysis of customhouse records in the American colonies added new understanding to the workings of *The English Navigation Laws*. But the archival and statistical riches of the modern era act as a magnet to younger historians who are in a hurry and who, in any event, are more interested in the modern than the medieval scene, while the relative scarcity of statistical data on, let us say, Carolingian demography or Icelandic civilization or literacy in the Germanies in the eighteenth century discourages investigation into those areas.

Yet modern science and technology can chalk up triumphs even in the most ancient fields. Willard Libby's stunning discovery, in 1947, that he could date organic matter with considerable exactitude as far back as forty thousand years by measuring with a Geiger counter the amount of radio-carbon that remained in it, was the greatest contribution to archaeology since those two remarkable Danes, C. J. Thomsen and J. J. A. Worsaae, first hit on the three-level system of prehistoric civilizations—the Stone Age, the Bronze Age, and the Iron Age—in the early years of the nineteenth century. And, just the other day, the IBM 705 managed to index, in a few weeks, some 30,000 words extracted from the Dead Sea Scrolls, a task that might otherwise have dragged on for a generation.

A fourth reservation about quantification has to do with style rather than substance. It associates itself eagerly with psycho-history, sociological history, and linguistics, and adopts a language, or a jargon, that is always difficult and sometimes incomprehensible. Here, for example, is Professor S. Sidney Ulmer discussing whether delegates to the Federal Convention of 1787 who acted together represented states with common characteristics:

273

> [the] procedure has been to tally the votes of the state delegations
> on 421 roll calls in the Convention. From this raw data, agreement-
> disagreement rates were calculated and the response pattern of each
> state was correlated with that of every other state. These correla-
> tions were then used to derive groupings or blocs of states using the
> techniques of Elementary Factor Analysis (EFA) developed by
> Louis McQuitty. EFA produced four sub-groups, as shown in Table
> 1. The extraction of four factors by the Principal Factor method re-
> vealed the same general result. The four principal factors and the
> correlation of each state with each factor subsequent to rotation are
> presented in Table 2. These four factors account for a little over 50
> per cent of the variance in the response to 421 issues.

As Jacques Barzun has said, "the reader neither can nor should have to go
into training before taking up a history. His curiosity about the past
should not commit him to a siege of *hineinstudieren* into a doctrine."

Finally, the most serious—and perhaps the most obvious—criticism of
quantification is that it acts as a kind of self-fulfilling prophecy; it almost
irresistibly channels historical research into those areas and toward those
problems that promise to lend themselves to the quantitative approach.
Thus in the realm of politics it produced not the *Federalist Papers* but
studies of voting patterns; thus in the realm of class relationships it produced not *Democracy in America* but Lee Benson's admirable but little-
read *Concept of Jacksonian Democracy;* thus in the realm of law it gave
us not Holmes's *Common Law*—still a classic almost one hundred years
later—but C. H. Pritchett's studies of the Roosevelt Court and the Vinson
Court. As Arthur Schlesinger has observed, the quantitative approach

> claims a false precision by the simple strategy of confining itself to
> the historical problems and materials with which quantitative tech-
> niques can deal, and ignoring all the others as trivial. The mystique
> of empirical social research, in short, leads its acolytes to accept as
> significant only the questions to which the quantitative magic can
> provide answers. As a humanist I am bound to reply that almost
> all important questions are important precisely because they are
> not susceptible to quantitative answers.

What is clear is that the tools and techniques of quantification have added
almost immeasurably to the tools of historical research; they are no substitute for the "conceiving imagination."

The most rewarding development in the "new" History—though as with
so many of the others, it is not really very new—is the emergence of what,
for want of a better term, we call cultural anthropology: a combination of

what the Germans, who have more names for these things, called *Kulturgeschichte* and *Sittengeschichte*. It is difficult to know whether cultural anthropology, as now cultivated, is closer to "culture" or to "anthropology." Both terms are, after all, so broad that they can be made to cover almost everything, for anthropology is defined as "the science of man," and culture as "the sum total of ways of living built up by human beings." Traditionally we have thought of anthropology as having to do with primitive or early man, and of culture in its older definition as "enlightenment" or "refinement." The eighteenth century, which really inaugurated cultural anthropology, did indeed conceive of its inquiry in this fashion: the Lafitaus, the Raynals, the Falconers, and their associates, in the discovery and interpretation of the peoples of New Worlds, were fascinated by the primitive and were primarily concerned with problems of "refinement" and "enlightenment." So, too, in a sense, more sophisticated historians such as Montesquieu and Voltaire and even Johann Gottfried von Herder either imposed a high degree of culture on their primitive peoples or rejected them if they had no culture to submit. But modern cultural anthropology does not judge primitive societies by those of modern Europe, nor does it seek out such formal aspects of culture as are to be found in literature, the arts, or politics. It is prepared to accept each culture, whether of the Trobriand Islanders, the Pueblo Indians, or the inhabitants of Haute-Savoie or of Akenfield in East Anglia, on its own merits, as sufficient, unique, and of equal interest to the student.

The philosophical roots of cultural anthropology are in the eighteenth century, its historical (and some of its scientific) roots in the nineteenth, and the methodological and technical in the twentieth. Each era—the Enlightenment, romanticism, the modern age—made its own contribution; and so did each of the great seminal ideas of the past two centuries—the idea of reason, the principle of progress, evolution, materialism, and—perhaps most influential of all—Freudian psychiatry.

Because the Enlightenment believed that men were (or should be) everywhere the same, they were ill-equipped to appreciate or sympathize with profound differences in the societies that their navigators and explorers revealed to them. Indeed, they imposed European standards upon those societies. Montesquieu's Persian (of the famous *Persian Letters*) was really only Montesquieu's alter ego; the Baron de Lahontan's Huron chief, Adario, was really a *philosophe,* as was Diderot's venerable Tahitian chief Orau, who confounded the seminarians with his wisdom; Macpherson's Ossian was a Celtic Homer, and when Sir Joseph Banks brought Omai from Tahiti to London, he dressed him in brown velvet and ruffled lace and taught him the arts of the courtier.

Not surprisingly, the Americans proved better able to understand and appreciate primitive peoples than did the Europeans; after all, they knew them not by some chance encounter or romantic fancy, but by daily and familiar intercourse. Lafitau's famous *Customs of the American Savages*

Compared to Those of Ancient Times, notwithstanding its romantic non-sense about the Greeks and the Trojans, nevertheless described the Hurons as they actually were and as they lived, with considerable faithfulness, as did the 73 volumes of the Canadian *Jesuit Relations,* which remain one of the great storehouses of cultural anthropology. Elsewhere, too, in the voluminous literature of eighteenth-century America—John Lawson's pioneering *New Voyage to Carolina* (1709), for example, or Cadwallader Colden's *History of the Five Indian Nations* (1775), or Alexander Henry's *Travels in Canada 1760–1766* (1809), or Jefferson's *Notes on Virginia,* written in 1781—we see realistic pictures of Indian life and society almost (though not wholly) free from Enlightenment preconceptions about either the primitiveness or the nobility of the savages.

More than any other commentator from the eighteenth century, it was Jean de Crèvecoeur who anticipated much of modern cultural anthropology with his analysis of the ways in which the European becomes an American: how he raises children who can marry whom they please, live where they please, work at what they please; how he discovers and then vindicates equality; how he finds happiness; how the frontier both liberates and brutalizes; how the conflict between Indian and white plunges even the best of men into barbarism.

Inspired by romanticism but disciplined by historical training, a new school of cultural history emerged in Germany and its neighboring countries in the middle years of the nineteenth century. Wilhelm Heinrich von Riehl was its leader and its spokesman. He had the perspicacity to see in the history of the primitive Germans the matrix for the highly sophisticated German civilization of modern times; he studied the folklore and folktales, the superstitions, faiths, and customs of the early Germans and saw what these had hinged on, consciously or unconsciously, through the centuries. At mid-century he produced his multivolumed *National History of the People as the Basis for German Social Politics.* In Switzerland, one of his followers, Otto Henne-am-Rhyn, turned out a prodigious number of scholarly studies in sociological history: cultural histories of women, of the Jews, of the Crusades, of the German people, a study of German folktales, and so forth. A few more years and the powerful Karl Lamprecht dominated the historical scene—Lamprecht, whose nineteen-volume *German History* purported to deal with "the collective work of humanity" in accordance with current sociological laws.

The most impressive and original contribution to cultural anthropology in the nineteenth century was doubtless Troels-Lund's fourteen volumes on *Daily Life in the North in the Sixteenth Century.* This great work, which combined scholarship, literary style, imagination, and skill, covered the whole range of those activities that went to make up the daily life of the common people: housing, clothing, food, religious beliefs, games and pastimes, birth, marriage, death. Based almost entirely on archival research, it did not inquire closely into such matters as sexual behavior, which loom so large in modern cultural anthropology, nor did it trace myths and superstitions into their current re-creations.

Even more profound and penetrating, though not so *consciously* in the realm of cultural anthropology, is the astonishing tour de force by Alexis de Tocqueville, *Democracy in America* (1835–40). How striking it is that this book which, by common consent, is the most profound ever written about America, should also be the very paradigm for so much of modern cultural anthropology—striking and paradoxical. For Tocqueville did not really know America; his interpretation was not inductive but deductive, and based on a visit of only six months or so. But he was supremely intelligent, and he had the perspicacity to seize upon a theme that was both central and pervasive: the principle of equality. This theme he pursued into every nook and cranny of American life that Victorian standards of reticence permitted him to investigate: language, law, the family, the position of women, the pampering of children, class divisions, the uses of history and of biography, social characteristics, national vanity, curiosity and conformism; attitudes toward war and peace and violence. In doing all this, he gathered just the kind of data that fascinates the modern cultural anthropologist.

These works indicated that the Enlightenment's conception of humanity was giving way to one that was both wider and more receptive. But it still (with a few exceptions such as Tocqueville's work) preferred the distant in time and space; it took refuge, more often than not, in deductive reasoning rather than observation; and it still scrupulously avoided subjects that might offend the somewhat rigid standards of good taste.

The breakthrough to modern cultural anthropology came around the turn of the century—that watershed for so many of the behavioral sciences—with the early editions of James Frazer's *Golden Bough* (the twelve-volume edition was not completed until 1915), William Graham Sumner's astonishing *Folkways* (1907), and the work of a new school of students of American Indian culture whose inspiration was Lewis Morgan (*Ancient Society*, 1877) and whose intellectual mentor was the great Columbia University savant, Franz Boas. From this pioneer group are descended most of the leading masters of the new science of the twentieth century: Bronislaw Malinowski, whose studies of the sexual life of the Trobriand Islanders in 1914–18 revolutionized field research; Alfred Kroeber, whose voluminous writings embraced the whole of anthropology for forty years; Ruth Benedict, who moved out from studies of the American Indian societies to analyze all *Patterns of Culture* (1934), and to write a classic interpretation of the Japanese character, *The Chrysanthemum and the Sword* (1946); Karl Llewellyn, who brought immense legal learning to the study of the legal practices and institutions of the Indians of the American southwest; and Margaret Mead, who more skillfully than any of her contemporaries has applied to American social mores the lessons she learned in New Guinea and Samoa and other primitive societies, as in *And Keep Your Powder Dry* and *Male and Female* (1942 and 1949).

What is new about the cultural anthropology of our day that distinguishes it from the social and cultural history of the past two centuries? First, perhaps, that at last it is doing what historians and sociologists long promised to do, but rarely did: depicting the daily lives of ordinary people at every level of civilization. Over a century ago Ralph Waldo Emerson said, in his address on the American Scholar:

> *I ask not for the great, the remote, the romantic . . . I embrace the common, I explore and sit at the feet of the familiar, the low. . . . What would we really know the meaning of? The meal in the firkin; the milk in the pan; the ballad in the street; the news of the boat; the glance of the eye; the form and the gait of the body . . . let me see every trifle bristling with the polarity that ranges it instantly on an eternal law; and the shop, the plough, and the ledger referred to the like cause by which light undulates and poets sing . . . .*[24]

Where the cultural historians of the past—and the attitude has not wholly disappeared—generally thought of culture in terms of Beautiful Letters, or Fine Art, or Profound Philosophy, or Higher Education, the new cultural anthropologists tend to ignore these activities entirely, and to concentrate rather on the simple, the homely, and the commonplace—the habits of nursing and of weaning babies, toilet training, play and games, the greatly varied relationships of children to parents and to siblings, the rites of puberty and the conventions of adolescence, sexual conventions and habits, food and cooking, shelter and sleeping habits, the division of labor, the treatment of the aged, the weapons and tools in daily use, art, ritual, superstition—these and a hundred similar experiences of all peoples.

Second, borrowing perhaps from Freudian psychiatry, the cultural anthropologists see in primitive peoples the intellectual and moral ancestors of modern or civilized societies, realize that what is overt and conscious in primitive society lingers on as covert and unconscious in the most sophisticated of peoples, and decide that therefore the study of primitive beliefs and superstitions illuminates and even explains the psychological life of individuals and societies in our own day. The most important contribution here was in the study of myth and superstition, a study firmly launched by Frazer in his classic, *The Golden Bough,* and now assiduously pursued by the most gifted of living students of primitive mythology, Claude Levi-Strauss.

Third, modern students of cultural anthropology do not differentiate between "primitive" and "civilized" societies, but accept each society as independent, unique, and possessed of a culture as self-sufficient as that of the highly sophisticated societies of the West. What this means is that the anthropologists neither condescend to the societies they study nor try to change them, but rather try to learn from them. What this customarily involves is a sharp departure from the library-oriented researches of a Troels-Lund or a Frazer. Ever since Malinowski—indeed for that matter since the American, Lewis Morgan—anthropologists get out into the field, live, sometimes for years, with their primitive tribes, and try to enter into their minds as they enter into their ways of life.

Fourth—and perhaps most profitable, as it is certainly most interesting— the cultural anthropologist of our time brings to the study of the character of Western societies the same insights, tools, and techniques that he (or more often she) employs for the study of primitive societies. It is here that cultural anthropology departs most dramatically from the cultural and intellectual History that obtained all through the nineteenth and twentieth centuries: the sort of thing familiar in Leslie Stephen's classic *English Thought in the Eighteenth Century,* or Georg Brandes' great six-volume study of *Main Currents in Nineteenth Century Literature,* or B. Sprague Allen's *Tides in English Taste,* or Paul Hazard's *European Thought in the Eighteenth Century* or Vernon L. Parrington's glowing *Main Currents in American Thought.* For the Ruth Benedicts and the Margaret Meads and the Geoffrey Gorers and their colleagues are not as interested in formal "thought" as they are in habits, customs, superstitions, and practices— in precisely those things that Emerson listed, but by no means only in those things. They are interested in the way the Russians and the Japanese raise their babies, in the differences in play patterns between American children and Chinese, in the significance of the "inner-directed" and the "outer-directed" individual, in the pressures that exaggerate individualism and competitiveness and those that discourage these traits, in dating patterns and sex patterns among the young (and among the old, too)—in these and a thousand similar indices to national character.

In all this inquiry segments of society heretofore neglected—children and women, the poor, the humble, the ignorant, even the delinquent—are accorded the place of honor, and the great and powerful and learned are regarded as interesting chiefly in relation to the deference or disdain with which society regards them. Many European visitors to America in the nineteenth century had the perspicacity to see something of the significance of the American attitude toward children; it has remained for the cultural anthropologists to place the child everywhere in the very center of the social stage, and a notable literature—ranging from Margaret Mead's *Growing Up in New Guinea* and *Coming of Age in Samoa* to Erik Erikson's profound study of *Childhood and Society;* from Philippe Ariès' *Centuries of Childhood* to Robert Coles's mordant volumes on the impact of poverty on American children of our own time, *Children of Crisis*—has emerged in the past two decades. And thanks in large part to the influence of Freud, and to the growing permissiveness of our society, subjects long excluded from polite literature, even scholarly literature, now command most conspicuous attention. Where Victorian educational literature, for all its preoccupation with the importance of physical culture and of the notion of *mens sana in corpore sano,* never mentioned sex or the reproductive system, much of the literature on childhood and adolescence today sometimes seems to mention nothing else. Sex provided the clue for Malinowski's studies of the people of the South Seas; sex was a prominent part of G. Stanley Hall's four volumes on *Adolescence;* sex was the chief theme of Margaret Mead's *Male and Female;* sex is pervasive for the interpretation of the American character in Francis K. Hsu's remarkable *Americans and Chinese* (1970). And it can be argued that the most influential and possibly the most valuable contribution to cultural anthropology of our time are the Kinsey reports that have been mentioned earlier.

V Philosophy and history

History has no philosophy, but historians do. Whatever philosophy is found in History has first been put there by some historian, or perhaps by some philosopher. When the historian purports to discover laws or principles of history, they invariably turn out to be laws and principles of his own making and application; when the philosopher reads some purpose into history, it is his own script that he is reading.

History, Denis Diderot said, is the other world of the philosopher. Turn this around and it is equally true: philosophy is the other world of the historian. Philosophy is to history what theology is to morals, and it has, too, much of the mystery, the complexity, and the special vocabulary of theology. Some historians yearn for this other world: they are perhaps the orthodox. Some merely toy with the possibility of its existence; they are the agnostics. Some are materialists who do not believe in any world not familiar to the sensations; they are the atheists. Some are dilettanti who simply do not care, one way or the other; they are the entertainers.

What is striking is that so few of those whom we think of as formal, orthodox, or professional historians have concerned themselves with the philosophy of history or, for that matter, with the methodology of history. The problems that agitated a Hegel, a Fichte, a Dilthey, a Croce, or a Karl Jaspers do not concern them, not consciously in any event. Even the sophisticated techniques and the self-conscious methods set forth in the shelf of handbooks that all students are supposed to ponder, they brush aside or ignore. Great historians like Macaulay, Lecky, Tocqueville, Guizot, Sybel, Troels-Lund, Parkman, and Henry Adams take what is called methodology in their stride, confident that it is simply the common sense of the matter—as indeed it is. Mostly they take the "philosophy of history" in their stride, too, confident that if there is any such thing it will emerge, in its own way, from what they write—as indeed it almost always does.

It is little wonder that almost all speculation about the philosophy of history comes from the philosophers rather than from historians, and that such speculation as does come from historians comes from those who do not write History or, as with Henry Adams, who begin to speculate only after they have abandoned the writing of History. If we fasten our attention on the great historical writers from Thucydides to Gibbon, from Mommsen to Churchill, we are impressed with how many of them got along without any formal historical philosophy and with how little they have to say about it. The great creative historians of the past took philosophy for granted. This is precisely what Professor Bernard Bailyn of Harvard University said of himself and his generation, that

> *in so far as my concern has been with understanding, teaching and writing about what has happened in the past, I have never once felt it necessary to work out precise answers to questions of objectivity and subjectivity, the nature of fact, etc., in order to advance my work in history. . . . Though I have discussed with other historians such matters (as the problems of the philosophy of history) I have never yet heard from them, either, a statement to the effect that their work in history has been affected one way or another by such considerations.*

This situation is by no means unique to history; it obtains generally where philosophers appear to impose themselves, or their importunate demands, upon practitioners. Great composers from Bach to Beethoven paid little attention to philosophers of music or even to musicologists. Practising artists from Giotto to the impressionists did not concern themselves greatly with what the philosophers of art submitted, though Joshua Reynolds with his annual *Discourses* on art, Whistler, or Robert Henri are of course exceptions. Poets and novelists, who are habituated to reading, doubtless read literary critics and philosophers, but it may be doubted that they conform to them or are greatly influenced by them. Clearly the situation in the social sciences is different. Economists and sociologists have long been fascinated by and dependent on theory and methodology; doubtless it is this very different training and discipline that accounts for their impatience with the current state of history.

In one sense, of course, all historians, like all thoughtful and articulate men, are philosophers. History, like religion, art, and literature, is imbued with philosophy, because all who think about it or contribute to it profess a point of view, an attitude, a body of convictions, or at least what William James called "can't help but believes." The trouble with talking about these is obvious enough: every thoughtful historian has his own "philosophy," and we cannot talk about all of them. We can, however, put some of them in groups and consider them collectively. Let us then put aside philosophies of history, which are the business of philosophers, and discuss the beliefs—call them philosophical if you will—that many historians actually hold.

Perhaps the historian is closer to the lawyer than to any other professional interpreter. The lawyer and the judge reconstruct the past, whether of an automobile accident, a crime, or a tort. They cannot recover the whole of the past, nor can any court or jury; all are confronted by gaps in the evidence, by witnesses who disagree or who are interested parties, or by stupidity or blundering. Neither lawyers nor judges can ever be really sure of their facts, or that they have all the relevant evidence. Like historians, they have to take a good deal on faith; they have to fill in the gaps from their own imagination; they have to make judgments about character; and they have to test evidence and arguments by precedents. What they finally arrive at is not ultimate justice or ultimate truth but an approximation of both. But unless both judge and jury are incompetent or corrupt, what they arrive at is usually acceptable and enables both the court and society to get on with the job. Yet all know that neither the findings nor even the principles that courts pronounce are final, that new evidence may crop up, that new points of view—philosophies if you will— will put a different face on many things, invalidate old opinions and create new ones. Clearly law is neither a science nor a philosophy; just as clearly it uses scientific methods, and incorporates the philosophies of judges and jurisprudents. And as the American experience has made clear, the best training for the law is not the study of legal theories or philosophies, but the case method.

Doubtless the quickest way to get at the philosophy of history is the same as that of getting at the philosophy of law—it is to turn to the thing itself. This is something that philosophers who write about the subject are loathe to do. It is only when historians such as Trevelyan, Nevins, Rowse, Marc Bloch, or C. V. Wedgwood turn their attention to historiography that *History* gets into the picture. It may be asserted that we cannot talk seriously about History until we know what it is, and that to discuss particular histories, such as those by Gibbon or Mommsen or Namier, is simply to beg the question. But this is a confession of bankruptcy, for on this principle we cannot talk about philosophy or education or art, or anything very important. Carry this principle to its logical conclusion, and young men and poets will be debarred from talking about love until they can define it.

When the historian reconstructs a chapter of the past he tries to be what he calls *scientific,* and sometimes he flatters himself that even if he has not achieved scientific accuracy he has achieved objectivity. The will-o-the-wisp of scientific History bemused the great Leopold von Ranke and his disciples for more than a hundred years. Needless to say, no historian is, or can be, truly scientific in the sense that a chemist or a physicist can be objective and scientific. Every historian is not only conditioned by but dominated by his own fate, and none has ever been able to surmount that fate. I have in mind not ostentatious prejudices, but built-in conditions. Almost every historian with whom we are acquainted, past or present, is civilized rather than primitive, European rather than Asian or African, white (or recently, in the United States, black) rather than red, yellow, or brown, and a product of the Christian-Judaic tradition. He was until recently male rather than female (is there a single memorable female historian before Madame de Stael?) and, of course, mature rather than young or adolescent. These basic conditions are as decisive in the interpretation of history as nationality or party, for all that they are mostly unconscious and taken for granted.

It is elementary considerations of this kind that make so many of the solemn philosophies of history irrelevant. After all, those who formulated such philosophies, which have presented history as the working out of the will of God, or of *Zeitgeist,* or of the principle of progress, were in every instance Western white men brought up in a particular—and therefore parochial—tradition. The God who guided the destinies of man turned out to be a Christian God, usually even a Catholic; the absolutes and universals of Hegel turned out to be not merely European but German; theories of progress were not based on a study of the Aztec or the Inca civilization or even of the Chinese but on that of western Europe. In the overwhelming majority of instances, universal History has been no more universal than our much-touted "world series" is really global. Almost alone among modern philosophers of history—perhaps of all philosophers of history—Arnold Toynbee has sought to embrace all civilizations in his theory. But the philosophers, alas, have no use for Mr. Toynbee.

The philosophy of history then turns out to be the philosophy of the historians who write it. Does this leave us with a thousand different philosophies of history? It does, indeed. Fortunately, historians, like critics and artists, tend to arrange themselves into somewhat disorderly patterns and we can deal with them as groups, ignoring the more pronounced idiosyncrasies. Carlyle and Michelet were not really alike, but they are forever linked together in studies of romanticism and of cultural nationalism, and so too with Prescott and Motley in the United States, or Sybel and Treitschke in Germany. We know that not all nineteenth-century German historians were followers of Ranke, and that not all modern English historians are disciples of Sir Lewis Namier—far from it—yet we speak of a Ranke school and a Namier school and, what is more, we can count on a pretty general understanding of these terms.

If we reject the notion that laws or philosophies are inherent in the stuff of history and embrace instead the assumption that groups, or schools, of historians display a preference for one or another approach to history, we can get on with the job. For now our inquiry is directed not to the hopeless task of discovering philosophies of history, but to the more rewarding task of finding attitudes toward history, and to understanding the uses that different schools or periods make of History—uses that illuminate the character and philosophy of the whole generation that is involved. This approach is familiar enough in belles lettres, let us say, or in art or music. It has been applied to historiography by a distinguished group of scholar-philosophers, including Cassirer, Croce, Dilthey, Max Weber, Meinecke, Collingwood, and Isaiah Berlin. With many of these men it has been subordinate to something else—literature or philosophy or sociology. But the study of historiography illuminates History itself; it not only interprets culture, it is part of the culture it interprets.

In a broad way we can discern two persistent and overarching *uses* of History from the beginnings of formal historical writing to our own time. The first and incomparably the oldest and the most distinguished is that which we associate with Dionysius of Halicarnassus: History as philosophy teaching by examples. The second, which has had many champions, and which was very much in the ascendent in the past century, as it is still in our own time, is History as the comprehensive reconstruction of the past.

There are, needless to say, many subsidiary conceptions of History. One of these held the field for some centuries without opposition or challenge: History as the unfolding of God's plan for man. Few are now prepared to entertain this theory in any but a symbolic sense, and even if it were true, there would be little to say about it except "Amen." A second merits only a word, but an amiable word: it is History as entertainment. This is the oldest use of literary History (as distinct from genealogical or dynastic tables), and it is one of the things that keeps History going. It is why children read History, usually in the form of poems or hero stories; it is why the majority of adults read History, too, usually in the form of historical novels like *Gone With the Wind* or plays like *Macbeth,* or why they listen to History through such television plays as those dealing with Queen Elizabeth or the wives of Henry VIII. Scorn not the popular History, the historical novel, the historical drama, the television re-creation of some great chapter of the past! Winston Churchill, one of the great historians of our age, said that he learned all of his English history from Shakespeare. While that of course was an exaggeration, the important thing is that he thought it worth saying.

But consider what has been the most persistent use of History: History as philosophy teaching by examples. According to this notion, the purpose and end of History was to discover those grand moral laws that man should know, and knowing, should obey. This was the search that sent the eighteenth-century historians and, in America especially, the statesmen, back to the ancient world and persuaded them to reflect on the rise and the decline of empires, the dangers of power, the fickleness of the public, and the inestimable value of freedom. It was what persuaded them to study the Orient, Europe, America, the islands of the Pacific, to contemplate primitive as well as civilized man. All particular histories were like tributaries, each carrying its own sediment of truth and morality and pouring it into the mainstream of history, where the historians could dredge it up. "The course of things has always been the same," wrote Lord Bolingbroke, who brought the axiom of Dionysius up to date. "National virtue and national vice have always produced national happiness and national misery." And the great David Hume added pontifically (as became him) that "mankind are so much the same, in all times and places, that history informs us of nothing new or strange in this particular. Its chief use is only to discover the constant and universal principles of human nature." [25]

Clearly the American Founding Fathers subscribed to this principle. All of them were immersed in history, especially the history of the ancient world. Almost all of them wrote History, though not under that rubric; they called their histories *Notes on Virginia* or the *Federalist Papers* or *The Rights of Man*. It was on history that they drew to justify independence, to guide them along the paths of federalism, to provide examples for every experiment and warnings against every danger that lurked in the shadows. Washington drew on history when he warned his fellow countrymen against the baleful influence of factions and parties; Jefferson when he denounced the tyranny of the Alien and Sedition laws, Madison when he undertook to justify and to illustrate the arguments of the *Federalist Papers*. Nor did this deep-engrained habit end with the generation of Jefferson. Lincoln began his Gettysburg Address with a reminder of what had happened four score and seven years ago, and Wilson was thinking as an historian when he called America "the world's best hope." And Winston Churchill tells us, in one of the most moving passages of his *Second World War*, that when he heard the news of the attack on Pearl Harbor, he knew that Britain would survive. "I had studied the American Civil War, fought out to the last desperate inch. . . . I went to bed and slept the sleep of the saved." [26]

The drawbacks and inadequacies of regarding History as philosophy whose business it is to teach by examples were serious ones. It meant that you studied history solely with a view to satisfying current interests, selecting from the great storehouse of the past only such events as you believed might throw a lurid light on the problems of the moment. It encouraged subjective interpretations of history, for the history it allowed you to select was the history that appealed to you, and it let you reject as trivial all that did not fit into the needs of the moment. It aggravated the almost universal inclination to partisanship and distortion, since it used History as polemic. It violated not only the canons of good scholarship but, curiously enough, of morality as well (curiously because its inspiration was moral), for it assumed that the end justified the means. If the end was *Ecraser l'infâme,* for example, or to prove that George III was a tyrant who proposed to subdue his loyal Americans to abject slavery, then you could play fast and loose with the facts with a clear conscience.

Nevertheless, History seems seldom if ever to have been able to get along without a moral dimension. Some of the greatest historical writing is evidence of this. Thucydides had moral aims, and so did Tacitus; Voltaire thought of History as a vehicle for teaching morality, and so did—far less zealously—Edward Gibbon. Our own day, as we shall see, is witnessing a curious revival of this moral aspect of History, which took one form of expression in Dilthey and Croce and Charles A. Beard, and a very different one in Arnold Toynbee.

Even as Voltaire and Gibbon were writing their great works of historical morality, two obscure historians, Giambattista Vico down in Naples and Justus Möser in the little town of Osnabrück in northern Germany, were laying the foundations for what was to be the dominant philosophy and method of History for the next two centuries. That was what came to be called historicism, or scientific History, or historical realism. Its purpose was simple enough: to reconstruct the past as it was, and to find out what actually happened; its method was to amass all the available source material that illuminated any one chapter of history—the history of Osnabrück for example—and then let the facts "speak for themselves"; its philosophy was to see the past through the eyes of the past, not through the eyes of the present, and to judge by the standards of the past, not of the present. And the "noble dream" that inspired this numerous and distinguished body of historians was that with these purposes and these methods they might lift History from the level of "mere" literature and raise it to the dignity of a science.

The driving force of much of this new historicism was the familiar and legitimate one of curiosity about the past—the same force that has motivated so much of scientific research from the beginnings of modern science. Out of the passion of the scientist to penetrate the secrets of nature and of the universe has come an increasing mastery of nature. Sometimes this results from a deliberate attack upon a single problem, as with the long and triumphant attack on the problem of poliomyelitis; sometimes it is an unexpected by-product of research, as in much of physics.

Needless to say, the new historical school, for all its affluent achievements, did not reduce History to a science, did not reconstruct the whole of the past as it actually happened, and did not solve the problem of causation. The failure was not in the historians, many of them men of towering scholarship and literary genius: Ranke himself, for example, "the cow from whom they drew all their milk"; or Mommsen, who encompassed the history of the whole of the ancient world with incomparable learning; or Frederic Maitland, who explained the origins of English law with marvelous learning and subtlety; or Henry Adams, whose nine volumes of the history of the Jefferson and Madison administrations set standards of literary scholarship not yet surpassed. No, the failure was inherent in the enterprise itself. It is impossible ever to reconstruct the whole of the past—impossible and undesirable, for a lifetime would not be sufficient to read all the thousands of millions of "facts" about the French Revolution alone. It is impossible for the past to reconstruct itself in meaningful patterns, for facts do not arrange themselves in any patterns at all: they are a chaos that only the historian, by a process of rigorous selection and of arbitrary organization, can whip into shape. It is impossible for facts to "speak for themselves." Facts never speak for themselves; they speak only through the historian who selects them, and no historian can overcome the limitations that the circumstances of his life, his time, his language, his race, his faith, have imposed upon him. And the problem of causation is as far from solution as it was when it bemused the philosophers of ancient Greece. Nor would History have survived as such if the problem had been solved. As Charles A. Beard, the severest American critic of the "noble dream" of scientific History once said:

> If a science of history were achieved it would, like the science of celestial mechanics, make possible the calculable prediction of the future in history. It would bring the totality of historical occurrences within a single field, and reveal the unfolding future to its last end, including all the apparent choices made and to be made. It would be omniscience. The creator of it would possess the attributes ascribed by the theologians to God. The future once revealed, mankind would have nothing to do but await its doom.

Beard's solution of this problem of what to do with History was even less satisfactory than that of the historicists whom he so lustily belabored. Let us recognize, he said, that all of History is controlled by the frame of reference in the mind of the historian. Let the historian acknowledge his frame of reference—that is, his bias and his values—and let him frankly use History to "throw light on the quandaries of our life today" and to facilitate "readjustment and reform." In this sense he agreed with Croce that all History is contemporary History because it exists in the mind of the historian, and that therefore the past that the historian sees or recreates is a contemporary view of the past. History then should use the past—

indeed it cannot avoid doing so—to understand and direct those great forces that will determine the future of man.

But is this not merely a sophisticated version of the familiar principle that History is philosophy teaching by examples? The moderns look with misgivings on the term *philosophy* (not Beard himself but most of his followers), and they reject the simplistic examples that can teach specific lessons, but like the Bolingbroke school they turn to the past to illuminate the present and to provide guidelines for the future. Like Voltaire and Montesquieu and Hume and John Adams, these moderns require that the past must be relevant—and indeed one may say that if all History is contemporary History, whatever history is studied is *per se* relevant. In all this they are immensely sophisticated. They are on their guard against the false analogy, they examine with scientific rigor the claims of the past, their attitudes are more critical, their techniques are more refined than those prevalent in the eighteenth century. But the ultimate purpose of the Croce-Dilthey-Beard school is not very different from that which animated the historians of the ancient world and of the Enlightenment.

We can turn now to a third use of History, one that differs fundamentally from the other two because it is not something formulated by historians to explain the past or to justify interest in the past, but an expression of the *Zeitgeist* in and through History. Since the eighteenth century, it is not only historians but educated people generally (and not always just the educated) who have used History to express their deepest interests, aspirations, and values. They have used History as they have used imaginative literature or art, to explain and to justify themselves. In this enterprise all forms of History are grist to their mill: History as song, story, drama, myth, biography, painting, polemic, or even, as with the Nazis, History as religion. Nowhere can students of the Enlightenment, for example, find better statements of what we call Enlightenment principles than in the vast body of historical writings—much of which would be excluded from that category today and assigned to more specialized categories of geography, ethnology, mythology, and philosophy. In their eagerness to exalt reason, establish order, and achieve happiness, they wrote (and of course read) histories or interpretations of China, Tahiti, and the American Indians, where—in dramatic contrast to the European world—reason flourished and order triumphed and men were happy. In their zeal to expose the infamy of church and the tyranny of government and the ruthlessness of the military and the immorality of the class system in their own lands, they conjured up ideal societies where religion was rational and government mild, where peace flourished and all men were equal. More often than not these societies were imaginary—in some curious land like *Australis Incognita* or on an island in the Pacific or on the moon or even underground—but the imagination not only illuminates history but is part of it. Increasingly these ideal societies were laid in or assigned to America, and increasingly Americans adopted the myths as real and even tried to live up to them and make them come true. In their passion for happiness the historians of the Enlightenment fashioned myths about a golden day, or the noble savage, or Utopia. They even concocted myths about the economy—the physiocratic myth about the relation of happiness and virtue to the soil, for example—or about childhood, as to which Rousseau was a myth-maker whose *Émile* would be transformed into reality by great educators from Johann Heinrich Pestalozzi and Friedrich Froebel to Jane Addams and John Dewey.

It is in History—if we remember to use that term broadly enough to embrace politics and law and science—better than elsewhere that we can read what Americans of Jefferson's generation thought of the nature of man and the relation of man to society and government. Almost all the Founding Fathers were historians, though none acknowledged that title: Jefferson with his *Notes on Virginia* and his great state papers, Tom Paine with *Common Sense* and *The Rights of Man,* John Adams with his voluminous *Defense of the Constitutions of Government of the United States,* Madison and Hamilton and Jay with the *Federalist Papers,* James Wilson with his lectures on the Constitution, Dr. Benjamin Rush with his medical essays, Noah Webster with his relentless stream of spellers and readers. It is in these and similar books that we can trace those theories of progress so different from the European, understand those ideas of freedom and justice so much bolder than any advanced in the Old World, and those hopes for frustrating the innate depravity of man and for eventually creating a social order that would nourish man's innate virtue. It is through their historical and political writings, too, that we come to understand the growth of the extraordinary notion that America was unique and therefore exempt from the vicissitudes and the ravages of history—an idea that has persisted and has contributed greatly to that curious combination of isolationism and imperialism that has been characteristic of American nationalism.

Students of romanticism can turn with even livelier expectations to the historians and their literature, for these not only recorded the spread of romanticism but contributed to it and were themselves an integral part of it; imagine writing about romanticism and leaving out Carlyle or Michelet! Those great romantic historians studied history only to come away with their deepest convictions about national and ethnic qualities confirmed by the evidence; they wrote History to indulge those convictions. They turned to the same past that had attracted Gibbon or Voltaire, but they read from it the lesson that Providence had intended men to organize into national states and to employ them as instruments for preserving the language, the culture, the law, the literature, the social institutions, and the moral principles peculiar to each people. The romantic historians studied the same art, literature, and philosophy that the *philosophes* had read, but unlike them, they discovered that men were not everywhere the same but everywhere different, and they concluded, *vive la différence!* They reflected not the static order of the Age of Reason, but the organic and dynamic order of Charles Lyell and Charles Darwin. Where their predecessors had been bemused by man, by society, and by humanity, they celebrated the individual.

One last word remains to be said about "technical" History. It is still too soon to know what the cultural historian will make of this, for it is only now developing its own character, as it were. Yet we can see already how naturally technical History fits into and mirrors our own era. It tends to reject meaning, design, and purpose at a time when much literature and art reject those things. It rejects the notion that History can or should wrest moral lessons from the past, because it does not really believe in moral lessons. It looks with scepticism on the notion of progress, as our age has questioned or even rejected that notion. It confesses an attachment to the technical, the mathematical, and the mechanical, and thus reflects the passion of our generation for processes, statistics, and machines. It is fascinated by impersonal processes, abstractions, and concepts rather than by actual events or actual people; it distrusts individual biography but delights in demographic studies. In all this it reflects something of our current psychology: the passion of art for the abstract and nonrepresentational; of literature for the non-novel, the non-hero, and the non-plot; of music for sounds that seem miscellaneous and chaotic rather than harmonious; of criticism that concentrates on grammar rather than on content; and of the films that have borrowed from Joyce and Virginia Woolf the once-popular stream-of-consciousness technique.

VI On causation

The problem of causation is the oldest in History, the most importunate, and the most inscrutable.

Felix qui potuit rerum cognoscere causas! Happy indeed, and as all men strive for happiness, all thinking men seek to find the causes of things. This is the *ignis fatuus* that glimmers forever before the eyes of the philosopher and the historian. This is what leads them down labyrinthine ways to seek out the curious, the fortuitous, the catastrophic, that they might somehow explain why things turned out as they have. This it is that persuades them to formulate great laws of history, laws that accommodate man to the will of Providence at one extreme, to the "forces of stellar universe" at the other—two accommodations that work out to be pretty much the same thing. Countless philosophers, over the centuries, have bemused themselves with the belief that they had indeed found the causes of things, but—since the Middle Ages, anyway—few have been able to persuade their fellows, much less future generations, that their findings are conclusive. Most students, certainly those of our own time, would subscribe to the confession of the great English historian H. A. L. Fisher:

> *One intellectual excitement has been denied me. Men wiser and more learned than I have discovered in history a plot, a rhythm, a predetermined pattern. These harmonies are concealed from me. I can see only one emergency following upon another as wave follows upon wave; only one great fact with respect to which, since it is unique, there can be no generalizations; only one safe rule for the historian, that he should recognize in the development of human destinies the play of the contingent and the unforeseen.*[27]

Clearly this does not mean that the historian should abandon the task of seeking the causes of things and take refuge either in the doctrine of fortuity or of determinism. As a greater and more profound historian than Fisher wrote, after a lifetime devoted first to writing, and then to interpreting history:

> *To the tired student, the idea that he must give it up seemed sheer senility. As long as he could whisper, he would go on as he had begun, bluntly refusing to meet his creator with the admission that the creation had taught him nothing. . . . Every man with self-respect enough to become effective . . . has had to account to himself for himself somehow, and to invent a formula of his own for his universe. . . .*[28]

The business of the historian, after all, is neither to entertain (important as that is) nor to describe (useful as that sometimes is). It is to ask questions and to try to answer them, or if not to answer, then to illuminate them. These questions occur at three levels of inquiry that are inextricably interrelated: what happened, how did it happen, and why did it happen? The vast majority of the questions are technical—how many people voted in a particular election? What were the casualties in the Civil War? At what age did girls marry in colonial Plymouth?—and designed to provide the basis for further inquiries. To answer them does not make either great History or a great historian, any more than to read a musical score accurately makes for great music or a great musician. Certain other questions, dealing with the "how" in history, require somewhat more sophistication, just as to put together the musical notes into the pattern of a sonata or a symphony requires sophistication. How did Napoleon plan the campaign of Waterloo? How did John Marshall use the courts to cement American nationalism? How did pioneers manage to recreate civilized societies on countless frontiers? Most of these questions can be answered to general if not universal satisfaction; that is really what we mean when we say that a particular piece of historical writing is "definitive."

The really interesting questions are those for which there are no "definitive" answers. Why were the Chinese a thousand years ahead of the West in civilization? Why did so few natives of America achieve any kind of civilization before the coming of Europeans in the fifteenth century? Why did the Roman Empire decline and "fall"; why were the Arabs able to conquer much of Africa and Europe, and why did Arab power decline so spectacularly after they had done so? What explains the rise of modern nationalism? Why did the Americans revolt against the mother country and how did they manage to set up an independent nation? Why did the Germans—the most civilized of peoples, one would suppose—embrace the barbarism of the Nazi regime? Why did Americans, with a long tradition of isolationism, plunge into Southeast Asia? And so on, almost *ad infinitum.*

As, in the nature of things, there can be no generally accepted answers to these and similar questions, it may be asserted that they are really not worth asking at all, and that historians should confine themselves to narrative, analysis, and reconstruction. This is fair enough, but it is irrelevant. There are no satisfactory answers to any of the great questions of "why"—questions of life and death, of good and evil, of beauty and truth. We do not know why man feels an irresistible compulsion to some form of worship or to express himself in art; we do not know why men have been willing, for centuries, to go to the stake for their beliefs or to fight and die for ideological abstractions; we do not know why we should cherish justice or freedom or charity. Religion often promises answers to these and similar questions, but the fact of 300 denominations, even in a single country, is sufficient commentary on the lack of general acceptance of the religious answers.

Yet if we cannot explain, in any ultimate way, why the Americans rebelled against the mother country, we can analyze the conditions that obtained in Britain and America and made the conduct of Americans reasonable. If we do not know precisely why the French Revolution began, we can point to certain things that help to explain why it caught on, and why, too, it was delivered into the hands of a Napoleon. If we cannot wholly explain either why the South rebelled against the United States or why the Confederacy lost the war, we can spell out the conditions for the rebellion and for ultimate defeat.

Those who are distressed at the looseness and vagueness of historical explanation make the mistake of supposing that it can, ideally, be like explanation in chemistry or in geology. They seem to think we can start with axioms, as we can in much of science, where two sides of a triangle will always be longer than the third side, and light invariably travels at a speed of 186,282 miles per second. But historical explanation is more like a moral or artistic explanation than a scientific one. It does not proceed from fixed truths. And this is because its data never stay put, as it were, and are never complete. It deals with the infinite vagaries of the human mind and spirit; it never has and never can have more than a small fragment of the facts; it cannot conduct experiments, as science can, by running history through some giant test tube; and its elements, or ingredients, can never be counted on to act in precisely the same way on any given number of occasions.

Baffled by the problem of causation, many students are tempted to take refuge in one of two extremes: what might be called the "Cleopatra's nose" theory and what might be called the "Rubáiyát" theory. "Had Cleopatra's nose been shorter," said Blaise Pascal, "the whole history of the world might have been different." This is the principle that appeals almost irresistibly to the uncritical mind: that all, really, depends on fortuity. But great events rarely if ever flow from accident or chance. Cleopatra fascinated Antony and Octavian, but the struggle for control of the East would have raged even without Cleopatra. Henry VIII lusted for Anne Boleyn, but that was not the reason he broke with the Church of Rome; the Reformation was already under way on the Continent, and would have come to England sooner or later. The winds scattered the Spanish Armada, but that was not why Spain failed to conquer England; no modern nation had ever conquered England. Washington surprised the Hessians at Trenton, and Benedict Arnold's plot to surrender West Point failed, but that was not why the Americans finally won their independence; even had the Hessians defeated Washington's ragged troops and Arnold's plot succeeded, the Americans would ultimately have won their independence. In 1784 Jefferson's attempt to bar slavery from the whole of the trans-Appalachian west failed by a single vote because one of the delegates from a key state was ill. It is difficult to believe that that was why slavery went into Alabama and Mississippi; no vote in the Continental Congress could have kept it out. Lee ordered Longstreet to attack at dawn on the fateful July 3, 1863; Longstreet procrastinated and the attack did not get under way until after Meade had moved his artillery onto the whole of Cemetery Ridge. That delay might have changed the outcome of Gettysburg, but not of the war; the explanation for the defeat of the Confederacy is rooted deeply in the existence of slavery itself.

These speculations about the "ifs" of history have bemused men for centuries. They are entirely natural. After all, this is the way most of us speculate about the past when we look back on it: what would have happened had I made this choice rather than that? These are not wholly

293

futile speculations, either, for they testify to the unwillingness of the mind to accept what happened as inevitable and they proclaim a faith that qualities of mind and character make a difference. They encourage a retroactive imagination that may function prospectively to the advantage of society, and a skepticism towards all those who would set history in rigid molds. Nor should our impatience with the escapism of fortuity blind us to the fact that chance does play a role in the fortunes of men. Chance is not—so we must believe—ultimately decisive, but again and again it breaks into the rhythm of history. England might well have gone over to the Reformation eventually; would it have gone over in the sixteenth century if it had not been for the willfulness of Henry VIII? The American colonies would doubtless have broken away from the mother country sooner or later; would they have won independence in 1781 had it not been for the resolution and courage and wisdom of George Washington? Britain might have withstood an invasion in 1941, and the United States might have come to her aid before she had been fatally weakened by bombardment and blockade, but it is difficult to see how the tide could have been turned and the war brought to a victorious conclusion without the indomitable courage and the inspired leadership of Winston Churchill. Speculations such as these seem even more valid when directed toward great occurrences of nature: surely the Black Death that swept Europe in the middle of the fourteenth century, the potato famine that afflicted Ireland in the 1840s, the blizzards that caught the Great Plains of the American west in an icy grip in the winter of 1888, left lasting marks on history.

But the "Rubáiyát" concept of historical causation is just as mistaken and perhaps more misleading than the Cleopatra's nose concept. We are all familiar with it:

> *The Moving Finger writes; and having writ,*
> *Moves on: nor all your Piety nor Wit*
> *Shall lure it back to cancel half a Line,*
> *Nor all your Tears wash out a Word of it.*[29]

True enough for the individual: William James made the same point in his wonderful essay on "Habit."[30] The trouble with determinism is that, embraced logically, it puts the historians (and for that matter the social scientists) out of business, for if everything is determined by climate and soil, social and economic forces, religious convictions or racial traits, or by fixed qualities in human nature and, presumably, in national character, then there is little use inquiring into causation in the past or speculating about the future. If the English peoples were bound to win out over the French or the Dutch or the Spanish in the "struggle for a continent," why devote twelve volumes to inquiring into the details of the victory, as Francis Parkman did? If the South was bound to lose the Civil War anyway, what is the point of the blow-by-blow account of every skirmish and every battle, every dispute between state and Confederate authorities, every step in the elaborate choreography of Confederate diplomacy?

But the objection to the principle of historical inevitability goes even deeper. It imposes, as it were, *ex post facto* rules on the past, judges its leading actors retroactively, and suggests that all those responsible for misreading the course of history were either fools or marplots. If, for example, it was clear from the beginning that the South had no chance of making good its bid for independence or for saving the anachronistic institution of slavery, how are we to explain why otherwise sensible, judicious, and honorable men like Jefferson Davis and Alexander Stephens and Judah P. Benjamin and Robert E. Lee were prepared to lead their "country" to certain defeat? If careful analysis—just such analysis as the historian makes today—proved beyond a doubt that defeat was inevitable, then those responsible for plunging the South into a hopeless war were guilty of criminal imbecility. But that is not only a mistaken conclusion, it is a worthless conclusion.

The sensible historian strikes a balance between these two explanations (or non-explanations) of history, and steers the barque of History between the Scylla of fortuity and the Charybdis of determinism. He rejects fortuity that would reduce History to a farrago of anecdote and gossip or hand his task over to some new Edward Johnson who can write a new *Wonder-Working Providence,* or to some new Michael Wigglesworth who can provide a new *Day of Doom.* He rejects determinism, which would reduce his task to that of recording the operation of great impersonal forces on a faceless and impotent society.

What the historian, like the dramatist, the novelist, the poet, the philosopher, is interested in is not so much ultimate causation, as explanation. Such explanation is to be found not in any one or even any four or five factors but in a combination of circumstances, considerations, influences, forces, so varied and so subtle that they almost elude recovery. The historian must blend these together with the skill and the patience and the imagination of the impressionist, rather than with a series of broad bravura strokes, allowing the light of knowledge and understanding to play on each of the thousands of touches of color that go to make the composite picture. He must take into account larger forces of geography, climate, natural resources; he must consider social institutions such as government, science, technology, church, and university; he must allow for accident and chance and fortuity; he must never neglect the individual, or groups of individuals, all with their infinite complexity; he may even be indulged in considering if not national "character," then national habits and traits. ("What kind of people does he take us for?" asked Winston Churchill when Hitler offered Britain peace without honor.)

All these and other ingredients provide the matrix in which History can take shape. Controlled, organized, and interpreted by a master craftsman—a Mommsen, let us say, a Maitland, a Parkman—such materials do not provide ultimate answers to all our questions, but they do provide a text that we can profitably read, and which will help us to formulate our own solutions.

That is the most we can do; that is also the least we can do. On this whole matter of seeking to know the causes of things, what Socrates said to Meno is still as valid as it was 2,500 years ago:

> *That we shall be better and braver and less helpless if we think that we ought to enquire, than we should have been if we indulged in the idle fancy that there was no knowing and no use in seeking to know what we do not know;—that is a theme upon which I am ready to fight, in word and deed, to the utmost of my power.*[31]

1 *The Education of Henry Adams* (New York: Random House, Modern Library, 1931), p. 382.

2 *History of the Peloponnesian War*, bk. 1; *GBWW*, Vol. 6, p. 354.

3 Henry Wadsworth Longfellow, "A Psalm of Life" (1839).

4 "Song of Myself," stanzas 37, 33 (1855).

5 William Wordsworth, "England, 1802," sonnet 4, "It is not thought."

6 In *The Greek Commonwealth*, trans. Alfred E. Zimmern, 2d ed. rev. (Oxford: The Clarendon Press, 1915), p. 202; cf. *GBWW*, Vol. 6, pp. 395–99.

7 Prologue to *Henry V; GBWW*, Vol. 26, p. 536.

8 *An Autobiography* (London: Longmans, Green and Co., 1949), p. 82.

9 *Pioneers of France in the New World* (Boston: Little, Brown and Co., 1865), Preface.

10 *The Maritime History of Massachusetts 1783–1860* (Boston: Houghton Mifflin Co., 1921), pp. 81–82.

11 *Le Morte D'Arthur*, 2 vols., ed. Janet Cowen (Harmondsworth, Middlesex: Penguin Books, 1969), 1:6.

12 "The Burden of History," in *History and Theory: Studies in the Philosophy of History*, ed. George H. Nadel, vol. 5 (Middletown, Conn.: Wesleyan University Press, 1966).

13 *Hawthorne* (London: The Macmillan Co., 1967), p. 57.

14 "Pioneers! O Pioneers!" (1865).

15 "Unguarded Gates" (1892).

16 Alexander Pope, epitaph for Sir Isaac Newton.

17 *Psychic Factors in Civilization* (1893).

18 *Capital,* pt. 4, chap. 15; *GBWW,* Vol. 50, p. 181.
19 *The Philosophy of History,* Introduction; *GBWW,* Vol. 46, p. 162.
20 *The German Ideology* (1846) in *The Varieties of History,* ed. Fritz Stern (Cleveland and New York: World Publishing Co., 1961), p. 149.
21 Introduction to *The Communist Manifesto; GBWW,* Vol. 50.
22 George E. Partridge, *The Genetic Philosophy of Education* (New York: The Macmillan Co., 1912).
23 *The Varieties of History,* p. 127.
24 *The American Scholar,* in *The Portable Emerson,* ed. Mark Van Doren (New York: Viking Press, 1946), pp. 43–44.
25 *An Enquiry Concerning Human Understanding; GBWW,* Vol. 35, p. 479.
26 *The Second World War,* vol. 3, *The Grand Alliance* (Boston: Houghton Mifflin Co., 1950), pp. 607–8.
27 *History of Europe,* 3 vols. (Boston: Houghton Mifflin Co., 1935), Introduction.
28 *The Education of Henry Adams,* p. 472.
29 *The Rubáiyát of Omar Khayyám,* trans. Edward FitzGerald, stanza 71 (1859).
30 See *The Principles of Psychology,* chap. 4; *GBWW,* Vol. 53, pp. 68–83.
31 *Meno; GBWW,* Vol. 7, p. 183.

NOTE TO THE READER

HISTORY is the subject of Chapter 34 of the *Syntopicon. See* the readings listed under Topic 1, which distinguish history from other human undertakings; under Topic 3, which are concerned with the writing of history, the determination and classification of fact, and the historian's treatment of causes; and under Topic 4, which have to do with the philosophy of history and theories of causation in the historical process. Readings under PHILOSOPHY 1*d* relate history to philosophy, myth, and poetry; those under PROGRESS 1–1*c* discuss the idea of progress in the philosophy of history.

Volume 6 of *GGB* contains a number of relevant shorter writings. Among them are J. B. Bury's essay, *Herodotus,* pp. 360–83; a selection from Crèvecoeur's *Letters From an American Farmer,* pp. 543–59; a chapter from Guizot's *History of Civilization in Europe,* pp. 299–317; Lucian on *The Way to Write History,* pp. 384–406; a selection from *The Crisis,* by Tom Paine, pp. 457–68; a chapter from *The Conquest of Mexico,* by W. H. Prescott, pp. 227–43; *The Life of Gnaeus Julius Agricola,* by Tacitus, pp. 271–98; a lengthy selection from Tocqueville's *Democracy in America,* pp. 560–690; and the description of the march to the sea from Xenophon's *Persian Expedition,* pp. 193–206.

PART THREE

A Special Feature

The Idea of Freedom

Part One

The Idea of Freedom — Part One

Charles Van Doren, Associate Director, Institute for Philosophical Research

Introduction

The essay that follows is the outgrowth of a study of the idea of freedom that was undertaken by the Institute for Philosophical Research some twenty years ago. The Institute was founded at that time by Mortimer J. Adler and several associates who had worked together in the production of *Great Books of the Western World*. Their intention, formed in the course of making the *Syntopicon,* was to take stock of Western thought on subjects that have been of continuing philosophical interest from the time of Plato to the present day. The full list of these subjects was acknowledged to be no shorter than that which is comprised by the *Syntopicon's* 102 Great Ideas—a number far in excess of any that the members of the Institute could hope to treat even if they supposed themselves capable of living several lifetimes. They sought to make a start, however, on a project that seemed to them worth all the time and energy they could devote to it.

The first idea chosen for the study was the idea of freedom or liberty. Liberty is the subject of Chapter 47 in the *Syntopicon*. Beginning on page 991 of the first volume of that work, the reader will find a review of the idea of liberty as it appears in the great books, and beginning on page 1001 of the same volume he will find a list of references to passages in those books where the subject is discussed in all its various aspects. So far as those books go, the references are complete and the subject is analyzed to the extent that such references require. But the Institute proposed to go beyond this. Not only was it thought proper to read the great books again and analyze them from a still wider point of view, it was considered necessary to examine a large number of additional works—ancient, medieval, and modern—and to take the views of their authors into account, so that something like a total context might be comprehended and the idea of freedom given what might fairly be called definitive treatment up to the present time.

This work occupied the Institute for eight years. The results of the research were written up by Dr. Adler and published as *The Idea of Freedom* in two volumes, the first of which appeared in 1958 and the second in 1961. These volumes (which have in subsequent years been followed by *The Idea of Happiness, The Idea of Progress, The Idea of Justice,* and *The Idea of Love,* written by other members of the Institute), are now out of print. Because of this, and because the nearly 1,500 pages of exhaustively annotated discussion they contain are in any case a formidable undertaking for most readers, the Institute some time ago determined to produce a shorter and more easily readable version of the work that might have a larger audience. This task was begun in 1970 and after a postponement is now complete. The result is a summary, the work of Charles Van Doren, Associate Director of the Institute, that seems likely to be of particular interest to readers of *The Great Ideas Today.* Accordingly, the editors have decided to publish it, though it has seemed best, because of its length, to do so in two segments, of which the first appears this year and the second will appear in 1973.

In its work on the idea of freedom, the Institute established, among other facts about the subject, that there are five (and only five) different kinds of freedom that have been discussed in the Western tradition. Three of these are basically different forms of freedom, and two are variants of the basic forms. In order to make the report of its studies precise and perspicuous, new names were given to these five kinds of freedom, to wit:

1. The circumstantial freedom of self-realization (SR)
2. The acquired freedom of self-perfection (SP)
3. The natural freedom of self-determination (SD)
4. Political liberty (PL—a variant of SR)
5. Collective freedom (CF—a variant of SP)

The first volume of *The Idea of Freedom* analyzes these five different forms or kinds of freedom each more or less in isolation, considering them one at a time and offering extensive documentary evidence of the views of Western philosophers and thinkers on the various aspects of the subject. The second volume of the work concentrates on a long list of issues among freedom authors that were identified in the course of the Institute's research.

This condensation of *The Idea of Freedom* is structured differently. It is in four chapters, of which only the first two appear in *The Great Ideas Today* this year. Chapter I, constituted by Sections 1–4, is concerned with the circumstantial freedom of self-realization and with the variant of it called political liberty. The last section of Chapter I, Section 4, treats the attack on self-realization freedom that is launched by the proponents of self-perfection freedom—in other words, analyzes the views of those authors who have maintained during the last 2,500 years that the circumstantial freedom of self-realization is not true freedom at all, or at least is only a secondary freedom, and that true or real freedom must be conceived differently. Analogously, Chapter II of the condensation treats self-perfection freedom, together with the variant of it called collective freedom, and ends—in Section 8—with an analysis of the counterattack, on the part of the self-realization authors, against the conception of freedom that we have called the acquired freedom of self-perfection.

Chapter III, to be published in *The Great Ideas Today 1973,* will treat the natural freedom of self-determination (a popular, though inaccurate, mnemonic for which is "free will"). Section 9 will deal with the meaning of this kind of freedom; Section 10, with the shape of the controversy among self-determination authors; Section 11, with the theological dimension of the problem of self-determination freedom; and Section 12, with the most interesting of all the issues in the discussion of freedom, the issue about the relation of freedom and responsibility. Chapter IV, also to be published next year, will then present the conclusions of the Institute's study of the idea of freedom. Section 13 will explain why there are three basic freedoms—no more, and no less. Section 14 will treat the underlying common notion of freedom that shows that the three basic freedoms are not absolutely equivocal but instead have certain notions in common. And Section 15 will be an epilogue, reviewing the work that has gone before and suggesting some of its implications.

Contents

Chapter I. The Freedom of Being Able to Do as One Wishes . . 303

   1. The circumstantial freedom of self-realization 303
   2. Individual liberty in relation to law 315
   3. Political liberty 321
   4. Liberty and license: the attack on self-realization freedom . 333

Chapter II. The Freedom of Being Able to Will as One Ought . . 342

   5. The acquired freedom of self-perfection 342
   6. Self-realization and self-perfection conjointly affirmed . . 358
   7. Collective freedom 370
   8. The counterattack against self-perfection freedom . . . 380

The Idea of Freedom — Part One

Chapter I. The Freedom of Being Able to Do as One Wishes

1. The circumstantial freedom of self-realization

Is there any sense in which it can be said with truth that an imprisoned man is free? Is a man free who, with a gun at his head, "voluntarily" reaches into his pocket for his wallet and removes his watch? Is the captain of a ship free when, in the midst of a terrible storm, he jettisons a valuable cargo in order to save his vessel, his crew, and his own life? Is the neurotic or psychopath—for example, the kleptomaniac—who is subject to an uncontrollable compulsion free? Are children and madmen, alcoholics and drug addicts free? Is an otherwise normal man free when he performs complicated actions on demand while in a hypnotic trance? Is a slave ever or in any sense free? Are men and women free, even when they possess all the normal and natural faculties and equipment that we expect in human beings, if their past and present environment is such that they are poor, or badly educated, or limited in the courses of action open to them because of prejudice or discrimination?

With a few exceptions, all of the writers in the Western tradition who affirm the circumstantial freedom of self-realization would answer most of these questions in the negative. These writers—they include, besides a large number of contemporary British and American writers, such disparate figures as Hobbes, Voltaire, Jonathan Edwards, Hume, Burke, Bentham, John Stuart Mill, Freud, Bertrand Russell, R. H. Tawney, Harold Laski, and A. J. Ayer—agree in holding that a man in prison is simply not free, even if, as some concede, there are different degrees of restraint exercised in different prisons, such that durance may be more or less vile. With one rather ambiguous exception, that of Hobbes, they agree that the man with the gun at his head and the captain of the storm-tossed ship are not truly free, even though the actions they perform out of fear (of being shot, or of losing all rather than only a part of their property) are from one point of view voluntary and the result of choice. On the whole, again with one or two exceptions, they agree that freedom is wrongly predicated of the neurotic or psychopath, on the one hand, or of the alcoholic or the addict, on the other, at least at such times as the victims are under the influence of their particular disease, drug, or the like (at other times such persons may be free). And most of these writers would also agree that an adequate education, a reasonable amount of wealth, and a relatively open social environment are conditions of this form of freedom. A man who is hindered in his actions by political, economic, and social circumstances beyond his control is not, in their view, truly or wholly free, even though he may enjoy some freedom.

These writers hold, in short, that freedom is largely if not entirely dependent on circumstances. To be free, in their conception of freedom, a man must be able to do as he pleases or wills; and he cannot do as he wills if circumstances, either external (the prison walls, the gun at the head) or internal (the drug or the alcohol in the blood, the neurotic compulsion), hinder or completely impede him. "Liberty," as Hobbes says, "is the absence of external impediments," for, as he adds, these impediments "take away part of a man's power to do what he would."[1] According to Jonathan Edwards,

> *the plain and obvious meaning of the words "freedom" and "liberty" in common speech, is power, opportunity or advantage that anyone has, to do as he pleases. Or in other words, his being free from hindrance or impediment in the way of doing, or conducting in any respect, as he wills. And the contrary to liberty, whatever name we call that by, is a person's being hindered or unable to conduct as he will, or being necessitated to do otherwise.*[2]

As Locke puts it, freedom consists in "our being able to act or not to act, according as we shall choose or will."[3] Freedom, in Russell's view of it, "means the absence of external obstacles to the realization of desires."[4] And for Harold Laski, freedom "implies power to expand, the choice by the individual of his own way of life without imposed prohibitions from without."[5]

The conception here adumbrated by these remarks—lengthy quotations from the many other writers who subscribe to it would do little to make it more precise—is, indeed, the typically modern conception of human freedom. Freedom, as most people understand it now and in fact have understood it for the last two or three hundred years, means acting as one wishes for the sake of the good as one sees it. A man is not free because someone *tells* him he is; he is free if and only if he *feels* himself to be free. He must not be hindered, obstructed, impeded. He must know what he wants to do and be able to do it. He must also, many people think, be able to have done otherwise if he had so wished—although this is a point on which not all authors concur.

"The circumstantial freedom of self-realization" is the term that we have adopted to describe this conception of freedom. We wish there were a simpler term, for in fact the conception itself is simple enough. Common usage indicates that most people believe that they enjoy freedom only if they are *free from* external obstacles to a desired course of action, and *free to* act (or not to act) as they choose. Indeed, it is a little hard to imagine any other sensible meaning of the term. How is it possible for a man to be really free if he is chained to the wall of a prison cell? How can it be reasonable to say that a person is free—or could be free—if he is under the "dominion" of a "repressive" law or rule? How can I be free if I *must* obey?

That such views have in fact been held, and argued for with force and eloquence, will become evident as we proceed. But before going on to outline the thinking of those who, in one way or another, oppose the conception of freedom that we are analyzing here, we must devote some attention to the words that make up the descriptive phrase "the circumstantial freedom of self-realization." In so doing we will not only throw light on the conception itself but also, and at the same time, show why such a long and cumbersome term is required to describe an apparently simple idea.

The meaning of circumstantial

The word *circumstantial,* as we will use it in this essay, describes one of three ways in which freedom is enjoyed by human beings, but it is not sufficient by itself to describe any one of the forms of freedom, more than one of which may be circumstantial—i.e., dependent on circumstances for its existence. The word by itself does not suffice to identify any of the subjects that men discuss in the name of freedom; it signifies the way in which a particular form of freedom is possessed, not what it consists in. It must, therefore, be combined with a second identifying term—such as *self-realization*—that characterizes the ability men have under certain circumstances. Nevertheless, it is possible to consider the meaning of *circumstantial* in isolation from the other terms we will relate to it.

Circumstantial, then, as we will use the word, refers to whatever external conditions affect human behavior insofar as that behavior consists in bodily movements. The external conditions may affect behavior *directly,* in two ways: either by preventing or facilitating such movements, or by contracting or expanding the opportunities for alternative courses of action. The external conditions may also affect behavior *indirectly,* by occasioning or inducing emotional or other mental reactions that inhibit or encourage impulses to act in certain ways. In the latter case, the external circumstances on which freedom depends include every sort of social and political impediment that hinders desired movement.

Some writers conceive freedom as dependent on external circumstances in all three of these ways; some, in only two of the three ways; and some, in only one of them.

The most usual and the simplest kind of external conditions are those that directly affect an individual's behavior and take away his freedom. "When employed without qualification," the philosopher Henry Sidgwick writes, " 'freedom' signifies primarily the absence of physical coercion or confinement: A is clearly not a free agent if B moves his limbs, and he is not free if he cannot get out of a building because B has locked the door."[6] I am obviously not free (in *this* conception of freedom) if I am physically held or impelled, or if I am confined in a limited space—although the size of the space might affect the degree or amount of freedom I have.

However, the notion of impediment or constraint is not limited to prison bars or chains. The word *coercion* is used by the writers who discuss this form of freedom to cover not only every kind of external force that directly compels or prevents a man's movements but also the indirect influence of threats on behavior: i.e., the duress exerted by fear of the consequences of acting in a certain way. Thus, for example, Moritz Schlick declares that a man "is unfree when he is locked up, or chained, or when someone forces him at the point of a gun to do what otherwise he would not do."[7] And F. A. Hayek feels that "freedom from coercion" means "freedom from the arbitrary power of other men, release from the ties which [leave] the individual no choice but obedience to the orders of a superior to whom he [is] attached."[8] A slave, in other words, even if at a given moment he is working at a distance from his master, perhaps even out of his master's sight, is nevertheless not free although his bodily movements are in a certain sense voluntary. He is doing what he does because he has to, not because he wants to.

It is useful to restrict the words *coercion* and *constraint* to the operation of external factors that exert direct physical force to compel an individual to do something he does not wish to do or to prevent him from doing what he wishes. *Duress,* then, may be used to refer to the operation of external factors that influence behavior indirectly or psychologically by threats or persuasion.

Coercion and duress may interfere with freedom not only by preventing a man from doing whatever he wants to do at the moment but also by closing off other courses of action that he might wish to resort to as alternatives. In the view of many writers, an individual is not free unless circumstances permit him to do the very opposite of what he actually does, or indeed anything else he may happen to desire. In this broad conception of circumstantial freedom, circumstances are not favorable to freedom unless they provide an open environment in which the individual has the opportunity of realizing any one of a number of alternative desires, in addition to the one he actually feels at the moment. Some writers go as far as to say that a man suffers compulsion if any one of the alternative courses of action is closed, while others regard the circumstances as more or less favorable to freedom in proportion as they expand or contract the number of alternatives that the environment leaves open.

Thus, for example, it may be maintained that even if a prisoner does not for the moment wish to leave his cell, he is nevertheless not free at that time, because if he had desired to leave he could not have done so. John Dewey makes the point in another way. "To say that a man is free to choose to walk," he wrote, "while the only walk he can take will lead him over a precipice is to strain words as well as facts."[9]

Circumstances unfavorable to freedom may not involve actual coercion or constraint through the direct application of physical force. They may only carry the threat of coercion, or involve other factors that exert duress by arousing fear of the consequences of acting or not acting in a certain way. In such cases, the fear is a factor that operates from within, not from without, but it is occasioned or induced by external circumstances.

The commonest example of duress in the sense in which we are using the word is the gun pointed at the head. The gun exerts no physical force until it is fired, and it may never be fired. But the man at whom it is pointed may fear that it will be and, consequently, may think it necessary to perform actions that he does not wish to perform. Another common example is the storm at sea that "forces" the captain to jettison his cargo. The word *forces* is in quotation marks because in fact the storm does not exert physical force on the captain, or not yet sufficient force (by definition) to destroy the ship and its cargo. But the captain is afraid it will exert such force, and (presumably) decides that his only chance is to destroy part of his property to save the rest.

In the latter case, the captain's action is from one point of view free, for it is obvious that he could have chosen not to throw the cargo overboard and to take the consequences. A similar observation could be made about the man with the gun at his head. He could refuse to act as directed by the gunman and once more take the consequences (guns, after all, have been known to misfire or even to be unloaded, and the gunman might lack the courage to pull the trigger). Indeed it is this quality of voluntariness about the victim's action that led one writer, Hobbes, to declare that "fear and liberty are consistent: as when a man throws his goods into the sea for *fear* the ship should sink, he doth it nevertheless very willingly, and may refuse to do it if he will; it is, therefore, the action of one that was *free*."[10] But Hobbes seems to be almost alone in holding thus; most if not all other writers on the subject maintain that the man in this situation is not free. He does what he wants to do in the circumstances, but, if the circumstances were otherwise, he would not want to do and would in fact not do it.

The philosopher A. J. Ayer raises another point when, in the context of asking, "In what circumstances can I legitimately be said to be constrained?" he writes that "if I suffered from a compulsion neurosis, so that I got up and walked across the room, whether I wanted to or not, or if I did so because somebody else compelled me, then I should not be acting freely."[11] Ayer gives another example as well. Constraint, he says, could also manifest itself in the actions of a kleptomaniac who "is not a free agent, in respect of his stealing, because he does not go through any process of deciding whether or not to steal. Or rather, if he does go through such a process, it is irrelevant to his behavior. Whatever he resolved to do, he would steal all the same."[12]

In these two cases—that of the neurotic compulsive and that of the psychopathic kleptomaniac—the circumstantial factors limiting freedom are not external, but internal. An internal factor—fear—is also operative in the case of the gun at the head and the storm at sea. But there the removal of the gun or the cessation of the storm will remove the external factors that produced the fear. The problems of the compulsive and the kleptomaniac are not so easily solved. In their case, an internal alteration is required, and this may have little or no relation to any exterior alterations. Strictly, therefore, the neurotic fears or obsessions in question are not circumstantial, even though it is undeniable that pathological conditions can, and perhaps often do, restrict the freedom of the individuals who suffer them. In addition, there are also many cases in which such conditions play a part, although not the whole part, in hindering the performance of desired actions. To take just one example, the person with an anxiety neurosis might be more inclined to act against his own wishes at the command of a gunman than a person with a more secure psychic makeup.

So far we have been suggesting that circumstances are favorable to freedom when they permit a man to act as he wishes and unfavorable when they prevent him from doing so. In this sense, favorable or permissive circumstances are negative, because they are constituted by the *absence* of coercion or duress. According to another view of the matter, circumstances are favorable to freedom in the sense that they are constituted by the *presence* of conditions that enable the individual to act as he wishes. They are facilitating, not merely permissive.

An illuminating example is given by the English historian R. H. Tawney, who asks whether a man is really free to dine at the Ritz if he lacks the money to do so; according to Tawney, he is not.[13] Another example is that of black Americans at the present day, who for one reason or another have failed to acquire as much education as white persons of the same age. It is all very well, the argument goes, to say that blacks are just as free as whites to find jobs in the marketplace, but if most jobs, and all of the best ones, require a certain level of education, and if most blacks do not have it, are they free? Liberal sociologists would say no. For many authors, indeed, the availability of such enabling means as money, the tools or implements necessary for performing a task, means of transportation or whatever physical facilities are needed by a man to accomplish his purposes constitute circumstances, or external conditions, favorable to freedom.

But what about the knowledge or skill or even the bodily strength a man may need to achieve whatever goals he sets himself? Consider the case of a mountaineer who is able to reach the top of Mont Blanc but is frustrated in all of his attempts to scale Mount Everest. Is it correct to say that he is "not free" to climb Mount Everest because he lacks the strength and stamina to do so? Such factors are enabling means, the lack of which is unfavorable to freedom. But are they properly called circumstances, within the meaning of the term that we have proposed here?

The answer would seem to be no. The point is similar to the one that was made earlier about fears and obsessions that are purely of neurotic origin and so are not directly induced by external circumstances of a threatening or compelling nature. Lack of health—physical or mental—may prevent a man from doing as he wishes just as effectively as coercion or duress. But in itself, health (or knowledge or skill) is not a circumstance in our sense of the term. Nor, unless such enabling means are directly tied to external conditions, are they circumstantial factors in freedom.

Only if freedom is held to depend *solely* on the acquirement of knowledge or skill, or on the attainment of mental health, is it non-circumstantial; for then, *under exactly the same external conditions or circumstances,* some men will be free and others unfree according as they have or lack the requisite state of mind or character. At this point, indeed, we encroach upon an entirely new and different form of freedom. We will return to it in Chapter II.

In the preceding pages we have mentioned a number of examples and cited a number of cases drawn from the works of writers who discuss circumstantial freedom. Many more examples and cases could also be cited, for writers of books on freedom use many terms to describe what they have in mind. They speak of "economic freedom," "political freedom," "civil liberty," "individual freedom," "the freedom of man in society," "freedom in relation to the state," "external freedom," and so forth. Sometimes their terms have a negative character: for example, "freedom from coercion or restraint," "freedom from restrictions," or "freedom from law"; and sometimes their terminology is positive: for example, "freedom of action," "freedom of spontaneity," or "freedom under law." Indeed, the whole range of social and economic conditions affords examples for authors who wish their readers to understand what they mean.

The term *circumstantial freedom* seems not to have been used by anyone before us. But this is an advantage in the present discussion, not a disadvantage, for it gives the term a degree of neutrality that it would not have if it had been used by some writers but not by others.

Whatever term is used, however, and whatever disagreements may exist among authors on minor points, the freedom in question is always the same. Circumstantial freedom is a freedom that the individual has *only under certain favorable circumstances.*

The meaning of self-realization

The meaning of the term *self-realization* has two parts, not just one. The first part is expressed by the statement that when unfavorable circumstances do not prevent it or when favorable circumstances permit it, the individual can enact his will, realize his desires, or carry out his plans and purposes, whatever they may be—in short, do what he wants to do. However, while this much is indispensable to the meaning of the term, it is not sufficient to express that meaning.

The reason why is of critical importance, for it points to the difference between the form of freedom we are identifying by the term *self-realization* and those other forms of freedom that only have a circumstantial *aspect*—that is, involve favorable and unfavorable circumstances. Just being able to translate one's will into overt action does not constitute self-realization. Something more is needed.

That something more is an emphasis on the singularity of the individual as such. A man's realization of his desires constitutes self-realization only when his desires represent his own personal bent or the path of life and the objectives he has set for himself. The self to be realized is his individual self, a self that may have much in common with the selves of other men but that, as individuals differ from one another, is always in the last analysis uniquely his own.

This additional point is the second part of the meaning of self-realization. It is expressed by the statement that through acting as he wishes, a man is able to realize for himself whatever he deems good because it is the object of *his* desires, that is, because *he* in fact desires it. Self-realization is thus not merely the realization of desires but the fulfillment of aspirations or purposes that constitute an individual's *own* estimate of what is good *for him*.

Individuals differ from one another in what they wish to do or to become—in the aims or purposes they seek to fulfill, in their immediate day-to-day objectives as well as in the ultimate goals they set themselves to achieve. One man's desires may be the very opposite of another's. But, with certain qualifications that will be noted in the next chapter, a man does not possess the form of freedom we are discussing here unless he is able to act, both in the short and the long term, as *he* wishes to act. He may in fact learn how he ought to act and to shape his life from some other person. But he is not truly free—in this conception of the word—if he is merely *told* how to act by others. He must himself feel that this is not only how he ought to act but also how he wants to act.

The phrase "doing as I please," which is sometimes used to express the meaning of self-realization, elliptically covers the two points. The translation of my intention into action is not enough by itself to constitute doing as I please; for I may will to do as I ought against strong desires to the contrary; and when that intention is executed the result may not please me at all. Hence two conditions, not just one, must be satisfied in order for me really to do as I please. These are *execution,* whereby my wish is translated into action; and *individual fulfillment,* wherein my own good as I see it is accomplished by the action performed.

We now see why, in the opinion of most writers on the subject, the captain of the storm-tossed ship and the man with the gun at his head are not free. When the captain throws his cargo overboard he executes his will of the moment—it is he who gives the order—but it is not what he really wants to do from the point of view of his overall or long-term good. If he survives the storm he will still have to suffer the unpleasant consequences of his action, in an ultimate loss of his own property or in blame being attached to him on the part of other property owners. The holdup victim is also translating his immediate wish into action, but he really does not want to give up his watch and his wallet. He would rather keep them even though, in the circumstances, he considers his life of more value than his money.

We also see why the child and the lunatic are not free in the sense we are discussing here. A child may desire, may indeed passionately desire, to eat more ice cream than is "good for him." One need not question the judgment of the adult who forbids it to recognize that even though the child is truly better off and is being "well taken care of," he does not do what he wants when he passes the ice cream by. He is not fulfilling or realizing his own desires even if, later on in his life, he may be grateful that he was not allowed to grow fat. And the lunatic who is restrained from harming himself is not free either. He must be restrained, and if he himself "knew better" he would want to be; but in fact he does not know better, and instead wants to hurt himself—or rather to perform actions that in the judgment (let us again assume that it is correct) of a sane person will in fact harm him.

These considerations, as well as others that have been mentioned in the preceding pages, raise the question of *degrees* of freedom. For since all of an individual's desires are seldom, if ever, realized or fulfilled, the freedom of self-realization is always subject to variation in degree.

The notion of degrees of freedom is not relevant to particular acts when these are said to be either completely free or completely unfree. But the notion is relevant when the behavior of a man over a period of time or his whole life is considered. The degrees of freedom may then be seen by considering men who, as compared with one another, are more or less free; or it may be seen that in the course of a single man's life there are periods when he enjoys greater freedom and periods when he enjoys less.

Sometimes, indeed, a single act is regarded as more or less free according as it is performed under conditions that allow for a wider or narrower range of alternatives. Hobbes thought that a man in a large prison cell should be considered freer than a man in a small one, although both were unfree compared to a man not in prison at all. Similarly, a wealthy man is said by some writers to be freer than a poor man (although both are "at liberty"), since his wealth increases his opportunities for action; and a man is said to be freer than a woman, because social and economic circumstances provide him with a more "open" environment.

Many writers have emphasized such variations in the amount or degree of freedom possessed either by a single individual at different periods of his life or by different individuals as compared to one another. Thus R. H. Tawney, for example, writes that "freedom is always, no doubt, a matter of degree; no man enjoys all the requirements of full personal development, and all men possess some of them."[14] Bertrand Russell observed that complete freedom in a whole life would be possible only for an omnipotent being. "Practicable freedom," he says, "is a matter of degree, dependent both upon external circumstances and upon the nature of our desires."[15] Voltaire, having said that freedom "is only the power of acting," explains that the sense in which a man is said to be free is "the same sense in which we use the words 'health,' 'strength,' and 'happiness.' Man is not always strong, healthy, or happy." And just as men are not always healthy or strong, even though in general or on the whole they may be so, so "neither are they always free."[16]

The concession that there are degrees of freedom does not lessen the emphasis placed by writers who discuss this form of freedom on the singularity of the individual. In their view, the individual is the final arbiter of what is good or bad, for that is relative to his temperament and tastes. Whether he calls his goal "happiness" or gives it some other name, it is an individual goal, a goal uniquely his own, in the sense that it has validity for him whether or not it is shared or approved by anyone else. Each man is judge of what is best for him. He can be mistaken about how to achieve it and, through error or misfortune, he may fail to achieve it; but he cannot be mistaken about the goal he seeks unless he misunderstands or miscalculates his own desires. Discovering this, the individual may alter his course; but it is he who has corrected himself, not someone else who tells him what he should seek.

Three points follow from these remarks. First, the desires that give content to the goal the individual seeks are the desires he actually has, not those he *should* have or *would* have if he were different than he is. Nor are they the innate tendencies or natural inclinations common to all men; for such desires, if they existed, would set the same goal for all men.

On the contrary, the goal of self-realization is an individual goal precisely because the desires it represents are an individual's conscious desires, reflecting his personal idiosyncrasies and temperament. The variety of goals involved in self-realization is, therefore, as great as the individual differences among men.

Second, what each individual deems to be good for himself is determined by what he himself actually and consciously desires. The good is that which pleases him or satisfies his desires. Hence, according as men differ in their desires, so they differ not only in their goals but also in their judgments about what is good and evil.

The individual's desires, in short, are subject to evaluation not by reference to what is good in general or for all men but only in terms of their importance to him as measured by their relative strength. This is to say, of course, that there is no goodness or value inherent in things apart from their being actually desired—no fixed order of *real* goods that all men *should* desire as contrasted with the *apparent* goods that each man orders according to his own scale of values.

Third, it follows from what was said in the last paragraph that the wish or desire whose enactment contributes to self-realization need not conform to standards of "right" desire or to "rules" of conduct that prescribe the things a man *should* desire or the actions he *ought to* perform, whether he wants to or not. Writers who think that an individual possesses freedom to the extent that circumstances permit him to realize his desires and the goal to which they lead and who, in addition, think this is the only freedom men can have, generally regard men as unfree to the extent that they act, not as they please for the good as they see it, but as they or others think they ought to act.

There is always the possibility, of course, that what an individual ought to do in obedience to some externally imposed moral law or obligation is something he wishes to do anyway, in which case conformity to the rule does not cancel his freedom. But if what others recommend, on grounds to which they attach moral sanctions, is contrary to what the individual desires, then his freedom of self-realization lies entirely in his pursuing the good *as he sees it* and not a good that is set for him as one that all men should strive to attain.

The universality of any moral standard or rule that prescribes what all men should do or seek is consequently antithetical to the individuality of self-realization. Whatever is universally mandatory, as a moral rule or obligation normally is, would seem, therefore, to oppose an individual's freedom to do as he pleases as much as physical constraint or coercion. But it does not oppose it in the same way.

Under physical constraint or coercion the individual *cannot* do as he wishes. In the absence of such compelling force he *can* do whatever he has the means and desires to do; but the individual may still refrain from some act in order to discharge some obligation. The question here is not whether he *can* do something, but rather, granted that he can, whether he *may* do it or *must* do it—that is, whether he is morally entitled or morally obliged to perform a certain act. When the individual acts, not in response to his own desire but only from fear of the consequences of violating a moral rule, then that rule or obligation interferes with his freedom of self-realization through the duress it exerts on him. He is like the man who, at the point of a gun, performs an act that, in other circumstances, he would prefer not to do.

The individual who manages to will as he thinks he ought is simply one who has been pleased to shape his desires in a direction prescribed by certain moral rules. That individual may wholeheartedly accept the rules as describing the general trend of his own inclinations, or as directing him in the pursuit of a goal to which he himself aspires. Nevertheless, such freedom of self-realization as he possesses comes from his doing as he wills to achieve what he deems good for himself, not from his willing as he ought to achieve a goal that all men should seek. His freedom is therefore no different from that of the man who, with quite contrary inclinations or goals, also does what he wills while not willing as he ought by any moral standard.

This is an important point because it raises an important further question. We see that there are two types of the circumstantial freedom of self-realization, or rather, two ways in which it is manifested. These two different types correspond to two different kinds of men. Both may be said to act as they please; but the one acts as he ought *because it pleases him,* and the other acts as he pleases whether he ought to act that way or not. From the strict point of view, both possess exactly the same freedom. But from the point of view of the moralist (as one may say), the first man is a "better" or more "responsible" man than the second.

The question that arises from these considerations is whether all men deserve to possess the freedom of self-realization, or whether some men deserve to possess it and some men do not. In the view of several of the leading writers on the subject of human freedom, the latter is true, not the former. St. Thomas Aquinas, for example, feels that there are standards of right desire or rules of conduct that prescribe the things a man should desire and, therefore, a man has no right to do as he pleases if what he wishes to do brings him into conflict with the moral law.

Aquinas concedes that there is a real deprivation of freedom suffered by men who are restrained by the law from doing what they please. Considering the case of a man whose will is inclined by undisciplined passions toward a merely *apparent* good, Aquinas writes that such a man "acts freely when he follows [his] passion or a corrupt habit; he acts slavishly, of course, if while his will remains such he—for fear of a law to the contrary—refrains from that which he wills."[17] The fact that, in Aquinas' view, this man has no right to the freedom of which he is deprived does not make the deprivation any less real, nor does it make the freedom he lacks any different in character from that of the limited self-realization to which men do have a right.

In other words, Aquinas has much the same conception of self-realization as those more modern writers who, unlike him, hold that it is the only form of freedom. For Aquinas and, doubtless, his many modern followers, self-realization is indeed a form of freedom, but it is only one form out of several, and not the most important one at that. The more characteristic modern view, however, is that self-realization is, even if not the only form of freedom, then immeasurably the most important.

It all goes back, perhaps, to the manacled man—the man not only in a prison cell but also manacled to the wall, so that he cannot move his hands and legs, much less engage in the manifold activities that those of us who are not bound take for granted. Aquinas would have said that the manacled man might enjoy a form of freedom, although he would not do so necessarily. Most modern writers would say that this was ridiculous. How can I be said to be free if I cannot even scratch my nose when it itches? To say nothing of realizing any and all goals, both proximate and ultimate, that I set for myself in my life?

The example of the manacled man, in fact, is the best possible one for making clear the form of freedom that is described by the term *self-realization,* and indeed by the extended term *the circumstantial freedom of self-realization.* The manacles are the *circumstances* that obstruct the freedom in question; remove them, and the man becomes by that very fact more free, if not yet totally so. And the manacles may also represent the very opposite of what self-realization means. For no one desires to be manacled, either in the short or in the long term. Not to be manacled is precisely what everyone wants, whether or not one desires other things as well. As Othello says,

> *I would not my unhoused free condition*
> *Put into circumscription and confine*
> *For the sea's worth.*[18]

2. Individual liberty in relation to law

We have seen that writers on freedom differ in their specification of the circumstances affecting freedom of action, that is, the circumstances that confer on an individual, or withhold from him, the ability to translate his desires, plans, or purposes into action. The most important difference of opinion has to do with whether unfavorable circumstances are limited to those exerting direct physical force to coerce or constrain, or whether they include circumstances that exert duress through the fears they arouse. We have also seen that writers are divided according as they maintain, on the one hand, that freedom of action is entirely dependent on external circumstances or, on the other hand, that it is also dependent on internal ones (health, strength, knowledge, skill, etc.).

In addition, we have seen that freedom of self-realization is attributed to individuals either in virtue of the particular acts by which they carry out their wishes or in virtue of the general tenor of their lives. Some writers tend to concentrate on the nature and circumstances of a single free act, while others try to comprehend the meaning of a *free life,* not merely as embracing a multiplicity of actions that are free, but also as fostered by general social, economic, and political conditions under which the individual develops, shares his purposes, and tries to fulfill them.

We noted, too, in the preceding section that writers on freedom of self-realization conceive it either as circumscribed by universal rules of conduct or as not limited in this way. This division of opinion gives rise to two types of the freedom of self-realization. The one that limits self-realization to those actions and goals that are permitted by moral standards or rules that are thought to be applicable to all men, we may call the *modified* type. In contrast, the other, or *pure* type, is one that acknowledges only individual standards or rules of conduct, which are often spoken of as an "individualist," "liberal," or "personal" ethic.

Among those whose theories embrace a freedom of self-realization, relatively few affirm the modified type of it (examples of those who do affirm such a modified type are Aquinas, John Locke, and Jacques Maritain). The preponderant number affirm self-realization in its pure form.

The purists may hold that self-realization is the only form of freedom that exists, or they may say that there are also other forms of freedom. But as far as self-realization goes, they deny that it is properly limited by any rules or sanctions that are thought to be applicable to all men. Freedom is freedom, in their view, and any and all hindrances or obstacles to it are deprivations thereof.

Nevertheless, they do not usually *recommend* absolute freedom of self-realization as a practical matter. That is, they do not assert that, practically, freedom of self-realization can mean the complete freedom to do whatever one pleases, in every situation.

When considering a single act of a single individual, they may indeed say this. In such a case, the freedom of self-realization is absolute; and any of the various kinds of circumstantial hindrances—either constraint or coercion or duress—represent deprivations of freedom, and as such are condemned. But even if it is possible to consider single acts in isolation, it is a sequence of acts that makes up a life; and human beings do not ordinarily live in total isolation from their fellows. It is therefore necessary to investigate the meaning of the freedom of self-realization in a social and political context. Only then does the idea come alive, as one might say, for that is the context in which most of us live.

In the preceding section we touched on the relation between this form of freedom and universal moral standards or rules. In the present section, then, we will consider its relation to the civil law—the positive and coercive regulations imposed by the state on its members. And in the following section we will examine the special variant of the circumstantial freedom of self-realization that we call political liberty.

Writers who affirm the pure type of the freedom of self-realization—i.e., who hold that this form of freedom cannot be limited by considerations of universal moral rules or standards—agree in maintaining that, in general, civil law is an obstacle to freedom and represents a deprivation of it. But agreeing on that, they differ on one important point. Some say that law and liberty are completely antithetical, while others feel that certain laws, in certain circumstances, are consonant with the liberty of the individual.

Freedom from government: law and liberty as antithetical

From one point of view, the law of the state always infringes on the individual's freedom to do as he pleases. Rules of law and the decrees of government represent the will of another—the will of a sovereign power, whether vested in the person of an absolute monarch, in the people as a whole, or in a majority. The law, therefore, represents a superior force that coerces and constrains those who disobey, or forestalls disobedience by its threat of coercion and constraint. Hence, insofar as the individual's conduct is controlled by law, it is not free; the spheres of law and liberty are mutually exclusive. The individual can do as he pleases only on matters on which the law is silent; and so the extent of his freedom depends on the degree to which his conduct is exempt from legal regulation or coercion.

Laws, says Hobbes, are "artificial chains." He concedes that no government could ever make laws regulating all the actions of men, and therefore men are free to do what they choose on all matters left unregulated; but in matters that are regulated, men are not free, for "obligation and liberty" are "inconsistent." Anarchy alone, it would appear, is compatible with unlimited liberty, "for the laws being removed, our liberty is absolute." [19]

But Hobbes does not recommend anarchy. Anarchy, he says, making an important point that has been made since by many others, is the equivalent of the state of nature, and that is the same as the state of war, in which each man (or nation) threatens or is threatened by the liberty of others insofar as their private wills conflict. It is absurd, says Hobbes, for men to demand the anarchic freedom that consists in total exemption from laws, since that liberty would make other men "masters of their lives." [20] The sword in the hand of the sovereign, enforcing civil law, may, in fact does, limit each individual's freedom; but it also protects him from the coercions or interferences he would suffer at the hands of other men if they were not restrained, like him, by the coercive force of law.

Many have agreed with Hobbes's analysis of the situation. They point out that an individual is unfree under two sets of circumstances: (1) when he is coerced or intimidated by law or government, and (2) when he is coerced or intimidated by other men who desire to impose their will on him. These two kinds of constraint can be seen as in conflict; and the question is whether a proper balance can be established between them. In fact this is so; for although laws take away some liberty, they may also create some; and it is even possible for the balance to be in favor of freedom when laws are made with this end in view. (Nevertheless, this qualification does not repudiate the proposition that laws *always* take away liberty.)

How should such a favorable balance be achieved? Answering this question, the English jurist and philosopher Jeremy Bentham makes another important point. The law ought to leave untouched all those acts, he argues, that, whether one approves of them or not, do no harm to other men or to the community as a whole. "The exercise of the rights allowed to and conferred upon each individual," he writes, "ought to have no other bounds set to it by law, than those which are necessary to enable it to maintain every other individual in the possession of such rights as . . . is consistent with the greatest good of the community."[21]

The point is important because it establishes a criterion for deciding which laws produce an increase in the total freedom of the members of a community and which do not. A number of English political philosophers have agreed with Bentham's position. Adam Smith, for instance, the great exponent of laissez-faire economics, advocates a system of liberty whereby "every man, as long as he does not violate the laws of justice, is left perfectly free to pursue his own interest in his own way."[22] This is to imply, of course, that some individuals will be hindered from doing their will. This deprives *them* of freedom, but since, by definition, *their* will, if exercised, would deprive others of even more freedom, the final result is a gain in the total amount of freedom. Men living together tend to encroach on one another's liberties. The freedom of each, therefore, has to be limited by law or custom to secure the maximum freedom possible for all.

However, according to these writers, the prevention of extralegal coercion or intimidation—for example, kidnapping or violence—although it mitigates, never removes the infringement of individual freedom by law and government. The freedom of self-realization, or doing as one pleases, is, therefore, always a freedom *from* law. Every law restricts individual freedom to some extent; and while the "true individualist" does not deny the necessity of coercive power on the part of the government, he does desire to limit it to those realms where it is indispensable, in order to reduce the total amount of coercion to the minimum.

Freedom from law and the conformity of laws and desires

From another point of view, the freedom to do as one pleases is not confined to conduct outside the sphere of law. In this view, the individual is free to do as he pleases not only in matters on which the law is silent (other circumstances permitting) but also when the law demands of him what he would willingly do anyway, in the course of realizing his own desires.

The individual can obey laws of this kind and not be deprived of his freedom, just as he is not deprived of it in acts that are not covered by laws at all. In other words, rules of positive law do not and need not *always* curtail the freedom of self-realization; and the degree to which they can be made to conform to individual desires depends on how they are made and whether the individual has an effective voice in their making.

Men are free, says Harold Laski, "when the rules under which they live leave them without a sense of frustration in realms they deem significant. They are unfree whenever the rules to which they have to conform compel them to conduct which they dislike and resent."[23] The point is not that all laws can or should conform to the wishes of every individual; there are types of conduct against which prohibitions are desirable. It is rather, as Laski says, "that any rule which demands from me something I would not otherwise give is a diminution of my freedom."[24]

But how can a man who is ruled by others remain master of himself and enjoy freedom even when he obeys regulations imposed from without? The answer given by Laski, and given also by many others, is that he can remain master of himself, not in obeying all laws, but in obeying those that represent his own will in the matter; and the extent to which he enjoys such freedom depends upon his having suffrage, or a share in the government.

The right to the suffrage, in short, is essential to liberty and a citizen excluded from it is unfree for the simple reason that the rulers of the state will not regard his will as entitled to consideration in making policy. To be free, as Laski says, "a people must be able to choose its rulers at stated intervals simply because there is no other way in which their wants, as they experience those wants, will receive attention."[25] Furthermore, through suffrage citizens have ways of maximizing their agreement with the law, that is, of increasing the number of laws they can willingly accept because those laws require of them only what they themselves desire.

Individuals cannot live together without common rules, according to this view, but an individual's liberty is not infringed by any rule that he himself accepts, any more than it is infringed by restraints he puts upon himself. Only when the individual is restrained by a will not his own is he subject to the kind of force that is imposed from without and is antithetical to freedom. Hence only those laws that do not win my consent, because they do not conform to my desires, invade my personality and abridge my freedom of self-realization.

At the same time, even though men are free to do as they please either in matters not regulated by law or in obeying laws that accord with their desires, they remain unfree insofar as they are (a) obligated or coerced by laws that contravene their individual wills, or (b) subject to forms of extralegal coercion or interference that law and government have failed to suppress.

That is why, in the opinion of most of the writers who hold this view, the primary—or an important—function of government is to prevent coercion and thus guarantee to every man the right to live his own life in terms of free association with his fellows. Law itself, of course, is coercive and is a restriction of individual freedom; it is justified only when it really adds more to freedom than it subtracts from it. But it *is* justified then. In that case, individual freedom, in the words of the philosopher Frank Knight, "is limited to conduct not regulated by law and to participation in activity directed to changing the law (and to law-breaking)." [26] This limitation, at least in an "open," "democratic" environment, need not be very stringent; the realm of freedom can be relatively large.

Even in the most open democracy, however, all of the members of a community will never agree on everything, and therefore some laws will always be made and enforced over individual dissents; and individuals will be free in their compliance not with all laws but only with those from which they do not dissent. An ideal or perfect democracy would be a different matter. There, as Knight remarks, complete agreement on all the concrete content of the law would exist, and there would be no need for law enforcement. Such complete agreement on every law would produce a situation in which each man was literally free, in the sense, as Knight says, in which Robinson Crusoe was the only individual in his world. But the point, of course, is that Robinson Crusoe was *alone,* and the perfect freedom he enjoyed reached its limit as soon as Friday entered his world.

The questions discussed in this section are far from being merely "abstract" or "academic"; in fact, they have been matters on which men have fought and, when not actually fighting, have deeply felt. Two hundred years ago their disagreements took the form of disputes about religious freedom; during the last century they divided mainly on political and economic freedom; today the arguments go on about the freedom to engage in activities of a personal nature, for example, sexual acts.

All countries in the West have laws on the books, though in many cases they are no longer enforced, against certain types of sexual activity—for example, laws forbidding homosexual acts or various "perversions." According to the first position outlined in this section, *all* such laws are repressive; according to the second position, they are repressive only if they forbid activities that individuals actually want to engage in. Recently, homosexual acts between "consenting adults" have been made legitimate in some countries. The arguments for such a change in the law have usually been in terms of the controversy as outlined here; it has been said that such acts harm no one, and that to forbid them is thus an unjustifiable abridgment of individual freedom. The continuing attack on such American laws by the editors of *Playboy* magazine has used these terms; the point is always made that laws against "perverse" sexual acts are unjustified because these acts do not hurt anyone, and the state has therefore no business interfering with such matters. (In an earlier age the keynote was "freedom of conscience," with which, it was said, the state had no business interfering.) The argument on the other side, of course, is that perversions really are harmful, and that the laws must in any event reflect the "conscience of the community" in this and other areas.

Gambling is another example of an activity that provokes disputes of this kind. There are many who feel that laws against gambling are repressive because the choice to gamble or not is an entirely individual matter, and the state has no business interfering in it. However, it is pointed out by those who advocate such laws that, first, gambling is often harmful to the person who engages in it—for gambling is a kind of disease, and the state is correct in protecting its citizens from any and all "epidemics"; second, even if gambling does not hurt the gambler, it does support otherwise harmful activities of criminals. Antigambling laws would be repressive in any event, for they would always impede the freedom of individuals, but they would be justified if their absence provided the opportunity for more coercion and intimidation than their promulgation would represent.

This section has considered the views of self-realization authors concerning the relation of liberty to law. We have seen that as far as strict self-realization authors are concerned—that is, authors who discuss or treat only this one kind of freedom—there are essentially two views: one, that *all* laws limit freedom; the other, that *some* laws, in *some* circumstances, do not. But the situation is in actuality more complex than that, for in discussing the relation of law and liberty a few authors, notably John Locke, inject a quite different conception of freedom itself. It will be more appropriate to discuss Locke's position in the matter in Section 6.

3. Political liberty

Let us suppose that I am over twenty-one years of age, that I voted in the last general election, and that I am taking a stroll in the streets of my city on a summer night. My attention is drawn to a commotion in the next street, and, moving in that direction, I see two young black men running, pursued by two policemen. The policemen capture their prey and force them, at gunpoint, to stand against the wall while they are "frisked." In the confusion, the policemen come to the mistaken conclusion that I am somehow involved, and I am also forced to stand against the wall and am searched. After about ten minutes I manage to convince the policemen that I am guiltless, after which I am allowed to go.

Let us suppose, furthermore, that I am unsympathetic with the law that permits the police to do this, not only to me but also to the blacks. I believe that the law is unfair, since it is directed mainly against blacks, who are more likely to be subjected to abuses under it than are whites; and I also believe it is unconstitutional, on the grounds that it abridges the freedoms guaranteed by the Fourth Amendment to the U.S. Constitution. That amendment reads:

> *The right of the people to be secure in their persons, houses, pa-*
> *pers, and effects, against unreasonable searches and seizures, shall*
> *not be violated, and no warrants shall issue, but upon probable*
> *cause, supported by oath or affirmation, and particularly describ-*
> *ing the place to be searched, the persons or things to be seized.*

Supposing all of these things to be so, then is there any sense in which I can be said to have been free during the ten minutes when I stood against the wall, with my hands raised, and with a gun at my head?

It is clear that all of the writers whose views were analyzed in the preceding section would say no. There would be no doubt in the minds of the first group of writers—those who hold that the only freedom men can enjoy with respect to law is in those areas where the law does not legislate, and that laws are always repressive and abridge freedom, even if it be conceded that they are sometimes necessary to control greater deprivations of freedom than they themselves represent. There would be no doubt in the minds of the second group, either—those who hold that one can obey, without losing freedom, a law of which one approves and with which one is in sympathy. For according to the supposed circumstances of the case, I am not sympathetic with the law in question, believe it unjust, and desire that it will be declared invalid.

In short, all of those who hold that freedom only exists outside the jurisdiction of the law, conjoined with those who maintain that I must accept a law if I am to be free when I obey it, would say that during those ten minutes when I was obviously under duress I was not free.

However, there is a small group of important writers on the subject of freedom who would say that, even in these circumstances, I was free—in a sense. But the freedom they have in mind is not the circumstantial freedom of self-realization. Instead, it is a special variety of that freedom, sufficiently different from it so that we must call it a distinct form. For purposes of identification, we will name this form of freedom *political liberty*.

Aristotle, Aquinas, Immanuel Kant, L. T. Hobhouse, Jacques Maritain, and Yves Simon are notable among the small group of writers who conceive political liberty as a distinct freedom, separate from other forms of freedom that they also affirm. It is a freedom that they attribute to men and women who enjoy a certain *status* in the political community— that of citizenship. Examination of their views will help us to understand the conception, and also to answer the question posed at the beginning of this section.

Before proceeding, one point should be stressed. In what follows, we will not use the term *political liberty* to refer to the freedom of communities, as opposed to that of individuals within communities. Some writers speak of independent or self-governing communities as "free," as contrasted with subjugated ones. While it is true that in subjugated states or colonies or in communities that are ruled by despots, no one enjoys the freedom of citizenship, it does not follow that all men enjoy that freedom in states that are politically independent or in communities in which there is some measure of self-government under the rule of law.

On the contrary, history is full of examples of conquered kingdoms that have managed to throw off the yoke of subjugation and to become "free states" without any of the kingdoms' subjects becoming politically free in the sense in which the citizen of a republic is free and the subject of an absolute monarch is not.

While a republic or any state that has attained some measure of constitutional government is politically free in the sense that it involves a form of government that creates a self-governing people, "the people," in this political sense, is seldom coextensive with the population. In most of the "free societies" of the past—in fact until very recently—large portions of the population, as distinguished from "the people," existed outside the pale of political life. They were excluded from suffrage and from the freedom that attaches to the status of citizenship. Hence they were deprived of political liberty in the sense in which we are here using that term: to signify a freedom belonging to the individual under certain political circumstances, not a freedom belonging to the state as such.

The fact that, in a community that has constitutional or republican government, some part of the population comprises "the people" and has political status should not obscure the distinction between the sense in which they as individuals enjoy the freedom that attaches to their status, and the sense in which the community as a whole is said to have a certain freedom in virtue of its form of government. While recognizing that the term *political liberty* is used for both of these freedoms, we are using it exclusively for one of them—the freedom of the individual man who is a citizen with suffrage. It is that freedom, and that alone, with which we are concerned in this section.

The freedom of citizenship

According to the writers listed above, men are politically free in relation to the state and civil government when they are admitted to the status of citizenship, with all its rights and privileges, especially the right of juridical appeal against the abuses of government and the right of suffrage. As full-fledged and active members of a self-governing community, they are politically free men.

Such political liberty is not possessed by those who live under absolute or despotic government, no matter how benevolent. Nor is it possessed by those who live under limited or constitutional government but are excluded from citizenship and suffrage. Under constitutional government, or a government of laws, those who are excluded from suffrage may have certain political rights, but without the franchise they are not full-fledged members of a self-governing people. It is a corollary of this that the extension of the suffrage does not alter the character of the political liberty that the enfranchised citizens possess; it merely alters the number of persons who possess it.

All of the writers listed conceive political liberty in terms of constitutional government and citizenship, but the earlier ones on the list are distinguished from the later by their insistence that not all men (and women) should enjoy this freedom. For Aristotle and Aquinas, "natural slaves," because of a defect that by definition cannot be overcome, should not enjoy political liberty; for Kant, it is mainly a question of education and experience. Refusing to assert that some human beings are slaves by nature, Kant nevertheless finds reasons for restricting suffrage, at least in his own day.

He is firm in stating that "only the united and consenting will of all the people . . . ought to have the power of enacting law in the state," but he also emphasizes that by "all the people" he means only those qualified for active citizenship.

> The capability of voting by possession of the suffrage properly constitutes the political qualification of a citizen as a member of the state. But this . . . presupposes the independence or self-sufficiency of the individual citizen among the people.[27]

In contrast to those who are active citizens in this sense, all the rest—"mere incidental parts of the commonwealth"—have only passive citizenship.

> The apprentice of a merchant or tradesman, a servant who is not in the employ of the state, a minor, . . . all women, and, generally, everyone who is compelled to maintain himself not according to his own industry, but as it is arranged by others (the state excepted), are without civil personality, and their existence is only, as it were, incidentally included in the state.[28]

Nevertheless, Kant adds (and it is at this point that we recognize that he is discussing a new and different form of freedom): "Such dependence on the will of others and the consequent inequality are . . . not inconsistent with the freedom and equality of the individuals *as men* helping to constitute the people."[29] The freedom to which Kant *here* refers is the circumstantial freedom of self-realization. Given propitious circumstances, all possess this, whether or not they also possess political liberty.

Referring to the "laws of natural freedom and equality," Kant goes on to assert the natural right of all men to political freedom and equality, even though under particular economic or cultural conditions that right cannot be immediately granted to those who are in a state of dependence.

> All they have a right in their circumstances to claim may be no more than that whatever be the mode in which the positive laws

are enacted, these laws must not be contrary to the natural laws that demand the freedom of all the people and the equality that is comfortable thereto; and it must therefore be made possible for them to raise themselves from this passive condition in the state to the condition of active citizenship.[30]

Kant thus envisages a progressive amelioration of society and with it the ultimate extension of suffrage to all its members. He looked forward to the time when all men would enjoy the political liberty that, in his own day, was restricted to the few—and, in his judgment, had to be.

Historically, it was in the context of struggles for the extension of the suffrage that spokesmen for equality identified political freedom with having a voice in the government. In 1647 the Levellers, led by Major William Rainborough and Sir John Wildman, raised the question of suffrage for the members of Oliver Cromwell's revolutionary army. Rainborough argues that "the poorest he that is in England hath a life to live, as the greatest he," and therefore "every man that is to live under a government ought first by his own consent to put himself under that government." He can see no reason "why any man that is born in England ought not to have his voice"—and an equal voice with every other—"in election of burgesses." Without a voice in their own government, he concludes, "the people of England have little freedom."[31]

Others spoke out to the same effect in later epochs. Tom Paine protests that those who do not have the right to vote for representatives are no better than slaves; for "he that has not a vote in the election of representatives is [in the same case as he who is] subject to the will of another."[32] J. S. Mill, arguing for universal suffrage on the grounds that "it is a personal injustice to withhold from any one . . . the ordinary privilege of having his voice reckoned in the disposal of affairs in which he has the same interest as other people,"[33] attributes political liberty only to those who, through suffrage and representation, exercise the "free agency" of self-government.[34] And, saying that "political freedom implies active citizenship,"[35] Hobhouse asserts that the individual is politically free only if he has "the right of contributing by voice and vote to the explicit decisions, laws and administrative acts, which bind the community."[36]

These remarks of Hobhouse were written in the early 1950s. According to Maritain, writing at about the same time, a philosophy that holds that "the human person as such is called upon to participate in political life" must claim "the right of suffrage for all adult citizens" as foremost among "the political rights of a community of free men."[37] The philosophy of Aristotle and Aquinas can, he thinks, be made to accord with the principle of universal suffrage, for this does not require any change in their conception of political liberty but only a more extended application of it. "The famous saying of Aristotle that man is a political animal," Maritain comments,

> *does not mean only that man is naturally made to live in society;*
> *it also means that man naturally asks to lead a political life and to*
> *participate actively in the life of the political community. It is*
> *upon this postulate of human nature that political liberties and*
> *political rights rest, and particularly the right of suffrage.*[38]

And like Maritain, Yves Simon also propounds a philosophy of democratic government based on principles to be found in Aristotle and Aquinas.

For all these writers, then, whatever their view of democracy and universal suffrage, political liberty is possessed by those and those alone who enjoy the status of citizenship and who, exercising the right of suffrage, participate in government, directly or through representation. As Simon sums it up, "the citizen is a free man." His freedom of self-government does not mean that he obeys himself alone and is subject to no authority except that of his own reason. Rather it means that "so far as the *ends* of action are concerned, the [citizen as] free man is not subject to authority, except for his own good and for the common good. . . . [and] so far as the *cause* of action is concerned, [he] retains, in his relation to authority, the character of an autonomous agent."[39]

The meaning of political liberty

That the special form of freedom we are discussing here is circumstantial is evident from the fact that it is possessed by individuals only under certain favorable circumstances—the fortunate circumstances of their living under constitutional government together with the good fortune of being enfranchised. Men who under less fortunate circumstances suffer subjection to the rule of despots are thereby deprived of political freedom, even if they are not enslaved by the despot's tyranny. Nor does the good fortune of living in republics save women from this deprivation as long as they are disfranchised—nor does it save disfranchised members of minority groups, or felons, or children.

However, although it is clearly circumstantial, the freedom in question is not one of self-realization; that is, it does not consist in the ability to realize one's desires by translating them into action. It does not exist simply wherever an individual has the means at his disposal for enacting his wishes and is exempt from physical coercion or constraint and from the duress of fear induced by threatening force. Nor does it derive from the opportunity, provided by an open environment, to take several alternative courses of action.

In none of these senses indicated can political liberty be simply equated with the freedom of self-realization. Each can exist without the other. Those who lack political liberty—children, slaves, the subjects of despots, disfranchised persons—may have, in varying degrees, the circumstantial ability to do as they please. Apart from the extremes of torture, no one is ever totally coerced and constrained. And, on the other hand, no citizen enjoying political liberty is totally exempt from coercion and constraint.

The fact that political liberty can remain the same while the freedom of self-realization varies in extent, together with the fact that the freedom of self-realization can exist in varying degrees for those who entirely lack political liberty, shows that the freedom Aristotle, Kant, Hobhouse, and the Thomists have in mind is quite distinct from the freedom we have identified as self-realization.

This becomes clearer when we reexamine the theories of individual liberty in relation to civil government and law held by certain writers who affirm the freedom of self-realization. With these before us, we shall be able to see that even for writers who regard living in a democracy and having citizenship with suffrage as circumstances highly favorable to an individual's ability to do as he wishes in spite of the coercive relations of government, these circumstances are *means to self-realization* rather than the elements of a special freedom.

In Section 2 we found that the self-realization writers fall into two groups according to the position they take on liberty in relation to law. Some maintain that individuals are free to do as they please only in areas of conduct not regulated by law; and some maintain that, in addition to such freedom, individuals are also free in matters regulated by law to whatever extent the prescriptions of law happen to coincide with their individual wishes.

The first group need not concern us here. Men like Hobbes and Bentham did not think that such political institutions as democracy, citizenship, or representation contribute to, much less establish, political liberty. For them, the extent of an individual's freedom in the state depends on one political circumstance and one alone, namely, the extent to which he is immune to coercive regulation by the laws of the state. If these writers consider democracy or citizenship at all, they dismiss it as of little importance for freedom. Herbert Spencer summarized this point of view when he said: "The liberty which a citizen enjoys is to be measured, not by the nature of the governmental machinery he lives under, whether representative or other, but by the relative paucity of the restraints it imposes on him."[40]

Harold Laski presents a harder case. Belonging to the second group of writers—those, that is, who believe that men are free in obeying laws that coincide with their individual wishes—he makes some statements that *appear* to express a conception of political liberty. One is: "The right . . . to the franchise is essential to liberty; and a citizen excluded from it is unfree."[41] Another is: "Everyone who considers the relation of liberty to the institutions of a State will, I think, find it difficult to resist the conclusion that without democracy there cannot be liberty."[42] But when we examine the reasons given in support of these statements we find that democratic institutions, citizenship, and suffrage are means for maximizing

327

the total amount of individual liberty possessed by the members of a political community who are subject to its coercive regulations. Political liberty is, therefore, not conceived as a freedom that is *inherent in the status of citizenship* and that is *actually enjoyed* whenever the citizen exercises his freedom. Rather, in Laski's view, the extent to which individuals can enjoy freedom of self-realization within the restrictions of the state depends on their having certain political rights and privileges that enable them to participate in lawmaking.

For liberty, according to Laski, "is essentially an absence of restraint . . . . [Men] are free when the rules under which they live leave them without a sense of frustration in realms they deem significant."[43] It is for this reason that Laski declares: "I do not think the average man can be made happy merely by living in a democracy; [but] I do not see how he can avoid a continual sense of frustration unless he does."[44] For, as Laski says, unless people are able to choose their rulers at stated intervals, there is no way in which their wants, as they experience them, will achieve attention. Furthermore, the rules under which I live should embody an experience I can, in general, accept; but if the rules are not generally acceptable to me, I will be compelled to endure "irksome restraints."[45] Therefore, Laski argues, "we must . . . find ways of maximizing our agreement with the law. . . . This maximization can only take place when the substance of law is continuously woven from the fabric of a wide consent."[46]

The critical point here is that, for Laski, men who are deprived of suffrage are not dispossessed of freedom altogether, but only in a degree. They are deprived of the means for getting their will embodied in the law, and consequently they will be subject to a larger number of rules that do not conform to their individual desires. As a group, they simply have less freedom of self-realization than those with political status and power. Or, making the same point in another way, all who have equal suffrage do not have freedom of self-realization to the same extent, since equal suffrage does not guarantee to all who exercise it that each will achieve the same amount of agreement with the law. This is confirmed by Laski's statement that "no merely mechanical arrangements will ever secure freedom in permanence to the citizens of a State. While there are certain constitutional forms which are . . . essential to freedom, their mere presence as forms will not, of themselves, suffice to make men free."[47]

Laski and others like him thus make participation in government a way of increasing the number of times the individual can act in accordance with his own desires while still obeying the enforceable rules of society. They in effect reduce democracy and citizenship to means whereby those who have suffrage may increase their freedom of self-realization.

In contradistinction, those who recognize a political liberty that is a distinct form of freedom regard the political machinery as conferring a special freedom on all who have a certain status, i.e., citizenship with suffrage.

That freedom does not depend on the objective rightness or justice of the law that is promulgated with the consent of the governed; it does not depend on the virtue or wisdom of the citizens who must obey it; nor does it vary in degree with the extent to which the law's prescriptions happen to coincide with the individual wishes of citizens. Instead, it is a freedom that only citizens possess, that all citizens possess equally if they have equal suffrage, and that each enjoys to the full when he exercises that suffrage, even though the result of the combined suffrage of all must always be adverse to the wishes of the minority.

The individual and the common good

We have seen that, although political liberty is possessed by individuals in a circumstantial manner, it nevertheless cannot be equated with the freedom of self-realization. Yet it does consist in individual freedom in relation to law and government. It involves having one's voice heard and one's will felt through active participation in political affairs—the making of laws and the formation of policies. In consequence of such participation the public or legislative will to which the citizen is subject is not a will wholly alien to his own. While it may not be identical with his own will in any particular instance, it always represents his own will together with that of all other citizens who have exercised their suffrage. Each has contributed to its formation, as those who are without suffrage have not and for whom, therefore, the public or legislative will is wholly the will of others.

Political liberty is thus in a very special sense a *variant of the freedom of individual self-realization*. This contention can be supported by examining some statements about the relation between the will of individuals and that of the community as a whole.

The exercise of suffrage by a body of citizens does not entirely remove a certain arbitrariness from the laws of the state and other positive institutions of government. What Kant calls the "united and consenting will" of the citizens, what Hobhouse calls the "social will," what Simon calls the "public will," and what others call the "legislative will," is still a will and not the voice of pure reason. Though it is a will to the formation of which each citizen contributes when he exercises suffrage, it must not be thought of as identical with his own will. As Hobhouse says, it is not because the social will is his own that the citizen is free but because in the process of its formation "he has [through suffrage] as much scope for expression as any one man can have if all are to have it." [48]

On the one hand, then, the freedom of a particular citizen, according to this conception of political liberty, does not depend on having the arbitrariness of the law express his own particular judgment or coincide with what he himself wills. But on the other hand, it does depend on the fact that the arbitrariness of the law does not represent a will that is wholly alien to his own, for his own will has participated in the formation of the public, social, or legislative will of the body politic, of which all citizens and only those who are citizens are full-fledged or active members.

While the law the citizen obeys is not wholly of his making, neither is it one in the making of which he has no—and can have no—part. The fact that other citizens try to shape the law in the light of their particular interests does not prevent him from bringing his own particular interests to bear on the formation of the law and other political institutions. Each citizen has the opportunity and power to say what is for the common good from the point of view of his own particular interests. His suffrage enables him to do that, and therein lies the special freedom that he has as a citizen.

Hence political liberty, as thus conceived, is a type of individual self-realization. It is not the self-realization of doing as one pleases in matters on which the law is silent, nor is it such freedom extended by democratic processes, which tend to make laws that please a larger number of individuals. Instead, it is self-realization of a different type. On its positive side, it is limited exclusively to the role that suffrage plays in enabling the individual self with its particular interests to give voice to those interests in lawmaking and so to have them taken into account in the determination of what is for the common good, which is not only the good of the whole but also the good of each individual person.

In a society where men are associated to lead a common life and to act in concert for a common good, the rules of law regulating their conduct and directing them to their common good cannot be instituted by the diverse wills of all concerned unless there is some way of unifying them. According to Aquinas, there are only two possible ways of obtaining such unification. One is to have the law proceed from the will of a "public personage" who as representative of the people is charged with the care of the community. The other is to have it instituted by the public will of the people as a whole.

In the latter case the unification of diverse private wills to create a single public will must be achieved *either* by unanimity *or* by giving authority, through the unanimous consent of all concerned, to the will of the preponderant number among those whose suffrages are consulted. It is only in the latter case, according to Yves Simon, that political authority is compatible with political liberty. A certain arbitrariness remains in what is thus willed. But it does not remove freedom, because all who consent to being ruled by a majority of themselves are subject to a public will that, while arbitrary, *is produced by themselves,* and not to one that is both arbitrary and *of alien origin.*

The question remains how laws made for the common good of the whole secure as well the good of the parts, precisely in those respects in which the individual good of one person differs from that of another. How can law take account of diverse individual interests of the variety of persons involved, so far as it is possible to reconcile these with one another and with the good of the community as a whole?

Following Aquinas, Simon answers this question by distinguishing between two ways in which the common good can be intended. It can be intended *materially,* in and of itself, as it is by those who are actually engaged in government. It can also be *formally* intended by private persons whose material desire is rather for particular goods, and this is so even when the particular goods that are desired, considered materially—that is, as ends—are in conflict with the common good. Such would be the case, Simon argues, in the following hypothetical example:

> *The wife of a murderer hates the prospect of her husband's being put to death; she is normally and virtuously concerned with the good of her family, and, from the standpoint which is and ought to be hers, the death of the murderer is an evil. On the other side, the judge, who stands for society, sees in the death of the murderer elements of the common good: justice and determent from crime. The common good, of course, shall prevail, but, significantly, Aquinas considers altogether sound and honest the opposition made to the requirements of the common good by the person in charge of the particular good. The common good itself demands that wives should want their husbands to survive, even though the latter happen to be criminals.* That particular goods be properly defended by particular persons matters greatly for the common good itself. *The wife of the murderer, as she fights for the life of the man whom the common good wants to put to death, does precisely what the common good wants her to do. It is in a merely material fashion that she disagrees with the requirements of the common good: by doing what the common good wants her to do, she formally desires the common good.*[49]

In a democratic society the individual citizen, in exercising his suffrage, is not called upon to consider the common good materially. He is not, as one citizen among many, a "public personage" who is charged with the care of the whole community. The suffrage of each private citizen, taken alone or by itself, is an instrument for expressing not the public will but his own private will, which, according to Simon, should not have the common good as its object except formally, in some abstract sense. What it should be directed to materially are goods of individual interest to himself. Society would be harmed, says Simon, if everyone intended the common good not only formally but materially. Particular persons and groups ought to intend particular goods. This, Simon urges, "is the keystone of the whole theory"; for the "common good cannot exist unless it does exist as the good of a multitude; but there is no good 'of a multitude' unless particular goods are intended by particular appetites and taken care of by particular agents."[50]

According to this theory of the use of the suffrage, it is a way in which the individual interests of the citizen, along with those of other citizens who favor the same or other means to the common good, can give direction to the public will that the combined suffrages of all produce. Suffrage enables each man to register his preference for things of particular interest to him as an individual and yet to regard them as means to the common good in which he as an individual shares. This enables him to influence the public will and to have his individual interests taken into consideration in the making of laws for the common good.

We see now how to answer the question posed at the beginning of this section. In the circumstances described—in which I stood with my hands against a wall and was searched at gunpoint—I had no individual freedom, that is, freedom of self-realization. But even in those restrictive circumstances I retained some freedom, namely the freedom of political liberty. This could not be taken from me unless I was disfranchised by the state and deprived of political rights, or unless I refused or otherwise failed to take advantage of my franchise. During the few minutes when I was deprived of the freedom of self-realization, I retained my political liberty and, barring extreme actions that are hardly ever taken in a democracy, would retain it for the rest of my life.

Simon's argument, as outlined in the previous pages, is relevant to the supposed circumstances of the case. It is to my interest, as it is to that of all citizens, to enjoy domestic tranquillity—what in recent years has more and more come to be called "law and order" (but should be called "peace and order"). Indeed, security of life and property in this sense is unquestionably a part of the common good, for it is one of the primary goods that men hope to achieve when they form associations and establish governments. But men may disagree about how to produce this kind of security. In the hypothetical case considered at the beginning of this section, I disagree with the majority of my fellow citizens on just this point. But even though I disagree with them on the *means* to domestic tranquillity, I agree with them on domestic tranquillity as an *end*. When I vote *against* a "stop and frisk" law, I do so for exactly the ultimate reasons that lead them to vote *for* it. And if I truly understand the common good and the way in which political liberty for all can help to attain it, I am willing to abide by the majority decision as to the means for attaining it. I may continue to try to change that decision—by voting, for example, in a later election, for candidates who share my view of the matter. But I do not lose my political liberty because I, or rather my candidates, lose an election.

Political liberty, as thus understood, is of the essence of democracy as it is conceived in the advanced industrial states of the West; in fact, political liberty and democracy are almost the same thing. The difference between seeking to effect improvements "within the democratic process" and trying to effect them by "confrontation" or "violent revolution" is the difference between retaining political liberty and discarding it. Clearly, for one who has been nurtured in the Western democratic tradition, to take the latter course is an act of political desperation. It might be justified in certain circumstances—circumstances that we will examine in the following sections—but it is not justifiable in terms of freedom when that is conceived as political liberty. On the face of it, this is obvious; and yet attempts to make such justifications are not rare at the present time.

4. Liberty and license: the attack on self-realization freedom

It may seem unquestionable to most readers that being able to do as one wills or wishes is genuinely freedom. While it may not appear equally obvious that, as many writers have maintained, this is man's *only* freedom, most readers may reasonably wonder how anyone could doubt that this is at least *one* of the freedoms that men normally want as much of as possible. Is not the freedom that we have called circumstantial self-realization the freedom that almost every child feels deprived of under parental regulation? Is it not the freedom that is taken away from every prisoner behind bars or from the slave who must do what another man wills? And when we think of the emancipation of children, prisoners, or slaves, is it not this freedom that we think of as being restored?

To these questions, the commonsense or everyday meaning of the word *freedom* would appear to require unqualifiedly affirmative answers. As the word is ordinarily used, it certainly connotes the absence of coercion, constraint, or other external interference that tends to prevent the individual from doing as he himself wishes. It would therefore appear to be farfetched or even preposterous to say that the meaning of the word in its most widely accepted usage is completely mistaken—that, in short, most people who use the word *freedom* in this ordinary sense are simply not speaking of freedom at all but of something else.

However, despite the apparent absurdity of this, it is exactly what some writers have maintained. In Book VIII of Plato's *Republic,* where the perverted forms of government and the analogous degradations in the human soul are being described, Socrates speaks of the life of the democratic man as having "neither law nor order; and this distracted existence he terms joy and bliss and freedom."[51] Such freedom, which thrives on the absence of laws, Socrates also refers to as "the libertinism of useless and unnecessary pleasures."[52] As democracy in its most extreme form inevitably degenerates into tyranny, according to Plato, so the licentious man or libertine becomes a slave. "The excess of liberty, whether in States or individuals, seems only to pass into excess of slavery."[53]

An even more explicit rejection of doing as one pleases occurs in Aristotle's *Politics,* again in the context of criticisms of democracy. "In democracies of the more extreme type," Aristotle writes, "there has arisen a false idea of freedom" held by those who think that "freedom means the doing what a man likes." Aristotle's own view is left in no doubt; concerning those democracies in which "every one lives as he pleases, or in the words of Euripides, 'according to his fancy,' " he asserts that "this is all wrong," adding pointedly that "men should not think it slavery to live according to the rule of the constitution."[54]

John Calvin shows himself in agreement with this position when he refers to "fanatics, who are pleased with nothing but liberty, or rather licentiousness without any restraint."[55] He dismisses those who give the title of freedom to a man's ability to do what he wants in the absence of restraint with the contemptuous question: "What end could it answer to decorate a thing so diminutive with a title so superb?"[56]

The same points were made by later writers. Jonathan Boucher, speaking against the revolutionary party in the American colonies, quotes with approval John Locke's statement that "where there is no law there is no freedom"; in Boucher's own view, "liberty consists in a subserviency to law." If there ever were men who existed in a completely lawless state of nature, they would have been, according to him, completely unfree. "The mere man of nature . . . has no freedom," even if he has the power, and circumstances allow him, to do as he pleases.[57]

For Rousseau, who in certain passages pictures the state of nature as completely lawless, natural liberty is at best an animal or brutish freedom. The individual's power to do as he pleases, which is limited only by his strength or cunning set against others, does not differ in any way from the kind of freedom the beasts of the jungle enjoy. When men deprive themselves of such freedom by entering into the social contract, they gain in its place the truly human freedom that, according to Rousseau, is at once a moral and a civil liberty. It is this, Rousseau says, "which alone makes [a man] truly master of himself; for the mere impulse of appetite is slavery, while obedience to a law which we prescribe to ourselves is liberty."[58] The transition from a state of nature to a state of civil society is, therefore, not to be interpreted as involving the exchange of one *kind* of human freedom for another, but rather as the elevation of man from a brutish to a human condition. Only then does man rise above the merely animal freedom of doing as he *pleases* and acquire the truly human freedom of doing as he *ought.* In Rousseau's view, "these two things are so different as to be mutually incompatible," and he suggested calling the former "independence" in sharp contradistinction to what is properly called "liberty."[59]

Hegel is on the same side. In his view, "the definition of freedom [as] ability to do what we please . . . can only be taken to reveal an utter immaturity of thought."[60] He regards self-indulgence or self-will (that is, doing as one pleases) as the very antithesis of freedom. The very things that restrain the individual from doing as he pleases are the indispensable conditions of his freedom. For example, the limitation imposed on the individual by the state "is a limitation of the mere brute emotions and rude instincts; as also, in a more advanced stage of culture, of the premeditated self-will of caprice and passion." But, as Hegel sees it, "this kind of constraint," far from being destructive of freedom, is necessary for the attainment of it "in its true—that is, its rational and ideal form." [61]

The passages quoted are offered to show that a number of important writers dismissed as no freedom at all a freedom that many other writers affirm, and a freedom, furthermore, that most modern readers would accept as patently genuine. The former speak of it as a false or illusory conception of freedom; they regard it as the antithesis of freedom—as virtual slavery; and they treat it as a freedom appropriate to animal but not to human life. Often, they oppose it to real freedom by calling it "license."

Unfortunately, though a useful mnemonic, the word *license* is used in many ways, like the word *freedom* itself. Some writers—among them those we have quoted above—deny that men are ever free by virtue of being able to do as they please, and use *license* to signify what they regard as an entirely false conception of freedom. But some writers who hold that doing as one pleases *is* genuinely human freedom, or even man's only freedom, nevertheless use *license* for a *part* of such freedom—the part that, in their opinion, society is justified in taking away from its members. There are, in addition, authors who appear to take a middle ground between these extremes. For them, acting as one wishes in contravention of the moral or civil law is license or a counterfeit of freedom, but in matters on which either kind of law is silent, a man's true freedom consists in being able to do as he pleases.

We will return to the various meanings of license below, in an attempt to clarify its ambiguities. For the moment, however, the terms *liberty* and *license* can serve as preliminary indications of the radical opposition between those who affirm the circumstantial freedom of self-realization and those who discard this as a totally false, and indeed dangerous, idea.

The attack on circumstantial self-realization

In general, arguments that doing as one pleases is not freedom under any conditions appeal to what we will call the *generic meaning* of freedom.* The effort to show that being able, under favorable circumstances, to act as one wishes for one's individual good as one sees it does not conform to this generic idea, according to which a man must have *in himself* the ability or power to make what he does his own action, and what he

---

* The generic meaning of freedom will be discussed in Section 14, after the groundwork is laid for a thorough analysis of it.

335

achieves his own property. If it can be shown that the formulation of what is common to all types of circumstantial self-realization does not fall under the most general formulation of what freedom is, this would provide adequate grounds for asserting that circumstantial self-realization is no freedom at all.

On the face of it, this line of argument might appear difficult to advance or sustain. The difficulty does not consist in establishing the relevance of the generic meaning of freedom to the question at issue. Just the contrary is the case; for supporters of circumstantial self-realization also refer to something they call the common or universal meaning of freedom. In fact, from their point of view, that common meaning clearly shows that every instance of circumstantial self-realization—doing as one pleases—*is* an instance of freedom; for in every such case the individual's action *proceeds from himself* rather than from another, and achieves for him *his own individual good,* something quite proper to himself.

How, then, can the generic or common understanding of freedom provide grounds for concluding that no instance of circumstantial self-realization is ever an instance of freedom, because in no case of acting as one wishes does the action represent the self, nor does such action achieve a good that is proper to the self?

The answer lies in the interpretation that is placed on the generic meaning by those who disavow circumstantial self-realization as true freedom. According to this interpretation, circumstantial self-realization fails to conform to the generic meaning on two counts. This gives rise to two arguments against circumstantial self-realization, one based on the nature of the *self,* the other on the very fact of *circumstantiality.* The arguments are as follows:

(1) The self that is the principle of freedom must be the *true* self, the self that *rightly* wills what is for the person's *real* good. The individual person as a whole includes forces or inclinations that are antagonistic to the true self and its real goods. These elements in a man's makeup lie outside his true self and constitute *the other within him* that the true self must control or dominate. Unless it does, he does not have self-mastery, that is, mastery by his true self over the rest of himself.

No one is free, it is agreed, who is not master of himself. But, so the argument runs, no one is master of himself *who does whatever he pleases,* for the true self is not in command when *any* wish or desire that the individual may have is the controlling source of his conduct. The true self is in command only when a person's conduct is controlled by what that self wills in accordance with the precepts of law or duty. Law or duty, not will or desire, is the principle of every action that flows from the true self and is directed toward that self's proper or real good. Hence, "doing as one pleases" expresses an utterly false notion of freedom, the very opposite of self-mastery, since it acknowledges wish or desire, *without any qualification,* to be the ultimate principle of action.

Self-realization only *appears* to conform to the generic meaning of freedom. The counterfeit takes on a certain plausibility precisely because it appears to make the self the principle of freedom. But, it is argued, the deception is unmasked as soon as we see that it is only the true self—the lawful or dutiful self—that can be the principle of true freedom. To use "self" as nothing but a covering or collective name for individual desires or wishes is to set up an imposter in place of the true self, and it is precisely this imposture that makes self-realization a counterfeit of genuine freedom.

(2) The additional fact that self-realization is dependent on external circumstances that are favorable to the enactment of an individual's wishes or desires furnishes another argument against its being genuine freedom. Here again the grounds lie in an appeal to the generic meaning of freedom. But now the argument turns on an interpretation that requires the *self* to be independent of the *other*. Freedom worthy of the name is not only self-mastery but also self-dependence, the opposite of which is dependence on the other.

No one is free so far as he depends on factors outside himself to make the things he does his own actions. But such a dependence, so this argument points out, is what those who maintain that freedom is a matter of self-realization always assert. For they say that the individual's ability to enact his desires or wishes depends wholly or partly on external circumstances. He does not have this ability through his own mind or character. Favorable circumstances confer on him the power to do as he pleases, unfavorable circumstances leave him powerless, and it is according as the one or the other set of circumstances prevails that he is said to be free or unfree.

The objection to this is that a man can hardly be called free or unfree in respect to those elements of his character that are controlled by things other than himself. The circumstantial character of self-realization deprives it of the self-dependence or independence that is required for freedom. To call "freedom" that which involves dependence on the other is to use the word in a fashion that contradicts its generic or common meaning. In violation of that meaning, circumstantial self-realization is, therefore, a false conception and represents the very opposite of true or genuine freedom.

Let us examine a few examples of these arguments as they are offered in the writings of philosophers who reject the genuineness of circumstantial self-realization.

The Roman Stoics of the century before and the century after the birth of Christ give a special turn to the argument by twisting the language of self-realization to their own purpose. Taking cognizance of expressions such as "doing what one pleases" or "living as one wishes," they first treat them as if they conveyed the most generic sense of what freedom is, and then proceed to exclude the sense of freedom that runs through all self-realization conceptions of it by the interpretation they place on the very phrases they borrow. Thus, for example, Cicero: "Who is it who has the power to live as he wishes, if not only those who follow right reason; whose pleasure consists in discharging their duties; who have planned their lives after giving much thought to it; and who, thereafter, never stray from this plan?" The question is obviously intended to elicit the answer that only such men have the power to live as they wish. "Such a person," as Cicero says, "has his actions and purposes rooted in his true self; and these actions never have an end aught but the true self. Such a person is truly master of himself." And only such a man, he concludes, "can truly be called free." [62]

Epictetus, the Greek slave in Rome, begins his discourse on freedom with a statement from which no self-realization author would dissent. "That man is free," he declares, "who lives as he wishes, who is proof against compulsion and hindrance and violence, whose impulses are untrammeled, who gets what he wills to get and avoids what he wills to avoid." [63] But who is this man? "Who is he," as Epictetus asks, "whom none can hinder?" He is not the man who desires things that are external to his true self, whose wishes are dependent on the other—in any sense of the other. Instead, he is "the man who fixes his aim on nothing that is not his own." The critical question, of course, as Epictetus realizes, is: "What does 'not his own' mean?" His answer:

> *All that does not lie in our power to have or not to have. . . . The body then does not belong to us, its parts do not belong to us, our property does not belong to us. If then you set your heart on one of these as though it were your own, you will pay the penalty deserved by him who desires what does not belong to him. The road that leads to freedom, the only release from slavery, is this, to be able to say with your whole soul: "Lead me, O Zeus, and lead me, Destiny, Whither ordained is by your decree."* [64]

The only thing that is wholly within man's power and entirely "his own," according to Epictetus, is a man's own will and the control it can exert over his judgments, impulses, and desires. Everything else is at the mercy of adventitious circumstances or can be hindered or controlled by the power of others. The man who sets his will on being able to walk unhindered in a certain direction can obviously be hindered; but it is only his body that is impeded, "as a stone is impeded." He has made the mistake of thinking that there is freedom in unimpeded bodily motion, but such things are not *within his power* nor are they *his own*. The same reasoning applies to other bodily conditions, pleasures of every sort, and all forms of worldly goods. "Am I not then to will to get health?"

The answer given by Epictetus summarizes his reasons for rejecting circumstantial self-realization as something lying entirely outside the sphere of true human freedom. "Certainly not," he writes, "nor anything else that is not your own."

> *For nothing is your own that it does not rest with you to procure or to keep when you will. Keep your hands far away from it; above all, keep your will away, or else you surrender yourself into slavery, and put your neck under the yoke, if you admire what is not your own, and set your heart on anything mortal, whatever it be, or anything that depends upon another.*[65]

That freedom involves independence is clearly the nerve of the argument. It is just the circumstantial character of self-realization that excludes it from being freedom. Whatever things shifting circumstances allow a man at one moment and take away at another cannot belong to his freedom. This argument restricts the sphere of freedom sharply—in the end, only one's thoughts are free, because only they cannot be taken away. But, in this limited sphere, freedom is absolute.

Writers such as Rousseau, Hegel, and Kant do not couch their arguments in terms of "living as one wishes" or "doing as one pleases." Their emphasis, instead, is on the independence of the *self*. The self is the principle of freedom only in that realm of acts in which it is sovereign and autonomous—dependent on nothing but itself, even for the law it obeys.

This form of the argument is implicit in Rousseau's statements to the effect that the free man, in obeying himself alone, is secure from all personal dependence on others. "Dependence on men," he writes, ". . . gives rise to every kind of vice, and through this master and slave become mutually depraved. If there is any cure for this social evil, it is to be found in the substitution of law for the individual; in arming the general will with a real strength beyond the power of any individual will."[66]

Those who obey the general will do not obey other men, but themselves alone, for they participate in the general will; and such "obedience to a law which we prescribe to ourselves is liberty."[67] Employing a famous phrase, Rousseau goes on to say that the man who is compelled to obey the general will is thereby "forced to be free," for he is thus secured "against all personal dependence."[68]

Speaking in terms of the will instead of the self, Hegel equates freedom and independence. "Only that will which obeys law is free," he writes, "for it obeys itself—it is independent and so free."[69] Circumstantial self-realization generally involves bodily motions for the enactment of the individual's wishes or the realization of his desires. But the physical realm of bodies in motion is one of dependent existences, each thing dependent for its being and its motions upon other things. Hence, according to Hegel, we cannot find any freedom there, but only in the realm of spirit, for "spirit is self-contained existence" and "this is freedom, exactly. For if I am dependent, my being is referred to something else which I am not; I cannot exist independently of something external. I am free, on the contrary, when my existence depends upon myself."[70]

To sum up: according to the English Hegelian Bernard Bosanquet, the argument against self-realization theories, as found in many writers from Plato to Hegel, gets at the truth about freedom as self-assertion and as absence of interference by others because it properly identifies the true self that is the principle of freedom. The *other,* from whose interference the *self* must be exempt, consists of all those forces within a man that stand in the way of his willing what is really for his good. What at first appears to be only a metaphorical version of freedom becomes upon closer examination the whole reality of freedom. This reality fully embodies the essential meaning of freedom. Circumstantial self-realization, which always involves "the absence of external constraint," is nothing but "an elementary type or symbol" of freedom—the appearance of it, in short, not the reality.[71]

We will return to the arguments advanced by self-realization theorists in support of their position and in opposition to the attack described here in Section 8.

Liberty and license: a clarification

We have noted that there are ambiguities in the use of the term *license* when it is opposed, in the literature of the subject, to the term *liberty*. The primary ambiguity is created by the fact that many writers who maintain—in contradistinction to the position outlined above— that doing as one pleases *is* truly freedom (or even that it is man's *only* freedom) also maintain that certain limits must be set to the exercise of such freedom on the part of individuals living together in society. When these writers condemn the attempts of some men to go beyond these limits, they are censuring what they regard as excessive freedom, but in their view such excesses are still truly freedom. They are simply saying that if some men arrogate too much freedom to themselves, the freedom of others will be infringed. They never mean that the man who has too much freedom or acts licentiously thereby becomes himself less free or unfree.

This is the sense of Jeremy Bentham's famous question: "Is not the liberty to do evil liberty?" Society must, of course, restrain men from the abuses of liberty, but in doing so does not society "take away liberty from idiots and bad men, because they abuse it?"[72] To say that what is being taken away is license, *not* liberty, is, from the point of view of Bentham and others like him, to mistake the distinction between a good and evil *use* of liberty for a distinction between what *is* freedom and what *is not*.

Declaring that "the liberty to kidnap or to engage in violence which the state represses is not a liberty which anyone would openly condone," the American legal philosopher Robert L. Hale nevertheless criticizes those "who say that when the state represses such activities, it is not repressing liberty at all, but license." What should be said, in his opinion, is that "the state . . . undertakes to repress [the] liberty to commit 'license' "—that use of liberty that, if permitted, would "destroy . . . liberties which ought to be protected."[73] The intent is similar in Frank Knight's remark that "freedom does not mean unregulated impulse, or 'license,' "[74] and in Bronislaw Malinowski's statement that "to speak about the criminal's freedom to murder, to rape, or to steal is simply an abuse of words," by which is meant no more than that "criminal tendencies to murder, to rape, and to steal should have no freedom."[75] The principle of limitation in these and many similar passages is one that draws a line between desires that society should permit men to realize and desires that it should restrain them from carrying out. When the restraint is successfully imposed by law or government, some men are deprived of freedom, whether or not it is also called "license," because it is a liberty that should be taken away from them.

Writers who conceive freedom as self-realization and who agree on the need for limiting freedom give somewhat different reasons for doing so. Some make the avoidance of injury the principle. Thus John Stuart Mill: "The sole end for which mankind are warranted, individually or collectively, in interfering with the liberty of action of any of their number, is self-protection."[76] Some look to the maximization of freedom itself—Bertrand Russell, for example: "There will be more liberty for all in a community where some acts of tyranny by individuals are forbidden, than in a community where the law allows each individual freely to follow his every impulse."[77] Knight maintains that no coercive law, restrictive of freedom, is justified unless "it really adds more to freedom in some way than it directly subtracts."[78] And Herbert Spencer feels that every man should be "free to do that which he wills, provided he infringes not the equal freedom of any other man."[79]

From the point of view of the writers who deny that there is any freedom in doing as one pleases, only those who have a false conception of freedom would give such reasons for limiting it. The point is made explicit in these words of Hegel:

> *Nothing has become . . . more familiar than the idea that each must* restrict *his liberty in relation to the liberty of others: that the state is a condition of such reciprocal restriction, and that the laws are restrictions. To such habits of mind liberty is viewed only as casual good-pleasure and self-will.*[80]

In this perspective, it is just as wrong to suppose that the individual is genuinely free in those cases in which no law governs his conduct, and so he can do what he wishes, as it is to suppose that any genuine freedom has been taken away from him in those cases in which some law prevents him from doing as he pleases.

Enough has been said here to indicate that the term *license* cannot be employed to formulate the precise issue between those who affirm circumstantial self-realization as a genuine freedom, those who reject it as illusory, and those who take a middle position. As we have seen, each of the typical parties to this issue would speak against license, just as each would speak for the limitation of freedom by law, *in some sense of these terms.*

What is involved here, in fact, is another, an entirely different, form of freedom. Before examining in greater detail the issue about liberty and license, and indeed the issue about the genuineness of self-realization itself, we must discuss this second basic form of freedom. We will do so in Chapter II.

Chapter II.   The Freedom of Being Able to Will as One Ought

5. The acquired freedom of self-perfection

For a large number of writers on freedom in the Western tradition there is a freedom to which all men should aspire but which only some men attain. However else these writers differ (and among them are such disparate figures as Plato, Epictetus, St. Augustine, Boethius, Aquinas, Luther, Calvin, Spinoza, Rousseau, Kant, Hegel, Maritain, Barth, and Tillich) about the nature of man, the good life, and the good society, they share the view that only persons who have developed a certain state of mind or character enjoy a certain freedom.

We have adopted the word *acquired,* as opposed to *circumstantial,* to signify the way in which *freedom is possessed* according to the conception of it under consideration here. And we have adopted the term *self-perfection* to name the mode of self that, as contrasted with *self-realization,* distinguishes the acquired freedom of being able to do as one ought from the circumstantial freedom of being able to do as one pleases.

The word *acquired,* as we shall use it, signifies the way in which freedom is possessed when it is based upon or follows from a change or development of human beings in terms of mind, character, or personality that differentiates them from other men. Whatever word is used to designate this difference—whether it be *good, wise, virtuous, righteous, holy, healthy, sound,* or whatever—the difference represents an improvement or the attainment of a superior condition, as measured on whatever scale of values is posited by the particular writer. Freedom, in other words, is thought to be possessed only in conjunction with a certain state of mind, character, or personality that marks one man as somehow better than another.

Many of the writers with whom we are now concerned use the word *perfection* to designate that state of the self in which a person has achieved or approximated the goal or ideal of human life—that state of the self that makes him "better" than others. Not all of them do. Some, indeed, speak of the attainment of the human goal or ideal as self-realization, a term that we are using in a quite different sense. But, here as always, what is at stake is not the mere words the writers use but the meaning their words express.

In the preceding chapter, we examined and analyzed two different forms of freedom: the circumstantial freedom of self-realization, and the variety of it that we called political liberty. We now are presented with a third: the acquired freedom of self-perfection. We will examine it in the same way we examined the others, that is, by analyzing the terms or phrases that describe it.

Before doing so, however, a few words should be said about the difference between *circumstantial* and *acquired,* on the one hand, and between *self-realization* and *self-perfection,* on the other hand.

The acquired is clearly distinct from the natural, for the natural is that which is somehow inherent in all men by virtue of their being human. But may not that which is acquired be dependent, at least in part, on favorable circumstances? The answer depends on the precise meaning of the question.

If what is being asked is whether certain circumstances are favorable and other external conditions are unfavorable to that human development or improvement with which freedom is acquired, many (though not all) of the writers that concern us here would say yes. But the affirmative answer does not make the freedom circumstantial rather than acquired; for men who enjoy the same favorable circumstances do not *all* attain the state of mind or character that not only marks them off as somehow "better" than other men but also confers freedom on them and them alone. If the freedom were circumstantial rather than acquired, all who enjoy the same favorable circumstances would thereby enjoy the freedom that such circumstances confer.

The question can also be interpreted as asking whether a freedom that is acquired is in any way dependent on favorable circumstances. That is, does the *exercise* of acquired freedom depend on the circumstances under which the individual lives? Here, writers divide according as they answer: (a) no, not at all, (b) yes, but not indispensably, or (c) yes, essentially. Nevertheless, this difference with regard to whether acquired freedom has a circumstantial *aspect* and, if it does, whether it is indispensable to the existence of freedom, leaves the common meaning of *acquired* unaffected.

Even in the extreme case in which favorable circumstances are thought to be essential to its existence, the kind of freedom we are discussing is thought to be acquired only insofar as, among the persons who enjoy such circumstances, there are some who have also attained a certain inner condition of mind or character. This understanding of *acquired* is shared by those who regard external circumstances as totally negligible or at least as not indispensable to the existence of acquired freedom.

So much for the distinction between *circumstantial* and *acquired*. As for the terms *self-realization* and *self-perfection,* at least one point of difference between them is immediately evident when we compare the discussion of freedom that occurs in what may be called self-realization authors with the discussion that is found in what may be called self-perfection authors. For the self-realization authors, without exception, freedom is destroyed by any form of external coercion or constraint that prevents a man from translating his will into overt action; and, except for a few writers, such as Hobbes (as we have seen), it is equally annulled by circumstances that exert duress through the fear they arouse. For self-perfection authors, however, the ability to enact what one wills is *never* by itself sufficient for freedom; and, again except for a few exceptions, freedom is not destroyed or annulled by any type of external circumstance that, in one way or another, prevents a man from translating his will into overt action.

Hence it is inaccurate to express the antithetical character of self-realization and self-perfection by saying that one consists in a man's ability to *act* as he *ought* and the other in a man's ability to *act* as he *pleases*. The words *ought* and *pleases* do express what is essential in the contrast; but the word *act* tends to blur it. For the typical self-perfection author, the antithesis is more sharply drawn by saying that self-perfection consists in a man's ability to *will* as he ought, and that so long as he has this ability he remains free whether or not he can *enact* what he wills.

According to the typical self-perfection author, the circumstances that make men prisoners or slaves do not deprive them of the freedom they have acquired if they are wise or good. "A wise man, though he be a slave, is at liberty," says St. Ambrose; "and from this it follows that, though a fool rule, he is in slavery."[81] That is, it is not through outer circumstances but through virtue and learning that the wise man is free. Boethius, who wrote his famous *Consolation of Philosophy* while a prisoner, made essentially the same point. The consolation of philosophy was her teaching him that even in prison, manacled to a wall, he was still free—for no jailer could deprive him of his inner or true freedom.

Statements of this sort indicate that the freedom of self-perfection has its locus in the moral or spiritual universe, not in the world of bodily motions or even in those realms of conduct in which men interact or impinge on one another. Such statements indicate that this freedom is held, not in relation to the power or wills of other men nor in relation to the impact of physical forces, but rather in the relation of a man's own will or mind to forces within himself, which he has the power to control or exert. Accordingly, it consists in being able to *will as we ought,* whether or not external circumstances permit us to *do as we will.*

Another important element in this kind of freedom is identified by Jacques Maritain. Referring to "all the sages, stoics, epicureans, and neo-platonists, yogis, rabbis, and sufis, spinozists, and nietzscheans" (not to mention the Christian theologians and modern psychiatrists) who have located this freedom at the very center of man's moral or spiritual life, he observes that "all have maintained that its achievement requires a certain measure of asceticism (interpreted in one or another of many different ways) and that it implies a state of perfection beyond ordinary reach."[82] Allowing, as Maritain does, for a wide latitude of interpretation, the word *asceticism* does carry, at the very least, the common connotation of self-control or self-discipline rather than self-realization or self-indulgence so far as desires or impulses of a certain sort are concerned. However, being able to resist or turn away from those pleasures or gratifications that are often referred to as "the world, the flesh, and the devil" is only the negative side of a freedom that, as Maritain also suggests, manifests itself positively in some degree of power to attain "a state of perfection beyond ordinary reach."

The meaning of acquired

The subject of discussion that we identify as acquired freedom is referred to under other names by the authors who are concerned with it. Most frequently they speak of "moral liberty" or "spiritual liberty," but some call it "terminal freedom" or "perfect freedom."

Christian theologians, both Catholic and Protestant, are at pains to distinguish between the freedom of the will to choose righteously and its freedom simply to choose. Beginning with Augustine, they employ the Latin word *libertas* to designate the one and the phrase *liberum arbitrium* for the other. The English phrase "Christian liberty" came to be used as a translation for *libertas;* in the theological context, acquired freedom is often referred to as "Christian liberty" and sometimes as "the freedom of the children of God."

In the language of modern psychiatry the point is expressed in medical rather than in ethical or religious terms. Among those who regard mental health or the integrated personality as the ideal of human development, the freedom men acquire when they have achieved a sound maturity is referred to as "freedom of the personality" or as the "freedom of the healthy adult," in contrast to the condition of the neurotic, infantile, and conflictful character. What psychiatrists have in mind when they speak,

345

negatively, of "freedom from conflict" is also sometimes expressed positively as a "freedom of harmony."

Though few writers actually call this freedom *acquired,* authors do use that word in writing about it, and many employ such verbs as *achieve, attain, obtain, become, develop,* and *grow* to signify the process of *coming to be.* Thus, for example, we find Aquinas saying that "the greatest thing is the acquiring of freedom, which is what knowledge of the truth causes in believers."[83] And Maritain: "Man is not born free unless in the basic potencies of his being: he becomes free, by warring upon himself . . . by the struggle of the spirit and virtue; by exercising his freedom he wins his freedom."[84]

From a different point of view, we find John Dewey saying that "we are free not because of what we statistically are, but in as far as we are becoming different from what we have been."[85] And in another place: "Actual or positive freedom is not a native gift or endowment, but is acquired."[86] "Experience has taught us," says Sigmund Freud, writing from still another point of view, "that psycho-analytic therapy—the liberation of a human being from his neurotic symptoms, inhibitions and abnormalities of character—is a lengthy business."[87] The emphasis in many of his writings is on the difficulty of this task, and on the fact that success in the effort is not assured.

Spinoza, like Freud and Maritain, thinks that the attainment of freedom is the reward (in the sense of it we are discussing here) of arduous effort and the termination of a prolonged pursuit. In the famous last paragraph of Part V of his *Ethics*—that part's title being "Of the Power of the Intellect, or of Human Liberty"—Spinoza asserts that the freedom that only the truly wise possess is difficult to attain. But, he adds, the path that leads to it "can nevertheless be found."

> *It must indeed be difficult since it is so seldom discovered; for if salvation lay ready to hand and could be discovered without great labour, how could it be possible that it should be neglected almost by everybody? But all noble things are as difficult as they are rare.*[88]

Dewey also makes the individual striving indispensable, but he, for one, denies the terminal character of freedom. Instead, we acquire it progressively as we progressively realize our native capacity for growth. All growth, Dewey reiterates, is for the sake of more growth. We must always "keep the avenues of growth open" and perpetually "fight against induration and fixity," for "we are actually free" only so long as we continue "to realize the possibilities of re-creation of our selves."[89]

From Plato to Dewey to Freud, there are many philosophers who regard the acquirement of freedom as an entirely natural development that occurs—or can occur—in the course of an individual life. But Christian theologians from Augustine to Calvin to Luther as well as Christian philosophers like Maritain, who regard the acquirement of freedom as essentially a supernatural event that is principally caused by the distribution of grace divine, necessarily take a different view.

While they by no means exclude the possibility that the conversion of a man toward God and God-given freedom may occur at some moment in his individual life, the doctrine of divine election or predestination obliges them to accept that a human being may from early childhood possess, through grace, a high degree of charity and spiritual freedom. Hence they regard it as possible that some men may enjoy *throughout life* the freedom that others attain only late in life and after arduous efforts to acquire it.

If the word *acquired* connotes a change or development that either gradually or instantaneously happens in the course of an individual life, it would seem difficult to apply it to a freedom with which some men may be blessed from the beginning. The difficulty is resolved by noting one of the points that is shared by those who give a *supernatural* as well as by those who give an entirely *natural* account of acquired freedom. For both, all men *can* acquire freedom, *but only some men do*. The explanation of this dictum may vary from the theological exegesis of the scriptural text that "many are called, but few are chosen" to Spinoza's sense of why the few discover and persevere in the path to wisdom, or to Freud's understanding of the difficulties of being an adult. But however divergent the explanations are, what is agreed is that only some men possess acquired freedom, whether throughout their life or for some part of it.

From the Christian point of view, the fact that only some members of the human race as a whole enjoy the freedom of sanctity is the sign that such freedom is acquired. From the point of view of the naturalists, the fact that only some individuals in any generation attain a freedom for which all men have the capacity by nature also shows that it is not native to man but acquired. Hence the word *acquired* retains a common core of meaning amidst the variety of theories about the manner in which acquired freedom is actually attained.

Authors who affirm a freedom that is acquired think the acquired state of mind or character that confers freedom on men also marks their achievement of a certain excellence in the scale of human values.

While the measure of excellence varies among the writers in question, they all look upon the attainment of freedom as something concurrent with the betterment of the individual. Such an individual is somehow "better" by reason of the change or development in his own person whereby he becomes free. In contrast, authors who affirm a freedom that is circumstantial look upon those who enjoy freedom through the good fortune of living under fortunate circumstances, not as "better," but as "better off" than other, less fortunate men.

If we can use the words *good* and *bad* to express judgments of human excellence on *any* scale of values, then we can say that, under favorable external conditions, circumstantial freedom may be enjoyed by bad men as well as good, and by both in the same way. In contrast, the possession of acquired freedom, according to all conceptions of it, is confined to the good—to those who have acquired the particular excellence of mind or character that is the source of freedom.

When freedom is thought to depend on favorable circumstances, it is also thought to consist in an individual's ability to execute or carry out in overt action whatever it is that he desires, wishes, or wills to do. But as we have already pointed out, when freedom is thought to depend on a person's attainment of certain excellence of mind or character, it is then thought to consist in his acquired ability to will as he ought. We can accentuate the difference between the two abilities if we describe the circumstantial ability as one that involves an individual's being able to act as he wishes for his own good as he sees it, and the acquired ability as one that involves a person's being able to live as he ought in accordance with the moral law or in conformity to an ideal befitting human nature.

In the statement just made, the critical words are *ought, moral law, ideal, conformity,* and *befitting.* They are subject to many variations in meaning as they occur in diverse theories of acquired freedom. We will consider some of these variations in a moment; for the present, we are concerned only with the variety of acquirements that diverse authors regard as the source of such ability. These fall into two main types according as the human excellence to be attained is measured (1) by standards of virtue or wisdom, or (2) by ideals of health or growth.

According to a large number of the older writers with whom we are here concerned, the acquirement on which freedom depends is virtue. But virtue is a word of many meanings. Thus Plato, for example, in explaining what it means for a man to be master of himself, lays it down that "temperance . . . is the ordering or controlling of certain pleasures and desires."[90] Plotinus seems to hold a similar view. "Virtue," he writes, "comes in to restore the disordered soul, taming passions and appetites," and by its entry into the soul "prepares freedom and self-disposal."[91]

Spinoza and Leibniz, together with such Stoic philosophers as Cicero, Seneca, Epictetus, and Marcus Aurelius, also regard the virtuous man as one in whom reason rules and in whom the passions are controlled and desires conquered. But for them—as perhaps also for Plato—the acquirement of virtue is inseparable from the acquirement of knowledge or wisdom. Only "in so far as we act with a distinct knowledge," as Leibniz puts it, are we "immune from bondage."[92]

In the tradition of Christian thought, from Augustine on, freedom comes with the acquirement of virtue, but the virtue requisite for freedom comes only with the acquirement of grace. In consequence, it is virtue of a different order from that treated by the philosophers who regard virtue as a purely natural acquirement. According to the theologians, such moral virtue and wisdom as men are able to achieve by the strength of their unaided reason or will may bring about some control of the passions and appetites, but they are not adequate to remove man's slavery to sin. That phrase, "slavery to sin," is reiterated in the writings of Augustine, Anselm, Aquinas, Calvin, and Luther; and with it we find a general concurrence with Augustine's summary statement that "no one is free to do right who has not been freed from sin."[93]

Authors who make the acquirement of virtue and freedom concurrent see this alteration in man's inner life as a victory of sanctity over sin, of the higher part of man's nature over the lower, of reason over the passions or appetites, of knowledge and wisdom over ignorance and folly, or of a sense of duty over sensuous impulses.

Freud, on the other hand, makes the acquirement of freedom concurrent with a strengthening of the ego in its conflicts with both the super-ego and the id. The aim of psychoanalysis, he declares, "is to strengthen the ego, to make it more independent of the super-ego, to widen its field of vision, and so to extend its organization that it can take over new portions of the id."[94] With this change in the organization of the psyche and shift in the balance of power among its component forces, there is a transition from an infantile to an adult condition; and with that a better approximation to the ideal of the integrated and healthy personality.

The ideal of growth, rather than the ideal of health, is for Dewey the necessary acquirement that is concurrent with freedom. In his view, the obstacles to freedom in the makeup of a person are "induration and fixity"—obstinate prejudices, fossilized habits, and all forms of inflexibility that are obstacles to growth; for the flexibility that favors growth also promotes freedom. Indeed, it is the acquirement of such flexibility that Dewey had in mind when he said that growth itself leads to further growth. Every step in the formation of a new self is "an experience of freedom." "If we state the moral law as the injunction to each self on every possible occasion to identify the self with a new growth that is possible, then," he declares, "obedience to law is one with moral freedom."[95]

The meaning of self-perfection

The fact that the translation of a man's intentions into overt action is all-important for self-realization but not for self-perfection helps to differentiate between these two freedoms. But it is neither the only difference they have nor the principal one. A deeper contrast between the two can be seen after we have first explored their similarities.

In both theories of freedom, a man is said to be free only if he acts voluntarily or willingly rather than under the compulsion of fear or force.

Hence, given a completely open environment in which men enjoy such favorable conditions that they can always translate their intentions into overt action, the man who lives as he ought, acts as he wishes, no less than the man whose voluntary behavior consists in doing as he pleases.

The analogy that exists between the two freedoms is further revealed by the following points:

> (1) Both the self-perfection authors and the self-realization authors hold that a goal or fulfillment of some sort is to be achieved.
>
> (2) Both groups hold that what the individual pursues is his good.
>
> (3) The self-perfection authors, no less than the self-realization authors, admit that if an obligation or rule represents a wholly external imposition or an entirely alien will that does not obtain or even solicit the individual's consent, then he is not free when he discharges that obligation or obeys that rule.
>
> (4) Hence it is clear that both groups make the self the principle of freedom. Both maintain that freedom must involve that which proceeds *from me* and that which achieves something *for me*. Whatever in my life merely happens to me or in me, but proceeds entirely from another, represents a compulsion rather than a freedom I enjoy.

It is against the background of these similarities that the basic differences between self-perfection and self-realization stand out. They turn on the meaning of the critical terms in the foregoing statement of the similarities. They are found by asking the following questions:

> (1) How does the meaning of *self* differ in the two cases?
>
> (2) How do the meanings of such words as *wish, desire, will,* and *intention* differ?
>
> (3) In the two cases, how do authors differ when they speak of what is good or right for the human person, or when they refer to man's goal or fulfillment?
>
> (4) What is the difference in the two cases between the forces or factors that make men unfree by preventing them from achieving their goals or fulfillment?

These questions can be answered by examining four points that are common to the understanding of freedom that is shared by all authors who affirm a freedom of self-perfection. These four points express the common and neutral meaning of the term *self-perfection,* which we have adopted to complete the identification of a freedom that we have already partially identified as acquired.

No one of these four points is shared by all self-realization authors; and no self-realization author subscribes to all four points but at most, in exceptional cases, to one or two of them.

The first point shared by all self-perfection authors is that the moral universe in which they regard some men as having the freedom to perfect themselves is one in which the principle of perfection is the *same for all human beings.* However these writers differ in their conception of the ultimate good for man or of human rectitude—and they differ widely on this matter—they hold that the distinction between good and evil or between right and wrong is objective rather than subjective; that it is grounded in the nature of things, in the universal dictates of reason, or in God's will; and that it is not finally determined by the preferences of the individual man.

If what is good or right is absolute in its universality rather than relative to individual differences, then no matter how individuals differ about what appears good to them or about what they deem to be right, what is really good or right for anyone is the same for all. Men may differ by fulfilling or not fulfilling their obligations, by achieving or not achieving their goal in life, by the degree to which they achieve it, or even in the way in which they achieve it, but the duty or goal that is the principle of their perfection does not differ from man to man.

Hence, according to self-perfection authors, a man is free through being able to live as every man ought to live, not through being able to give vent to his individual desires, predilections, or caprice. It is not the good or right as he himself sees it that is relevant to his freedom, but rather that which is objectively good and right in itself. The good or right relevant to the freedom of self-perfection is absolute in the sense that it determines what a man ought to seek or admire, not relative in the sense that it is determined by each man according to his individual tendencies or tastes.

This contrast between the absolute or objective good and the relative or subjective good is sometimes made in terms of what is in fact good for all men *whether or not they actually judge it to be so,* and what each individual deems to be good for himself *whether or not it is in fact good for him.* That which is good independently of individual judgment or desire is called the "real" good in contrast to the merely "apparent" good—that which appears good to an individual whose judgment is influenced by his own desire.

Some self-perfection authors, such as Leibniz and Kant, think of man's desires or appetites as sensuous inclinations or the promptings of passions, and set them against the judgments of his reason or his rational will. For them, whatever a man wills by his reason is always the good or the right. But other writers often use the terms *will, wish,* or *desire* interchangeably. While they recognize that a man experiences many desires that run counter to his better judgment, they distinguish such impulses from the wishes that spring from virtue or wisdom. What the wise or virtuous man wishes for himself, in their view, is that which is really right or good.

The third point shared by all self-perfection authors involves the assertion of a duality in the structure or makeup of the human person. This assertion is of basic significance for the meaning of self-perfection that is common among authors who conceive human freedom as an acquired ability to will what is right or to direct one's life toward the attainment of its fullest good. For if there were no duality of principles in man, if man's whole being or nature tended of itself toward its real good or was inherently incapable of swerving from the path of right, human life might still be a temporal process of self-perfection, but there would be no need to *acquire* a power to work for or achieve that goal. There would be no distinction between men of wisdom, virtue, or rectitude who have acquired some measure of such power and freedom, and those who, lacking such acquirements, also lack freedom. The fact that self-perfection authors divide men into two categories is thus seen to be connected with the fact that these writers also assert *a division within man himself.*

We have already observed two ways in which these writers advert to the divided nature or being of man. One is the distinction they make between the real and the merely apparent good, or between the truth about what is objectively right for all men and false opinions or mistaken judgments about it. The other is the distinction they make between conflicting tendencies in man—his rational will and sensuous desires; or his natural or right desires, on the one hand, and all his contrary impulses, on the other. These two distinctions are connected, for of the conflicting tendencies in man, one directs him toward the true good or what is objectively right, and the other turns him away from it or misdirects him to a merely apparent good or that which is in fact wrong.

To these two distinctions a third must be added to complete the picture of the duality in man that the self-perfection authors hold and in terms of which they discuss man's acquired freedom. This third distinction is implied by the first two. If there are conflicting tendencies in man, there is not only a division within him, but he is also divided against himself. Hence it becomes necessary to identify that part of man that *is the self* that tends toward human perfection, and to distinguish it from that part of him, that *other within him,* that tends on the contrary toward human imperfection.

We see here one of the clearest differences between the self-perfection authors and the self-realization authors. The latter identify the self with *the individual as a whole* and set that self against an other that is wholly external to the individual—either other men or impinging forces in the physical and social environment. The circumstantial freedom of self-realization is then conceived, positively, in terms of actions that flow from that self and redound to the fulfillment of its desires and, negatively, in terms of exemption from coercion and constraint by that other and for its benefit, or at least not for one's own.

The self-perfection authors, on the contrary, never identify the self for which freedom is sought with the individual as a whole; nor do they ever conceive freedom as being won for a self that is confronted by an external other that, by dominating it, crushes its freedom. The struggle for freedom, for them, occurs within the person; and the parties involved are the parts of the human person that are represented by the conflicting tendencies we have just examined.

The fourth and last common point that we need to examine involves the assertion—or the recognition—by all self-perfection authors that there is a deep conflict within man. There is a split between the true, better, or higher self and the other, lower, or opposite part of his nature. And this split radically transforms the meaning of "as I please" and "as I ought."

For the self-realization authors, the word *ought* always expresses an external imposition that is as antithetical to freedom as coercive force is. Whether that imposition is a rule or an obligation, it represents the will or pleasure of another, not the will or pleasure of the individual who is subject to it and who complies with it only to avoid what, from his point of view, are less desirable consequences.

But for the self-perfection authors, the word *ought* expresses what man's true, better, or higher self wills or wishes. The law, duty, or ideal it signifies is, therefore, not an external imposition, and is in no sense antithetical to the freedom of the real self that has its goal in the perfection to which man is directed by moral law, obligations, or ideals. It does, however, exert compulsion or restraint upon the other part of himself, whose desires or impulses must be frustrated when they are antagonistic to what is truly right or really good.

Hence when a man is able to live as he ought in conformity with the moral law or ideal, his lower nature *is not* free to do as it pleases, but his true or better self *is* free to do as it will or wishes. For the self-perfection authors, the good man takes pleasure in living as he ought, or as Kant would prefer saying, finds contentment in so doing. Only the bad man regards what he ought to do as unqualifiedly inimical to his pleasure.

The self-perfection authors differ among themselves about the way in which the good man resolves the conflict within himself between (a) desires or impulses that run counter to what he ought to do and (b) his will or wish to do that which will lead him to the perfection of happiness, equanimity, or blessedness. But whether they think that the righteous or the integrated person has completely subdued or even eliminated the opposing forces within himself, or whether they hold that the wise or virtuous man has only gained the upper hand over those forces and must retain his mastery by continually disciplining them, they all acknowledge the existence of the conflict at some stage of the moral life.

For all of them the acquirement of freedom is coincident with some mode of resolving the conflict, which results in the government of a man's

life by his true, better, or higher self. For all of them the degree of freedom acquired is proportionate to the completeness with which that self
dominates or to the firmness with which it holds the reins. For all of them
freedom is won not by a momentary victory on the battlefield, which can
be reversed at the next moment, but only by a relatively stable conquest
or by enduring peace.

The preceding paragraph makes use of a number of dramatic metaphors; they are metaphors that are often used by self-perfection authors.
It is important to recognize, especially in the last third of the twentieth
century, that these metaphors, at least when they occur in the writings
of self-perfection authors, are not mere poetic license. The two selves in
man, the two parties to the conflict within him, are in a sense the *dramatis
personae* of that conflict, but they are not conceived as mythical. They
are as real as the struggle itself in which they are engaged. When these
authors describe that struggle in terms of war, victory, and conquest or
peace, or when they use the terms *master* or *slave* to describe the relation
between one part of man and another, they refer to what they consider
to be real factors actually operating within the individual.

In their view, the man who is held back by his undisciplined passions
from doing what is right suffers from constraint and the man who is
driven by his uncontrolled impulses suffers from coercion quite as literally
as the individual does who is prevented by chains from doing as he pleases
or who is compelled by superior force—the gun at the head—to act contrary to his own wishes. The man who is able to discipline his own passions or control his own impulses in the interest of what is really good
or right possesses a power that literally liberates him from bondage to
those forces within him and literally gives him mastery over them.

In the foregoing, we examined four points that all self-perfection authors
hold in common. But there are differences among these authors, too.
The differences among them do not invalidate our contention that the
freedom they affirm is the same for all. But according as they differ on
certain critical points, self-perfection takes different forms for them.

Three such critical points require consideration here. The first concerns
the autonomy of the self that has attained to some degree the perfection that is the goal of human life.

The autonomous individual is somehow the sponsor of the very law he
obeys. Being thus self-regulated, he is free in living lawfully as every man
ought. To the extent that he is the sponsor of the law, he has spontaneity
or freedom in obeying it. The fact that he is somehow a law unto himself does not mean that the moral law he obeys is subjective or fails to be
binding on all other men of good will. But even when an absolute and
objective law is affirmed, there is still room for wide differences of opinion
as to its source and authority. Accordingly the autonomy that the virtu-

ous or righteous man has in his freedom will be differently conceived.

Two other words—*independence* and *self-sufficiency*—are closely related to *autonomy*. When the individual acquires the freedom of self-perfection he achieves a certain independence. His life has a quality of wholeness or completeness. But the wholeness or self-sufficiency may be greater or less. It is obviously limited when the perfection that the free man enjoys involves his participation in a perfection other than his own—that of the state, of nature, or of God. When the goal does not involve such participation, the independence or self-sufficiency is, of course, much greater.

That the free man has *some measure* of autonomy is the common opinion of all the authors who affirm a freedom of self-perfection. These writers, like those who affirm a freedom of self-realization, hold that moral rules or obligations are inimical to freedom *when they are externally imposed without our consent or by an alien will.* But the two groups of writers place quite divergent interpretations on the italicized words.

According to the self-realization authors, externally imposed moral rules or obligations interfere with freedom when they constrain men to obey them from fear of the consequences and to forego the satisfaction of their individual desires. According to the self-perfection authors, such rules and obligations militate against freedom only when the individual is not able to give his full consent to them. The opposition to freedom in the first case comes from outside; in the second, from within.

Freedom of self-perfection is never found in mere obedience to rules or mere compliance with standards. It lies rather in the willingness to obey or comply, which springs only from assent to the right or love of the good. Since such willingness *is not motivated by fear of the consequences of transgression,* the moral rule or obligation exerts no coercion or duress. It may express a will that is external, but never one that is alien or despotic.

This is to say no more than that the self is the principle of freedom and that just as physical coercion destroys freedom *because* what I do under coercion proceeds from another rather than from myself, so moral obligation or regulation destroys freedom *if* what I do at its behest in no way springs from my own will, my moral commitments or aspirations. Though I am compelled in both cases, there is a crucial difference. Physical coercion is always incompatible with my spontaneity (that is, my freedom of self-realization). Moral obligation is *not* always incompatible with my autonomy (that is, my freedom of self-perfection). But when moral obligation subordinates the self to something that transcends the individual, that which transcends the self may be the principle or sine qua non of its freedom. When, for example, the individual willingly prescribes to himself what is laid down in the moral law, he not only gains some measure of the autonomy essential to freedom but he also allies the author of the moral law with his higher or better self in its struggle against recalcitrant or obstructive forces in his own nature.

The second critical difference of opinion among self-perfection authors can be summarized by saying that for certain authors the freedom of self-perfection takes a purely *personal* form, while for other writers it takes an essentially *social* form. To understand what is and is not at stake in this diversity, we must be clear that the dependence of this freedom on the individual's relation to society does not make it circumstantial rather than acquired. This mistake is avoided by observing that society or the state plays, in certain theories, a role analogous to God in other theories.

The fact that Christian theologians maintain that men acquire the freedom of autonomy under divine law only through God's grace does not make such freedom "circumstantial" in our sense of the term. That it is acquired is plainly indicated by the fact that, according to Christian theology, men become free only with the radical change that is produced when their sinful nature is rectified by healing and sanctifying grace. Their freedom depends upon a change in themselves, not a change in the external circumstances of their lives.

When, in certain theories, the state plays a role analogous to God, the consequences are analogous. Certain authors—for example, Rousseau—maintain that men acquire the freedom of self-perfection only with the help of a beneficent state. For them, the state performs an educative function, transforming wild men into civilized ones. But this does not make the state a favorable circumstance enabling men to act as they wish. Though the state is an indispensable adjunct to the acquirement of freedom, the freedom itself results from an inner change that is produced in the self that is humanized and civilized by the state.

Whether it is personal or social in form, the freedom of self-perfection remains an acquired freedom. This is decisively indicated by the fact that under identical circumstances in a given society only good men are free. However, we find that when self-perfection takes a social form it always has a circumstantial aspect, in that the freedom extends beyond intention to action. It may also have a circumstantial aspect when it takes a personal form, but this does not hold for all writers who conceive self-perfection as personal in form, as it does hold for all those who conceive it as social in form.

Indeed, these remarks raise the third critical point of difference to which we have referred. While some writers hold the view that the virtuous man is completely free even if external circumstances prevent him from doing as he ought, others maintain that the free man must also be able to carry out what he wills. Still others take the position that while circumstances preventing a man from doing as he wills cannot destroy the freedom of self-perfection, they can render it incomplete.

On the question whether a slave, all of whose actions are at the command of his owner, can be regarded as free, self-perfection authors thus divide into three groups.

(1) In the first group are those such as Rousseau, Hegel, and Dewey, who would say that a man in this condition, no matter how virtuous or wise he may be, is not free. For example, Rousseau's famous statement that "whoever refuses to obey the general will shall be compelled to do so by the whole body" (which "means nothing less than that he will be forced to be free") applies only to the *acts* of the recalcitrant individual, not to his *intentions*. The benign institutions of a republic whose laws express the general will may cultivate and support the freedom that good men carry in their hearts, but nothing can *force* men to *will* as they ought in conformity to the general will. Hence when those who are neither good men nor good citizens are compelled to obey just laws, they are forced to conform to the general will. But such men are not free. Hence we see that for Rousseau two things are requisite for freedom— a *right will* and *right action*. Either without the other results in a counterfeit of freedom.

(2) At the opposite extreme, such writers as Philo, the Stoics, Augustine, and Kant would reply that if the slave is a man of good will, then his being enslaved neither destroys nor attenuates his freedom of self-perfection.

For the Stoics, as many passages from their writings show, circumstances are excluded as totally irrelevant. The freedom of self-perfection for them is wholly a matter of man's inner moral life and so remains unaffected by external conditions that either permit or prevent overt action. The virtuous man who cannot express his will in physical motions is no less free than the virtuous man who can.

Kant, with certain reservations, may be associated with the Stoics in this respect. He is concerned, he tells us, "only with the determination of the will and the determining principles of its maxims as a free will, not at all with the result. For, provided only that the *will* conforms to the law of pure reason, then let its *power* in execution be what it may."[96] And in another place we find him saying, "A good will is good not because of what it performs or effects, not by its aptness for the attainment of some proposed end, but simply by virtue of the volition; that is, it is good in itself."[97] And again:

> *Even if it should happen that, owing to special disfavor of fortune, or the niggardly provision of a step-motherly nature, this will should wholly lack power to accomplish its purpose, if with its greatest efforts it should yet achieve nothing . . . then, like a jewel, it would still shine by its own light, as a thing which has its whole value in itself. Its usefulness or fruitfulness can neither add nor take away anything from this value.*[98]

Nor, according to Kant, can it add or take away anything from its freedom.

(3) Finally, writers such as Aquinas, Spinoza, Montesquieu, and Maritain would say that while a man who has acquired the freedom of self-perfection can never be deprived of it by unfortunate circumstances of the sort that might exist under a despotism or tyranny, yet such circumstances would have some effect upon his freedom. The effect they would have would be to diminish that freedom by confining it to an internal or private exercise, as, on the other hand, favorable circumstances would enlarge it by extending it to the domain of external conduct.

This view of the matter thus finds middle ground as between the position taken by Rousseau and that which would be taken by Kant and the Stoics. It should be emphasized, however, that those who take this middle ground do not maintain that the favorable circumstances of good government can by themselves bestow a freedom of self-perfection on man, but only that they add, when present, a circumstantial aspect to the acquired freedom that is already possessed by men who, through virtue, interiorize such laws and obey them willingly. By the same token, of course, such men are superior to circumstantial constraints. As the seventeenth-century English poet Richard Lovelace put it, in some famous lines written while he was imprisoned on political charges:

> *Stone walls do not a prison make,*
> *Nor iron bars a cage;*
> *Minds innocent and quiet take*
> *That for an hermitage;*
> *If I have freedom in my love*
> *And in my soul am free,*
> *Angels alone, that soar above,*
> *Enjoy such liberty.*

6. Self-realization and self-perfection conjointly affirmed

We have completed the identification of two distinct kinds of freedom, as well as two distinct subjects of controversy—one, a circumstantial freedom of self-realization; the other, an acquired freedom of self-perfection. These identifications are constructions of our own. In terms of them, we have in each case interpreted a number of authors as sharing a certain minimal common understanding of freedom. This topical agreement does not prevent them from disagreeing with one another about the freedom thus identified. On the contrary, it makes such disagreement possible.

The two identifications not only distinguish two subjects of controversy but also divide authors who discuss freedom into two groups—a group of self-perfection authors, on the one hand, and a group of self-realization authors, on the other. The members of each group, apart from some interesting exceptions to be discussed, appear to affirm only one of these two freedoms. They do not mention the other freedom at all; or, if they do, they deny its reality or deny that it is truly or properly a freedom for man. So far as this is the case, there would appear to be a genuine disagreement about freedom between the members of one group and the members of the other, in addition to such disagreements as may occur within each group about the freedom that all of its members affirm.

The self-realization authors are most clearly and typically represented by such writers as Hobbes, Bentham, J. S. Mill, and Laski; the self-perfection authors, by such writers as Plato, the Stoics, Spinoza, and Kant. There is no doubt about which group the authors just mentioned belong in. And we can be almost as certain about the position of many other writers, so far as the two freedoms we have identified are concerned.

The following tabulation presents a threefold division of authors who have written significant works about the idea of freedom. The first two columns list writers who, on the evidence, belong exclusively to one or the other group. The third column lists the exceptions already referred to—authors who cannot be placed in either group because they affirm both freedoms.

Authors who affirm only a circumstantial freedom of self-realization	*Authors who affirm only an acquired freedom of self-perfection*
HOBBES	PLATO
VOLTAIRE	CICERO
EDWARDS	PHILO
HUME	SENECA
ADAM SMITH	EPICTETUS
BURKE	MARCUS AURELIUS
BENTHAM	PLOTINUS
CALHOUN	AMBROSE
J. S. MILL	AUGUSTINE
SPENCER	BOETHIUS
HOBHOUSE	ANSELM
TAWNEY	LUTHER
MALINOWSKI	CALVIN
KNIGHT	SPINOZA
LASKI	LEIBNIZ
AYER	ROUSSEAU
	KANT
	HEGEL
	WHITEHEAD
	SANTAYANA
	BARTH
	TILLICH

> *Authors who affirm both a circumstantial*
> *freedom of self-realization and an acquired*
> *freedom of self-perfection*

> AQUINAS
> LOCKE
> MONTESQUIEU
> FREUD
> DEWEY
> RUSSELL
> MARITAIN
> SIMON

In view of the fact that the greatest number of authors affirm self-realization or self-perfection to the exclusion or neglect of the other, we are called upon to examine some of the theories that affirm both. When both are affirmed by an author, is either conception altered or modified by its conjunction with the other? If so, in what manner?

Before we turn to this problem we must first deal with a prior one. In theories of freedom that take account of both circumstances and acquirements, how can we tell whether what is affirmed is *one* freedom with both a circumstantial and an acquired aspect or *two* freedoms, one of which is circumstantial, the other acquired? Only after solving this problem can we see how, in those theories that affirm two conceptions of freedom, the two are related.

One conception of freedom or two: the diagnostic signs

We saw in the preceding section that authors who affirm an acquired freedom of self-perfection differ about whether the ability to will as one ought is, by itself, sufficient for such freedom. They fall into three subgroups according as they maintain (1) that the virtuous man is completely free even if external circumstances prevent him from acting as he ought; (2) that circumstances that prevent the good man from doing as he wills cannot destroy his freedom but can render it incomplete; or (3) that the virtuous man must be able to carry out what he wills in addition to willing as he ought.

The self-perfection authors who take the first view hold that there is a freedom entirely beyond circumstances; those who take the second view hold that freedom is incomplete insofar as action is impeded by circumstances; and those who take the third view hold that circumstances favorable to execution are essential to freedom. Philo, Plotinus, the Stoic philosophers, and Kant represent clear cases of the first view; Aquinas, Spinoza, and Montesquieu, clear cases of the second view; Rousseau, Hegel, and Dewey, clear cases of the third.

The following table summarizes the division of opinion with regard to the effect of circumstances upon the freedom of self-perfection.

Effect of Circumstances	*Typical Authors*
1. None	Philo, Plotinus, Stoics, Kant
2. Can render freedom incomplete by preventing action	Aquinas, Spinoza, Montesquieu
3. Can nullify freedom entirely by preventing action	Rousseau, Hegel, Dewey

The foregoing table requires two comments. First, Dewey differs from Rousseau and Hegel in that his theory not only conceives freedom as having both a circumstantial and an acquired aspect but also fuses self-realization and self-perfection. These are not distinct freedoms for him. Secondly, whereas for Aquinas, Spinoza, and Montesquieu the acquired freedom of self-perfection has a circumstantial aspect, Aquinas and Montesquieu, unlike Spinoza, also affirm circumstantial self-realization as a distinct freedom. Their theories combine it with an acquired freedom of self-perfection. Hence, for Aquinas and Montesquieu, the effect of circumstances must be represented as follows:

Effect of Circumstances

On freedom of self-perfection	Can prevent the completion of freedom by preventing action
On freedom of self-realization	Determines existence or non-existence of freedom according as conditions are favorable or unfavorable

It will be remembered that all self-realization theories of freedom conceive it as dependent on favorable circumstances; and that all self-perfection theories of freedom conceive it as dependent on the acquirement of virtue, wisdom, or other traits of personality, mind, or character. But whereas some self-perfection theories of freedom make it dependent on circumstances, others do not. And, whereas a few self-realization theories of freedom make it dependent on the acquirement of knowledge or skill, most of them do not.

Circumstances and acquirements, therefore, do not always indicate whether an author's theory includes one freedom or two. If his theory pays no attention to circumstances, then we know, of course, that it does not include a freedom of self-realization. If it pays no attention to acquirements of any sort, we know that it does not include a freedom of self-perfection. But if it pays attention to both circumstances and acquirements we cannot know from this fact alone whether it includes two distinct conceptions of freedom, or only one, that somehow combines the circumstantial and the acquired mode of possession.

We propose the following diagnostic signs for telling whether a theory is either the freedom of self-realization or the freedom of self-perfection, but not both.

(a) When a theory maintains or implies that the free man need not be virtuous, and that the laws enforced by the state are compatible with individual liberty only when they are consonant with what the individual wishes to do anyway, then we know the theory in question affirms a freedom of self-realization, and that it excludes a freedom of self-perfection.

(b) When, on the contrary, a theory affirms that good men alone are free, and that virtue or wisdom leads to a willing compliance with whatever rules, moral or legal, prescribe what all men ought to do, then we know that the theory in question conceives freedom as self-perfection and excludes freedom as self-realization.

But, while the relations of liberty to law give us clear signs for detecting theories that affirm *either* self-realization *or* self-perfection, they do not help us to discern theories that include *both* a freedom of self-realization *and* one of self-perfection. How, then, shall we tell whether a theory, especially one that pays attention to *both* circumstances and acquirements, includes both conceptions of freedom and keeps them distinct?

To answer this question we must take account of the following possibilities. When both freedoms are included in a single theory, (a) one may be modified by its relation to the other, though remaining distinct from it; (b) both may remain distinct and intact, with neither modifying the other; and (c) they may be fused into a single freedom. Let us examine these three possibilities in turn.

The subordination of self-realization to self-perfection:
Aquinas, Locke, etc.

If we find an author maintaining that men are free in submitting to the moral law or to just laws of the state when they are able to do so willingly and virtuously, we know that author affirms a freedom of self-perfection. If in addition we find him maintaining that men are also free when they act as they wish in regard to all matters not regulated by law, we know that his theory includes a distinct freedom of self-realization. If these diagnostic signs are present, then there is good reason to believe that the author in question relates self-realization to self-perfection by subordinating the former to the latter; for clearly such an author circumscribes the freedom of self-realization when he limits it to matters not regulated by the civil or the moral law. What has just been said applies to the positions taken by Aquinas, Jacques Maritain, and Yves Simon, and also, albeit with complications, to those taken by Montesquieu and Locke.

We are dealing here with theories that subordinate a circumscribed freedom of self-realization *outside the sphere of law* to a freedom of self-perfection *under law*. The first (that is, freedom outside the sphere of law) requires favorable circumstances. Under such circumstances it can be enjoyed by good and bad men alike, even though good men and bad men may not use this freedom in the same way. The second (that is, freedom under law) can be enjoyed only by men of wisdom or virtue. In their case favorable circumstances may render the freedom they possess more complete by permitting them to translate their virtuous, law-abiding intentions into action.

There can be no doubt that Aquinas, Maritain, and Simon affirm a freedom of self-perfection. In their view, the virtuous man, by submission to the moral or civil law, becomes free through interiorizing the law and making its precepts the maxims of his own conduct. What Aquinas says about the liberty of the children of God (that is, that when led by the Spirit of God, they are no longer under the coercion of law but are freely in harmony with it, because, by virtue of grace and supernatural love, they follow their own inclinations in doing the will of God) applies equally to virtuous men as subject to the law of the state. The good man acts from the promptings of his own virtue or justice when he obeys just laws; and even if the particular law is questionable and can be improved, his devotion to the common good may cause him to respect it if prudence recommends that obedience rather than disobedience serves the end his own justice leads him to seek.

The only question we face here is whether Aquinas and his Thomist followers also affirm a circumstantial freedom of self-realization, open to good and bad men alike, yet one that is circumscribed in the case of the virtuous by the moral and civil law, and so is subordinate to the liberty the good man enjoys in doing everything the law prescribes. Is there evidence for thinking that the Thomists hold that in all things not prescribed or prohibited by law, men should have the freedom of doing as they individually wish—a freedom that is circumstantially theirs to the extent that they are not constrained by arbitrary force on the part of government or of other men?

An affirmative answer to this question is supplied by the following Thomistic doctrine.

The moral law leaves many alternatives open to individual discretion. For example, it contains certain precepts concerning marriage, but it does not command anyone to marry; and though it may eliminate certain persons as unfit to wed, it does not, among all those who are eligible, direct the choice of any particular one. The individual should be free, therefore, to marry or not to marry, and to marry the eligible person of his choice. A father who tries to compel his son to marry against his will, or a state that interferes with the individual's choice of a mate, unjustly limits the freedom everyone should have.

There are many matters that the moral law leaves to be decided by individual discretion, in which the individual should be free from interference. They include such things as selecting and using any one of several alternative means, all of which are morally flawless ways of attaining the same good end. Thus, for example, since a certain amount of relaxation is morally sound, the individual should be free to do this or that for his amusement, on condition, of course, that the alternatives in question are each without the taint of iniquity or corruption. Similarly, the individual should be free to dress or adorn himself in any number of ways; for while the moral law prohibits nudity and immodest attire, it does not prescribe how these two prohibitions shall be respected. The latitude of such freedom even extends to what the theologians call an *actus remissus,* in which the individual does what is good, but what is less good than something else he might have done.

The controlling principle in all such matters, according to Aquinas, is that it belongs to the perfection of liberty that the individual should be able to elect various means that indifferently, or even more or less adequately, serve his pursuit of the good end that all men should strive for. Among actions that are morally acceptable because of their ordination to the right end, the moral law permits the individual to choose one rather than another. External circumstances are, therefore, favorable to a freedom of self-realization insofar as they permit him to act on his choice and do as he pleases.

What is true of matters not prescribed by the moral law holds *a fortiori* with regard to all matters that are not or should not be subject to regulation by the positive law of the state. Not only are there many particulars that are not and cannot be regulated by civil government, such as the multitude of things that fall within the sphere of a man's private life, but, in addition, Aquinas points out, it does not belong to the positive law to prescribe the acts of all the virtues or to prohibit the acts of all the vices, but only those that are affected with the public interest or concern the common good. In the whole area of conduct that is left unprescribed by the natural moral law as well as by the positive law of the state, men are free to do as they please to the extent that external circumstances afford them the opportunity of realizing their individual desires.

Aquinas, Maritain, and Simon think that all men should have such liberty, even though the vicious will abuse it so that it becomes license. When not so abused, it is the morally and legally circumscribed liberty of individual actions that is proper to the virtuous man and subordinate to his freedom of self-perfection under law.

Arising in a somewhat different context, John Locke's position is nevertheless similar to that of the Thomists. When Locke distinguishes two ways in which man in civil society can be free in relation to the laws of the state, he is in effect presenting us with the two distinct conceptions of freedom that are being discussed in this section. One of these freedoms is the freedom that men have in areas where the law does not reach—what we may call freedom *from* law. The other is the freedom that men *can* have when they willingly comply with the law—what we may call freedom *under* law. The freedom men have to do as they please in matters *not regulated by law* is a freedom of self-realization. But the freedom men have under law and through a *willing compliance with its demands* is not a freedom of self-realization but one of self-perfection.*

In order to understand this, we must recognize that Locke's theory of individual freedom in relation to law, as expressed in his own terms, has two major tenets. The first is that men are free to do as they please in all matters not regulated by law. In holding this, Locke is in accord with those authors who affirm only a freedom of self-realization. The second is that men are free when they comply with any law that has been made with their general consent and so is virtually, if not actually, an expression of their own will. In holding this, Locke seems again to be in accord with certain self-realization authors who are discussed in Section 2. It is only with Locke's further explanation of this second tenet that we see that he crosses the line that divides the freedom of doing as one pleases (self-realization) from the freedom of doing as one ought (self-perfection).

"Freedom," he maintains, is not merely "what Sir Robert Filmer tells us: 'A liberty for every one to do what he lists, to live as he pleases, and not to be tied by any laws.'" Rather it depends, at least in part, on having "a standing rule to live by, common to every one of that society, and made by the legislative power erected in it."[99] When men are in a state of nature and have only natural law to govern them, they are much more subject to "restraint and violence from others," who may act in contravention of the natural law, than they are when they live under a civil government and have the coercive force of its laws as a safeguard against extralegal coercion. "The end of law," Locke consequently says, "is not to abolish or restrain, but to preserve and enlarge freedom," and for all "beings, capable of laws, where there is no law there is no freedom."[100]

Even as described here, however, Locke's position does not appear to be essentially different from that of several authors discussed in Section 2, who maintain that some laws, in some circumstances, do not infringe on an individual's circumstantial freedom of self-realization. But on further consideration we see that Locke goes beyond them. In the first

---

* Locke also holds a third conception of freedom, the variant of self-realization freedom that we have called political liberty. Political liberty was discussed in Section 3.

place, he carefully distinguishes, as they do not, between liberty and license, and maintains that in a state of nature man's freedom is true liberty rather than license *only* if the individual's actions accord with the law of nature, or the rules of reason, *which are the same for all men.* This is the first diagnostic point that tells us that Locke's position is different from that of the authors treated in Section 2. In the second place, Locke asserts that "law in its true notion, is not so much the *limitation* as the *direction* of a free and intelligent agent to his *proper interest.*"[101] We can interpret his use of the words "proper interest" to mean that civil law, in its "true notion," directs individuals to pursue interests they ought to have, whether or not in fact they do have them. Thus Locke, in his theory of freedom under law, does not conceive that freedom as one of self-realization, according to the common understanding of that kind of freedom shared by self-realization authors. Instead, the freedom that Locke conceives as having its foundation in law is a freedom of self-perfection.

The theory of freedom held by such authors as Aquinas and Locke can, therefore, be sharply contrasted with that of writers like Hobbes, Bentham, J. S. Mill, and Laski, on the one hand, and with that of writers like Plato, Spinoza, Rousseau, and Hegel, on the other. The latter either deny or neglect the possibility of a circumstantial freedom of doing as the individual pleases in regard to all matters not prescribed by law. The former reject the distinction between the freedom only good men acquire and a freedom all men possess under favorable circumstances; likewise, they deny that there is any liberty in relation to law except under circumstances in which the individual does—lawfully or unlawfully—as he himself wishes.

In contrast, the Thomists and Locke affirm both an acquired freedom of harmony with law and also a circumstantial freedom for the individual to do as he pleases where law does not prescribe; and they do so consistently by circumscribing the latter, and thus subordinating a limited self-realization to the fullness of self-perfection.

Self-realization and self-perfection distinct and unrelated: Freud

If we find an author maintaining that only men who have acquired a certain moral excellence of mind or character are free, we know that the author in question affirms a freedom of self-perfection. And if we also find him maintaining that under certain favorable circumstances any individual is in addition free to whatever extent such circumstances permit him to act as he wishes, we know that his theory includes a distinct freedom of self-realization. If these diagnostic signs are present and we can find no explicit evidence that the author connects the two freedoms, we can do no more than note that he affirms both freedoms and fails to relate them.

What has just been said applies to Freud, whose theory of freedom as a result represents a rather special case in this discussion, and also, though secondarily, to Bertrand Russell.

That Freud affirms a freedom of self-perfection is clear, although "moral excellence" may not be the most apt phrase to describe the acquired trait of mind or character that is necessary for this freedom to be enjoyed. "Health" in general, "mental health" in particular, might be a better term; but this does not mean that Freud's conception of mental health is very far from the conception of moral excellence that other writers hold. Thus, for example, we find Freud saying of a woman patient that

> *to achieve this* mastery of herself *she must be taken through the primordial era of her mental development and in this way reach* that greater freedom within the mind *which distinguishes conscious mental activity—in the systematic sense—from unconscious.*[102]

He speaks of "the liberation of a human being from his neurotic symptoms, inhibitions and abnormalities of character,"[103] emphasizes the difficulties of being an adult, which make normality an ideal achieved by few and neurosis the "normal" condition of most men, and makes the acquirement of freedom concurrent with a strengthening of the ego in its conflict with both the id and the super-ego.

> *From the point of view of morality, the control and restriction of instinct, it may be said of the id that it is totally non-moral, of the ego that it strives to be moral, and of the super-ego that it can be hyper-moral and then becomes as ruthless as only the id can be.*[104]

In short, there seems to be no question that Freud regards the mental health of an integrated and adult personality as the ideal of human perfection toward which every man should strive, though few if any fully achieve it. Thoroughly cognizant of individual differences, as well as appreciative of their significance for the individual character of the struggle to live sanely and well, Freud nevertheless looks upon health as a goal that can be generally recommended to men as worthy of their effort. The medical ideal of health, no less than the ethical ideal of happiness or virtue, is conceived in terms of human nature or the structure of the human psyche.

To this extent Freud holds views that are at least analogous to those of the moral philosophers and theologians we have considered. But Freud's language is different. He does not speak of a *duty* or *obligation* to be healthy, nor does he censure the neurotic who fails to achieve the freedom of mental health. Yet he recommends, as necessary for freedom, the achievement of an integrated, balanced, and well-adjusted personality, and offers therapeutic prescriptions, if not moral rules, as guidance to this end.

At the same time, it seems clear that Freud also affirms the freedom of self-realization. "The liberty of the individual is not a benefit of culture," he writes in a famous passage in *Civilization and Its Discontents*. "It was greatest before any culture. . . . Liberty has undergone restrictions through the evolution of civilization."[105] Just as J. S. Mill, an indubitable self-realization author, regards "the despotism of culture" as everywhere hostile to "the spirit of liberty," so Freud regards civilization or culture as its enemy. "The cry for freedom," he writes in the same book, "is directed either against particular forms or demands of culture or else against culture itself," because each man, unwilling to submerge himself in the group, as insects do, "will always . . . defend his claim to individual freedom against the will of the multitude."[106]

Freud therefore affirms both self-realization and self-perfection as distinct human freedoms, one circumstantial and the other acquired. But his theory of freedom does not modify self-realization to accommodate self-perfection; it asserts self-realization in its pure form. The scope of this kind of freedom is not limited, in Freud's view, by reference to the universally applicable precepts of the moral law (or to the universal characteristics of mental health). He does, of course, assert that the amount of the freedom of self-realization that a man may enjoy changes as circumstances change, for example as civilization advances. But that is not the same as a modification of the conception of one freedom by the other.*

The fusion of self-realization and self-perfection: Dewey

We have found only one author, John Dewey, who takes the position that self-realization and self-perfection are fused into a single freedom, both of the elements of which, however, are conceived in nontraditional ways. The distinguishing mark of the freedom that results is the fact that no instance of it involves self-realization without also involving self-perfection; and conversely, no instance of it involves self-perfection without also involving self-realization.

"The commonest mistake made about freedom," Dewey writes, "is . . . to identify it with freedom of movement, or with the external or physical side of activity."[107] Such freedom, he maintains, should be treated not as an end in itself but as a means to the freedom that lies in the trained power of growth.

---

* Russell appears to take much the same position as Freud in his essay "A Free Man's Worship."

> *Freedom from restriction . . . is to be prized only as a means to a freedom which is power: power to frame purposes, to judge wisely, to evaluate desires by the consequences which will result from acting upon them; power to select and order means to carry chosen ends into operation.*[108]

Dewey insists that freedom requires something more than a harmonization of conflicting desires or impulses, effected by the individual himself. It requires something more, he says, than the opportunity afforded by external circumstances to realize desires. Dewey maintains that unless the individual has acquired the power to control and change his desires in the light of his changing experiences, his circumstantial ability to realize them may give him the illusion of freedom, but it will be the mere outer shell of self-realization with no self-perfection at its center to make it genuine freedom.

Nevertheless, from Dewey's point of view, the opposite error can also be made. While freedom does not lie in "external unconstraint of movements" alone, neither can it "develop without a fair leeway of movements in exploration, experimentation, application" whereby the individual tests his plans and fulfills his purposes.[109] This statement, together with the statement that the "external and physical side of activity cannot be separated from the internal side of activity; from freedom of thought, desire, and purpose"[110] indicates that while in Dewey's view these aspects of freedom are distinguishable, circumstantial self-realization is, *as freedom,* inseparable from acquired self-perfection.

At the same time, Dewey—like Freud—rejects the notion of fixed ends or final goals, in the attainment of which men can rest. "*The* end is growth itself," Dewey asserts; "to make an end a final goal is but to arrest growth."[111] In another place he writes: "Not perfection as a final goal, but the ever-enduring process of perfecting, maturing, refining is the aim in living."[112] The ultimate goal for man is living itself, when it is fully understood that "life is development, and that developing, growing, is life."[113]

At various places in his works, however, Dewey speaks directly of freedom in relation to a moral law, and with references to the goodness and badness of men. "If we state the moral law," he writes, "as the injunction to each self on every occasion to identify the self with a new growth that is possible, then obedience to law is one with moral freedom."[114] For him, "it is impossible for the self to stand still"; it either becomes better through growth or deteriorates through failure to grow.[115] "The bad man is the man who no matter how good he *has* been is beginning to deteriorate. . . . The good man is the man who no matter how morally unworthy he *has* been is moving to become better."[116]

Dewey summed up his position in the following words:

> *The possibility of freedom is deeply grounded in our very beings.*
> *It is one with our individuality, our being uniquely what we are*
> *and not imitators or parasites of others. But like all other possi-*
> *bilities, this possibility has to be actualized; and, like all others,*
> *it can only be actualized through interaction with objective*
> *conditions.*[117]

We conclude that while such writers as Freud, to say nothing of Rousseau and Hegel, separate self-realization quite clearly from self-perfection,
and while authors like Aquinas and Maritain modify one in relation to
the other, Dewey fuses the two into one freedom. Dewey's theory is best
described as the affirmation of a single, complexly constituted freedom,
which is circumstantial in one aspect and acquired in another. It involves obeying a single law, that of personal growth, which permits and
encourages the fullest realization of *individual* desires and needs.

Thus Dewey, like Freud, is a very special case in the literature of
freedom.

7. Collective freedom

We have employed the term *political liberty* to designate a distinct freedom that is affirmed by certain writers and not by others, and we will
adopt the term *collective freedom* to designate a distinct subject of discussion that still remains to be identified.

The discussion of this subject is found in the writings of Auguste
Comte, Mikhail Bakunin, Karl Marx, and Friedrich Engels. While philosophical anarchists, such as Kropotkin and those whom Marx calls "utopian socialists"—Saint-Simon, Proudhon, and Fourier—have certain affin-
ities with the four authors mentioned, we shall take these four as the
typical exponents of the freedom with which we are concerned in this
section. This freedom requires special consideration because, like political liberty, it cannot be equated either with the freedom of self-realization or with the freedom of self-perfection, as these subjects of controversy have already been identified.

At an earlier point in this essay, we proposed as an hypothesis that
political liberty can be identified as a variant of circumstantial self-
realization. The evidence presented in Section 3 seemed sufficient to
justify our thus assimilating political liberty to the freedom of self-
realization while at the same time preserving it as something distinct.

The hypothesis we propose with respect to collective freedom is that
it can be identified as a variant of acquired self-perfection. We are led
to this hypothesis by the following facts: (1) We do not find in Comte,
Bakunin, Marx, or Engels any evidence that they affirm a freedom to do
as one pleases under circumstances that permit the individual to realize

his own desires. (2) We find no evidence that they affirm a freedom possessed by good men alone, who through virtue or wisdom are able to live as they ought in conformity to the moral law. (3) On the contrary, we find evidence that they reject these freedoms and in place of them advocate a freedom that the human race will enjoy *collectively* in the future when it has achieved the ideal mode of association that is the goal of mankind's historical development.

The theories of freedom advanced by Comte, Bakunin, Marx, and Engels do not stem from the same philosophical background. Their several conceptions of collective freedom differ in significant respects. But this is also true of such writers as Aristotle, Aquinas, Locke, Montesquieu, and Kant, all of whom nevertheless share a minimal common understanding of political liberty that constitutes their topical agreement about that subject. That, in spite of their differences, Comte, Bakunin, Marx, and Engels similarly share a minimal common understanding of collective freedom is indicated, in a preliminary way, by the points mentioned above: they all project a freedom that will be achieved in the future and that will be attained by mankind, socially or collectively, in proportion as it is able to approximate the ideal form of association that is the ultimate goal on earth of the human race.*

In the pages that follow we will develop our hypothesis in detail by explaining why we think collective freedom can be assimilated to the freedom of self-perfection, yet in such a way that it remains a distinct freedom. We will first state a number of negative points that are common to the theories of collective freedom—the ways in which these theories deem men unfree when they are deprived of collective freedom. After elucidating the significance of these negative points we will develop our hypothesis about the positive character of collective freedom as a variant of acquired self-perfection.

The deprivation of collective freedom

Auguste Comte holds before us the vision of an ideal society, brought into being by the acceptance of the positive philosophy and by the consequent rejection of religious superstition and metaphysical speculation. He sometimes calls this ideal condition, to which humanity will ultimately progress, the "positive state." When mankind has evolved from its infancy, spent under the domination of religion, and from its childhood, spent under the domination of metaphysical speculations or myths, "man will no longer be the slave of man."[118]

The ideal condition of society is not for Comte a condition of political

---

* Unlike the writers who advance conceptions of political liberty as a distinct freedom, the advocates of collective freedom reject or ignore all other conceptions of freedom. This not only gives collective freedom a drastic and revolutionary character but also requires us to preserve its distinctness from the various freedoms that other writers affirm.

anarchy. In his view it is not attended by the abolition of government, as it is for Bakunin, or by the withering away of the state, as it is for Marx and Engels. "Society can no more exist without a government," he writes, "than government can exist without a society."[119] Nevertheless, in his view, the nearer humanity approaches the positive state, "the more free will our conduct become from arbitrary command or servile obedience."[120] What Comte calls "true liberty" begins only when all arbitrariness has been eliminated from human life and society.

According to Saint-Simon and his followers—the so-called utopian socialists—the domination of the physical environment by science and industry will progressively emancipate men, not merely from want and insecurity but also from the domination of some men by others. They are like Comte in thinking that the development of natural science and its applications in industry will bring about this change; but, unlike Comte, they do not go beyond asserting that the freedom that is to accrue will consist simply in exemption from arbitrary rule. They do not picture the positive state of freedom, in which the scientific laws of human behavior and of social action will govern mankind instead of the juridical regulations foisted upon society in its earlier religious and metaphysical stages.

For the anarchist Bakunin, however, as for Comte, the negative point leads to the positive one. With regard to the negative point, Bakunin holds that all man-made rules of conduct are in their very nature authoritarian and arbitrary. Freedom will never exist until men have completely overthrown all "the political and juridical laws which are imposed by men on other men, whether with the right of might, violently or hypocritically, in the name . . . of the fiction, the democratic lie, which is called universal suffrage."[121]

Bakunin does not limit his attack on man-made law to the ordinances of civil government. He includes as well, because equally authoritarian and arbitrary, the moral and religious precepts "which the privileged classes have established in the course of history, always in the interest of the exploitation of the work of the working masses, with the only end to muzzle the liberty of these masses, laws which, under the pretext of a fictitious morality, have always been the source of the profoundest immorality." They can all be lumped together, since "from the negative point of view [liberty is] the complete independence of the will of each from the will of others."[122]

But authoritarianism or arbitrariness, as embodied in the state as well as in public morality, is not the only source of human slavery, from which mankind as a whole must be emancipated. Another obstacle to freedom must be eliminated. It is man's dependence on nature for his subsistence and comfort. "The chains of slavery which nature places on all of her children" include such things as "hunger, privations of all kinds, pain, the influence of climate, the seasons, and, in general, the thousand conditions of animal life which maintain the human being in a quasi-absolute dependence on the environment which surrounds him. . . . In a word, [man] does not lack any element of the most absolute slavery."[123] Here the remedy, according to Bakunin, lies in man's effort "to transform the surface of the globe into an environment more and more favorable to the development of humanity."[124] This is a remedy that Marx and Engels develop in much greater economic detail.

In their view, as man passes from primitive communism to a society based on slavery, and then to feudalism, capitalism, and socialism, there occurs a progressive expansion of technology and productivity, and the economic foundation is laid for both abundance and leisure. The realm of human freedom, Marx declared, has "the shortening of the working day [as] its fundamental premise."[125] Until the productive forces at man's disposal have reached the point where all men can enjoy substantial free time as well as ample subsistence, society will be divided into those who control the means of production for their own benefit and those whose labor they exploit to this end.

It is the mode of production that, according to Marx and Engels, determines the antagonistic class relations and the political, legal, and cultural forms that exist in every society except the primitive communism and the communism of abundance at the beginning and end of man's economic development. The oppressing class, whether slaveowners, feudal lords, or industrial masters, are compelled to use every means, direct or indirect, to maintain their ascendancy and their "way of life" against the claims of the oppressed classes. And, so long as the class-divided society and its political embodiment in the state persist, the full freedom that is possible for mankind cannot be achieved. It will be achieved only when "class distinctions have disappeared and all production has been concentrated in the hands of a vast association of the whole nation." Then "the public power will lose its political character" and the state will wither away.[126] The ideal society toward which history inevitably leads will be economically as well as politically classless, for all the means of production will be socially, or publicly, owned and operated. Under advanced technological conditions the emancipation of one class from oppression by another will be accompanied by the emancipation of mankind as a whole from the need of grinding toil to satisfy its wants.

The first stage of the communist revolution, brought about by the dictatorship of the proletariat, is *immediately aimed* at emancipating them from their slavery under capitalist oppression. But its *ultimate aim* goes beyond that. It looks to the emancipation of all men, even those who were formerly the oppressors and members of the ruling class. This complete emancipation, this full freedom of mankind as a whole, will be achieved only when the communist society emerges from the dictatorship of the proletariat. In that final stage of the revolution man will enter for the first time into a real community—a completely classless society.

The dictatorship of the proletariat is thus seen as only a stage on the road toward the communist or classless society, in which alone the full freedom of mankind will exist. Under the dictatorship of the proletariat the state will not yet have completely withered away, nor will all class antagonism have yet disappeared. But according to Marx and Engels,

> *if the proletariat during its contest with the bourgeoisie is com-*
> *pelled by the force of circumstances to organize itself as a class;*
> *if by means of a revolution it makes itself the ruling class and, as*
> *such, sweeps away by force the old conditions of production, then*
> *it will, along with these conditions, have swept away the condi-*
> *tions for the existence of class antagonisms and of classes gener-*
> *ally, and will thereby have abolished its own supremacy as a class.*

Consequently,

> *in place of the old bourgeois society, with its classes and class an-*
> *tagonisms, we shall have an association in which the free develop-*
> *ment of each is the condition for the free development of all.*[127]

What is this freedom that is predicted for mankind when the ideal society is achieved—Marx's ideal of the classless society, Comte's ideal of the positive state, or Bakunin's ideal of human fellowship in the anarchic community?

To regard the freedom these authors are prophesying for a still-to-be achieved future condition of humanity as one that men can possess when, in the absence of coercion or duress, they are able to act as they wish, is to make no sense of the revolution in human affairs these writers posit as indispensable to freedom. Nor does it make sense of the futurity they all insist upon. In all past and present societies the master class, the arbitrary and authoritarian rulers, have been and are able to do as they please for the most part. But according to Comte, Bakunin, Marx, and Engels, there never has been and there is as yet no real freedom in any historic society. The members of the ruling class may appear to be free; but, as Marx explicitly points out, their so-called personal freedom is illusory.

It is equally difficult to regard the freedom of the future as one that virtuous or wise men, and only they, can possess when by overcoming obstacles within themselves they are able to live as they ought in conformity with the moral law or an ethical ideal. For one thing, the prediction is that all mankind will come into the possession of freedom by a radical reform in society. Even if this transforms human nature or actualizes potentialities it has always possessed, the resultant freedom is not one some individual men acquire or conquer by a perfection of themselves. Furthermore, Comte, Bakunin, Marx, and Engels, far from thinking the divine law or the moral law to be the ideal or the norm of human self-perfection, look upon the dogmas of traditional religion and morality as deceits imposed by the historic ruling class or as vain substitutes to meet needs that society does not satisfy. So far as the good life is concerned, Bakunin expresses a point of view that is shared by the others when he says: "there is no good outside liberty, and liberty is the source and absolute condition of all good which really deserves that name, the good being nothing else than liberty."[128]

Let us see then, what is common to the understanding of freedom in the passages from Comte, Bakunin, Marx, and Engels that we have so far examined. With one exception, they appear to share four points, all of them negative in that they state what freedom is an exemption or emancipation from. The four points are:

(1) Emancipation from the arbitrary rule of other men.

(2) Emancipation from compulsory toil by which mankind satisfies its economic wants, together with emancipation from degrading poverty, long hours of labor, and economic insecurity.

(3) Emancipation of human labor from economic servitude and exploitation, that is, from organizations of production in which the conditions of work are determined by a master class who own the means of production, and in which the fruits of work are alienated from workers to the benefit of their masters.*

(4) Complete emancipation from the state or political community as that has so far existed in the history of mankind, that is, from the essential features of all past and present societies.

Of these four negative points, no one of the first three is by itself distinctive of theories of collective freedom. Each is to be found in other theories, yet with altered meaning when it is not associated with the fourth point, which sets forth the one emancipation that is uniquely called for in the theories of such authors as Comte, Bakunin, Marx, and Engels. The fourth point is thus not only distinctive but is the one point that gives us any clue as to the positive character of the collective freedom that these authors project.

The positive character of collective freedom

That collective freedom is a variant of the acquired freedom of self-perfection is indicated by the following considerations.

According to Comte, Bakunin, Marx, and Engels, it is a freedom under

---

* The one exception mentioned above applies to points (2) and (3). Auguste Comte's theory does not include these two points of economic emancipation.

law and through law, not a freedom from law or in spite of law. For all these writers the law that lies at the heart of liberty is natural law. By "natural law" or "the laws of nature," these authors do not mean the natural moral law of the jurists, the theologians, or the philosophers, but the laws of the physical world, human nature, and social phenomena, which science has discovered or will discover.

Such laws are descriptions, not prescriptions or directions for the behavior of men or things, which whoever or whatever is subject to the law may or may not obey and take the consequences. They do not prescribe what *should* be done because it is right and proper. Rather, in the view of the authors we are considering, they describe what *is* done—that is to say, what happens—in the physical and human world, according to inviolable rule. They are statements of the natural necessities by which the behavior of all things is in fact governed.

According to the self-realization authors, freedom does not consist in man's voluntary compliance with necessities. But, as we have seen, such compliance is involved in freedom for the self-perfection authors. The rules of divine, moral, or juridical law, in prescribing what men ought to do, lay down the duties men *must* unconditionally discharge in order to be virtuous, or the path they *must* follow if they are to achieve the happiness they seek. In either case, virtue consists in a voluntary compliance with such necessities, as wisdom consists in understanding and acknowledging them; and precisely because the compliance is voluntary, being subject to necessity is not incompatible with the freedom of the virtuous man who is able to will as he ought.

At this point we must note two differences between self-perfection authors and the writers whose conception of collective freedom we are trying to identify by comparison with their views. (1) For the self-perfection authors, the rules of human conduct that prescribe moral necessities are always *violable;* otherwise compliance with them could not be voluntary. And as a consequence (2) some men acquire freedom and some men do not, according as their possession of virtue enables them to comply or the lack of it allows the opposing forces within them to prevent such compliance.

But according to the theory of collective freedom, (1) the physical or psychological necessities described by the scientific laws of nature are *inviolable*. Whatever or whoever is subject to them complies with them of necessity, not voluntarily. Hence, as a consequence, (2) free men are not distinguished from unfree men by their individual acquirement of virtue or by whatever development of moral character enables them to will as they ought.

It follows, therefore, that collective freedom cannot be equated with the freedom of self-perfection. But it still remains possible for collective freedom to be regarded as a variant of it, just as political liberty, which cannot be equated with the freedom of self-realization, can be regarded as a *variant* of that freedom. The two considerations which follow seem to justify this way of identifying collective freedom.

(1) At first glance it might seem as if collective freedom is circumstantial, for it is said to exist only under the ideal conditions of the positive state (Comte), of the anarchic community (Bakunin), or of the classless society (Marx and Engels). But upon closer examination the requirement of an ideal society does not make collective freedom circumstantial any more than, in the theories of Rousseau and Hegel, the requirement of a well-constituted society makes the freedom of self-perfection circumstantial. That requirement, as we have seen, only makes the self-perfection of virtuous men social rather than personal in form.

Is it, then, acquired; and if so, who acquires it? In the several theories of collective freedom the answer to these questions is that it is acquired by the human race or mankind, or humanity, not by the individual human person. These writers approach the problem of human freedom in terms of the history or development of the human race as a whole. As they look back upon that history or consider the condition of mankind in the present, they find evidence for maintaining that collective freedom has not yet been acquired by the human race because of all the opposing factors within the structure of human society, which have been and are still operative. It will be acquired in the future when mankind or humanity—that "Great Being," in the language of Comte— is liberated from these factors by a radical transformation in the structure of society itself.

The statement that mankind or humanity is the acquirer or possessor of collective freedom is susceptible of certain misunderstandings that must be avoided. When Comte, Bakunin, Marx, and Engels speak of humanity or mankind, they clearly do not have in mind the individual person, to whom other authors attribute freedom, but it is equally clear that they are not speaking of an abstraction.* They have in mind something as concrete as the individual human being, namely, the associated multitude of men that constitutes the human race at any moment in history. Under all historic forms of association this multitude lacks freedom. Mankind in all its past and present societies is not free. The human race as a whole will acquire freedom only when human society is thoroughly reformed and renovated. It is appropriate, therefore, to speak of the freedom it will then acquire as the collective freedom of the human race—a freedom possessed by the human multitude in an ideal association of man with man.

---

* If anything, it is the individual man, considered apart from society, that is an abstraction in the view of the collective-freedom authors. Man does not exist as man except in society, and his nature varies with the form of social organization in which he exists as part of the whole. Human nature is, therefore, perfectible with the progress of human society from less to more perfect forms of organization.

Seen in this light, the collectively acquired freedom of mankind and the individually acquired freedom of self-perfection seem to have significant points in common. In both cases the obstacles to freedom lie within the being or structure of that which becomes free. Such things as poverty, despotism, class divisions, and exploitation operate within the social whole as sin, the passions, or inordinate desires operate within the makeup of the individual person. Just as the individual person must overcome these obstacles in order to achieve his self-perfection and live in accordance with the will of his higher or better self, so mankind as a whole must overcome these obstacles in its social structure in order to achieve its self-perfection and live in accordance with the best of which humanity is capable.

When the freedom of self-perfection is attributed to individual persons, men living at the same time and even in the same society can be divided into those who have acquired it through the right resolution of their inner conflict and those who remain subject to that conflict and so remain unfree. Analogously, in the case of collective freedom, the human race as a whole, viewed not one at a time but over the whole course of its history, can be divided into two temporal phases. In that long period of time that represents the whole of human history so far, mankind is unperfected and unfree because of the conflicts and defects in its social structure that have not yet been overcome. The freedom of mankind as a whole belongs to that future epoch in human affairs when, these conflicts having been resolved and these defects transcended, human nature itself will be perfected with the perfection of human society.

Another misunderstanding of the statement that the human race as a whole acquires and possesses collective freedom would be to suppose that individual men as such do not enjoy this freedom. The language of Comte, Bakunin, Marx, and Engels suggests the very opposite. Thus, for example, Comte says that "the action of the Great Being [that is, humanity] has for its main object the perfecting of the order of man's world, for the individual as well as for society."[129] For Bakunin, liberty consists in "the full development of all the material, intellectual, and moral powers latent in every man."[130] And with the dawn of the classless society, according to Marx, "we shall have an association in which the free development of each is the condition for the free development of all."[131]

The claim that individual men will enjoy freedom in the ideal society does not negate the proposition that collective freedom belongs to mankind as a whole. Since each man is related to society and to the human race as the part is to the whole, each naturally participates in the freedom of the whole when, with its perfection under ideal conditions, such freedom is acquired. Each individual shares in the perfection of human nature that is consequent upon the transformation of human society.

(2) This brings us to the second of the two considerations that support

the identification of collective freedom as a variant of the acquired freedom of self-perfection.

In the case of the latter, what is acquired by the individual is always a moral perfection, such as virtue, righteousness, sanctity, or personal growth. Even when wisdom is said to be the principal acquirement needed for freedom, wisdom is understood as comprehending moral virtue. It is not mere knowledge, certainly not knowledge of a scientific character, that can be possessed by morally good and bad men alike. When it is said that only the wise man is free it is understood that none but the wise can be good, and that no one who is wise can be evil.

According to the theories of collective freedom, what is acquired by mankind is scientific knowledge, knowledge of the natural necessities that pervade all phenomena, social as well as physical. The acquirement does not consist in knowledge alone, however, important as that is, but also in the developed ability to put it to social use. As Comte, Bakunin, Marx, and Engels discuss this point, it is the *social use of knowledge* that is acquired. What must be achieved is not simply a recognition of the necessities under which men must live but also the conduct of human life in accordance with those necessities. The ideal society to which these writers look forward will for the first time put knowledge of necessity to use for the sake of freedom, by applying it, without distortion or restriction, to the control of the environment and the management of human affairs. Society thereby perfects itself and its members. With this self-perfection the collective freedom of humanity is acquired.

Our hypothesis that collective freedom is a variant of the acquired freedom of self-perfection can, therefore, be summarized in the proposition that collective freedom is *acquired* with a use of knowledge that *enables* mankind to govern itself in accordance with *necessity*. The following additional facts must be noted: (1) that the freedom accrues to individuals only when it is acquired by mankind; (2) that it is acquired through the perfecting of human association rather than through the moral development of the individual in any social context; (3) that the laws with which liberated humanity is in harmony are the scientific formulations of how things *do* behave, rather than theologically, morally, or juridically declared rules of how men *should* behave; (4) that such laws are inviolable and, therefore, can either be put to beneficial use or not, but never disobeyed, in contrast to ethical prescriptions, which are violable and may or may not be voluntarily obeyed. These facts do not invalidate the hypothesis. They show why collective freedom cannot be equated with the freedom of self-perfection; but they also show why it can be regarded as a variant of such freedom.*

---

* For an analysis of the works of Comte, Bakunin, Marx, and Engels, educing evidence for the foregoing interpretation of their position, see *The Idea of Freedom*, Vol. 1, pp. 390–99.

8. The counterattack against self-perfection freedom

In Chapter I we considered the circumstantial freedom of self-realization. Section 1 was concerned with the meaning of that kind of freedom; its relation to law was discussed in Section 2; and in Section 3 we described a variant of that freedom which we called political liberty. In the last section of Chapter 1, Section 4, we then analyzed the attack on the circumstantial freedom of self-realization that is mounted by a group of prestigious authors in behalf of another major kind of freedom, the acquired freedom of self-perfection. The latter has been discussed in Chapter II. Section 5 considered the meaning of that freedom; the joint affirmation of both freedoms (self-realization and self-perfection) was treated in Section 6; and Section 7 contained the analysis of a variant of the acquired freedom of self-perfection which we called collective freedom. To complete the discussion of these two major freedoms, together with the two variants thereof, it remains for us to consider the counterattack against the freedom of self-perfection that is mounted by the self-realization authors, either explicitly, or implicitly by virtue of their assertion that self-realization is the only true freedom, the only freedom worthy of the name.

We recall that with few exceptions, the authors who affirm an acquired freedom of self-perfection also assert the existence of moral obligations or duties, moral standards or rules, and ethical ideals or goals, all of which have their foundation in universal laws of reason, of nature, or of God. They hold certain typical views about a fundamental conflict in man, between his reason and passions, between a sense of duty and sensuous inclinations, or between his higher and lower nature. To be able to will or live as one ought depends, in their view, upon having the power to follow the dictates of reason or duty and to overcome the promptings of passion or appetite. Hence, for them only the morally good man —the man who has attained virtue or wisdom—has the self-mastery in which the acquired freedom of self-perfection consists. A freedom so conceived is subject to attack on two quite distinct grounds.

As in the case of circumstantial self-realization, the question can be raised whether or not acquired self-perfection fits the common understanding or the generic meaning of freedom.* To say that it does not is to reject a whole family of conceptions as false conceptions of freedom, to say, in effect, that what·is·being conceived is not freedom at all, but something mistaken for freedom. The conceptual issue that would result from this type of rejection is not only like the issue

---

* We note here, as we did in Section 4, that the generic meaning of freedom will be discussed in greater detail in Section 14, after the groundwork is laid for a thorough analysis of the conception.

concerning self-realization treated in Section 4, it is also in large part the reverse face of that issue, and it involves the same arguments in reverse perspective.

Acquired self-perfection, however, unlike circumstantial self-realization, is also subject to another kind of attack. Questions can be raised about the validity of its ethical and psychological presuppositions. If these are not valid, then conceptions of freedom as acquired self-perfection are conceptions of a freedom that simply has no existence in human life, man and the world being what they are. If, in other words, there are no universal laws of reason, of nature, or of God that give rise to moral obligations, standards, precepts, or goals that are the same for all men and binding on all in the same way, then to say that men are free when they are able to comply willingly with moral requirements having such origin is to propound a mythical or fictitious freedom, not one that has reality or existence in the world as it is. To reject acquired self-perfection on such grounds is to reject a whole family of conceptions as existentially false—in effect, to deny that anything corresponding to the conceptions in question actually exists.

When the ground of rejection is the meaning of freedom itself, the resultant issue is conceptual; when it is the nonexistence of things stipulated or presupposed by a conception of freedom, it is existential. In the first part of this section we will deal with the existential issue concerning acquired self-perfection. In the second part we will deal with the conceptual issue. In a final part we will give the self-perfection authors a chance to respond.

The existential issue

Let us begin by stating as neutrally as possible all of the presuppositions common to typical conceptions of acquired self-perfection. The first supposition concerns the *ought*. It asserts the existence of moral obligations that are the same for all men and are binding on all in the same way. These moral rules or laws prescribe specific conduct and require a definite way of life. They define duties to be performed or virtues to be developed and practised. The moral standards they establish, it is claimed, are not relative to the institutions of particular societies, the customs of particular cultures, or the temperamental differences of particular human beings. They are not offered merely as pragmatic or utilitarian recommendations of things that it may be expedient to do, subject always to the individual judgment of what *appears* to be right, good, or pleasant in particular cases. On the contrary, what is being asserted is that, regardless of how they may appear to the individual, certain things are right or wrong, good or bad, and that the individual can be morally judged by reference to them.

The second presupposition concerns *willing as one ought*. It asserts the existence in man of a *rational* will or a *natural* desire to do or seek the very things that are morally obligatory or prescribed by the moral law. What every man ought to do or seek is something that each individual, *as rational,* wills to do, or that, by tendencies inherent in his nature, he desires to attain. It is not asserted that every man always acts in accordance with his rational will or his natural desire, but only that there exists in every human being a principle that makes it possible for him to act as he ought *willingly*.

The third presupposition concerns *being able to will as one ought*. It involves a twofold assertion. The first assertion is the existence in all men of conflicting elements, variously designated as reason and the passions, a sense of duty and sensuous inclinations, the higher and the lower nature, and so forth; of these, the second one named in each case represents the source of impulses to act as a man ought not. The second assertion is the existence in some human beings—the wise, the virtuous, the righteous, the holy—of an acquired power to resist or overcome the impulses to violate or transgress the rules of the moral life. Since this acquired power gives predominant strength to a will that is rational or that accords with natural desires, it enables those who possess it not only to will as they ought but also to do so willingly and, hence, freely.

Unless these three suppositions are valid, that is, unless what they assert to exist does exist in fact, typical conceptions of acquired self-perfection do not correspond to anything real in life. But it is clear from the divergent approaches and doctrinal differences we find in the fields of ethics and psychology that the validity of each of these presuppositions common to all typical theories of acquired self-perfection is open to doubt. Indeed, each of them has at some point or other been flatly denied.

The famous statement by Pythagoras, for example, that "man is the measure of all things" represents an approach to morals that, early in the tradition of Western thought, challenged the view that judgments of right and wrong or good and bad can be more than personal opinions relative to the individual or to the society in which he lives. "Fire burns in Greece as it does in Persia," the Sophists are often quoted as saying, "but the laws and customs of the Greeks differ from those of the Persians." This again represents the familiar doctrine of the Sophists that opinions about the good or the right vary with time and place and that there is no criterion for deciding which, among such opinions, is objectively and universally true. It was against this skeptical view on the part of the Sophists that Plato and Aristotle advanced the distinction between the real and the apparent good, specifying the things in which human happiness really consists, and arguing for universal principles of justice and other virtues as providing a moral code that is the measure of the good man and the good life.

The foregoing example suggests one approach to moral questions that denies the validity of the first of the three existential presuppositions of acquired self-perfection. It is the approach that Montaigne, centuries later, found congenial to his general skepticism; and in our own day it has been widely adopted by sociologists and anthropologists, who, on the basis of much more detailed evidence of the diversity of tribal customs, maintain that the *mores* of one social group do not provide any valid standard for judging the values enshrined in the customs of another. Still another variation on this point of view is to be found in the sharp distinction that is often made between value judgments and judgments of fact, accompanied by a declaration that the former, unlike the latter, cannot be scientifically tested or empirically verified, and must therefore be treated, in part at least, as expressions of emotional prejudice or purely personal predilection.

Anyone who takes some variety of the skeptical approach to moral matters would deny the existence of moral obligations or moral laws that are the same for all men and binding on all in the same way. He would deny the existence of moral standards that are not relative to the institutions of particular societies, or to the customs of particular cultures, or to the temperamental differences of particular men. If, in addition, he were acquainted with the typical self-perfection view that, since all men are duty-bound to behave in certain specific ways, those alone are free who are able to discharge their moral obligations willingly, he would reject the freedom described in this way as mythical or nonexistent.

It would be possible to draw up a fairly long list of authors in the Western tradition who, taking the approach indicated here, would deny the first (that is, the ethical) presupposition common to all typical conceptions of acquired self-perfection. In the case of such authors as Thomas Hobbes, J. S. Mill, L. T. Hobhouse, Harold Laski, and Frank Knight, we have already given documentary evidence (in Section 1) that they share a conception of the circumstantial freedom of self-realization that involves them in the requisite denials. They hold views, as has been shown, that are incompatible with one or more of the presuppositions common to typical conceptions of acquired self-perfection, especially the first (or ethical) presupposition. Moreover, at least two of the authors mentioned—Hobhouse and Laski—advance arguments that can be interpreted as denying all the existential presuppositions of acquired self-perfection. Passages from their writings, some of which have been quoted in previous sections, reveal that their view of the roles played by reason and desire in human life and their insistence on the integrity of the self (that is, on the unity of the individual as a whole, comprising all his tendencies and aspirations) deny the existence in man of principles (such as a rational will or natural desires) that, when made to prevail over lower impulses by the power of virtue, enable the individual willingly to will as he ought. Here, then, we have evidence of denials of the second and third presuppositions involved in conceptions of acquired self-perfection.

The conceptual issue

Those who affirm that being able to will as one ought is genuinely freedom assert this without any qualifications. Those who deny that men are free when they bring their will into line with duty or with law also enter this denial without any qualifications. Hence, the conceptual issue is a relatively simple one. It involves a two-sided disagreement stemming from contradictory positions, namely, the affirmative and negative answers to the question: "Is acquired self-perfection a kind of freedom?"

On the affirmative side of the issue could be listed all of the authors who have been discussed in Chapter II as exponents of acquired self-perfection and who either maintain that it is man's only freedom or that it is one of the freedoms man possesses. Among these authors are Plato, Epictetus, Marcus Aurelius, Augustine, Aquinas, Luther, Calvin, Spinoza, Locke, Leibniz, Montesquieu, Rousseau, Kant, Hegel, Freud, and Maritain. In such an enumeration, the typical varieties of acquired self-perfection are well represented: the Platonic and Stoic conceptions in antiquity; the Christian conception, not only in the Middle Ages but also in modern times; and in modern times such divergent conceptions as the Spinozist, the Kantian, and the Hegelian.

But there are also many authors whom we can construe, with varying degrees of assurance, as taking the negative side of the issue. Among them are Hobbes, Voltaire, David Hume, Jeremy Bentham, J. S. Mill, Herbert Spencer, R. H. Tawney, Bronislaw Malinowski, and Harold Laski. These assert that circumstantial self-realization is the only freedom possessed by human beings, and thus they take, or they would be obliged to take, a negative position on the issue in question. To their number might be added the names of Descartes, William James, Jean-Paul Sartre, and Edmund Burke, as well as Comte, Bakunin, Marx, and Engels, all of whom, though for different reasons and in different ways, deny the validity of an acquired freedom of self-perfection.

In the case of many of the authors mentioned, the evidence is indirect, and we must rely on more or less oblique intepretations of their positions. But some of them take cognizance of acquired self-perfection, explicitly reject it, and argue against it on conceptual grounds—on the grounds, in short, that it violates the universally accepted sense of the term *freedom*.

All conceptions of freedom stress the *self* as against the *other* and regard only such acts as free that flow from the self rather than from the other. Each of the two major conceptions of freedom that we see in conflict here specifies in a different way the self, which is the principle of freedom, and also the other, which can be the source of unfreedom. Neither of these specifications, in itself, excludes the other. But that fact does not prevent the authors who affirm a conception of freedom in which *self* and *other* are specified in a certain way from excluding other specifications of those terms as untenable.

Thus, some self-perfection authors argue against the specification of self and other involved in the self-realization conception of freedom on the ground that the self referred to is not the real or true self.* The answer to that is clear. It is provided by arguments in which some self-realization authors maintain, on their part, that no tenable distinction can be drawn between the individual's actual self, as constituted by his whole person, and some part of him which is elevated to the status of his "real" or "true" self.

The argument runs thus. To describe the so-called virtuous man, as the self-perfection authors do, as an individual whose true self or rational will is able to follow its own bent in the direction of the *ought* (because, having overcome contrary impulses or inclinations, it is exempt from the inner coercion they exercise in the opposite direction) is to concoct an image of freedom in the inner contest between "self" and "other" that does no more than bear a similitude to the fact of freedom in the world of external relations between individual things. It is the *fact* of freedom, the argument insists, that gives the word its literal meaning. This of course is another way of saying that the only actual freedom an individual has is in relation to others wholly external to himself—other men or natural forces.

While it can be maintained, authors who hold this conception admit, that there may be something *like* freedom in the inner life of a human being, or at least that there may be some poetic truth in the metaphorical attribution of freedom to one part of an individual as against coercion from another part of himself, concern for the scientific or philosophical truth of the matter requires the metaphor to be plainly labeled as such. When that is done, no one will mistake virtue for freedom merely because the power it confers on a man in his inner life is thought to resemble the freedom that favorable circumstances confer on him in the outer world of his actions.

Granting all the ethical and psychological presuppositions of the self-perfection authors, but excluding their metaphorical use of the term *freedom,* the critics contend in effect that the literal description of the man who is able to will as he ought would be that he is wise, or virtuous, or righteous, or dutiful, but never that he is, as such, free. Since these other terms are available for the self-perfection authors to use in expressing their various conceptions of the morally good man, there is no excuse, it is held, for their misuse of the term *freedom* in this connection. And the argument in this form usually concludes by adding that the misuse not only puts a counterfeit conception of freedom into circulation

---

* These arguments were set forth in Section 4.

but also leads to practical recommendations and policies that are deeply inimical to the cause of freedom.

As Barbara Wootton has said in a book published after World War II, "We deny the validity . . . of any distinction between what people want to do, and what they 'really' want to do. Any such distinction," she continued,

> *is extremely dangerous, and may be the cloak for some of the most wicked, because the most insidious, attacks upon freedom. For sooner or later what I "really" want to do turns out to be a polite paraphrase for what you think I ought to want to do. But freedom means freedom to do what I want, and not what anybody else wants me to want*—or else it has no meaning at all. *How my wants come to be what they are is, no doubt, the result of a complex social and personal process which had best be left to the psychologist to explore.* So far as freedom is concerned, what people want to do must be taken as something to be discovered, not changed.[132]

Similarly Malinowski, who insists that, as measured by the standard or generally accepted meaning of the term, "freedom as willing submission to restraint—any restraint and every restraint—is obviously a perverted concept."[133] And Hobhouse takes the same tack. Criticizing Bosanquet's use of the term "real will" to give *willing as one ought* the appearance of *willing as one really wishes*, Hobhouse maintains that strictly, or literally, "there is no part in me which is more real than any other part." Only by using words rhetorically can "freedom" be said to lie in what a man "really" wills, as contrasted to what he actually wishes. It is "mere words" to say that, in willing as I ought, I am free because "the compulsion is exercised by myself upon myself."[134]

Following Hobhouse, Laski argued in the same vein against what he called the "idealist view of liberty" to be found in Rousseau and Hegel and their modern apologists. As such authors use words, Laski observed, there is no sense to the problem of individual liberty, as that is ordinarily understood. They regard the individual as "free" when he is required to fulfill his obligations, because they hold that when he "is constrained in this way he is in fact willing only what his true self desires." But to say this is to play with words, for in ordinary speech the accepted meaning of freedom is that any experience of restraint marks a loss of liberty. Those who try to tell a man "that he is made free when he is prevented from fulfilling the purpose he regards as the *raison d'être* of his existence . . . deprive words of all their meaning."[135] And Robert M. MacIver has gone even further. He would not object if such writers as Rousseau and Hegel were to say, on the one hand, that willing as one ought is good and, on the other hand, that liberty is good, and then "seek for some relation between them." But when "they say the one *is* the other," MacIver charges them with misappropriating the term *freedom* for an ulterior purpose. Instead of speaking "of men being 'forced to be free,' " Rousseau should have said " 'forced to be good,' 'forced to be rational,' " for thus he could have avoided a paradoxical, or, worse, a perverse use of terms. Such writers, MacIver concluded,

> *will not face the issue that they value other things more highly than liberty and that they reject liberty for the sake of those other things. That position would at least be honest. Instead, they pervert the universal meaning of liberty in order to deny the most obvious of facts. They would destroy the meaning of liberty because they are afraid to admit its meaning. They call it something else, hoping that thus no one will claim it for what it is.*[136]

The arguments in rebuttal

Are there any arguments in rebuttal—in defense of the acquired freedom of self-perfection and against the attack on it by the self-realization authors? There are such arguments, we have found, although few authors explicitly voice them, mainly because the explicit attacks are quite recent. Of the twenty-five or so authors who can clearly be construed as taking an affirmative stand on the conceptual issue being analyzed in this section, only Bosanquet and T. H. Green reply to the argument that being able to will as one ought does not conform to the generally recognized meaning of freedom. Only they meet the charge that the self-perfection authors are using the term in a metaphorical sense without acknowledging their substitution of it for the literal meaning of freedom, which is exemplified in the conception of it as circumstantial self-realization. And Green alone defends a wide variety of representative authors on the affirmative side of the issue—Plato, St. Paul, the Stoics, and Kant, as well as Rousseau and Hegel.

Green's argument is subtle and cannot be examined in any detail here.* The nub of it, however, is easy enough to state. Conceding that being able to do as one pleases in the absence of external constraints is the commonly accepted meaning of freedom and the only one employed in everyday speech, and admitting furthermore that other uses of the term *freedom* are to some extent metaphorical, Green nevertheless feels that there is a justifiable extension of the term from the individual's outer relation to other men to the relation of factors within his inner life. "After all," he has written,

---

* For a detailed analysis see *The Idea of Freedom*, Vol. 2, pp. 123–29.

> *this extension does but represent various stages of reflection upon the self-distinguishing, self-seeking, self-asserting principle, of which the establishment of freedom, as a relation between man and man, is the expression. The reflecting man is not content with the first announcement which analysis makes as to the inward condition of the free man, viz., that he can do what he likes, that he has the power of acting according to his will or preference. In virtue of the same principle which led him to assert himself against others, and thus to cause there to be such a thing as (outward) freedom, he distinguishes himself from his preference, and asks how he is related to it.*[137]

What is of importance to note in this statement is that Green is here appealing to the generic meaning of freedom as against the commonly accepted sense of it in ordinary speech. His reference to the self-asserting principle is a reference to the generic meaning, according to which the assertion of the self as against the other is the principle of freedom. In the light of this principle, he then proceeds to argue that the common-sense meaning of freedom involves the "self-asserting principle" and participates in the generic meaning of freedom *neither more nor less* than does the meaning of freedom which develops from philosophical reflection.

When this is seen, the fact that the commonsense meaning may be earlier in the order of development of our notions of freedom does not give it primacy among the various conceptions, all of which conform equally to the generic meaning of freedom; nor need we concern ourselves any longer with the propriety of using the word *freedom* in a sense different from that employed in everyday speech.

Still other arguments to this effect seem possible, although we cannot say that we have found them in the writings of other authors. One such argument would commence, forseeably, with a thorough analysis of the connection between the ideas of *freedom* and *responsibility*. It would require an examination of the issues that arise out of the various relationships that exist between those two ideas. It would require also a consideration of the third basic form of freedom, the freedom we have called the natural freedom of self-determination, which we have not so far discussed, and which would lead in turn to a concept we have not yet had occasion to treat, though it is of the greatest importance in the literature on freedom in the West—the concept we refer to when we use the term *free will*. We shall take up these matters in Chapter III of this essay, which will be published next year.

---

1 *Leviathan,* pt. 1. chap. 14; *GBWW,* Vol. 23, p. 86.

2 *Freedom of the Will,* ed. Paul Ramsey (New Haven: Yale University Press, 1957), p. 163.

3 *An Essay Concerning Human Understanding,* bk. 2, chap. 21; *GBWW,* Vol. 35, p. 184.

4 "Freedom in Society," in *Sceptical Essays* (London: George Allen & Unwin, 1952), p. 169.

5 *Liberty in the Modern State* (Harmondsworth, Middlesex: Penguin Books, 1937), p. 49.

6 *The Elements of Politics,* 4th ed. (London: Macmillan & Co., 1919), p. 45.

7 *Problems of Ethics,* trans. David Rynin (New York: Prentice-Hall, 1939), p. 150.

8 *The Road to Serfdom* (Chicago: University of Chicago Press, 1950), p. 25.

9 *Human Nature and Conduct: An Introduction to Social Psychology* (New York: Random House, Modern Library, 1922), p. 304.

10 *Leviathan,* pt. 1, chap. 21; *GBWW,* Vol. 23, p. 113.

11 "Freedom and Necessity," in *Philosophical Essays* (London: Macmillan & Co., 1954), p. 281.

12 Ibid., p. 280.

13 "We Mean Freedom," in *The Attack and Other Papers* (New York: Harcourt, Brace and Co., 1953), p. 83.

14 *Equality* (New York: Harcourt, Brace & Co., 1931), p. 223.

15 "Freedom and Government," in *Freedom: Its Meaning,* ed. Ruth Nanda Anshen (New York: Harcourt, Brace and Co., 1940), p. 251.

16 "Free-Will," in *A Philosophical Dictionary,* in *The Works of Voltaire,* trans. William F. Fleming, 42 vols. (Paris: E. R. Dumont, 1901), 5:130.

17 *(Summa Contra Gentiles) On the Truth of the Catholic Faith,* bk. 4, trans. Charles J. O'Neil (New York: Hanover House, 1957), p. 127.

18 *Othello,* act 1, sc. 2; *GBWW,* Vol. 27, p. 207.

19 *Leviathan,* pt. 2, chap. 21, pt. 1, chap. 14 (*GBWW,* Vol. 23, pp. 113, 86); idem, *Philosophical Rudiment Concerning Government and Society,* in *The English Works of Thomas Hobbes,* ed. W. Molesworth, 11 vols. (London: John Bohn, 1839–45), 2:186.

20 *Leviathan,* pt. 2, chap. 21; *GBWW,* Vol. 23, p. 113.

21 *The Works of Jeremy Bentham,* ed. J. Bowring, 11 vols. (Edinburgh: William Tait, 1838–45), 2:505–6.

22 *The Wealth of Nations,* bk. 4, chap. 9; *GBWW,* Vol. 39, p. 300.

23 *Liberty in the Modern State,* p. 49.

24 Ibid.

25 Ibid., p. 67.

26 *Freedom and Reform* (New York: Harper and Brothers, 1947), p. 215.

27 *The Science of Right,* pt. 2; *GBWW,* Vol. 42, p. 436.

28 Ibid., p. 437.

29 Ibid.

30 Ibid.

31 In *The People Shall Judge,* ed. The Staff, Social Sciences I, the College of the University of Chicago, 2 vols. (Chicago: University of Chicago Press, 1953), 1:41–43.

32 "Dissertation on First Principles of Government," in *Common Sense and Other Political Writings,* ed. Nelson F. Adkins (New York: Liberal Arts Press, 1953), p. 165.

33 *Representative Government; GBWW,* Vol. 43, p. 382.

34 Ibid., p. 348.

35 *The Metaphysical Theory of State* (London: George Allen & Unwin, 1951), p. 61.

36 *The Elements of Social Justice* (London: George Allen & Unwin, 1949), p. 88.

37 *Christianity and Democracy,* trans. D. C. Anson (New York: Charles Scribner's Sons, 1950), pp. 69–70.

38 *The Rights of Man and Natural Law,* trans. D. C. Anson (New York: Charles Scribner's Sons, 1951), p. 84.

39 *Philosophy of Democratic Government* (Chicago: University of Chicago Press, 1951), pp. 74–75.

40 "The Man Versus the State," in *A Collection of Essays by Herbert Spencer,* ed. Truxton Beale (New York: Mitchell Kennerley, 1916), p. 26.

41 *Liberty in the Modern State,* p. 66.

42 Ibid.

43 Ibid., p. 49.

44 Ibid., pp. 66–67.

45 *A Grammar of Politics,* 2d ed. (New Haven: Yale University Press, 1931), pp. 142–43.

46 *Liberty in the Modern State,* p. 160.

47 Ibid., p. 64.

48 *The Metaphysical Theory of State,* p. 61.

49 *Philosophy of Democratic Government,* pp. 41–42.

50 Ibid., pp. 51, 55.

51 *GBWW,* Vol. 7, p. 411.

52 Ibid.

53 Ibid., p. 412.

54 *GBWW,* Vol. 9, p. 512.

55 *Institutes of the Christian Religion,* ed. and trans. John Allen, 2 vols. (Grand Rapids, Mich.: Wm. B. Eerdmans Publishing Co., 1949), 2:771.

56 Ibid., 1:287.

57 *A View of the Causes and Consequences of the American Revolution, in Thirteen Discourses* (London: G. G. and J. Robinson, 1797), Discourse 12, p. 509.

58 *The Social Contract,* bk. 1, chap. 8; *GBWW,* Vol. 38, p. 393.

59 *Letters from the Mountain,* in vol. 7, *Oeuvres Complètes de J. J. Rousseau,* ed. P. R. Auguis (Paris: Dalibon, 1824), Letter 8, pp. 437–38.

60 *The Philosophy of Right; GBWW,* Vol. 46, p. 16.

61 *The Philosophy of History; GBWW,* Vol. 46, p. 172.

62 *Paradoxa Stoicorum,* in *De Oratore,* trans. H. Rackham, 2 vols., Loeb Classical Library (Cambridge, Mass.: Harvard University Press, 1948), 2:284–86.

63 *Discourses,* bk. 4, chap. 1; *GBWW,* Vol. 12, p. 213.

64 Ibid., p. 220.

65 Ibid., p. 217.

66 *Emile, or Education,* trans. Barbara Foxley (New York: E. P. Dutton & Co., Everyman's Library, 1950), p. 49.

67 *The Social Contract,* bk. 1, chap. 8; *GBWW,* Vol. 38, p. 393.

68 Ibid., chap. 7, p. 393.

69 *The Philosophy of History; GBWW,* Vol. 46, p. 171.

70 Ibid., p. 160.

71 Bernard Bosanquet, *The Philosophical Theory of the State* (London: Macmillan and Co., 1930), pp. 128–36.

72 *The Theory of Legislation,* ed. C. K. Odgen, translated from the French of Etienne Dumont by Richard Hildreth (London: Routledge & Kegan Paul, 1950), pp. 94–95.

73 *Freedom Through Law: Public Control of Private Governing Power* (New York: Columbia University Press, 1952), pp. 3–4.

74 *Freedom and Reform,* p. 372.

75 *Freedom and Civilization* (London: George Allen & Unwin, 1947), p. 82.

76 *On Liberty,* chap. 1; *GBWW,* Vol. 43, p. 271.

77 *Roads to Freedom,* 3d ed. (London: George Allen & Unwin, 1939), p. 123.

78 *Freedom and Reform,* p. 196.

79 *Principles of Ethics,* 2 vols. (New York: D. Appleton & Co., 1898), 2:46.

80 *Philosophy of Mind,* trans. William Wallace (Oxford: Clarendon Press, 1894), p. 265.

81 *Letters,* trans. Sister Mary Melchior Beyenka, O.P., in *The Fathers of the Church,* vol. 26 (New York: Fathers of the Church, Inc., 1954), p. 295.

82 *Freedom in the Modern World,* trans. R. O'Sullivan (New York: Charles Scribner's Sons, 1936), p. 31.

83 (*Commentary on St. John*) *Sancti Thomae Aquinatis in Joannem Evangelistam Exposito*, in vol. 10, *Opera Omnia* (New York: Musurgia Publishers, 1949), chapter 8, lecture 4.

84 "The Conquest of Freedom," in *Freedom: Its Meaning*, p. 639.

85 *Philosophy and Civilization* (New York: Minton, Balch & Co., 1931), p. 291.

86 *Ethics* (with James H. Tufts), rev. ed. (New York: Henry Holt & Co., 1952), p. 340.

87 *Collected Papers*, trans. Joan Riviere et al., 5 vols. (London: Hogarth Press and the Institute of Psychoanalysis, 1950), 5:316.

88 *GBWW*, Vol. 31, p. 463.

89 *Ethics*, p. 340.

90 *Republic*, bk. 4; *GBWW*, Vol. 7, p. 348.

91 *Sixth Ennead*, tractate 8; *GBWW*, Vol. 17, p. 345.

92 *Theodicy*, ed. Austin Farrer, trans. E. M. Huggard (New Haven: Yale University Press, 1952), p. 303.

93 (*Enchiridion*) *Faith, Hope and Charity*, trans. Bernard M. Peebles, in *The Fathers of the Church*, vol. 2 (New York, Fathers of the Church, Inc., 1950), p. 395.

94 *New Introductory Lectures on Psychoanalysis*, lecture 31; *GBWW*, Vol. 54, p. 840.

95 *Ethics*, p. 342.

96 *Critique of Practical Reason*, pt. 1, bk. 1; *GBWW*, Vol. 42, p. 309.

97 *Fundamental Principles of the Metaphysic of Morals; GBWW*, Vol. 42, p. 256.

98 Ibid.

99 *Second Essay Concerning Civil Government*, chap. 4; *GBWW*, Vol. 35, p. 29.

100 Ibid., chap. 6; *GBWW*, Vol. 35, p. 37.

101 Ibid.

102 *Collected Papers*, 2:390.

103 Ibid., 5:316.

104 *The Ego and the Id; GBWW*, Vol. 54, p. 715.

105 *GBWW*, Vol. 54, p. 780.

106 Ibid., pp. 780–81.

107 *Experience and Education* (New York: The Macmillan Co., 1959), p. 69.

108 Ibid., p. 74.

109 *Democracy and Education: An Introduction to the Philosophy of Education* (New York: The Macmillan Co., 1917), p. 357.

110 *Experience and Education*, p. 69.

111 *Ethics*, p. 340.

112 *Reconstruction in Philosophy* (Boston: Beacon Press, 1948), p. 177.

113 *Democracy and Education*, p. 59.

114 *Ethics*, p. 342.

115 Ibid., p. 340.

116 *Reconstruction in Philosophy*, p. 176.

117 *Philosophy and Civilization*, pp. 297–98.

118 *System of Positive Polity*, trans. J. H. Bridges et al., 4 vols. (London: Longmans, Green & Co., 1875–77), 1:296.

119 Ibid., 2:162.

120 Ibid., 1:296.

121 *Oeuvres*, 6 vols. (Paris: P. V. Stock, 1895–1913), 3:213–14.

122 Ibid., 5:158.

123 Ibid., 1:110–11.

124 Ibid., 1:112.

125 *Capital: A Critique of Political Economy*, ed. Friedrich Engels, trans. Ernest Untermann, vol. 3 (Chicago: Charles H. Kerr & Co., 1909), p. 955.

126 *The Communist Manifesto*, chap. 2; *GBWW*, Vol. 50, p. 429.

127 Ibid.

128 *Oeuvres*, 1:206.

129 *Positive Polity*, 4:35.

130 *The Political Philosophy of Bakunin: Scientific Anarchism*, ed. G. P. Maximoff (Glencoe, Ill.: The Free Press, 1953), p. 270.

131 *The Communist Manifesto*, chap. 2; *GBWW*, Vol. 50, p. 429.

132 *Freedom Under Planning* (Chapel Hill: University of North Carolina Press, 1945), p. 5.

133 *Freedom and Civilization,* p. 47.

134 *The Metaphysical Theory of State,* p. 59.

135 *The State in Theory and Practice* (New York: The Viking Press, 1935), p. 44.

136 "The Meaning of Liberty and Its Perversions," in *Freedom: Its Meaning,* pp. 286–87.

137 *Lectures on the Principles of Political Obligation* (New York: Longmans, Green & Co., 1950), pp. 9–10.

NOTE TO THE READER

The discussion of the idea of freedom in GBWW is extensive. Much of the ground covered by the foregoing essay (as distinct from those aspects of the subject that will be taken up in Part Two) is indicated by the references listed in Chapter 47 of the *Syntopicon,* LIBERTY, under Topic 1c, which deals with the relation between liberty and personal development; under Topic 1e, which is concerned with liberty and license; and under Topic 3c, where virtue is considered as the discipline of free choice. But *see,* in addition, the readings listed under NECESSITY AND CONTINGENCY 5a(3), which discuss human freedom as the acceptance of necessity, and those at WILL 5a(2), 5b(2), and 8a, which are concerned with relevant aspects of the freedom of the will.

In *GGB,* the *Enchiridion* of Epictetus, which appears in Vol. 10, pp. 234–54, gives the Stoic position on freedom. Further relevant readings are Emerson's essay *Self-Reliance,* also in Vol. 10, at pp. 525–45, and the various *Great Documents* of liberty and human rights that are reprinted in Vol. 6, pp. 407–56.

PART FOUR

Additions
to the
Great Books Library

The Duration of Life

August Weismann

Editor's Introduction

Everything that is born also dies; that is what, accident apart, we call the condition of its being—something of which stones are incapable and to which angels are immune. But what really is the necessity we recognize, or think we recognize, when we say this? Is it a matter of external regulation, a law of God or nature such as men of old conceived of when they said that they were subject to an appointed term of three-score years and ten? Or do we have in mind an outcome regulated by a sort of internal clock within each organism, as the modern biologist might prefer to argue, which is wound by some initial genetic force for an interval, and when the interval is done, runs no more? Are we sure that what we are talking about is not something quite different, such as an accommodation made long ago by all existent species with the biological order, whose convenience it may be supposed to serve? And if it came about in that way, what lottery determined that some species would live longer than others, as seems to have been decided at the outset?

These and similar questions are taken up in the following essay by August Weismann, one of the great biologists of the nineteenth century, who propounded the theory of the germ plasm, laying the basis for modern genetics. Weismann was led to contemplate such questions by his researches into this essential form of matter, which he regarded as a separate, hereditary substance (he knew nothing of chromosomes) that unlike somatoplasm, the perishable body of the individual organism, is passed on from generation to generation and constitutes the life of the species. One of the great problems such a vital principle created was how death could enter into the organism's existence, since the germ plasm by which it was given life was itself in some sense immortal.

Weismann was born in Frankfurt am Main in 1834. He studied medicine at Göttingen from 1852 to 1856, and after some early work in insect embryology, which he was forced to give up owing to the deterioration of his eyesight, he settled at the University of Freiburg. There he devoted himself to theoretical problems and was eventually made professor of zoology, a position from which he retired in 1912, only two years before his death. Throughout most of his career, which was spent in research, in lectures, and in writing, he was known as a follower of Darwin, who contributed an introduction to the English translation of one of his books, *Studies in the Theory of Descent* (1882), and whose own theory of natural selection Weismann upheld with special fervor against the followers of Lamarck, who thought adaptation of species came about through the transmission of acquired characteristics. It was, indeed, his discovery of the germ plasm that validated Darwin's theory, Weismann believed, since it indicated that heredity was determined by a substance that was not subject to modification by the environment. And although this is now thought to have been accomplished rather by the researches of Mendel and Hugo de Vries, among others, it has been acknowledged by later writers that Weismann established the distinction that we now recognize as lying between modifications and mutations.

In his effort to account for the fact that the duration of life varies in different species and to suggest how and why it is that, from a biological point of view, death occurs at all, Weismann made statements about the longevity of certain species that were erroneous. It is not true, for example, that "whales live for some hundreds of years," or that "elephants live 200 years"; the correspondence Weismann noted between size and longevity, though it holds good up to a point, does not project to any such extremes.

Nor did Weismann sufficiently appreciate, so far as appears, how much was unknown (and is still unknown) about just what the life span is for most species of animals, at least as they exist in nature, and how difficult it is even to define such a thing in many kinds of plants. Animals kept in captivity are exposed to far fewer hazards than they would face if left to move about in the wild, where it is almost impossible to keep track of them. Plants, on the other hand, while easy enough to observe, have such important structural differences as compared with animals that it is difficult to include them within the same concept of a life cycle. Even among the kinds of plants, as mosses, algae, ferns, and bacteria, differences are so great that no single notion of life span can be conceived for them.

Admitting such defects, however, and allowing for the great advances in biology that have been made since Weismann's time that have rendered some of his terminology obsolete and have greatly extended and refined the experimental evidence on which he relied, it may fairly be said that the views he set forth on this subject are consistent with current ideas of it. And really they are more than current. For there is a kind of philosophical seriousness to Weismann's discussion, a visible determination to state—a willingness to believe it may be possible to state—an important truth about the terms of existence, which nowadays is rarely found in scientific writing, and which makes the piece a classic of its kind.

The essay was first published in 1881. It is reprinted here from a two-volume collection of Weismann's shorter writings translated into English and published ten years later as *Essays Upon Heredity and Kindred Biological Problems*. A lengthy appendix dealing with the particular species, chiefly insects, has been omitted.

The Duration of Life

With your permission, I will bring before you to-day some thoughts upon the subject of the duration of life. I can scarcely do better than begin with the simple but significant words of Johannes Müller: "Organic bodies are perishable; while life maintains the appearance of immortality in the constant succession of similar individuals, the individuals themselves pass away." *

Omitting, for the time being, any discussion as to the precise accuracy of this statement, it is at any rate obvious that the life of an individual has its natural limit, at least among those animals and plants which are met with in every-day life. But it is equally obvious that the limits are very differently placed in the various species of animals and plants. These differences are so manifest that they have given rise to popular sayings. Thus Jacob Grimm mentions an old German saying, "A wren lives three years, a dog three times as long as a wren, a horse three times as long as a dog, and a man three times as long as a horse, that is eighty-one years. A donkey attains three times the age of a man, a wild goose three times that of a donkey, a crow three times that of a wild goose, a deer three times that of a crow, and an oak three times the age of a deer."

If this be true a deer would live 6,000 years, and an oak nearly 20,000 years. The saying is certainly not founded upon exact observation, but it becomes true if looked upon as a general statement that the duration of life is very different in different organisms.

The question now arises as to the causes of these great differences. How is it that individuals are endowed with the power of living long in such very various degrees?

One is at first tempted to seek the answer by an appeal to the differences in morphological and chemical structure which separate species from one another. In fact all attempts to throw light upon the subject which have been made up to the present time lie in this direction.

All these explanations are nevertheless insufficient. In a certain sense it is true that the causes of the duration of life must be contained in the organism itself, and cannot be found in any of its external conditions or circumstances. But structure and chemical composition—in short the physiological constitution of the body in the ordinary sense of the words—are not the only factors which determine duration of life. This conclusion forces itself upon our attention as soon as the attempt is made to explain existing facts by these factors alone: there must be some other additional cause contained in the organism as an unknown and invisible part of its constitution, a cause which determines the duration of life.

---

* Johannes Peter Müller (1801–58), one of the founders of modern physiology, who as an author and teacher was influential in several branches of science during the nineteenth century.

The size of the organism must in the first place be taken into consideration. Of all organisms in the world, large trees have the longest lives. The Adansonias of the Cape Verde Islands are said to live for 6,000 years. The largest animals also attain the greatest age. Thus there is no doubt that whales live for some hundreds of years. Elephants live 200 years, and it would not be difficult to construct a descending series of animals in which the duration of life diminishes in almost exact proportion to the decrease in the size of the body. Thus a horse lives forty years, a blackbird eighteen, a mouse six, and many insects only a few days or weeks.

If however the facts are examined a little more closely it will be observed that the great age (200 years) reached by an elephant is also attained by many smaller animals, such as the pike and carp. The horse lives forty years, but so does a cat or a toad; and a sea anemone has been known to live for over fifty years. The duration of life in a pig (about twenty years) is the same as that in a crayfish, although the latter does not nearly attain the hundredth part of the weight of a pig.

It is therefore evident that length of life cannot be determined by the size of the body alone. There is, however, some relation between these two attributes. A large animal lives longer than a small one because it is larger; it would not be able to become even comparatively large unless endowed with a comparatively long duration of life.

Apart from all other reasons, no one could imagine that the gigantic body of an elephant could be built up like that of a mouse in three weeks, or in a single day like that of the larva of certain flies. The gestation of an elephant lasts for nearly two years, and maturity is only reached after a lapse of about twenty-four years.

Furthermore, to ensure the preservation of the species, a longer time is required by a large animal than by a small one, when both have reached maturity. Thus Leuckart*

and later Herbert Spencer have pointed out that the absorbing surface of an animal only increases as the square of its length, while its size increases as the cube; and it therefore follows that the larger an animal becomes, the greater will be the difficulty experienced in assimilating any nourishment over and above that which it requires for its own needs, and therefore the more slowly will it reproduce itself.

But although it may be stated generally that the duration of the period of growth and length of life are longest in the largest animals, it is nevertheless impossible to maintain that there is any fixed relation between the two; and Flourens† was mistaken when he considered that the length of life was always equivalent to five times the duration of the period of growth. Such a conclusion might be accepted in the case of man if we set his period of growth at twenty years and his length of life at a hundred; but it cannot be accepted for the majority of other Mammalia. Thus the horse lives from forty to fifty years, and the latter age is at least as frequently reached among horses as a hundred years among men; but the horse becomes mature in four years, and the length of its life is thus ten or twelve times as long as its period of growth.

The second factor which influences the duration of life is purely physiological: it is the rate at which the animal lives, the rapidity with which assimilation and the other vital processes take place. Upon this point Lotze‡ remarks in his *Mikrokosmus:* "Active and restless mobility destroys the organized body: the swift-footed animals hunted by man, as also dogs, and even apes, are inferior in length of life to man and the larger beasts of prey, which satisfy their needs by a few vigorous efforts. The inert-

----

* K. G. F. R. Leuckart (1822–98), German zoologist, noted for his studies of parasites.
† M. F. P. Flourens (1794–1867), French physiologist, noted for his studies of the brain.
‡ R. H. Lotze (1817–81), noted German physician and psychologist.

ness of the Amphibia is, on the other hand, accompanied by relatively great length of life."

There is certainly some truth in these observations, and yet it would be a great mistake to assume that activity necessarily implies a short life. The most active birds have very long lives, as will be shown later on: they live as long as and sometimes longer than the majority of Amphibia which reach the same size. The organism must not be looked upon as a heap of combustible material, which is completely reduced to ashes in a certain time the length of which is determined by size, and by the rate at which it burns; but it should be rather compared to a fire, to which fresh fuel can be continually added, and which, whether it burns quickly or slowly, can be kept burning as long as necessity demands.

The connection between activity and shortness of life cannot be explained by supposing that a more rapid consumption of the body occurs, but it is explicable because the increased rate at which the vital processes take place permit the more rapid achievement of the aim and purpose of life, viz. the attainment of maturity and the reproduction of the species.

When I speak of the aim and purpose of life, I am only using figures of speech, and I do not mean to imply that nature is in any way working consciously.

When I was speaking of the relation between duration of life and the size of the body, I might have added another factor which also exerts some influence, viz. the complexity of the structure. Two organisms of the same size, but belonging to different grades of organization, will require different periods of time for their development. Certain animals of a very lowly organization, such as the Rhizopoda, may attain a diameter of 5 mm. and may thus become larger than many insects' eggs. Yet under favourable circumstances an Amoeba can divide into two animals in ten minutes, while no insect's egg can develop into the young animal in a less period than twenty-four hours. Time is required for the development of the immense number of cells which must in the latter case arise from the single egg-cell.

Hence we may say that the peculiar constitution of an animal does in part determine the length of time which must elapse before reproduction begins. The period before reproduction is however only part of the whole life of an animal, which of course extends over the total period during which the animal exists.

Hitherto it has always been assumed that the duration of this total period is solely determined by the constitution of the animal's body. But the assumption is erroneous. The strength of the spring which drives the wheel of life does not solely depend upon the size of the wheel itself or upon the material of which it is made; and, leaving the metaphor, duration of life is not exclusively determined by the size of the animal, the complexity of its structure, and the rate of its metabolism. The facts are plainly and clearly opposed to such a supposition.

How, for instance, can we explain from this point of view the fact that the queen-ant and the workers live for many years, while the males live for a few weeks at most? The sexes are not distinguished by any great difference in size or complexity of body, or in the rate of metabolism. In all these three particulars they must be looked upon as precisely the same, and yet there is this immense difference between the lengths of their lives.

I shall return later on to this and other similar cases, and for the present I assume it to be proved that physiological considerations alone cannot determine the duration of life. It is not these which alone determine the strength of the spring which moves the machinery of life; we know that springs of different strengths may be fixed in machines of the same kind and quality. This metaphor is however imperfect, because we cannot imagine the existence of any special force in an organism which determines the duration of its life; but it is nevertheless useful because it emphasises the fact that the duration of life is forced upon the organism by causes outside itself, just as the spring is fixed in its place by forces outside the machine, and not only fixed in its place, but chosen of a certain strength so that it will run down after a certain time.

To put it briefly, I consider that duration of life is really dependent upon adaptation to external conditions, that its length, whether longer or shorter, is governed by the needs of the species, and that it is determined by precisely the same mechanical process of regulation as that by which the structure and functions of an organism are adapted to its environment.

Assuming for the moment that these conclusions are valid, let us ask how the duration of life of any given species can have been determined by their means. In the first place, in regulating duration of life, the advantage to the species, and not to the individual, is alone of any importance. This must be obvious to any one who has once thoroughly thought out the process of natural selection. It is of no importance to the species whether the individual lives longer or shorter, but it is of importance that the individual should be enabled to do its work towards the maintenance of the species. This work is reproduction, or the formation of a sufficient number of new individuals to compensate the species for those which die. As soon as the individual has performed its share in this work of compensation, it ceases to be of any value to the species, it has fulfilled its duty and may die. But the individual may be of advantage to the species for a longer period if it not only produces offspring, but tends them for a longer or shorter time, either by protecting, feeding, or instructing them. This last duty is not only undertaken by man, but also by animals, although to a smaller extent; for instance, birds teach their young to fly, and so on.

We should therefore expect to find that, as a rule, life does not greatly outlast the period of reproduction except in those species which tend their young; and as a matter of fact we find that this is the case.

All mammals and birds outlive the period of reproduction, but this never occurs among insects except in those species which tend their young. Furthermore, the life of all the lower animals ceases also with the end of the reproductive period, as far as we can judge.

Duration of life is not however determined in this way, but only the point at which its termination occurs relative to the cessation of reproduction. The duration itself depends first upon the length of time which is required for the animal to reach maturity—that is, the duration of its youth, and, secondly, upon the length of the period of fertility—that is the time which is necessary for the individual to produce a sufficient number of descendants to ensure the perpetuation of the species. It is precisely this latter point which is determined by external conditions.

There is no species of animal which is not exposed to destruction through various accidental agencies—by hunger or cold, by drought or flood, by epidemics, or by enemies, whether beasts of prey or parasites. We also know that these causes of death are only apparently accidental, or at least that they can only be called accidental as far as a single individual is concerned. As a matter of fact a far greater number of individuals perish through the operation of these agencies than by natural death. There are thousands of species of which the existence depends upon the destruction of other species; as, for example, the various kinds of fish which feed on the countless minute Crustacea inhabiting our lakes.

It is easy to see that an individual is, *ceteris paribus*, more exposed to accidental death when the natural term of its life becomes longer; and therefore the longer the time required by an individual for the production of a sufficient number of descendants to ensure the existence of the species, the greater will be the number of individuals which perish accidentally before they have fulfilled this important duty. Hence it follows, first, that the number of descendants produced by any individual must be greater as the duration of its reproductive period becomes longer; and, secondly, the surprising result that nature does not tend to secure the longest possible life to the adult individual, but, on the contrary, tends to shorten the period of reproductive activity as far as possible, and with this the duration of life; but these conclusions only refer to the animal and not to the vegetable world.

All this sounds very paradoxical, but the facts show that it is true. At first sight numerous instances of remarkably long life seem to refute the argument, but the contradictions are only apparent and disappear on closer investigation.

Birds as a rule live to a surprisingly great age. Even the smallest of our native singing birds lives for ten years, while the nightingale and blackbird live from twelve to eighteen years. A pair of eider ducks were observed to make their nest in the same place for twenty years, and it is believed that these birds sometimes reach the age of nearly one hundred years. A cuckoo, which was recognised by a peculiar note in its call, was heard in the same forest for thirty-two consecutive years. Birds of prey, and birds which live in marshy districts, become much older, for they outlive more than one generation of men.

Schinz mentions a bearded vulture which was seen sitting on a rock upon a glacier near Grindelwald, and the oldest men in Grindelwald had, when boys, seen the same bird sitting on the same rock. A white-headed vulture in the Schönbrunn Zoological Gardens had been in captivity for 118 years, and many examples are known of eagles and falcons reaching an age of over 100 years. Finally, we must not forget Humboldt's Atur parrot from the Orinoco, concerning which the Indians said that it could not be understood because it spoke the language of an extinct tribe.[1]

It is therefore necessary to ask how far we can show that such long lives are really the shortest which are possible under the circumstances.

Two factors must here be taken into consideration; first, that the young of birds are greatly exposed to destructive agencies; and, secondly, that the structure of a bird is adapted for flight and therefore excludes the possibility of any great degree of fertility.

Many birds, like the stormy petrel, the diver, guillemot, and other sea-birds, lay only a single egg, and breed (as is usually the case with birds) only once a year. Others, such as birds of prey, pigeons, and humming-birds, lay two eggs, and it is only those which fly badly, such as jungle fowls and pheasants, which produce a number of eggs (about twenty), and the young of these very species are especially exposed to those dangers which more or less affect the offspring of all birds. Even the eggs of our most powerful native bird of prey, the golden eagle, which all animals fear, and of which the eyrie, perched on a rocky height, is beyond the reach of any enemies, are very frequently destroyed by late frosts or snow in spring, and, at the end of the year in winter, the young birds encounter the fiercest of foes, viz. hunger. In the majority of birds, the egg, as soon as it is laid, becomes exposed to the attacks of enemies; martens and weasels, cats and owls, buzzards and crows are all on the look out for it. At a later period the same enemies destroy numbers of the helpless young, and in winter many succumb in the struggle against cold and hunger, or to the numerous dangers which attend migration over land and sea, dangers which decimate the young birds.

It is impossible directly to ascertain the exact number which are thus destroyed; but we can arrive at an estimate by an indirect method. If we agree with Darwin and Wallace in believing that in most species a cer-

---

[1] Alexander von Humboldt, *Ansichten der Natur* [Perspectives on Nature] (1807).

tain degree of constancy is maintained in the number of individuals of successive generations, and that therefore the number of individuals within the same area remains tolerably uniform for a certain period of time; it follows that, if we know the fertility and the average duration of life of a species, we can calculate the number of those which perish before reaching maturity. Unfortunately the average length of life is hardly known with certainty in the case of any species of bird. Let us however assume, for the sake of argument, that the individuals of a certain species live for ten years, and that they lay twenty eggs in each year; then of the 200 eggs which are laid during the ten years, which constitute the lifetime of an individual, 198 must be destroyed, and only two will reach maturity, if the number of individuals in the species is to remain constant. Or to take a concrete example; let us fix the duration of life in the golden eagle at 60 years, and its period of immaturity (of which the length is not exactly known) at ten years, and let us assume that it lays two eggs a year; then a pair will produce 100 eggs in 50 years, and of these only two will develop into adult birds; and thus on an average a pair of eagles will only succeed in bringing a pair of young to maturity once in fifty years. And so far from being an exaggeration, this calculation rather under-estimates the proportion of mortality among the young; it is sufficient however to enforce the fact that the number of young destroyed must reach in birds a very high figure as compared with the number of those which survive.

If this argument holds, and at the same time the fertility from physical and other grounds cannot be increased, it follows that a relatively long life is the only means by which the maintenance of the species of birds can be secured. Hence a great length of life is proved to be an absolute necessity for birds.

I have already mentioned that these animals demonstrate most clearly that physiological considerations do not by any means

suffice to explain the duration of life. Although all vital processes take place with greater rapidity and the temperature of the blood is higher in birds than in mammals, yet the former greatly surpass the latter in length of life. Only in the largest Mammalia—the whales and the elephants—is the duration of life equal to or perhaps greater than that of the longest lived birds. If we compare the relative weights of these animals, the Mammalia are everywhere at a disadvantage. Even such large animals as the horse and bear only attain an age of fifty years at the outside; the lion lives about thirty-five years, the wild boar twenty-five, the sheep fifteen, the fox fourteen, the hare ten, the squirrel and the mouse six years; but the golden eagle, though it does not weigh more than from nine to twelve pounds, and is thus intermediate as regards weight between the hare and the fox, attains nevertheless an age which is ten times as long. The explanation of this difference is to be found first in the much greater fertility of the smaller Mammalia, such as the rabbit or mouse, and secondly in the much lower mortality among the young of the larger Mammalia. The minimum duration of life necessary for the maintenance of the species is therefore much lower than it is among birds. Even here, however, we are not yet in possession of exact statistics indicating the number of young destroyed; but it is obvious that Mammalia possess over birds a great advantage in their intra-uterine development. In Mammalia the destruction of young only begins after birth, while in birds it begins during the development of the embryo. This distinction is in fact carried even further, for many mammals protect their young against enemies for a long time after birth.

It is unnecessary to go further into the details of these cases, or to consider whether and to what extent every class of the animal kingdom conforms to these principles. Thus to consider all or even most of the classes of the animal kingdom would be quite impossible at the present time, because our knowledge of the duration of life among animals is very incomplete. Biological problems have for a long time excited less interest than morphological ones. There is nothing or almost nothing to be found in existing zoological text-books upon the duration of life in animals; and even monographs upon single classes, such as the Amphibia, reptiles, or even birds, contain very little on this subject. When we come to the lower animals, knowledge on this point is almost entirely wanting. I have not been able to find a single reference to the age in Echinodermata, and very little about that of worms, Crustacea, and Coelenterata. The length of life in many molluscan species is very well known, because the age can be determined by markings on the shell. But even in this group, any exact knowledge, such as would be available for our purpose, is still wanting concerning such necessary points as the degree of fertility, the relation to other animals, and many other factors.

Data the most exact in all respects are found among the insects, and to this class I will for a short time direct your special attention. We will first consider the duration of larval life. This varies very greatly, and chiefly depends upon the nature of the food, and the ease or difficulty with which it can be procured. The larvae of bees reach the pupal stage in five to six days; but it is well known that they are fed with substances of high nutritive value (honey and pollen), and that they require no great effort to obtain the food, which lies heaped up around them. The larval life in many *Ichneumonidae* is but little longer, being passed in a parasitic condition within other insects; abundance of accessible food is thus supplied by the tissues and juices of the host. Again, the larvae of the blow-fly become pupae in eight to ten days, although they move actively in boring their way under the skin and into the tissues of the dead animals upon which they live. The life of the leaf-eating caterpillars of butterflies and moths lasts for six weeks or longer, corresponding to the lower nutritive value of their food

and the greater expenditure of muscular energy in obtaining it. Those caterpillars which live upon wood, such as *Cossus ligniperda,* have a larval life of two to three years, and the same is true of hymenopterous insects with similar habits, such as *Sirex.*

Furthermore, predaceous larvae require a long period for attaining their full size, for they can only obtain their prey at rare intervals and by the expenditure of considerable energy. Thus among the dragon-flies larval life lasts for a year, and among many may-flies even two or three years.

All these results can be easily understood from well-known physiological principles, and they indicate that the length of larval life is very elastic, and can be extended as circumstances demand; for otherwise carnivorous and wood-eating larvae could not have survived in the phyletic development of insects. Now it would be a great mistake to suppose that there is any reciprocal relation between duration of life in the larva and in the mature insect, or imago; or, to put it differently, to suppose that the total duration of life is the same in insects of the same size and activity, so that the time which is spent in the larval state is, as it were, deducted from the life of the imago, and *vice versa.* That this cannot be the case is shown by the fact already alluded to, that among bees and ants larval life is of the same length in males and females, while there is a difference of some years between the lengths of their lives as imagos.

The life of the imago is generally very short, and not only ends with the close of the period of reproduction, as was mentioned above, but this latter period is also itself extremely short.

The larva of the cockchafer devours the roots of plants for a period of four years, but the mature insect with its more complex structure endures for a comparatively short time; for the beetle itself dies in about a month after completing its metamorphosis. And this is by no means an extreme case. Most butterflies have an even shorter life, and among the moths there are many species (as in the *Psychidae*) which only live for a few days, while others again, which reproduce by the parthenogenetic method, only live for twenty-four hours. The shortest life is found in the imagos of certain may-flies, which only live four to five hours. They emerge from the pupa-case towards the evening, and as soon as their wings have hardened, they begin to fly, and pair with one another. Then they hover over the water; their eggs are extruded all at once, and death follows almost immediately.

The short life of the imago in insects is easily explained by the principles set forth above. Insects belong to the number of those animals which, even in their mature state, are very liable to be destroyed by others which are dependent upon them for food; but they are at the same time among the most fertile of animals, and often produce an astonishing number of eggs in a very short time. And no better arrangement for the maintenance of the species under such circumstances can be imagined than that supplied by diminishing the duration of life, and simultaneously increasing the rapidity of reproduction.

This general tendency is developed to very different degrees according to conditions peculiar to each species. The shortening of the period of reproduction, and the duration of life to the greatest extent which is possible, depends upon a number of co-operating circumstances, which it is impossible to enumerate completely. Even the manner in which the eggs are laid may have an important effect. If the larva of the may-fly lived upon some rare and widely distributed food-plant instead of at the bottom of streams, the imagos would be compelled to live longer, for they would be obliged—like many moths and butterflies—to lay their eggs singly or in small clusters, over a large area. This would require both time and strength, and they could not retain the rudimentary mouth which they now possess, for they would have to feed in order to acquire sufficient strength for long flights; and—whether they were carnivorous like

dragon-flies, or honey-eating like butterflies—their feeding would itself cause a further expenditure of both time and strength, which would necessitate a still further increase in the duration of life. And as a matter of fact we find that dragon-flies and swift-flying hawk-moths often live for six or eight weeks and sometimes longer.

We must also remember that in many species the eggs are not mature immediately after the close of the pupal stage, but that they only gradually ripen during the life of the imago, and frequently, as in many beetles and butterflies, do not ripen simultaneously, but only a certain number at a time. This depends, first, upon the amount of reserve nutriment accumulated in the body of the insect during larval life; secondly, upon various but entirely different circumstances, such as the power of flight. Insects which fly swiftly and are continually on the wing, like hawk-moths and dragon-flies, cannot be burdened with a very large number of ripe eggs. In these cases the gradual ripening of the eggs becomes necessary, and involves an increase in the duration of life. In Lepidoptera, we see how the power of flight diminishes step by step as soon as other circumstances permit, and simultaneously how the eggs ripen more and more rapidly, while the length of life becomes shorter, until a minimum is reached. Only two stages in the process of transformation can be mentioned here.

The strongest flyers—the hawk-moths and butterflies—must be looked upon as the most specialised and highest types among the Lepidoptera. Not only do they possess organs for flight in their most perfect form, but also organs for feeding—the characteristic spiral proboscis or "tongue."

There are certain moths (among the Bombyces) of which the males fly as well as the hawk-moths, while the females are unable to use their large wings for flight, because the body is too heavily weighted by a mass of eggs, all of which reach maturity at the same time. Such species, as for instance *Aglia tau,* are unable to distribute their eggs over a wide area, but are obliged to lay them all in a single spot. They can however do this without harm to the species, because their caterpillars live upon forest trees, which provide abundant food for a larger number of larvae than can be produced by the eggs of a single female. The eggs of *Aglia tau* are deposited directly after pairing, and shortly afterwards the insect dies at the foot of the tree among the moss-covered roots of which it has passed the winter in the pupal state. The female moth seldom lives for more than three or four days; but the males which fly swiftly in the forests, seeking for the less abundant females, live for a much longer period, certainly from eight to fourteen days.[2]

The females of the *Psychidae* also deposit all their eggs in one place. The grasses and lichens upon which their caterpillars live grow close at hand upon the surface of the earth and stones, and hence the female moth does not leave the ground, and generally does not even quit the pupa-case, within which it lays its eggs; as soon as this duty is finished, it dies. In relation to these habits the wings and mouth of the female are rudimentary, while the male possesses perfectly developed wings.

The causes which have regulated the length of life in these cases are obvious enough, yet still more striking illustrations are to be found among insects which live in colonies.

The duration of life varies with the sex in bees, wasps, ants, and termites: the females have a long life, the males a short one; and there can be no doubt that the explanation of this fact is to be found in adaptation to external conditions of life.

The queen-bee—the only perfect female in the hive—lives two to three years, and often as long as five years, while the male bees or drones only live four to five months. Sir John Lubbock* has succeeded in keeping female and working ants alive for seven years—a great age for insects—while the males only lived a few weeks.

These last examples become readily intel-

ligible when we remember that the males neither collect food nor help in building the hive. Their value to the colony ceases with the nuptial flight, and from the point of view of utility it is easy to understand why their lives should be so short. But the case is very different with the female. The longest period of reproduction possible, when accompanied by very great fertility, is, as a rule, advantageous for the maintenance of the species. It cannot however be attained in most insects, for the capability of living long would be injurious if all individuals fell a prey to their enemies before they had completed the full period of life. Here it is otherwise: when the queen-bee returns from her nuptial flight, she remains within the hive until her death, and never leaves it. There she is almost completely secure from enemies and from dangers of all kinds; thousands of workers armed with stings protect, feed, and warm her; and in short there is every chance of her living through the full period of a life of normal length. And the case is entirely similar with the female ant. In neither of these insects is there any reason why the advantages which follow from a lengthened period of reproductive activity should be abandoned.

That an increase in the length of life has actually taken place in such cases seems to be indicated by the fact that both sexes of the saw-flies—the probable ancestors of bees and ants—have but a short life. On the other hand, the may-flies afford an undoubted instance of the shortening of life. Only in certain species is life as short as I have indicated above; in the majority it

---

[2] This estimate is derived from observation of the time during which these insects are to be seen upon the wing. Direct observations upon the duration of life in this species are unknown to me.

* (1834–1913), English banker and naturalist, author of, among other works, *Ants, Bees and Wasps* (1882). E. B. Poulton, the translator of Weismann's essay, notes here that Lubbock subsequently kept a queen ant alive for nearly 15 years.

lasts for one or more days. The extreme cases, with a life of only a few hours, form the end of a line of development tending in the direction of a shortened life. This is made clear by the fact that one of these may-flies (*Palingenia*) does not even leave its pupa-skin, but reproduces in the so-called sub-imago stage.

It is therefore obvious that the duration of life is extremely variable, and not only depends upon physiological considerations, but also upon the external conditions of life. With every change in the structure of a species, and with the acquisition of new habits, the length of its life may, and in most cases must, be altered.

In answering the question as to the means by which the lengthening or shortening of life is brought about, our first appeal must be to the process of natural selection. Duration of life, like every other characteristic of an organism, is subject to individual fluctuations. From our experience with the human species we know that long life is hereditary. As soon as the long-lived individuals in a species obtain some advantage in the struggle for existence, they will gradually become dominant, and those with the shortest lives will be exterminated.

So far everything is quite simple; but hitherto we have only considered the external mechanism, and we must now further inquire as to the concomitant internal means by which such processes are rendered possible.

This brings us face to face with one of the most difficult problems in the whole range of physiology—the question of the origin of death. As soon as we thoroughly understand the circumstances upon which normal death depends in general, we shall be able to make a further inquiry as to the circumstances which influence its earlier or later appearance, as well as to any functional changes in the organism which may produce such a result.

The changes in the organism which result in normal death—senility so-called—have been most accurately studied among men.

We know that with advancing age certain alterations take place in the tissues, by which their functional activity is diminished; that these changes gradually increase, and finally either lead to direct or so-called normal death, or produce indirect death by rendering the organism incapable of resisting injuries due to external influences. These senile changes have been so well described from the time of Burdach and Bichat to that of Kussmaul,* and are so well known, that I need not enter into further details here.

In answer to an inquiry as to the causes which induce these changes in the tissues, I can only suggest that the cells which form the vital constituents of tissues are worn out by prolonged use and activity. It is conceivable that the cells might be thus worn out in two ways; either the cells of a tissue remain the same throughout life, or else they are being continually replaced by younger generations of cells, which are themselves cast off in their turn.

In the present state of our knowledge the former alternative can hardly be maintained. Millions of blood corpuscles are continually dying and being replaced by new ones. On both the internal and external surfaces of the body countless epithelial cells are being incessantly removed, while new ones arise in their place; the activity of many and probably of all glands is accompanied by a change in their cells, for their secretions consist partly of detached and partly of dissolved cells; it is stated that even the cells of bone, connective tissue and muscle undergo the same changes, and nervous tissue alone remains, in which it is doubtful whether such a renewal of cells takes place. And yet as regards even this

---

* K. F. Burdach (1776–1847), German physiologist specializing in studies of the nervous system; M. F. X. Bichat (1771–1802), French physiologist, regarded as the founder of scientific histology and pathological anatomy; Adolf Kussmaul (1822–1902), German physician, regarded as one of the outstanding clinicians of his day.

tissue, certain facts are known which indicate a normal, though probably a slow renewal of the histological elements. I believe that one might reasonably defend the statement—in fact, it has already found advocates —that the vital processes of the higher (i.e. multicellular) animals are accompanied by a renewal of the morphological elements in most tissues.

This statement leads us to seek the origin of death, not in the waste of single cells, but in the limitation of their powers of reproduction. Death takes place because a worn-out tissue cannot for ever renew itself, and because a capacity for increase by means of cell-division is not everlasting, but finite. This does not however imply that the immediate cause of death lies in the imperfect renewal of cells, for death would in all cases occur long before the reproductive power of the cells had been completely exhausted. Functional disturbances will appear as soon as the rate at which the worn-out cells are renewed becomes slow and insufficient.

But it must not be forgotten that death is not always preceded by senility, or a period of old age. For instance, in many of the lower animals death immediately follows the most important deed of the organism, viz. reproduction. Many Lepidoptera, all may-flies, and many other insects die of exhaustion immediately after depositing their eggs. Men have been known to die from the shock of a strong passion. Sulla* is said to have died as the result of rage, whilst Leo X succumbed to an excess of joy. Here the psychical shock caused too intense an excitement of the nervous system. In the same manner the exercise of intense effort may also produce a similarly fatal excitement in the above-mentioned insects. At any rate it is certain that when, for some reason, this effort is not made, the insect lives for a somewhat longer period.

It is clear that in such animals as insects we can only speak figuratively of normal death, if we mean by this an end which is not due to accident. In these animals an accidental end is the rule, and is therefore, strictly speaking, normal.

Assuming the truth of the above-mentioned hypothesis as to the causes of normal death, it follows that the number of cell-generations which can proceed from the egg-cell is fixed for every species, at least within certain limits; and this number of cell-generations, if attained, corresponds to the maximum duration of life in the individuals of the species concerned. Shortening of life in any species must depend upon a decrease in the number of successive cell-generations, while conversely, the lengthening of life depends upon an increase in the number of cell-generations over those which were previously possible.

Such changes actually take place in plants. When an annual plant becomes perennial, the change—one in every way possible—can only happen by the production of new shoots, i.e. by an increase in the number of cell-generations. The process is not so obvious in animals, because in them the formation of young cells does not lead to the production of new and visible parts, for the new material is merely deposited in the place of that which is worn out and disappears. Among plants, on the other hand, the old material persists, its cells become lignified, and it is built over by new cells which assume the functions of life.

It is certainly true that the question as to the necessity of death in general does not seem much clearer from this point of view than from the purely physiological one. This is because we do not know why a cell must divide 10,000 or 100,000 times and then suddenly stop. It must be admitted that we can see no reason why the power of cell-multiplication should not be unlimited, and why the organism should not therefore be endowed with everlasting life. In the same manner, from a physiological point of view, we might admit that we can see no reason why the functions of the organism should ever cease.

---

* *See* Plutarch, *Lives; GBWW,* Vol. 14, p. 387.

It is only from the point of view of utility that we can understand the necessity of death. The same arguments which were employed to explain the necessity for as short a life as possible, will with but slight modification serve to explain the common necessity of death.[3]

Let us imagine that one of the higher animals became immortal; it then becomes perfectly obvious that it would cease to be of value to the species to which it belonged. Suppose that such an immortal individual could escape all fatal accidents, through infinite time—a supposition which is of course hardly conceivable. The individual would nevertheless be unable to avoid, from time to time, slight injuries to one or another part of its body. The injured parts could not regain their former integrity, and thus the longer the individual

lived, the more defective and crippled it would become, and the less perfectly would it fulfil the purpose of its species. Individuals are injured by the operation of external forces, and for this reason alone it is necessary that new and perfect individuals should continually arise and take their place, and this necessity would remain even if the individuals possessed the power of living eternally.

From this follows, on the one hand, the necessity of reproduction, and, on the other, the utility of death. Worn-out individuals are not only valueless to the species, but they are even harmful, for they take the place of those which are sound. Hence by the operation of natural selection, the life of our hypothetically immortal individual would be shortened by the amount which was useless to the species. It would be re-

---

[3] At this point, E. B. Poulton, Weismann's translator, notes: "After reading these proofs Dr. A. R. Wallace kindly sent me an unpublished note upon the production of death by means of natural selection, written by him some time between 1865 and 1870. The note contains some ideas on the subject, which were jotted down for further elaboration, and were then forgotten until recalled by the argument of this Essay. The note is of great interest in relation to Dr. Weismann's suggestions, and with Dr. Wallace's permission I print it in full below."

The Action of Natural Selection in Producing Old Age, Decay, and Death

Supposing organisms ever existed that had not the power of natural reproduction, then since the absorptive surface would only increase as the square of the dimensions while the bulk to be nourished and renewed would increase as the cube, there must soon arrive a limit of growth. Now if such an organism did not produce its like, accidental destruction would put an end to the species. Any organism therefore that, by accidental or spontaneous fission, could become two organisms, and thus multiply itself indefinitely without increasing in size beyond the limits most favourable for nourishment and existence, could not be thus exterminated: since the individual only could be accidentally destroyed, the race would survive. But if individuals did not die they would soon multiply inordinately and would interfere with each other's healthy existence. Food would become

scarce, and hence the larger individuals would probably decompose or diminish in size. The deficiency of nourishment would lead to parts of the organism not being renewed; they would become fixed, and liable to more or less slow decomposition as dead parts within a living body. The smaller organisms would have a better chance of finding food, the larger ones less chance. That one which gave off several small portions to form each a new organism would have a better chance of leaving descendants like itself than one which divided equally or gave off a large part of itself. Hence it would happen that those which gave off very small portions would probably soon after cease to maintain their own existence while they would leave a numerous offspring. This state of things would be in any case for the advantage of the race, and would therefore, by natural selection, soon become established as the regular course of things, and thus we have the origin of *old age, decay,* and *death;* for it is evident that when one or more individuals have provided a sufficient number of successors they themselves, as consumers of nourishment in a constantly increasing degree, are an injury to those successors. Natural selection therefore weeds them out, and in many cases favours such races as die almost immediately after they have left successors. Many moths and other insects are in this condition, living only to propagate their kind and then immediately dying, some not even taking any food in the perfect and reproductive state.

duced to a length which would afford the most favourable conditions for the existence of as large a number as possible of vigorous individuals, at the same time.

If by these considerations death is shown to be a beneficial occurrence, it by no means follows that it is to be solely accounted for on grounds of utility. Death might also depend upon causes which lie in the nature of life itself. The floating of ice upon water seems to us to be a useful arrangement, although the fact that it does float depends upon its molecular structure and not upon the fact that its doing so is of any advantage to us. In like manner the necessity of death has been hitherto explained as due to causes which are inherent in organic nature, and not to the fact that it may be advantageous.

I do not however believe in the validity of this explanation; I consider that death is not a primary necessity, but that it has been secondarily acquired as an adaptation. I believe that life is endowed with a fixed duration, not because it is contrary to its nature to be unlimited, but because the unlimited existence of individuals would be a luxury without any corresponding advantage. The above-mentioned hypothesis upon the origin and necessity of death leads me to believe that the organism did not finally cease to renew the worn-out cell material because the nature of the cells did not permit them to multiply indefinitely, but because the power of multiplying indefinitely was lost when it ceased to be of use.

I consider that this view, if not exactly proved, can at any rate be rendered extremely probable.

It is useless to object that man (or any of the higher animals) dies from the physical necessity of his nature, just as the specific gravity of ice results from its physical nature. I am quite ready to admit that this is the case. John Hunter,* supported by his experiments on *anabiosis*, hoped to prolong the life of man indefinitely by alternate freezing and thawing; and the Veronese

Colonel Aless. Guaguino made his contemporaries believe that a race of men existed in Russia, of which the individuals died regularly every year on the 27th of November, and returned to life on the 24th of the following April. There cannot however be the least doubt, that the higher organisms, as they are now constructed, contain within themselves the germs of death. The question however arises as to how this has come to pass; and I reply that death is to be looked upon as an occurrence which is advantageous to the species as a concession to the outer conditions of life, and not as an absolute necessity, essentially inherent in life itself.

Death, that is the end of life, is by no means, as is usually assumed, an attribute of all organisms. An immense number of low organisms do not die, although they are easily destroyed, being killed by heat, poisons, etc. As long, however, as those conditions which are necessary for their life are fulfilled, they continue to live, and they thus carry the potentiality of unending life in themselves. I am speaking not only of the Amoebae and the low unicellular Algae, but also of far more highly organized unicellular animals, such as the Infusoria.

The process of fission in the Amoeba has been recently much discussed, and I am well aware that the life of the individual is generally believed to come to an end with the division which gives rise to two new individuals, as if death and reproduction were the same thing. But this process cannot be truly called death. Where is the dead body? What is it that dies? Nothing dies; the body of the animal only divides into two similar parts, possessing the same constitution. Each of these parts is exactly like its parent, lives in the same manner, and finally also divides into two halves. As far as these organisms are concerned, death can only be spoken of in the most figurative sense.

There are no grounds for the assumption

---

* (1728–93), English surgeon, anatomist, and physiologist.

that the two halves of an Amoeba are differently constituted internally, so that after a time one of them will die while the other continues to live. Such an idea is disproved by a recently discovered fact. It has been noticed in *Euglypha* (one of the Foraminifera) and in other low animals of the same group, that when division is almost complete, and the two halves are only connected by a short strand, the protoplasm of both parts begins to circulate, and for some time passes backwards and forwards between the two halves. A complete mingling of the whole substance of the animal and a resulting identity in the constitution of each half is thus brought about before the final separation.

The objection might perhaps be raised that, if the parent animal does not exactly die, it nevertheless disappears as an individual. I cannot however let this pass unless it is also maintained that the man of to-day is no longer the same individual as the boy of twenty years ago. In the growth of man, neither structure nor the components of structure remain precisely the same; the material is continually changing. If we can imagine an Amoeba endowed with self-consciousness, it might think before dividing "I will give birth to a daughter," and I have no doubt that each half would regard the other as the daughter, and would consider itself to be the original parent. We cannot however appeal to this criterion of personality in the Amoeba, but there is nevertheless a criterion which seems to me to decide the matter: I refer to the continuity of life in the same form.

Now if numerous organisms, endowed with the potentiality of never-ending life, have real existence, the question arises as to whether the fact can be understood from the point of view of utility. If death has been shown to be a necessary adaptation for the higher organisms, why should it not be so for the lower also? Are they not decimated by enemies? Are they not often imperfect? Are they not worn out by contact with the external world? Although they are certainly destroyed by other animals, there is nothing comparable to that deterioration of the body which takes place in the higher organisms. Unicellular animals are too simply constructed for this to be possible. If an infusorian is injured by the loss of some part of its body, it may often recover its former integrity, but if the injury is too great it dies. The alternative is always perfect integrity or complete destruction.

We may now leave this part of the subject, for it is obvious that normal death, that is to say, death which arises from internal causes, is an impossibility among these lower organisms. In those species at any rate in which fission is accompanied by a circulation of the protoplasm of the parent, the two halves must possess the same qualities. Since one of them is endowed with a potentiality for unending life, and must be so endowed if the species is to persist, it is clear that the other exactly similar half must be endowed with equal potentiality.

Let us now consider how it happened that the multicellular animals and plants, which arose from unicellular forms of life, came to lose this power of living for ever.

The answer to this question is closely bound up with the principle of division of labour which appeared among multicellular organisms at a very early stage, and which has gradually led to the production of greater and greater complexity in their structure.

The first multicellular organism was probably a cluster of similar cells, but these units soon lost their original homogeneity. As the result of mere relative position, some of the cells were especially fitted to provide for the nutrition of the colony, while others undertook the work of reproduction. Hence the single group would come to be divided into two groups of cells, which may be called somatic and reproductive—the cells of the body as opposed to those which are concerned with reproduction. This differentiation was not at first absolute, and indeed it is not always so to-day. Among the lower

Metazoa, such as the polypes, the capacity for reproduction still exists to such a degree in the somatic cells, that a small number of them are able to give rise to a new organism—in fact new individuals are normally produced by means of so-called buds. Furthermore, it is well known that many of the higher animals have retained considerable powers of regeneration; the salamander can replace its lost tail or foot, and the snail can reproduce its horns, eyes, etc.

As the complexity of the Metazoan body increased, the two groups of cells became more sharply separated from each other. Very soon the somatic cells surpassed the reproductive in number, and during this increase they became more and more broken up by the principle of the division of labour into sharply separated systems of tissues. As these changes took place, the power of reproducing large parts of the organism was lost, while the power of reproducing the whole individual became concentrated in the reproductive cells alone.

But it does not therefore follow that the somatic cells were compelled to lose the power of unlimited cell-production, although in accordance with the law of heredity, they could only give rise to cells which resembled themselves, and belonged to the same differentiated histological system. But as the fact of normal death seems to teach us that they have lost even this power, the causes of the loss must be sought outside the organism, that is to say, in the external conditions of life; and we have already seen that death can be very well explained as a secondarily acquired adaptation. The reproductive cells cannot lose the capacity for unlimited reproduction, or the species to which they belong would suffer extinction. But the somatic cells have lost this power to a gradually increasing extent, so that at length they became restricted to a fixed, though perhaps very large number of cell-generations. This restriction, which implies the continual influx of new individuals, has been explained above as a result of the impossibility of entirely pro-

tecting the individual from accidents, and from the deterioration which follows them. Normal death could not take place among unicellular organisms, because the individual and the reproductive cell are one and the same: on the other hand, normal death is possible, and as we see, has made its appearance, among multicellular organisms in which the somatic and reproductive cells are distinct.

I have endeavoured to explain death as the result of restriction in the powers of reproduction possessed by the somatic cells, and I have suggested that such restriction may conceivably follow from a limitation in the number of cell-generations possible for the cells of each organ and tissue. I am unable to indicate the molecular and chemical properties of the cell upon which the duration of its power of reproduction depends: to ask this is to demand an explanation of the nature of heredity—a problem the solution of which may still occupy many generations of scientists. At present we can hardly venture to propose any explanation of the real nature of heredity.

But the question must be answered as to whether the kind and degree of reproductive power resides in the nature of the cell itself, or in any way depends upon the quality of its nutriment.

Virchow, in his *Cellular Pathology,* has remarked that the cells are not only nourished, but that they actively supply themselves with food.[*] If therefore the internal condition of the cell decides whether it shall accept or reject the nutriment which is offered, it becomes conceivable that all cells may possess the power of refusing to absorb nutriment, and therefore of ceasing to undergo further division.

Modern embryology affords us many proofs, in the segmentation of the ovum, and in the subsequent developmental changes, that the causes of the different forms of reproductive activity witnessed in

---

[*] Rudolf Virchow (1821–1902), the founder of cellular pathology. See *GBWW*, Vol. 3, p. 1213.

cells lie in the essential nature of the cells themselves. Why does the segmentation of one half of certain eggs proceed twice as rapidly as that of the other half? Why do the cells of the ectoderm divide so much more quickly than those of the endoderm? Why does not only the rate, but also the number of cells produced (so far as we can follow them) always remain the same? Why does the multiplication of cells in every part of the blastoderm take place with the exact amount of energy and rapidity necessary to produce the various elevations, folds, invaginations, etc., in which the different organs and tissues have their origin, and from which finally the organism itself arises? There can be no doubt that the causes of all these phenomena lie within the cells themselves; that in the ovum and the cells which are immediately derived from it, there exists a tendency towards a certain determined (I might almost say specific) mode and energy of cell-multiplication. And why should we regard this inherited tendency as confined to the building up of the embryo? Why should it not also exist in the young, and later in the mature animal? The phenomena of heredity which make their appearance even in old age afford us proofs that a tendency towards a certain mode of cell-multiplication continues to regulate the growth of the organism during the whole of its life.

The above-mentioned considerations show us that the degree of reproductive activity present in the tissues is regulated by internal causes, while the natural death of an organism is the termination—the hereditary limitation—of the process of cell-division, which began in the segmentation of the ovum.

Allow me to suggest a further consideration which may be compared with the former. The organism is not only limited in time, but also in space: it not only lives for a limited period, but it can only attain a limited size. Many animals grow to their full size long before their natural end: and although many fishes, reptiles, and lower animals are said to grow during the whole of their life, we do not mean by this that they possess the power of unlimited growth any more than that of unlimited life. There is everywhere a maximum size, which, as far as our experience goes, is never surpassed. The mosquito never reaches the size of an elephant, nor the elephant that of a whale.

Upon what does this depend? Is there any external obstacle to growth? Or is the limitation entirely imposed from within?

Perhaps you may answer, that there is an established relation between the increase of surface and mass, and it cannot be denied that these relations do largely determine the size of the body. A beetle could never reach the size of an elephant, because, constituted as it is, it would be incapable of existence if it attained such dimensions. But nevertheless the relations between surface and mass do not form the only reason why any given individual does not exceed the average size of its species. Each individual does not strive to grow to the largest possible size, until the absorption from its digestive area becomes insufficient for its mass; but it ceases to grow because its cells cannot be sufficiently nourished in consequence of its increased size. The giants which occasionally appear in the human species prove that the plan upon which man is constructed can also be carried out on a scale which is far larger than the normal one. If the size of the body chiefly depends upon amount of nutriment, it would be possible to make giants and dwarfs at will. But we know, on the contrary, that the size of the body is hereditary in families to a very marked extent; in fact so much so that the size of an individual depends chiefly upon heredity, and not upon amount of food.

These observations point to the conclusion that the size of the individual is in reality pre-determined, and that it is potentially contained in the egg from which the individual develops.

We know further that the growth of the individual depends chiefly upon the multiplication of cells and only to a slight extent upon the growth of single cells. It is therefore clear that a limit of growth is imposed by a limitation in the processes by which cells are increased, both as regards the number of cells produced and the rate at which they are formed. How could we otherwise explain the fact that an animal ceases to grow long before it has reached the physiologically attainable maximum of its species, without at the same time suffering any loss of vital energy?

In many cases at least, the most important duty of an organism, viz. reproduction, follows upon the attainment of full size—a fact which induced Johannes Müller to reject the prevailing hypothesis which explained the death of animals as due to "the influences of the inorganic environment, which gradually wear away the life of the individual." He argued that, if this were the case, "the organic energy of an individual would steadily decrease from the beginning," while the facts indicate that this is not so.[4]

If it is further asked why the egg should give rise to a fixed number of cell-generations, although perhaps a number which varies widely within certain limits, we may now refer to the operation of natural selection upon the relation of surface to mass, and upon other physiological necessities which are peculiar to the species. Because a certain size is the most favourable for a certain plan of organization, the process of natural selection determined that such a size should be within certain variable limits, characteristic of each species. This size is then transmitted from generation to generation, for when once established as normal for the species, the most favourable size is potentially present in the reproductive cell from which each individual is developed.

If this conclusion holds, and I believe that no essential objection can be raised against it, then we have in the limitation in space a process which is exactly analogous to the limitation in time, which we have already considered. The latter limita-

tion—the duration of life—also depends upon the multiplication of cells, the rapid increase of which first gave rise to the characteristic form of the mature body, and then continued at a slower rate. In the mature animal, cell-reproduction still goes on, but it no longer exceeds the waste; for some time it just compensates for loss, and then begins to decline. The waste is not compensated for, the tissues perform their functions incompletely, and thus the way for death is prepared, until its final appearance by one of the three great *Atria mortis*.

I admit that facts are still wanting upon which to base this hypothesis. It is a pure supposition that senile changes are due to a deficient reproduction of cells: at the same time this supposition gains in probability when we are enabled to reduce the limitations of the organism in both time and space to one and the same principle. It cannot however be asserted under any circumstances that it is a pure supposition that the ovum possesses a capacity for cell-multiplication which is limited both as to numbers produced and rate of production. The fact that each species maintains an average size is a sufficient proof of the truth of this conclusion.

Hitherto I have only spoken of animals and have hardly mentioned plants. I should not have been able to consider them at all, had it not happened that a work of Hildebrand's* has recently appeared, which has, for the first time, provided us with exact observations on the duration of plant-life.

The chief results obtained by this author agree very well with the view which I have brought before you to-day. Hildebrand shows that the duration of life in plants also is by no means completely fixed, and that it may be very considerably altered through the agency of the external conditions of life. He shows that, in course of time, and under changed conditions of life,

---

[4] *Physiologie* (1840), vol. 1, p. 40.
* J. M. Hildebrand (1807–81), German traveler and botanist.

an annual plant may become perennial, or *vice versa*. The external factors which influence the duration of life are here however essentially different, as indeed we expect them to be, when we remember the very different conditions under which the animal and vegetable kingdoms exist. During the life of animals the destruction of mature individuals plays a most important part, but the existence of the mature plant is fairly well secured; their chief period of destruction is during youth, and this fact has a direct influence upon the degree of fertility, but not upon the duration of life. Climatic considerations, especially the periodical changes of summer and winter, or wet and dry seasons, are here of greater importance.

It must then be admitted that the dependence of the duration of life upon the external conditions of existence is alike common to plants and animals. In both kingdoms the high multicellular forms with well-differentiated organs contain the germs of death, while the low unicellular organisms are potentially immortal. Furthermore, an undying succession of reproductive cells is possessed by all the higher forms, although this may be but poor consolation to the conscious individual which perishes. Johannes Müller is therefore right, when in the sentence quoted at the beginning of my lecture, he speaks of an "appearance of immortality" which passes from each individual into that which succeeds it. That which remains over, that which persists, is not the individual itself—not the complex aggregate of cells which is conscious of itself—but an individuality which is outside its consciousness, and of a low order, an individuality which is made up of a single cell, which arises from the conscious individual. I might here conclude, but I wish first, in a few words, to protect myself against a possible misunderstanding.

I have repeatedly spoken of immortality, first of the unicellular organism, and secondly of the reproductive cell. By this word I have merely intended to imply a duration of time which appears to be endless to our human faculties. I have no wish to enter into the question of the cosmic or telluric origin of life on the earth. An answer to this question will at once decide whether the power of reproduction possessed by these cells is in reality eternal or only immensely prolonged, for that which is without beginning is, and must be, without end.

The supposition of a cosmic origin of life can only assist us if by its means we can altogether dispense with any theory of spontaneous generation. The mere shifting of the origin of life to some other far-off world cannot in any way help us. A truly cosmic origin in its widest significance will rigidly limit us to the statement—*omne vivum ex vivo*—to the idea that life can only arise from life, and has always so arisen, to the conclusion that organic beings are eternal like matter itself.

Experience cannot help us to decide this question; we do not know whether spontaneous generation was the commencement of life on the earth, nor have we any direct evidence for the idea that the process of development of the living world carries the end within itself, or for the converse idea that the end can only be brought about by means of some external force.

I admit that spontaneous generation, in spite of all vain efforts to demonstrate it, remains for me a logical necessity. We cannot regard organic and inorganic matter as independent of each other and both eternal, for organic matter is continually passing, without residuum, into the inorganic. If the eternal and indestructible are alone without beginning, then the noneternal and destructible must have had a beginning. But the organic world is certainly not eternal and indestructible in that absolute sense in which we apply these terms to matter itself. We can, indeed, kill all organic beings and thus render them inorganic at will. But these changes are not the same as those which we induce in a piece of chalk by pouring sulphuric acid upon it; in this case we only change the form, and the inorganic matter remains. But when we pour sulphuric acid upon a worm, or when we burn an oak tree, these organisms are not changed into some other animal and tree, but they disappear entirely as organized beings and are resolved into inorganic elements. But that which can be completely resolved into inorganic matter must have also arisen from it, and must owe its ultimate foundation to it. The organic might be considered eternal if we could only destroy its form, but not its nature.

It therefore follows that the organic world must once have arisen, and further that it will at some time come to an end. Hence we must speak of the eternal duration of unicellular organisms and of reproductive cells in the Metazoa and Metaphyta in that particular sense which signifies, when measured by our standards, an immensely long time.

Yet who can maintain that he has discovered the right answer to this important question? And even though the discovery were made, can any one believe that by its means the problem of life would be solved? If it were established that spontaneous generation did actually occur, a new question at once arises as to the conditions under which the occurrence became possible. How can we conceive that dead inorganic matter could have come together in such a manner as to form living protoplasm, that wonderful and complex substance which absorbs foreign material and changes it into its own substance, in other words grows and multiplies?

And so, in discussing this question of life and death, we come at last—as in all provinces of human research—upon problems which appear to us to be, at least for the present, insoluble. In fact it is the quest after perfected truth, not its possession, that falls to our lot, that gladdens us, fills up the measure of our life, nay! hallows it.

NOTE TO THE READER

LIFE AND DEATH is the subject of Chapter 48 of the *Syntopicon*. The readings listed under Topic 6a, "the life span of plants and animals, and of different species of plants and animals," and Topic 6c, "the biological characteristics of the stages of life," are especially relevant. There is a brief but interesting discussion of Weismann's essay in Freud, *Beyond the Pleasure Principle, GBWW*, Vol. 54, pp. 655–56.

Benito Cereno

Herman Melville

Editor's Introduction

Benito Cereno, like *Billy Budd, Bartleby the Scrivener,* and one or two other pieces of similar length, may be fairly described as an example of Melville's second-best work. That is to say, it is not, nor are those other tales, of the order and magnitude of *Moby Dick;* but it is something more, as they are, than either the casual romances of travel and adventure, such as *Typee* and *Omoo,* or the imperfect allegories, like *Mardi* and *Pierre,* that Melville wrote at other times. In such works he was not able to combine successfully the two great talents he had, for storytelling and for speculation, so that they either skim the surface or lose themselves in the depths of his intention; whereas in these shorter tales, as of course in *Moby Dick* itself, he struck a balance between his gifts, or at least made room for them both, and achieved results that are both striking and profound. *Benito Cereno* is at once an absorbing story, ominous with suspense, and a statement, only a little too much underscored, of genuinely philosophic dimensions.

Its theme is one to which Melville returned again and again—that of a man involved in circumstances that imply the existence of a moral order that at best is arbitrary and at worst malign, and that he finds himself unable or unwilling to accept. The resulting conflict is of cosmic proportions in *Moby Dick,* where Ahab, crippled and enraged by the great white whale, pursues it as the embodiment of all that is evil. At the opposite extreme is the quiet resistance of the clerk, Bartleby, to the blank monotony of his everyday tasks—a resistance, amounting at last to absolute refusal, which is explained only by his mysterious, mild remark that he "would prefer not to." Benito Cereno stands somewhere between these two figures. His situation, though terrible, is more limited than Ahab's, but unlike Bartleby he can make no resistance at all.

It is easy to see such figures as projections of Melville himself. He was descended from a line of Scottish Calvinists whose strict doctrine, which provided harsh but definite answers to questions about the existence of evil, the justness of God, and the rebellious human heart, had become inadequate for the complexities and the aspirations of the century in which he lived. It is appropriate that he was a wanderer in his youth, a sailor in ships, as the world knew from his stories, in search—as the same stories implied—of a faith. The search was not successful, yet Melville did not give it up. Endlessly he talked of it with the one kindred spirit he thought he had found, Nathaniel Hawthorne, who listened sympathetically but could not sustain the intense kind of friendship that Melville wanted—that his restless nature demanded. "He can neither believe, nor be comfortable in his unbelief," Hawthorne noted of him, "and he is too honest and courageous not to try to do one or the other." We can suppose that this honesty bore some relation to Ahab's fierce quest, and we can surmise where for Melville that quest may finally have led (we do not know as much as we should like about his private life, owing to the deliberate obscurity in which his last years were passed, and the absence of any private journal or extensive correspondence) when we contemplate the despair of Don Benito and the resignation of Bartleby.

But if we find Melville in each of these protagonists, we must find him also, it would appear, in the observers through whose eyes we are in each case allowed to see them, and whose part it is to comprehend their fate without sharing it. Such an observer is Ishmael, in *Moby Dick;* in *Bartleby,* it is Bartleby's employer; in *Benito Cereno* it is the Yankee captain, Amasa Delano. And if we consider the role these observers play, and the recognition and resolution that are required of them, we perceive that for Melville it was ultimately the comprehension that mattered. For he could not really *be* Ahab or Bartleby or Benito Cereno, nor could he sanely wish to be; he could only *know* them and offer them to be known, suggesting as he did so how great the cost might be of seeing or not seeing what it is that, morally speaking, they represent. How hard he found it to compute this cost, or even to decide where it should rightly lie, is shown in *Benito Cereno.* The paradox of Captain Delano is that his failure to understand the situation in which he finds himself is both the source of mortal danger to him and the reason he survives it. Yet he does survive, unlike Don Benito, as a strong will may outlast a stricken spirit.

Benito Cereno was first published serially, without Melville's name, in *Putnam's Monthly Magazine* for October, November, and December 1855, and was subsequently included in the volume called *The Piazza Tales* (1856). The substance of the story was provided by an episode that Melville had read of in a work by a real Captain Amasa Delano called *Narrative of Voyages and Travels . . . Round the World . . .* (1817). Melville added the oakum-pickers, the Ashanti hatchet-polishers, the ruined magnificence of the Spanish ship, and certain other details. He ignored the real Captain Delano's expressions of sympathy for the slaves, and his excuses for their conduct. Such sentiments, which Melville was likely to have shared, were nevertheless foreign to his purpose, which was to construct an allegory of good and evil, and to consider the workings of justice not in social but in moral terms.

Benito Cereno

In the year 1799, Captain Amasa Delano, of Duxbury, in Massachusetts, commanding a large sealer and general trader, lay at anchor with a valuable cargo, in the harbour of Santa Maria—a small, desert, uninhabited island toward the southern extremity of the long coast of Chile. There he had touched for water.

On the second day, not long after dawn, while lying in his berth, his mate came below, informing him that a strange sail was coming into the bay. Ships were then not so plenty in those waters as now. He rose, dressed, and went on deck.

The morning was one peculiar to that coast. Everything was mute and calm; everything grey. The sea, though undulated into long roods of swells, seemed fixed, and was sleeked at the surface like waved lead that has cooled and set in the smelter's mould. The sky seemed a grey surtout. Flights of troubled grey fowl, kith and kin with flights of troubled grey vapours among which they were mixed, skimmed low and fitfully over the waters, as swallows over meadows before storms. Shadows present, foreshadowing deeper shadows to come.

To Captain Delano's surprise, the stranger, viewed through the glass, showed no colours; though to do so upon entering a haven, however uninhabited in its shores, where but a single other ship might be lying, was the custom among peaceful seamen of all nations. Considering the lawlessness and loneliness of the spot, and the sort of stories, at that day, associated with those seas, Captain Delano's surprise might have deepened into some uneasiness had he not been a person of a singularly undistrustful good nature, not liable, except on extraordinary and repeated incentives, and hardly then, to indulge in personal alarms, any way involving the imputation of malign evil in man. Whether, in view of what humanity is capable, such a trait implies, along with a benevolent heart, more than ordinary quickness and accuracy of intellectual perception, may be left to the wise to determine.

But whatever misgivings might have obtruded on first seeing the stranger, would almost, in any seaman's mind, have been dissipated by observing, that the ship, in navigating into the harbour, was drawing too near the land; a sunken reef making out off her bow. This seemed to prove her a stranger, indeed, not only to the sealer, but the island; consequently, she could be no wonted freebooter on that ocean. With no small interest, Captain Delano continued to watch her—a proceeding not much facilitated by the vapours partly mantling the hull, through which the far matin light from her cabin streamed equivocally enough; much like the sun—by this time hemisphered on the rim of the horizon, and, apparently in company with the strange ship entering the harbour—which, wimpled by the same low, creeping clouds, showed not unlike a Lima intriguante's one sinister eye peering across the Plaza from the Indian loop-hole of her dusk *saya-y-manto*.

It might have been but a deception of the vapours, but, the longer the stranger was watched the more singular appeared her manœuvres. Ere long it seemed hard to decide whether she meant to come in or no—

what she wanted, or what she was about. The wind, which had breezed up a little during the night, was now extremely light and baffling, which the more increased the apparent uncertainty of her movements.

Surmising, at last, that it might be a ship in distress, Captain Delano ordered his whale-boat to be dropped, and, much to the wary opposition of his mate, prepared to board her, and, at the least, pilot her in. On the night previous, a fishing party of the seamen had gone a long distance to some detached rocks out of sight from the sealer, and, an hour or two before daybreak, had returned, having met with no small success. Presuming that the stranger might have been long off soundings, the good captain put several baskets of the fish, for presents, into his boat, and so pulled away. From her continuing too near the sunken reef, deeming her in danger, calling to his men, he made all haste to apprise those on board of their situation. But, some time ere the boat came up, the wind, light though it was, having shifted, had headed the vessel off, as well as partly broken the vapours from about her.

Upon gaining a less remote view, the ship, when made signally visible on the verge of the leaden-hued swells, with the shreds of fog here and there raggedly furring her, appeared like a whitewashed monastery after a thunder-storm, seen perched upon some dun cliff among the Pyrenees. But it was no purely fanciful resemblance which now, for a moment, almost led Captain Delano to think that nothing less than a ship-load of monks was before him. Peering over the bulwarks were what really seemed, in the hazy distance, throngs of dark cowls; while, fitfully revealed through the open portholes, other dark moving figures were dimly descried, as of Black Friars pacing the cloisters.

Upon a still nigher approach, this appearance was modified, and the true character of the vessel was plain—a Spanish merchantman of the first class, carrying negro slaves, amongst other valuable freight, from one colonial port to another. A very large, and,

in its time, a very fine vessel, such as in those days were at intervals encountered along that main; sometimes superseded Acapulco treasure-ships, or retired frigates of the Spanish king's navy, which, like superannuated Italian palaces, still, under a decline of masters, preserved signs of former state.

As the whale-boat drew more and more nigh, the cause of the peculiar pipe-clayed aspect of the stranger was seen in the slovenly neglect pervading her. The spars, ropes, and great part of the bulwarks, looked woolly, from long unacquaintance with the scraper, tar, and the brush. Her keel seemed laid, her ribs put together, and she launched, from Ezekiel's Valley of Dry Bones.

In the present business in which she was engaged, the ship's general model and rig appeared to have undergone no material change from their original warlike and Froissart pattern. However, no guns were seen.

The tops were large, and were railed about with what had once been octagonal net-work, all now in sad disrepair. These tops hung overhead like three ruinous aviaries, in one of which was seen perched, on a ratlin, a white noddy, a strange fowl, so called from its lethargic, somnambulistic character, being frequently caught by hand at sea. Battered and mouldy, the castellated forecastle seemed some ancient turret, long ago taken by assault, and then left to decay. Toward the stern, two high-raised quarter-galleries—the balustrades here and there covered with dry, tindery sea-moss—opening out from the unoccupied state-cabin, whose dead-lights, for all the mild weather, were hermetically closed and calked—these tenantless balconies hung over the sea as if it were the grand Venetian canal. But the principal relic of faded grandeur was the ample oval of the shield-like stern-piece, intricately carved with the arms of Castile and Leon, medallioned about by groups of mythological or symbolical devices; uppermost and central of which was a dark satyr in a mask, holding his foot on the prostrate neck of a writhing figure, likewise masked.

Whether the ship had a figure-head, or

only a plain beak, was not quite certain, owing to canvas wrapped about that part, either to protect it while undergoing a refurbishing, or else decently to hide its decay. Rudely painted or chalked, as in a sailor freak, along the forward side of a sort of pedestal below the canvas was the sentence, *"Seguid vuestro jefe,"* (follow your leader); while upon the tarnished headboards, near by, appeared, in stately capitals, once gilt, the ship's name, "SAN DOMINICK," each letter streakingly corroded with tricklings of copper-spike rust; while, like mourning weeds, dark festoons of sea-grass slimily swept to and fro over the name, with every hearse-like roll of the hull.

As, at last, the boat was hooked from the bow along toward the gangway amidship, its keel, while yet some inches separated from the hull, harshly grated as on a sunken coral reef. It proved a huge bunch of conglobated barnacles adhering below the water to the side like a wen—a token of baffling airs and long calms passed somewhere in those seas.

Climbing the side, the visitor was at once surrounded by a clamorous throng of whites and blacks, but the latter outnumbering the former more than could have been expected, negro transportation-ship as the stranger in port was. But, in one language, and as with one voice, all poured out a common tale of suffering; in which the negresses, of whom there were not a few, exceeded the others in their dolorous vehemence. The scurvy, together with the fever, had swept off a great part of their number, more especially the Spaniards. Off Cape Horn they had narrowly escaped shipwreck; then, for days together, they had lain tranced without wind; their provisions were low; their water next to none; their lips that moment were baked.

While Captain Delano was thus made the mark of all eager tongues, his one eager glance took in all faces, with every other object about him.

Always upon first boarding a large and populous ship at sea, especially a foreign one, with a nondescript crew such as Lascars or Manila men, the impression varies in a peculiar way from that produced by first entering a strange house with strange inmates in a strange land. Both house and ship—the one by its walls and blinds, the other by its high bulwarks like ramparts—hoard from view their interiors till the last moment; but in the case of the ship there is this addition: that the living spectacle it contains, upon its sudden and complete disclosure, has, in contrast with the blank ocean which zones it, something of the effect of enchantment. The ship seems unreal; these strange costumes, gestures, and faces, but a shadowy tableau just emerged from the deep, which directly must receive back what it gave.

Perhaps it was some such influence, as above is attempted to be described, which, in Captain Delano's mind, heightened whatever, upon a staid scrutiny, might have seemed unusual; especially the conspicuous figures of four elderly grizzled negroes, their heads like black, doddered willow tops, who, in venerable contrast to the tumult below them, were couched, sphynx-like, one on the starboard cat-head, another on the larboard, and the remaining pair face to face on the opposite bulwarks above the main-chains. They each had bits of unstranded old junk in their hands, and, with a sort of stoical self-content, were picking the junk into oakum, a small heap of which lay by their sides. They accompanied the task with a continuous, low, monotonous chant; droning and drooling away like so many grey-headed bagpipers playing a funeral march.

The quarter-deck rose into an ample elevated poop, upon the forward verge of which, lifted, like the oakum-pickers, some eight feet above the general throng, sat along in a row, separated by regular spaces, the cross-legged figures of six other blacks; each with a rusty hatchet in his hand, which, with a bit of brick and a rag, he was engaged like a scullion in scouring; while between each two was a small stack of hatchets, their rusted edges turned forward awaiting a like operation. Though occasionally the four oakum-pickers would briefly address some person or persons in the crowd below, yet the six hatchet-polishers neither spoke to others, nor breathed a whisper among themselves, but sat intent upon their task, except at intervals, when, with the peculiar love in negroes of uniting industry with pastime, two and two they sideways clashed their hatchets together, like cymbals, with a barbarous din. All six, unlike the generality, had the raw aspect of unsophisticated Africans.

But that first comprehensive glance which took in those ten figures, with scores less conspicuous, rested but an instant upon them, as, impatient of the hubbub of voices, the visitor turned in quest of whomsoever it might be that commanded the ship.

But as if not unwilling to let nature make known her own case among his suffering charge, or else in despair of restraining it for the time, the Spanish captain, a gentlemanly, reserved-looking, and rather young man to a stranger's eye, dressed with singular richness, but bearing plain traces of recent sleepless cares and disquietudes, stood passively by, leaning against the main-mast, at one moment casting a dreary, spiritless look upon his excited people, at the next an unhappy glance toward his visitor. By his side stood a black of small stature, in whose rude face, as occasionally, like a shepherd's dog, he mutely turned it up into the Spaniard's, sorrow and affection were equally blended.

Struggling through the throng, the American advanced to the Spaniard, assuring him of his sympathies, and offering to render whatever assistance might be in his power. To which the Spaniard returned for the present but grave and ceremonious acknowledgments, his national formality dusked by the saturnine mood of ill-health.

But losing no time in mere compliments, Captain Delano, returning to the gangway, had his baskets of fish brought up; and as the wind still continued light, so that some hours at least must elapse ere the ship could be brought to the anchorage, he bade his men return to the sealer, and fetch back as much water as the whale-boat could carry, with whatever soft bread the steward might have, all the remaining pumpkins on board, with a box of sugar, and a dozen of his private bottles of cider.

Not many minutes after the boat's pushing off, to the vexation of all, the wind entirely died away, and the tide turning, began drifting back the ship helplessly seaward. But trusting this would not long last, Captain Delano sought, with good hopes, to cheer up the strangers, feeling no small satisfaction that, with persons in their condition, he could—thanks to his frequent voyages along the Spanish main—converse with some freedom in their native tongue.

While left alone with them, he was not long in observing some things tending to heighten his first impressions; but surprise was lost in pity, both for the Spaniards and blacks, alike evidently reduced from scarcity of water and provisions; while long-continued suffering seemed to have brought out the less good-natured qualities of the negroes, besides, at the same time, impairing the Spaniard's authority over them. But, under the circumstances, precisely this condition of things was to have been anticipated. In armies, navies, cities, or families, in nature herself, nothing more relaxes good order than misery. Still, Captain Delano was not without the idea, that had Benito Cereno been a man of greater energy, misrule would hardly have come to the present pass. But the debility, constitutional or induced by hardships, bodily and mental, of the Spanish captain, was too obvious to be overlooked. A prey to settled dejection, as if long mocked with hope he would not now indulge it, even when it had ceased to be a mock, the prospect of that day, or evening at furthest, lying at anchor, with plenty of water for his people, and a brother captain to counsel and befriend, seemed in no perceptible degree to encourage him. His mind appeared unstrung, if still more seriously affected. Shut up in these oaken walls, chained to one dull round of command, whose unconditionality cloyed him, like some hypochondriac abbot he moved slowly about, at times suddenly pausing, starting, or staring, biting his lip, biting his finger-nail, flushing, paling, twitching his beard, with other symptoms of an absent or moody mind. This distempered spirit was lodged, as before hinted, in as distempered a frame. He was rather tall, but seemed never to have been robust, and now with nervous suffering was almost worn to a skeleton. A tendency to some pulmonary complaint appeared to have been lately confirmed. His voice was like that of one with lungs half gone—hoarsely suppressed, a husky whisper. No wonder that, as in this state he tottered about, his private servant apprehensively followed him. Sometimes the negro gave his master his arm, or took his handkerchief out of his pocket for him; performing these and similar offices with that affectionate zeal which transmutes into something filial or fraternal acts in themselves but menial; and which has gained for the negro the repute of making the most pleasing body-servant in the world; one, too, whom a master need be on no stiffly superior terms with, but may treat with familiar trust; less a servant than a devoted companion.

Marking the noisy indocility of the blacks in general, as well as what seemed the sullen inefficiency of the whites, it was not without humane satisfaction that Captain Delano witnessed the steady good conduct of Babo.

But the good conduct of Babo, hardly more than the ill-behaviour of others, seemed to withdraw the half-lunatic Don Benito from his cloudy languor. Not that such precisely was the impression made by the Spaniard on the mind of his visitor. The Spaniard's individual unrest was, for the present, but noted as a conspicuous feature in the ship's general affliction. Still, Captain Delano was not a little concerned at what he could not help taking for the time to be Don Benito's unfriendly indifference towards himself. The Spaniard's manner, too, conveyed a sort of sour and gloomy disdain, which he seemed at no pains to disguise. But this the American in charity ascribed to the harassing effects of sickness, since, in former instances, he had noted that there are peculiar natures on whom prolonged physical suffering seems to cancel every social instinct of kindness; as if, forced to black bread themselves, they deemed it but equity that each person coming nigh them should, indirectly, by some slight or affront, be made to partake of their fare.

But ere long Captain Delano bethought him that, indulgent as he was at the first, in judging the Spaniard, he might not, after all, have exercised charity enough. At bottom it was Don Benito's reserve which displeased him; but the same reserve was shown towards all but his faithful personal attendant. Even the formal reports which, according to sea-usage, were, at stated times, made to him by some petty underling, either a white, mulatto or black, he hardly had patience enough to listen to, without betraying contemptuous aversion. His manner upon such occasions was, in its degree, not unlike that which might be supposed to have been his imperial countryman's, Charles V, just previous to the anchoritish retirement of that monarch from the throne.

This splenetic disrelish of his place was evinced in almost every function pertaining to it. Proud as he was moody, he condescended to no personal mandate. Whatever special orders were necessary, their delivery was delegated to his body-servant, who in turn transferred them to their ultimate destination, through runners, alert Spanish boys or slave boys, like pages or pilot-fish within easy call continually hovering round Don Benito. So that to have beheld this undemonstrative invalid gliding about, apathetic and mute, no landsman could have dreamed that in him was lodged a dictatorship beyond which, while at sea, there was no earthly appeal.

Thus, the Spaniard, regarded in his reserve, seemed the involuntary victim of mental disorder. But, in fact, his reserve might, in some degree, have proceeded from design. If so, then here was evinced the unhealthy climax of that icy though conscientious policy, more or less adopted by all commanders of large ships, which, except in signal emergencies, obliterates alike the manifestation of sway with every trace of sociality; transforming the man into a block, or rather into a loaded cannon, which, until there is call for thunder, has nothing to say.

Viewing him in this light, it seemed but a natural token of the perverse habit induced by a long course of such hard self-restraint, that, notwithstanding the present condition of his ship, the Spaniard should still persist in a demeanour, which, however harmless, or, it may be, appropriate, in a well-appointed vessel, such as the *San Dominick* might have been at the outset of the voyage, was anything but judicious now. But the Spaniard, perhaps, thought that it was with captains as with gods: reserve, under all events, must still be their cue. But probably this appearance of slumbering dominion might have been but an attempted disguise to conscious imbecility—not deep policy, but shallow device. But be all this as it might, whether Don Benito's manner was designed or not, the more Captain Delano noted its pervading reserve, the less he felt uneasiness at any particular manifestation of that reserve towards himself.

Neither were his thoughts taken up by the captain alone. Wonted to the quiet orderliness of the sealer's comfortable family of a crew, the noisy confusion of the *San Dominick's* suffering host repeatedly challenged his eye. Some prominent breaches, not only of discipline but of decency, were observed. These Captain Delano could not but ascribe, in the main, to the absence of those subordinate deck-officers to whom, along with higher duties, is intrusted what may be styled the police department of a populous ship. True, the old oakum-pickers appeared at times to act the part of monitorial constables to their countrymen, the blacks; but though occasionally succeeding in allaying trifling outbreaks now and then between man and man, they could do little or nothing toward establishing general quiet. The *San Dominick* was in the condition of a transatlantic emigrant ship, among whose multitude of living freight are some

individuals, doubtless, as little troublesome as crates and bales; but the friendly remonstrances of such with their ruder companions are of not so much avail as the unfriendly arm of the mate. What the *San Dominick* wanted was, what the emigrant ship has, stern superior officers. But on these decks not so much as a fourth-mate was to be seen.

The visitor's curiosity was roused to learn the particulars of those mishaps which had brought about such absenteeism, with its consequences; because, though deriving some inkling of the voyage from the wails which at the first moment had greeted him, yet of the details no clear understanding had been had. The best account would, doubtless, be given by the captain. Yet at first the visitor was loth to ask it, unwilling to provoke some distant rebuff. But plucking up courage, he at last accosted Don Benito, renewing the expression of his benevolent interest, adding, that did he (Captain Delano) but know the particulars of the ship's misfortunes, he would, perhaps, be better able in the end to relieve them. Would Don Benito favour him with the whole story?

Don Benito faltered; then, like some somnambulist suddenly interfered with, vacantly stared at his visitor, and ended by looking down on the deck. He maintained this posture so long, that Captain Delano, almost equally disconcerted, and involuntarily almost as rude, turned suddenly from him, walking forward to accost one of the Spanish seamen for the desired information. But he had hardly gone five paces, when, with a sort of eagerness, Don Benito invited him back, regretting his momentary absence of mind, and professing readiness to gratify him.

While most part of the story was being given, the two captains stood on the after part of the main-deck, a privileged spot, no one being near but the servant.

"It is now a hundred and ninety days," began the Spaniard, in his husky whisper, "that this ship, well officered and well manned, with several cabin-passengers—some fifty Spaniards in all—sailed from Buenos

Ayres bound to Lima, with a general cargo, hardware, Paraguay tea and the like—and," pointing forward, "that parcel of negroes, now not more than a hundred and fifty, as you see, but then numbering over three hundred souls. Off Cape Horn we had heavy gales. In one moment, by night, three of my best officers, with fifteen sailors, were lost, with the main-yard; the spar snapping under them in the slings, as they sought, with heavers, to beat down the icy sail. To lighten the hull, the heavier sacks of maté were thrown into the sea, with most of the water-pipes lashed on deck at the time. And this last necessity it was, combined with the prolonged detentions afterwards experienced, which eventually brought about our chief causes of suffering. When——"

Here there was a sudden fainting attack of his cough, brought on, no doubt, by his mental distress. His servant sustained him, and drawing a cordial from his pocket placed it to his lips. He a little revived. But unwilling to leave him unsupported while yet imperfectly restored, the black with one arm still encircled his master, at the same time keeping his eye fixed on his face, as if to watch for the first sign of complete restoration, or relapse, as the event might prove.

The Spaniard proceeded, but brokenly and obscurely, as one in a dream.

—"Oh, my God! rather than pass through what I have, with joy I would have hailed the most terrible gales; but——"

His cough returned and with increased violence; this subsiding, with reddened lips and closed eyes he fell heavily against his supporter.

"His mind wanders. He was thinking of the plague that followed the gales," plaintively sighed the servant; "my poor, poor master!" wringing one hand, and with the other wiping the mouth. "But be patient, Señor," again turning to Captain Delano, "these fits do not last long; master will soon be himself."

Don Benito reviving, went on; but as this portion of the story was very brokenly delivered, the substance only will here be set down.

It appeared that after the ship had been many days tossed in storms off the Cape, the scurvy broke out, carrying off numbers of the whites and blacks. When at last they had worked round into the Pacific, their spars and sails were so damaged, and so inadequately handled by the surviving mariners, most of whom were become invalids, that, unable to lay her northerly course by the wind, which was powerful, the unmanageable ship, for successive days and nights, was blown north-westward, where the breeze suddenly deserted her, in unknown waters, to sultry calms. The absence of the water-pipes now proved as fatal to life as before their presence had menaced it. Induced, or at least aggravated, by the more than scanty allowance of water, a malignant fever followed the scurvy; with the excessive heat of the lengthened calm, making such short work of it as to sweep away, as by billows, whole families of the Africans, and a yet larger number, proportionably, of the Spaniards, including, by a luckless fatality, every remaining officer on board. Consequently, in the smart west winds eventually following the calm, the already rent sails, having to be simply dropped, not furled, at need, had been gradually reduced to the beggars' rags they were now. To procure substitutes for his lost sailors, as well as supplies of water and sails, the captain, at the earliest opportunity, had made for Valdivia, the southernmost civilized port of Chile and South America; but upon nearing the coast the thick weather had prevented him from so much as sighting that harbour. Since which period, almost without a crew, and almost without canvas and almost without water, and, at intervals, giving its added dead to the sea, the *San Dominick* had been battledored about by contrary winds, inveigled by currents, or grown weedy in calms. Like a man lost in woods, more than once she had doubled upon her own track.

"But throughout these calamities," huskily continued Don Benito, painfully turning in the half embrace of his servant, "I have to

thank those negroes you see, who, though to your inexperienced eyes appearing unruly, have, indeed, conducted themselves with less of restlessness than even their owner could have thought possible under such circumstances."

Here he again fell faintly back. Again his mind wandered; but he rallied, and less obscurely proceeded.

"Yes, their owner was quite right in assuring me that no fetters would be needed with his blacks; so that while, as is wont in this transportation, those negroes have always remained upon deck—not thrust below, as in the Guineamen—they have, also, from the beginning, been freely permitted to range within given bounds at their pleasure."

Once more the faintness returned—his mind roved—but, recovering, he resumed:

"But it is Babo here to whom, under God, I owe not only my own preservation, but likewise to him, chiefly, the merit is due, of pacifying his more ignorant brethren, when at intervals tempted to murmurings."

"Ah, master," sighed the black, bowing his face, "don't speak of me; Babo is nothing; what Babo has done was but duty."

"Faithful fellow!" cried Captain Delano. "Don Benito, I envy you such a friend; slave I cannot call him."

As master and man stood before him, the black upholding the white, Captain Delano could not but bethink him of the beauty of that relationship which could present such a spectacle of fidelity on the one hand and confidence on the other. The scene was heightened by the contrast in dress, denoting their relative positions. The Spaniard wore a loose Chile jacket of dark velvet, white small-clothes and stockings, with silver buckles at the knee and instep; a high-crowned sombrero, of fine grass; a slender sword, silver mounted, hung from a knot in his sash—the last being an almost invariable adjunct, more for utility than ornament, of a South American gentleman's dress to this hour. Excepting when his occasional nervous contortions brought about disarray, there was a certain precision in his attire curiously

at variance with the unsightly disorder around; especially in the belittered Ghetto, forward of the main-mast, wholly occupied by the blacks.

The servant wore nothing but wide trousers, apparently, from their coarseness and patches, made out of some old topsail; they were clean, and confined at the waist by a bit of unstranded rope, which, with his composed, deprecatory air at times, made him look something like a begging friar of St. Francis.

However unsuitable for the time and place, at least in the blunt-thinking American's eyes, and however strangely surviving in the midst of all his afflictions, the toilette of Don Benito might not, in fashion at least, have gone beyond the style of the day among South Americans of his class. Though on the present voyage sailing from Buenos Ayres, he had avowed himself a native and resident of Chile, whose inhabitants had not so generally adopted the plain coat and once plebeian pantaloons; but, with a becoming modification, adhered to their provincial costume, picturesque as any in the world. Still, relatively to the pale history of the voyage, and his own pale face, there seemed something so incongruous in the Spaniard's apparel, as almost to suggest the image of an invalid courtier tottering about London streets in the time of the plague.

The portion of the narrative which, perhaps, most excited interest, as well as some surprise, considering the latitudes in question, was the long calms spoken of, and more particularly the ship's so long drifting about. Without communicating the opinion, of course, the American could not but impute at least part of the detentions both to clumsy seamanship and faulty navigation. Eyeing Don Benito's small, yellow hands, he easily inferred that the young captain had not got into command at the hawse-hole, but the cabin-window; and if so, why wonder at incompetence, in youth, sickness, and gentility united?

But drowning criticism in compassion, after a fresh repetition of his sympathies,

Captain Delano, having heard out his story, not only engaged, as in the first place, to see Don Benito and his people supplied in their immediate bodily needs, but, also, now further promised to assist him in procuring a large permanent supply of water, as well as some sails and rigging, and, though it would involve no small embarrassment to himself, yet he would spare three of his best seamen for temporary deck-officers; so that without delay the ship might proceed to Concepcion, there fully to refit for Lima, her destined port.

Such generosity was not without its effect, even upon the invalid. His face lighted up; eager and hectic, he met the honest glance of his visitor. With gratitude he seemed overcome.

"This excitement is bad for master," whispered the servant, taking his arm, and with soothing words gently drawing him aside.

When Don Benito returned, the American was pained to observe that his hopefulness, like the sudden kindling in his cheek, was but febrile and transient.

Ere long, with a joyless mien, looking up towards the poop, the host invited his guest to accompany him there, for the benefit of what little breath of wind might be stirring.

As during the telling of the story, Captain Delano had once or twice started at the occasional cymballing of the hatchet-polishers, wondering why such an interruption should be allowed, especially in that part of the ship, and in the ears of an invalid; and moreover, as the hatchets had anything but an attractive look, and the handlers of them still less so, it was, therefore, to tell the truth, not without some lurking reluctance, or even shrinking, it may be, that Captain Delano, with apparent complaisance, acquiesced in his host's invitation. The more so, since, with an untimely caprice of punctilio, rendered distressing by his cadaverous aspect, Don Benito, with Castilian bows, solemnly insisted upon his guest's preceding him up the ladder leading to the elevation; where, one on each side of the last step, sat for armorial supporters and sentries two of the ominous file. Gingerly enough stepped good Captain Delano between them, and in the instant of leaving them behind, like one running the gauntlet, he felt an apprehensive twitch in the calves of his legs.

But when, facing about, he saw the whole file, like so many organ-grinders, still stupidly intent on their work, unmindful of everything beside, he could not but smile at his late fidgety panic.

Presently, while standing with his host, looking forward upon the decks below, he was struck by one of those instances of insubordination previously alluded to. Three black boys, with two Spanish boys, were sitting together on the hatches, scraping a rude wooden platter, in which some scanty mess had recently been cooked. Suddenly, one of the black boys, enraged at a word dropped by one of his white companions, seized a knife, and, though called to forbear by one of the oakum-pickers, struck the lad over the head, inflicting a gash from which blood flowed.

In amazement, Captain Delano inquired what this meant. To which the pale Don Benito dully muttered, that it was merely the sport of the lad.

"Pretty serious sport, truly," rejoined Captain Delano. "Had such a thing happened on board the *Bachelor's Delight*, instant punishment would have followed."

At these words the Spaniard turned upon the American one of his sudden, staring, half-lunatic looks; then, relapsing into his torpor, answered, "Doubtless, doubtless, Señor."

Is it, thought Captain Delano, that this hapless man is one of those paper captains I've known, who by policy wink at what by power they cannot put down? I know no sadder sight than a commander who has little of command but the name.

"I should think, Don Benito," he now said, glancing towards the oakum-picker who had sought to interfere with the boys, "that you would find it advantageous to keep all your blacks employed, especially the younger ones, no matter at what useless task, and no matter what happens to the ship. Why, even with my little band, I find such a course indispensable. I once kept a crew on my quarter-deck thrumming mats for my cabin, when, for three days, I had given up my ship—mats, men, and all—for a speedy loss, owing to the violence of a gale, in which we could do nothing but helplessly drive before it."

"Doubtless, doubtless," muttered Don Benito.

"But," continued Captain Delano, again glancing upon the oakum-pickers and then at the hatchet-polishers, near by, "I see you keep some, at least, of your host employed."

"Yes," was again the vacant response.

"Those old men there, shaking their pows from their pulpits," continued Captain Delano, pointing to the oakum-pickers, "seem to act the part of old dominies to the rest, little heeded as their admonitions are at times. Is this voluntary on their part, Don Benito, or have you appointed them shepherds to your flock of black sheep?"

"What posts they fill, I appointed them," rejoined the Spaniard, in an acrid tone, as if resenting some supposed satiric reflection.

"And these others, these Ashantee conjurors here," continued Captain Delano, rather uneasily eyeing the brandished steel of the hatchet-polishers, where, in spots, it had been brought to a shine, "this seems a curious business they are at, Don Benito?"

"In the gales we met," answered the Spaniard, "what of our general cargo was not thrown overboard was much damaged by the brine. Since coming into calm weather, I have had several cases of knives and hatchets daily brought up for overhauling and cleaning."

"A prudent idea, Don Benito. You are part owner of ship and cargo, I presume; but not of the slaves, perhaps?"

"I am owner of all you see," impatiently returned Don Benito, "except the main company of blacks, who belonged to my late friend, Alexandro Aranda."

As he mentioned this name, his air was heart-broken; his knees shook; his servant supported him.

Thinking he divined the cause of such unusual emotion, to confirm his surmise, Captain Delano, after a pause, said: "And may I ask, Don Benito, whether—since a while ago you spoke of some cabin-passengers—the friend, whose loss so afflicts you, at the outset of the voyage accompanied his blacks?"

"Yes."

"But died of the fever?"

"Died of the fever. Oh, could I but——" Again quivering, the Spaniard paused.

"Pardon me," said Captain Delano, lowly, "but I think that, by a sympathetic experience, I conjecture, Don Benito, what it is that gives the keener edge to your grief. It was once my hard fortune to lose, at sea, a dear friend, my own brother, then supercargo. Assured of the welfare of his spirit, its departure I could have borne like a man; but that honest eye, that honest hand—both of which had so often met mine—and that warm heart; all, all—like scraps to the dogs—to throw all to the sharks! It was then I vowed never to have for fellow-voyager a man I loved, unless, unbeknown to him, I had provided every requisite, in case of a fatality, for embalming his mortal part for interment on shore. Were your friend's remains now on board this ship, Don Benito, not thus strangely would the mention of his name affect you."

"On board this ship?" echoed the Spaniard. Then, with horrified gestures, as directed against some spectre, he unconsciously fell into the ready arms of his attendant, who, with a silent appeal toward Captain Delano, seemed beseeching him not again to broach a theme so unspeakably distressing to his master.

This poor fellow now, thought the pained American, is the victim of that sad superstition which associates goblins with the deserted body of man, as ghosts with an abandoned house. How unlike are we made! What to me, in like case, would have been a solemn satisfaction, the bare suggestion, even, terrifies the Spaniard into this trance. Poor Alexandro Aranda! what would you say could you here see your friend—who, on former voyages, when you, for months, were left behind, has, I dare say, often longed, and longed, for one peep at you—now transported with terror at the least thought of having you anyway nigh him.

At this moment, with a dreary grave-yard toll, betokening a flaw, the ship's forecastle bell, smote by one of the grizzled oakum-pickers, proclaimed ten o'clock, through the leaden calm; when Captain Delano's attention was caught by the moving figure of a gigantic black, emerging from the general crowd below, and slowly advancing towards the elevated poop. An iron collar was about his neck, from which depended a chain, thrice wound round his body; the terminating links padlocked together at a broad band of iron, his girdle.

"How like a mute Atufal moves," murmured the servant.

The black mounted the steps of the poop, and, like a brave prisoner, brought up to receive sentence, stood in unquailing muteness before Don Benito, now recovered from his attack.

At the first glimpse of his approach, Don Benito had started, a resentful shadow swept over his face; and, as with the sudden memory of bootless rage, his white lips glued together.

This is some mulish mutineer, thought Captain Delano, surveying, not without a mixture of admiration, the colossal form of the negro.

"See, he waits your question, master," said the servant.

Thus reminded, Don Benito, nervously averting his glance, as if shunning, by anticipation, some rebellious response, in a disconcerted voice, thus spoke:

"Atufal, will you ask my pardon, now?" The black was silent.

"Again, master," murmured the servant, with bitter upbraiding eyeing his countryman. "Again, master; he will bend to master yet."

"Answer," said Don Benito, still averting his glance, "say but the one word, *pardon,* and your chains shall be off."

Upon this, the black, slowly raising both arms, let them lifelessly fall, his links clanking, his head bowed; as much as to say, "No, I am content."

"Go," said Don Benito, with inkept and unknown emotion.

Deliberately as he had come, the black obeyed.

"Excuse me, Don Benito," said Captain Delano, "but this scene surprises me; what means it, pray?"

"It means that that negro alone, of all the band, has given me peculiar cause of offence. I have put him in chains; I——"

Here he paused; his hand to his head, as if there were a swimming there, or a sudden bewilderment of memory had come over him; but meeting his servant's kindly glance seemed reassured, and proceeded:—

"I could not scourge such a form. But I told him he must ask my pardon. As yet he has not. At my command, every two hours he stands before me."

"And how long has this been?"

"Some sixty days."

"And obedient in all else? And respectful?" "Yes."

"Upon my conscience, then," exclaimed Captain Delano, impulsively, "he has a royal spirit in him, this fellow."

"He may have some right to it," bitterly returned Don Benito, "he says he was king in his own land."

"Yes," said the servant, entering a word, "those slits in Atufal's ears once held wedges of gold; but poor Babo here, in his own land, was only a poor slave; a black man's slave was Babo, who now is the white's."

Somewhat annoyed by these conversational familiarities, Captain Delano turned curiously upon the attendant, then glanced inquiringly at his master; but, as if long wonted to these little informalities, neither master nor man seemed to understand him.

"What, pray, was Atufal's offence, Don Benito?" asked Captain Delano; "if it was

not something very serious, take a fool's advice, and, in view of his general docility, as well as in some natural respect for his spirit, remit him his penalty."

"No, no, master never will do that," here murmured the servant to himself, "proud Atufal must first ask master's pardon. The slave there carries the padlock, but master here carries the key."

His attention thus directed, Captain Delano now noticed for the first time, that, suspended by a slender silken cord, from Don Benito's neck, hung a key. At once, from the servant's muttered syllables, divining the key's purpose, he smiled and said:— "So, Don Benito—padlock and key—significant symbols, truly."

Biting his lip, Don Benito faltered.

Though the remark of Captain Delano, a man of such native simplicity as to be incapable of satire or irony, had been dropped in playful allusion to the Spaniard's singularly evidenced lordship over the black; yet the hypochondriac seemed some way to have taken it as a malicious reflection upon his confessed inability thus far to break down, at least, on a verbal summons, the entrenched will of the slave. Deploring this supposed misconception, yet despairing of correcting it, Captain Delano shifted the subject; but finding his companion more than ever withdrawn, as if still sourly digesting the lees of the presumed affront abovementioned, by and by Captain Delano likewise became less talkative, oppressed, against his own will, by what seemed the secret vindictiveness of the morbidly sensitive Spaniard. But the good sailor, himself of a quite contrary disposition, refrained, on his part, alike from the appearance as from the feeling of resentment, and if silent, was only so from contagion.

Presently the Spaniard, assisted by his servant, somewhat discourteously crossed over from his guest; a procedure which sensibly enough, might have been allowed to pass for idle caprice of ill-humour, had not master and man, lingering round the corner of the elevated skylight, begun whispering together in low voices. This was unpleasing. And more: the moody air of the Spaniard, which at times had not been without a sort of valetudinarian stateliness, now seemed anything but dignified; while the menial familiarity of the servant lost its original charm of simple-hearted attachment.

In his embarrassment, the visitor turned his face to the other side of the ship. By so doing, his glance accidentally fell on a young Spanish sailor, a coil of rope in his hand, just stepped from the deck to the first round of the mizzen-rigging. Perhaps the man would not have been particularly noticed, were it not that, during his ascent to one of the yards, he, with a sort of covert intentness, kept his eye fixed on Captain Delano, from whom, presently, it passed, as if by a natural sequence, to the two whisperers.

His own attention thus redirected to that quarter, Captain Delano gave a slight start. From something in Don Benito's manner just then, it seemed as if the visitor had, at least partly, been the subject of the withdrawn consultation going on—a conjecture as little agreeable to the guest as it was little flattering to the host.

The singular alternations of courtesy and ill-breeding in the Spanish captain were unaccountable, except on one of two suppositions—innocent lunacy, or wicked imposture.

But the first idea, though it might naturally have occurred to an indifferent observer, and, in some respect, had not hitherto been wholly a stranger to Captain Delano's mind, yet, now that, in an incipient way, he began to regard the stranger's conduct something in the light of an intentional affront, of course the idea of lunacy was virtually vacated. But if not a lunatic, what then? Under the circumstances, would a gentleman, nay, any honest boor, act the part now acted by his host? The man was an impostor. Some low-born adventurer, masquerading as an oceanic grandee; yet so ignorant of the first requisites of mere gentlemanhood as to be betrayed into the present remarkable indecorum. That strange ceremoniousness, too, at other times evinced, seemed not uncharacteristic of one playing a part above his real level. Benito Cereno— Don Benito Cereno—a sounding name. One, too, at that period, not unknown, in the surname, to supercargoes and sea captains trading along the Spanish Main, as belonging to one of the most enterprising and extensive mercantile families in all those provinces; several members of it having titles; a sort of Castilian Rothschild, with a noble brother, or cousin, in every great trading town of South America. The alleged Don Benito was in early manhood, about twenty-nine or thirty. To assume a sort of roving cadetship in the maritime affairs of such a house, what more likely scheme for a young knave of talent and spirit? But the Spaniard was a pale invalid. Never mind. For even to the degree of simulating mortal disease, the craft of some tricksters had been known to attain. To think that, under the aspect of infantile weakness, the most savage energies might be couched—those velvets of the Spaniard but the silky paw to his fangs.

From no train of thought did these fancies come; not from within, but from without; suddenly, too, and in one throng, like hoar frost; yet as soon to vanish as the mild sun of Captain Delano's good nature regained its meridian.

Glancing over once more towards his host —whose side-face, revealed above the sky-light, was now turned towards him—he was struck by the profile, whose clearness of cut was refined by the thinness, incident to ill-health, as well as ennobled about the chin by the beard. Away with suspicion. He was a true off-shoot of a true hidalgo Cereno.

Relieved by these and other better thoughts, the visitor, lightly humming a tune, now began indifferently pacing the poop, so as not to betray to Don Benito that he had at all mistrusted incivility, much less duplicity; for such mistrust would yet be proved illusory, and by the event; though, for the present, the circumstance which had provoked that distrust remained unexplained. But when that little mystery should have been cleared up, Captain Delano thought he might extremely regret it, did he allow Don Benito to become aware that he had indulged in ungenerous surmises. In short, to the Spaniard's black-letter text, it was best, for a while, to leave open margin.

Presently, his pale face twitching and overcast, the Spaniard, still supported by his attendant, moved over towards his guest, when, with even more than his usual embarrassment, and a strange sort of intriguing intonation in his husky whisper, the following conversation began:

"Señor, may I ask how long you have lain at this isle?"

"Oh, but a day or two, Don Benito."

"And from what port are you last?"

"Canton."

"And there, Señor, you exchanged your sealskins for teas and silks, I think you said?"

"Yes. Silks, mostly."

"And the balance you took in specie, perhaps?"

Captain Delano, fidgeting a little, answered—

"Yes; some silver; not a very great deal, though."

"Ah—well. May I ask how many men have you, Señor?"

Captain Delano slightly started, but answered—

"About five-and-twenty, all told."

"And at present, Señor, all on board, I suppose?"

"All on board, Don Benito," replied the Captain, now with satisfaction.

"And will be to-night, Señor?"

At this last question, following so many pertinacious ones, for the soul of him Captain Delano could not but look very earnestly at the questioner, who, instead of meeting the glance, with every token of craven discomposure dropped his eyes to the deck; presenting an unworthy contrast to his servant, who, just then, was kneeling at his feet, adjusting a loose shoe-buckle; his disengaged face meantime, with humble curiosity, turned openly up into his master's downcast one.

The Spaniard, still with a guilty shuffle, repeated his question:

"And—and will be to-night, Señor?"

"Yes, for aught I know," returned Captain Delano—"but nay," rallying himself into fearless truth, "some of them talked of going off on another fishing party about midnight."

"Your ships generally go—go more or less armed, I believe, Señor?"

"Oh, a six-pounder or two, in case of emergency," was the intrepidly indifferent reply, "with a small stock of muskets, sealing-spears, and cutlasses, you know."

As he thus responded, Captain Delano again glanced at Don Benito, but the latter's eyes were averted; while abruptly and awkwardly shifting the subject, he made some peevish allusion to the calm, and then, without apology, once more, with his attendant, withdrew to the opposite bulwarks, where the whispering was resumed.

At this moment, and ere Captain Delano could cast a cool thought upon what had just passed, the young Spanish sailor, before mentioned, was seen descending from the rigging. In act of stooping over to spring inboard to the deck, his voluminous, unconfined frock, or shirt, of coarse woollen, much spotted with tar, opened out far down the chest, revealing a soiled undergarment of what seemed the finest linen, edged, about the neck, with a narrow blue ribbon, sadly faded and worn. At this moment the young sailor's eye was again fixed on the whisperers, and Captain Delano thought he observed a lurking significance in it, as if silent signs, of some Freemason sort, had that instant been interchanged.

This once more impelled his own glance in the direction of Don Benito, and, as before, he could not but infer that himself formed the subject of the conference. He paused. The sound of the hatchet-polishing fell on his ears. He cast another swift sidelook at the two. They had the air of conspirators. In connection with the late questionings, and the incident of the young sailor, these things now begat such return of involuntary suspicion, that the singular guilelessness of the American could not endure it. Plucking up a gay and humorous expression, he crossed over to the two rapidly, saying:—"Ha, Don Benito, your black here seems high in your trust; a sort of privy-counsellor, in fact."

Upon this, the servant looked up with a good-natured grin, but the master started as from a venomous bite. It was a moment or two before the Spaniard sufficiently recovered himself to reply; which he did, at last, with cold constraint: "Yes, Señor, I have trust in Babo."

Here Babo, changing his previous grin of mere animal humour into an intelligent smile, not ungratefully eyed his master.

Finding that the Spaniard now stood silent and reserved, as if involuntarily, or purposely giving hint that his guest's proximity was inconvenient just then, Captain Delano, unwilling to appear uncivil even to incivility itself, made some trivial remark and moved off; again and again turning over in his mind the mysterious demeanour of Don Benito Cereno.

He had descended from the poop, and, wrapped in thought, was passing near a dark hatchway, leading down into the steerage, when, perceiving motion there, he looked to see what moved. The same instant there was a sparkle in the shadowy hatchway, and he saw one of the Spanish sailors, prowling there, hurriedly placing his hand in the bosom of his frock, as if hiding something. Before the man could have been certain who it was that was passing, he slunk below out of sight. But enough was seen of him to make it sure that he was the same young sailor before noticed in the rigging.

What was that which so sparkled? thought Captain Delano. It was no lamp—no match—no live coal. Could it have been a jewel? But how come sailors with jewels?—or with silk-trimmed under-shirts either? Has he been robbing the trunks of the dead cabin-passengers? But if so, he would hardly wear one of the stolen articles on board ship here. Ah, ah—if, now, that was, indeed, a secret sign I saw passing between this suspicious fellow and his captain awhile since; if I could only be certain that, in my uneasiness, my senses did not deceive me, then——

Here, passing from one suspicious thing to another, his mind revolved the strange questions put to him concerning his ship.

By a curious coincidence, as each point was recalled, the black wizards of Ashantee would strike up with their hatchets, as in ominous comment on the white stranger's thoughts. Pressed by such enigmas and portents, it would have been almost against nature, had not, even into the least distrustful heart, some ugly misgivings obtruded.

Observing the ship, now helplessly fallen into a current, with enchanted sails, drifting with increased rapidity seaward; and noting that, from a lately intercepted projection of the land, the sealer was hidden, the stout mariner began to quake at thoughts which he barely durst confess to himself. Above all, he began to feel a ghostly dread of Don Benito. And yet, when he roused himself, dilated his chest, felt himself strong on his legs, and coolly considered it—what did all these phantoms amount to?

Had the Spaniard any sinister scheme, it must have reference not so much to him (Captain Delano) as to his ship (the *Bachelor's Delight*). Hence the present drifting away of the one ship from the other, instead of favouring any such possible scheme, was, for the time, at least, opposed to it. Clearly any suspicion, combining such contradictions, must need be delusive. Besides, was it not absurd to think of a vessel in distress —a vessel by sickness almost dismanned of her crew—a vessel whose inmates were parched for water—was it not a thousand times absurd that such a craft should, at present, be of a piratical character; or her commander, either for himself or those under him, cherish any desire but for speedy relief and refreshment? But then, might not general distress, and thirst in particular, be affected? And might not that same undiminished Spanish crew, alleged to have perished off to a remnant, be at that very moment

lurking in the hold? On heart-broken pretence of entreating a cup of cold water, fiends in human form had got into lonely dwellings, nor retired until a dark deed had been done. And among the Malay pirates, it was no unusual thing to lure ships after them into their treacherous harbours, or entice boarders from a declared enemy at sea, by the spectacle of thinly manned or vacant decks, beneath which prowled a hundred spears with yellow arms ready to upthrust them through the mats. Not that Captain Delano had entirely credited such things. He had heard of them—and now, as stories, they recurred. The present destination of the ship was the anchorage. There she would be near his own vessel. Upon gaining that vicinity, might not the *San Dominick*, like a slumbering volcano, suddenly let loose energies now hid?

He recalled the Spaniard's manner while telling his story. There was a gloomy hesitancy and subterfuge about it. It was just the manner of one making up his tale for evil purposes, as he goes. But if that story was not true, what was the truth? That the ship had unlawfully come into the Spaniard's possession? But in many of its details, especially in reference to the more calamitous parts, such as the fatalities among the seamen, the consequent prolonged beating about, the past sufferings from obstinate calms, and still continued suffering from thirst; in all these points, as well as others, Don Benito's story had corroborated not only the wailing ejaculations of the indiscriminate multitude, white and black, but likewise—what seemed impossible to be counterfeit—by the very expression and play of every human feature, which Captain Delano saw. If Don Benito's story was, throughout, an invention, then every soul on board, down to the youngest negress, was his carefully drilled recruit in the plot: an incredible inference. And yet, if there was ground for mistrusting his veracity, that inference was a legitimate one.

But those questions of the Spaniard. There, indeed, one might pause. Did they not seem put with much the same object with which the burglar or assassin, by daytime, reconnoitres the walls of a house? But, with ill purposes, to solicit such information openly of the chief person endangered, and so, in effect, setting him on his guard; how unlikely a procedure was that? Absurd, then, to suppose that those questions had been prompted by evil designs. Thus, the same conduct, which, in this instance, had raised the alarm, served to dispel it. In short, scarce any suspicion or uneasiness, however apparently reasonable at the time, which was not now, with equally apparent reason, dismissed.

At last he began to laugh at his former forebodings; and laugh at the strange ship for, in its aspect, someway siding with them, as it were; and laugh, too, at the odd-looking blacks, particularly those old scissors-grinders, the Ashantees; and those bed-ridden old knitting women, the oakum-pickers; and almost at the dark Spaniard himself, the central hobgoblin of all.

For the rest, whatever in a serious way seemed enigmatical, was now good-naturedly explained away by the thought that, for the most part, the poor invalid scarcely knew what he was about; either sulking in black vapours, or putting idle questions without sense or object. Evidently, for the present, the man was not fit to be intrusted with the ship. On some benevolent plea withdrawing the command from him, Captain Delano would yet have to send her to Concepcion, in charge of his second mate, a worthy person and good navigator—a plan not more convenient for the *San Dominick* than for Don Benito; for, relieved from all anxiety, keeping wholly to his cabin, the sick man, under the good nursing of his servant, would, probably, by the end of the passage, be in a measure restored to health, and with that he should also be restored to authority.

Such were the American's thoughts. They were tranquillizing. There was a difference between the idea of Don Benito's darkly pre-ordaining Captain Delano's fate, and Captain Delano's lightly arranging Don Benito's. Nevertheless, it was not without something of relief that the good seaman presently perceived his whale-boat in the distance. Its absence had been prolonged by unexpected detention at the sealer's side, as well as its returning trip lengthened by the continual recession of the goal.

The advancing speck was observed by the blacks. Their shouts attracted the attention of Don Benito, who, with a return of courtesy, approaching Captain Delano, expressed satisfaction at the coming of some supplies, slight and temporary as they must necessarily prove.

Captain Delano responded; but while doing so, his attention was drawn to something passing on the deck below: among the crowd climbing the landward bulwarks, anxiously watching the coming boat, two blacks, to all appearances accidentally incommoded by one of the sailors, violently pushed him aside, which the sailor someway resenting, they dashed him to the deck, despite the earnest cries of the oakum-pickers.

"Don Benito," said Captain Delano quickly, "do you see what is going on there? Look!"

But, seized by his cough, the Spaniard staggered, with both hands to his face, on the point of falling. Captain Delano would have supported him, but the servant was more alert, who, with one hand sustaining his master, with the other applied the cordial. Don Benito restored, the black withdrew his support, slipping aside a little, but dutifully remaining within call of a whisper. Such discretion was here evinced as quite wiped away, in the visitor's eyes, any blemish of impropriety which might have attached to the attendant, from the indecorous conferences before mentioned; showing, too, that if the servant were to blame, it might be more the master's fault than his own, since, when left to himself, he could conduct thus well.

His glance called away from the spectacle of disorder to the more pleasing one before him, Captain Delano could not avoid again congratulating his host upon possessing such

a servant, who, though perhaps a little too forward now and then, must upon the whole be invaluable to one in the invalid's situation.

"Tell me, Don Benito," he added, with a smile—"I should like to have your man here, myself—what will you take for him? Would fifty doubloons be any object?"

"Master wouldn't part with Babo for a thousand doubloons," murmured the black, overhearing the offer, and taking it in earnest, and, with the strange vanity of a faithful slave, appreciated by his master, scorning to hear so paltry a valuation put upon him by a stranger. But Don Benito, apparently hardly yet completely restored, and again interrupted by his cough, made but some broken reply.

Soon his physical distress became so great, affecting his mind, too, apparently, that, as if to screen the sad spectacle, the servant gently conducted his master below.

Left to himself, the American, to while away the time till his boat should arrive, would have pleasantly accosted some one of the few Spanish seamen he saw; but recalling something that Don Benito had said touching their ill conduct, he refrained; as a ship-master indisposed to countenance cowardice or unfaithfulness in seamen.

While, with these thoughts, standing with eye directed forward towards that handful of sailors, suddenly he thought that one or two of them returned the glance and with a sort of meaning. He rubbed his eyes, and looked again; but again seemed to see the same thing. Under a new form, but more obscure than any previous one, the old suspicions recurred, but, in the absence of Don Benito, with less of panic than before. Despite the bad account given of the sailors, Captain Delano resolved forthwith to accost one of them. Descending the poop, he made his way through the blacks, his movement drawing a queer cry from the oakum-pickers, prompted by whom, the negroes, twitching each other aside, divided before him; but, as if curious to see what was the object of this deliberate visit to their Ghetto,

closing in behind, in tolerable order, followed the white stranger up. His progress thus proclaimed as by mounted kings-at-arms, and escorted as by a Kaffir guard of honour, Captain Delano, assuming a good-humoured, off-handed air, continued to advance; now and then saying a blithe word to the negroes, and his eye curiously surveying the white faces, here and there sparsely mixed in with the blacks, like stray white pawns venturously involved in the ranks of the chess-men opposed.

While thinking which of them to select for his purpose, he chanced to observe a sailor seated on the deck engaged in tarring the strap of a large block, a circle of blacks squatted round him inquisitively eyeing the process.

The mean employment of the man was in contrast with something superior in his figure. His hand, black with continually thrusting it into the tar-pot held for him by a negro, seemed not naturally allied to his face, a face which would have been a very fine one but for its haggardness. Whether this haggardness had aught to do with criminality, could not be determined; since, as intense heat and cold, though unlike, produce like sensations, so innocence and guilt, when, through casual association with mental pain, stamping any visible impress, use one seal—a hacked one.

Not again that this reflection occurred to Captain Delano at the time, charitable man as he was. Rather another idea. Because observing so singular a haggardness combined with a dark eye, averted as in trouble and shame, and then again recalling Don Benito's confessed ill opinion of his crew, insensibly he was operated upon by certain general notions which, while disconnecting pain and abashment from virtue, invariably link them with vice.

If, indeed, there be any wickedness on board this ship, thought Captain Delano, be sure that man there has fouled his hand in it, even as now he fouls it in the pitch. I don't like to accost him. I will speak to this other, this old Jack here on the windlass.

He advanced to an old Barcelona tar, in ragged red breeches and dirty night-cap, cheeks trenched and bronzed, whiskers dense as thorn hedges. Seated between two sleepy-looking Africans, this mariner, like his younger shipmate, was employed upon some rigging—splicing a cable—the sleepy-looking blacks performing the inferior function of holding the outer parts of the ropes for him.

Upon Captain Delano's approach, the man at once hung his head below its previous level; the one necessary for business. It appeared as if he desired to be thought absorbed, with more than common fidelity, in his task. Being addressed, he glanced up, but with what seemed a furtive, diffident air, which sat strangely enough on his weather-beaten visage, much as if a grizzly bear, instead of growling and biting, should simper and cast sheep's eyes. He was asked several questions concerning the voyage— questions purposely referring to several particulars in Don Benito's narrative, not previously corroborated by those impulsive cries greeting the visitor on the first coming on board. The questions were briefly answered, confirming all that remained to be confirmed of the story. The negroes about the windlass joined in with the old sailor; but, as they became talkative, he by degrees became mute, and at length quite glum, seemed morosely unwilling to answer more questions, and yet, all the while, this ursine air was somehow mixed with his sheepish one.

Despairing of getting into unembarrassed talk with such a centaur, Captain Delano, after glancing round for a more promising countenance, but seeing none, spoke pleasantly to the blacks to make way for him; and so, amid various grins and grimaces, returned to the poop, feeling a little strange at first, he could hardly tell why, but upon the whole with regained confidence in Benito Cereno.

How plainly, thought he, did that old whiskerando yonder betray a consciousness of ill desert. No doubt, when he saw me coming, he dreaded lest I, appraised by his captain of the crew's general misbehaviour, came with sharp words for him, and so down with his head. And yet—and yet, now that I think of it, that very fellow, if I err not, was one of those who seemed so earnestly eyeing me here awhile since. Ah, these currents spin one's head round almost as much as they do the ship. Ha, there now's a pleasant sort of sunny sight; quite sociable, too.

His attention had been drawn back to a slumbering negress, partly disclosed through the lacework of some rigging, lying, with youthful limbs carelessly disposed, under the lee of the bulwarks, like a doe in the shade of a woodland rock. Sprawling at her lapped breasts, was her wide-awake fawn, stark naked, its black little body half-lifted from the deck, crosswise with its dam's; its hands, like two paws, clambering upon her; its mouth and nose ineffectually rooting to get at the mark; and meantime giving a vexatious half-grunt, blending with the composed snore of the negress.

The uncommon vigour of the child at length roused the mother. She started up, at a distance facing Captain Delano. But as if not at all concerned at the attitude in which she had been caught, delightedly she caught the child up, with maternal transports, covering it with kisses.

There's naked nature, now; pure tenderness and love, thought Captain Delano, well pleased.

This incident prompted him to remark the other negresses more particularly than before. He was gratified with their manners: like most uncivilized women, they seemed at once tender of heart and tough of constitution; equally ready to die for their infants or fight for them. Unsophisticated as leopardesses; loving as doves. Ah! thought Captain Delano, these, perhaps, are some of the very women whom Ledyard saw in Africa, and gave such a noble account of.

These natural sights somehow insensibly deepened his confidence and ease. At last he looked to see how his boat was getting on; but it was still pretty remote. He turned to see if Don Benito had returned; but he had not.

To change the scene, as well as to please himself with a leisurely observation of the coming boat, stepping over into the mizzenchains, he clambered his way into the starboard quarter-gallery—one of those abandoned Venetian-looking water-balconies previously mentioned—retreats cut off from the deck. As his foot pressed the half-damp, half-dry sea-mosses matting the place, and a chance phantom cats-paw—an islet of breeze, unheralded, unfollowed—as this ghostly cats-paw came fanning his cheek; as his glance fell upon the row of small, round dead-lights—all closed like coppered eyes of the coffined—and the state-cabin door, once connecting with the gallery, even as the dead-lights had once looked out upon it, but now calked fast like a sarcophagus lid; and to a purple-black, tarred-over panel, threshold, and post; and he bethought him of the time, when that state-cabin and this state-balcony had heard the voices of the Spanish king's officers, and the forms of the Lima viceroy's daughters had perhaps leaned where he stood—as these and other images flitted through his mind, as the cats-paw through the calm, gradually he felt rising a dreamy inquietude, like that of one who alone on the prairie feels unrest from the repose of the noon.

He leaned against the carved balustrade, again looking off toward his boat; but found his eye falling upon the ribbon grass, trailing along the ship's water-line, straight as a border of green box; and parterres of seaweed, broad ovals and crescents, floating nigh and far, with what seemed long formal alleys between, crossing the terraces of swells, and sweeping round as if leading to the grottoes below. And overhanging all was the balustrade by his arm, which, partly stained with pitch and partly embossed with moss, seemed the charred ruin of some summer-house in a grand garden long running to waste.

Trying to break one charm, he was but becharmed anew. Though upon the wide sea, he seemed in some far inland country;

prisoner in some deserted château, left to stare at empty grounds, and peer out at vague roads, where never wagon or way-farer passed.

But these enchantments were a little disenchanted as his eye fell on the corroded main-chains. Of an ancient style, massy and rusty in link, shackle and bolt, they seemed even more fit for the ship's present business than the one for which she had been built.

Presently he thought something moved nigh the chains. He rubbed his eyes, and looked hard. Groves of rigging were about the chains; and there, peering from behind a great stay, like an Indian from behind a hemlock, a Spanish sailor, a marlingspike in his hand, was seen, who made what seemed an imperfect gesture towards the balcony, but immediately, as if alarmed by some advancing step along the deck within, vanished into the recesses of the hempen forest, like a poacher.

What meant this? Something the man had sought to communicate, unbeknown to any one, even to his captain. Did the secret involve aught unfavourable to his captain? Were those previous misgivings of Captain Delano's about to be verified? Or, in his haunted mood at the moment, had some random, unintentional motion of the man, while busy with the stay, as if repairing it, been mistaken for a significant beckoning?

Not unbewildered, again he gazed off for his boat. But it was temporarily hidden by a rocky spur of the isle. As with some eagerness he bent forward, watching for the first shooting view of its beak, the balustrade gave way before him like charcoal. Had he not clutched an outreaching rope he would have fallen into the sea. The crash, though feeble, and the fall, though hollow, of the rotten fragments, must have been overheard. He glanced up. With sober curiosity peering down upon him was one of the old oakum-pickers, slipped from his perch to an outside boom; while below the old negro, and, invisible to him, reconnoitring from a port-hole like a fox from the mouth of its den, crouched the Spanish sailor again. From something suddenly suggested by the man's air, the mad idea now darted into Captain Delano's mind, that Don Benito's plea of indisposition, in withdrawing below, was but a pretence: that he was engaged there maturing his plot, of which the sailor, by some means gaining an inkling, had a mind to warn the stranger against; incited, it may be, by gratitude for a kind word on first boarding the ship. Was it from foreseeing some possible interference like this, that Don Benito had, beforehand, given such a bad character of his sailors, while praising the negroes; though, indeed, the former seemed as docile as the latter the contrary? The whites, too, by nature, were the shrewder race. A man with some evil design, would he not be likely to speak well of that stupidity which was blind to his depravity, and malign that intelligence from which it might not be hidden? Not unlikely, perhaps. But if the whites had dark secrets concerning Don Benito, could then Don Benito be any way in complicity with the blacks? But they were too stupid. Besides, who ever heard of a white so far a renegade as to apostatize from his very species almost, by leaguing in against it with negroes? These difficulties recalled former ones. Lost in their mazes, Captain Delano, who had now regained the deck, was uneasily advancing along it, when he observed a new face; an aged sailor seated cross-legged near the main hatchway. His skin was shrunk up with wrinkles like a pelican's empty pouch; his hair frosted; his countenance grave and composed. His hands were full of ropes, which he was working into a large knot. Some blacks were about him obligingly dipping the strands for him, here and there, as the exigencies of the operation demanded.

Captain Delano crossed over to him, and stood in silence surveying the knot; his mind, by a not uncongenial transition, passing from its own entanglements to those of the hemp. For intricacy, such a knot he had never seen in an American ship, nor indeed any other. The old man looked like an Egyptian priest, making Gordian knots for the temple of Ammon. The knot seemed a combination of double-bowline-knot, treble-crown-knot, back-handed-well-knot, knot-in-and-out-knot, and jamming-knot.

At last, puzzled to comprehend the meaning of such a knot, Captain Delano addressed the knotter:

"What are you knotting there, my man?"

"The knot," was the brief reply, without looking up.

"So it seems; but what is it for?"

"For some one else to undo," muttered back the old man, plying his fingers harder than ever, the knot being now nearly completed.

While Captain Delano stood watching him, suddenly the old man threw the knot towards him, saying in broken English— the first heard in the ship—something to this effect: "Undo it, cut it, quick." It was said lowly, but with such condensation of rapidity, that the long, slow words in Spanish, which had preceded and followed, almost operated as covers to the brief English between.

For a moment, knot in hand, and knot in head, Captain Delano stood mute; while, without further heeding him, the old man was now intent upon other ropes. Presently there was a slight stir behind Captain Delano. Turning, he saw the chained negro, Atufal, standing quietly there. The next moment the old sailor rose, muttering, and, followed by his subordinate negroes, removed to the forward part of the ship, where in the crowd he disappeared.

An elderly negro, in a clout like an infant's, and with a pepper and salt head, and a kind of attorney air, now approached Captain Delano. In tolerable Spanish, and with a good-natured, knowing wink, he informed him that the old knotter was simple-witted, but harmless; often playing his odd tricks. The negro concluded by begging the knot, for of course the stranger would not care to be troubled with it. Unconsciously, it was handed to him. With a sort of congé, the negro received it, and, turning his back, ferreted into it like a detective custom-house officer after smuggled laces. Soon, with some African word, equivalent to pshaw, he tossed the knot overboard.

All this is very queer now, thought Captain Delano, with a qualmish sort of emotion; but, as one feeling incipient sea-sickness, he strove, by ignoring the symptoms, to get rid of the malady. Once more he looked off for his boat. To his delight, it was now again in view, leaving the rocky spur astern.

The sensation here experienced, after at first relieving his uneasiness, with unforeseen efficacy soon began to remove it. The less distant sight of that well-known boat—showing it, not as before, half blended with the haze, but with outline defined, so that its individuality, like a man's, was manifest; that boat, *Rover* by name, which, though now in strange seas, had often pressed the beach of Captain Delano's home, and, brought to its threshold for repairs, had familiarly lain there, as a Newfoundland dog; the sight of that household boat evoked a thousand trustful associations, which, contrasted with previous suspicions, filled him not only with lightsome confidence, but somehow with half humorous self-reproaches at his former lack of it.

"What, I, Amasa Delano—Jack of the Beach, as they called me when a lad—I, Amasa; the same that, duck-satchel in hand, used to paddle along the water-side to the school-house made from the old hulk—I, little Jack of the Beach, that used to go berrying with cousin Nat and the rest; I to be murdered here at the ends of the earth, on board a haunted pirate-ship by a horrible Spaniard? Too nonsensical to think of! Who would murder Amasa Delano? His conscience is clean. There is some one above. Fie, fie, Jack of the Beach! you are a child indeed; a child of the second childhood, old boy; you are beginning to dote and drool, I'm afraid."

Light of heart and foot, he stepped aft, and there was met by Don Benito's servant, who, with a pleasing expression, responsive

to his own present feelings, informed him that his master had recovered from the effects of his coughing fit, and had just ordered him to go present his compliments to his good guest, Don Amasa, and say that he (Don Benito) would soon have the happiness to rejoin him.

There now, do you mark that? again thought Captain Delano, walking the poop. What a donkey I was. This kind gentleman who here sends me his kind compliments, he, but ten minutes ago, dark-lantern in hand, was dodging round some old grindstone in the hold, sharpening a hatchet for me, I thought. Well, well; these long calms have a morbid effect on the mind, I've often heard, though I never believed it before. Ha! glancing towards the boat; there's *Rover;* good dog; a white bone in her mouth. A pretty big bone though, seems to me. What? Yes, she has fallen afoul of the bubbling tide-rip there. It sets her the other way, too, for the time. Patience.

It was now about noon, though, from the greyness of everything, it seemed to be getting towards dusk.

The calm was confirmed. In the far distance away from the influence of land, the leaden ocean seemed laid out and leaded up, its course finished, soul gone, defunct. But the current from landward, where the ship was, increased; silently sweeping her further and further towards the tranced waters beyond.

Still, from his knowledge of those latitudes, cherishing hopes of a breeze, and a fair and fresh one, at any moment, Captain Delano, despite present prospects, buoyantly counted upon bringing the *San Dominick* safely to anchor ere night. The distance swept over was nothing; since, with a good wind, ten minutes' sailing would retrace more than sixty minutes' drifting. Meantime, one moment turning to mark *Rover* fighting the tide-rip, and the next to see Don Benito approaching, he continued walking the poop.

Gradually he felt a vexation arising from the delay of his boat; this soon merged into

443

uneasiness; and at last—his eye falling continually, as from a stage-box into the pit, upon the strange crowd before and below him, and, by and by, recognizing there the face—now composed to indifference—of the Spanish sailor who had seemed to beckon from the main-chains—something of his old trepidations returned.

Ah, thought he—gravely enough—this is like the ague: because it went off, it follows not that it won't come back.

Though ashamed of the relapse, he could not altogether subdue it; and so, exerting his good nature to the utmost, insensibly he came to a compromise.

Yes, this is a strange craft; a strange history, too, and strange folks on board. But—nothing more.

By way of keeping his mind out of mischief till the boat should arrive, he tried to occupy it with turning over and over, in a purely speculative sort of way, some lesser peculiarities of the captain and crew. Among others, four curious points recurred:

First, the affair of the Spanish lad assailed with a knife by the slave boy; an act winked at by Don Benito. Second, the tyranny in Don Benito's treatment of Atufal, the black; as if a child should lead a bull of the Nile by the ring in his nose. Third, the trampling of the sailor by the two negroes; a piece of insolence passed over without so much as a reprimand. Fourth, the cringing submission to their master, of all the ship's underlings, mostly blacks; as if by the least inadvertence they feared to draw down his despotic displeasure.

Coupling these points, they seemed somewhat contradictory. But what then, thought Captain Delano, glancing towards his now nearing boat—what then? Why, Don Benito is a very capricious commander. But he is not the first of the sort I have seen; though it's true he rather exceeds any other. But as a nation—continued he in his reveries—these Spaniards are all an odd set; the very word Spaniard has a curious, conspirator, Guy-Fawkish twang to it. And yet, I dare say, Spaniards in the main are as good

folks as any in Duxbury, Massachusetts. Ah good! At last *Rover* has come.

As, with its welcome freight, the boat touched the side, the oakum-pickers, with venerable gestures, sought to restrain the blacks, who, at the sight of three gurried water casks in its bottom, and a pile of wilted pumpkins in its bow, hung over the bulwarks in disorderly raptures.

Don Benito, with his servant, now appeared; his coming, perhaps, hastened by hearing the noise. Of him Captain Delano sought permission to serve out the water, so that all might share alike, and none injure themselves by unfair excess. But sensible, and, on Don Benito's account, kind as this offer was, it was received with what seemed impatience; as if aware that he lacked energy as a commander, Don Benito, with the true jealousy of weakness, resented as an affront any interference. So, at least, Captain Delano inferred.

In another moment the casks were being hoisted in, when some of the eager negroes accidentally jostled Captain Delano, where he stood by the gangway; so that, unmindful of Don Benito, yielding to the impulse of the moment, with good-natured authority he bade the blacks stand back; to enforce his words making use of a half-mirthful, half-menacing gesture. Instantly the blacks paused, just where they were, each negro and negress suspended in his or her posture, exactly as the word had found them—for a few seconds continuing so—while, as between the responsive posts of a telegraph, an unknown syllable ran from man to man among the perched oakum-pickers. While the visitor's attention was fixed by this scene, suddenly the hatchet-polishers half rose, and a rapid cry came from Don Benito.

Thinking that at the signal of the Spaniard he was about to be massacred, Captain Delano would have sprung for his boat, but paused, as the oakum-pickers, dropping down into the crowd with earnest exclamations, forced every white and every negro back, at the same moment, with gestures friendly and familiar, almost jocose, bidding

him, in substance, not be a fool. Simultaneously the hatchet-polishers resumed their seats, quietly as so many tailors, and at once, as if nothing had happened, the work of hoisting in the casks was resumed, whites and blacks singing at the tackle.

Captain Delano glanced towards Don Benito. As he saw his meagre form in the act of recovering itself from reclining in the servant's arms, into which the agitated invalid had fallen, he could not but marvel at the panic by which himself had been surprised, on the darting supposition that such a commander, who, upon a legitimate occasion, so trivial, too, as it now appeared, could lose all self-command, was, with energetic iniquity, going to bring about his murder.

The casks being on deck, Captain Delano was handed a number of jars and cups by one of the steward's aids, who, in the name of his captain, entreated him to do as he had proposed—dole out the water. He complied, with republican impartiality as to this republican element, which always seeks one level, serving the oldest white no better than the youngest black; excepting, indeed, poor Don Benito, whose condition, if not rank, demanded an extra allowance. To him, in the first place, Captain Delano presented a fair pitcher of the fluid; but, thirsting as he was for it, the Spaniard quaffed not a drop until after several grave bows and salutes. A reciprocation of courtesies which the sight-loving Africans hailed with clapping of hands.

Two of the less wilted pumpkins being reserved for the cabin table, the residue were minced up on the spot for the general regalement. But the soft bread, sugar, and bottled cider, Captain Delano would have given the whites alone, and in chief Don Benito; but the latter objected; which disinterestedness not a little pleased the American; and so mouthfuls all around were given alike to whites and blacks; excepting one bottle of cider, which Babo insisted upon setting aside for his master.

Here it may be observed that as, on the first visit of the boat, the American had not permitted his men to board the ship, neither did he now; being unwilling to add to the confusion of the decks.

Not uninfluenced by the peculiar good-humour at present prevailing, and for the time oblivious of any but benevolent thoughts, Captain Delano, who, from recent indications, counted upon a breeze within an hour or two at furthest, dispatched the boat back to the sealer, with orders for all the hands that could be spared immediately to set about rafting casks to the watering-place and filling them. Likewise he bade word be carried to his chief officer, that if, against present expectation, the ship was not brought to anchor by sunset, he need be under no concern; for as there was to be a full moon that night, he (Captain Delano) would remain on board ready to play the pilot, come the wind soon or late.

As the two Captains stood together, observing the departing boat—the servant, as it happened, having just spied a spot on his master's velvet sleeve, and silently engaged rubbing it out—the American expressed his regrets that the *San Dominick* had no boats; none, at least, but the unseaworthy old hulk of the long-boat, which, warped as a camel's skeleton in the desert, and almost as bleached, lay pot-wise inverted amid-ships, one side a little tipped, furnishing a subterraneous sort of den for family groups of the blacks, mostly women and small children; who, squatting on old mats below, or perched above in the dark dome, on the elevated seats, were descried, some distance within, like a social circle of bats, sheltering in some friendly cave; at intervals, ebon flights of naked boys and girls, three or four years old, darting in and out of the den's mouth.

"Had you three or four boats now, Don Benito," said Captain Delano, "I think that, by tugging at the oars, your negroes here might help along matters some. Did you sail from port without boats, Don Benito?"

"They were stove in the gales, Señor."

"That was bad. Many men, too, you lost then. Boats and men. Those must have been hard gales, Don Benito."

"Past all speech," cringed the Spaniard.

"Tell me, Don Benito," continued his companion with increased interest, "tell me, were these gales immediately off the pitch of Cape Horn?"

"Cape Horn?—who spoke of Cape Horn?"

"Yourself did, when giving me an account of your voyage," answered Captain Delano, with almost equal astonishment at this eating of his own words, even as he ever seemed eating his own heart, on the part of the Spaniard. "You yourself, Don Benito, spoke of Cape Horn," he emphatically repeated.

The Spaniard turned, in a sort of stooping posture, pausing an instant, as one about to make a plunging exchange of elements, as from air to water.

At this moment a messenger-boy, a white, hurried by, in the regular performance of his function carrying the last expired half-hour forward to the forecastle, from the cabin time-piece, to have it struck at the ship's large bell.

"Master," said the servant, discontinuing his work on the coat sleeve, and addressing the rapt Spaniard with a sort of timid apprehensiveness, as one charged with a duty, the discharge of which, it was foreseen, would prove irksome to the very person who had imposed it, and for whose benefit it was intended, "master told me never mind where he was, or how engaged, always to remind him, to a minute, when shaving-time comes. Miguel has gone to strike the half-hour afternoon. It is *now*, master. Will master go into the cuddy?"

"Ah—yes," answered the Spaniard, starting, as from dreams into realities; then turning upon Captain Delano, he said that ere long he would resume the conversation.

"Then if master means to talk more to Don Amasa," said the servant, "why not let Don Amasa sit by master in the cuddy, and master can talk, and Don Amasa can listen, while Babo here lathers and strops."

"Yes," said Captain Delano, not unpleased with this sociable plan, "yes, Don Benito, unless you had rather not, I will go with you."

"Be it so, Señor."

As the three passed aft, the American could not but think it another strange instance of his host's capriciousness, this being shaved with such uncommon punctuality in the middle of the day. But he deemed it more than likely that the servant's anxious fidelity had something to do with the matter; inasmuch as the timely interruption served to rally his master from the mood which had evidently been coming upon him.

The place called the cuddy was a light deck-cabin formed by the poop, a sort of attic to the large cabin below. Part of it had formerly been the quarters of the officers; but since their death all the partitionings had been thrown down, and the whole interior converted into one spacious and airy marine hall; for absence of fine furniture and picturesque disarray of odd appurtenances, somewhat answering to the wide, cluttered hall of some eccentric bachelor-squire in the country, who hangs his shooting-jacket and tobacco-pouch on deer antlers, and keeps his fishing-rod, tongs, and walking-stick in the same corner.

The similitude was heightened, if not originally suggested, by glimpses of the surrounding sea; since, in one aspect, the country and the ocean seem cousins-german.

The floor of the cuddy was matted. Overhead, four or five old muskets were stuck into horizontal holes along the beams. On one side was a claw-footed old table lashed to the deck; a thumbed missal on it, and over it a small, meagre crucifix attached to the bulk-head. Under the table lay a dented cutlass or two, with a hacked harpoon, among some melancholy old rigging, like a heap of poor friars' girdles. There were also two long, sharp, ribbed settees of Malacca cane, black with age, and uncomfortable to look at as inquisitors' racks, with a large, misshapen arm-chair, which, furnished with a rude barber's crotch at the back, working with a screw, seemed some grotesque engine of torment. A flag-locker

447

was in one corner, open, exposing various coloured bunting, some rolled up, others half unrolled, still others tumbled. Opposite was a cumbrous washstand, of black mahogany, all of one block, with a pedestal, like a font, and over it a railed shelf, containing combs, brushes, and other implements of the toilet. A torn hammock of stained grass swung near; the sheets tossed, and the pillow wrinkled up like a brow, as if whoever slept here slept but illy, with alternate visitations of sad thoughts and bad dreams.

The further extremity of the cuddy, overhanging the ship's stern, was pierced with three openings, windows or port-holes, according as men or cannon might peer, socially or unsocially, out of them. At present neither men nor cannon were seen, though huge ring-bolts and other rusty iron fixtures of the woodwork hinted of twenty-four-pounders.

Glancing towards the hammock as he entered, Captain Delano said, "You sleep here, Don Benito?"

"Yes, Señor, since we got into mild weather."

"This seems a sort of dormitory, sitting-room, sail-loft, chapel, armoury, and private closet all together, Don Benito," added Captain Delano, looking round.

"Yes, Señor; events have not been favourable to much order in my arrangements."

Here the servant, napkin on arm, made a motion as if waiting his master's good pleasure. Don Benito signified his readiness, when, seating him in the Malacca arm-chair, and for the guest's convenience drawing opposite one of the settees, the servant commenced operations by throwing back his master's collar and loosening his cravat.

There is something in the negro which, in a peculiar way, fits him for avocations about one's person. Most negroes are natural valets and hair-dressers; taking to the comb and brush congenially as to the castanets, and flourishing them apparently with almost equal satisfaction. There is, too, a smooth tact about them in this employment, with a marvellous, noiseless, gliding briskness, not ungraceful in its way, singularly pleasing to behold, and still more so to be the manipulated subject of. And above all is the great gift of good-humour. Not the mere grin or laugh is here meant. Those were unsuitable. But a certain easy cheerfulness, harmonious in every glance and gesture; as though God had set the whole negro to some pleasant tune.

When to this is added the docility arising from the unaspiring contentment of a limited mind, and that susceptibility of blind attachment sometimes inhering in indisputable inferiors, one readily perceives why those hypochondriacs, Johnson and Byron—it may be, something like the hypochondriac Benito Cereno—took to their hearts, almost to the exclusion of the entire white race, their serving men, the negroes, Barber and Fletcher. But if there be that in the negro which exempts him from the inflicted sourness of the morbid or cynical mind, how, in his most prepossessing aspects, must he appear to a benevolent one? When at ease with respect to exterior things, Captain Delano's nature was not only benign, but familiarly and humorously so. At home, he had often taken rare satisfaction in sitting in his door, watching some free man of colour at his work or play. If on a voyage he chanced to have a black sailor, invariably he was on chatty and half-gamesome terms with him. In fact, like most men of a good, blithe heart, Captain Delano took to negroes, not philanthropically, but genially, just as other men to Newfoundland dogs.

Hitherto, the circumstances in which he found the *San Dominick* had repressed the tendency. But in the cuddy, relieved from his former uneasiness, and, for various reasons, more sociably inclined than at any previous period of the day, and seeing the coloured servant, napkin on arm, so debonair about his master, in a business so familiar as that of shaving, too, all his old weakness for negroes returned.

Among other things, he was amused with an odd instance of the African love of bright colours and fine shows, in the black's informally taking from the flag-locker a great piece of bunting of all hues, and lavishly tucking it under his master's chin for an apron.

The mode of shaving among the Spaniards is a little different from what it is with other nations. They have a basin, specifically called a barber's basin, which on one side is scooped out, so as accurately to receive the chin, against which it is closely held in lathering; which is done, not with a brush, but with soap dipped in the water of the basin and rubbed on the face.

In the present instance salt-water was used for lack of better; and the parts lathered were only the upper lip, and low down under the throat, all the rest being cultivated beard.

The preliminaries being somewhat novel to Captain Delano, he sat curiously eyeing them, so that no conversation took place, nor, for the present, did Don Benito appear disposed to renew any.

Setting down his basin, the negro searched among the razors, as for the sharpest, and having found it, gave it an additional edge by expertly stropping it on the firm, smooth, oily skin of his open palm; he then made a gesture as if to begin, but midway stood suspended for an instant, one hand elevating the razor, the other professionally dabbling among the bubbling suds on the Spaniard's lank neck. Not unaffected by the close sight of the gleaming steel, Don Benito nervously shuddered; his usual ghastliness was heightened by the lather, which lather, again, was intensified in its hue by the contrasting sootiness of the negro's body. Altogether the scene was somewhat peculiar, at least to Captain Delano, nor, as he saw the two thus postured, could he resist the vagary, that in the black he saw a headsman, and in the white a man at the block. But this was one of those antic conceits, appearing and vanishing in a breath, from which, perhaps, the best regulated mind is not always free.

Meantime the agitation of the Spaniard had a little loosened the bunting from around him, so that one broad fold swept curtain-like over the chair-arm to the floor, revealing, amid a profusion of armorial bars and ground-colours—black, blue, and yellow—a closed castle in a blood-red field diagonal with a lion rampant in a white.

"The castle and the lion," exclaimed Captain Delano—"why, Don Benito, this is the flag of Spain you use here. It's well it's only I, and not the King, that sees this," he added, with a smile, "but,"—turning towards the black—"it's all one, I suppose, so the colours be gay," which playful remark did not fail somewhat to tickle the negro.

"Now, master," he said, readjusting the flag, and pressing the head gently further back into the crotch of the chair; "now, master," and the steel glanced nigh that throat.

Again Don Benito faintly shuddered.

"You must not shake so, master. See, Don Amasa, master always shakes when I shave him. And yet master knows I never yet have drawn blood, though it's true, if master will shake so, I may some of these times. Now, master," he continued. "And now, Don Amasa, please go on with your talk about the gale, and all that; master can hear, and, between times, master can answer."

"Ah, yes, these gales," said Captain Delano; "but the more I think of your voyage, Don Benito, the more I wonder, not at the gales, terrible as they must have been, but at the disastrous interval following them. For here, by your account, have you been these two months and more getting from Cape Horn to Santa Maria, a distance which I myself, with a good wind, have sailed in a few days. True, you had calms, and long ones, but to be becalmed for two months, that is, at least, unusual. Why, Don Benito, had almost any other gentleman told me such a story, I should have been half disposed to a little incredulity."

Here an involuntary expression came over the Spaniard, similar to that just before on the deck, and whether it was the start he gave, or a sudden gawky roll of the hull in the calm, or a momentary unsteadiness of the servant's hand, however it was, just then the razor drew blood, spots of which stained the creamy lather under the throat: immediately the black barber drew back his steel, and, remaining in his professional attitude, back to Captain Delano, and face to Don Benito, held up the trickling razor, saying, with a sort of half humorous sorrow, "See, master—you shook so—here's Babo's first blood."

No sword drawn before James the First of England, no assassination in that timid King's presence, could have produced a more terrified aspect than was now presented by Don Benito.

Poor fellow, thought Captain Delano, so nervous he can't even bear the sight of barber's blood; and this unstrung, sick man, is it credible that I should have imagined he meant to spill all my blood, who can't endure the sight of one little drop of his own? Surely, Amasa Delano, you have been beside yourself this day. Tell it not when you get home, sappy Amasa. Well, well, he looks like a murderer, doesn't he? More like as if himself were to be done for. Well, well, this day's experience shall be a good lesson.

Meantime, while these things were running through the honest seaman's mind, the servant had taken the napkin from his arm, and to Don Benito had said—"But answer Don Amasa, please, master, while I wipe this ugly stuff off the razor, and strop it again."

As he said the words, his face was turned half round, so as to be alike visible to the Spaniard and the American, and seemed, by its expression, to hint that he was desirous, by getting his master to go on with the conversation, considerately to withdraw his attention from the recent annoying accident. As if glad to snatch the offered relief, Don Benito resumed, rehearsing to Captain Delano, that not only were the calms of unusual duration, but the ship had fallen in with obstinate currents; and other things he added, some of which were but repetitions of former statements, to explain how it came to pass that the passage from Cape Horn to Santa Maria had been so exceed-

ingly long; now and then mingling with his words, incidental praises, less qualified than before, to the blacks, for their general good conduct. These particulars were not given consecutively, the servant, at convenient times, using his razor, and so, between the intervals of shaving, the story and panegyric went on with more than usual huskiness.

To Captain Delano's imagination, now again not wholly at rest, there was something so hollow in the Spaniard's manner, with apparently some reciprocal hollowness in the servant's dusky comment of silence, that the idea flashed across him, that possibly master and man, for some unknown purpose, were acting out, both in word and deed, nay, to the very tremor of Don Benito's limbs, some juggling play before him. Neither did the suspicion of collusion lack apparent support, from the fact of those whispered conferences before mentioned. But then, what could be the object of enacting this play of the barber before him? At last, regarding the notion as a whimsy, insensibly suggested, perhaps, by the theatrical aspect of Don Benito in his harlequin ensign, Captain Delano speedily banished it.

The shaving over, the servant bestirred himself with a small bottle of scented waters, pouring a few drops on the head, and then diligently rubbing; the vehemence of the exercise causing the muscles of his face to twitch rather strangely.

His next operation was with comb, scissors, and brush; going round and round, smoothing a curl here, clipping an unruly whisker-hair there, giving a graceful sweep to the temple-lock, with other impromptu touches evincing the hand of a master; while, like any resigned gentleman in barber's hands, Don Benito bore all, much less uneasily, at least, than he had done the razoring; indeed, he sat so pale and rigid now, that the negro seemed a Nubian sculptor finishing off a white statue-head.

All being over at last, the standard of Spain removed, tumbled up, and tossed back into the flag-locker, the negro's warm breath blowing away any stray hair which might have lodged down his master's neck; collar and cravat readjusted; a speck of lint whisked off the velvet lapel; all this being done, backing off a little space, and pausing with an expression of subdued self-complacency, the servant for a moment surveyed his master, as, in toilet at least, the creature of his own tasteful hands.

Captain Delano playfully complimented him upon his achievement; at the same time congratulating Don Benito.

But neither sweet waters, nor shampooing, nor fidelity, nor sociality, delighted the Spaniard. Seeing him relapsing into forbidding gloom, and still remaining seated, Captain Delano, thinking that his presence was undesired just then, withdrew, on pretence of seeing whether, as he had prophesied, any signs of a breeze were visible.

Walking forward to the main-mast, he stood awhile thinking over the scene, and not without some undefined misgivings, when he heard a noise near the cuddy, and turning, saw the negro, his hand to his cheek. Advancing, Captain Delano perceived that the cheek was bleeding. He was about to ask the cause, when the negro's wailing soliloquy enlightened him.

"Ah, when will master get better from his sickness; only the sour heart that sour sickness breeds made him serve Babo so; cutting Babo with the razor, because, only by accident, Babo had given master one little scratch; and for the first time in so many a day, too. Ah, ah, ah," holding his hand to his face.

It is possible, thought Captain Delano; was it to wreak in private his Spanish spite against this poor friend of his, that Don Benito, by his sullen manner, impelled me to withdraw? Ah, this slavery breeds ugly passions in man. Poor fellow!

He was about to speak in sympathy to the negro, but with a timid reluctance he now re-entered the cuddy.

Presently master and man came forth; Don Benito leaning on his servant as if nothing had happened.

But a sort of love-quarrel, after all, thought Captain Delano.

He accosted Don Benito, and they slowly walked together. They had gone but a few paces, when the steward—a tall, rajah-looking mulatto, orientally set off with a pagoda turban formed by three or four Madras handkerchiefs wound about his head, tier on tier—approaching with a salaam, announced lunch in the cabin.

On their way thither, the two captains were preceded by the mulatto, who, turning round as he advanced, with continual smiles and bows, ushered them on, a display of elegance which quite completed the insignificance of the small bare-headed Babo, who, as if not unconscious of inferiority, eyed askance the graceful steward. But in part, Captain Delano imputed his jealous watchfulness to that peculiar feeling which the full-blooded African entertains from the adulterated one. As for the steward, his manner, if not bespeaking much dignity of self-respect, yet evidenced his extreme desire to please; which is doubly meritorious, as at once Christian and Chesterfieldian.

Captain Delano observed with interest that while the complexion of the mulatto was hybrid, his physiognomy was European —classically so.

"Don Benito," whispered he, "I am glad to see this usher-of-the-golden-rod of yours; the sight refutes an ugly remark once made to me by a Barbados planter; that when a mulatto has a regular European face, look out for him; he is a devil. But see, your steward here has features more regular than King George's of England; and yet there he nods, and bows, and smiles; a king, indeed— the king of kind hearts and polite fellows. What a pleasant voice he has, too."

"He has, Señor."

"But tell me, has he not, so far as you have known him, always proved a good, worthy fellow?" said Captain Delano, pausing, while with a final genuflexion the steward disappeared into the cabin; "come, for the reason just mentioned, I am curious to know."

"Francesco is a good man," rather sluggishly responded Don Benito, like a phlegmatic appreciator, who would neither find fault nor flatter.

"Ah, I thought so. For it were strange, indeed, and not very creditable to us white-skins, if a little of our blood mixed with the African's, should, far from improving the latter's quality, have the sad effect of pouring vitriolic acid into black broth; improving the hue, perhaps, but not the wholesomeness."

"Doubtless, doubtless, Señor, but,"—glancing at Babo—"not to speak of negroes, your planter's remark I have heard applied to the Spanish and Indian intermixtures in our provinces. But I know nothing about the matter," he listlessly added.

And here they entered the cabin.

The lunch was a frugal one. Some of Captain Delano's fresh fish and pumpkins, biscuit and salt beef, the reserved bottle of cider, and the *San Dominick's* last bottle of Canary.

As they entered, Francesco, with two or three coloured aids, was hovering over the table giving the last adjustments. Upon perceiving their master they withdrew, Francesco making a smiling congé, and the Spaniard, without condescending to notice it, fastidiously remarking to his companion that he relished not superfluous attendance.

Without companions, host and guest sat down, like a childless married couple, at opposite ends of the table, Don Benito waving Captain Delano to his place, and, weak as he was, insisting upon that gentleman being seated before himself.

The negro placed a rug under Don Benito's feet, and a cushion behind his back, and then stood behind, not his master's chair, but Captain Delano's. At first, this a little surprised the latter. But it was soon evident that, in taking his position, the black was still true to his master; since by facing him he could the more readily anticipate his slightest want.

"This is an uncommonly intelligent fellow of yours, Don Benito," whispered Captain Delano across the table.

"You say true, Señor."

During the repast, the guest again reverted to parts of Don Benito's story, begging further particulars here and there. He inquired how it was that the scurvy and fever should have committed such wholesale havoc upon the whites, while destroying less than half the blacks. As if this question reproduced the whole scene of plague before the Spaniard's eyes, miserably reminding him of his solitude in a cabin where before he had had so many friends and officers round him, his hand shook, his face became hueless, broken words escaped; but directly the sane memory of the past seemed replaced by insane terrors of the present. With starting eyes he stared before him at vacancy. For nothing was to be seen but the hand of his servant pushing the Canary over towards him. At length a few sips served partially to restore him. He made random reference to the different constitutions of races, enabling one to offer more resistance to certain maladies than another. The thought was new to his companion.

Presently Captain Delano, intending to say something to his host concerning the pecuniary part of the business he had undertaken for him, especially—since he was strictly accountable to his owners—with reference to the new suit of sails, and other things of that sort; and naturally preferring to conduct such affairs in private, was desirous that the servant should withdraw; imagining that Don Benito for a few minutes could dispense with his attendance. He, however, waited awhile; thinking that, as the conversation proceeded, Don Benito, without being prompted, would perceive the propriety of the step.

But it was otherwise. At last catching his host's eye, Captain Delano, with a slight backward gesture of his thumb, whispered, "Don Benito, pardon me, but there is an interference with the full expression of what I have to say to you."

Upon this the Spaniard changed countenance; which was imputed to his resenting the hint, as in some way a reflection upon his servant. After a moment's pause, he assured his guest that the black's remaining with them could be of no disservice; because since losing his officers he had made Babo (whose original office, it now appeared, had been captain of the slaves) not only his constant attendant and companion, but in all things his confidant.

After this, nothing more could be said; though, indeed, Captain Delano could hardly avoid some little tinge of irritation upon being left ungratified in so inconsiderable a wish, by one, too, for whom he intended such solid services. But it is only his querulousness, thought he; and so filling his glass he proceeded to business.

The price of the sails and other matters were fixed upon. But while this was being done, the American observed that, though his original offer of assistance had been hailed with hectic animation, yet now, when it was reduced to a business transaction, indifference and apathy were betrayed. Don Benito, in fact, appeared to submit to hearing the details more out of regard to common propriety, than from any impression that weighty benefit to himself and his voyage was involved.

Soon, his manner became still more reserved. The effort was vain to seek to draw him into social talk. Gnawed by his splenetic mood, he sat twitching his beard, while to little purpose the hand of his servant, mute as that on the wall, slowly pushed over the Canary.

Lunch being over, they sat down on the cushioned transom; the servant placing a pillow behind his master. The long continuance of the calm had now affected the atmosphere. Don Benito sighed heavily, as if for breath.

"Why not adjourn to the cuddy?" said Captain Delano. "There is more air there." But the host sat silent and motionless.

Meantime his servant knelt before him, with a large fan of feathers. And Francesco coming in on tiptoes, handed the negro a little cup of aromatic waters, with which at intervals he chafed his master's brow; smoothing the hair along the temples as a nurse does a child's. He spoke no word. He only rested his eye on his master's, as if, amid all Don Benito's distress, a little to refresh his spirit by the silent sight of fidelity.

Presently the ship's bell sounded two o'clock; and through the cabin windows a slight rippling of the sea was discerned; and from the desired direction.

"There," exclaimed Captain Delano, "I told you so, Don Benito, look!"

He had risen to his feet, speaking in a very animated tone, with a view the more to rouse his companion. But though the crimson curtain of the stern-window near him that moment fluttered against his pale cheek, Don Benito seemed to have even less welcome for the breeze than the calm.

Poor fellow, thought Captain Delano, bitter experience has taught him that one ripple does not make a wind, any more than one swallow a summer. But he is mistaken for once. I will get his ship in for him, and prove it.

Briefly alluding to his weak condition, he urged his host to remain quietly where he was, since he (Captain Delano) would with pleasure take upon himself the responsibility of making the best use of the wind.

Upon gaining the deck, Captain Delano started at the unexpected figure of Atufal, monumentally fixed at the threshold, like one of those sculptured porters of black marble guarding the porches of Egyptian tombs.

But this time the start was, perhaps, purely physical. Atufal's presence, singularly attesting docility even in sullenness, was contrasted with that of the hatchet-polishers, who in patience evinced their industry; while both spectacles showed, that lax as Don Benito's general authority might be, still, whenever he chose to exert it, no man so savage or colossal but must, more or less, bow.

Snatching a trumpet which hung from the bulwarks, with a free step Captain Delano advanced to the forward edge of the poop, issuing his orders in his best Spanish.

The few sailors and many negroes, all equally pleased, obediently set about heading the ship towards the harbour.

While giving some directions about setting a lower stu'n-sail, suddenly Captain Delano heard a voice faithfully repeating his orders. Turning, he saw Babo, now for the time acting, under the pilot, his original part of captain of the slaves. This assistance proved valuable. Tattered sails and warped yards were soon brought into some trim. And no brace or halyard was pulled but to the blithe songs of the inspired negroes.

Good fellows, thought Captain Delano, a little training would make fine sailors of them. Why see, the very women pull and sing too. These must be some of those Ashantee negresses that make such capital soldiers, I've heard. But who's at the helm? I must have a good hand there.

He went to see.

The *San Dominick* steered with a cumbrous tiller, with large horizontal pulleys attached. At each pulley-end stood a subordinate black, and between them, at the tiller-head, the responsible post, a Spanish seaman, whose countenance evinced his due share in the general hopefulness and confidence at the coming of the breeze.

He proved the same man who had behaved with so shame-faced an air on the windlass.

"Ah, it is you, my man," exclaimed Captain Delano—"well, no more sheep's eyes now; look straight forward and keep the ship so. Good hand, I trust? And want to get into the harbour, don't you?"

The man assented with an inward chuckle, grasping the tiller-head firmly. Upon this, unperceived by the American, the two blacks eyed the sailor intently.

Finding all right at the helm, the pilot went forward to the forecastle, to see how matters stood there.

The ship now had way enough to breast the current. With the approach of evening, the breeze would be sure to freshen.

Having done all that was needed for the present, Captain Delano, giving his last orders to the sailors, turned aft to report affairs to Don Benito in the cabin; perhaps additionally incited to rejoin him by the hope of snatching a moment's private chat while the servant was engaged upon deck.

From opposite sides, there were, beneath the poop, two approaches to the cabin; one further forward than the other, and consequently communicating with a longer passage. Marking the servant still above, Captain Delano, taking the nighest entrance—the one last named, and at whose porch Atufal still stood—hurried on his way, till arrived at the cabin threshold, he paused an instant, a little to recover from his eagerness. Then, with the words of his intended business upon his lips, he entered. As he advanced toward the seated Spaniard, he heard another footstep, keeping time with his. From the opposite door, a salver in hand, the servant was likewise advancing.

"Confound the faithful fellow," thought Captain Delano; "what a vexatious coincidence."

Possibly, the vexation might have been something different, were it not for the brisk confidence inspired by the breeze. But even as it was, he felt a slight twinge, from a sudden indefinite association in his mind of Babo with Atufal.

"Don Benito," said he, "I give you joy; the breeze will hold, and will increase. By the way, your tall man and time-piece, Atufal, stands without. By your order, of course?"

Don Benito recoiled, as if at some bland satirical touch, delivered with such adroit garnish of apparent good breeding as to present no handle for retort.

He is like one flayed alive, thought Captain Delano; where may one touch him without causing a shrink?

The servant moved before his master, adjusting a cushion; recalled to civility, the Spaniard stiffly replied: "You are right. The slave appears where you saw him, according to my command; which is, that if at the given hour I am below, he must take his stand and abide my coming."

"Ah now, pardon me, but that is treating the poor fellow like an ex-king indeed. Ah, Don Benito," smiling, "for all the licence you permit in some things, I fear lest, at bottom, you are a bitter hard master."

Again Don Benito shrank; and this time, as the good sailor thought, from a genuine twinge of his conscience.

Again conversation became constrained. In vain Captain Delano called attention to the now perceptible motion of the keel gently cleaving the sea; with lack-lustre eye, Don Benito returned words few and reserved.

By and by, the wind having steadily risen, and still blowing right into the harbour, bore the *San Dominick* swiftly on. Rounding a point of land, the sealer at distance came into open view.

Meantime Captain Delano had again repaired to the deck, remaining there some time. Having at last altered the ship's course, so as to give the reef a wide berth, he returned for a few moments below.

I will cheer up my poor friend, this time, thought he.

"Better and better, Don Benito," he cried as he blithely re-entered: "there will soon be an end to your cares, at least for a while. For when, after a long, sad voyage, you know, the anchor drops into the haven, all its vast weight seems lifted from the captain's heart. We are getting on famously, Don Benito. My ship is in sight. Look through this side-light here; there she is; all a-taunt-o! The *Bachelor's Delight,* my good friend. Ah, how this wind braces one up. Come, you must take a cup of coffee with me this evening. My old steward will give you as fine a cup as ever any sultan tasted. What say you, Don Benito, will you?"

At first, the Spaniard glanced feverishly up, casting a longing look towards the sealer, while with mute concern his servant gazed into his face. Suddenly the old ague of coldness returned, and dropping back to his cushions he was silent.

"You do not answer. Come, all day you have been my host; would you have hos-

pitality all on one side?"

"I cannot go," was the response.

"What? It will not fatigue you. The ships will lie together as near as they can, without swinging foul. It will be little more than stepping from deck to deck; which is but as from room to room. Come, come, you must not refuse me."

"I cannot go," decisively and repulsively repeated Don Benito.

Renouncing all but the last appearance of courtesy, with a sort of cadaverous sullenness, and biting his thin nails to the quick, he glanced, almost glared, at his guest, as if impatient that a stranger's presence should interfere with the full indulgence of his morbid hour. Meantime the sound of the parted waters came more and more gurglingly and merrily in at the windows; as reproaching him for his dark spleen; as telling him that, sulk as he might, and go mad with it, nature cared not a jot; since, whose fault was it, pray?

But the foul mood was now at its depth, as the fair wind at its height.

There was something in the man so far beyond any mere unsociality or sourness previously evinced, that even the forbearing good-nature of his guest could no longer endure it. Wholly at a loss to account for such demeanour, and deeming sickness with eccentricity, however extreme, no adequate excuse, well satisfied, too, that nothing in his own conduct could justify it, Captain Delano's pride began to be roused. Himself became reserved. But all seemed one to the Spaniard. Quitting him, therefore, Captain Delano once more went to the deck.

The ship was now within less than two miles of the sealer. The whale-boat was seen darting over the interval.

To be brief, the two vessels, thanks to the pilot's skill, ere long in neighbourly style lay anchored together.

Before returning to his own vessel, Captain Delano had intended communicating to Don Benito the smaller details of the proposed services to be rendered. But, as it was, unwilling anew to subject himself to rebuffs,

he resolved, now that he had seen the *San Dominick* safely moored, immediately to quit her, without further allusion to hospitality or business. Indefinitely postponing his ulterior plans, he would regulate his future actions according to future circumstances. His boat was ready to receive him; but his host still tarried below. Well, thought Captain Delano, if he has little breeding, the more need to show mine. He descended to the cabin to bid a ceremonious, and, it may be, tacitly rebukeful adieu. But to his great satisfaction, Don Benito, as if he began to feel the weight of that treatment with which his slighted guest had, not indecorously, retaliated upon him, now supported by his servant, rose to his feet, and grasping Captain Delano's hand, stood tremulous; too much agitated to speak. But the good augury hence drawn was suddenly dashed, by his resuming all his previous reserve, with augmented gloom, as, with half-averted eyes, he silently reseated himself on his cushions. With a corresponding return of his own chilled feelings, Captain Delano bowed and withdrew.

He was hardly midway in the narrow corridor, dim as a tunnel, leading from the cabin to the stairs, when a sound, as of the tolling for execution in some jail-yard, fell on his ears. It was the echo of the ship's flawed bell, striking the hour, drearily reverberated in this subterranean vault. Instantly, by a fatality not to be withstood, his mind, responsive to the portent, swarmed with superstitious suspicions. He paused. In images far swifter than these sentences, the minutest details of all his former distrusts swept through him.

Hitherto, credulous good-nature had been too ready to furnish excuses for reasonable fears. Why was the Spaniard, so superfluously punctilious at times, now heedless of common propriety in not accompanying to the side his departing guest? Did indisposition forbid? Indisposition had not forbidden more irksome exertion that day. His last equivocal demeanour recurred. He had risen to his feet, grasped his guest's hand, motioned toward his hat; then, in an instant, all was eclipsed in sinister muteness and gloom. Did this imply one brief, repentant relenting at the final moment, from some iniquitous plot, followed by remorseless return to it? His last glance seemed to express a calamitous, yet acquiescent farewell to Captain Delano forever. Why decline the invitation to visit the sealer that evening? Or was the Spaniard less hardened than the Jew, who refrained not from supping at the board of him whom the same night he meant to betray? What imported all those day-long enigmas and contradictions, except they were intended to mystify, preliminary to some stealthy blow? Atufal, the pretended rebel, but punctual shadow, that moment lurked by the threshold without. He seemed a sentry, and more. Who, by his own confession, had stationed him there? Was the negro now lying in wait?

The Spaniard behind—his creature before: to rush from darkness to light was the involuntary choice.

The next moment, with clenched jaw and hand, he passed Atufal, and stood unharmed in the light. As he saw his trim ship lying peacefully at anchor, and almost within ordinary call; as he saw his household boat, with familiar faces in it, patiently rising and falling on the short waves by the *San Dominick's* side; and then, glancing about the decks where he stood, saw the oakum-pickers still gravely plying their fingers; and heard the low, buzzing whistle and industrious hum of the hatchet-polishers, still bestirring themselves over their endless occupation; and more than all, as he saw the benign aspect of nature, taking her innocent repose in the evening; the screened sun in the quiet camp of the west shining out like the mild light from Abraham's tent; as charmed eye and ear took in all these, with the chained figure of the black, clenched jaw and hand relaxed. Once again he smiled at the phantoms which had mocked him, and felt something like a tinge of remorse, that, by harbouring them even for a moment, he should, by implication, have betrayed an atheist doubt of the ever-watchful Providence above.

There was a few minutes' delay, while, in obedience to his orders, the boat was being hooked along to the gangway. During this interval, a sort of saddened satisfaction stole over Captain Delano, at thinking of the kindly offices he had that day discharged for a stranger. Ah, thought he, after good actions one's conscience is never ungrateful, however much so the benefited party may be.

Presently, his foot, in the first act of descent into the boat, pressed the first round of the side-ladder, his face presented inward upon the deck. In the same moment, he heard his name courteously sounded; and, to his pleased surprise, saw Don Benito advancing—an unwonted energy in his air, as if, at the last moment, intent upon making amends for his recent discourtesy. With instinctive good feeling, Captain Delano, withdrawing his foot, turned and reciprocally advanced. As he did so, the Spaniard's nervous eagerness increased, but his vital energy failed; so that, the better to support him, the servant, placing his master's hand on his naked shoulder, and gently holding it there, formed himself into a sort of crutch.

When the two captains met, the Spaniard again fervently took the hand of the American, at the same time casting an earnest glance into his eyes, but, as before, too much overcome to speak.

I have done him wrong, self-reproachfully thought Captain Delano; his apparent coldness has deceived me; in no instance has he meant to offend.

Meanwhile, as if fearful that the continuance of the scene might too much unstring his master, the servant seemed anxious to terminate it. And so still presenting himself as a crutch, and walking between the two captains, he advanced with them towards the gangway; while still, as if full of kindly contrition, Don Benito would not let go the hand of Captain Delano, but retained it in his, across the black's body.

Soon they were standing by the side, looking over into the boat, whose crew turned up their curious eyes. Waiting a moment for the Spaniard to relinquish his hold, the now embarrassed Captain Delano lifted his foot, to overstep the threshold of the open gangway; but still Don Benito would not let go his hand. And yet, with an agitated tone, he said, "I can go no further; here I must bid you adieu. Adieu, my dear, dear Don Amasa. Go—go!" suddenly tearing his hand loose, "go, and God guard you better than me, my best friend."

Not unaffected, Captain Delano would now have lingered; but catching the meekly admonitory eye of the servant, with a hasty farewell he descended into his boat, followed by the continual adieus of Don Benito, standing rooted in the gangway.

Seating himself in the stern, Captain Delano, making a last salute, ordered the boat shoved off. The crew had their oars on end. The bowsman pushed the boat a sufficient distance for the oars to be lengthwise dropped. The instant that was done, Don Benito sprang over the bulwarks, falling at the feet of Captain Delano; at the same time calling towards his ship, but in tones so frenzied, that none in the boat could understand him. But, as if not equally obtuse, three sailors, from three different and distant parts of the ship, splashed into the sea, swimming after their captain, as if intent upon his rescue.

The dismayed officer of the boat eagerly asked what this meant. To which, Captain Delano, turning a disdainful smile upon the unaccountable Spaniard, answered that, for his part, he neither knew nor cared; but it seemed as if Don Benito had taken it into his head to produce the impression among his people that the boat wanted to kidnap him. "Or else—give way for your lives," he wildly added, starting at a clattering hubbub in the ship, above which rang the tocsin of the hatchet-polishers; and seizing Don Benito by the throat he added, "this plotting pirate means murder!" Here, in apparent verification of the words, the servant, a dagger in his hand, was seen on the rail overhead, poised, in the act of leaping, as if with desperate fidelity to befriend his master to the last; while, seemingly to aid the black, the three white sailors were trying to clamber into the hampered bow. Meantime, the whole host of negroes, as if inflamed at the sight of their jeopardized captain, impended in one sooty avalanche over the bulwarks.

All this, with what preceded, and what followed, occurred with such involutions of rapidity, that past, present, and future seemed one.

Seeing the negro coming, Captain Delano had flung the Spaniard aside, almost in the very act of clutching him, and, by the unconscious recoil, shifting his place, with arms thrown up, so promptly grappled the servant in his descent, that with dagger presented at Captain Delano's heart, the black seemed of purpose to have leaped there as to his mark. But the weapon was wrenched away, and the assailant dashed down into the bottom of the boat, which now, with disentangled oars, began to speed through the sea.

At this juncture, the left hand of Captain Delano, on one side, again clutched the half-reclining Don Benito, heedless that he was in a speechless faint, while his right foot, on the other side, ground the prostrate negro; and his right arm pressed for added speed on the after oar, his eye bent forward, encouraging his men to their utmost.

But here, the officer of the boat, who had at last succeeded in beating off the towing sailors, and was now, with face turned aft, assisting the bowsman at his oar, suddenly called to Captain Delano, to see what the black was about; while a Portuguese oarsman shouted to him to give heed to what the Spaniard was saying.

Glancing down at his feet, Captain Delano saw the freed hand of the servant aiming with a second dagger—a small one, before concealed in his wool—with this he was snakishly writhing up from the boat's bottom, at the heart of his master, his countenance lividly vindictive, expressing the centered purpose of his soul; while the Spaniard, half-choked, was vainly shrinking away, with husky words, incoherent to all but the Portuguese.

That moment, across the long-benighted mind of Captain Delano, a flash of revelation swept, illuminating, in unanticipated clearness, his host's whole mysterious demeanour, with every enigmatic event of the day, as well as the entire past voyage of the *San Dominick*. He smote Babo's hand down, but his own heart smote him harder. With infinite pity he withdrew his hold from Don Benito. Not Captain Delano, but Don Benito, the black, in leaping into the boat, had intended to stab.

Both the black's hands were held, as, glancing up towards the *San Dominick*, Captain Delano, now with scales dropped from his eyes, saw the negroes, not in misrule, not in tumult, not as if frantically concerned for Don Benito, but with mask torn away, flourishing hatchets, and knives, in ferocious piratical revolt. Like delirious black dervishes, the six Ashantees danced on the poop. Prevented by their foes from springing into the water, the Spanish boys were hurrying up to the topmost spars, while such of the few Spanish sailors, not already in the sea, less alert, were descried, helplessly mixed in, on deck, with the blacks.

Meantime Captain Delano hailed his own vessel, ordering the ports up, and the guns run out. But by this time the cable of the *San Dominick* had been cut; and the fag-end, in lashing out, whipped away the canvas shroud about the beak, suddenly revealing, as the bleached hull swung round towards the open ocean, death for the figure-head, in a human skeleton; chalky comment on the chalked words below, *"Follow your leader."*

At the sight, Don Benito, covering his face, wailed out: "'Tis he, Aranda! my murdered, unburied friend!"

Upon reaching the sealer, calling for ropes, Captain Delano bound the negro,

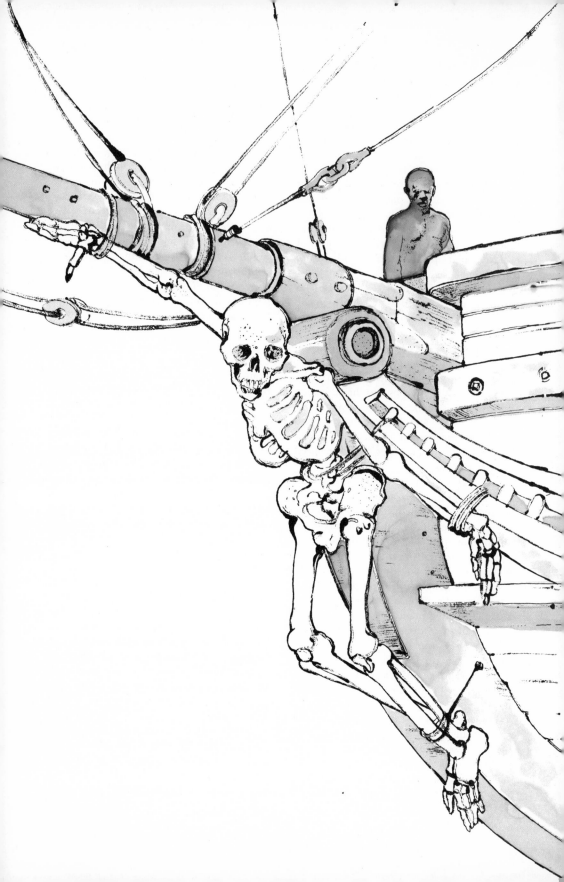

who made no resistance, and had him hoisted to the deck. He would then have assisted the now almost helpless Don Benito up the side; but Don Benito, wan as he was, refused to move, or be moved, until the negro should have been first put below out of view. When, presently assured that it was done, he no more shrank from the ascent.

The boat was immediately dispatched back to pick up the three swimming sailors. Meantime, the guns were in readiness, though, owing to the *San Dominick* having glided somewhat astern of the sealer, only the aftermost one could be brought to bear. With this, they fired six times; thinking to cripple the fugitive ship by bringing down her spars. But only a few inconsiderable ropes were shot away. Soon the ship was beyond the gun's range, steering broad out of the bay; the blacks thickly clustering round the bowsprit, one moment with taunting cries towards the whites, the next with upthrown gestures hailing the now dusky moors of ocean—cawing crows escaped from the hand of the fowler.

The first impulse was to slip the cables and give chase. But, upon second thoughts, to pursue with whale-boat and yawl seemed more promising.

Upon inquiring of Don Benito what fire-arms they had on board the *San Dominick*, Captain Delano was answered that they had none that could be used; because, in the earlier stages of the mutiny, a cabin-passenger, since dead, had secretly put out of order the locks of what few muskets there were. But with all his remaining strength, Don Benito entreated the American not to give chase, either with ship or boat; for the negroes had already proved themselves such desperadoes, that, in case of a present assault, nothing but a total massacre of the whites could be looked for. But, regarding this warning as coming from one whose spirit had been crushed by misery, the American did not give up his design.

The boats were got ready and armed. Captain Delano ordered his men into them. He was going himself when Don Benito grasped his arm.

"What! have you saved my life, Señor, and are you now going to throw away your own?"

The officers also, for reasons connected with their interests and those of the voyage, and a duty owing to the owners, strongly objected against their commander's going. Weighing their remonstrances a moment, Captain Delano felt bound to remain; appointing his chief mate—an athletic and resolute man, who had been a privateer's-man—to head the party. The more to encourage the sailors, they were told, that the Spanish captain considered his ship good as lost; that she and her cargo, including some gold and silver, were worth more than a thousand doubloons. Take her, and no small part should be theirs. The sailors replied with a shout.

The fugitives had now almost gained an offing. It was nearly night; but the moon was rising. After hard, prolonged pulling, the boats came up on the ship's quarters, at a suitable distance lying upon their oars to discharge their muskets. Having no bullets to return, the negroes sent their yells. But, upon the second volley, Indian-like, they hurled their hatchets. One took off a sailor's fingers. Another struck the whale-boat's bow, cutting off the rope there, and remaining stuck in the gunwale like a woodman's axe. Snatching it, quivering from its lodgment, the mate hurled it back. The returned gauntlet now stuck in the ship's broken quarter-gallery, and so remained.

The negroes giving too hot a reception, the whites kept a more respectful distance. Hovering now just out of reach of the hurtling hatchets, they, with a view to the close encounter which must soon come, sought to decoy the blacks into entirely disarming themselves of their most murderous weapons in a hand-to-hand fight, by foolishly flinging them, as missiles, short of the mark, into the sea. But, ere long, perceiving the stratagem, the negroes desisted, though not before many of them had to replace their lost hatchets with handspikes;

an exchange which, as counted upon, proved, in the end, favourable to the assailants.

Meantime, with a strong wind, the ship still clove the water; the boats alternately falling behind, and pulling up, to discharge fresh volleys.

The fire was mostly directed towards the stern, since there, chiefly, the negroes, at present, were clustering. But to kill or maim the negroes was not the object. To take them, with the ship, was the object. To do it, the ship must be boarded; which could not be done by boats while she was sailing so fast.

A thought now struck the mate. Observing the Spanish boys still aloft, high as they could get, he called to them to descend to the yards, and cut adrift the sails. It was done. About this time, owing to causes hereafter to be shown, two Spaniards, in the dress of sailors, and conspicuously showing themselves, were killed; not by volleys, but by deliberate marksman's shots; while, as it afterwards appeared, by one of the general discharges, Atufal, the black, and the Spaniard at the helm likewise were killed. What now, with the loss of the sails, and loss of leaders, the ship became unmanageable to the negroes.

With creaking masts, she came heavily round to the wind; the prow slowly swinging into view of the boats, its skeleton gleaming in the horizontal moonlight, and casting a gigantic ribbed shadow upon the water. One extended arm of the ghost seemed beckoning the whites to avenge it.

"Follow your leader!" cried the mate; and, one on each bow, the boats boarded. Sealing-spears and cutlasses crossed hatchets and handspikes. Huddled upon the longboat amidships, the negresses raised a wailing chant, whose chorus was the clash of the steel.

For a time, the attack wavered; the negroes wedging themselves to beat it back; the half-repelled sailors, as yet unable to gain a footing, fighting as troopers in the saddle, one leg sideways flung over the

bulwarks, and one without, plying their cutlasses like carters' whips. But in vain. They were almost overborne, when, rallying themselves into a squad as one man, with a huzza, they sprang inboard, where, entangled, they involuntarily separated again. For a few breaths' space, there was a vague, muffled, inner sound, as of submerged swordfish rushing hither and thither through shoals of black-fish. Soon, in a reunited band, and joined by the Spanish seamen, the whites came to the surface, irresistibly driving the negroes toward the stern. But a barricade of casks and sacks, from side to side, had been thrown up by the main-mast. Here the negroes faced about, and though scorning peace or truce, yet fain would have had respite. But, without pause, overleaping the barrier, the unflagging sailors again closed. Exhausted, the blacks now fought in despair. Their red tongues lolled, wolf-like, from their black mouths. But the pale sailors' teeth were set; not a word was spoken; and in five minutes more, the ship was won.

Nearly a score of the negroes were killed. Exclusive of those by the balls, many were mangled; their wounds—mostly inflicted by the long-edged sealing-spears, resembling those shaven ones of the English at Preston Pans, made by the poled scythes of the Highlanders. On the other side, none were killed, though several were wounded; some severely, including the mate. The surviving negroes were temporarily secured, and the ship, towed back into the harbour at midnight, once more lay anchored.

Omitting the incidents and arrangements ensuing, suffice it that, after two days spent in refitting, the ships sailed in company for Concepcion, in Chile, and thence for Lima, in Peru; where, before the vice-regal courts, the whole affair, from the beginning, underwent investigation.

Though, midway on the passage, the ill-fated Spaniard, relaxed from constraint, showed some signs of regaining health with free-will; yet, agreeably to his own foreboding, shortly before arriving at Lima, he relapsed, finally becoming so reduced as to be carried ashore in arms. Hearing of his story and plight, one of the many religious institutions of the City of Kings opened an hospitable refuge to him, where both physician and priest were his nurses, and a member of the order volunteered to be his one special guardian and consoler, by night and by day.

The following extracts, translated from one of the official Spanish documents, will, it is hoped, shed light on the preceding narrative, as well as, in the first place, reveal the true port of departure and true history of the *San Dominick's* voyage, down to the time of her touching at the island of Santa Maria.

But, ere the extracts come, it may be well to preface them with a remark.

The document selected, from among many others, for partial translation, contains the deposition of Benito Cereno; the first taken in the case. Some disclosures therein were, at the time, held dubious for both learned and natural reasons. The tribunal inclined to the opinion that the deponent, not undisturbed in his mind by recent events, raved of some things which could never have happened. But subsequent depositions of the surviving sailors, bearing out the revelations of their captain in several of the strangest particulars, gave credence to the rest. So that the tribunal, in its final decision, rested its capital sentences upon statements which, had they lacked confirmation, it would have deemed it but duty to reject.

I, DON JOSÉ DE ABOS AND PADILLA, *His Majesty's Notary for the Royal Revenue, and Register of this Province, and Notary Public of the Holy Crusade of this Bishoprick, etc.*

Do certify and declare, as much as is requisite in law, that, in the criminal cause commenced the twenty-fourth of the month of September, in the year seventeen hundred and ninety-nine, against the negroes

of the ship San Dominick, *the following declaration before me was made:*

Declaration of the first Witness, DON BENITO CERENO.

The same day and month and year, His Honour, Doctor Juan Martinez de Rozas, Councillor of the Royal Audience of this Kingdom, and learned in the law of this Intendency, ordered the captain of the ship San Dominick, *Don Benito Cereno, to appear; which he did in his litter, attended by the monk Infelez; of whom he received the oath, which he took by God, our Lord, and a Sign of the Cross; under which he promised to tell the truth of whatever he should know and should be asked; and being interrogated agreeably to the tenor of the act, commencing the process, he said, that on the twentieth of May last, he set sail with his ship from the port of Valparaiso, bound to that of Callao; loaded with the produce of the country beside thirty cases of hardware and one hundred and sixty blacks, of both sexes, mostly belonging to Don Alexandro Aranda, gentleman, of the City of Mendoza; that the crew of the ship consisted of thirty-six men, beside the persons who went as passengers; that the negroes were in part as follows:*

[Here, in the original, follows a list of some fifty names, descriptions, and ages, compiled from certain recovered documents of Aranda's and also from recollections of the deponent, from which portions only are extracted.]

*—One, from about eighteen to nineteen years, named José, and this was the man that waited upon his master, Don Alexandro, and who speaks well the Spanish, having served him four or five years; * * * a mulatto, named Francesco, the cabin steward, of a good person and voice having sung in the Valparaiso churches, native of the province of Buenos Ayres, aged about thirty-five years. * * * A smart negro, named*

Dago, who had been for many years a grave-
digger among the Spaniards, aged forty-six
years. * * * Four old negroes, born in
Africa, from sixty to seventy, but sound,
calkers by trade, whose names are as follows:
the first was named Mure, and he was killed
(as was also his son named Diamelo); the
second, Nacta; the third, Yola, likewise
killed; the fourth, Ghofan; and six full-
grown negroes, aged from thirty to forty-
five, all raw, and born among the Ashantees
—Matinqui, Yau, Lecbe, Mapenda, Yambaio,
Akim, four of whom were killed; * * * a
powerful negro named Atufal, who being
supposed to have been a chief in Africa, his
owner set great store by him. * * * And a
small negro of Senegal, but some years
among the Spaniards, aged about thirty,
which negro's name was Babo; * * * that
he does not remember the names of the
others, but that still expecting the residue of
Don Alexandro's papers will be found, will
then take due account of them all, and remit to the court; * * * and thirty-nine
women and children of all ages.

[The catalogue over, the deposition goes
on:]

* * * That all the negroes slept upon
deck, as is customary in this navigation, and
none wore fetters, because the owner, his
friend Aranda, told him that they were all
tractable; * * * that on the seventh day after leaving port, at three o'clock in the
morning, all the Spaniards being asleep except two officers of the watch, who were the
boat-swain, Juan Robles, and the carpenter, Juan Bautista Gayete, and the helms-
man and his boy, the negroes revolted suddenly, wounded dangerously the boat-swain
and the carpenter, and successively killed
eighteen men of those who were sleeping
upon deck, some with handspikes and
hatchets, and others by throwing them alive
overboard, after tying them; that of the
Spaniards upon deck, they left about seven,
as he thinks, alive and tied, to manœuvre
the ship, and three or four more, who hid

themselves, remained also alive. Although
in the act of revolt the negroes made themselves masters of the hatchway, six or seven
wounded went through it to the cockpit,
without any hindrance on their part; that
during the act of revolt, the mate and another person, whose name he does not recollect, attempted to come up through the
hatchway, but being quickly wounded, were
obliged to return to the cabin; that the
deponent resolved at break of day to come
up the companion-way, where the negro
Babo was, being the ringleader, and Atufal,
who assisted him, and having spoken to
them, exhorted them to cease committing
such atrocities, asking them, at the same
time, what they wanted and intended to
do, offering, himself, to obey their commands; that notwithstanding this, they
threw, in his presence, three men, alive
and tied, overboard; that they told the deponent to come up, and that they would
not kill him; which having done, the negro
Babo asked him whether there were in those
seas any negro countries where they might
be carried, and he answered them, No; that
the negro Babo afterwards told him to carry
them to Senegal, or to the neighbouring
islands of St. Nicholas; and he answered,
that this was impossible, on account of the
great distance, the necessity involved of
rounding Cape Horn, the bad condition of
the vessel, the want of provisions, sails, and
water; but that the negro Babo replied to
him he must carry them in any way; that
they would do and conform themselves to
anything the deponent should require as to
eating and drinking; that after a long conference, being absolutely compelled to please
them, for they threatened to kill all the
whites if they were not, at all events, carried to Senegal, he told them that what was
most wanting for the voyage was water; that
they would go near the coast to take it, and
thence they would proceed on their course;
that the negro Babo agreed to it; and the
deponent steered towards the intermediate
ports, hoping to meet some Spanish or foreign vessel that would save them; that

within ten or eleven days they saw the land, and continued their course by it in the vicinity of Nasca; that the deponent observed that the negroes were now restless and mutinous, because he did not effect the taking in of water, the negro Babo having required, with threats, that it should be done, without fail, the following day; he told him he saw plainly that the coast was steep, and the rivers designated in the maps were not to be found, with other reasons suitable to the circumstances; that the best way would be to go to the island of Santa Maria, where they might water easily, it being a solitary island, as the foreigners did; that the deponent did not go to Pisco, that was near, nor make any other port of the coast, because the negro Babo had intimated to him several times, that he would kill all the whites the very moment he should perceive any city, town, or settlement of any kind on the shores to which they should be carried: that having determined to go to the island of Santa Maria, as the deponent had planned, for the purpose of trying whether, on the passage or near the island itself, they could find any vessel that should favour them, or whether he could escape from it in a boat to the neighbouring coast of Arauco, to adopt the necessary means he immediately changed his course, steering for the island; that the negroes Babo and Atufal held daily conferences, in which they discussed what was necessary for their design of returning to Senegal, whether they were to kill all the Spaniards, and particularly the deponent; that eight days after parting from the coast of Nasca, the deponent being on the watch a little after day-break, and soon after the negroes had their meeting, the negro Babo came to the place where the deponent was, and told him that he had determined to kill his master, Don Alexandro Aranda, both because he and his companions could not otherwise be sure of their liberty, and that to keep the seamen in subjection, he wanted to prepare a warning of what road they should be made to take did they or any of them oppose him; and that, by means of

the death of Don Alexandro, that warning would best be given; but, that what this last meant, the deponent did not at the time comprehend, nor could not, further than that the death of Don Alexandro was intended; and moreover the negro Babo proposed to the deponent to call the mate Raneds, who was sleeping in the cabin, before the thing was done, for fear, as the deponent understood it, that the mate, who was a good navigator, should be killed with Don Alexandro and the rest; that the deponent, who was the friend, from youth, of Don Alexandro, prayed and conjured, but all was useless; for the negro Babo answered him that the thing could not be prevented, and that all the Spaniards risked their death if they should attempt to frustrate his will in this matter, or any other, that, in this conflict, the deponent called the mate, Raneds, who was forced to go apart, and immediately the negro Babo commanded the Ashantee Matinqui and the Ashantee Lecbe to go and commit the murder; that those two went down with hatchets to the berth of Don Alexandro; that, yet half alive and mangled, they dragged him on deck; that they were going to throw him overboard in that state, but the negro Babo stopped them, bidding the murder be completed on the deck before him, which was done, when, by his orders, the body was carried below, forward; that nothing more was seen of it by the deponent for three days; * * * that Don Alonzo Sidonia, an old man, long resident at Valparaiso, and lately appointed to a civil office in Peru, whither he had taken passage, was at the time sleeping in the berth opposite Don Alexandro's; that awakening at his cries, surprised by them, and at the sight of the negroes with their bloody hatchets in their hands, he threw himself into the sea through a window which was near him, and was drowned, without it being in the power of the deponent to assist or take him up; * * * that a short time after killing Aranda, they brought upon deck his cousin-german, of middle-age, Don Francisco Masa, of Mendoza, and the young Don Joaquin, Marques de Aramboa-laza, then lately from Spain, with his Spanish servant Ponce, and the three young clerks of Aranda, José Morairi, Lorenzo Bargas, and Hermenegildo Gandix, all of Cadiz; that Don Joaquin and Hermenegildo Gandix, the negro Babo, for purposes hereafter to appear, preserved alive; but Don Francisco Masa, José Morairi, and Lorenzo Bargas, with Ponce the servant, beside the boat-swain, Juan Robles, the boat-swain's mates, Manuel Viscaya and Roderigo Hurta, and four of the sailors, the negro Babo ordered to be thrown alive into the sea, although they made no resistance, nor begged for anything else but mercy; that the boat-swain Juan Robles, who knew how to swim, kept the longest above water, making acts of contrition, and, in the last words he uttered, charged this deponent to cause mass to be said for his soul to our Lady of Succour; * * * that, during the three days which followed, the deponent, uncertain what fate had befallen the remains of Don Alexandro, frequently asked the negro Babo where they were, and, if still on board, whether they were to be preserved for interment ashore, entreating him so to order it; that the negro Babo answered nothing till the fourth day, when at sunrise, the deponent coming on deck, the negro Babo showed him a skeleton, which had been substituted for the ship's proper figure-head —the image of Cristobal Colon, the discoverer of the New World; that the negro Babo asked him whose skeleton that was, and whether from its whiteness, he should not think it a white's; that, upon discovering his face the negro Babo, coming close, said words to this effect: "Keep faith with the blacks from here to Senegal, or you shall in spirit, as now in body, follow your leader," pointing to the prow; * * * that the same morning the negro Babo took by succession each Spaniard forward, and asked him whose skeleton that was, and whether, from its whiteness, he should not think it a white's; that each Spaniard covered his face; that then to each the negro Babo re-

peated the words in the first place said to the deponent; * * * that they (the Spaniards), being then assembled aft, the negro Babo harangued them, saying that he had now done all; that the deponent (as navigator for the negroes) might pursue his course, warning him and all of them that they should, soul and body, go the way of Don Alexandro, if he saw them (the Spaniards) speak or plot anything against them (the negroes), a threat which was repeated every day; that, before the events last mentioned, they had tied the cook to throw him overboard, for it is not known what thing they heard him speak, but finally the negro Babo spared his life, at the request of the deponent; that a few days after, the deponent, endeavouring not to omit any means to preserve the lives of the remaining whites, spoke to the negroes peace and tranquillity, and agreed to draw up a paper, signed by the deponent and the sailors who could write, as also by the negro Babo, for himself and all the blacks, in which the deponent obliged himself to carry them to Senegal, and they not to kill any more, and he formally to make over to them the ship, with the cargo, with which they were for that time satisfied and quieted. * * * But the next day, the more surely to guard against the sailors' escape, the negro Babo commanded all the boats to be destroyed but the long-boat, which was unseaworthy, and another, a cutter in good condition, which knowing it would yet be wanted for towing the water casks, he had it lowered down into the hold. * * *

[Various particulars of the prolonged and perplexed navigation ensuing here follow, with incidents of a calamitous calm, from which portion one passage is extracted, to wit:]

—That on the fifth day of the calm, all on board suffering much from the heat, and want of water, and five having died in fits, and mad, the negroes became irritable, and for a chance gesture, which they deemed suspicious—though it was harmless—made by the mate, Raneds, to the deponent in the act of handing a quadrant, they killed him; but that for this they afterwards were sorry, the mate being the only remaining navigator on board, except the deponent.

* * *

—That omitting other events which daily happened, and which can only serve uselessly to recall past misfortunes and conflicts, after seventy-three days' navigation, reckoned from the time they sailed from Nasca, during which they navigated under a scanty allowance of water, and were afflicted with the calms before mentioned, they at last arrived at the island of Santa Maria, on the seventeenth of the month of August, at about six o'clock in the afternoon, at which hour they cast anchor very near the American ship, Bachelor's Delight, which lay in the same bay, commanded by the generous Captain Amasa Delano; but at six o'clock in the morning, they had already descried the port, and the negroes became uneasy, as soon as at distance they saw the ship, not having expected to see one there; that the negro Babo pacified them, assuring them that no fear need be had; that straightway he ordered the figure on the bow to be covered with canvas, as for repairs, and had the decks a little set in order; that for a time the negro Babo and the negro Atufal conferred; that the negro Atufal was for sailing away, but the negro Babo would not, and, by himself, cast about what to do; that at last he came to the deponent, proposing to him to say and do all that the deponent declares to have said and done to the American captain; * * * that the negro Babo warned him that if he varied in the least, or uttered any word, or gave any look that should give the least intimation of the past events or present state, he would instantly kill him, with all his companions, showing a dagger, which he carried hid, saying something which, as he understood it, meant that that dagger would be alert as his eye; that the negro Babo then announced the plan to all his companions, which pleased them; that he then, the better to disguise the truth, devised many expedients, in some of them uniting deceit and defense; that of this sort was the device of the six Ashantees before named, who were his bravoes; that them he stationed on the break of the poop, as if to clean certain hatchets (in cases, which were part of the cargo), but in reality to use them, and distribute them at need, and at a given word he told them; that, among other devices, was the device of presenting Atufal, his right hand man, as chained, though in a moment the chains could be dropped; that in every particular he informed the deponent what part he was expected to enact in every device, and what story he was to tell on every occasion, always threatening him with instant death if he varied in the least: that, conscious that many of the negroes would be turbulent, the negro Babo appointed the four aged negroes who were calkers, to keep what domestic order they could on the decks; that again and again he harangued the Spaniards and his companions, informing them of his intent, and of his devices, and of the invented story that this deponent was to tell; charging them lest any of them varied from that story; that these arrangements were made and matured during the interval of two or three hours, between their first sighting the ship and the arrival on board of Captain Amasa Delano; that this happened about half-past seven o'clock in the morning, Captain Amasa Delano coming in his boat, and all gladly receiving him; that the deponent, as well as he could force himself, acting then the part of principal owner, and a free captain of the ship, told Captain Amasa Delano, when called upon, that he came from Buenos Ayres, bound to Lima, with three hundred negroes; that off Cape Horn, and in a subsequent fever, many negroes had died; that also, by similar casualties, all the sea-officers and the greatest part of the crew had died.

* * *

[And so the deposition goes on, circumstantially recounting the fictitious story dictated to the deponent by Babo, and through the deponent imposed upon Captain Delano; and also recounting the friendly offers of Captain Delano, with other things, but all of which is here omitted. After the fictitious story, etc., the deposition proceeds:]

—*That the generous Captain Amasa Delano remained on board all the day, till he left the ship anchored at six o'clock in the evening, deponent speaking to him always of his pretended misfortunes, under the forementioned principles, without having had it in his power to tell a single word, or give him the least hint, that he might know the truth and state of things; because the negro Babo, performing the office of an officious servant with all the appearance of submission of the humble slave, did not leave the deponent one moment; that this was in order to observe the deponent's actions and words, for the negro Babo understands well the Spanish; and besides, there were thereabout some others who were constantly on the watch, and likewise understood the Spanish; * * * that upon one occasion, while deponent was standing on the deck conversing with Amasa Delano, by a secret sign the negro Babo drew him (the deponent) aside, the act appearing as if originating with the deponent; that then, he being drawn aside, the negro Babo proposed to him to gain from Amasa Delano full particulars about his ship, and crew, and arms; that the deponent asked "For what?" that the negro Babo answered he might conceive; that, grieved at the prospect of what might overtake the generous Captain Amasa Delano, the deponent at first refused to ask the desired questions, and used every argument to induce the negro Babo to give up this new design; that the negro Babo showed the point of his dagger; that, after the information had been obtained, the*

negro Babo again drew him aside, telling him that that very night he (the deponent) would be captain of two ships, instead of one, for that, great part of the American's ship's crew being to be absent fishing, the six Ashantees without any one else, would easily take it; that at this time he said other things to the same purpose; that no entreaties availed; that, before Amasa Delano's coming on board, no hint had been given touching the capture of the American ship; that to prevent this project the deponent was powerless; * * * that in some things his memory is confused, he cannot distinctly recall every event; * * * that as soon as they had cast anchor at six o'clock in the evening, as has before been stated, the American Captain took leave, to return to his vessel; that upon a sudden impulse, which the deponent believes to have come from God and his angels, he, after the farewell had been said, followed the generous Captain Amasa Delano as far as the gunwale, where he stayed, under pretence of taking leave, until Amasa Delano should have been seated in his boat; that on shoving off, the deponent sprang from the gunwale into the boat and fell into it, he knows not how, God guarding him; that—

[Here, in the original, follows the account of what further happened at the escape, and how the *San Dominick* was retaken, and of the passage to the coast; including in the recital many expressions of "eternal gratitude" to the "generous Captain Amasa Delano." The deposition then proceeds with recapitulatory remarks, and a partial renumeration of the Negroes, making record of their individual part in the past events, with a view to furnishing, according to command of the court, the data whereon to found the criminal sentences to be pronounced. From this portion is the following:]

—*That he believes that all the negroes, though not in the first place knowing to the design of revolt, when it was accomplished, approved it. * * * That the negro José,* eighteen years old, and in the personal service of Don Alexandro, was the one who communicated the information to the negro Babo about the state of things in the cabin, before the revolt; that this is known, because, in the preceding nights, he used to come from his berth, which was under his master's, in the cabin, to the deck where the ringleader and his associates were, and had secret conversations with the negro Babo, in which he was several times seen by the mate; that one night, the mate drove him away twice; * * * that this same negro José was the one who, without being commanded to do so by the negro Babo, as Lecbe and Matinqui were, stabbed his master, Don Alexandro, after he had been dragged half-lifeless to the deck * * * that the mulatto steward, Francesco, was of the first band of revolters, that he was, in all things, the creature and tool of the negro Babo; that, to make his court, he, just before a repast in the cabin, proposed, to the negro Babo, poisoning a dish for the generous Captain Amasa Delano; this is known and believed, because the negroes have said it; but that the negro Babo, having another design, forbade Francesco; * * * that the Ashantee Lecbe was one of the worst of them; for that, on the day the ship was retaken, he assisted in the defence of her, with a hatchet in each hand, with one of which he wounded, in the breast, the chief mate of Amasa Delano, in the first act of boarding; this all knew; that, in sight of the deponent, Lecbe struck with a hatchet, Don Francisco Masa, when, by the negro Babo's orders, he was carrying him to throw him overboard alive, beside participating in the murder, before mentioned, of Don Alexandro Aranda, and others of the cabin-passengers; that, owing to the fury with which the Ashantees fought in the engagement with the boats, but this Lecbe and Yau survived; that Yau was bad as Lecbe; that Yau was the man who, by Babo's command, willingly prepared the skeleton of Don Alexandro, in a way the negroes afterwards told the deponent, but which he, so long as reason is left him, can never divulge; that Yau and Lecbe were the two who, in a calm by night, riveted the skeleton to the bow; this also the negroes told him; that the negro Babo was he who traced the inscription below it; that the negro Babo was the plotter from first to last; he ordered every murder, and was the helm and keel of the revolt; that Atufal was his lieutenant in all; but Atufal, with his own hand, committed no murder; nor did the negro Babo; * * * that Atufal was shot, being killed in the fight with the boats, ere boarding; * * * that the negresses of age, were knowing to the revolt, and testified themselves satisfied at the death of their master, Don Alexandro; that, had the negroes not restrained them, they would have tortured to death, instead of simply killing, the Spaniards slain by command of the negro Babo; that the negresses used their utmost influence to have the deponent made away with; that, in the various acts of murder, they sang songs and danced—not gaily, but solemnly; and before the engagement with the boats, as well as during the action, they sang melancholy songs to the negroes, and that this melancholy tone was more inflaming than a different one would have been, and was so intended; that all this is believed, because the negroes have said it; that of the thirty-six men of the crew, exclusive of the passengers (all of whom are now dead), which the deponent had knowledge of, six only remained alive, with four cabin-boys and ship-boys, not included with the crew; * * * —that the negroes broke an arm of one of the cabin-boys and gave him strokes with hatchets.

[Then follow various random disclosures referring to various periods of time. The following are extracted:]

—That during the presence of Captain Amasa Delano on board, some attempts were made by the sailors, and one by

Hermenegildo Gandix, to convey hints to him of the true state of affairs; but that these attempts were ineffectual, owing to fear of incurring death, and furthermore, owing to the devices which offered contradictions to the true state of affairs, as well as owing to the generosity and piety of Amasa Delano, incapable of sounding such wickedness; * * * that Luys Galgo, a sailor about sixty years of age, and formerly of the King's navy, was one of those who sought to convey tokens to Captain Amasa Delano; but his intent, though undiscovered, being suspected, he was, on a pretence, made to retire out of sight, and at last into the hold and there was made away with. This the negroes have since said; * * * that one of the ship-boys feeling, from Captain Amasa Delano's presence, some hopes of release, and not having enough prudence, dropped some chance word respecting his expectations, which being overheard and understood by a slave-boy with whom he was eating at the time, the latter struck him on the *head with a knife, inflicting a bad wound, but of which the boy is now healing; that likewise, not long before the ship was brought to anchor, one of the seamen, steering at the time, endangered himself by letting the blacks remark some expression in his countenance, arising from a similar cause to the above; but this sailor, by his heedful after conduct, escaped; * * * that these statements are made to show the court that from the beginning to the end of the revolt, it was impossible for the deponent and his men to act otherwise than they did; * * * —that the third clerk, Hermenegildo Gandix, who before had been forced to live among the seamen, wearing a seaman's habit, and in all respects appearing to be one for the time, he, Gandix, was killed by a musket ball fired through mistake from the boats before boarding; having in his fright run up the mizzen-rigging, calling to the boats—"don't board," lest upon their boarding the negroes should kill him; that this inducing the Americans to believe he some way favoured the cause of the negroes, they fired two balls at him, so that he fell wounded from the rigging, and was drowned in the sea; * * * —that the young Don Joaquin, Marques de Aramboalaza, like Hermenegildo Gandix, the third clerk, was degraded to the office and appearance of a common seaman; that upon one occasion when Don Joaquin shrank, the negro Babo commanded the Ashantee Lecbe to take tar and heat it, and pour it upon Don Joaquin's hands; * * * —that Don Joaquin was killed owing to another mistake of the Americans, but one impossible to be avoided, as upon the approach of the boats, Don Joaquin, with a hatchet tied edge out and upright to his hand, was made by the negroes to appear on the bulwarks; whereupon, seen with arms in his hands, and in a questionable attitude, he was shot for a renegade seaman; * * * that on the person of Don Joaquin was found secreted a jewel, which, by papers that were discovered, proved to have been meant for the shrine of our Lady of Mercy in Lima; a votive offering, before-*

hand prepared and guarded, to attest his gratitude, when he should have landed in Peru, his last destination for the safe conclusion of his entire voyage from Spain; * * * —that the jewel, with the other effects of the late Don Joaquin, is in the custody of the Hospital de Sacerdotes, awaiting the disposition of the honourable court; * * * —that, owing to the condition of the deponent, as well as the haste in which the boats departed for the attack, the Americans were not forewarned that there were, among the apparent crew, a passenger and one of the clerks disguised by the negro Babo; * * * —that, beside the negroes killed in the action, some were killed after the capture and reanchoring at night, when shackled to the ring-bolts on deck; that these deaths were committed by the sailors, ere they could be prevented. That so soon as informed of it, Captain Amasa Delano used all his authority, and in particular with his own hand, struck down Martinez Gola, who, having found a razor in the pocket of an old jacket of his, which one of the shackled negroes had on, was aiming it at the negro's throat; that the noble Captain Amasa Delano also wrenched from the hand of Bartholomew Barlo a dagger, secreted at the time of the massacre of the whites, with which he was in the act of stabbing a shackled negro, who, the same day, with another negro, had thrown him down and jumped upon him; * * * —that, for all the events befalling through so long a time, during which the ship was in the hands of the negro Babo, he cannot here give account; but that, what he has said is the most substantial of what occurs to him at present, and is the truth under the oath which he has taken; which declaration he affirmed and ratified, after hearing it read to him.

He said that he is twenty-nine years of age, and broken in body and mind; that when finally dismissed by the court, he shall not return home to Chile, but betake himself to the monastery on Mount Agonia without; and signed with his honour, and crossed himself, and, for the time, departed

as he came, in his litter, with the monk
Infelez, to the Hospital de Sacerdotes.
BENITO CERENO. DR. ROZAS.

If the Deposition have served as the key
to fit into the lock of the complications
which precede it, then, as a vault whose door
has been flung back, the *San Dominick's*
hull lies open to-day.

Hitherto the nature of this narrative, besides rendering the intricacies in the beginning unavoidable, has more or less required that many things, instead of being
set down in the order of occurrence, should
be retrospectively, or irregularly given; this
last is the case with the following passages,
which will conclude the account.

During the long, mild voyage to Lima,
there was, as before hinted, a period during
which the sufferer a little recovered his
health, or, at least in some degree, his tranquillity. Ere the decided relapse which came,
the two captains had many cordial conversations—their fraternal unreserve in singular contrast with former withdrawments.

Again and again it was repeated, how
hard it had been to enact the part forced
on the Spaniard by Babo.

"Ah, my dear friend," Don Benito once
said, "at those very times you thought me
so morose and ungrateful, nay, when, as
you now admit, you have thought me plotting your murder, at those very times my
heart was frozen; I could not look at you,
thinking of what, both on board this ship
and your own, hung, from other hands,
over my kind benefactor. And as God lives,
Don Amasa, I know not whether desire for
my own safety alone could have nerved me
to that leap into your boat, had it not been
for the thought that, did you, unenlightened,
return to your ship, you, my best friend,
with all who might be with you, stolen
upon, that night, in your hammocks, would
never in this world have wakened again.
Do but think how you walked this deck,
how you sat in this cabin, every inch of
ground mined into honey-combs under you.
Had I dropped the least hint, made the

least advance towards an understanding between us; death, explosive death—yours as
mine—would have ended the scene."

"True, true," cried Captain Delano, starting, "you have saved my life, Don Benito,
more than I yours; saved it, too, against my
knowledge and will."

"Nay, my friend," rejoined the Spaniard,
courteous even to the point of religion,
"God charmed your life, but you saved
mine. To think of some things you did—
those smilings and chattings, rash pointings
and gesturings. For less than these, they
slew my mate, Raneds; but you had the
Prince of Heaven's safe-conduct through all
ambuscades."

"Yes, all is owing to Providence, I know:
but the temper of my mind that morning
was more than commonly pleasant, while
the sight of so much suffering, more apparent than real, added to my good-nature,
compassion, and charity, happily interweav-
ing the three. Had it been otherwise, doubtless, as you hint, some of my interferences
might have ended unhappily enough. Besides, those feelings I spoke of enabled me
to get the better of momentary distrust, at
times when acuteness might have cost me
my life, without saving another's. Only at
the end did my suspicions get the better of
me, and you know how wide of the mark
they then proved."

"Wide, indeed," said Don Benito, sadly;
"you were with me all day; stood with me,
sat with me, talked with me, looked at me,
ate with me, drank with me; and yet, your
last act was to clutch for a monster, not only
an innocent man, but the most pitiable of
all men. To such degree may malign mach-
inations and deceptions impose. So far
may even the best man err, in judging the
conduct of one with the recesses of whose
condition he is not acquainted. But you
were forced to it; and you were in time
undeceived. Would that, in both respects,
it was so ever, and with all men."

"You generalize, Don Benito; and mourn-
fully enough. But the past is passed; why
moralize upon it? Forget it. See, yon bright

sun has forgotten it all, and the blue sea, and the blue sky; these have turned over new leaves."

"Because they have no memory," he dejectedly replied; "because they are not human."

"But these mild trades that now fan your cheek, do they not come with a human-like healing to you? Warm friends, steadfast friends are the trades."

"With their steadfastness they but waft me to my tomb, Señor," was the foreboding response.

"You are saved," cried Captain Delano, more and more astonished and pained; "you are saved: what has cast such a shadow upon you?"

"The negro."

There was silence, while the moody man sat, slowly and unconsciously gathering his mantle about him, as if it were a pall.

There was no more conversation that day.

But if the Spaniard's melancholy sometimes ended in muteness upon topics like the above, there were others upon which he never spoke at all; on which, indeed, all his old reserves were piled. Pass over the worst, and, only to elucidate, let an item or two of these be cited. The dress, so precise and costly, worn by him on the day whose events have been narrated, had not willingly been put on. And that silver-mounted sword, apparent symbol of despotic command, was not, indeed, a sword, but the ghost of one. The scabbard, artificially stiffened, was empty.

As for the black—whose brain, not body, had schemed and led the revolt, with the plot—his slight frame, inadequate to that which it held, had at once yielded to the superior muscular strength of his captor, in the boat. Seeing all was over, he uttered no sound, and could not be forced to. His aspect seemed to say, since I cannot do deeds, I will not speak words. Put in irons in the hold, with the rest, he was carried to Lima. During the passage, Don Benito did not visit him. Nor then, nor at any time after would he look at him. Before the tribunal he refused. When pressed by the judges he fainted. On the testimony of the sailors alone rested the legal identity of Babo.

Some months after, dragged to the gibbet at the tail of a mule, the black met his voiceless end. The body was burned to ashes; but for many days, the head, that hive of subtlety, fixed on a pole in the Plaza, met, unabashed, the gaze of the whites; and across the Plaza looked towards St. Bartholomew's church, in whose vaults slept then, as now, the recovered bones of Aranda: and across the Rimac bridge looked towards the monastery, on Mount Agonia without; where, three months after being dismissed by the court, Benito Cereno, borne on the bier, did, indeed, follow his leader.

NOTE TO THE READER

Details of Melville's life are given in *GBWW*, Vol. 48, which contains *Moby Dick*. *Billy Budd* is in *GGB*, Vol. 3, pp. 27–98. Among readings that are suggested by *Benito Cereno*, see those listed in the *Syntopicon* under GOOD AND EVIL, especially Topics 6*a* and 6*b*, which are concerned with the relation between being good and knowing what is good, and the need for experience of evil; also those listed in the first topic under SLAVERY, devoted to the nature of enslavement; and those too on the subject of the pathology of the will, which appear under WILL 9*b*. The implications of Don Benito's remark at the end of the story to the effect that only men have memories are developed in the readings under MEMORY 4*a* and 4*b* about the function of memory in the life of both the individual and the race.

PICTURE CREDITS

—FRONTISPIECE * Wallraf-Richartz Museum, Cologne, Germany; © A.D.A.G.P. **—6** Bonnie Freer/Rapho Guillumette **—8** Charles Harbutt/Magnum **—10** Paul Sequeira **—12** Doug Wilson/Black Star **—14** Thomas England **—16** Lawrence Frank/Rapho Guillumette **—20** * City of New York Police Department **—27** (t.) Culver **—27** (c.l.) Burt Glinn /Magnum **—27** (c.r.) Mati Maldre **—27** (b.l.) Bob Combs/Rapho Guillumette **—27** (b.r.) Mati Maldre **—29** (t.) Hella Hammid/ Rapho Guillumette **—29** (l.) Dennis Brack/ Black Star **—29** (r.) Warren Jorgensen/Medical World News **—33** (l.) Bob Combs/Rapho Guillumette **—33** (t.) Heinz Kluetmeier/LIFE Magazine © Time Inc. **—33** (b.) Charles Harbutt/Magnum **—38** Bob Combs/Rapho Guillumette **—43** Hiroji Kubota/Magnum **—48** Wide World **—49** UPI/Compix **—50** Paul Sequeira **—55** Leonard Freed/Magnum **—60** Burt Glinn/Magnum **—62** Paul Sequeira **—63** Lawrence Frank/Rapho Guillumette **—65** Dennis Brack/Black Star **—67** Thomas England **—69** Martin J. Dain/Magnum **—71** UPI/Compix **—74** Jerry N. Uelsmann **—78–79** Gamma/Pix from Publix **—82** (t.) Thomas England **—82** (b.) Popperfoto/Pictorial Parade **—86** * Presse und Informationsamt der Bundesregierung, Bonn, Germany **—88** * Institut Belge d'Information et Documentation, Brussels **—157** Harvey Stein **—160** Jack Jaffee/Black Star **—161** (t.) Charles Harbutt/Magnum **—161** (b.) Erich Hartmann/Magnum **—168** Marion Bernstein /Editorial Photocolor Archives **—169** (t.) Ron Benvenisti/Magnum **—169** (b.) George Zimbel/Photo Researchers **—181** Hella Hammid/ Rapho Guillumette **—182** (t.) Bruce Roberts/ Rapho Guillumette **—182** (b.) Van Bucher/ Photo Researchers **—184** (t.) Joseph Nettis **—184** (b.) Harvey Stein **—194** (t.) Rene Burri/Magnum **—194** (b.) Harvey Stein **—194–95** Black Star **—201** * Art Institute of Chicago **—202** Ron Sherman/Nancy Palmer Agency **—203** Thomas England **—205** Ted Spiegel/Rapho Guillumette **—212–13** Paul Sequeira **—213** (t., b.) Bruce Roberts/Rapho Guillumette **—222** Werner Wolff/Black Star **—228** * Amherst College **—394** Bettmann Archive **—416** * Harvard College Library **—421, 427, 432, 438, 445, 456, 460, 470** illustrations by Ron Villani

The type for this book was set primarily by SSPA Typesetting, Inc., Carmel, Indiana, and the book was printed and bound by R. R. Donnelley & Sons Company, Crawfordsville, Indiana.